A History of Modern Syria

BY THE SAME AUTHOR

Occupying Syria under the French Mandate: Insurgency, Space and State Formation (CUP, 2012)

A History of Modern Syria

DANIEL NEEP

ALLEN LANE
an imprint of
PENGUIN BOOKS

ALLEN LANE

UK | USA | Canada | Ireland | Australia
India | New Zealand | South Africa

Allen Lane is part of the Penguin Random House group of companies whose addresses can be found at global.penguinrandomhouse.com.

Penguin Random House UK
One Embassy Gardens, 8 Viaduct Gardens, London SW11 7BW

penguin.co.uk

Penguin Random House UK

First published in Great Britain by Allen Lane 2025
001

Set in 11.9/16pt Sabon Next LT Pro
Typeset by Six Red Marbles UK, Thetford, Norfolk
Printed and bound in Great Britain by Clays Ltd, Elcograf S.p.A.

The authorized representative in the EEA is Penguin Random House Ireland, Morrison Chambers, 32 Nassau Street, Dublin D02 YH68

A CIP catalogue record for this book is available from the British Library

ISBN: 978-0-241-00329-9

Penguin Random House is committed to a sustainable future for our business, our readers and our planet. This book is made from Forest Stewardship Council® certified paper.

FSC www.fsc.org MIX Paper | Supporting responsible forestry FSC® C018179

It seems that the complicated entanglement between the local struggle against tyranny and religious, sectarian and ethnic conflicts, along with all the complex and intertwined international interventions, constitute as a whole what could be called the Syria Question.

[The Syria Question] reflects the agency of the powerful in history, which transforms human history into an inescapably convoluted and ugly narrative whose characters are professional criminals, thieves, murderers and liars.

Yet history also has another face: the face of revolutions and rebellions of the weak.

Yassin al-Hajj Salih, 2016[1]

الدين لله و الوطن للجميع

Religion belongs to God,
but the Nation belongs to All.

Arab nationalist slogan, nineteenth century

Contents

List of Illustrations ix
List of maps xi
Preface xiii
Acknowledgements xxiii
Note on Transliteration xxv

1 Of Peasants and Grand Families: The Lands of Syria, 1800s–1860s 1
2 Reforms and Regionalism: The Late Ottoman Empire, 1860s–1920 53
3 From Kingdom to Colonialism, 1920–1927 97
4 Liberal Nationalism and Popular Politics, 1927–1946 133
5 Liberalism Implodes, 1946–1949 175
6 Military Reform, 1949–1954 217
7 Radicals and Liberals, 1954–1958 253
8 Unity, Freedom, Socialism, 1958–1970 297
9 Building Assad's Syria, 1970–1982 359
10 Seasons of Discontent, 1982–2003 405
11 From Social Market to Civil War, 2003–2014 453
12 New Divisions, New Beginnings: An Overview, 2015–2025 507

Notes 531
Bibliography 587
Index 623

List of Illustrations

Photographic acknowledgments are shown in italics.

1. West minaret of the Umayyad Mosque, Damascus, c.1867–1899. *Maison Bonfils via Library of Congress, https://www.loc.gov/pictures/item/2004670443/*
2. Cemal Pasha, Ottoman governor of Syria (1915–1918), riding through the streets of Damascus on 17 July 1917. *Hulton Archive/Getty Images.*
3. Rebels in the Great Syrian Revolt against the French Mandate, 1925–1927. *Markaz al-Watha'iq al-Tarikhiyya, Damascus, Syria.*
4. Nationalist politician Abd al-Rahman Shahbandar addresses Syrians protesting against French rule on 23 January 1939. *Associated Press/ Alamy.*
5. Syrian President Shukri al-Quwwatli, 1948. *-/AFP via Getty Images.*
6. General Adib al-Shishakli, Syrian president (1953–54) on 7 July 1953. © *Keystone/ZUMA Press/Bridgeman Images.*
7. Automobile showrooms at the Damascus International Fair, 1957. *Private collection of Sami Moubayed.*
8. Syrian President Shukri al-Quwwatli with Egyptian President Gamal Abd al-Nasser during his visit to Damascus in March 1958. *Keystone/ Getty Images.*
9. Syrian President Hafiz al-Assad (1971–2000) with his wife Anisa Makhlouf and their children (from left): Basil, Bushra, Maher, Majd and Bashar on 4 June 1974. *Alexandra DE BORCHGRAVE/Gamma-Rapho via Getty Images.*
10. Poster from 1999 with the images of Syrian President Hafiz al-Assad with his sons Basil (left), who died in a car crash in 1994, and Bashar

(right), who succeeded his father to the presidency in 2000. *Barry Iverson/Getty Images.*

11. A Syrian boy buys a portrait of President Bashar al-Assad (2000–2024) from a shop in Damascus on 26 May 2007 before the presidential referendum. *HASSAN AMMAR/AFP via Getty Images.*
12. A destroyed street in the city of Homs in 2022. *Ali Wannous via Pexels.*

List of Maps

Map 1. Geographical regions of the Arab East xxvii
Map 2. Ottoman provinces of Bilad al-Sham, 1800 xxviii
Map 3. Post-Tanzimat Ottoman provinces of the Middle East, 1914 xxix
Map 4. Early boundaries of the French Mandate Territories in the Levant, 1921 xxx
Map 5. Territorial control in Syria, June 2015 xxxi
Map 6. Territorial control in Syria, July 2020 xxxii

Preface

In December 2024, the regime of the Assads that had brutally dominated Syria for over fifty years suddenly collapsed during a lightning advance by rebel forces. This turn of events was unexpected, to say the least. The regime had survived thirteen years of vicious and chaotic conflict, albeit at the terrible cost of half a million deaths, fourteen million refugees and displaced people and the utter devastation of entire city neighbourhoods, and uncounted villages and towns. The last four years of the regime were marked by an uneasy stalemate with rebels who had been corralled into the north-western region of Idlib behind a largely static frontline. The self-evident staying power of the Assad regime had even begun to reconcile some governments in Europe and the Arab world to pragmatic arguments for normalizing diplomatic relations with Syria after years of censure and sanctions. Then, in late November 2024, a coalition of rebels suddenly broke through the Idlib frontline and in just two days captured Aleppo, Syria's second-largest city. In an astonishingly swift offensive, the rebels turned south to take the central cities of Hama and Homs. The Syrian army buckled in the face of their gains. On 8 December, the rebels reached Damascus. Bashar al-Assad, who had inherited the presidency of the republic from his father in 2000, fled the country for Russia. In less than two weeks, the regime of the Assads had gone.

If the regime's implosion had been impossible to foresee just two weeks earlier, the scale of the uprising that broke out in early 2011 was equally unthinkable in advance. Bashar al-Assad's father, Hafiz, had quelled the rebellion of the late 1970s and early 1980s so ruthlessly that the opposition had been eradicated inside the country. Whereas regime opponents in such countries as Egypt could organize and compete in elections around this time (even if the outcomes of those elections were tightly controlled), in Assad's Syria all opposition was rooted out and harshly repressed by security forces known for their brutality. Unlike Tunisia and Egypt, where popular uprisings ousted incumbent rulers in January 2011, Syria lacked recent experience of protest and political organization. Yet just months after the first small-scale protests, tens of thousands of ordinary Syrians across the country took to the streets calling for dignity and freedom. Such calls were not made for any single party, political organization or social group, but for *all* Syrians. That well-known slogan of the 2010–11 Arab uprisings 'The people want the fall of the regime!' notably invokes the collective sovereignty of *the people* against political tyranny.

In the aftermath of the regime's defeat in 2024, Syrians found themselves faced with the monumental task of rebuilding their country – quite literally, given the scale of the destruction. Yet in addition to the desperately needed economic reconstruction, the prospect of Syria's *political* reconstruction was now open to debate for the first time in over half a century. What kind of constitution would post-Assad Syria adopt? Who would be empowered to write that constitution? What electoral system should be in place? Should power be concentrated in the central state, as in the past, or devolved to the regions? Should the economy be opened to international investment or collectively controlled by the government on behalf of the people? Would Syria's current de facto rulers, members of the Islamist rebel group Hay'at Tahrir al-Sham (HTS), impose their own puritanical sensibilities on a religiously diverse population? After 2024, Syrians could consider such inherently political questions openly for the first time since the Arab Ba'th Socialist Party had come to power in 1963. The civil war had torn Syria apart to the point that many observers had doubted its continued viability as a sovereign state. Yet by 2025, the breaking of Syria seemed less likely a possibility than its *remaking*. Syrians lived in a world of new possibilities.

Despite the recent devastation, the prospect of remaking Syria was not entirely unprecedented in the history of the country. In many respects, debates over the future of Syria in the mid-2020s mirrored the same political preoccupations with which successive generations of Syrians had been grappling for over two hundred years. Taking a long-term historical and sociological perspective reveals how the lands of Syria were shaped by fitful bursts of repression and protest, tyranny and rebellion, as different would-be rulers sought to impose their political vision on Syria. The difficulty of imposing that vision was compounded not only by the country's ethnic, religious and sectarian diversity, but also by the sheer speed of political change and social transformation in Syria over this time. From the Ottoman Empire to French colonialism to post-independence experiments with liberalism, socialism and military dictatorship, Syrians have struggled to control the direction of their country while navigating sea changes in the global economy, tempestuous geopolitical rivalries and frantic competition between domestic political forces scrabbling for control over resources, status and power. The sedimented legacies of such struggles mean that each generation may have to remake Syria, but never under conditions of their own choosing. Although the origins of modern Syria are often erroneously attributed to the colonial machinations of Britain and France during the First World War, its foundations go much deeper.

At the beginning of the nineteenth century, the eastern Mediterranean coast and interior stretching from the fringes of the Taurus Mountains in the north to Palestine in the south, was generally known by its Arabic-speaking inhabitants as the 'lands of Damascus' (*Bilad al-Sham*). In the decades that followed, these lands were reshaped by concentrated bursts of infrastructure development, institution building, economic breakdown and social restructuring. Cities that had been only loosely bound in the past came to find that the rapid expansion of roads and railways, ports and telegraph lines, not only gave them unprecedented connections within the region, but also opened new avenues for the centralization of political power, the import of cheap foreign goods from overseas and the intrusive hand of imperialism. By the 1860s, these new connections had forged the early foundations of a shared regional identity, which would come to be symbolized by the name of 'Syria' – a revival of the ancient Greek term for the Roman province in the area. Originally reintroduced by European diplomats in their geopolitical intrigues with the Ottoman Empire, the name of 'Syria' (rendered in Arabic as *Suriya*) was nevertheless quickly embraced by Arab intellectuals and reformers, in whose writings the term came to resonate with a new cultural meaning. Although the older term *Bilad al-Sham* continued to be used, the linguistic emergence of *Suriya* marked a shift in how the region's identity was understood and imagined.

Perhaps surprisingly, for proponents of the new Syria the question of geographical boundaries only rarely appeared during the late nineteenth and early twentieth centuries. It was not until the crumbling of the Ottoman Empire during the First World War that Syria's relationship with the wider world came to the fore. As the Ottoman provinces of Anatolia came to be dominated by Turkish nationalists, primarily Arabic-speaking Syria was faced with the question of how to relate to the adjacent Arabic-speaking lands of Arabia, Iraq and Egypt. Should Syria join a loose confederation of independent Arab states or form a subordinate part of a much larger Arab polity? For many inhabitants of Syria, such questions invariably touched upon deeply held notions of community, identity and belonging. Yet even when based on claims about identity, visions of the future were difficult to express without broaching explicitly political issues. Alignment with the equally new neighbouring states of Iraq or Jordan, for example, would imply alignment with the conservative, Westward orientation of their monarchical regimes. Later, alignment with Egypt, the regional powerhouse, offered a different direction: under the charismatic leadership of Gamal Abd al-Nasser in the 1950s, Egypt would become a radical pioneer of Arab nationalism and socialism. In the middle years of the twentieth century, Syrians grappled with many of the same political debates that raged across the newly decolonized Middle East, Africa and Asia. Should the state or private sector take responsibility for generating employment? How actively should government provide welfare to its citizens? Could the legacies of class division and regional inequality be overcome? In post-independence Syria, arguments about sovereignty and relations with other Arab states were entangled with domestic concerns, especially the controversial debates over inequality between communities, classes and regions within the country. From the 1930s to the 1970s, arguments over identity, foreign policy and economics intersected in complex and often unexpected ways, creating extreme polarization between right and left. As state institutions were consumed by partisanship, constitutional political life broke down, opening a door for domination by the army and one-party rule.

That those debates died down in the 1970s owes much to the ruthless pragmatism of Hafiz al-Assad, president from 1971 to 2000, whose regime brought roads, electricity, water and employment to Syria's neglected rural masses, and who responded to dissent with astonishing brutality. During this time, Syria remained something of an outlier in the Arab world. Not only did Assad's Syria resist the tentative steps towards political pluralism that many Middle Eastern regimes had started to take in the 1980s and 1990s, but the country also largely withstood global pressures to introduce privatization, liberalization and the free-market principles that had displaced state-led development as the new economic orthodoxy. It was left for the regime headed by his son Bashar al-Assad to attempt to articulate a Syrian version of this new global liberalism.

In principle, the Social Market Economy introduced in the mid-2000s was supposed to allow space for private business to usher in a golden age of prosperity without jeopardizing the gains that had been won for peasants and workers in previous decades. In practice, the opening gave rise to collusion between the next generation of the regime and the super-rich. The sudden influx of foreign capital sparked a speculative boom in construction and services that dramatically reshaped the country's urban geography and exacerbated long standing inequalities between Syria's diverse regions.

The protests that broke out in 2011 were initially more about changing this deeply uneven system than they were about overthrowing the regime. Over the following decade, Syria was torn apart by violence, torture and destruction. As the warring parties proliferated, so too did their rival visions for Syria. Polarization, radicalization and foreign entanglement once again went hand in hand. What emerged from the civil war of the 2010s was a Syria divided – but one whose fractures bore little resemblance to the regionalism of the past. This book seeks to explain how the most recent remaking of Syria has been built on stratified layers of earlier makings and remakings, the first traces of which can be excavated as far back as the early 1800s.

A History of Modern Syria departs significantly from conventional accounts of the subject in several respects. The narrative most commonly encountered about Syrian history relates to its putative origins as part of the division of the Near East secretly negotiated by Britain and France during the First World War in the Sykes–Picot Accord. For many commentators, especially in the media, the external imposition of Syria's modern borders, grouping together disparate religious, sectarian and ethnic communities, lies at the heart of the ongoing conflict. Yet, as already suggested, such a narrative overlooks the pre-colonial foundations for modern Syria that were undertaken by reformers, infrastructure builders and identity entrepreneurs in the late Ottoman Empire. It also neglects the role that Syrians themselves played in determining the precise course of these borders, many of which were at best tentatively plotted, and also fairly porous, for several decades. While the logic of the Sykes–Picot narrative would ultimately suggest that smaller, more homogenous states might provide greater stability in the Near East, this argument is largely proposed by journalists and think-tank researchers in the West. Rather than pushing for smaller polities, local opponents of the existing borders have more often advocated the merger of post-Ottoman governments into a single, much larger regional superstate. Even at the height of the civil war in the 2010s, Syrians fought among themselves to control the country; only groups from outside sought to unravel it.

The issue of ethnic and sectarian identity in Syria must also be treated with circumspection. The fact of Syria's diverse population – comprised of Sunni and Shia Muslims, Greek and Syriac Christians, Druze and Alawis, Arabs and Kurds, Circassians and Armenians, not to mention urbanites, rural villagers and tribesmen – does not mean that these identities have existed, static and unchanging, since ancient times. As this book attests, such identities have themselves been formed and transformed in the crucible of social, political and economic change the region has undergone since the nineteenth century. Since then, sectarianism has manifested at various points as bouts of communal violence, as a deliberate strategy of political mobilization, and as a product of impersonal structural biases in government institutions. Given the diverse forms that 'sectarianism' can take, this book seeks to unpack its incarnations to better understand their varying contexts and causes. Sectarianism is rarely about religious difference in the theological sense; it is instead a manifestation of identity politics.

Often, the history of Syria has been told as a story primarily involving external actors, whether the colonial machinations of Britain or France, the geopolitical competition between the United States and the Soviet Union or intra-Arab rivalries between Iraq and Egypt. That the international struggle for Syria re-emerged with a vengeance during the civil war of the 2010s can also not be denied. This book, however, tells a slightly different story than that reconstructed from diplomatic schemes hatched in corridors of power from Washington, D.C., to Tehran. *A History of Modern Syria* seeks to explain the interplay between different 'Syria-making' episodes and contemporary regional and even global processes. Time and time again, we see how developments in Syria are never determined by purely domestic factors but are shaped by the powerful forces responsible for restructuring international relations more generally. This formulation draws attention not only to the usual suspects of European colonialism, American imperialism and Soviet expansionism, but also to the seemingly impersonal economic currents that have produced alternating bouts of expansion and contraction, globalization and protectionism, from the nineteenth century to the twenty-first. Whether they unfolded in 1873, 1929 or 2008, international financial crises have played a crucial yet often overlooked role in remaking modern Syria, as well as in remaking the non-Western world more generally.

In a book of this length, I have necessarily drawn on a wide range of sources, from French and British archives to the revisionist scholarship in Ottoman historiography to political science research on the 2010s civil war. But as much as possible, I tell this story using sources written by Syrians, usually in Arabic, including politicians' memoirs, officer autobiographies, philosophical essays, newspapers, magazines, literary musings, films and soap operas. My analysis is also informed by the rich Arabic language scholarship on Syria. (Note to the Western academy: Syrians also write history!). If my account of Syria differs from that familiar to anglophone readers, it is perhaps for these reasons.

The first two chapters of the book offer a broad overview of revolts, reforms and regionalism in the late Ottoman lands of Syria. Chapter 3 covers the overthrow of the first independent Arab Kingdom of Syria by French forces, which then waged a war of occupation against local rebels. Chapter 4 explains how, with the military option exhausted, Syria's political elite sought to use negotiation to obtain independence from France – much to the annoyance of the next generation, who pushed for more radical, direct action. Chapter 5 examines Syria's short-lived experience, after independence in 1946, of liberal parliamentary democracy, which failed largely because the elite sacrificed the issues of social reform, regional inequality and the question of Palestine to maintain the inherited privilege of the establishment. Chapters 6 and 7 explore the polarization of the 1950s and early 1960s, as discontented radicals fought back, battling conservatives over economic policy and foreign affairs, and struggling for dominance over the government and armed forces. The radicals' victory saw them launch new political experiments – union with Egypt, socialist egalitarianism – that, as Chapter 8 explains, ultimately ended in repression, authoritarianism and division. Chapter 9 recounts the new unity forcefully imposed on Syria by Hafiz al-Assad and the terrible price exacted by his regime to achieve its monopoly over power. In a break from the usual periodization, Chapter 10 looks at the stalled economic and political reforms that were first launched in the late 1980s, frozen in the 1990s and thawed in the early 2000s under the newly inaugurated president, Bashar al-Assad. Chapter 11 charts the path from Assad's Social Market Economy to the outbreak of the uprising and the subsequent descent into civil war. Given the difficulties of writing not simply contemporary history, but the contemporary history of a warzone, Chapter 12 offers instead a bird's-eye view of the most important developments in Syria after the Russian military intervention in 2015, during which zones of territorial control had largely stabilized, and concludes with the unexpected fall of the regime in December 2024.

I write this book with the hope that the name of 'Syria' will once again viably stand as an ecumenical, pluralist and civic identity for the inhabitants of this remarkable country. 'Religion belongs to God,' says an old Arab nationalist slogan, first popularized after a bloody episode of sectarian conflict in the late nineteenth century, 'but the Nation belongs to All.'

Acknowledgements

Over a decade of research and writing I have incurred several lifetimes' worth of debt to the librarians and archivists whose largely unseen labour sustains academic inquiry. I would therefore like to offer my deepest thanks to the staff at the Institut Français du Proche Orient in Damascus and Beirut; the former Assad Library, Damascus; Markaz al-Watha'iq al-Tarikhiya, Damascus; Jafet Library, American University of Beirut; Centre des Archives Diplomatiques, Nantes; Service Historique de l'Armée de Terre, Paris; Woodrow Wilson Center Library, Washington, D.C.; Lauinger Library, Georgetown University; Brandeis University Library; Gelman Library, George Washington University; and the Library of Congress, Washington, D.C.

I am grateful for the fellowships and awards I received that collectively made this book possible, including those from the Public Scholar Program, National Endowment for the Humanities; Woodrow Wilson Center for International Scholars; American Druze Foundation; Crown Center for Middle East Studies, Brandeis University; the British Academy; and the Council for British Research in the Levant (CBRL).

Time spent at the Crown Center for Middle East Studies, Brandeis University, offered a uniquely warm and engaging cross-disciplinary intellectual community in which to write, think and discuss my work. The Crown Center serves as a beacon for Middle East Studies in North America. The Center for Arab and Middle East Studies at the American University of Beirut welcomed me as a visiting researcher for a semester in 2015, for which I am deeply appreciative. I would like to thank students who took my graduate seminar on the politics of Syria at the Center for Contemporary Arab Studies at Georgetown University. I hope you will see in these pages your impact on how I think about the making of modern Syria. I also thank my research assistants, Craig Browne and Carlo Darouni, for their invaluable support in the early stages of the project.

For their comments on draft chapters and workshop presentations, invitations to speak and hearty encouragement during often difficult years of research and writing, I would like to express my appreciation to Fida Adely, Hayal Akarsu, Maryam Alemzadeh, Catherine Batruni, Eva Bellin, Rochelle Davies, Toby Dodge, Yazan Doughan, Jennifer Dueck, Aula Hariri, Sarah El-Kazaz, Neil Ketchley, Marc Lynch, Kevin Mazur, Pascal Menoret, David Patel, Gary Samore, Jillian Schwedler, Amy Singer, Naghmeh Sohrabi, Rebecca Thompson, Charles Tripp, Mike Williams, Jonathan Wyrzten and Hind Ahmad Zaki. I especially thank my editor at Allen Lane, Simon Winder, and my agent, Jonathan Pegg, for their faith in this project.

To my rock, M.S.A., who keeps me focused on what is, and our children, Z. and A., who keep me focused on what will be, all I can say is: (i) I love you; (ii) thank you for your patience; and (iii) yes, the book is finished now.

Note on Transliteration

In the main text of the book, I transliterate Arabic words using a simplified version of the IJMES system, without diacritical marks. I retain diacritics in the footnotes to help readers track down the original Arabic sources that I cite.

I use the standard English names for major cities and countries (for example, Damascus, Aleppo, Homs, Syria, Iraq, Lebanon, etc.) and personal names (for example, Bashar al-Assad, not Bashshar al-Asad). Arabic family names with the prefix *al-* are provided where I give an individual's first name (for example, Shukri al-Quwwatli), but without the prefix when I refer to them by their family name alone (Quwwatli). Transliterations of colloquial Arabic and less-well-known place names may reflect local pronunciation.

All translations from Arabic and French are mine unless otherwise noted.

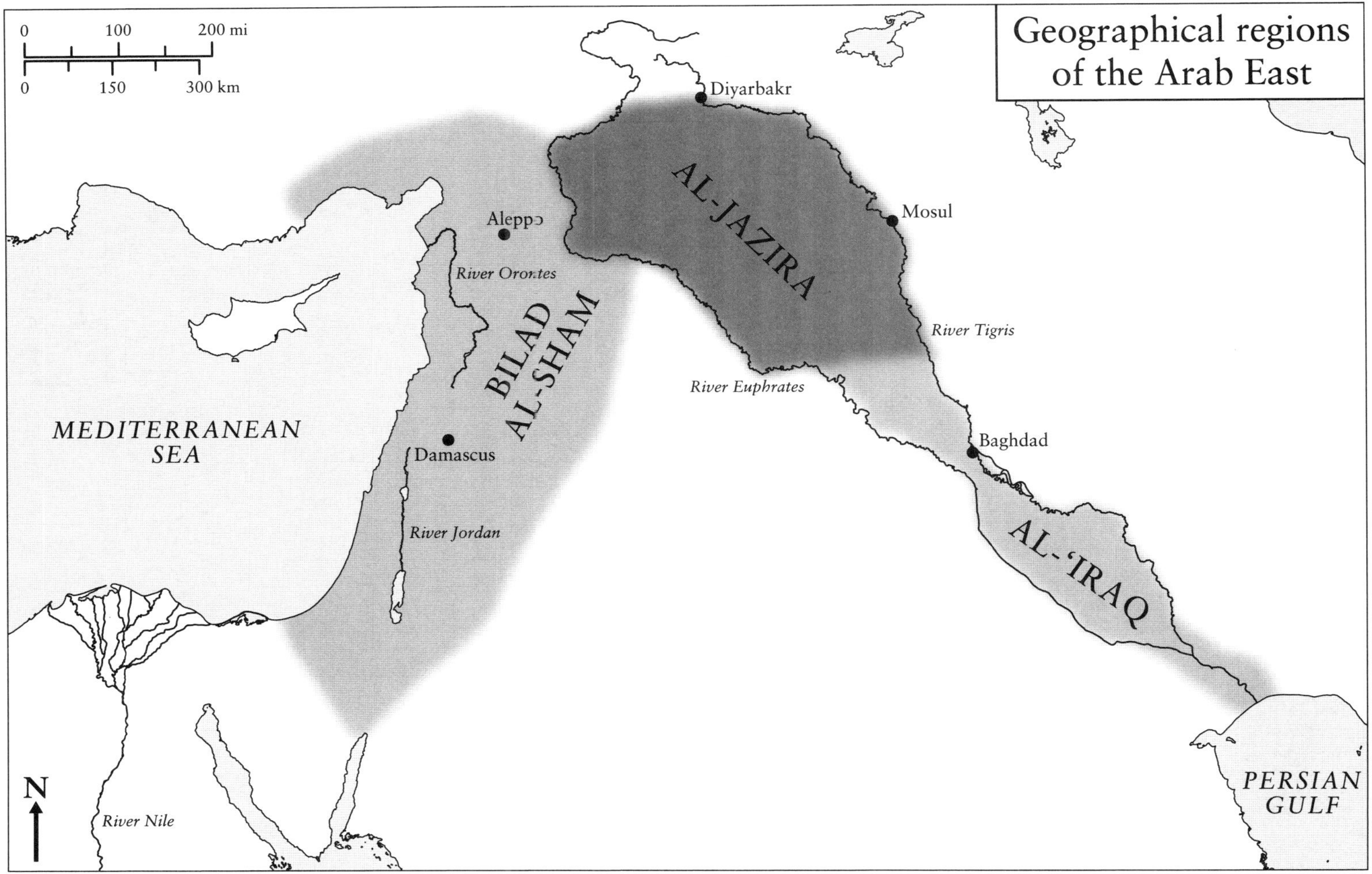
Geographical regions
of the Arab East
0
100
200 mi
0
150
300 km
MEDITERRANEAN
SEA
Aleppo
River Orontes
BILAD
AL-SHAM
Damascus
River Jordan
AL-JAZIRA
Diyarbakr
Mosul
River Tigris
River Euphrates
Baghdad
AL-'IRAQ
PERSIAN
GULF
River Nile
N

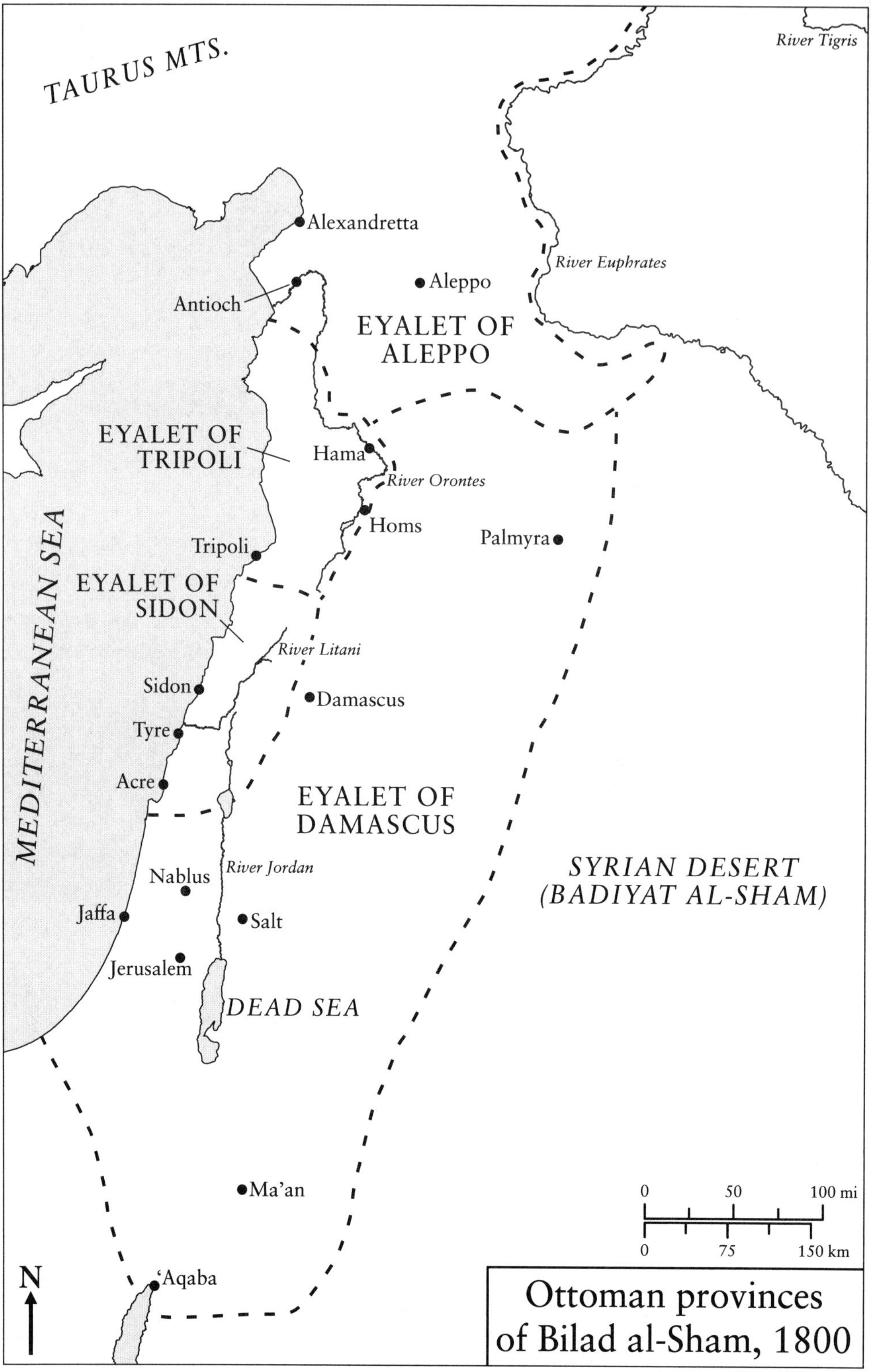

Ottoman provinces of Bilad al-Sham, 1800

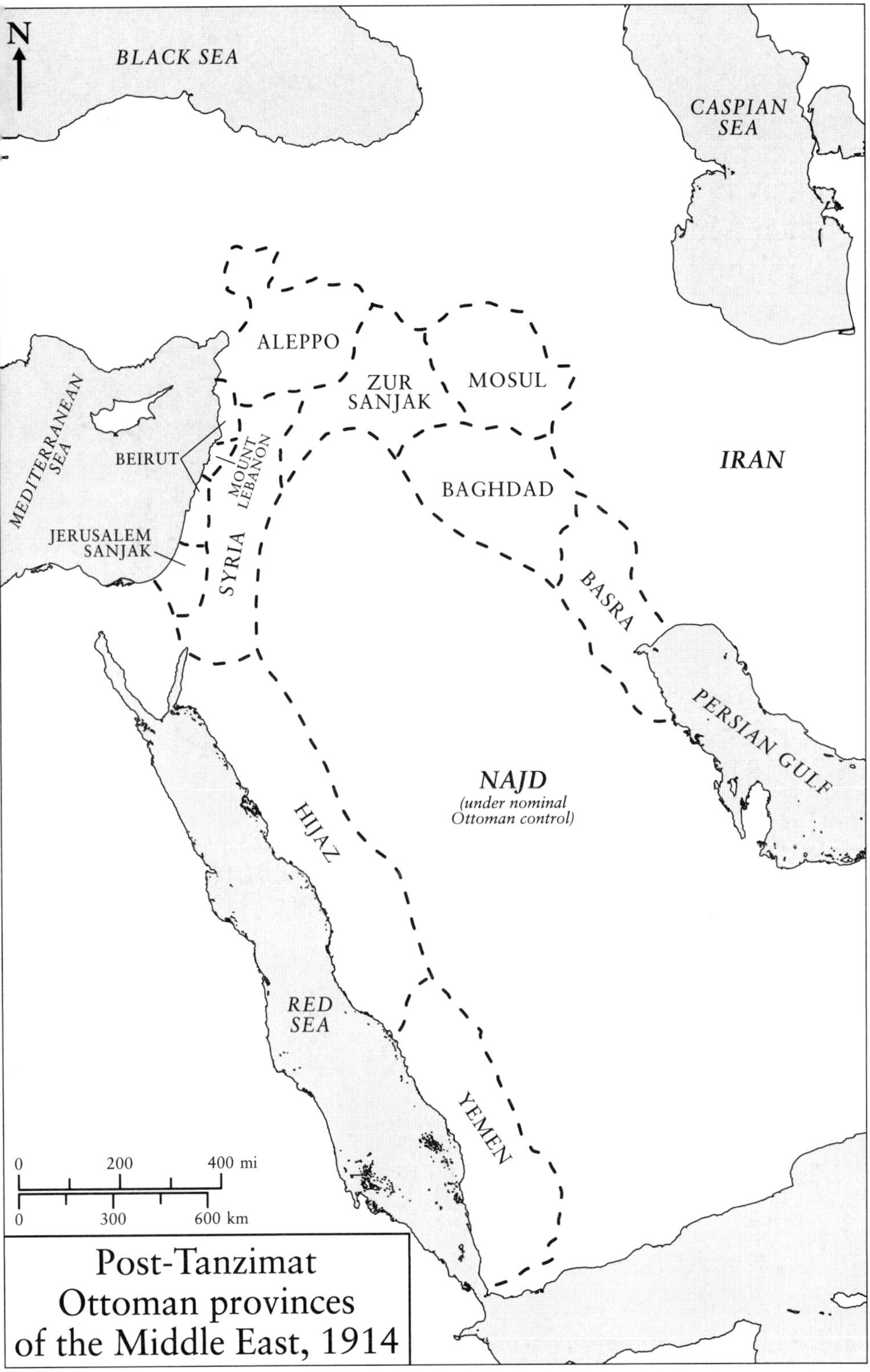

Post-Tanzimat Ottoman provinces of the Middle East, 1914

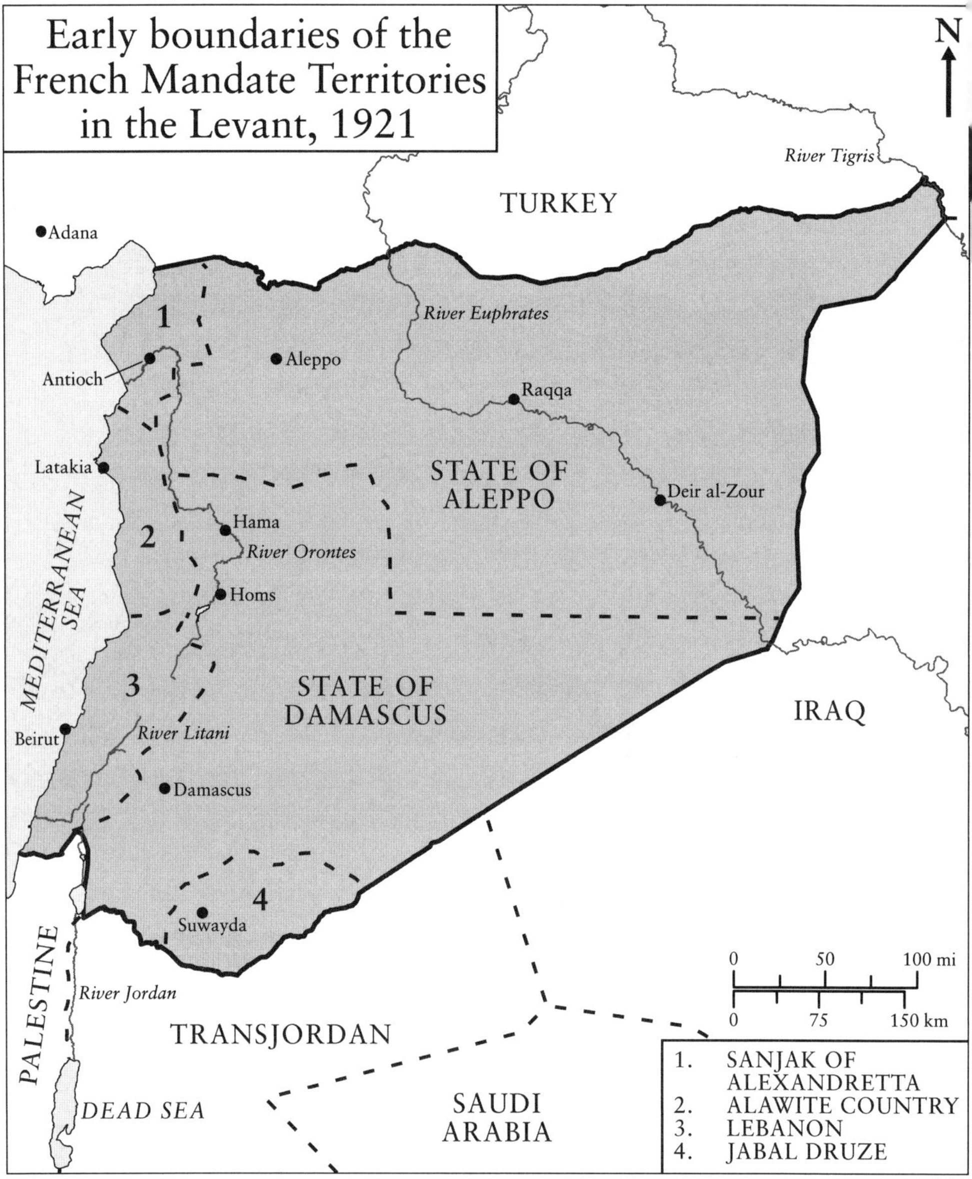

Early boundaries of the French Mandate Territories in the Levant, 1921
N
TURKEY
River Tigris
Adana
1
River Euphrates
Aleppo
Antioch
Raqqa
Latakia
STATE OF ALEPPO
Deir al-Zour
Hama
2
River Orontes
MEDITERRANEAN SEA
Homs
3
STATE OF DAMASCUS
IRAQ
Beirut
River Litani
Damascus
4
Suwayda
PALESTINE
River Jordan
0 50 100 mi
0 75 150 km
TRANSJORDAN
DEAD SEA
SAUDI ARABIA
1. SANJAK OF ALEXANDRETTA
2. ALAWITE COUNTRY
3. LEBANON
4. JABAL DRUZE

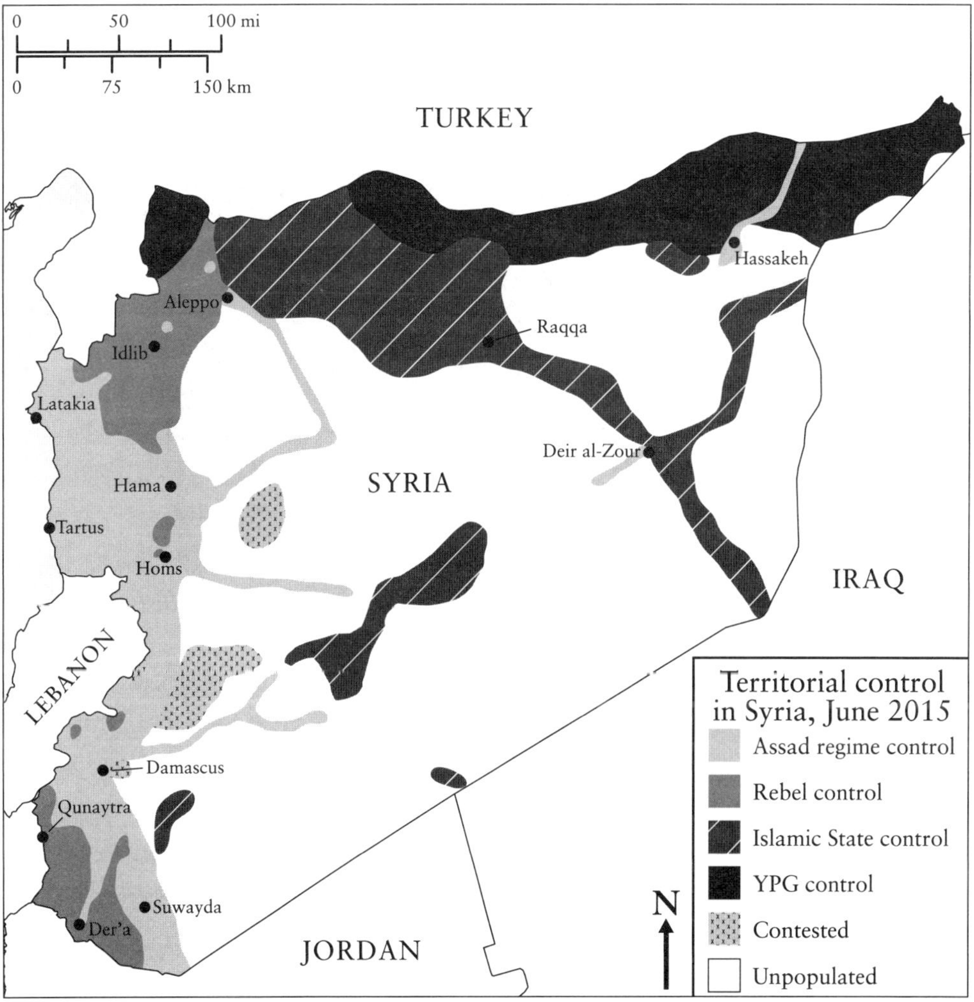
0
50
100 mi
0
75
150 km
TURKEY
Aleppo
Idlib
Latakia
Hama
Tartus
Homs
LEBANON
Damascus
Qunaytra
Suwayda
Der'a
JORDAN
SYRIA
Raqqa
Hassakeh
Deir al-Zour
IRAQ
N
Territorial control in Syria, June 2015
Assad regime control
Rebel control
Islamic State control
YPG control
Contested
Unpopulated

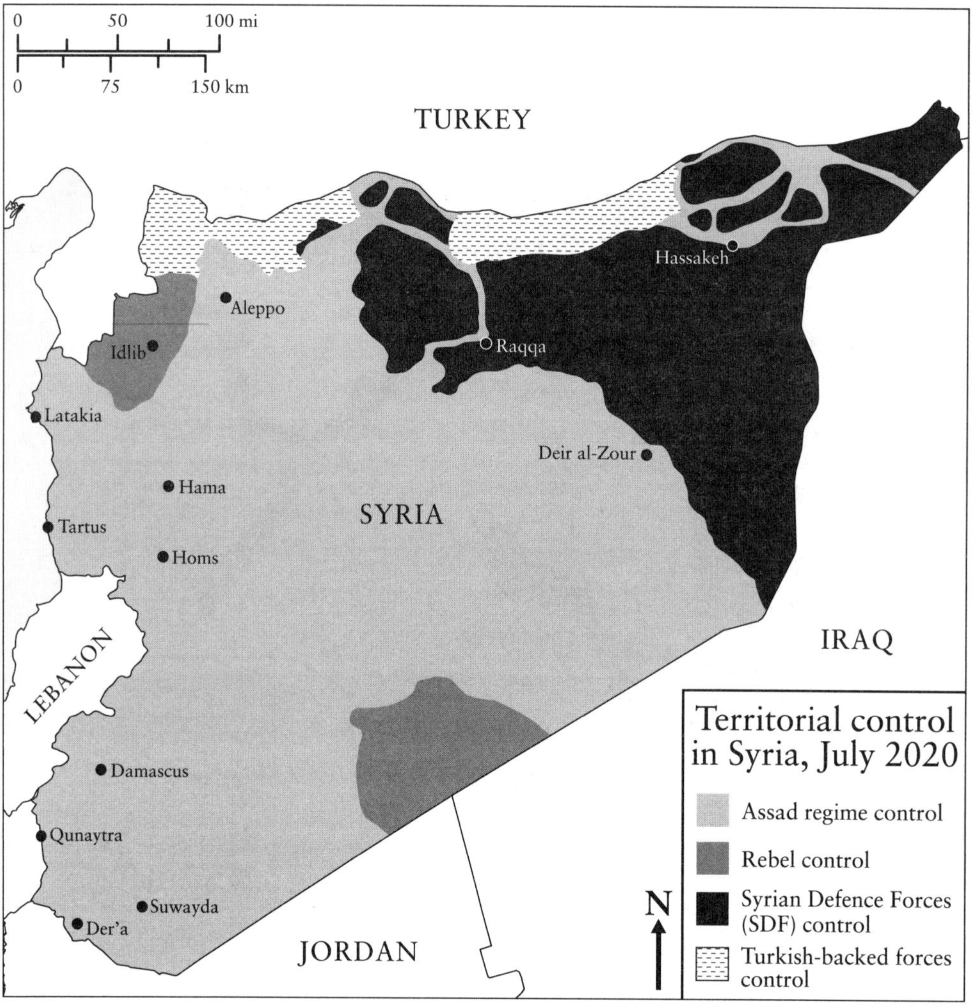
0
50
100 mi
0
75
150 km
TURKEY
Hassakeh
Aleppo
Idlib
Raqqa
Latakia
Deir al-Zour
Hama
Tartus
SYRIA
Homs
IRAQ
LEBANON
Territorial control in Syria, July 2020
Damascus
Assad regime control
Qunaytra
Rebel control
Suwayda
Syrian Defence Forces (SDF) control
Der'a
N
JORDAN
Turkish-backed forces control

A History of Modern Syria

413. Damas. Minaret de l'ouest. Syrie
Bonfils

1

Of Peasants and Grand Families: The Lands of Syria, 1800s–1860s

At the beginning of the nineteenth century, the Ottomans controlled one of the largest empires on the planet. From the imperial capital of Istanbul, the Ottoman sultan claimed authority over a swathe of territory that stretched from Algeria in the west to Iraq in the east, from the southern tip of Yemen up along the Arabian Peninsula, across the lands of Syria and all the way north to Anatolia, the Balkans and south-east Europe. This sprawling, multicultural empire was home to some thirty million souls: Greeks and Turks, Albanians and Armenians, Arabs and Kurds, Serbs and Bulgarians, Slavs and Circassians. Yet most inhabitants of the empire paid little heed to these ethnic identities, which, when they were acknowledged at all, were less important than religion, language and social class.[1]

Most of the sultan's subjects followed the traditions of Sunni Islam, but there was considerable variety in how these traditions were practised. Religious scholars adhered to one of four Sunni schools of Islamic law, while Sufi spiritual brotherhoods were popular in many towns and folk traditions held sway in rural areas. Significant numbers of Shia Muslims lived in some parts of the empire, especially Iraq and the Persian Gulf, as well as isolated pockets of smaller sects – Druze, Ismailis, Alevis, Alawis and Ahl-e

Haqq, among others – whose beliefs included esoteric elements that had long diverged from mainstream Islam. Ottoman Christians displayed a similar diversity and belonged to an assortment of churches, mostly Eastern Orthodox, but also Roman Catholic, Assyrian and Coptic. The empire's Jewish community, in contrast, was smaller and largely urban.

For the most part, Ottoman rulers granted substantial autonomy to their subjects. Muslims, Christians and Jews were allowed to follow their own legal frameworks for marriage, inheritance and other personal affairs as deemed appropriate by their communal religious tradition. In return for this freedom, Christian and Jewish leaders of the *millets*, as these religious–legal communities were known, collected a special tax levied on non-Muslim subjects of the empire. The heterodox Islamic sects, in contrast, had no independent legal standing and for administrative purposes could be treated as Sunnis, despite the lack of social integration.

Turkish, Arabic and Greek were widely spoken across different parts of the empire and helped to bridge misunderstandings in what could be a cacophony of local languages. Formal, Classical Arabic provided a lingua franca for Muslim scholars, like Latin in medieval Europe, although regional dialects dominated the daily lives of Arabic speakers. Ottoman Turkish was the official language of government and law, but it was a baroque and artificial construction, effectively incomprehensible to ordinary people as it borrowed heavily from the lofty, literary vocabularies of Arabic and Persian, as well as from European vernaculars such as Venetian Italian and French. For the most part, Ottoman subjects spoke the language – or languages – most useful to them in their daily lives, without any interference from or reference to the government. This fluidity meant that language was more a useful tool than a marker of identity.

Ethnic as well as linguistic boundaries were rather more

malleable than we might think of them today. First, the empire's major cities had been influenced by centuries of cosmopolitanism. Much of the ruling elite of Cairo had ancestral roots in the northern Caucasus, for example, while the high society of Aleppo had long married into Turkish families, and spoke Turkish at home as often as they spoke Arabic. Even purely Arabic-speaking inhabitants of Damascus, Cairo and Baghdad would not consider themselves as 'Arab', an epithet that was then reserved for the unruly nomadic Bedouin tribes of Arabia. Although they might allude to their ancestry by referring to themselves as *awlad al-'arab*, or 'descendants of the Arabs', their common language conveyed no collective identity. In the cities of the Syrian interior, these families with Arab roots had been joined by similarly wealthy land owning families of Kurdish origins, with whom they had slowly become socially and culturally indistinguishable within a shared urban culture that was alien to desert life. Beyond the cities, in the isolated peripheries of the Ottoman Empire, the lines between ethnicity, religion and language were even more hazy. In the south-east of present-day Turkey, for example, there lived tribes who were originally turcophone, but had adopted one of the local Kurdish languages and had, for all intents and purposes, become Kurds. As late as the nineteenth century, there are examples of rural Armenians converting from Christianity to Islam and thereafter describing themselves as Kurds.[2] In the nineteenth century, identity was a product of shared local culture, not genetics. For its part, the Ottoman Empire had little interest in the ethnicity of the general populace as long as they respected the ultimate authority of the sultan.

Compared to governments of the twentieth and twenty-first centuries, the Ottoman Empire of the early nineteenth century seems strangely incurious about the identities, lives and daily affairs of the population living in its territory. Across most of its lands, Ottoman rule was surprisingly indirect and decentralized. The functions of government were typically sub-contracted from Istanbul to elites who were able to enforce their power in the provinces – officially on behalf of the sultan, but in reality with a great degree of autonomy from the imperial capital. In practice, decentralizing power to regional elites was an effective way of overcoming the challenges of governing diverse and relatively independent communities that had over the centuries developed distinct local characteristics that outsiders found difficult to penetrate. The job of collecting taxes, for example, was not carried out by employees of the central state, but by prominent local figures who were permitted to appropriate a portion of this revenue for their own personal profit. In previous centuries, the right to collect taxes had often been a reward for loyal military service and could be handed down from father to son. However, mounting pressure on state finances meant that the right to collect taxes from peasants in a particular area came to be sold off to the highest bidder at auction. During the eighteenth century, a number of provincial families accumulated enough 'tax-farming' rights from the government to amass considerable independent wealth.

The prominent Azm family of central Syria, for example, used income from their tax farms in Hama, Homs and Ma'rrat al-Nu'man to finance their meteoric social and economic ascent. The Azms went on to purchase properties in Damascus and later monopolized the position of city governor for nearly fifty years. The most famous member of the family, As'ad Pasha, was responsible for building caravanserais, mosques and schools, as well as such impressive architectural landmarks as the Azm Palace, located in the very heart of the Old City of Damascus.[3] In the Syrian towns of the empire, grand families of notables (*a'yan*) such as the Azms essentially acted as intermediaries between the local population and the central Ottoman authorities. The unusual ability to adapt imperial governance to fit the nuances of local context allowed the Ottomans to maintain and successfully hold a vast transcontinental empire for hundreds of years.[4]

Skirting the eastern edge of the Mediterranean Sea, from the mountains of Anatolia in the north to the Sinai Desert in the south, was an arc of human settlement known to Arabic speakers as *Bilad al-Sham*, 'the lands of the north' – or, more literally, 'the lands of the left hand', given their location relative to someone facing the rising sun in Arabia. (The moniker of 'the lands of the right hand', in contrast, was reserved for territories in the south: *al-Yaman*, known in English as Yemen). Nurtured by Mediterranean rains, the patchwork of hills, mountains, valleys and farmlands that made up *Bilad al-Sham* was sufficiently rich to produce food to sustain the development of sophisticated urban culture in the cities of Aleppo, Sidon, Tripoli, Nablus, Jerusalem and Damascus. The prominence of this last city – which centuries ago had been the seat of the Ummayyad dynasty – was such that Damascus was often simply referred to as *al-Sham*. The benefits of law and order grew thinner with distance from the cities, as the relatively hospitable Mediterranean coast gave way to steppe and desert to the east. Here, agriculture grew hazardous under the double shadows of Bedouin tribal raids and harsh climatic conditions. The fertile lands that stretched east of Aleppo, along the southern edge of the Taurus Mountains all the way to Mosul, were politically and socially disconnected from the coast. Medieval Arab geographers called this region *al-Jazira* (the 'island' or 'peninsula') in reference to the mighty Euphrates and Tigris rivers that separated the Jazira from *Bilad al-Sham* to the west and *al-'Iraq* (Iraq) to the south-east (see Map 1).[5]

In practical terms, there was little integration between the component parts of *Bilad al-Sham*. The littoral of the eastern

Mediterranean was effectively an archipelago of semi-autonomous regions centred on cities like Damascus, Aleppo or Nablus, and remote, self-contained mountain redoubts such as Jabal al-Duruz (on the edge of the desert south-east of Damascus), Jabal al-Ansariya (along the coast behind Latakia) and Mount Lebanon (overshadowing the tiny seaside village of Beirut).

For administrative purposes, the Ottomans divided *Bilad al-Sham* into four provinces (*eyalat*) – Aleppo, Damascus, Sidon and Tripoli[6] (see Map 2) – but they had abandoned dispatching governors from the capital and instead recognized whichever local notable was capable of consolidating or imposing power for himself. Provincial governors such as the Azms were largely left to their own devices; for the most part, they busied themselves with intriguing against one another and extracting tax revenues from the impoverished peasantry. In terms of external relations, trade routes connected Aleppo to the silks and spices of the East, and Damascus to the pilgrimage caravans bound south to Mecca and Medina, rather than linking the two cities to one other. Around the year 1800, the local population would have recognized they inhabited the same region of the world, but there were few functional networks that rendered this name meaningful in terms of community, politics or economics. The name *Bilad al-Sham* conveyed little more than a rough sense of physical location.

Despite this inauspicious beginning, over the next hundred years *Bilad al-Sham* was transformed from a patchwork of governance structures into a more integrated and increasingly coherent geographical zone. As the eastern Mediterranean was rocked by disruptive waves of trade with Europe, Egyptian military expansionism and the reassertion of Ottoman authority from Istanbul, the inhabitants of *Bilad al-Sham* came to articulate a new-found sense of belonging to their rapidly changing region. Older understandings of place gradually gave way to an emerging sense of identity that, by the late nineteenth century, expressed itself in the adoption of an Arabized version of the Greek name for the old Roman province that had once existed in the region – *Suriya* – or, as English speakers were also starting to call it, 'Syria'.

Early markers of regionalism in the eastern Mediterranean

The first signs of a new geographical consciousness were articulated in the interstices of Ottoman provincial government. Early in the decade, of the 1800s a local strongman, Emir Bashir II, consolidated his position as leader of Mount Lebanon, which was dominated by grand families of Druze and Maronite landowners. Over the next four decades, Bashir II made significant headway in transforming the mountain into a regional powerhouse, skilfully exploiting local geopolitical tensions to advance his agenda. The Ottoman governor of Sidon, Sulayman Pasha, realized that Emir Bashir's peasant army, bound to him by quasi-feudal fealties, was more reliable than his own mercenary troops, a fact that had the potential to tip the balance in the governor's rivalry with the neighbouring province of Damascus. In 1810, the joint forces of Sulayman Pasha and Bashir II entered Damascus, ostensibly to defend the city from the Wahhabi forces of the Arabian Peninsula that had turned to raiding Iraq and Syria after capturing the holy cities of Mecca and Medina several years earlier. After repelling the Wahhabis, Sulayman Pasha displaced the incumbent governor and was given responsibility for administering the province of Damascus in addition to that of Sidon.

The de facto unification of two of the four provinces of *Bilad al-Sham* lasted only a year. Nevertheless, Bashir's new-found influence as the governor's right-hand man immeasurably strengthened his position in Mount Lebanon. First, Bashir dislodged the Druze families from their dominant positions on the mountain and empowered the Maronite Christian elite to take their place. With an eye to the growing taste for silk in Europe, Bashir encouraged his Maronite supporters to cultivate mulberry trees and move into the export business. Coupled with the European preference for trading with fellow Christians (whose Church was in this instance affiliated to Roman Catholicism), Maronite families began to accumulate wealth more quickly than their Druze counterparts. These new merchants began to export grain, tobacco and cotton, in addition to silk. To meet rising demand in France and Britain, many such entrepreneurs turned to suppliers in the Syrian hinterland, both Muslim and Christian. This trade expansion allowed several smaller towns to enjoy their heyday: by 1840, Deir al-Qamar, the emir's centre of operations, had doubled in size, while the population of Zahlé, an interior trade hub in the Biqaa Valley, swelled tenfold in just fifty years.[7] These towns became the epicentres of trading networks that connected merchants across the interior of *Bilad al-Sham* to the ports of the Mediterranean coast.

With taxes from this growing prosperity, Bashir II invested in bridges and roads; he also expanded his administration and sponsored a minor cultural and literary revival. Several decades later, intellectuals across the region would look back on this episode of prosperity as forging the economic and cultural connections that formed the basis for the emergence of a distinctly Syrian identity. These later generations would ruefully speculate what might have happened had the emirate survived 1840, when Bashir was sent into exile. 'His descendants might have ruled every corner of Syria and Lebanon,' mused historian Mikhail Mishaqa (1800–88), 'just as the grandsons of Mehmed Ali Pasha rule the Valley of the Nile.'[8]

Somewhat ironically, it was the very success of this same Mehmed Ali that ended Bashir's experiment at proto-state-building in *Bilad al-Sham*. Under Mehmed Ali's leadership, Egypt became a rising power whose rapid territorial expansion not only turned *Bilad al-Sham* into an arena for conflict between Cairo and Istanbul, but also brought the region to the attention of the great powers of Britain, France and Russia for the first time. To understand this nascent geopolitical struggle, we must first trace how France's invasion of Egypt had set in motion a train of events that in turn led to Egypt's invasion of the lands of Syria.

From the rise of Egypt to the occupation of Syria

In 1798, France launched an occupation of Egypt that would last three years. A force of 50,000 men – including scholars, scientists and engineers, in addition to soldiers – led by the young Napoleon Bonaparte had intended not only to conquer Egypt, but also to bring the torch of liberty and the blessings of modern civilization to a corner of the world considered backward and benighted. In the words of Jean-Baptiste Fourier, a brilliant mathematician who was part of the expedition, the objectives of Napoleon's mission were:

> to abolish the tyranny of the Mamlukes [Egypt's Ottoman military rulers], to extend irrigation and cultivation, to open a constant communication between the Mediterranean and the Arabian Gulf, to form commercial establishments, to offer the Orient the useful example of European industry, finally, to render the constitution of the inhabitants softer and to procure them all the advantages of a perfected civilisation.[9]

To this end, Napoleon's men concocted ambitious plans to modernize Egypt by introducing private property, replacing tax farmers with tax collectors and abolishing an Arabic alphabet they considered irrational in favour of Latin letters they thought to be more capable of expressing modern scientific thought. These visions of development – however ludicrous – illustrate that the French expedition was not simply a military endeavour: the occupation was also intended to plant the seeds of conquest in the realms of science, culture and even the economy. Although the term was not coined until the 1870s, Napoleon's expedition was France's first colonial venture to be couched in the values of *la mission civilisatrice*, the 'civilizing mission'.

The Egyptians themselves were sceptical that the foreigners' military superiority necessarily extended to other domains of civilized life. 'Whenever a Frenchman has to perform an act of nature,' wrote Abd al-Rahman al-Jabarti, the famed chronicler of Napoleon's campaign, in a tone of hushed scandal, 'he does so wherever he happens to be, even in full view of people, and he goes away as he is, without washing his private parts after defecation.'[10] Jabarti was also appalled by the poor quality of foreign experts on the Middle East, whose 'incoherent words and vulgar constructions' revealed their inadequate command of the Arabic language. French efforts to modernize Egypt largely remained confined to the page.

Weakened by disease, wearied by local uprisings and harried by the threat of an Ottoman counter-attack, the last French soldiers and scholars departed Egypt in 1801. Although Napoleon failed to transform Egypt in line with his vision of modern civilization, the French withdrawal left a political vacuum in which previously unknown actors could swiftly rise to prominence. Among the soldiers dispatched to reassert control of the country, Mehmed Ali, a Turkish-speaking Albanian officer, waged a successful military campaign against the old Mamluke elites, and for his efforts was rewarded by Istanbul with the title of Governor of Egypt. In 1811 he cemented his authority by inviting several hundred surviving Mamlukes to a lavish dinner at the citadel of Cairo, then promptly slaughtering them and systematically hunting down their followers. His prowess as a military commander earned him the attention of successive sultans in Istanbul, on whose behalf he undertook campaigns to invade (and effectively annex) Sudan, repress rebellions in the Greek provinces of the empire and reconquer the holy cities of Mecca and Medina that had been captured by Wahhabi rebels.

Mehmed Ali's massacre of the Mamlukes did more than remove his political adversaries: it also eradicated any vested interests that might oppose the radical reforms he was keen to introduce. In 1821–22, he imposed the novel policy of conscription and created the first mass-based army of the Ottoman Empire – much to the chagrin of the Egyptian peasantry, who were forcibly taken from their villages and harshly disciplined to transform them into professionally trained soldiers.[11] Impressed by the speed and scale of Napoleon Bonaparte's advances across Europe, as well as an earlier example of Ottoman military reforms in Istanbul that had stalled due to internal opposition,[12] Mehmed Ali imported French military advisors; he also arranged for delegations of scholars to study science, the arts and languages in Paris, and, on their return to Cairo, to translate their newly acquired knowledge into Arabic. He contemplated a path of rapid development that would transform Egypt into a modern state that would take its rightful place in world affairs alongside the great powers of France, Britain and Russia.

To fund his costly revolution in military affairs, Mehmed Ali pioneered two ground-breaking economic policies. First, he ended the inefficient system of tax farming and introduced the direct collection of taxes by salaried government officials. Second, he abolished the private market for agricultural goods and replaced it with a state monopoly. Peasants were forced to sell to the government their cereals, rice, sugar and beans at prices fixed by the state, which would then sell the crops for much higher prices on the international market. The nationalization of agriculture brought an influx of wealth into state coffers that was used to expand the irrigation system (to which peasants were also forced to contribute their unpaid labour), finance the introduction of long-staple cotton (better suited for modern textile weaving than Egyptian varieties) and support the creation of indigenous textile manufacturing through the founding of some thirty state-run factories (several of which were equipped with precisely the same kinds of advanced industrial technology that could be found in the English cotton mills of Lancashire). Mehmed Ali also established modern arms factories to make muskets, cannons and other munitions, and founded a naval yard at Alexandria to build warships.[13] While Egyptian factories may not have been as efficient as their British counterparts, he set in motion the beginnings of an impressive fiscal–military–industrial machine, fuelled by the state's appropriation of agricultural profits from the peasantry.

In the late 1820s, Mehmed Ali asked for his exemplary record of military service to the sultan to be recognized by granting him the additional right to govern the rich forests and agricultural lands of *Bilad al-Sham*. His request was refused. In response, he turned his conscript army northwards, and in 1831 launched an invasion to take the region for himself. His conquest advanced relentlessly. One after another, Jaffa, Haifa, Acre, Jerusalem, Beirut, Damascus and Tripoli fell or surrendered to his forces. Mehmed Ali's son Ibrahim Pasha defeated the Ottoman battalions sent to halt his advance and swept forward, victorious, all the way to the edge of Anatolia before a truce was finally brokered: Istanbul granted Mehmed Ali rule over its Levantine provinces. From 1833 to 1840, the whole of *Bilad al-Sham* – from the towns of Jaffa and Jerusalem all the way north to Aleppo and the district of Adana – were for the first time unified under one governor, Ibrahim Pasha. The Egyptian administration of this new province of *Arabistan*, as it was officially known, presided over a period of surprising prosperity and delivered palpable improvements in governance, economic activity and rural security. At the same time, Ibrahim Pasha's policies upset the delicate balance of power between different social groups across the Syrian lands, in some places provoking unforeseen resistance or stoking the fire of communal tensions.

Ibrahim Pasha experimented with introducing to *Bilad al-Sham* the same kind of modernizing reforms that his father had pioneered in Egypt. The immediate motivation was to raise funds to sustain the tens of thousands of Egyptian troops stationed in the region. Although it proved impossible to replace tax farming with salaried government tax collectors as in Egypt, the overall fiscal situation was improved by auctioning off tax-farming rights for much higher amounts and increasing tax rates in general. In addition, a new individual poll tax was to be collected from Muslims, Christians and Jews alike. In every city, Ibrahim Pasha established a consultative assembly comprised of the governor and local notables, with the power to oversee laws governing economic and criminal activities that had previously been dealt with by Islamic courts. These initiatives represented an unprecedented shift towards secularism and representative government.

The heavy presence of so many soldiers brought security to rural areas, allowing peasants to cultivate land further from home with less fear of brigandage or Bedouin raids. Ibrahim Pasha also granted land rights and tax exemptions to Bedouin shaykhs to entice them to leave their nomadic ways and adopt a sedentary life in the Euphrates Valley, southern Palestine and the Jordan

Valley. These measures were remarkably successful at resettling parts of rural *Bilad al-Sham* that had long been abandoned. A report prepared for Ibrahim Pasha in 1836, for example, noted that eighty-five villages had already been rebuilt in the countryside east of Aleppo, and the reconstruction of a further eighty-five was planned.[14] Ibrahim Pasha's reach extended far beyond the safe confines of the settled Mediterranean coast. In 1835, Ibrahim Pasha founded a garrison in the village of Deir al-Zour, on the distant Euphrates River in the sparsely populated eastern desert, partly to defend against Wahhabi incursions from the Arabian Peninsula. The new garrison provided security that allowed for a steady resettlement of hamlets along the Euphrates Valley.

Reactions to these developments were mixed. The notable families of Damascus welcomed Ibrahim Pasha's arrival, which forced out an Ottoman-appointed governor towards whom their goodwill had long dissipated. Emir Bashir II of Mount Lebanon went further and supplied troops to Ibrahim Pasha to assist his campaign. The significant presence of Maronites in Bashir's militia, not to mention the fact that Christians were for the first time allowed a formal seat in government on Ibrahim Pasha's new consultative assembly and were invited to play prominent roles in his administration, won the Egyptians many supporters from the various Christian communities. The Sunni Muslim religious hierarchy, in contrast, was concerned that the privileges newly accorded to Christians seemed to come at their expense. 'The government has turned into a state for Christians,' went the common complaint. 'The Islamic state is over!' Opposition to Ibrahim Pasha among some religious scholars was pronounced: Shaykh Muhammad Amin ibn Abidin, for example, went to the extreme of declaring that the Ottoman ruler in Istanbul was not simply a sultan (a term denoting political authority) but a caliph – the ruler of all Muslims, against whom rebellion was forbidden by religion.[15] In making this claim, Shaykh Ibn Abidin was essentially proclaiming that Ibrahim Pasha's policies could only be those carried out by an infidel – a stark rejection of his rule.

Outside the cities, peasants took advantage of the opportunity to expand cultivation only under the ever present risk of conscription into the Egyptian army.[16] Many young men fled their villages to seek refuge in the hills, among the Bedouin, or in the lands of the Jazira that lay beyond the reach of Egyptian rule.[17] Conversely, rural peripheries with strong local elites – including the Jabal al-Duruz, Jabal al-Ansariya and the Palestinian hills around Nablus – mounted armed resistance to preserve their independence from Ibrahim Pasha's central government.[18] In 1838, the Druze of the Hawran notably launched an insurrection against Egyptian rule that attracted their disaffected co-religionists from Mount Lebanon. After defeating several Egyptian expeditions, Druze rebels closed on Damascus and incited local villagers to join them against the occupation; the rebellion then spread to Wadi al-Taym in present-day Lebanon, where it was defeated only with the help of the army of Emir Bashir II. By relying on Bashir's Maronite forces to repress a Druze uprising, Ibrahim Pasha inadvertently exacerbated the animosity of an aggrieved population already suspicious of his Christian sympathies. At the same time, the Egyptian concern for order led them to insist that even the Maronites disarm, a move that was interpreted as a prelude to forced conscription and caused the Maronite elite to withdraw their support. At this point the Maronites turned against their erstwhile commander, Bashir – who was now dismissed as a mere Egyptian vassal – and reconciled with the Druze in joint opposition to Ibrahim Pasha. In June 1840, a cross-communal insurrection swept Mount Lebanon and its surrounds, which echoed with calls to end conscription, disarmament, forced labour and excessive taxation. Ibrahim Pasha could defeat this mounting insurgency only by harsh methods, namely a blockade that starved the area of fresh supplies of food and weaponry.[19] With local resistance unable to dislodge his rule, Ibrahim Pasha seemed unstoppable.

Had the Egyptian occupation continued, Ibrahim Pasha might eventually have introduced to *Bilad al-Sham* the kind of drastic reforms that had transformed the face of Egypt and reoriented its economy towards agricultural exports and industrial production. However, the rise of Egypt threatened to unsettle the balance of power between the great powers, who swiftly intervened to end this novel political experiment. Britain, Prussia and Russia considered the Ottoman Empire to provide a useful bulwark against one another's territorial aspirations: any significant internal fracturing of Ottoman power therefore required buttressing to prevent a general great power land grab. In 1838, Mehmed Ali began openly to discuss independence from Istanbul, and *Bilad al-Sham* found itself thrust into the international limelight as the great powers sought to contain Egypt. Lacking an equivalent term for the lands of Damascus in their native languages, French and British diplomats fell back on the name of an old Roman province – Syria – that overlapped with much of the region. Ottoman officials subsequently began to refer to *Bilad al-Sham* with the same name (*Suriye* in Ottoman Turkish) in their return correspondence to Paris and London.

As Palmerston, the British foreign secretary, noted, the objective of putting Mehmed Ali back in his box was entirely self-interested:

> Coercion of Mehemet [Mehmed] Ali by England if war broke out might appear partial and unjust; but we *are* partial [emphasis added . . .] The maintenance of the Turkish empire [. . .] is essential for the preservation of peace, and for the upholding of the independence of Eastern Europe. A partition of Turkey would be fatal to the independence of Austria and Prussia

> [...] and it could not be accomplished without a general war. No ideas therefore of fairness towards Mehemet ought to stand in the way of such great and paramount interests.[20]

To secure these 'great and paramount interests', in 1840, the three powers pressured the adolescent Ottoman Sultan Abdülmecid I to issue an ultimatum: Mehmed Ali would be granted governorship over Egypt and the Palestinian district of Acre in southern Syria for life, in exchange for relinquishing the rest of the lands currently held by his son Ibrahim Pasha. France backed Mehmed Ali and Ibrahim Pasha, whom they saw as viable replacements for ineffective sultans in Istanbul but stayed out of the negotiations: its strategic vision could not be reconciled with the French monarchy's ideological claim to be the worldwide protector of Catholics, given the widespread Maronite opposition to Egyptian rule in Mount Lebanon. The other great powers took advantage of French wavering to supply the insurrection with arms and win back Maronite support. When Mehmed Ali refused to accept Istanbul's ultimatum, the British navy bombarded Beirut and a joint force of over 8,000 Ottoman, British and Austrian troops landed on the coast. The allied forces occupied town after town; the Egyptian army retreated before its advances. By November, Ibrahim Pasha had begun to withdraw from the Syrian provinces. His henchman Bashir II promptly fled Mount Lebanon and hopped on a British ship to carry him in exile to Malta.

The intervention of the great powers did more than simply eject Mehmed Ali from Syria. In 1838, Britain had pressured the sultan to accept the Anglo-Turkish Commercial Convention, which both enforced free trade and abolished monopolies throughout the empire. The convention thus outlawed the economic motor that had powered Mehmed Ali's military expansion in the first place; it now ensured that Egypt would never attain great power status.[21] Britain's imposition of free trade also removed the tariffs that had protected Ottoman markets from foreign competition, effectively guaranteeing that any effort to build up a local industrial base would be wrecked by a flood of cheap imports from overseas.

For its part, *Bilad al-Sham* was negatively affected by the withdrawal of Egyptian troops in 1840. The Ottoman appointees who returned to govern the Syrian provinces lacked both the military and the economic power needed to replicate the Egyptian model. Land owning notable families recommenced their exploitation of the tax-farming system and consolidated their positions by taking over the newly established town councils. Villages were abandoned, Bedouin tribes returned to nomadism and roads once again became unsafe; uncultivated fields on the fringes of the settled lands were swallowed by the advancing desert. Not until the 1860s was the reform agenda taken up again. This time, its effects would prove irreversible.

The Tanzimat reforms (1839–1876)

After territorial losses to Russia in the 1770s and the challenge of Mehmed Ali in the 1830s, Istanbul felt the need for change more urgently than ever. In the mid-nineteenth century, Ottoman officials inaugurated a new age of reforms collectively known as the Tanzimat. Launched by the gloriously named Noble Edict of the Rose Chamber (*Gülhane Hatt-ı Şerif*) of 1839 and the more prosaically named Imperial Edict (*Hatt-ı Hümayun*) of 1856, the Tanzimat aimed to overhaul Ottoman law, administration and finances to bring the empire up to date with the other great powers of the day, especially France and Britain. These reforms were numerous and multi-faceted – and highly unsettling for the status quo across the empire.

In terms of their impact on *Bilad al-Sham*, two components of the Tanzimat proved particularly consequential. First, all inhabitants of the empire were guaranteed equality before the law, regardless of religion or sect. This secularizing trend continued in 1869, when a new law of nationality declared that Muslim, Christian and Jewish communities were henceforth 'Ottomans' of equal standing, rather than religious groups with different rights and duties. Ottoman subjects were incorporated into a single legal jurisdiction (apart from the domain of family affairs, which remained under the authority of each *millet*). A new system of universally applicable law was systematically detailed in the *Majalla*, a colossal intellectual undertaking comprising sixteen volumes of codified laws and regulations that outlived the Ottoman Empire and remained in force in Syria – and across much of the Middle East – during British and French rule after the First World War. What these secularizing reforms meant for the empire's established elites was not at the time self-evident. The upper classes of cities such as Damascus and Aleppo had long legitimized their position and prestige, after all, on the grounds that they were Muslims living in an Islamic empire.

The second crucial component of the Tanzimat came in the Land Code of 1858. This law officially abolished the widespread practice of communal land tenure and replaced it with a system of individual property rights in which ownership would be recorded in official government registers. The new system was intended to reproduce the shift from common land to private property that had occurred in Britain in the previous century, when the 'enclosure of the commons' had been credited with inspiring an agricultural revolution. Ottoman reformers believed that when individuals were granted permanent legal title to their land, they would similarly come to consider agriculture a productive business rather than a mere source of subsistence. Landowners would then invest in long-term improvements such as irrigation, to raise agricultural productivity. The new registers of land deeds would also facilitate government taxation of agriculture, the main economic activity across the empire. These enhanced revenues would then feed back into Istanbul's ongoing military modernization and deepening administrative reforms.

The reforms of the Tanzimat were intended to meet multiple objectives. Besides raising revenue to fund military modernization, they injected an element of secular modernity that enabled the Ottoman Empire to assert its credentials as a legitimate player in the European state system, alongside France and Britain, Austria and Russia. Guaranteeing equality to all inhabitants of the empire regardless of religion, for example, helped Istanbul defend against claims that Christians were discriminated against by Muslims and needed international intervention to guarantee their protection. In 1856, the Ottoman Empire was admitted to the Concert of Europe, and its territorial integrity was recognized by co-signatories to the Treaty of Paris that ended the Crimean War. Nevertheless, over the following years, European powers repeatedly invoked fears of sectarian conflict to justify their continuing interference in the domestic affairs of the empire.

Although the reforms were inspired by what were thought to be the best practices of rival great powers – France's rationalized administrative system, Austria's absolutist bureaucracy, Britain's enclosure of the commons – mid-century Ottomans did not see the Tanzimat as Westernization. Instead, they considered reform a technocratic device by means of which they could engineer a stronger and more efficient state. There was no particular sense of a civilization divide between 'East and West' or 'Islam and Christianity': the Ottoman elite saw themselves as members of the same category of civilized countries as Britain, France and Russia. Much as such countries as Spain or Sweden – or even

Russia – were adopting from Paris and London the most modern techniques of warfare and administration, the Ottomans saw themselves as engaged in a similar process of intergovernmental learning, not inter-civilizational borrowing.

This point is illustrated in the work of the prolific Egyptian intellectual Rif'at al-Tahtawi, who had been part of Mehmed Ali's scholarly delegation to Paris. In his famous 1848 account of his travels, Tahtawi observed that the world contains three stages of human development.[22] The first is that of 'savages' (*al-mutawahhishun*), such as are found in sub-Saharan Africa. The second stage is 'barbarism' (*al-barabira*), of which the Arab Bedouin tribes provide the prime example. The most elevated stage of humanity is highly cultured, refined, civilized and urbanized (*ahl al-adab wa'l-zarafa wa'l-tahaddur wa'l-tamaddun wa'l-tamassur al-mutatarrifin*) and is concentrated in Europe, Egypt, Syria, Anatolia, Yemen, Persia and – opined Tahtawi – 'parts of' North America and Oceania. Tahtawi and other learned men of the Ottoman provinces identified themselves as belonging not to a backwards or underdeveloped country, but to a broader civilization that was global in scale and expansive in scope.

From Tahtawi's perspective, the presence of 'savage' populations in Ottoman lands outside the cities inhabited by the privileged elite by no means disqualified the empire from its claim to be part of modern civilization. The presence of native tribes in North America, after all, did not mean that the United States was pre-modern. Even the modernizing elites of Western Europe, it should be remembered, would at this time regard the impoverished inhabitants of their own rural areas with something akin to abject disgust. A French landowner in 1865, for example, colourfully described the peasants of Limousin as 'animals with two feet, hardly resembling a man. [The peasant's] clothes are filthy; under his thick skin one cannot see the blood flow. The wild, dull gaze betrays no flicker of thought in the brain of this being, morally and physically atrophied.' Other observers opined that schoolchildren in Brittany were 'like those of countries where civilization has not penetrated: savage, dirty, and don't understand a word of the language.'[23] In sociological terms, urban elites in different countries often saw themselves as having more in common with their foreign counterparts than with their own rural compatriots.

Sophisticated urban Ottomans would similarly look at rural populations like the Maronite Christians or Druze of Mount Lebanon as little more than barbarians. Indeed, the Ottoman Sultan Abdulhamid was once heard to remark that Anatolia was home to 'people whose comportment was similar to savage tribes in America'.[24] Arab and Kurdish tribes were considered so wild that they required 'civilizing' through state-led campaigns of sedentarization, education and religious schooling as, in the words of Ottoman officials, they lived 'in a state of nomadism and savagery'.[25] More remote parts of the empire, such as Yemen, were viewed as so underdeveloped that Ottoman reformers even contemplated installing European-style colonies there, to spread civilization to the rebellious subjects of Arabia Felix. The Egyptian modernizer Mehmed Ali adopted a similar position vis-à-vis the recently conquered Sudanese, who were enslaved to work in the army and agriculture. In the nineteenth century, nothing was more emblematic of cutting-edge modernity than cultural supremacy and settler colonialism.

The Tanzimat reforms are sometimes described as if they were undertaken in blind imitation of the West, as if the Ottomans were importing European policies into new territories. This portrayal is misleading. Alongside the Ottoman Empire, much of Europe was itself involved in a similar process of reforming their pre-modern kingdoms, principalities and empires in response to the new ideas of equality and citizenship that had been unleashed by the American, French and Haitian revolutions and the fast-paced evolution of capitalism after the Industrial Revolution. The Ottoman Tanzimat are best conceived not as the Middle East attempting to catch up with the West, but as part of a generalized reconfiguration of relations between state, society and economy that swept the world in the nineteenth century.

The Ottoman Land Code of 1858 finds parallels, for example, in Mexico's *Ley de desamortización* of 1856, the British proclamation of 1858 in Northern India and the Dutch Agrarian Land Law in Indonesia of 1870, all of which sought to replace communal systems of land tenure with individual property rights. As political scientist Joel Migdal observes: 'Legislation and administrative decrees changing proprietary and social relationships to the land could be found from South America to East Asia [. . .] As if in a flash, government after government came to see the hidden potential of changing landholding rights.'[26] Similarly, deliberate nation-building efforts such as the French state's nineteenth-century campaign to 'civilize' its peasantry by forcibly refashioning their regional identities into the homogenized category of 'Frenchmen', or British efforts to 'educate' its recalcitrant Welsh fringe, were replicated by Ottoman modernizers in their own rural and nomadic peripheries. Rather than being divided by any putative clash of civilizations, Ottoman reformers saw themselves, alongside British and French urban elites, as members of a unitary civilization that was slowly spreading from the orderly, educated realm of the city to the wild, savage and unregulated rural reaches beyond.

Perhaps inevitably, the success of such ambitious reforms was incomplete. State-led modernization rarely followed the original plan, but was typically resisted or subverted by local actors, or else encountered the quirks of pre-existing patterns of social organization and economic activity in ways that shaped the implementation of the reforms in complex and unpredictable ways. Although the Tanzimat reforms were in theory to be applied consistently throughout the empire to create a regular and standardized system, the diverse conditions of the Ottoman provinces meant that it was impossible to control the implementation of the reforms. Even within such a relatively small part of the empire as *Bilad al-Sham*, the implementation of the Tanzimat produced an uneven array of highly localized consequences. The Tanzimat reforms accelerated the pace of social transformation, prompting waves of communal violence and peasant uprisings that shook the status quo, both generating new divisions and forging new connections across the lands of Syria.

Upsetting the status quo: reforms, economy, violence (1840s–1860s)

After the Egyptian withdrawal in 1840, Ottoman authority needed to be reasserted before the Tanzimat could be implemented in the Syrian provinces. The northern city of Aleppo was the first to return to the fold. Since at least the sixteenth century, Aleppo had been autonomous from Damascus and was an administrative centre in its own right: the city acted as an economic hub for southern Anatolia, had its own trade ties with the East and was for these reasons largely uninvolved with the south of *Bilad al-Sham*. After the departure of Ibrahim Pasha, Ottoman troops re-entered Aleppo, and, a year later, the newly appointed Ottoman governor revealed to the townsfolk the contents of the 1839 Noble Edict of the Rose Chamber, which stipulated that Christians were considered loyal subjects under the protection of the sultan. Buoyed by this support, the Christian community in Aleppo became more confident and visible, prompting concern among the local Muslim elite that Christian empowerment would come at their expense.

In this context, the introduction of a new, egalitarian poll tax proved provocative. In the past only Jewish and Christians had been obliged to pay the special poll tax, but now it seemed that Muslims had lost their privileged status. In October 1850, a sizeable crowd rallied around the Ottoman governor's residence in Aleppo to protest against the reintroduction of conscription that many feared would follow the poll tax. When the governor fled the city, the crowd turned its anger against shops and Christian neighbourhoods, the residents of which were identified as sympathizers to the Tanzimat cause. A day of looting saw twenty dead and a hundred injured, as well as the destruction of several churches.

The international community of the day – including Britain, Russia, Germany and France – protested at this treatment of Christians. In response, the Ottoman army suppressed the protests by heavily shelling neighbourhoods of Aleppo with modern artillery recently supplied by Britain. Over 3,000 inhabitants of Aleppo were killed in the bombing. Far from expressing outrage, the international community applauded what they saw as an unusually decisive Ottoman response. As the British Consul in Aleppo put it, 'this lesson will serve to make the Islams [*sic*] generally in the north of Syria obedient' to a government he described as usually 'rather too mild [...] for such barbarians'.[27]

Southern *Bilad al-Sham* did not fully return to Ottoman control until a decade after the reconquest of Aleppo, when a severe episode of communal violence broke out. The 1860 Damascus massacre was partly a reaction to the changing relative status of social groups in uncertain economic times, just as it had been in Aleppo. In Damascus, the position of Muslim notables appeared to be in relative decline for three reasons. First, Christians and Jews had benefitted more than Muslims from the expansion of international trade as European merchants preferred to use their co-religionists as their agents. Although the expansion of European industry and trade spelled declining markets for Damascene textiles in general, Christian merchants were able to retain a greater market share than their Muslim counterparts thanks to their closer contacts with overseas buyers. Second, Christians and Jews were granted representation on the local council in Damascus. Third, the economic decline of southern Syria after the Egyptian withdrawal had led to a steep decline in tax revenues. The governor of Damascus had therefore sought to finance government activities by issuing short-term bonds, many of which had been purchased by local Christian and Jewish financiers. In lieu of earning interest on the bonds, the cash-strapped local government granted bondholders the right to collect taxes from certain villages. Once again, the new economic power accruing to Christians and Jews set them in competition with the better-established Muslim families, who feared these newcomers might acquire rival tax-farming rights. Tension was further heightened by harvest failures in 1859 and 1860, which caused the price of bread to soar.

While communal violence can never be entirely attributed merely to declining economic fortunes, the context of the changing socio-economic positions of Christian and Muslim elites is essential for understanding the outbreak of eight days of violence in which an estimated 8,000 people were killed, primarily in Bab Touma, the Christian quarter of the Old City of Damascus. Widespread looting and destruction also targeted looms and textiles workshops owned by Christians.[28] Although Muslim notables were reluctant or perhaps powerless to influence the mobs, local leaders in the vibrant commercial neighbourhood of the Maydan did speak out to protect their Christian neighbours in Bab Musalla from attack.[29]

In response to this violence, 4,000 Ottoman troops belonging to the Fifth Army Corps marched into Damascus to restore calm. As in Aleppo, this decisive move was motivated less by concerns over the loss of human life than by the desire to preempt Britain, France and Russia from invoking Christian massacres once again as a pretext to intervene in the empire's domestic affairs and to impose settlements favourable to their own strategic interests. The Ottoman governor, Fu'ad Pasha, executed 170 men and ordered Muslim notables to compensate the Christians for their financial losses. Several members of the local Muslim elite were also exiled to Cyprus as a warning to their peers to uphold more energetically the responsibility to protect should a similar conflict break out again in future. The second-tier leaders of the Maydan, in contrast, were rewarded for their bravery with additional seats on the city administrative council, alongside the established aristocratic families of the Old City.

The renewed army presence in Damascus and Aleppo allowed security to extend to the surrounding regions. With the desert fringes once again secured against Bedouin raids, a series of new villages and farms were founded: east of Aleppo, along the Euphrates River, in the countryside east of Homs and Hama and in the Hawran and northern Transjordan. Several prominent towns and villages trace their origins to this time. The village of Salamiyya, on the edge of the desert south-east of Hama, was resettled by Isma'ili migrants from the coastal mountains and grew large enough to be named the centre of a new administrative district in 1883. The previously abandoned town of Raqqa was similarly resettled in the 1850s. By 1870, even the still largely uninhabited and unsettled Euphrates Valley, in which the Egyptians had situated a garrison, was sufficiently pacified to merit elevation to a new administrative district. What had once been a mere military outpost at Deir al-Zour was now growing into a large town in its own right.

The expansion of settlements and cultivation was also fed by refugee inflows from the Caucasus, seized from the Ottomans by Russia in the 1870s. Some 30,000 Circassians, Chechens and Daghestanis were resettled near to Qunaytra, south-west of Damascus, and further south, in Transjordan, as well as in the countryside north-east of Homs and along the coast south of Latakia. It was in the context of this self-reinforcing expansion in population, cultivation and security – and the resulting expansion in the tax base of the Syrian provinces – that the Ottoman authorities started to implement arguably the most important of all the Tanzimat reforms: individual property rights.

Privatizing property: the Land Code of 1858

Before modern property rights were rolled out across the Levant, much agricultural land was farmed according to a communal system known as *musha'*. Villages would divide the nearby farmland into rectangular strips, assign the right to farm the strips to different families and then periodically rotate the assignment to balance out any inequalities in soil, irrigation or exposure. The precise way in which the assignment and rotation of fields was organized varied from place to place, depending on crops, climate and family relations in the village. *Musha'* was flexible, reflecting both local geographical conditions and the social balance of power.[30]

One advantage of *musha'* was that it spread risk among all the members of the community. In much of Syria, the combination of erratic rainfall and lack of irrigation meant that harvests were often hostage to the whim of the climate: drought was a perennial concern. Ottoman reformers nevertheless maintained that communal land ownership made cultivators disinclined to make long-term investments in the land and compounded the difficulties of taxing agriculture. The 1858 Land Code therefore introduced a compulsory system of land registration: individual peasants were to henceforth record their legal claims in land registers maintained by the government (*defterkhane*), strengthening individual property rights, as well as the state's ability to calculate and pursue tax collection. The reforms fell short of guaranteeing the absolute right of private property as had become common in Western Europe and its colonies, even though this category of land ownership (*mulk*) did exist under Ottoman law and was common in cities. Instead, the 1858 Land Code granted peasants the right of usufruct over state-owned rural land, meaning that their ownership rights to registered land was conditional upon its continued cultivation; abandoned land could be reclaimed by the state. Nevertheless, the Land Code enacted the first step of a process that would, by the mid-twentieth century, eventually develop into the legal institution of fully fledged private property in Syria.

Although the 1858 Land Code was intended to guarantee individual property rights, ironically it produced almost exactly the opposite effect. Instead of breaking the power of the local elites who mediated between the peasantry and the central state, the reforms accelerated the concentration of land in the hands of a small number of wealthy families who exercised over their tenant farmers a new level of social control so complete that it almost resembled feudalism. In only a small part of the country were peasants able to resist the expropriation of their communal land rights by notable families. The variations in this pattern can best be explored by focusing on five regions: (i) the Syrian interior, from Aleppo in the north to Damascus in the south; (ii) Mount

Lebanon; (iii) the Hawran region, south of Damascus; (iv) Jabal al-Ansariya, the mountains along Syria's Mediterranean coast; and (v) the lands to the east of *Bilad al-Sham*, including the Jazira and the desert.

The Syrian interior: Damascus, Aleppo, Homs, Hama

Given that their previous encounters with the Ottoman state had invariably involved either taxation or conscription, peasants were understandably suspicious of government institutions and did not necessarily grasp the legal implications of the 1858 Land Code. Notable families, in contrast, were quick to register lands formally in their own name. In some cases, they promised to deal with the red tape and safeguard the peasants against the predations of the state; in others, they purchased lands forfeited by smallholders who could no longer afford the continuing costs of debt or bad harvests. The new system of land registration provided a vehicle for what was effectively the legal robbery of the peasantry. Growing numbers of peasants became tenants of the legal landowner who lived in the city but accumulated sizeable tracts – often entire villages – of surrounding agricultural land. These absentee landlords would extract every ounce of profit from the peasants who now laboured on their farms as tenant sharecroppers.

The terms of the sharecropping arrangement varied across the Syrian interior. One common agreement saw the landowner provide the peasant with a house, land and seed in exchange for three-quarters of the harvest; the peasant and his family would have to survive on the remaining quarter. In Hama, the landowner contributed a house and land and paid half the cost of taxes and seeds, leaving the peasant to pay the other half; the harvest was then split half and half. Elsewhere, a 70:30 ratio split in favour of the landlord could be encountered. Given the erratic rainfall and high chance of harvest failure, the terms of the deal often left peasant families penniless and starving.

As Syrian historian Abdullah Hanna has pointed out, sharecropping left peasants constantly fearful of hunger, eviction and even death: the all-powerful landowner could evict them and their families arbitrarily and without prior notice.[31] To mitigate the uncertainty of the harvest, peasants had little choice but to borrow from moneylenders to feed their families or buy seed to sow the following year. These crisis loans came with usurious rates of interest, from 9 to 20 per cent, or even 40 or 45 per cent at times of widespread crop failure. In some parts of the interior, most notoriously in the countryside around Hama, the economic power of the landowner was translated into oppressive social control: landowners dominated every dimension of peasants' lives. They would decide which crops the peasants should plant and when the peasants should harvest them; they would requisition peasants' unpaid labour for the upkeep of their own fields and luxurious mansions; their consent would even be required before peasants were permitted to marry.

In the villages, order was maintained by thuggish strongmen in the pay of the notables, who preferred to maintain their urban residences and rarely visited their farms. The tenuous economic situation of the peasantry also manifested itself in an engrained deference towards their ostensible social superiors, in whose hands their fate rested. Critics of the oppressive ties between notables and peasants described this relationship as akin to that binding the serfs of medieval Europe to their aristocratic lords and masters. This Levantine form of feudalism (*iqta'*) was remarkably well entrenched and endured well into the 1940s and 1950s, until the emergence of a Syrian leftist movement that sought to liberate the peasantry from the strictures of feudal patterns of land tenure. In the meantime, a handful of landowning families rose to social and economic prominence in the four towns of the Syrian interior.

In Damascus, the most famous of these grand families included the Azm, Mardam-Beg, Quwwatli, Sham'a, Barudi, 'Ajlani, Ghazzi and Kaylanis. In Aleppo, the Jabiri, Mudarris, Qudsi and Kayyali were all prominent names; Homs was home to the prestigious Atasi family, along with the Rifa'i and Jundi families. The hold of feudal landowners was especially strong in Hama, which was dominated by just four families: Azm, Tayfur, Kilani and Barazi. The wealth and pomp of Hama's notables was captured by British traveller Gertrude Bell, who visited in 1906:

> Four powerful Mohammadan families are reckoned as the aristocracy of that town, that of Azam Zadeh, Teifur, Killani and Barazi . . . The combined income of each family is probably about £6000 a year, all derived from land and villages, there being little trade in Hamah. Before the Ottoman government was established as firmly as it is now, these four families were the lords of Hamah and the surrounding districts; they are still of considerable weight in the administration of the town, and the officials of the Sultan let them go pretty much their own way . . . I went to the house of Khalid Beg Azam, which is the most beautiful in the city, as beautiful as the famous Azam house in Damascus . . . The Killani I visited also in their charming house by the Orontes, the Tekyah Killaniyyeh. It contains a mausoleum, where three of their ancestors are buried.[32]

In contrast to the grand families' income of £6,000, Bell estimated that the poorest peasant families earned just £7 to £11 each year.

Not every town's agricultural hinterland was characterized by the stark economic inequalities witnessed by Bell. Peasants tending the fruit orchards in the Ghouta oasis surrounding Damascus, for example, benefitted from the commercial viability of their produce, especially apricots, which they would process at home into a paste for sale across southern *Bilad al-Sham* and Egypt. The extra revenue insulated them from some of the pressures of debt and repossession, which meant that smallholdings were more common.[33] However, the distance between the grand families and the rest of the population was generally so wide that the noble scions of these families could, even decades later, rely on their family name (not to mention family fortune) to support their political careers. Many of the notable families who dominated Syrian politics well into the mid-twentieth century owed their position and prominence to opportunities granted by the 1858 Land Code. By the beginning of the twentieth century, these landowning families had consolidated their collective position thanks to intermarriages, mutual alliances and common interests. While the Ottoman authorities would still nominate the official governors of Damascus and Aleppo, notable families otherwise formed the social, economic and political elites of these towns.

Other parts of *Bilad al-Sham* were less hospitable to the *iqta'* system. Peasants in these regions proved less acquiescent to elite efforts to accumulate economic power, leading to a series of intense and sustained political struggles that aimed at a more equitable division of wealth. These dynamics were especially visible in Mount Lebanon and the Hawran.

Mount Lebanon

Behind the port of Beirut stretch the verdant yet difficult-to-access slopes of Mount Lebanon, inhabited by a mixed population of Druze and Maronite Christians. The evolution of the very particular situation of this mountain had important ramifications for the rest of the region. In contrast to the Syrian interior, feudalism never really found its footing on Mount Lebanon. In part, simple geography explains this divergence: fragmented parcels of mountainous terrain are more difficult to exploit, expropriate and consolidate than grain-producing farmlands and orchards in the lowlands. But international economics also played a role. The silk industry originally incubated by Emir Bashir II underwent a colossal expansion after the 1850s, owing to prodigious investments from French businessmen. This influx of capital provided local peasants and entrepreneurs with a source of income outside the control of the Maronite and Druze elites, who consequently found it difficult to enforce their traditional rights to tax collection, due deference and social obligation. In addition, the sway of the notables was threatened by political challenge from below.

In 1858–59, Maronite commoners rose up against the notable families that controlled the Kisrawan district of Mount Lebanon. Although the peasants initially protested excessive taxation, their demands soon escalated to include equality with the notables and formal representation in government. The peasants chased the prominent Khazin family off their land, looted their homes, and seized back their harvests. The rebels invoked the Tanzimat reforms in justification of their rebellion, although the Ottomans had only intended their support for equality *between* religious sects, not *within* them: the notion of redistributing resources from rich to poor was alien to even the most ardent Ottoman modernizer. Similarly, the Maronite notables of Mount Lebanon found unthinkable the suggestion that the Maronite peasantry should play an active part in political life. The rebels had other ideas. Calling themselves 'the people [*ahali*] of Kisrawan', this grassroots movement broke new historical ground by making one of the first appeals to the notion of popular sovereignty in the Middle East.[34]

Despite its progressive dimensions, the Kisrawan uprising rapidly acquired sectarian connotations as its initial focus on Maronite notables expanded to include Druze areas. Just as the changing balance of power between religious communities in a context of rapid socio-economic change had provoked communal clashes in Aleppo in 1850, and subsequently in Damascus in 1860, so too did Mount Lebanon find it impossible to avoid communal violence between its Christian and Druze inhabitants. The resulting clashes were more intense than anywhere in the Syrian interior: during the winter and spring of 1860, thousands of people were killed and as many as two hundred villages destroyed.

The scale of the fighting prompted the European powers to force the Ottoman Empire to instate a special administrative status in Mount Lebanon, the *Règlement organique* of 1861, that was intended to safeguard Christian autonomy. A Catholic governor (*mutasarrif*) would be appointed to the mountain, advised by a twelve-man council whose seats were initially divided equally between the different sects (Catholic, Greek Orthodox, Shia and Sunni, in addition to Maronite and Druze), but subsequently readjusted in closer reflection of what was argued to be demographic reality (four to the Maronites, three to the Druze, two for the Greek Orthodox and Greek Catholic, and one for the smaller Sunni and Shia populations). In this way, the 1861 *Règlement* inscribed confessionalism, mediated through the elites of each religious community, into the formal institutions of Lebanese government.[35] The *Règlement* also formally abolished the institution of tax farming – the only place in *Bilad al-Sham* where this was true – thereby preventing the grand families of Mount Lebanon from exploiting this particular method of accumulating wealth.[36] Over time, the elites turned their attention away from feudal-style agriculture to commerce and finance, helping to construct Lebanon's reputation as an outward-looking republic of traders.[37] Because of this early inhibition of the landowning class, the trajectory of Lebanese politics after independence was marked more by intra-elite confessional struggles than by the quest for social justice through land reform that would shape the face of neighbouring Syria for the next hundred years.

The Hawran Plain and Mountain

Rural uprisings against the consolidation of landholdings by the elite were rare in the Syrian interior, with the notable exception of the Hawran region, south of Damascus. This region was comprised of two distinct areas: the sparsely populated Hawran plain, which stretched from east of the Sea of Galilee all the way to north-western Jordan (including the governorate of Der'a that exists in Syria today); and the adjoining elevated volcanic plateau to the east that underwent several changes of name over the years, but was known until the 1850s as Jabal Hawran (Mount Hawran, roughly corresponding to today's governorate of Suwayda).

Jabal Hawran had been settled in the seventeenth and eighteenth centuries by Druze from the Shouf and Wadi al-Taym in present-day Lebanon, and later waves of migrants from the Galilee, Mount Carmel and, near Aleppo, Jabal al-A'la. These Druze newcomers displaced local Sunni families such as the Suwaydan and al-Zu'bi, who retreated west to the plains, although a small number of Christians continued to live on the Mountain. Although the Druze in the Jabal maintained relations with their co-religionists across *Bilad al-Sham*, they habitually interacted more closely with the Bedouin who lived on the eastern fringes of the mountain, and, over time, the social structure and customs of the Druze of the Jabal were strongly influenced by those of the tribes.

By the mid-nineteenth century, each village in Jabal Hawran had its own shaykh, who decided the distribution of agricultural land. The village shaykh enjoyed the privilege of taking one-quarter of the village's land for himself before assigning the remainder as he saw fit, usually based on personal loyalty, the willingness of families to work on his lands or their ability to pay taxes. Peasants would provide the village shaykh with one day of unpaid labour each week but could also volunteer their time beyond this lower limit, or offer gifts, to curry favour. Although the language of tribal obligation served to disguise what was essentially exploitation, respect for tradition prevented the shaykhs from making excessive demands on the peasantry – especially as labour was scarce given the Jabal's low population.[38]

Village shaykhs belonged to one of the ten to fifteen prominent families of the Jabal, each of which was also led by its own head shaykh. These noble, shaykhly families were collectively known as *al-khassa* ('the elite') but were ranked according to an explicit social hierarchy. The chief of the leading family of the day held the title of shaykh al-mashayikh – 'Chief of Chiefs' – and wielded ultimate authority among the Druze. Beyond these tribal notables were the peasantry, who comprised the *'amma* – 'the commoners'. Druze religious affairs, meanwhile, were overseen by a parallel structure of 'spiritual shaykhs' drawn from just three prestigious families. At the bottom of the social hierarchy was a relatively small subaltern class of impoverished landless peasants, the *falīta*.[39]

This well-articulated social structure allowed the Druze villages to create a tight-knit, self-governing community that, although by no means immune from internal conflict, pulled together to defend their collective autonomy against incursions by government authorities. As we have seen, during the Egyptian occupation of the 1830s, the Druze of the Jabal chafed at Ibrahim Pasha's demands to supply men for his army and incited a rebellion that cut across regional lines. Druze notables were quick to see the advantages of working with opponents of Ibrahim Pasha elsewhere in the country and liaised for this purpose with religious and secular leaders from the Damascene neighbourhood of Maydan, whose merchants were at this time becoming important intermediaries for the export of wheat from the Hawran.[40] In later years, the commercial relationship between Maydani merchants and Druze notables would provide a foundation for solid social and political ties between Damascus and the Jabal. The rebellion against the Egyptians resulted in a series of concessions made to the Druze, including exemptions from conscription, forced labour and disarmament. They were also promised that no garrisons would be built in the Jabal – a crucial component of Druze demands for autonomy from the central state.

While Egyptian reforms made little headway into Jabal Hawran, the authority of the shaykhs was shaken by the 1860 conflict between Maronites and Druze in Mount Lebanon, which prompted several thousand Druze peasants to leave their homes and seek refuge in the Hawran. This population influx prompted the region to be renamed from Jabal Hawran to *Jabal al-Duruz* – the 'Druze Mountain'. The new arrivals brought new life to the south of the Jabal, rebuilding abandoned villages and cultivating fields that had long been left untilled. This population boom revived the fortunes of the notable Atrash family that held authority over this hitherto sparsely populated area. The Atrash shaykh, Isma'il, gained support from secondary families and peasants because he had voiced support for their discontent with some of the more unpopular rights of the village shaykhs, such as their right to demand unpaid labour or to evict farmers from their land.[41] In 1869, Isma'il al-Atrash built on this success by wresting the title 'Chief of Chiefs' from the Hamdan family, who had held the position for decades.[42] The Atrash became rich from agricultural lands forfeited by the Hamdans but failed to live up to these commitments to reform and soon started acting in a manner more befitting feudal landowners than the Druze tradition of tribal chiefs.

The changing demography of the Jabal facilitated power being concentrated in the hands of the Atrash, who were able to exploit villages inhabited by multiple families of recent migrants; in contrast, rival shaykhs further north were constrained by the small size of their villages and the greater historical accumulation of ties of marriage or reciprocal social obligations, which inhibited any tendency to despotism. The expansion of agricultural production came at a time of unprecedented demand for grain on the international market. The combination of increased taxation and higher export prices in the 1870s only accelerated the growing inequality between the Atrash and the ordinary peasantry, a growing number of whom found themselves reduced to working as sharecroppers.[43] While the Druze notables were never absentee landlords like their counterparts in Damascus, Aleppo or Hama, this shifting economic balance led less prominent families to question the status quo. In the mid-1870s, peasants held a series of meetings across the south of Jabal al-Duruz to discuss the situation.[44] These meetings laid much of the groundwork for a fully fledged uprising a decade later.

In the meantime, the leading Druze shaykhs responded to peasant concerns by greater recourse to coercion. Ismail passed on the title 'Chief of Chiefs' to his son, Ibrahim al-Atrash, who bolstered his power by cooperating with the Ottoman authorities. Ibrahim was officially appointed governor of the Jabal in 1882. Ibrahim seem to revel in his adoption of Ottoman culture, eschewing the traditional Druze dress in favour of a glamorous fez and European-style suit, and collecting taxes on behalf of the central state (a good portion of which he would retain for himself) as if he were a regular Ottoman tax farmer, rather than the defender of the special status that the recalcitrant Jabal had historically demanded from the authorities. Ibrahim personalized his role as *shaykh al-mashayikh* to an unprecedented extent, insisting that even marriages not be contracted without his express approval.[45] Other shaykhs followed suit: Ibrahim's relative, Najm al-Atrash, shaykh of the village of 'Urman, reportedly ordered a camel to be burned alive to punish its owner's refusal to follow orders, while peasants were admonished for transgressing the traditional preserves of shaykhly privilege, such as wearing red shoes, slaughtering animals to welcome honoured guests or simply drinking coffee, considered the exclusive and inviolable symbol of the shaykh's hospitality.[46]

Under the weight of this oppression, in April 1888 peasants from four southern villages – 'Urman, Malah, Imtan and al-Huwayya – called a secret meeting in the ruined settlement of Majdal. They drafted a statement of protest against what they described as the ongoing moral and material assault on the very peasants who had transformed the southern slopes of the Jabal into cultivated land. Many of the eighty-two signatories to the statement had settled the area following the 1860 conflict in Mount Lebanon, leading to the intriguing hypothesis that they acted as channels for the culture of revolt to travel from the Kisrawan to the Hawran. Although the Majdal al-Shur Declaration, as the statement came to be known, did not propose specific measures to rectify the injustices against the peasantry, it nevertheless provided the Syrian interior with its first, vivid articulation of the principle of peasant rights.[47]

The Majdal al-Shur Declaration circulated throughout the Jabal, raising awareness of the common plight of the peasantry, and no doubt feeding into the first armed clashes that began in the village of Malah but soon spread as the shaykhs of nearby villages rallied to support their peers. The conflict reached the capital of Suwayda and even extended to the northern villages beyond the control of the Atrash. The mounting number of casualties prompted some members of the Atrash family to seek protection in the nearby Ottoman garrison at al-Mazra'a; others fled for the safety of the Hawran plain or Damascus.

Over summer 1888, the revolt of the commoners – the 'Ammiyya Revolt – articulated several concrete demands. The first was that the village shaykhs should forfeit half of their customary property and henceforth control just an eighth rather than a quarter of village lands. The second was that land-ownership rights should be systematically recognized. Third, they insisted that peasants should have the right to consultation in village and municipal affairs. Although some voices in the 'Ammiyya movement advocated all the shaykhs be expelled and their lands redistributed to the peasantry, the radicals were in a minority. The brother and rival of the chief of chiefs, the poet Shibli al-Atrash, was relatively sympathetic to the movement and refused to work against them, although he had prudently abandoned the Jabal for his own safety. Shibli expressed the political programme of the 'Ammiyya in his distinctive vernacular verse:

The decision was taken that we should flee our country;
We fled and abandoned our every necessity.
The first demand, they said, was the quarter of the shaykh,
For the shaykhs themselves were no longer necessary!
The second demand, they said, was their right to the citadel,
For our shaykhs were obsolete!
The third demand, they said, was everything they wished,
For the shaykh was a cowardly tyrant!

Much like the rebels of Kisrawan before them, the 'Ammiyya expressed support for the Tanzimat project as a way to undermine the power of the shaykhs and protect themselves from arbitrary eviction and exploitation. Despite this, the Ottoman authorities considered that the uprising risked spreading the contagion of disorder. They dispatched a sizeable military force to occupy Jabal al-Duruz, expel the rebels and restore the Atrash to power. This goal was accomplished in the summer of 1890, but the Atrash were unable to resume their position without making significant concessions to the peasants. They agreed to pay financial compensation to all victims of the conflict, both shaykhs and 'Ammiyya, and to redistribute half their lands to the peasants and half to the dispossessed *falīta*, leaving them with only land they had inherited from the displaced Hamdans. Limits were placed on the right of shaykhs to evict or demand unpaid labour from the peasantry, and the shaykhs were obliged to concede that working the land was the equivalent to owning the land: the logic of the feudal *iqta'* system was now effectively superseded by the principle of individual rights.[48]

Although the overall aims of the 'Ammiyya were less radical than those of the earlier uprising in Mount Lebanon, the events of 1889–90 had a profound effect on Jabal al-Duruz. Although the Atrash family continued to wield prestige and influence, sizeable numbers of small and medium-sized farms granted Druze peasants more economic security than their counterparts in the Syrian interior. Even decades later, property ownership in the Jabal was considerably more equitable than in regions where notables had accumulated large swathes of farmland without meeting peasant resistance. Moreover, this early confrontation between notables and peasantry permitted a rebalancing of power that largely allowed the Jabal to avoid the more vicious class-based conflicts that were to rack the rest of the country in the mid-twentieth century.

Jabal al-Ansariya

In contrast to rebellious Mount Lebanon and Jabal al-Duruz, the mountains along Syria's Mediterranean coast experienced no significant upheavals during the late Ottoman years – despite the fact the economic situation of the population living there was in many ways much more precarious. Although such coastal towns as Latakia, Baniyas and Jablah were largely Sunni, the mountains themselves were home to a mixed population of Christians, Ismailis and Alawis in the south, with a higher preponderance of Alawis further north. Outsiders often called Alawis 'Nusayris', a name derived from the controversial ninth-century religious luminary Ibn Nusayr, whose teachings the community was alleged to follow. By Ottoman times, the coastal mountains were commonly known as Jabal al-Ansariya in reference to their 'Nusayri' inhabitants.

The villagers eked out a living from the difficult highland terrain, although from the eighteenth century onwards some began to descend to settle the plains and swamps that lapped the eastern and southern slopes of the mountains as well as the district of Adana to the north. The vast majority of Alawis in the lands of Syria lived in desperate poverty. In the mountains the soil was poor, the topography broken and the paths difficult to navigate. The Alawi population was overwhelmingly rural and did not begin any significant migration to Syria's cities – even to the towns of the coast – until much later in the twentieth century.

The territorial concentration of the Alawis in these coastal hills has led scholars of Syria to classify them, along with the Druze, as 'compact minorities'. But while the Druze of the Hawran had developed a fairly cohesive set of social relations, the Alawis were deeply fragmented. Alawi villagers were scattered across a wide, disconnected stretch of hills, plains and swamps, working on land belonging to mostly Sunni and Christian notables; their isolated hamlets were small and sparsely populated, usually holding no more than two or three hundred people. As this pattern of settlement had not changed for hundreds of years, Alawis had clustered into a number of highly localized social structures rather than developing into a single over-arching community in its own right.

Over the centuries, alliances and intermarriages between the leading Alawi families had coalesced into a relatively stable set of four leading tribes: the Kalbiyyah, the Khayyatin, the Matawira and the Haddadin. The origins of this system are obscure. Each tribe recounts its own genealogical myths, and claims descent from particular historical leaders and specific birthplaces, but the historical record suggests the tribes may have formed as late as the eighteenth century around a number of Alawi families that had begun to accumulate wealth through tax farming.[49] Alawi tribes are thus a relatively recent historical phenomenon, encouraged by an Ottoman state seeking to identify local intermediaries, not an expression of ancient genealogical identity.

Alawi tribes were sprawling, loose-knit extended families rather than closely bonded units. Relationships between the tribes shifted unpredictably between confrontation and cooperation, while relations within the same tribal confederations were rarely entirely harmonious: ad hoc alliances and neighbourly feuds were the order of the day. In the 1850s, an English missionary, Samuel Lyde, spent six years in the mountains and used his experience to become the first European to write a book about Alawi religion and society. Lyde's work describes a near-constant stream of intra-Alawi conflict, including one clash between the Kalbiyyah and Muhalibah tribes in which ten people were killed.

'The fight had been brewing for some time,' remarked Lyde, 'but the immediate cause was a battle about a cucumber.'[50] In an environment of material scarcity, tribal identity provided a basis for organizing conflict as well as a ready-made cooperative association for mutual assistance.

A similar kind of fragmentation also manifested itself in the religion of the Alawis, which combined Shia religious philosophy with fragments of Gnosticism, neo-Platonism and local folk beliefs. As a mystery cult, the secrets of which were only revealed to the select few, the Alawi faith was largely practised rather than debated, although local variations had coalesced into two distinct spiritual traditions, the Shamsi and the Qamari, named after the sun and the moon. (A third branch, constructed around the mystical, charismatic figure of a man named Suleiman al-Murshid, emerged in the 1920s.) The geographical dispersal, poverty and illiteracy of the Alawi population, as well as the esoteric nature of the faith, meant that the religious shaykhs neither disseminated their doctrine publicly nor asserted their power as a distinct class. Theology consequently shaped Alawi society much less than village, family and tribe.

Overviews of Middle East history often maintain that the Alawis retreated to the mountains between the eleventh and fourteenth centuries to escape persecution from Sunni Muslims who looked askance at their unorthodox religious practices. The reality is more complicated. In medieval times, the periodic intrusions of state power into Jabal al-Ansariya were aimed at collecting taxes from the Alawis, not punishing or converting them. In the eighteenth century, a handful of Alawi families became tax farmers, profiting from the region's increasing export trade in tobacco and enjoying an elevated social and economic status. Around this time, the Ottoman authorities also began to overlook Alawi 'heresies', describing Alawi banditry in secular rather than sectarian terms, allowing Alawis access to Islamic courts to settle disputes and even referring to them in official documents as Alawis rather than the pejorative 'Nusayris'.[51] It was this new-found prominence that in the 1810s perhaps encouraged the Ottoman governor of Tripoli, Barbar Mustafa, to collect taxes from Alawi villages with unprecedented brutality, devastating the countryside.[52] Just as sectarian identity came to play a crucial political role in Mount Lebanon after the 1830s, so too in Jabal al-Ansariya did social tensions increasingly express themselves in overtly sectarian terms.

Although far from the political and cultural currents that would transform urban life in the nineteenth century, the Alawis were not entirely insulated from the encroachments of the modern state that were seen in the Syrian interior. A handful of Alawis left the mountains to pursue successful careers in the Ottoman bureaucracy, even attaining such impressive appointments as governor of Aleppo or grand admiral of the Ottoman navy. Alawis of more modest means were able to find employment working for Mehmed Ali's state-building project in Cairo or its expansion into the lands of Syria.[53] As a rule, though, Alawis opposed unwanted state intrusion into the hills. The attempted conscription and disarmament of Alawi villagers during Egyptian rule in the 1830s, for example, provoked fierce resistance that was only quelled when Ibrahim Pasha sent in Druze irregulars from Mount Lebanon. Unrest continued in the 1850s after the Ottoman Reconquista, in reaction to the efforts of central government to expand taxation, conscription and census-taking into the coastal mountains.

The difficulty of penetrating the rugged Jabal al-Ansariya meant that the central authorities found it expedient to use local strongmen as intermediaries. In 1853, an Alawi chief named Ismail Khayr Bek seized control of the district of Safita; having little alternative, Istanbul pragmatically recognized this achievement as a fait accompli. Khayr Bek was granted the official title of Governor and for the next five years ruled – rather brutally – over the Alawi, Christian and Sunni villages in the district. At that point, Ottoman troops finally moved against him. Before the military expedition could reach Khayr Bek, he was pre-emptively decapitated by a disapproving uncle, which solved the Ottomans' problem for them.[54]

The endemic poverty in Jabal al-Ansariya meant that, in some parts of the country, the word 'Alawi' was effectively interchangeable with the word 'peasant'.[55] However, a small number of families – the 'Abbas in the Akkar, the Junayd in the Ghab and the Arsuzi in Antakya, for example – began to expand their landholdings in a manner very similar to that of the notable families of the urban interior. Indeed, some Alawi landowners exploited their peasants with much the same gusto as the great notable families of Hama. On several occasions, Alawi notables even colluded with Sunni and Christian landlords to maintain the landowners' collective control over Alawi peasants.[56] In cases such as this, pragmatic class interest proved stronger than common religious identity.

Owing to their economic differentiation, geographical dispersion and harsh living conditions, Alawis in the Ottoman Empire never spoke or acted as an independent, coherent community. Their collective experience comprised occasional bouts of state-sponsored brutality, alternating with moments of tolerant pragmatism that punctured persistent periods of entrenched misery. The ongoing marginalization of Alawis was to outlive both the Ottoman Empire and the French Mandate, with profound implications for Syria's post-independence politics.

Eastern Syria: The Euphrates Valley, the Jazira, the Desert

For the first half of the nineteenth century, there were few permanent settlements very far east of the road from Aleppo to Damascus. Here, cultivated lands (*al-ma'moura*) gave way to the desert spaces of the vast Syrian steppe (*al-badiya*), the eastern edge of which was delimited by the Euphrates River as it flowed south-east into Iraq; to the south, it eventually merged into the deserts of Arabia. Its arid expanses were inhabited by Arabic-speaking tribesmen, usually referred to as the *A'raab* (Arabs) or the *Badu* ('desert-dwellers', of which the singular form, *badawi*, came into English as Bedouin), In the Syrian steppe, tribes who raised camels were considered the most noble and would roam far in the course of the year, while the less mobile sheep-herding tribes would cross into the *ma'moura* to graze their animals, often causing great damage to farm crops. The tribes themselves were numerous: the Mawali had once dominated the northern steppe but were now largely confined to the area between Aleppo and Hama, owing to pressures from newcomers of the Anaza tribal grouping. The Fid'an tribe ranged eastwards from Aleppo, which they would raid from time to time. The Sba' were often found around Palmyra, while the great Ruwala tribe had moved north from the Najd in the Arabian Peninsula to graze in southern Syria and the Hawran.[57]

In the past, the tribes had experienced only intermittent contact with the Ottoman authorities, typically when local governors sought to mitigate the effects of their raiding. Yet even far from the cities, from the mid-nineteenth century the Bedouin also came to find themselves navigating a social and political landscape that was being reshaped according to the new contours of modernizing state power. Just as the Ottomans reasserted control over the Syrian interior in the 1850s and 1860s, they also extended the territorial reach of the central state into the desert by means including military expeditions, subsidies to shaykhs and interference in intertribal intrigue. Army outposts were built along the Euphrates Valley, culminating in the establishment of a garrison at Deir al-Zour in 1864. By the 1890s, the Ottoman securitization of the desert was so thorough that tribal shaykhs could sometimes be induced to pay taxes, or to settle in villages (at least temporarily), although attempts to conscript their men would still provoke resistance or, more simply, flight to the depths of the steppe. Indeed, many tribes removed themselves from the orbit of state power and retreated to the far north-eastern corner of Syria, the Jazira, which remained beyond the reach of the central authorities. As they did so, the Euphrates Valley east and south-east of Aleppo was rendered secure, prompting an agricultural and economic revival the impact of which was vividly described by the British aristocrat Mark Sykes, who travelled the region in the early 1900s.

'Wealth, business, movement, and traffic have increased beyond all expectation,' wrote Sykes. '[T]he progress in every direction may, I think, be attributed to one cause – the general revival of agriculture in the plains to the east of the city [. . .] On the way from Haleb [Aleppo] to Meskene, as far as the eye can see, there stretches a glorious tract of corn-bearing land, spotted with brown mud villages, containing a mixed race of people who reply equally readily in Turkish, Kurdish or Arabic [. . .] Many of these villages are the property of wealthy citizens of Haleb [. . .] the continual influx of industrious peoples is steadily regenerating the land.'[58]

The ethnic and linguistic ambiguity described by Sykes – who would go on to negotiate a secret agreement between Britain and France to divide up the Middle East after the First World War – could also be found in the north-eastern Jazira, a sparsely populated yet fertile region that held great untapped potential for agriculture. The Jazira was inhabited by a mixture of Kurds, whose ancestors had descended from the mountains of present-day Turkey to avoid the expanding power of the Ottomans centuries earlier, and sheep-farming Arab tribes such as the Baggara, the Tayy and the Uqaydat, who were regarded with some condescension by the great camel tribes of the Anaza and the Shammar.

As we have already seen, the lines between tribes and ethnicities were especially porous along the unpoliced frontiers of the empire. Sykes recounts his memorable encounter with the Adwan, who, he explains, were originally a sub-tribe of the mighty Arab Anaza that had migrated to the Jazira early in the nineteenth century. 'Since then,' noted Sykes, the Adwan tribe 'has gradually fallen away from its Arab neighbours and has grown more closely associated with the Kurdish clans, so that now, by intermarriage, in the process of time it has become almost entirely Kurdish. The men are broadly built and coarse-featured, the women tall and independent. Its Shaykh is a certain Mahmud Agha, who can only talk Arabic with difficulty.'[59] Much as the seemingly certain line demarcating the cultivated lands of the *ma'moura* from the wild steppe of the *badiya* would slowly recede or advance according to variations in climate or human cultivation, so too were the cultural lines distinguishing Arab from Kurd more an uncharted frontier than a fixed border.

The sheer remoteness and wildness of the Jazira – not to mention the distinct lack of roads to connect it to Aleppo or the coast – meant that this part of the country was largely unaffected by either the Tanzimat reforms or the closer contact with the European economy that was having such a tumultuous impact nearer the Mediterranean. Not until French troops eventually penetrated this far-flung corner in the late 1920s would the Jazira begin its integration with the rest of Syria. In the meantime, the rapid pace of social and economic transformation further west began to forge new connections between cities and villages, accelerating the flow of goods, people and ideas in ways that would reshape the familiar cultural landscape of the Ottoman Empire and lay the infrastructure for the emergence of a distinctly *Syrian* territorial identity.

2

Reforms and Regionalism: The Late Ottoman Empire, 1860s–1920

Across the lands of Syria, the package of administrative reforms known as the Tanzimat unsettled the status quo as peasants and notables jockeyed for position in the new social and economic order. Yet, in addition to reshaping social relations within these lands, the Tanzimat also began to forge new relationships *between* them. In this way, the foundations were laid for the loosely connected *Bilad al-Sham* to cohere into a distinct, increasingly integrated geographical region in its own right.

As part of their modernization drive, the Ottoman authorities redrew internal borders, created new provinces – including the newly named province of 'Syria' – and experimented with contemporary forms of representative government. An innovative system of modern, secular schooling was rolled out across the region to educate a generation of bureaucrats and army officers who considered themselves first and foremost 'Ottomans' – servants of the empire above and beyond their local identities. A flurry of investment in road building and railways dramatically accelerated the flow of people and goods between towns that had previously been distant or dangerous to reach. Telegraphs, postal services and newspapers revolutionized the speed of communication and the spread of information. Even traditional urban architecture was overhauled: chaotic souqs turned into avenues of orderly shops, grand edifices of brick and stone were built to house town halls and hospitals and streets hummed with the hitherto unfamiliar buzz of tramways and electric lamps.

These novel forms of representation, education and communication came to open new horizons for the people of the lands of Syria. On the one hand, these government-led initiatives had the potential to create an unprecedented sense of integration in the wider Ottoman Empire. On the other, the drive to realign the diverse peoples of the region with the central state's united, standardized vision of what it meant to be Ottoman risked provoking a backlash from provinces that had historically enjoyed considerable autonomy from Istanbul. This tension between centralization and devolution would provide the crucible for the emergence of new cultural understandings of identity in the late Ottoman Empire – as well as the catalyst for questioning whether Istanbul was best suited to govern a population that, between the 1860s and the 1920s, increasingly came to consider itself as not merely Ottoman, but also as distinctively *Arab*.

Connecting the provinces

The colonial settlement imposed on the Levant after the First World War is often blamed for drawing new borders without reference to pre-existing patterns of politics, economics or demography. However, even prior to the arrival of Britain and France, Ottoman reform initiatives had already begun experimenting with new governance structures. Upon reclaiming the lands of Syria after 1840, the Ottomans reinstated three of the *eyalat* ('provinces') that predated the Egyptian occupation – Damascus, Aleppo and Sidon – but abolished the fourth province, Tripoli, whose lands were now mostly assigned to Sidon. Other changes affected the province of Damascus, which gained the Biqaa Valley but in Palestine lost Nablus and Gaza, also to Sidon.[1] The coastal town of Alexandretta, meanwhile, was transferred from the *eyalat* of Aleppo to that of Adana, in present-day Turkey.

These new provincial boundaries did not remain in place for very long. Tanzimat reformers soon introduced what they considered to be a modern, rational system of local government to replace the more flexible administrative divisions that had customarily been used across different parts of the empire. In 1864, the *eyalat* system was replaced with a new administrative structure, the *wilaya*.

The province of Damascus was renamed the province of Syria (*wilayat Suriya* in Arabic), a classical name for the region that had been revived by European officials and travellers and popularized as the Levant became a focus for geopolitical contest in the 1830s. The adoption of this name first by the Ottoman authorities, and then by Arabic-speaking intellectuals across the eastern Mediterranean, symbolized the extent to which European strategic interests were already acting as catalysts to redefine the political geography of the Ottoman Empire even before the onset of colonial occupation. The newly minted 1864 province of Syria stretched all the way from Karak (in modern-day Jordan) in the south to Hama in the north; to the west, it included lands previously part of the former coastal province of Sidon as well as the three Palestinian districts of Acre, Nablus and Jerusalem. The boundaries of the province of Aleppo moved further north and east, to encompass parts of Anatolia and the Jazira.

Several modifications to the new system followed. First, in 1872, the district of Jerusalem was detached from the province of Syria and granted special administrative status – from this time it was governed directly from Istanbul. Second, the notables of

Beirut lobbied for their city to be upgraded to a provincial capital, given its rising prominence as a trading hub.[2] In 1888, Beirut was elevated to become centre of a new province which stretched along the coast all the way from Latakia in the north to Nablus, Acre and Jaffa in the south, but excluded Beirut's immediate hinterland of Mount Lebanon. This exclusion came in response to pressure from France and Britain, whose professed concern for the fate of Christians and other minorities afforded them a useful justification for continuing geopolitical intervention in the domestic affairs of the empire. Mount Lebanon retained the special autonomous status granted after the 1860 civil conflict. Third, in the far-eastern interior of Syria, the growing population and stability of the once unsettled Euphrates Valley led to the establishment, in 1871, of an additional subdistrict based at Deir al-Zour. These administrative arrangements then largely remained in place until the First World War (see Map 3).

The *wilaya* system did more than designate geographical jurisdictions: it also specified an orderly hierarchy of administrative units. Each *wilaya* was divided into several *sanjak*s; each *sanjak* was subdivided into *qada*s; and each *qada* was subdivided into *nahiya*s, which might contain a town or a handful of villages. At these lower levels, each town had its own municipal authority and each village was headed by an official named a *mukhtar*, a local figure who was nominated by the village, but who received a government salary.[3] Inspired by the French model of *départements* that had been introduced after the 1789 Revolution, this top-down structure was similarly intended to allow the authority of the central state to flow all the way down from the imperial capital to the smallest rural hamlet. The changes were intended to replace what had been a confusing, uneven array of diverse local arrangements with a predictable, rationalized system that was universally applied across the empire. Much as the Tanzimat reformers proposed that Ottomans should be equal citizens before the law, regardless of their religion, so too were all the spaces of the empire to be equally governed by parallel institutions. The glaring irregularity within this secular system came from the special status granted – under British and French pressure – to Christian-dense territories such as Mount Lebanon and Jerusalem, which persisted like archaic vestiges of a less egalitarian age.

The first Ottoman parliament, convened in 1876, embodied the same rational logic of geographical representation. The parliament soon became a forum for lively political debate: members would voice the concerns and perspectives of the province that had nominated them, but largely without regard for ethnic or religious distinctions. Representatives from the provinces of Syria and Aleppo included younger members from some of the most prominent grand families, who were quick to criticize the government for its shortcomings as well as to lobby for improvements to their home regions.[4] So vociferous were the proceedings of this first Ottoman experiment in deliberative politics in fact that Abdulhamid II, who became sultan also in 1876, just two years later suspended both the parliament and the newly written constitution. After banishing these young troublemakers from the capital, Abdulhamid spent the next three decades trying to reconsolidate the territories of the empire under his personal control, while also fighting the three principal threats of the day: foreign expansionism, external intervention and financial insolvency.

To assert his authority, Abdulhamid reinvigorated the power and prestige of his religious position as caliph in addition to his secular position as sultan. In deference to Islamic tradition, which discouraged the display of human images, Abdulhamid ordered his portraits be removed from public places and replaced with banners that read 'Long live the Sultan!' Fridays became occasions for pomp and splendour: each week Abdulhamid headed a royal procession that would wend its way to midday prayers escorted by contingents of liveried guards and observed by curious crowds and tourists. Military bands and morning coats began to appear during the sultan's public ceremonies. The arrival of Abdulhamid's silver jubilee was celebrated by constructing clock towers emblazoned with his coat of arms in towns across the empire.[5] Although ostensibly undertaken to reinforce the sultan's Islamic credentials, these displays of public pageantry were in fact recent political innovations. Just as Queen Victoria and other European monarchs and emperors were inventing new traditions to bolster their legitimacy in the face of rising popular and democratic pressures, so too did Sultan Abdulhamid embrace the power of the royal spectacle to shore up his rule against the forces of constitutionalism.[6]

While earlier sultans had largely been content to ignore the spiritual practices of Muslim subjects who remained loyal to the empire, Abdulhamid introduced religious orthodoxy as a central component of his new state ideology. The Hanafi school of Islamic law was codified and imposed above all other interpretations of the Sharia. Heterodox communities such as the Alawis, as well as populations considered impious, like the nomadic Bedouin tribes of *Bilad al-Sham*, were at this time singled out for correctional instruction in religious affairs or targeted by campaigns of outright conversion.[7]

Abdulhamid implemented one further move from the playbook of Victorian state builders. From Britain and France to Russia and Japan, mass education had come to be recognized by the late nineteenth century as an important instrument not merely for transmitting knowledge, but also for shaping the values of the broader citizenry in line with the worldview of the political and social elite. In much the same way, new state schools were now constructed across the empire with the aim of producing a modern generation of Ottomans in whom had been instilled a deep sense of belonging to the imperial project. These government-run educational establishments were also intended to provide a defensive bulwark against the inroads made by Christian missionaries from France, Britain and the United States, who had founded a worryingly large number of schools along the eastern coast of the Mediterranean.[8] The Ottoman authorities deemed missionary schools such as the Syrian Protestant College (later renamed the American University of Beirut) as potential vectors of subversion, a particular concern given the penchant of foreign powers for interfering in the empire's domestic affairs.

By the 1890s, some nineteen elite high schools had been founded in cities such as Damascus, Beirut, Aleppo, Tripoli and Jerusalem. Here, the region's best students were drilled in multiple languages (Turkish, Arabic, French and Persian), instructed in moral philosophy and the Islamic sciences (especially the Hanafi school of law) and taught mathematics, geometry, history and geography. A parallel system of military schools prepared students for careers in the imperial army.[9] Supposedly wayward rural populations such as the Bedouin and Druze were also granted access to the new system: in 1892, the *Asiret Mektebi Humayun* – the Imperial School for Tribes – opened its doors in Istanbul to educate the sons of prominent shaykhs.[10] So popular was this school that Kurdish and Alawi tribal leaders – whose families were not initially offered places – also clamoured for their right to participate in such a prestigious establishment. By the end of the nineteenth century, a new generation of notables was finding that a modern, secular Ottoman education unlocked the door to an exciting and cosmopolitan career in the imperial civil service or army, with postings that could rotate across Anatolia, the Balkans or Iraq, as well as the lands of Syria.[11]

The new educational and bureaucratic networks forged during

the reign of Abdulhamid II were reinforced by a series of technological innovations that further integrated the Arab provinces. The introduction of the telegraph greatly accelerated the flow of state power across the eastern Mediterranean. By the late 1860s, Aleppo, Damascus, Beirut and Latakia were already connected to Istanbul; by the late 1870s, the telegraph network reached even such small towns as Jableh (between Latakia and Tripoli) and Mzayrib (in the Hawran). By the late 1880s, telegraph posts dotted the landscape as far south as Haifa, Bethlehem and Salt. In allowing intelligence about bandits and tribal raids to be swiftly transmitted between different areas, telegraph communications did much to improve rural policing, but they also exerted more subtle effects. The communications revolution helped the central authorities to standardize prices and weights across the empire, for example, and even to synchronize the beginning and end of Ramadan across its far-flung reaches, rather than leaving that decision to local initiative as had been the case in the past.[12] The banal authority of the state thus began to insinuate itself almost imperceptibly into the routines and rhythms of everyday life.

Regional connectivity was markedly improved by two further infrastructural developments. First, new roads that were suitable for vehicles came to replace the meandering caravan paths that had previously linked settlements. The road from Beirut to Damascus, for example, took a French company seven years to build, but its completion in 1863 reduced the journey between the two cities from an arduous three or four days to a mere thirteen hours. With Beirut's port now offering this swift access to the Syrian interior, the city flourished at the expense of such maritime rivals as Haifa and Tripoli. The second development was the coming of the railway. In the 1890s, French investors financed the first railway lines to connect the Hawran to Damascus and Beirut. In response, Sultan Abdulhamid II launched his own prestige project in the form of the Hijaz Railway, completed in 1908, which linked Damascus to Der'a and Haifa before going on to the holy city of Medina, where it asserted the power of the empire in the face of both local elites in the Hijaz and potential Wahhabi challengers from the neighbouring desert of central Arabia.[13] To symbolize the grandeur of this ambitious project, an opulent station was built at the railway's starting point in Damascus. In 1903, a third, German-financed initiative began constructing a railway to link Konya to Aleppo and then eastwards to Baghdad and Basra. In the meantime, the French-built railway system continued to expand, connecting Homs, Hama, Aleppo and, by 1911, Tripoli. The new roads and railways provided unprecedented links from the Syrian interior to the south and to the Mediterranean coast, which then connected by sea to Europe. In the process, the Syrian provinces' international trade was decisively reoriented away from Asian markets in the east. Vast amounts of grain, cotton and wool began to stream out of Syria and into the industrializing powerhouses of Britain and France, ravenous for raw materials.

Much as today, the impact of this wave of globalization was neither evenly distributed nor unambiguously beneficial. Disruptive trade patterns and financial flows gradually transformed the Syrian interior, just as new ideas about culture, politics and society began to circulate in the common intellectual space created by modern education, newspapers and informed public debate. Between the late nineteenth and early twentieth centuries, these new developments unleashed forces that checked Sultan Abdulhamid's tendencies to impose Ottomanism from the top-down, and accelerated the centrifugal pressures from the empire's Arab provinces, against which the imperial capital fitfully struggled to maintain itself as a centre of gravity.

From boom to bust: *Bilad al-Sham* and the world economy

Between 1846 and 1873, what was in effect a vast free trade zone came into being on an almost global scale; centred on Western Europe, it had frontiers that reached Russia, the Ottoman Empire, India, the Americas and even Australia. Countries such as Britain, France, Belgium and Italy one by one eliminated barriers to commerce, slashed customs tariffs, liberalized labour laws and opened their economies to exports, to a degree that would not be repeated until the globalization of the 1990s. In just twenty years, global trade expanded by 260 per cent.[14] Goods, capital and people were shipped around the world with little regulation, oversight or bureaucracy; freedom of movement – in any direction – neither attracted political controversy nor provoked social angst.

Britain's ideological commitment to free trade had a calamitous impact on the rest of the world. Wheat was shipped out of starving Ireland, killing thousands; narcotics were exported to China, producing a generation of addicts; territories were incorporated into Britain's 'informal empire' through unfair terms of trade just as surely as if they had been conquered by military force.[15] For its part, the Ottoman Empire buttressed its heartlands against these external pressures, even at the expense of abandoning the peripheries. In the meantime, the acceleration of trade with Europe had significant social and economic consequences within the Syrian provinces.

Initially, some sections of the population of *Bilad al-Sham* were well placed to benefit from the new commercial opportunities granted by improved sea and land communications. By the mid-nineteenth century, rapid industrialization and urbanization had left Britain for the first time unable to feed its population from domestic agriculture; consequently, in 1846, the country decided to repeal its long-standing ban on grain imports. This decision by the global economic powerhouse of the day created a demand for wheat so vast that, almost overnight, agricultural produce around the world was siphoned away from local markets and redirected to feeding the apparently insatiable appetites of buyers in London and Liverpool. In *Bilad al-Sham*, the grain merchants – or *buwaykis* – of Damascus swiftly positioned themselves as intermediaries to supply Britain with Syrian wheat.

Concentrated in the Maydan quarter of Damascus, *buwaykis* procured high-quality varieties of wheat grown in southern Syria specifically for export to Britain.[16] Maydani families like the Mahaynis, 'Abids, Nuris and Sabbaghs thus developed strong commercial and personal ties with Druze shaykhs who controlled agriculture in the Hawran. These Damascene traders maintained second homes in Druze villages in the Jabal, provided hospitality to Druze shaykhs at their homes and even gave lodgings to the sons of those shaykhs when they attended Ottoman schools in Damascus.[17] Such linkages served to bind together the prominent families of Jabal al-Duruz with the commercial elites of the Maydan in a close-knit relationship of mutual benefit. By the 1860s, these *buwaykis* had accumulated enough wealth from exporting wheat to start ascending the city's social hierarchy, where they would sit alongside the more established prominent families of Damascus. In the meantime, the sons of the merchants and the Druze shaykhs received a modern education intended to prepare them for productive lives as good and loyal Ottoman citizens. This next generation forged meaningful bonds of youthful camaraderie that would remain strong over the years. Common interest in the grain trade thus provided the basis for elite networks that for the first time transcended regional and sectarian particularisms.

The 1850s and 1860s were also good for two further exports from the Levant: silk and cotton. The silk industry was particularly strong in Mount Lebanon, where it had been established under Emir Bashir II some fifty years earlier: roughly half the population now earned a living from cultivating cocoons and tending the mulberry trees upon which the silkworms depended for sustenance.[18] Silk exports provided an important source of income for peasants on the mountain and helped prevent the excessive concentration of wealth in the hands of large absentee landowners, in contrast to the rural areas around Damascus, Aleppo and Hama. Syrian cotton, on the other hand, was mostly cultivated near Latakia. Cotton traders benefitted from exceptionally high prices in the 1860s, when civil war interrupted exports from the United States, and Britain turned to other producers, including those in Syria.[19]

Although the newly built commodity chains of wheat, silk and cotton connected Syrian traders with the profits to be generated from the international economy centred on the British Empire, the flourishing of exports also made the Syrian interior vulnerable to fluctuations in world prices over which they had no control. After the boom of the 1860s, international links allowed economic crisis to spread from overseas to infect the lands of Syria. The worldwide downturn from 1873 to 1896 was so pronounced that English speakers at the time called it the 'Great Depression', until they decided that term was better suited to those even more miserable years following 1929, when the earlier episode was renamed the 'Long Depression'. In Europe, the Long Depression led to the retreat of free trade, the reintroduction of protectionism and the reinvigoration of imperial rivalries that contributed to the outbreak of the First World War. In the Ottoman Empire, the same global downturn contributed to the collapse of state finances, the decimation of local industry and the revival of provincial resistance to the project of state centralization.

For contemporary observers, the immediate cause of the Long Depression was the international financial crisis that hit in 1873. In central Europe, investors had been ebullient about the potential for growth after the unification of Germany and, anticipating huge profits, took advantage of new mortgages on offer from a booming financial services industry to direct vast amounts of capital into railway expansion and construction. In May 1873, the bubble burst. The Vienna Stock Exchange crashed: listed construction companies saw their share price plummet by 74 per cent in just a few months, while 58 per cent was wiped off the value of listed banks, setting off a chain reaction of losses and bankruptcies that swept central Europe.[20] As credit dried up and interest rates increased, Continental investors also pulled out of North American railroads, which had been part of a separate speculative bubble, similarly fuelled by unsustainable borrowing. When a major US railroad company proved unable to meet its repayment schedule in September 1873, investors rushed to withdraw their money from what now seemed like such a risky endeavour, sparking a major panic that swiftly spread to other companies and sectors. Over the next few years, hundreds of US banks closed, factories ground to a halt and unemployment skyrocketed.[21]

While the causes of the 1873 crisis seemed specific to central Europe and North America, they also reflected the unseen vulnerabilities that had been created as by-products of the new global system of free trade. The first of these hidden vulnerabilities stemmed from a worldwide shift in the nature of money itself. During the 1870s, countries around the world had gradually abandoned the use of silver-based money and adopted the common gold standard, in which currencies were pegged to the price of gold at a fixed rate. In the short term, this move stabilized the relative value of currencies and facilitated international trade, but in the longer term it produced a wave of deflation. Because countries were unable to devalue their currencies, and because the planet has only a finite amount of gold, long-term systemic pressures would induce prices to lower until they eventually corresponded to the amount of gold in circulation. By the 1880s, the painful, deflationary impact of the gold standard was being felt across the world.[22]

The second unforeseen consequence of nineteenth-century globalization was the disruption caused to established agricultural producers when wheat started to be supplied from such previously untapped sources as the American Midwest, Australia, India and Russia. The sheer volume of grain produced by these new suppliers, its export now viable thanks to cheaper shipping costs and more efficient agricultural technologies, flooded the world market and forced down prices that were already in freefall thanks to deflationary monetary pressures.[23] Together, these factors help explain why the depression of 1873 to 1896 was quite so 'Long'.

Historians of the nineteenth century only rarely connect what is usually described as the decline of the Ottoman Empire to the vicissitudes of the world economy. The usual story of the 'Sick Man of Europe' is one of wasteful spending, inefficient resource allocation and excessive reliance on debt to plug the parlous state of Ottoman finances. It is true that between 1854 and 1874 the Ottoman Empire took out some fourteen loans to fund its programme of administrative and military reform, acquiring a total debt of £232 million sterling for which repayments devoured over half of the empire's entire annual budget. At this point, we are told, the empire fell precipitously into the debt trap and in 1875 declared itself bankrupt.[24] Foreign creditors swept in to secure their interests and, in 1881, created the Ottoman Public Debt

Administration, which directly supervised the empire's finances to ensure their debts were repaid rather than spent on expanding infrastructure, education or the armed forces. For Istanbul, this imposed financial austerity was a palpable attack on Ottoman state sovereignty.[25]

What is remarkable about traditional historical narratives is that they overlook the fact that the Ottoman Empire's declaration of bankruptcy was not simply a reflection of its inability to balance the books.[26] After all, since taking out its first loan in 1854, the Ottoman Empire had never found it difficult meet its repayment schedule: European banks were only too happy to keep supplying additional credit in an arrangement that proved immensely profitable for French and British bankers.[27] Not only did these loans carry high interest rates, usually in the range of 9 to 12 per cent, but they were often accompanied by exorbitant commission fees that swallowed up nearly half the face value of the loan. Only in the wake of the European credit crunch after the 1873 financial crisis did it become harder to secure more loans. From this perspective, the Ottoman Empire's 1875 declaration of bankruptcy – which prompted Britain and France to seize control of its finances – is not simply an isolated episode of foolish third-world economic policy-making (to indulge in an anachronism), but part of a much wider story of capital flows and speculative bubbles that produced one of the first financial crises in the modern international system.[28]

In *Bilad al-Sham*, the wheat growers of the Hawran were hit hard by the Long Depression. Peasants were plunged ever further into debt and poverty, in many cases losing their land to the rich families of Damascus.[29] Rural unrest in the south peaked in the Ammiyya revolt of the 1880s, which, as we have seen, demanded a more equitable distribution of land and wealth in Jabal al-Duruz. For their part, Syrian grain merchants who suffered from the collapse in world prices blamed their misfortune on neither the global depression nor the roads and railways that allowed vast amounts of grain to be moved out of the region with unprecedented speed. Instead, they simply blamed the sheer backwardness of Syrian peasants. 'Despite the fact that the best lands for the cultivation of wheat are in the Ottoman Empire,' opined an Arabic-language newspaper in 1898, 'the prices of our [native] wheat flour in Beirut are now [as high as] those in London and Paris. The reason for this is that our peasants are lazy, stupid and irresponsible.'[30] The nouveau-riche Damascene *buwaykis*, on the other hand, were suspected by more established families of having contributed to the economic crisis by hoarding, speculation and generally unfair business practices.[31]

Trade between Europe and the lands of Syria was by no means one way. British consumer goods (especially textiles), manufactured cheaply and efficiently with the latest industrial technologies, quickly found their way into the Syrian interior. Facilitated by the low customs tariff that Britain had imposed on the Ottoman Empire in 1838, by the late nineteenth century cheap British imports had begun to undermine the livelihoods of traditional artisanal producers. A unique insight into the rapidity of social and economic change in Damascus comes from a book entitled the *Dictionary of Damascene Industries* (*Qamus al-Sina'at al-Shamiyya*). Compiled between 1890 and 1905, this treasure trove provides detailed eye-witness descriptions of 437 occupations that were traditionally practised in the city. Some of these crafts, such as those of the mason or mirror-maker, are familiar. Other vocations filled a narrow niche: the *hawalsili* sold nothing but wood, the *qabaqibi* made clogs while the *mikabbati* devoted his days to manufacturing lids for food containers. The *Dictionary* provides evidence of how some of these traditional crafts were already suffering from the impact of foreign competition.

'Cloths imported from European countries astound the mind,' observes the *Dictionary*. 'This craft used to be very profitable in Damascus, but now, due to the imports of printed cloth of all patterns and kinds from foreign countries, this industry has reached the point of stagnation. Its practitioners are few in Damascus. No one desires printed cloth any longer.'[32] Other jobs, such as needle-making and porcelain-mending, were also becoming obsolete. Although the authors of the *Dictionary of Damascene Industries* were alarmed by the unprecedented pace of change, Syrian artisans proved surprisingly resilient in the face of British competition. Weavers, for example, ingeniously encouraged new fashions and styles of embroidery that Lancashire's textile mills found difficult to mimic, prompting a revival of their fortunes by the turn of the century.[33] Nevertheless, Syrian artisans ultimately lacked the financial resources to replace traditional methods of tanning leather, spinning cotton or making soap with more efficient modern technologies. Foreign capital had no interest in industrializing the non-European world and only sought out investment opportunities in infrastructure. The rich families of Syria, meanwhile, preferred to use their wealth to accumulate land, where the profits to be made by squeezing the peasantry were, despite the uncertainties of the world market, nevertheless easier than investing in the risky, untested and unprestigious sector of productive industry.

Contemporary observers such as the authors of the *Dictionary of Damascene Industries* found it difficult to escape the sensation that the familiar contours of social life were being reshaped before their eyes. This feeling also extended into the domain of culture: individuals who received modern educations from either missionaries or Ottomans were coming to see their world – and the changes it was undergoing – in a very different light from their predecessors. In this sense, the project of intellectual reform launched by Egypt's Mehmed Ali was continued by the efforts of educated individuals in Syria as they grappled with the uncertain consequences of state centralization, secularization and globalization. In wrestling with these issues and the backlash that they provoked, between the 1860s and the 1880s, a new generation of writers and thinkers found inspiration that sustained a literary boom and the advent of modern journalism. In the process, these pioneers revived the Arabic language from an ossified corpus of legal and religious terminology and rendered it a vibrant repertoire of communication capable of expressing the latest, cutting-edge ideas in science, philosophy and politics that were sweeping the world. This wave of cultural innovation produced a movement known as the *Nahda*, heralded by later generations as the intellectual cornerstone of an authentic Arab modernity.

The *Nahda*: the Arab Renaissance

The *Nahda* – a term that literally means 'getting up' or 'rising up' but is usually translated as 'renaissance' or 'revival' – defies any easy explanation in terms of origins, geography or content.[34] The thinkers of the *Nahda* were secular as well as religious, spiritual as well as scientific, creatives as well as chroniclers. The genealogy of the *Nahda* can be traced back to Egypt, from where Mehmed Ali first dispatched scholars to Paris to learn the ways of the *Afranj* ('the Franks'), introduced the printing press to Cairo and founded the first news bulletins covering government affairs. Yet its origins can also be found in the Mount Lebanon of Bashir II, where graduates of recently established Maronite colleges formed the core of a nascent intelligentsia who had mastered Classical Arabic and composed poetry that, rather predictably, lavished praise upon the wisdom and benevolence of their political patron.[35] From about

1860 onwards, the next generation of graduates from Maronite and missionary schools broke away from the ornate, baroque style of Classical Arabic in favour of a clearer, more direct form of writing that had the potential to reach a mass audience. Taking advantage of the new printing technologies, writers of the *Nahda* produced newspapers, scientific journals and literary works in which they pushed forward intellectual boundaries. In parallel with these efforts, religious scholars in Cairo and Damascus contributed to an ongoing Islamic reform movement that had first emerged in the eighteenth century, but now sought to reconcile European scientific advancement with Islamic knowledge; their quest to find a balance between reason and faith resonated with secular concerns. Rather than representing a unitary current of modern Arabic thought, the *Nahda* had a variety of intellectual tributaries and streams.

The cultural agility of the *Nahda* is exemplified in the trajectories of some of its best-known writers. Ahmad Faris al-Shidyaq (1804–87) of Mount Lebanon was born a Maronite but converted to Protestantism and – after incurring the wrath of the Maronite patriarch – worked his way to Cairo then Malta, London, Oxford, Paris and Istanbul as a translator and *littérateur*. Shidyaq was an advocate of women's equality ('there will be no liberation nor renaissance of the East,' he said, 'without the liberation and renaissance of the Oriental woman'), a critic of the English class system (which concentrated land ownership in the hands of the aristocracy, he observed, leaving the English peasantry just as miserable as their equivalents on Mount Lebanon) and an author of what is sometimes considered to be the first Arabic novel.[36] Shidyaq was also the founder of *al-Jawa'ib*, one of the Ottoman Empire's most influential Arabic-language newspapers, published in Istanbul from 1861 to 1883. It was here that Shidyaq first translated the term 'socialism' into Arabic; his neologism of choice, *ishtirakiya*, has since become the accepted standard.[37] Although Shidyaq was an avowed secularist, this did not prevent him from translating the Bible, studying with religious scholars at al-Azhar University and undertaking a second religious conversion, to Islam, and possibly even a third upon his deathbed, this time to Catholicism. Shidyaq's concern for the modernization of the Arabic language was typical of *Nahda* writers, but he also revelled in rhetorical flourishes and erudite ridiculousness, at one time rather joyfully listing over 250 literary euphemisms for 'penis', 'vagina' and 'sexual intercourse'.[38] Shidyaq further espoused a critical perspective on economic and social inequality that is largely absent from the writings of his contemporaries. Shidyaq's character may have been quixotic, but his idiosyncrasies were very much those of the new age in which he lived.

A second pioneer of the *Nahda* was Butrus al-Bustani (1819–83), who received an expansive modern education in a prestigious Maronite school in Mount Lebanon but converted to Protestantism and worked as a teacher and translator for American missionaries in Beirut. Bustani's fierce intelligence propelled him to the forefront of Beirut's emerging intellectual scene. He was a founding member of the Syrian Society for the Arts and Sciences, the author of a comprehensive dictionary of modern Arabic, *Muhit al-Muhit* ('Ocean of the Oceans'), and the first Arabic encyclopedia, *Da'irat al-Ma'arif* ('The Scope of Knowledge'). He founded numerous newspapers and journals that brought to an Arabic readership the latest news in politics, culture and science. In response to Mount Lebanon's sectarian conflict between Christians and Druze in 1860, Bustani expounded a vision for a secular civil society in which individuals would relate to one other not through their family or religious community, but through their common membership in a single nation.

'You have tried civil war time after time,' Bustani wrote. 'But what have you gained? . . . What has been the consequence of violence? Widowhood, orphanhood and poverty? Degradation, earthly and spiritual destruction and humiliation? Belittlement of native sons in the eyes of rational men and foreigners? . . . Exchange your blind prejudice – which is nothing but a kind name for excessive self-love – with love for the nation and inter-confessional friendship. The success of the country is achieved only through concord and unity.'[39]

Bustani and his contemporaries now explicitly identified this nation as 'Syria' (*Suriya*), taking up the name of the former Roman province in part of the region that had become common among French and British diplomats and missionaries as well as Ottoman officials. The boundaries of Syria did not coincide with the new Ottoman province created in 1865 with Damascus as its capital, they were careful to point out, but essentially overlapped with the already familiar *Bilad al-Sham*. 'Syria lies between the River Euphrates in the east and the Mediterranean Sea to the west, between the Arabian Peninsula to the south and Anatolia to the north,' as an 1866 article in the *Hadiqat al-Akhbar* newspaper explained to its readers.[40] The first book in Arabic to feature the name 'Syria' in its title had appeared a little earlier, in 1860: Khalil al-Khuri's *Kharabat Suriya* ('Ruins of Syria') was a gazetteer of ancient archaeological sites that mapped a common regional history. Subsequent books such as Ilyas Matar's *The Pearl Necklace of the Syrian Kingdom* (1874), Jurji Yanni's *History of Syria* (1881), and Yusuf al-Dibs' ten-volume *History of Syria* (1893-1905) did not simply narrate the history of an old Roman province, a loose-knit *Bilad al-Sham* or an Ottoman administrative experiment, but established a new meaning for 'Syria' as the common home of its people.

Calls for cultural renewal were disseminated across the lands of Syria by a proliferation of Arabic newspapers. In the 1860s and 1870s, a new wave of Beirut-based publications such as *Hadiqat al-Akhbar* ('The Garden of News', established 1858), *al-Jinan* ('The Garden', established 1870), *Thamarat al-Funun* ('The Fruit of Knowledge', established 1875) and *al-Muqtataf* ('The Digest', established 1876) were avidly perused by educated elites as far away as Damascus and Aleppo, Homs and Hama.[41] In addition to the latest political developments in Europe and the Ottoman Empire, these newspapers introduced the theories of Darwin, debated the need for women's liberation and showcased avant-garde Arabic fiction in the form of the serialized novel.[42] The intellectual scope of the *Nahda* was truly remarkable.

While *Nahda* intellectuals called for the renewal of a nation they identified as Syrian, and Arabic speaking, their project was exclusively cultural and linguistic, and rarely trespassed into the domain of government. These writers espoused principles of equality, civility and renewal that were initially consistent with the overall framework of Ottomanism. Nevertheless, this position proved more difficult to maintain after 1876, when Sultan Abdulhamid II suspended the constitution, reasserted his Islamic credentials and introduced strict censorship to counter criticism. The flourishing Arabic press scene found itself struggling for air. To escape the reach of Abdulhamid's despotism, a steady stream of Syrian intellectuals, along with their newspapers, abandoned Istanbul and Beirut for Cairo, where they found a more hospitable and even more cosmopolitan environment under Khedive Ismail, grandson of Mehmed Ali. Syrian immigrants went on to play a prominent role in the Egyptian press, including the founding of the prominent *al-Ahram* ('The Pyramids') newspaper. By the 1880s, Cairo had overtaken Beirut as the capital of Arab journalism.

Although Beirut had become the centre for secular thought in the *Nahda*, it was Cairo that was the locus of an explicitly Islamic strand of the movement. Religious scholars and activists such as Jamal al-Din al-Afghani and Muhammad Abduh maintained that spiritual as well as social renewal was a precondition for restoring Islam to its rightful place in the world. This argument identified Islam not merely as a religion, but as a civilization.[43] Abduh's outspoken criticism of British interference and occupation in Egypt earned him imprisonment and exile, three years of which he spent teaching in Beirut where his calls to reconcile religious law and rational thought fell on fertile ground. Abduh soon became the most prominent voice in the Islamic modernism of the *Nahda*, a stream of thought which also included Damascus-based scholar Tahir al-Jaza'iri and Tripoli's Rashid Rida.[44] In this way, the Islamic as well as secular currents of the *Nahda* rippled across both Egypt and Syria.

While exiled in Egypt or in Europe, both secular and religious thinkers from the Syrian provinces developed their critique of the sultan's departure from constitutionalism. In doing so, they contributed to a growing opposition against the despotism of Sultan Abdulhamid and helped build the foundations of what would later become alternative political visions for their homeland.

Fragmenting the empire: Ottomans, Young Turks and Arabists

Towards the end of the nineteenth century, mounting opposition to the policies of Sultan Abdulhamid propelled dissidents to create secret political organizations across and beyond the empire. In 1889, Istanbul students founded a group that formed the nucleus of the Committee of Union and Progress (CUP), which then agitated against the sultan from Europe. Around the same time, similar opposition groups in London and Paris were founded by Salim Faris, son of the noted *Nahda* intellectual

Ahmad Faris al-Shidyaq, and Amin Arslan, a Druze emir from Mount Lebanon. These groups became collectively known as the Young Turks, a somewhat misleading term given the leading role played in the movement by individuals from Arabic-speaking provinces of the Ottoman lands; the Young Turks also included many Kurds and Albanians in their number.[45] Importantly, the Young Turks opposed only the autocracy of Sultan Abdulhamid II: they called for constitutional reforms within the framework of the Ottoman Empire, not for its abolition. To escape the Ottoman censor, the Young Turks spread their message through journals and newspapers based in Paris, London and Cairo, which were smuggled into the Ottoman lands and read widely. Ironically, the Young Turks' message proved popular with graduates of those same elite government schools that had been established to produce government officials loyal to the over-arching Ottoman Empire. Dispatched across the provinces in the course of their careers, these officers and administrators became vectors for transmitting Young Turk criticism of the sultan across Syria, Iraq and even the Hijaz of coastal Arabia.

Of all the cities of the Syrian provinces, Damascus proved perhaps most surprisingly receptive to the ideas of the Ottoman opposition. Unlike Beirut, Damascus had not yet become home to a flourishing newspaper scene: the few journals published there very much echoed the official government line. However, the recent wave of modern schools had produced a small elite readership for the intellectual production of the *Nahda*. Many members of the new educated class of Damascus were shaped by the influence of Tahir al-Jaza'iri, religious scholar and educational reformer. Throughout the 1890s and early 1900s, al-Jaza'iri became the hub of a thriving intellectual circle that brought together disaffected Ottoman reformers and Islamic modernizers. This new generation of students had been raised in the climate of the *Nahda*, which emphasized the achievements of the Arabic language and culture as part of its programme for cultural renewal. This education predisposed these individuals to begin thinking of themselves not merely as Arabic speakers, but as something new: *Arabs*.

Producing an ethnically 'Arab' identity out of a linguistically 'Arabic' culture was a complex and contingent process. The revivalism of the *Nahda*, both secular and religious, stimulated an interest in the Arabic language that necessarily redirected attention to the classical Arab-Islamic age that had preceded both Ottoman rule and European encroachment. This attention to the historical centres of earlier Islamic polities – Mecca, Medina, Damascus and Baghdad – highlighted the seminal importance of the Arabian Peninsula from which Islam and the Arabs had originated. Travelling to Istanbul from cities such as Damascus, individuals with this Arab-Islamic worldview were shocked to see that the cultural capital they had acquired from immersion in the *Nahda* meant little to their Turkish Ottoman educators. Students from the Syrian provinces were treated like second-rate provincial hicks in the imperial schools, while the sons of high-ranking officials from Istanbul – inevitably not native Arabic speakers – received an array of special privileges: better food, nicer lodgings, even separate classes. Despite the promise of an 'Ottoman' national identity that bridged diverse communities, Syrian students encountered a reality in which their cultural orientation towards Arabic marked out their second-class status at the very heart of the empire.

Around the turn of the century, Arabic-speaking intellectuals started to frame debates about the ills of Sultan Abdulhamid's rule not only as a critique of political despotism, but increasingly as a critique of the cultural decay that had eroded Islamic civilization under the Ottoman dynasty. For some, the solution was to restore the vitality of Islam by looking back to Arabia, where the religion was still pure and untouched by the corrupting influence of either Ottomans or Europeans. This revalorization of the Arabian Peninsula marked an abrupt break with prevailing ideas about the desert, which urban communities had historically considered to be uncivilized, irreligious and, quite frankly, dangerous. The only part of Arabia touched by Ottoman government was the western coastal region of the Hijaz, which maintained a certain cosmopolitanism thanks to trade and pilgrimage routes to Mecca. Arabia's arid interior was home to a puritanical revivalist movement, the Wahhabis, and their political allies, the Saudis, whose hostile takeovers of Ottoman-claimed lands had prompted military intervention from Istanbul on numerous occasions since the mid-eighteenth century. Further afield, the distant province of Yemen was considered so far removed from civilization that imperial reformers mooted sending Ottoman colonists there to end its state of savagery. Although Ottoman sovereignty in principle extended to the eastern coast of the Peninsula, in practice Istanbul's authority barely extended far south of the province of Basra.

One of the earliest expressions of Arabia's political rehabilitation came from Aleppo-born writer Abd al-Rahman al-Kawakibi, whose 1898–99 *Umm al-Qura* ('The Mother of Towns', an epithet of Mecca) was perhaps the first book to celebrate the cultural significance of the Bedouin tribes for modern Arab-Islamic civilization.[46] In Cairo, the religious scholar Rashid Rida disseminated Kawakibi's ideas in the pages of his *al-Manar* newspaper and voiced similar arguments in his own works.[47] Although unthinkable for earlier generations, the idea spread that the tribes of Arabia maintained noble values, free from the taint of foreign influence, that could provide the resources for civilizational renewal. Despite its novelty, this line of argument initially sought to reorient only religion and culture, not politics. Not until the First World War was this criticism of the Ottoman Empire repurposed to serve the new and explicitly insurrectionary agenda of political independence for the Arabs.

In July 1908, an Ottoman army revolt in the Balkans pressured Abdulhamid to finally restore the constitution. Just a year later, Young Turk elements deposed him from office. The dominant Committee of Union and Progress (CUP) faction now played a prominent role in shaping the government agenda. With parliament restored and censorship restrictions lifted, there was a resurgence of political and intellectual life across the Arab provinces. Unlike the earlier *Nahda*, this wave of activity was not concentrated in Beirut. Over the next few years, Damascus and Aleppo – which until then produced only three newspapers between them – published no fewer than sixty-two new periodicals. The pages of *al-Muqtabas*, perhaps the most renowned newspaper of its kind, became a focus for a new generation of Damascene intellectuals, schooled in the reformist thought of the *Nahda*. Under the leadership of its editor, the famed thinker Muhammad Kurd 'Ali, *al-Muqtabas* published articles by such individuals as Shukri al-'Asali, Abd al-Rahman al-Shahbandar and Fakhri al-Baroudi, many of whom went on to become prominent political figures in Syria well into the 1930s and 1940s. The boom in journalism also swept Palestine, where thirty-four new newspapers were founded, and Iraq, which produced seventy new publications. Even in distant Hijaz, six new journals came into being. In total, over 355 Arabic-language newspapers were published across the empire between 1908 and the First World War. This unprecedented expansion of the space for public debate represents what Ami Ayalon has described as a 'unique chapter in the story of Arab journalism'.[48]

In this newly charged political environment, deputies from

across the Arab provinces converged on Istanbul to serve in the restored parliament. Unlike in the short-lived 1876 chamber, this time there were efforts to bring together the representatives from Syria, Iraq, Libya and the Hijaz to articulate a common Arab agenda. A deputy from Jerusalem raised concerns about the plans of Zionist settlers to establish a Jewish state in Palestine, concerns shared by a representative from Damascus who had previously served as an administrator in Nazareth.[49] Although a firm intra-Arab coalition never really took shape, the deputies did push for improved representation for the Arab provinces in parliament and the civil service. In the process, they developed a more antagonistic relationship with the CUP, which was seeking to bolster the power of central government over the provinces. Notably, the CUP's policy of centralization was accompanied by a renewed emphasis on Turkish as the common language of government and schooling. The extent to which 'Turkification' was actually implemented is still debated,[50] but the question became a source of friction between the CUP in Istanbul and Syrian urban elites.

Rural Syria too chafed at the infringements of centralization. In 1910–11, the Druze and Bedouin of the Hawran and Transjordan took up arms to protest against efforts to carry out a new census (with its associated dangers of conscription and taxation): they deliberately targeted the Hijaz Railway as the symbolic as well as material expression of state authority. The Ottoman authorities dispatched a huge force of thirty battalions to quell the revolt and sentenced as many as 150 Druze and Bedouin leaders to forced labour, imprisonment and execution.[51] Among their number were members of the Atrash and 'Amir families of Jabal al-Duruz, who were hanged publicly in Damascus. The gruesome scene caused great consternation among the intelligentsia of *al-Muqtabas*, who took up the cause of the great injustice visited upon their Druze brothers and campaigned on their behalf. By

1912, petitions were being sent to Istanbul co-signed by prominent Druze, Damascene and even Bedouin leaders, indicating the emergence of growing political connections and consensus.[52] These urban intellectuals had come to identify the Druze, much like the Bedouin, as reservoirs of authentic Arab culture: 'All are Arabs, of the Arabs and for the Arabs.'[53] By this point, political opposition to the centralization programme advocated by the CUP had started to acquire a distinctly ethnic tone. Secret societies and literary clubs such as *al-Fatat* ('Youth') and *al-'Ahd* ('The Covenant') became popular among Arab officers in the Ottoman army as well as among the urban elites of Syria and Iraq. These societies facilitated the ongoing flow of Arabist ideas, which became only more popular as Istanbul clamped down on political activity and purged Arabs from the Ottoman armed forces.

Even at this stage, 'Arabism' (*al-'uruba*) was not incompatible with continued loyalty to the Ottoman Empire. An Arab Congress held in Paris in June 1913, for example, brought together opposition figures from the lands of Syria and beyond, but once again called for reform within the Ottoman Empire, not for its dissolution. Nevertheless, the Arabist cause did imply a degree of autonomy that placed it on a potential collision course with Istanbul. It was at this point that the Ottoman Empire, already under strain from these internal pressures, launched itself into the maelstrom of global warfare.

The First World War: Cemal Pasha, *safarbarlik* and the Arab Revolt

The Ottoman Empire entered the Great War in November 1914 in alliance with the German Empire, which – unlike the French and British – had no history of assaulting Ottoman territorial or financial sovereignty. In the eyes of the CUP, moreover, the Ottoman Empire had already been involved in fighting across south-eastern Europe for several decades. An expansion of the war effort would surely bestow a new sense of purpose and unity to the empire as a whole.[54]

To implement this policy in an important region of the home front, the Ottomans sent to Damascus Cemal Pasha, who in the course of his career had governed Baghdad and Istanbul, and also served as Ottoman minister for the navy and for public works. Cemal Pasha's responsibilities were straightforward: to strengthen Ottoman control over the Syrian provinces, which would be used as a springboard to retake Egypt from the British. To achieve this goal, Cemal was granted full military and civilian authority over all the lands of Syria, from Aleppo to Palestine. A zealous modernizer, Cemal believed it the duty of government to save the peoples of the Ottoman Empire from their own backwardness. He considered that his mission in Syria required him to reassert the authority of the central Ottoman state, which could then get back to the business of producing modern Ottoman citizens through education, conscription and the state-sponsored media. Given the empire's recent territorial losses in the Balkans and Libya, Cemal Pasha – much like the rest of the CUP – had no tolerance for opposition or dissent. In his view, expressions of local identity, whether Arab or Armenian, Christian or Zionist, required harsh repression if they implied any autonomy from Istanbul. His position effectively reversed not only CUP efforts over the previous two years to undermine the appeal of Arabism by recruiting more Arabs into the government bureaucracy, but also other concessions made after the 1913 Arab Congress in Paris. In contrast to these initiatives, Cemal Pasha now imposed a more radical, hardline approach. If we 'break the heads of these damn people,' Cemal wrote in his private correspondence, 'there would be no Arab question to emerge.'[55]

Cemal Pasha's first step was to purge his administration of many local officials suspected of harbouring Arabist sympathies; he replaced them with well-qualified Turks, new to the region, whom he therefore considered more capable of governing the Syrian provinces objectively. The second step came in August 1915, when he ordered the hanging of eleven prominent Arabists who had entertained the possibility of collaborating with Britain should the Ottoman Empire collapse during the war. The investigation of what Cemal Pasha perceived as treasonous opposition expanded further over the following months: In May 1916, fourteen more Arabists were hanged in Beirut and a further seven in Damascus. Many more Arabists were arrested, exiled or imprisoned, their properties confiscated, their families persecuted. In total as many as 5,000 people were deported from the country to Anatolia or beyond.[56]

The hangings of the Arabists created anger and disbelief that etched themselves indelibly into local collective memory.[57] Cemal Pasha earned himself the sobriquet *al-Saffah*, 'the butcher'; the Arabists who had been hanged were canonized as martyrs for the cause; and al-Merjeh Square in Damascus, where the gallows had been built, was popularly renamed *Sahat al-Shuhada*, 'Martyrs' Square'. The next generation of the Syrian political leadership – those active in the 1920s and 1930s – would later describe how outrage at the deaths of the martyrs had ignited their adolescent political consciousness and won them over to the Arabist cause.[58] Ironically, Cemal Pasha's ruthless persecution of Arabism drove a wider wedge between Istanbul and the Syrian provinces and produced an enduring symbol for later Arab nationalists.

Although Cemal Pasha's draconian repression of the Arabist movement became a cornerstone of Syria's narrative of independence, less well known are his efforts to eliminate other forms of local autonomy and foreign interference from the region. Cemal

Pasha ordered Armenian refugees fleeing genocidal violence in Anatolia to be scattered across the towns of Syria, where they could become 'harmless minorities' rather than congregating in one place to form a new power bloc. He reasserted the empire's authority over the Greek Catholic and Maronite clergy, which he considered too independent and too close to Russia and France. He considered Zionist settlers in Palestine to be dangerous European fifth columnists, who sought to undermine imperial sovereignty by building independent, self-governing communities on Ottoman land. Cemal Pasha deported from the area prominent Zionists who had not acquired Ottoman citizenship and clamped down on the movement's political leadership. French-owned railways and ports were nationalized, foreign capitulations cancelled and many French, British and Russian citizens – including subjects of their empires, among them Algerians and Indians – were also deported. Cemal Pasha's suspicion of French infiltration even extended to prominent Christian families of Beirut, who were deemed too Francophile and summarily expelled. French schools and orphanages were closed or 'Ottomanized', a euphemism for being taken over by the state. This expansion of state education, along with increased conscription, served a dual purpose: to fuel the war effort, certainly, but also to eradicate foreign influence and restore a distinct Ottoman identity to the Syrian lands.

As if Syrians were not already suffering enough from Cemal Pasha's top-down state-building, the First World War was accompanied by food shortages that rapidly escalated to the point of famine. Suffering the effects of wartime hoarding and speculation, drought and locust invasion, not to mention a British and French naval blockade that mercilessly cut off food supplies, the Syrian provinces began to starve. Concerned that a revolt would break out in the Hijaz – which was similarly blockaded – Cemal Pasha ordered already scarce Syrian grain to be exported to Medina, which plunged *Bilad al-Sham* even further into misery. Desperate people ate vermin, emaciated children filled orphanages and the corpses of the destitute decayed on the roadside. Hundreds of thousands of people across the Syrian provinces died from hunger, typhoid and malaria. Some survived by turning to prostitution and crime; many more fled conscription, disease and despotism by leaving their homeland to seek a better life in Europe, the Americas or West Africa.[59] Syrians adopted a new name for the cataclysm they lived through during these years: *safarbarlik*. This was originally the empire's official term for wartime mobilization, but was now requisitioned and repurposed by ordinary people to capture the trauma they collectively endured.[60] *Safarbarlik* became synonymous with families lost, lives shattered and homes abandoned. While in Europe the horrors of the First World War were visited upon soldiers in the trenches, in the lands of Syria they were inflicted upon civilians. During the dark years of *safarbarlik*, the region became depopulated, impoverished and deeply traumatized.

Cemal Pasha lost his gamble that exporting food from starving Syria would prevent unrest sweeping the Hijaz. In June 1916, an uprising broke out against Ottoman troops in Arabia that met with surprising success. The uprising was led by Sharif Husayn ibn Ali al-Hashimi, a prominent notable whose importance as a local intermediary had been recognized by the sultan in 1908 with the title Emir of Mecca. Although originally a loyal Ottoman, Sharif Husayn was deeply suspicious of centralization policies emanating from Istanbul. The recently completed extension of the Hijaz Railway to Medina, for example, already threatened to strengthen Istanbul's administrative and military authority at the expense of local autonomy.

To bolster his position, Sharif Husayn had opened lines of communication with the British high commissioner in Cairo,

Sir Henry McMahon, and had also sent his son Faysal to liaise with Arabists in Damascus. Between July 1915 and March 1916, Sharif Husayn negotiated with McMahon over potential British support for an Arab polity independent from Istanbul. McMahon agreed to recognize the sovereignty of Arab rule in Arabia and Syria, although he stipulated three conditions. The first was that districts west of the line of Damascus, Homs, Hama and Aleppo would be excluded (that is, the Mediterranean coast of Mount Lebanon, Jabal al-Ansariya and Alexandretta) on the grounds they were ostensibly 'not purely Arab'. The second was that the Ottoman provinces of Baghdad and Basra would require a special administrative status to reflect existing and future British interests. Third, sovereignty would be recognized only inasmuch as Britain was able to act 'without detriment to the interests of her ally, France' and without prejudice to existing treaties with other Arab shaykhs. This final condition could be used to exclude British protectorates such as Kuwait and Bahrain, as well as to absolve London of its subsequent failure to honour the deal for the sake of its wartime alliance with Paris. Despite these caveats, the promise of independence – along with material support and an end to the naval blockade preventing food supplies from reaching the Hijaz via the Red Sea – was enough to persuade Sharif Husayn to take up arms against the Ottomans.

Running on a diet of 'guns, grain and gold' supplied by Britain, a nucleus of tribal forces led by Sharif Husayn's son Faysal swept out of Arabia, seizing control of Aqaba and Jerusalem in late 1917 and thereby clearing the advance of British troops entering Palestine from Egypt.[61] Reinforced with defected Ottoman officers and Arab prisoners-of-war who had been held in Egypt, Iraq and India, the Arab Revolt acted as a guerrilla force along the right flank of the British army. At first, the revolt adopted the language of religion rather than Arabism. Compared to *Bilad al-Sham*, after all, the Hijaz had been much less profoundly touched by the cultural revival of the *Nahda*, secular education or accelerated contact with Europe.[62] Yet as victories propelled it northwards, the ranks of the revolt swelled with Arab army officers and activists from *al-'Ahd*, *al-Fatat* and other Arab secret societies, not to mention local tribes who threw their lot in with the rebels.[63] The ideas of Arabism usefully legitimized the extension into Syria of a political authority the centre of which lay in distant Arabia. From its beginnings in the Hijaz to its arrival at the gates of Damascus, the revolt grew from a core of just a few thousand to a popular movement in which as many as 20,000 or 30,000 people had participated.

By 1918, the Ottoman administration in Syria was under severe strain as it defended itself against the advancing forces of Britain and Sharif Husayn, a starving population and a collapsing currency.[64] In September that year, British forces commanded by General Allenby followed a significant victory in northern Palestine by taking Der'a, Damascus and, a month later, Aleppo. Soon after, when hostilities between Britain, France and the Ottoman Empire ended with the Armistice of Mudrus, a coalition of anti-Ottoman forces that included Syrian journalists, Iraqi officers and Sharif Husayn's son Faysal found themselves in a position to conduct an unprecedented political experiment in Damascus: government by Arabs, for Arabs. But it was an experiment that was not to last long.

From Arab Government to Faysal's kingdom, 1918–1920

The fortunes of the Arab Government in Damascus were shaped by no fewer than five competing forces, each with their own political vision for Syria. The first was Faysal himself, who believed that the best hope of independence lay with trusting Britain, which had after all committed itself to an independent Arab Kingdom in the region. Faysal's preoccupation with a negotiated diplomatic settlement led him to spend weeks and months in Paris and London, where he was increasingly distant from changing public opinion in Syria. A second force emerged to fill this gap that took a more radical, less compromising position on independence: this group's numbers included Arabist army officers and younger intellectuals. A third, including many notables and elite families, resented the fact that Faysal's government had been imposed upon them by British force of arms and looked to retain the privileged position they had enjoyed under the Ottomans. The fourth party was France, which was determined to advance its interests in the Levant more aggressively in the wake of the losses it had suffered during the Great War. While initially focused on Mount Lebanon, the French government and business community now aspired to bring the Syrian interior into its sphere of influence. The fifth was Britain, which sought to navigate a path through its competing wartime commitments to France (the Sykes–Picot Accord), the Zionists (the 1917 Balfour Declaration, which promised a 'national home' for the Jewish people in Palestine) and Sharif Husayn (the Husayn–McMahon correspondence). The eventual solution involved London satisfying the first two of these and reneging on the understanding that had been reached with Sharif Husayn.

Although geopolitical competition ultimately determined the trajectory of the post-war Levant, its political landscape was nevertheless deeply shaped by currents of contention within Syria itself. Faysal arrived in Damascus to find he had been beaten to establishing an independent Arab government: two notables from the Jaza'iri family had already raised the flag of the Arab Revolt and declared themselves in charge. However, the Jaza'iris had few links with the Arabist movement and were expelled from the city at Faysal's request. On 5 October, Faysal officially declared the establishment of an independent, constitutional government in the name of Sharif Husayn, encompassing 'all of the Syrian lands'. The flag of the Arab Revolt was swiftly raised in Aleppo, Hama, Homs, Latakia and Beirut, and committees of local government established by Faysal's supporters.[65] Faysal explicitly guaranteed the rights of Muslims, Jews and Christians within the new polity.

Faysal's geographical expansiveness clashed with British and French plans for the lands of Syria. Much to his annoyance, Faysal was pressured to have his flag taken down from Beirut less than a month after he had declared the coast part of the independent Arab government. Threatening to resign, Faysal was able to regain control of a narrow tranche of the Biqaa Valley, albeit temporarily, and the British recognized his political authority over the Arab-administered interior, where Faysal's ally Ali Rida al-Rikabi – a member of *al-Fatat* and a former Ottoman officer originally from Damascus – effectively served as his prime minister.

The territory granted to Faysal corresponded to the former Ottoman provinces of Damascus (which reached as far south as Aqaba) and Aleppo: the British called this area 'Occupied Enemy Territory: North'. The former Ottoman districts of Jerusalem, Acre and Nablus, west of the Jordan River in Palestine ('Occupied Enemy Territory: South') were placed under direct British occupation. By late 1919, Britain had ceded control of the former Ottoman province of Beirut, Mount Lebanon and the former *sanjak* of Latakia on the Mediterranean coast, as well as lands to the interior that reached to the town of Zahleh in the Biqaa, to a force of some 19,000 French troops. This zone was known as 'Occupied Enemy Territory: West'. After French forces moved north from Beirut in December 1918 to forcefully occupy the region of Cilicia, the former Ottoman province of Adana became 'Occupied Enemy Territory: North'.

In November 1918, Faysal departed for Europe to lobby the Paris Peace Conference for an independent Arab state in all the lands of Syria. A flurry of political organizing took place during his absence. Under Rikabi's supervision, the old institutions of Ottoman government had been reinvigorated by an influx of new civil servants, British experts and Syrian specialists, several of whom had already worked in colonial administration for Britain in Egypt and Sudan.[66] A chronic lack of funds – which in any case came mostly from British subsidy – meant this administration was limited; in practice, its reach did not extend far beyond Damascus. Directorates were nevertheless established to govern portfolios including Finance, Justice, War, Health, Education, Public Works, and Agriculture and Tribes (although not foreign relations, which were conducted through the British). The Baghdad-born Yasin al-Hashimi, who had served with distinction as an officer in the Ottoman army, was made head of the War Council and tasked with overseeing the irregular forces of the Arab Revolt transition into a regular Arab army. Hashimi recruited more professional officers into the Arab Army, most of whom had not in fact defected from the Ottoman Empire until after the Armistice was signed.[67] Many of these former Ottoman officers originally came from Iraq.

The Arabist secret societies of *al-'Ahd* and *al-Fatat* had now come out into the open, although the Iraqi-dominated *al-'Ahd* had been alienated by Faysal's efforts to gain independence for Syria by cooperating with Britain, which was now also an occupying force in Iraq. A new organization, *al-Nadi al-'Arabi* ('The Arab Club'), began life as a cultural association, but soon attracted a younger generation of political activists with an uncompromising vision for independence and a taste for rowdiness. Several new political parties were also founded around this time. The popular *Hizb al-Istiqlal* (Independence Party) called for Arab independence within a decentralized, federal system, while the *Hizb al-Ittihad al-Suri* (Syrian Union Party) was primarily a vehicle for Syrian radicals who had returned from Egypt after the Ottoman defeat. The Syrian Union was notably the first party to call for a commission to ascertain the wishes of Syrians from Gaza to Aleppo for their own political future. By the time Faysal returned to Damascus in April 1919, the political scene had shifted dramatically from the one he had left behind.

Faysal brought news that he had not succeeded in persuading Britain and France to recognize his government's sovereignty in Syria. On the contrary, the Paris Peace Conference had agreed the Charter of the League of Nations, Article 22 of which stated that what it referred to as the former Turkish territories should receive 'administrative advice and assistance' from a so-called 'mandatory' power 'until such time as they are able to stand alone'. It was unclear quite how long this time of 'tutelage' was supposed to last or the extent of colonial control this 'advice' would in practice convey.

Faysal nevertheless seized on language in Article 22 noting that 'the wishes of these communities must be a principal consideration in the selection of the mandatory'. Faysal consequently declared a national congress would be held to voice the wishes of the Syrian people. Over eighty congressmen were elected from across the region controlled by Faysal; Britain and France blocked elections in Palestine and the coast, then argued the congress was unrepresentative and therefore illegitimate.[68]

The Syrian congress was nevertheless established in time to meet with the King–Crane Commission, sent by US President Woodrow Wilson to determine the degree of civilization to be found in the former Ottoman territories. The congress presented the King–Crane Commission with a unified programme that rejected the Sykes–Picot Accord and the Balfour Declaration and called for full independence for all of Syria, from Anatolia to the Red Sea, the Euphrates to the Mediterranean. The congress further proposed Faysal as constitutional monarch, supported by international assistance from the United States – or from Britain as a second choice – although without an official mandate. This position mirrored the stance of Faysal himself, whose dismissive treatment from Paris had convinced him that tutelage from Britain was the only obstacle standing between Syria and French military occupation. Most petitions from across the region received by the King–Crane Commission echoed the appeals of the Syrian congress. The Commission consequently recommended a limited American Mandate to govern the lands of Syria and a rejection of British and French territorial designs on the region.[69] The Commission's recommendations were never acted upon. The prospect of any international support for Syria's independence receded beyond the horizon.

Under financial pressure to demobilize the quarter million soldiers it had stationed in the Middle East, in September 1919 Britain decided to withdraw both from the Syrian interior north of Transjordan and from Cilicia, the Mediterranean edge of Anatolia that, according to the agreement with Paris, fell under French jurisdiction. The departure of British troops was accompanied by the withdrawal of British subsidies, which left the Arab government in Damascus with neither protection against France's territorial ambitions nor support for its budget. When Faysal turned once again to diplomacy to achieve the goal of independence, the more radical nationalist camp began to train part-time militias to defend against the occupation by France they believed to be imminent. Anti-French protestors took to the streets, often bearing arms, in Damascus, Aleppo and even such small towns as

Idlib, Membij and Salamiya. Grassroots activists formed a Higher National Committee, in which most of the main nationalist parties were represented, to coordinate self-defence and 'take all means necessary to preserve the unity of the Syrian land, support its independence and resist any initiative to introduce a foreign national consciousness [*qawmiyya ghariba*] that threatens the political existence of the country'.[70] The Higher National Committee acted as an umbrella for a network of smaller Popular Committees, organized at the neighbourhood level, which gathered the urban lower middle class, in contrast to the Syrian congress that was dominated by notables and the intelligentsia.[71]

This unusual expression of mass political participation alienated many established notables. Elites in Damascus and Aleppo, as well as the Jabal al-Duruz and even some of the Bedouin tribes, broke with the nationalist consensus and put their own best interests first. As British troops withdrew from northern Syria, members of these local elites requested that Paris provide them with protection and autonomy given what seemed to them the forgone conclusion of occupation.

Across the lands of Syria, opposition to foreign rule gave rise to a series of insurrections. Loose knit bands of rebels took up arms against the French forces that had already begun to advance north and east from Beirut. In Cilicia, today part of Turkey, the campaign was led by Mustafa Kemal (better known as Atatürk). When this conflict spilled over into sectarian violence in which thousands of Armenians were killed, France feared similar scenes in the Syrian interior, unless they moved to intervene. As they advanced from Latakia into the Jabal al-Ansariya mountains, an Alawi chief named Salih al-Ali sought to fend off the invasion. In December, French forces marched east from Beirut into the Biqaa Valley, occupying territory that Britain had temporarily given to Faysal. Here too their forces were harried by bands of irregulars.

In the meantime, rebel forces led by Ramadan al-Shallash, a former Ottoman officer, captured the eastern town of Deir al-Zour from Britain in the name of the Arab government in Damascus. This move came as a surprise to Faysal, who denied all knowledge, apologized to the British and ordered Shallash arrested (albeit to no avail). In the meantime, the Arab government argued that Britain was wrong to insist that the border between Syria and Iraq should be demarcated by the Khabour River, as this line would artificially split the 'Uqaydat tribe who lived on both its banks.[72] Damascus therefore insisted the border be moved further east. Eventually the British conceded and pulled their forces back along the Euphrates, past the town of Albu Kamal. Today, this point still marks the border between Syria and Iraq.

Faced with the risk of losing the initiative to these men of action and uncompromising nationalists in the Syrian congress alike, Faysal took steps to outflank them. To counter the weight of the more radical parties, Faysal rallied his own grouping of notables, the Syrian Patriotic Party (*al-Hizb al-Watani al-Suri*), and, in March 1920, reassembled the Syrian congress in Damascus. He delivered a rousing address in which he declared Syria had every right to independence: he now called upon congress to decide the form of Syrian government and write its constitution.

The head of the grassroots-based Higher National Committee, Shaykh Kamal al-Qassab, was quick to endorse Faysal's initiative. 'The independence of Syria,' Qassab reminded the congress, 'is the cornerstone of independence for [all] the Arab countries [...] We urge [the members of the Congress] to fulfil their duty as brave footmen, for they know that there is no nation without an army, and no independence without a people to carry out its will.'[73] Riding on the crest of this new-found determination, the Syrian congress declared the independence of Syria within not only the territories granted to Faysal (whom they confirmed as constitutional monarch), but also the Syrian coast and Palestine then occupied, respectively, by France and Britain.[74]

In this defiant declaration of independence, the processes of imperial fragmentation and regional integration that had been launched during the late Ottoman Empire reached their culmination. Where *Bilad al-Sham* once lay, on 8 March 1920, the Kingdom of Syria now stood.

3

From Kingdom to Colonialism, 1920–1927

The Syrian congress's declaration of independence in March 1920 was an act of defiance. By claiming sovereignty over the entirety of Syria, including Mount Lebanon and Palestine, the Arab Kingdom explicitly rejected the plans for the region that Britain and France had set in motion. More concretely, the declaration of independence called for the evacuation of the 15,000 French troops fighting Alawi and Turkish rebels along the Mediterranean coast, as well as the 100,000 British soldiers in Palestine. While Britain was eager to scale back its wartime presence in the region, France had its eye set on expanding into the Syrian interior.

Despite this ominous geopolitical setting, a government was quickly formed in Damascus with Rikabi as prime minister. A new flag was raised (the black, green, white and red flag of the Arab Revolt, with the addition of a seven-pointed star), new stamps were issued, and King Faysal's name was added to Friday prayers. The Syrian congress assumed the functions of a legislature, its members clustering into two loose-knit camps: the Progressives (who were closer to Faysal's more moderate stance) and the Democrats (who were less willing to compromise their nationalist ideals). After much debate, the congress put together a constitution of 147 articles that declared Damascus to be the capital of the Syrian Arab Kingdom, defined as a 'civilian parliamentary monarchy' with Arabic as its official language. The constitution guaranteed civil liberties and reserved around a third of seats in the Chamber of Deputies for minorities.[1] This new document thus continued the egalitarian principles of late Ottoman constitutionalism, although its secularizing tendencies were arguably stronger: other than specifying that the monarch should be a Muslim, mention of Islam was notably absent from its articles.

Despite the grand political vision of the Arab Kingdom, the new polity lacked the expertise and institutions to deal with the economic situation, which had continued to deteriorate since the end of the war. The sheer size of the British and French armies continued to drain food from the broader region's already depleted supplies: military spending also exacerbated inflation, causing everyday prices to rocket. Just a few days after the declaration of independence, usually quiescent Hama was shaken by bread riots that brought the urgency of the problem to centre stage, while workers in Damascus organized a wave of strikes. The Arab government banned wheat exports from the interior to the coast, but even regular inspections of railways and roads could not stamp out all smuggling. Hoping to cut out the profiteers, the government itself began to purchase and mill wheat from the Hawran.[2] Faysal's government had been forced to implement severe spending cuts with the end of the subsidy from Britain; now, it tried to replace that revenue by doubling taxes, auctioning off tax-farming rights and banning the circulation of the 'Syrian pound' (pegged to the franc) that the French had started to issue in Beirut. (A new Syrian Arab currency, the dinar, was hastily created by fiat for government accounts, although its coins were never minted or exchanged). The decision to expand conscription was almost as unpopular as the increase in tax rates, provoking open resistance in Damascus and the Hawran.[3]

Besides alienating the popular classes, Faysal's government caused ambivalence among the urban elites. Damascene notables were alarmed by the mounting disorder, while their counterparts in Aleppo – who had always been culturally as well as geographically closer to the centre of the Ottoman Empire – looked to the successes of Atatürk's military campaign against the French as evidence that traditional ties with Turkey might yet be revived.

As French forces moved into northern Syria, Aleppo's Committee of National Defence continued to funnel money and supplies to the guerrilla forces led by Ibrahim Hananu, which now stood several hundred strong. Hananu's network not only coordinated resistance against French forces advancing from the coast into the region of Idlib, it also founded revolutionary courts, municipal governments and other structures of rebel governance across the territories it had liberated west of Aleppo.[4] The coastal town of Latakia strongly supported King Faysal, while the highlands of Jabal al-Ansariya were held by Alawi insurgents commanded by Salih al-Ali and sustained with weapons and money from the Arab government.[5] Loyalist rebel bands even appeared in the Biqaa Valley, west of Damascus, prior to any French advance into the interior, prompting some local Christian villagers to flee to the Lebanese coast for security.

Far from the fray of battle, the notables of Jabal al-Duruz sought to safeguard their autonomy within the framework of the Syrian Arab Kingdom. In 1919 Faysal had already recognized the authority of the most important family in the Jabal by appointing Salim al-Atrash as its governor. The Atrash were also represented in the Syrian congress by a young firebrand named Sultan al-Atrash, who had participated in the Arab Revolt against the Ottomans. The Atrash family had, moreover, gone on record to the American King–Crane Commission as being in favour of full independence for the whole of Syria. Nevertheless, a significant number of Druze notables believed that accepting a French Mandate to safeguard their autonomy would be preferable to an independent Arab state that would risk bringing the Jabal under the direct rule of Damascus – a fact that they had indeed communicated to French officials.[6]

The situation in Mount Lebanon – claimed by Faysal, but effectively excluded from his zone of influence by the occupying French forces – was even more complicated. The prominent Maronite Christian families of the region were already sympathetic to the prospect of French rule; over the previous few years they had also begun to be swayed by the voices of Maronite expatriates who argued for the novel idea that Mount Lebanon's religious and demographic specificity merited its full independence from the rest of Syria. Although the elite Druze families of the area were unmotivated by such sentiments of nascent nationalism, they too came to believe that Paris offered a better chance for autonomy than Damascus. In practice, however, the realities of French military administration and heavy-handedness meant that the debates about relations with Faysal's kingdom remained ongoing among both Maronites and Druze.

Faced with such diverse internal politics, entangled in the geopolitical rivalries of the post-war world, and unable to rebuild its shattered economy, Faysal's Syrian Arab Kingdom had little room for manoeuvre.

Public opinion hardened further when news broke of the agreement made by Britain and France at the San Remo Conference in April 1920. Ignoring the Arab Kingdom's claim to the lands of Syria, the conference severed British-held from French-held Syria, and bestowed London and Paris with the authority of mandatory powers. The essence of the mandates was to recognize the independence of these former Ottoman areas only provisionally, the condition being they were administered by France and Britain until such point as they were considered capable of governing themselves. The areas would be governed under the provisions of Article 22 of the covenant of the new League of Nations that had come into force just a few months earlier, affording a degree of international oversight and accountability that would ostensibly distinguish the new mandates from old-fashioned colonial rule. Britain was granted mandates over both Iraq and Palestine (which included Transjordan), while France received the mandate over the rest of a truncated Syria which encompassed the remaining territory of Faysal's Arab Kingdom. Britain assured Faysal that his kingdom's independence would be honoured under the mandate, albeit conditionally.

France had other ideas. After severe resistance from Turkish-organized rebels forced a partial withdrawal from the northern region of Cilicia, the commander of French troops in the Levant – who was also the newly appointed high commissioner in charge of the Mandate for Syria – redirected his attention towards Damascus. In July 1920, General Gouraud issued an ultimatum to Faysal: accept the French Mandate, approve the 'Syrian' currency issued by France, abandon conscription, accept French control of Syrian railways and punish any hostile actions targeting French forces. Gouraud gave Faysal four days to comply. As Faysal quite characteristically sought to negotiate the terms of the agreement, Gouraud pressed his advantage and demanded more concessions. Faysal felt he had no choice but to conform. His move provoked mass protests in Damascus that could only be repressed by turning the Arab army against its own civilians: hundreds of people were killed or wounded. Ironically, official notification of Faysal's compliance never reached Gouraud, who marched on Damascus with a force of 12,000 soldiers equipped with modern artillery, tanks and airpower. Anticipating immediate occupation, the Arab government ordered its army and civilian militias to confront the French army as they advanced to Khan Maysaloun, just outside the city.

On 24 July, the two sides clashed. Outmanned and outgunned, the Syrian Arab forces led by Faysal's minister of war Yusuf al-Azma suffered total defeat. Damascus fell quickly before Gouraud's troops. Aleppo, for its part, had been occupied the previous day without undue resistance. Faysal was expelled from the mandated territories claimed by the French and sought protection from the British in Palestine. He later resurrected his political career as the new Hashemite monarch of Iraq (under British supervision). In the meantime, the Syrian Arab Kingdom was at an end; the French Mandate had begun.

Foundations of the French Mandate

With French forces firmly in control of Aleppo, Damascus and Latakia, in addition to Mount Lebanon and the Biqaa Valley, High Commissioner Gouraud was faced with two distinct challenges: how to govern the cities of Syria, which were for the most part calm, and how to repress the ongoing rural insurgencies in the coastal mountains and the contested frontier between northern Aleppo and what would become southern Turkey. Rather than tackling these problems as separate military and political objectives, French officials ambitiously sought to fuse armed force, cultural understanding and institution building to facilitate their occupation of the region. While in strategic importance the lands of Syria were secondary to North Africa, French advocates of colonialism argued that historical links to the Christians of the Levant, the commitment to the civilizing mission and – rather surprisingly – the local population's great love for France made long-term French rule in the region all but inevitable. Whereas Britain was quick to pay lip service to the letter of the new mandates system, finding local proxies who would rule in their interests, French officials were more sceptical of the need to accept Wilsonian principles of self-determination. Their strategy in the Levant thus built on an older formula that France had tested out on colonized peoples around the world over more than a hundred years.

The first pillar of this strategy was the French doctrine of colonial warfare that had emerged in the 1890s in reaction to domestic criticism over the brutal and inhumane excesses of violence that had been inflicted in Algeria.[7] Instead of a scorched-earth campaign to shatter the morale of indigenous populations, French colonial officers in Indo-China, Madagascar and Morocco elaborated a new theory and practice of occupation that proposed to achieve victory by transforming local society in a way that would cause the enemy to recognize the benefits of occupation. Joseph-Simon Galliéni and his disciple Hubert Lyautey decided they would no longer destroy conquered villages but build markets and schools there; instead of crushing the economy, they would construct roads and bridges to revitalize local trade. They called this the *tache d'huile* ('oil stain') principle: just as specks of oil would spread out across a pool of water and eventually form a layer over the whole surface, the civilizing force of colonialism would calmly pacify society as it issued forth from multiple points of military conquest. Once the natives had crossed the threshold of 'civilization' in this way, they could in principle be allowed to govern themselves.[8]

French officials in Syria drew explicitly on their earlier experience of implementing this novel method of colonial occupation in Morocco, where Lyautey himself had been made resident-general in 1912. Lyautey was less convinced than Galliéni that those he considered to be primitive peoples could be transformed into civilized populations just by social engineering. Lyautey had therefore relied on Moroccan elites, especially tribal chiefs, to act as intermediaries for French rule, and established a specialist body of colonial intelligence officers combining the skill sets of anthropologists, explorers and spies to provide vital insights into the workings of Moroccan society, insights that could then be exploited by the colonial authorities.

In the event, the local knowledge supplied by the officers of the *Service des affaires indigènes* did not accurately reflect Morocco's complex social and political dynamics. Their analysis was filtered through the assorted cultural biases, racist stereotypes and erroneous received wisdoms that French colonialism had cultivated about the Orient over long decades. The French concluded alliances with individuals they had identified as powerful tribal chiefs (the *grands caïds*, for example), but often it was French recognition that had empowered these individuals in the first place. French authorities built a whole policy around the assumption that 'Arab' and 'Berber' were mutually exclusive ethnic groups, when these categories were much more fluid. French efforts to catalogue, preserve and enforce 'Berber traditions' actually lent them a coherence, unity and appearance of timelessness that they did not otherwise possess.[9] Morocco had its own sultan, whom the French understood to be the local equivalent of European royalty. The French therefore obliged the sultan to take up permanent resident in Rabat as befitting a king, rather than moving his court between four cities, as in the past. This hugely unpopular monarchy was kept immobile, toothless and isolated by the French in the name of cultural preservation, as if it were a prize exhibit in a living museum.

Far from respecting local tradition, Lyautey's approach tended to misinterpret Moroccan reality, establish that misinterpretation as the norm and insulate his inventions against any threat of social change. Even Lyautey's apparent desire to conserve the traditional architecture of Moroccan cities followed this logic. Colonial policy left urban neighbourhoods unmodernized and Moroccans prevented from moving into the newly built communities that enjoyed all the benefits of rational city planning. Instead, Europeans typically filled these modern developments, which were segregated in all but name from the sprawling and chaotic neighbourhoods of informal housing inhabited by Moroccans. This policy turned Rabat into what has been famously described as a city of apartheid.[10] For all Lyautey's celebration of the need to understand Moroccan society, that understanding was thin and instrumental. More importantly, despite its cultural trappings, French rule was always underwritten by the ready recourse to violence. In this doctrine of colonial warfare, brute force and subtle cultural knowledge were not alternative strategies of occupation, but two sides of the same coin.

Lyautey's Morocco provided the training ground for many colonial officials whose careers later took them to Syria and Lebanon. High Commissioner Gouraud had himself been posted in Morocco and was close to Lyautey, before being reassigned to the battlefields of the First World War, where he lost his right arm. Gouraud consciously drew on his Moroccan experience when setting up the French Mandate in Syria: many French officers in his administration had also been trained in Lyautey's methods in North Africa.[11] These officials thought they could straightforwardly import the model ostensibly perfected in Morocco across the Mediterranean to Syria. Perhaps unsurprisingly, reality proved them wrong.

Divide-and-rule: Syria as a 'mosaic society'

The religious, ethnic and socio-economic diversity of Syria presented mandatory officials with an abundance of options for fostering divisions and co-opting local elites, as prescribed by the Moroccan formula. Indeed, so diverse was the Levant that the French came to understand its society as lacking any real unity – in fact, they maintained, it could not in good conscience be called a society. French officials saw the Levant as little more than a chaotic patchwork of sects and tribes, who constantly feuded and fought one another in a state of permanent upheaval and anarchy. This notion of a 'mosaic society' – richly tessellated yet profoundly fragmented – was never far from the minds of colonial officials as they sought to navigate Syrian society. After militarily defeating the rural insurgencies within the first couple of years of the mandate, the French began to cultivate supporters in the regions of Jabal al-Ansariya and Jabal al-Duruz to balance the political opposition in the urban interior. Time and time again, the French justified this divide-and-rule strategy by referring to what they saw as sectarian fault lines in Syrian society. Without a strong French hand to protect Christians and other sects, they proclaimed, the Muslim majority would inevitably start a massacre, as had supposedly happened in the nineteenth century. Ignoring the fact that earlier episodes of communal violence came during times of rapid social change and foreign interference, France decided that the best solution was to divide Syria along broadly ethno-religious lines.[12]

High Commissioner Gouraud quickly consolidated control of Damascus and Aleppo. Ardent nationalists from Faysal's government were expelled from Syria, typically relocating to British-controlled Iraq, Transjordan or Egypt. To replace them, individuals from notable families willing to fill the political vacuum were found to collaborate with the French administration. By the end of the year, Gouraud had authorized the creation of two new political units – the State of Aleppo and the State of Damascus – and named local governors, who were quick to put their supporters and family members on the payroll.

The territory of these new statelets was greatly reduced from their previous incarnations as Ottoman provinces. In addition to the earlier loss of Palestine, Damascus was now detached from the less developed lands south of the Hawran, over which Britain was awarded a mandate the following year. Britain named this new state 'Transjordan' and installed Faysal's brother Abdullah there as king. To the north, Aleppo lost a large swathe of its economic hinterland in 1921 when France and the newly independent state of Turkey agreed a border which bisected the old Ottoman province. In the far north-western corner of the territories under the French Mandate, Turkey also laid claim to two additional districts of the former province – Alexandretta and Antioch. Given the mixed Turkish- and Arabic-speaking populations of this region, France bestowed a special administrative status on what it called the Sanjak of Alexandretta, loosely attached to the State of Aleppo in 1923.

In the meantime, a third new state, Greater Lebanon, was created to give the French-leaning Maronite Christian community of Mount Lebanon (which had largely refused to support Faysal's kingdom) a viable economic hinterland, by expanding it to absorb much of the former Ottoman province of Beirut (from the highlands south of Sidon to the Akkar plains north of Tripoli) and part of the old province of Damascus (the Biqaa Valley). Here too French strategic interests trumped the wishes of those who lived in the region. The decision to create Greater Lebanon followed no consultation with local leaders; its borders were based on a French military map drawn eighty years earlier. Thus, all three of the mini-states that initially constituted the territories under the French Mandate – Damascus, Aleppo and Greater Lebanon – had borders that could at best be described as loosely defined (see Map 4).

By 1921, the French felt sufficiently established to issue an amnesty to the exiled nationalists, who, upon their return, promptly resumed political activities. In Damascus, one of Faysal's former ministers, Abd al-Rahman al-Shahbandar, secretly organized the Iron Hand Society to oppose French rule. Agitation in Aleppo was coordinated by Sa'dallah al-Jabiri, scion of one of the city's most prestigious landowning families. The following year, Shahbandar took advantage of the return of Charles Crane, co-chair of the King–Crane Commission, to publicly denounce the occupation. The outcry at his subsequent arrest took the French by surprise: thousands of people took to the streets in repeated protest, each time marching through the Souq al-Hamidiya to be dispersed with increasing violence by French troops. Shahbandar was subsequently imprisoned on the island of Arwad, off the coast of Tartous, while other nationalists were jailed or exiled. These harsh sentences temporarily spelled an end to dissidence in the cities of the Syrian interior.

Episodes such as this confirmed what the French *thought* they knew about the Sunni Muslims of the towns: that is, although they were passive and weak, they were also the main political threat to French rule given their receptivity to supposedly radical ideologies such as Arab nationalism and Islamic fanaticism. Colonial officials furthermore believed that Britain actively stoked what they called the anti-French 'xenophobia' of urban Sunnis to support their own agenda – a suspicion they considered borne out by Britain's longstanding support for King Faysal and his followers. As they saw it, the problem was not France's heavy-handed occupation, but the fact that Syria's primitive populations were by nature unruly and hated all forms of authority: whatever France did to stop the natives killing one another, Syrians would always be rebellious. As General Clément-Grandcourt, commander of French troops in southern Syria, observed:

> Whether [Syria's ruling] authority be cruel or kind, regressive or liberal, it will always be detested by the majority, and especially by the Muslim masses, because it represents order and will seek to prohibit the internal struggle of races and religions which has torn apart Syria for so long – and which will tear it apart tomorrow if the Syrians were left to their own devices. With the exception of the Maronites, the Djebel Ansariyeh [i.e. the Alawis], and islands of Circassians and Christians in the interior, Syrians (at least the Syrians of the towns) will always consider their master to be an enemy, even if – as was the case with France – it was the desire of the overwhelming majority to invite him.[13]

The Syrian propensity for conflict provided a handy explanation for why the French occupation faced such seemingly irrational resistance, despite what colonial officials saw as the indisputable benefits of occupation by a civilizing force.

The 'Moroccan formula' initially appeared well-suited to the Jabal al-Duruz at least, where the leading family, the Atrash, stepped forward to negotiate autonomy for the Mountain. In 1921, the Atrash reached an agreement with General George Catroux, who had absorbed the spirit of Lyautey's approach to colonial affairs during his service in Morocco. The agreement with Catroux guaranteed them a Druze governor (Salim al-Atrash, who had held the same position under Faysal), an elected advisory council, an administrative commission and – importantly – an exemption from conscription. In exchange, French forces were given the right to install military forces and civilian advisors in the Jabal, which was constituted as an autonomous governorate independent of the states of Damascus and Aleppo. The agreement also specified that the governorate of Jabal al-Duruz forfeit the right to reunify with the rest of the territories under the French Mandate.[14]

While the tactic of collaborating with a stronger outside power to ensure local autonomy under their leadership was part of a playbook that the Druze notables had used successfully many times in the past, some of the younger generation saw things differently. In 1922, Sultan al-Atrash rallied his supporters and waged guerrilla warfare against the French in the Jabal. With the nationalists in Damascus in disarray, however, the sultan's efforts lacked support and he was obliged to accept an uneasy truce with the mandatory power the following year.

To the north, the revolts of Salih al-Ali and Hananu had also subsided by 1922, strangled by a combination of the loss of support from Atatürk and ongoing repression from French forces. For the French, the Alawis seemed to be a viable ethnic group that might be played against urban Sunni nationalists, but their fragmented social structure and underdeveloped collective consciousness limited their utility in that regard. The colonial authorities therefore sought to transform the Alawis from a dispersed population into a more unified cultural bloc that would conform to French expectations of how a proper communal group should behave. Government institutions were therefore repurposed to become incubators of Alawi identity.

In July 1922, the French created yet another new state centred on the Syrian coastal mountains. Sandwiched between the State of Greater Lebanon and the Sanjak of Alexandretta, these lands had previously been part of the Ottoman province of Beirut. They named this area the Territory of the Alawites (Alaouites, as the French called the Alawis), a designation that purposefully overlooked the region's mixed religious composition in the search to create allies in Syria's most impoverished and marginalized community. Alawis were guaranteed a majority of seats on the Representative Council, the statelet's equivalent of a parliament, which was headed by members of prominent Alawi families such as the Abbas and the Kinj. The region's French military governor, Colonel Paul Niéger, established an official system of religious courts staffed by Alawi shaykhs. That Alawis could for the first time have legal claims judged by their co-religionists represented another break with the past. In the preceding decades, conversely, there had been incremental steps towards integration in the context of both Ottoman reforms and Alawi shaykhs' own efforts to move closer to the main currents of Islam (especially to centres of Shia learning in the south of the new Greater Lebanon). Now Alawi spiritual leaders were suddenly thrust into positions of worldly authority based on the premise that they were distinct, *un*integrated components of what France saw as the ethnological mosaic of the Levant. Measures such as these gave leading Alawi families their first collective taste of the institutional power of the modern state. The changes also established the principle that Alawis' access to power came not from wealth or social standing, as it had in the past, but from their identities as Alawis. Under the French Mandate it became possible to speak about a collective self-awareness of Alawis as a distinct ethno-religious community in a way that was that very different from the loose-knit, scattered population of the nineteenth century.

The Moroccan model of divide-and-rule was not successful everywhere across Syria. French officers repeatedly concluded what they thought were serious negotiations with Bedouin chiefs, who promised to provide desert security in exchange for French money and guns. To the chagrin of these officers,

Syrian tribal shaykhs could not – or would not – make good their word. Officers who had served in Morocco bitterly complained that Syria's Bedouin lacked the nobility, honour and martial skill of their North African counterparts, who were also much better at navigating the desert.[15] As one French official lamented, 'our Bedouin chiefs have nothing of Morocco's *grands caïds* [great chiefs], who are warchiefs and pure-bred aristocrats. In general – and without exception – they are vulgar sellers of sheep and camels, whose mentalities they share.'[16] Several French officers argued for a separate Bedouin state in the Syrian desert under military control,[17] but colonial power was concentrated in the west of the country and the trackless desert difficult to police.

Despite their efforts to cultivate suitable local allies, French officials were disappointed to discover that Syrians would sometimes simply feign support for their own reasons, without becoming loyal supporters. Even military force was less effective in the Levant than in North Africa, they complained. 'When we attack a village,' noted General Gamelin, military commander of the French troops, 'some hope for our arrival, others meet us with gunshots. We cannot even trust those who have surrendered and, more importantly, use them, as we do in Africa. Treachery and deceit are everywhere.' Clearly, lessons from the Moroccan experience did not travel well to the politically complex eastern Mediterranean. In another twist, the new legal framework of the mandates system meant French colonial policy could not be as unfettered as it had been in the past. According to the League of Nations, the responsibility to build a modern state was now an integral component of the French occupation.

The colonial state in Syria

The League of Nations Mandate officially tasked France with tutoring Syria in the arts of self-government, a charge that necessitated a certain amount of institution building by successive high commissioners. In response to the nationalist upheaval of 1922, the states of Damascus and Aleppo were federated, along with the Territory of the Alawites. Directorates of Finance, Justice, Public Works, Higher Education and so forth, were built on institutions from the Ottoman and Faysal eras to create the skeleton of a fully fledged national bureaucracy within each statelet, a replication of functions that proved a huge drain on finances. Each statelet had its own administrative council, from the ranks of which representatives were drawn to form a new Federal Council. Although meetings were supposed to alternate between Damascus and Aleppo on an annual basis, in 1923, the seat of the Federal Council moved permanently to Damascus, much to the irritation of its Aleppine members. The notables of Aleppo already resented that the federal budget used resources from their city's more resilient economy to support the budgets of Damascus and the impoverished coastal region, not to mention the fact that nearly half of the states' revenue was taken by the French as a contribution to the occupation's security costs.

Concerns over these mounting costs prompted France to lighten its military footprint in the Levant. At its peak in 1921, the *Armée du Levant* had comprised 70,000 soldiers, mostly from other French colonies such as Morocco, Senegal and Madagascar. By 1924, it had been reduced to just 15,000. In addition, the French created the *Troupes spéciales*, a local force of 6,500 in 1924. Relative to their overall proportion in the population, Christians, Alawis, Ismailis, Kurds and Circassians were distinctly over-represented in the *Troupes spéciales.* Cultivating these 'minorities' (as they routinely came to be called by the French in the 1930s) against urban Sunni nationalists was a mainstay of the occupation.

The worsening financial situation was exacerbated by the collapse of the French franc in early 1924. The federal system broke down in dysfunction. The mandatory power sought to curry favour with the public with a limited concession to Syrian unity. The French high commissioner decreed the unification of Aleppo and Damascus into a single State of Syria. The Alawi territory was excluded from the union; its administrative detachment from Syria was accompanied by renaming it the State of the Alawites. The Sanjak of Alexandretta was part of the State of Syria, although now detached from Aleppo; the Jabal al-Duruz remained autonomous.

Initially, the higher echelons of government were filled with the elites of Damascus and Aleppo, many of whom had served under the Ottomans and considered exploiting public office for the benefit of themselves, their friends and their families to be a perk of the job.[18] But Syrian nationalists then took advantage of the electoral system reinstated in 1923 to advocate their pro-independence agenda. Even so, Syrian governments had limited power: legal authority was vested in the Beirut office of the French high commissioner for the Levant. In every government directorate, French advisors oversaw and habitually over-ruled Syrian officials. Although France had begun the process of constructing the formal apparatus of a modern state in Syria, the autonomy of these institutions was deliberately and consistently undermined by a parallel system of informal colonial rule.

In comparison with today's norms, the colonial state in Syria looks oddly hollowed out. Between 1923 and 1940, 63.5 per cent of the national budget was devoted to security and administration, meaning that the colonial state made little headway in providing healthcare, education and other public services.[19] Owing to constant French interference, the Syrian state bureaucracy had relatively little opportunity to learn self-government and administration: the civil service was inefficient, poorly coordinated and fragmented. These fragile state institutions lost much of their already limited effectiveness the further they reached from urban centres. Isolated rural areas, such as the interior of the State of the Alawites, distant outposts in the north-eastern Jazira and eastern Deir al-Zour and the sparsely populated reaches of the Syrian steppe were for the most part impervious to routine operations of government regulation.

Outside the cities, the most active instruments of colonial power were French intelligence officers. In keeping with Lyautey's conviction that colonial rule should exploit both military force and local cultural knowledge, the *Service des renseignements* (SR) was established in 1921 as a leaner – and less well-funded – version of Morocco's famous colonial intelligence organization. The Syrian SR was responsible for gathering military and political intelligence, and for assembling detailed knowledge about local society, from topography and economy to local customs, genealogics and historics.[20] A similar organization, the *Contrôle Bédouin* (CB), was given responsibility for the Bedouin tribes. With their intimate knowledge of local politics, tribal disputes and family feuds, SR and CB officers in the field were supposed to exploit the intricacies of rural society to smooth the workings of colonial rule. Liberated from the chains of bureaucratic hierarchy, routine discipline and parliamentary oversight, the SR officer was intended to use personal discretion and initiative to solve problems on the ground without having his hands tied by a cumbersome chain of authority that stretched back to the high commissioner in Beirut or government ministers back in Paris.

This romantic image of the expert intelligence officer, roaming from village to village and outwitting the natives through his superior understanding of their own society, was at odds with the principles of self-government that the mandates system was supposed to introduce to the Levant. Although SR officers were formally tasked only with advising Syrian officials in small towns and villages, they recurrently undermined the workings of local government by taking it upon themselves to act as judge and jury, provincial governor and village headman. Journalist Munir al-Rayyis described the situation in the town of Misyaf in 1921:

> It became clear that the Special Service Officer had the last word in the region of the State of the Alawis and that the *qa'imaqam* [the administrative head of the district] – whose position should make him the highest official of the district in the Syrian interior – was merely an employee of the French councillor in that state. He could not accept a complaint from the people without first submitting it to the councillor's office for agreement, so that he could consider it first, or keep it with him, or ignore it, or personally intervene in the immediate situation. Similarly, before each day's session of court, the head of the court would explain to the intelligence officer the cases before him and listen to his personal opinion of the parties involved. The word of the councillor sometimes went beyond the [limits of] the law, but woe to whomever opposed him![21]

The unaccountability and sheer arbitrariness of colonial power was especially evident at its peripheries, which helps explain why it was rural areas rather than cities that mounted the strongest resistance to French rule. Shahbandar and his fellow nationalists did benefit from a second amnesty in 1924 and returned to political opposition, founding a new People's Party (*Hizb al-Sha'b*) that included such well-known names as Faris al-Khouri, Jamil

Mardam and Lutfi al-Haffar. The People's Party proved hugely popular: its call for an independent state within Syria's natural boundaries attracted over a thousand members in Damascus alone. Despite this resurgence of the urban opposition, it was Jabal al-Duruz – not Damascus – that produced the largest and most sustained challenge to French rule.

The Great Syrian Revolt 1925–1927

In 1925, a coordinated uprising took place across several regions of Syria that seriously threatened the French occupation and, for a time, even looked set to liberate Damascus. The Great Revolt began as a local affair in the Jabal al-Duruz, but quickly swept north throughout the countryside, encircling and attempting to wrest from French control the cities of Damascus and Hama. The immediate cause of the revolt was the brutal behaviour and unchecked excesses of the French governor of the Jabal, Captain Gabriel Carbillet.

Carbillet's appointment to the Jabal was wildly controversial, as it contravened the Catroux–Druze Accords' promise of a Druze governor in the Mountain. After the Druze could not agree a successor to their first governor, Salim al-Atrash, who died in 1923, the High Commission assigned a French officer to take his place. Once appointed to the position, Carbillet sought to implement Lyautey's vision of colonial transformation with an uncommon zeal. He ordered thirty-two schools, five museums and many miles of roads to be built throughout the Jabal, and constructed new shops, markets and the first clinic in the regional capital of Suwaida.[22] A committed leftist, Carbillet sought to replicate in the Jabal al-Duruz a miniaturized version of the experience of late-nineteenth-century nation-building in France, where the strong, centralized state of the Third Republic had – rather despotically – built a new physical infrastructure as the basis for radical social changes that would inculcate a new political consciousness among a French peasantry seen as backward and unmodernized.[23] As a good French republican, Carbillet considered it his duty to implement the universal promise of *liberté, égalité* and *fraternité* by liberating benighted Druze peasants from the exploitation of leaders whom he identified as their feudal masters. 'Should I leave these chiefs to continue their oppression of a people who dream of liberty?' Carbillet appealed to his superiors. 'Should I renounce the traditions of France?'[24]

Carbillet described Druze social arrangements as the equivalent of European feudalism, which the French Revolution had ended. His analogy was off the mark. The 'Ammiyya uprising thirty years earlier had already curbed the power of the landowning shaykhs;[25] in reality, patterns of landholding in the Jabal al-Duruz were more equitable than they were elsewhere in the French Mandate territories. This fact meant little to Carbillet. His determination to eradicate exploitation drove him to extreme measures in his efforts to break down traditional social hierarchies.

Lacking the manpower for his ambitious programme of public works, Carbillet imposed a system of forced labour, backed up by a harsh regime of arbitrary justice. He ordered Druze men from prestigious families to break rocks alongside common peasants, punished dissenters by imprisoning them in his infamous 'coal cellar' (a tight, dank and lightless confine where the ceiling was too low to permit standing), and imported Christians from Lebanon to teach in schools and serve as his eyes and ears in the local community. Carbillet also angered Druze religious shaykhs by brazenly interfering in family affairs such as marriages and inheritances. His taste for alcohol and young men, moreover, was as objectionable to the local population as his disproportionality, such as the time he imposed a heavy fine on the townsfolk of Suwayda after a French officer's pet cat went missing.[26]

Carbillet saw his ready recourse to coercion not as a sign of incompetence or loss of control, but as evidence of how deeply he understood the local culture. Carbillet lionized his leading opponent in the Jabal, the rebellious Sultan al-Atrash, who continued to resist French rule and to whose effortless, charismatic authority among the Druze Carbillet seemed to aspire. Sultan Pasha, Carbillet wrote in his memoirs, is 'he who one must obey, or else face severe punishment. It is he who rallies doubters with his threats, as they know he will carry them out. [...] In the Jabal, only he is capable of making his chiefs obey him, by reason of his forcefulness which does not hesitate to use every means available to impose his will.'[27] In Carbillet's mind, his measures were not violent, but merely emulated Druze traditions of leadership.

Rumours of anger with the excesses of Carbillet's rule in Jabal al-Duruz eventually reached Beirut. In spring 1925, the recently appointed high commissioner, General Maurice Sarrail, temporarily withdrew Carbillet from his post, but refused to meet with Druze representatives to discuss their concerns. Undeterred, a delegation of twenty-nine Druze notables travelled to Damascus and presented a visiting French senator with a petition in which they called for freedom of speech, due judicial process and Carbillet's removal. Their petition reaffirmed the principle of Syrian unity and called for the autonomous Jabal to rejoin the rest of the country. 'The Jabal Druze is an integral part of Syria through deeply ingrained common language, common nationality and common economic relations,' the petition stated. 'Damascus gets its food from the Jabal and the Jabal procures all its supplies from Damascus. These relations between them date from the distant past.'[28]

The high commissioner disregarded these protests. Sarrail

also dismissed warnings of an imminent revolt in the south from other French officials, whom he suspected of belittling Carbillet's sterling achievements to enhance their own career prospects. Rather than deploying military reinforcements, Sarrail sent his own warning. He invited several members of the Atrash family to meet him for negotiations, then promptly arrested them and imprisoned them in distant Palmyra. This final insult was all it took to provoke an uprising.

Sultan al-Atrash and his entourage toured the south and east of the Jabal to rally Druze villagers; their growing band was joined by Bedouin tribesmen who lived on the edge of the steppe. On 19 July, a pair of reconnaissance aeroplanes spotted the amassed rebel forces, who shot one of the planes out of the sky and took its pilot hostage. The next day, Sultan Pasha's insurgents seized the town of Salkhad. Still unable or unwilling to grasp the scale of the uprising, the French sent a small force of 200 men led by General Normand to rescue the pilot and retake Salkhad. After rebuffing Sultan's offer of talks, the Normand column was overwhelmed at the village of al-Kafr and massacred by what the few survivors described as thousands of Druze fighters, although Syrian accounts suggest a much smaller number.[29] Emboldened by this success, Sultan went on to seize Suwayda, confining the French forces there to the city's citadel where they were besieged for two months.

French reinforcements came in the form of a second, heavier military column, including machine guns and artillery batteries, under the leadership of General Michaud. Its progress faltered amid the sweltering August heat and the rocky terrain of the Jabal. Once its defensive formation was broken, Michaud's column proved an easy target for Druze snipers hidden among the rocks and ravines, who pilfered the column's provisions. Exhausted and demoralized, the French troops panicked and fled when they were attacked head-on by Druze fighters, who seized their weapons and ammunition. A month later, a third, even heavier armed column led by General Gamelin was sent to retake Suwayda, but upon arrival found the town had been abandoned and its water supply sabotaged. Gamelin had no choice but to retreat without inflicting even a minor defeat on the rebels. By this point, the Druze insurgents' spectacular success had gained the attention of the whole of Syria.

Over the summer of 1925, the atmosphere in Damascus grew hot and tense. Wild rumours about the uprising in the Jabal raced through the city, causing consternation among the foreigners and putting Shahbandar and his nationalists in a quandary. Should they support the uprising? Should the People's Party gamble the political freedoms it had only recently been granted by the French – no matter how limited – on the risky and uncertain outcome of the rebellion? Although nationalist politicians wanted an end to French rule, this desire did not necessarily mean they would endorse an armed uprising. As men of education, family wealth and high social standing, their interests largely inclined them towards an orderly transition of power that would safeguard rather than upset the status quo.

However, a small, more radical wing of this elite was ready to make common cause with the rebellion. Even before the outbreak of the revolt, Abd al-Rahman al-Shahbandar had held regular meetings in Damascus with influential Druze notables to discuss current affairs. In the course of these conversations, many of these chiefs had begun to frame their problems with Carbillet in the Jabal as local symptoms of an illness that afflicted the nation as a whole.[30] Over the summer, Sultan al-Atrash sent letters to Shahbandar through the intermediary of Nasib al-Bakri – a Damascene who had worked to advance the cause of Arab nationalism in the Jabal during the last years of the Ottoman Empire and

Faysal's Syrian Arab Kingdom – to exchange news of the latest developments and coordinate strategy. This cooperation between Druze notables and Damascene nationalists was not novel: it built upon well-established social and business relationships that stretched back for years. As we have seen, provincial notables from the Jabal had long sent their sons to be educated alongside the sons of the elites of Damascus and Aleppo in the administrative, military and tribal schools of the Ottoman Empire. A surprising number of rebel leaders of the Great Revolt had shared formative moments together in the classroom, in state administration or on battlefields in far-flung stretches of the Ottoman Empire.[31] As the uprising spread across Syria, these old friendships were rekindled and served as bridges to unite men from different regions, villages and religious communities. Ramadan al-Shallash, for example – who had earlier conquered Deir al-Zour in the name of Faysal – took up arms during the Great Revolt alongside Ali al-Atrash of Suwayda, a former classmate at the Tribal School in Istanbul.

Even before the revolt, these networks of friendships had proved useful to Syrian political activists. During the First World War, many young Arab nationalists seeking to escape Ottoman persecution had fled Damascus for the safety of the Jabal al-Duruz. A decade later, several of the same individuals – who had since become members of Shahbandar's People's Party – now travelled south to join Sultan al-Atrash and fight in Druze rebel bands. These social connections between the urban and provincial elites of the next generation were crucial in transforming the revolt from a merely local affair to one that threatened colonial rule across all the territories under the French Mandate. They also provided a vital means of rallying support for the Great Revolt at the grassroots level.[32] These relationships made it natural for Druze leaders such as Sultan al-Atrash to work with Damascene notables such as Shahbandar to extend the rebellion beyond the Jabal.

Despite their intertwined history, Druze insurgents and Damascene nationalists failed in their first attempt to bring the revolt to the city. French troops and planes forced Druze forces led by Muhammad Izz al-Din al-Halabi to retreat before they reached Damascus, and French authorities arrested leading nationalist leaders in the city. Shahbandar and his associates narrowly escaped this round-up and fled south to the insurgent-held Jabal. Rebel bands were now forming across southern Syria and the countryside around Damascus in response to patriotic calls to arms that were being circulated across towns and villages in the name of Sultan al-Atrash. The next significant episode of the Great Revolt came from an unexpected quarter: the town of Hama.

In the months preceding the Great Revolt, a man named Fawzi al-Qawuqji had secretly organized an anti-colonial movement in Hama that he had named *Hizbullah* ('Party of God'); although the name gave a nod to the town's conservative milieu, the party espoused no religious agenda. Another well-connected graduate of the Ottoman military school in Istanbul, Qawuqji was serving at the time as an army officer in France's *Troupes spéciales*. By education and temperament he was inclined to become an early supporter of armed uprising against the French and liaised with Sultan al-Atrash for this purpose.

Skilfully marshalling the support of the popular neighbourhoods of Hama, the leading families of the town and Bedouin from the Mawali tribe outside the city, Qawuqji launched a surprise attack against French forces on 4 October 1925.[33] For a time, his men had the upper hand, but the next morning French aeroplanes bombed the city, causing widespread destruction. In a petition to the Permanent Mandates Commission of the League of Nations, Syrian nationalists would later report that French planes killed 377 men, women and children, and destroyed 115 homes that day.[34] Alarmed by the scale of the bombing, representatives of prominent Hama families such as the Barazis and Kilanis, who had initially supported the uprising, persuaded Qawuqji to withdraw.[35]

With the Hama revolt quelled, the mandatory authorities concluded that the bombing of the city had been a great success and dismissed Syrian reports of the number of civilian deaths as being exaggerated for political purposes. The French made plans to repeat the bombing strategy if the rebels ever made a serious attempt at taking Damascus, which they did just two weeks later.

By mid-October, local rebel bands were active throughout the villages of the Ghouta, the expanse of fertile farmland that encircles Damascus, where they conducted hit-and-run raids against French forces too slow and cumbersome to apprehend them. French troops began to target the non-combatant populations that the rebels passed through, looting and burning villages including the mainly Druze settlement of Jaramana, where the family of Nasib al-Bakri were important landowners. The French executed rebel sympathizers and, as a macabre warning, exhibited their corpses in al-Merjeh Square in central Damascus, where the Ottomans had notoriously hanged Syrian Arabists just a decade earlier.

Alice Poulleau, a French civilian living in Syria who was fiercely critical of the conduct of the colonial troops, described the scene at al-Merjeh in uncompromising terms:

> All around the square were soldiers, guns in hand. In the middle were gendarmes, their hands in their pockets, the chief of police in his cravat and civilian and military officials. On the ground were long trails of blood. It was a Dantesque horror: the corpses' shoes were scattered all about; they had tragic faces, their arms outstretched. One, so very young, still had his mouth open, as if he were crying something out.

> Bloodied brains, guts spilling from open stomachs – it was a scene of human carnage.[36]

In contrast to Poulleau's moral outrage, French officials observing how Syrians reacted to the scene dispassionately reported back that 'the psychological effect seems to have been considerable'.[37]

On 18 October, Nasib al-Bakri launched a daring yet foolhardy attempt to capture High Commissioner Sarrail, who was mistakenly believed to be at the Azm Palace, a beautiful complex of courtyards and fountains in the heart of the Old City of Damascus, just a stone's throw from the ancient Umayyad Mosque. Too impatient to await reinforcements, Bakri coordinated bands of local men from the Maydan neighbourhood of Damascus and Druze from Jaramana, who staged a loud and jubilant incursion into the popular quarters of the city, attacking and pillaging police stations and gendarme posts along the way. Many Damascenes welcomed the rebels and joined them in the streets; others assembled to protect the Christian and Jewish quarters from attack by angry bands that might target these groups for their suspected sympathy with the occupying power.

As evening fell, the French military began a full-scale bombardment of Damascus. Over the next two days, French planes dropped more than 300 bombs in nearly forty separate sorties.[38] The destruction they inflicted was vast. Although the mandatory authorities declared that the bombing had killed only 150 Syrians, Syrian officials counted 1,146 dead, including 336 women and children.[39] An entire section of the Old City of Damascus, between the two famous souqs of al-Hamidiya and Midhat Pasha, had been levelled by bombs and eaten by flames. Locals renamed this neighbourhood al-Hariqa ('the burnt quarter') in memory of this incendiary destruction, a name that the area still bears to this day. Bombs and shells had etched a black scar of ashes and rubble that stretched from the Old City to the Maydan: hundreds of houses and shops had been destroyed, including the homes of notable families who were opposed to the French. Faced with this onslaught, the rebels had no choice but to withdraw from Damascus to the Ghouta countryside.

The bombing of Damascus provoked an outcry from the international community, although this was less due to the casual deaths of hundreds of civilians than to the fact that resident diplomats were not warned to evacuate prior to the bombardment. The French maintained that the bombing had been an unavoidable necessity. General Gamelin justified the strategy by observing that 'subsequent developments have proven that it was an efficient means: it saved our troops, as well as all the Europeans [resident in Damascus] from a massacre.'[40] The French used the notion of military necessity quite liberally over the coming months, as increasing coordination between rebel bands allowed them to escalate their attacks to the level of fully fledged guerrilla warfare.

Over the autumn of 1925, the rebels took over the entire Ghouta, effectively cutting off Damascus from the outside world during the winter months. Rebel forces now roamed freely from the Jabal al-Duruz and Hawran all the way north to al-Qalamoun and al-Nabak, halfway to Homs. These forces were loose-knit bands of fighters, whose numbers varied from a couple of dozen to a couple of hundred, who mostly came from popular urban quarters and rural villages destroyed or looted by French forces. Each band would be led by a charismatic figure, who usually came from the same village or neighbourhood. One of the best-known rebel leaders, Hasan al-Kharrat, had been a simple night-watchman in the Shaghour quarter of Damascus before taking up arms. Kharrat's son Fakhri would be publicly hanged by the French at al-Merjeh Square in early 1926. Another band was led by three Akkash brothers from the Ghouta village of Dummar, while a third was mainly made up of volunteers from the Maydan in Damascus and led by a member of the Sukkar family from the same neighbourhood.[41]

Although mostly lacking formal education, band leaders and their men received instruction in military tactics from their comrades who had graduated from the Ottoman Military Academy. Rather than simply learning how to fight on the job, the bands adopted a fairly sophisticated doctrine of guerrilla warfare that had been taught at the Academy under the moniker of *Harb al-'Isabat*, the 'War of the Bands'. In his memoirs, the journalist Munir al-Rayyis recalled how the art of insurgency was taught in the rebel band he had joined:

> Colonel Yahya al-Hayati . . . advised us to adopt the rules of the *'isaba* . . . which were taught as a science at military schools. Armed *'isabat* [bands] did not stay in one place for more than a night and they camped away from roads, which regular campaigns and their weaponry could traverse with ease. It was better not to stay in villages with populations which were linked by paved roads, but to avoid them, and to place guards at locales which we sought refuge in, so that the *'isabat* knew the enemy's weak points. [We should] attack at unexpected times and withdraw quickly, without leaving behind any evidence of the place in which we should hide. He said the first condition of the success of *Harb al-'Isabat* in any region was the loyalty of the inhabitants: an *'isaba* could not continue its work in a region whose inhabitants were not loyal to it.[42]

The rebels' doctrine of guerrilla warfare provided detailed information about surprise attacks, camouflage, terrain and even targeting French aeroplanes, which the bands soon discovered were highly vulnerable to well-aimed rifle fire if lured down to low altitudes.[43] For their part, French forces soon found their technological superiority did not automatically translate into an easy victory over the rebels, whom they dismissed as little more than uneducated bandits. Rural insecurity was, the French reasoned, in any event endemic to this part of the world. 'How could it be otherwise,' mused General Gamelin, 'in this land where so many racial and religious rivalries meet, with not one of them being able to concede the superiority of the next?'[44] Yet these nimble 'bandits' proved highly adept at avoiding the slow-moving, heavily armoured French military columns that patrolled the Ghouta, stumbling over the many streams and orchards of the agricultural oasis and presenting easy targets for hit-and-run raids.[45] French efforts to 'pacify' Syrian villages by imposing heavy fines, setting fire to homes or taking hostages from local families generally backfired, and drove yet more peasants to join the rebels. Insurgents roamed throughout the region, raiding French outposts, cutting telephone lines and sabotaging railway tracks.

Although speed, fluidity and improvisation were the watchwords of *Harb al-'Isabat*, several rebels concluded that greater discipline and coordination was needed for the revolt to continue. Prominent leaders convened at the village of Saqba in November 1925 to discuss concerns that some rebels were more interested in pillaging villages than advancing the cause. Rebels with formal military training had already blamed the failure to take Damascus on the fact that Nasib al-Bakri and the Druze warriors were neither sufficiently trained in *Harb al-'Isabat* nor sufficiently self-controlled to avoid the temptation of plundering more than they needed to survive.[46] To prevent this problem from getting worse, in subsequent meetings the rebels agreed to elect a government to oversee the revolt, to forbid individualistic activities by band leaders, to establish a revolutionary court to punish spies and to create an accounting and tax collection system to raise funds from villages according to their ability to pay. They released a public statement declaring that 'pillage and plunder and demanding money are forbidden to all. The blood of anyone who crosses villages with weapons is forfeit. So that these particulars are known to all, spread this message to all the respectable inhabitants of the Ghouta.'[47]

Despite these orders, some bands continued to impose arbitrary 'fines' on villagers or to jeopardize the success of military missions because of ill discipline. Rebel leaders tussled for power at the meetings of the Revolutionary Council, trading accusations of behaviour unbecoming of the movement. In December 1925, Ramadan al-Shallash was officially expelled from the revolt on these grounds, although several rebels who were present believed the allegations had been manufactured for political reasons.[48] Raids on Christian villages were vociferously condemned by the leadership. In response to a raid on the village of Ma'loula, band leader Sa'id al-'As wrote:

> This work was not legitimate, and the revolt was exposed to doubt by their attack and their hostility . . . This alienated the hearts of the Christian sons of the nation, our brothers in nationalism and the homeland . . . It was the work of a group of simple souls who had adopted the revolt as a means of satisfying their desire and their greed for pillage and plunder.[49]

Far from being primitive bandits, as the French described them, the rebels elaborated a distinctly political vision of both their fight against colonialism and the Syrian nation they were seeking to liberate.

The Great Revolt began to wane in 1926, after French forces adopted a new counter-insurgency strategy. First, rather than using heavy armoured columns, the French started to organize small units of Syrian partisans (as always, disproportionately from 'minority' communities such as Ismailis, Circassians, Druze, Kurds and even Bedouin) who were commanded by French intelligence officers of the *Service des renseignements* to pursue the rebels. These units were able to mimic the guerrillas' speed and fluidity, possessed a deep knowledge of nearby villages and their inhabitants and intuitively understood the hidden paths and byways that marked the local geography. SR officers began to compile detailed, almost encyclopedic files about local areas, and employed this knowledge to gain a better understanding of the bands and their movements.[50]

Second, the French army ordered the construction of a wall of iron, concrete and gunfire to seal Damascus off from the rebel-infested Ghouta. In January and February 1926, 1,500 Syrian workers built what eventually became twelve kilometres of barbed-wire fences and machine-gun outposts all around the perimeter of the city.[51] Attempts were made to electrify the fence, but without success.[52] With Damascus secure, the French flooded the Ghouta with a surge of troops redeployed from the recently ended Rif War in Morocco who then 'cleansed' the region of rebels. Most of the survivors were forced to retreat to the Jabal. Suffering from attrition and exhaustion, by spring 1927, the Great Revolt finally petered out where it had first begun. The few remaining recalcitrant rebels evaded pursuit by slipping across the border into British-held Transjordan.

France's repression of the Great Syrian Revolt involved previously unimaginable levels of violence. An estimated 6,000 rebels were killed and over 100,000 people displaced from their homes.[53] Entire neighbourhoods were destroyed, villages burned, rebels shot or hanged and their corpses exhibited in public to impress upon the population the futility of rebellion against the mandatory power. In one respect, this strategy worked. The human cost of the uprising was so shocking that, in all the remaining years of the mandate, Syrians never again took up arms in the name of fighting colonialism. Over the next two decades, Syrians sought to achieve independence by negotiation, not insurrection. Despite its failure, the Great Revolt established that, regardless of region, sect or social status, Syrians *as Syrians* could be engaged in a common struggle against colonial rule. The Revolt made it possible to imagine a future in which the Syrian people would be united in independence.

4

Liberal Nationalism and Popular Politics, 1927–1946

After intense international criticism of its handling of the Great Revolt, France softened its stance in Syria. The poor judgement of General Sarrail ensured that he was the last military high commissioner; his successors were all civilian appointees. Henri Ponsot, a French diplomat who had served in Indochina and Canada, replaced Sarrail in late 1926 and spent a year reviewing the situation, listening to local concerns and consulting with Paris before finally making a long-overdue policy statement. In July 1927, Ponsot broke his silence to announce that France would honour its obligations under the terms of the mandate treaty, but that he would rejoin the Jabal al-Duruz and the State of the Alawites with the rest of the country, and devolve greater power to the Syrian government. Ponsot gave no indication that France would consider withdrawing from the region or reuniting the State of Syria with the State of Lebanon, which remained detached from Damascus. However limited, Ponsot's concessions nevertheless created a new political terrain for Syrian nationalists to navigate.

Negotiating independence: the years of 'honourable cooperation'

The Syrian political elite had been divided by the Great Revolt, both ideologically and geographically. Ardent supporters of the armed uprising remained in exile: Sultan al-Atrash remained in Transjordan, and Abd al-Rahman al-Shahbandar in Transjordan and Egypt, until France granted amnesty in 1937. Fawzi al-Qawuqji's visceral hatred of colonialism would later lead him to join revolts against the British in Palestine in 1936 and Iraq in 1941, as well as the 1948 war against the newly declared State of Israel. Less radical opponents of the mandate were granted an amnesty and returned to Syria the following spring. Moderates were now the dominant force inside the country. At a conference in Beirut, they issued a statement that condemned the inadequacy of Ponsot's gestures, but also affirmed the necessity of 'collaboration' between French and Syrians 'based on the reciprocity of interests and the determination of mutual obligations'.[1] In March 1928, they held a second conference in Damascus and announced that they would participate in the elections for the new Constituent Assembly that Ponsot had announced. After what they saw as the chaos and violence of the Great Revolt, the tone of these pronouncements was welcomed by numerous members of the elites of Damascus and Aleppo, who soon joined the ranks of the reformed nationalist movement.

Unlike the earlier Iron Hand Society or People's Party of Shahbandar, this new coalition was decidedly quietist and anti-insurrectionary. Its members came from the upper echelons of society. They were well educated, having studied at Ottoman colleges or universities in Lebanon and Europe: lawyers, doctors and other modern professionals were well represented in their ranks, alongside the usual landowners and merchants.

By 1930, this group was sufficiently identifiable to acquire its own name: *al-Kutla al-Wataniyya*, the National Bloc. Ironically, the Bloc was hardly representative of the nation as a whole. Its leaders were 80 per cent from Damascus and Aleppo, while the rest came from Homs and Hama. Provincial elites from the Jabal, who had been so prominent in the Great Revolt, were entirely absent, as were Alawi notables from the coast.[2] Peasants of all ethnicities, religions and regions were similarly excluded. Nevertheless, a handful of names associated with the leadership of the National Bloc – Hashim al-Atasi, Lutfi al-Haffar, Jamil Mardam, Husni al-Barazi and Sa'dallah al-Jabiri – played recurring roles in Syrian politics throughout the rest of the French Mandate and well into the 1950s.

Although the high commissioner had instructed elections be held according to the Ottoman system since 1923, it was after the failure of the Great Revolt that national elections were reinvigorated as a site for nationalist politics. In 1928, the National Bloc won a third of the seats, with the remainder going to independent nationalists, tribal shaykhs and French-sponsored politicians, many of whom were as corrupt as they were incompetent. The more professional and better-organized National Bloc soon dominated parliamentary proceedings, much to the surprise of High Commissioner Ponsot, who reopened the controversial question of restoring the Syrian throne to sow dissent among their ranks. Ponsot was once again surprised to discover that the Syrian political elite had lost enthusiasm for the return of the monarchy. The incumbent political elite reasoned that if Faysal and his entourage were to return to Syria from Iraq, they would themselves surely lose their official positions and much of their political influence in the ensuing reshuffle. Perhaps counter intuitively, as historian

Philip Khoury observes, 'these highly educated and sophisticated politicians were avowedly republican by this time, ironically inspired by the democratic system of the French republic and the liberal bourgeois ideals of the French revolution'.[3] Although independence would later revive debates about unification with the monarchies of either Iraq or Transjordan, the attachment to Syria's existence as a *republic* was deeply felt as early as the late 1920s.

The 1928 Constituent Assembly drafted a new constitution that identified Syria as a parliamentary republic with a single chamber elected by universal suffrage in two stages of elections. Freedom of religion was enshrined in the draft constitution, although echoing the 1920 Constitution of the Syrian congress, which stated the king should be a Muslim, the new draft document made similar stipulations for the president of the republic. The French struck down the clauses that referred to the 'indivisible' territory of Syria, which included the State of Greater Lebanon as well as the mandated territories of Palestine and Transjordan under British jurisdiction. France also removed articles that attributed to the Syrian president rights and duties held to be the exclusive preserve of the high commissioner: there was a limit to how far the mandatory power would allow this constitutional experiment to progress, after all. Under pressure from France to enforce the red lines of acceptable political debate, Ponsot suspended the assembly for six months. The decision caused great anger in Syria. Yet, in keeping with their policy of honourable cooperation, the National Bloc quelled public dissent and kept the situation calm. Truly, this was a world removed from the days of popular uprisings and rural revolts.

After many deliberate delays, national elections were held in late 1931 and early 1932 in an atmosphere of high tension as French intelligence officers, collaborators and the National

Bloc competed in a campaign of dirty tricks and vote-rigging. Gangs of their supporters clashed in the streets. The Bloc did well in Damascus, as expected, and also in Homs, where Hashim al-Atasi benefitted from his family's traditional position of local leadership. But in Aleppo, the Bloc was defeated by the fraudulent voting campaign waged by pro-French politicians and their partners in the colonial administration. Acrimony turned to violence and even the odd assassination attempt. Once parliament finally entered session, its discussions were scarred with bitterness, recrimination and distrust.

For the next few years, one issue preoccupied Syrian politicians more than any other: the prospect of a treaty with France. In 1932 Britain set a powerful precedent by ending its League of Nations Mandate and recognizing Iraq's independence, albeit after having extracted a treaty which safeguarded British airbases and military transit rights in the country. Despite the claims of some Iraqi nationalists that the lingering military presence of the former colonial power was incompatible with the true meaning of independence, their Syrian counterparts called on France to concede to a similar treaty. The new, left-leaning French government that had been elected in 1932 seemed more receptive to the idea than the previous incumbents, and Ponsot signalled his willingness to commence treaty negotiations.

The National Bloc was divided by this proposal. One wing, in which Jamil Mardam was a significant player, was happy to enter talks without preconditions, in adherence to the policy of honourable cooperation. A second wing, headed by former guerrilla leader Ibrahim Hananu, was unconvinced of France's sincerity and wanted prior guarantees that the deal would meet the minimum standards set by the Anglo-Iraqi Treaty. After much wrangling, the Bloc agreed to allow Mardam to begin preliminary discussions with the high commissioner. However, Mardam's position was undermined the following spring when Ponsot declared that the State of the Alawites, the Jabal al-Duruz and Lebanon would be excluded from any future treaty arrangements, in light of what he described as their political underdevelopment. Furious, the Bloc reaffirmed its commitment to the national unity of the whole of Syria, and Mardam was pressured to resign his seat in parliament.

Treaty discussions dragged on. Ponsot was replaced as high commissioner by Charles de Martel, a suave aristocrat who sought to secure an agreement favourable to France by variously manipulating, bribing and dividing the Syrian political elite. A familiar pattern soon emerged: the High Commission would draft treaty proposals with terms unacceptable to the National Bloc, the Bloc would vote against them in parliament and then parliament would be suspended by the mandatory authorities. Initial support for a treaty in France dissipated amid a series of domestic political crises, rapid changes in government and unrelated unrest. With the Syrian parliament suspended and government entrusted to non-nationalist politicians, the two wings of the National Bloc coalesced to adopt a firm position of refusing to negotiate with the occupying power. Mardam was rehabilitated by the Bloc and regained his position of prominence, albeit after apologizing for his overly ardent pursuit of the diplomatic option. By 1935, the National Bloc's policy of honourable cooperation had reached an impasse.

Coupled with an important series of social and economic changes that had been unfolding under colonial rule, this impasse was about to give way to a more confrontational style of politics in which the Syrian public would once again play a critical role.

Outside parliament: economics, agriculture and industry

The mandated territories of French Syria and Lebanon suffered profound economic dislocation with the onset of colonial rule. The new borders were not just imaginary lines on the map; they were made real with import restrictions, customs tariffs, and the increasingly protectionist economist policies adopted across the region from Turkey to the French and British mandates. What had once been a wide-ranging economic area of some forty or fifty million people was suddenly truncated to some three million inhabitants enclosed within the French Mandate. Aleppo, the largest industrial centre under French control, was cut off from its long-established markets in Anatolia and northern Iraq, which meant the city's traders had to reorient their activities to towns of the Syrian interior where they previously had few business connections. To the south, French Syria had lost access to the port of Haifa and could turn only to Beirut for essential access to the Mediterranean. New borders obstructed Damascus's long-standing trade and pilgrimage routes south to the Hijaz, while access to Palestine – a major market for Syrian goods – became ever more difficult.

In addition to this downsizing of the Levantine market, France introduced a new currency, the Syro-Lebanese pound. Its value was established at a fixed rate of twenty French francs, but this exchange rate proved ruinous for the Syrian population as the French franc itself fluctuated wildly throughout the 1920s: the currency peg exported France's inflation and price volatility across the Levant. Many Syrians consequently preferred to keep using their old Turkish pounds, albeit illegally, rather than gamble with a new currency that so rapidly lost its value.

The mandates opened Syria to foreign business interests, ushering in a period of rather one-sided globalization. Although the mandates were originally conceived as a way to introduce an 'open-door' economic model for the collective benefit of the world's major powers, the colonial authorities in Syria and Lebanon deliberately discriminated against their competitors. They granted preferential treatment to French exporters and reserved the lion's share of government concessions for French businesses, which were soon running Syria's electricity and transport networks. The colonial power's economic policy was not simply about plundering Syrian resources to enrich the French private sector, although this element was certainly present. Where Lyautey's doctrine of colonial warfare had sought to achieve pacification through social transformation, the mandatory authorities also sought to 'modernize' Syrian society – and, not uncoincidentally, eliminate its nationalist opposition – through an ambitious and far-reaching programme of agricultural reform.

French agricultural policy was shaped by the widespread yet exaggerated impression of Syria's agricultural richness. Although Syria had been known in classical times as the breadbasket of Rome, its bountiful harvests of wheat and barley were hostage to the vagaries of rainfall, which varied unpredictably from year to year. Nevertheless, the First World War had driven home the need to secure reliable supply lines to keep France from starving if another conflict broke out in Europe. Syria's apparently vast agricultural potential made it an ideal candidate for rapid development of its primary resources, an approach that the French called *mise en valeur*.[4] In the Levant, this approach was most thoroughly implemented by Edouard Achard, a French engineer and agronomist who became the architect of colonial agricultural policy during more than a decade of service in the region.

Achard argued that Syria's potential could be achieved with

three steps. First, the irrigation system should be expanded with major infrastructure projects to build new dams, reservoirs and canals. Second, new crops should be planted that were in high demand on the world market, such as cotton. Achard's third and most controversial argument (as the Syrian establishment saw it, at least) was that the large landowning families that dominated much of the countryside were obstacles to economic development. Absentee landowners exploited the peasantry to such an extent that neither landlord nor peasant had any incentive to improve productivity. Landowners were parasites who lived off the rent from their rural properties, while the peasants slaved in the fields trying to feed their families. Nevertheless, as Achard pointed out, attempts to impose modernization from above would only alienate the notables, as had happened in the Great Revolt. French authorities should therefore resort to the conventional legal mechanism of purchasing land from the notables and distributing it to the peasantry. In doing so, France would create a class of independent smallholders and family farmers whose interests would lead them to support the mandatory power rather than the nascent nationalist movement.[5]

Although this analysis shaped French policy for the duration of the mandate, by the eve of independence little progress had been made towards any of the goals Achard had outlined. Not only were Syrian peasants disinclined to abandon their communal farming practices to become smallholding entrepreneurs, but the whole plan was hindered by the fact that much of Syria's land was neither mapped nor officially registered. Although the French initiated a cadastral survey to remedy the situation, by 1939, the survey had only covered half of the country's cultivable territory. Similarly, the grand irrigation projects proposed by Achard proved to be too large and too costly for the limited budget of the mandatory authorities. Experiments in cotton farming ended in ruin after the Great Depression saw the collapse of the world market. However, despite its limited success, French agricultural policy did set the tone for later developments: successive post-independence governments in the 1950s and 1960s revived originally French plans for irrigation schemes; cotton indeed became a staple crop across the country.[6] At the same time, the rising political awareness of the peasantry saw the emergence of new, radical critiques of traditional patterns of land inequality that echoed French descriptions of the propertied classes as lazy, self-enriching parasites. After independence, antagonism over land reform came to polarize Syrian politics as conservatives and radicals became locked in bitter struggle.

If French officials were quick to recognize the importance of developing Syria's agriculture, they were uninterested in its industrial potential. Of course, this was entirely consonant with the policy of *mise en valeur*, which considered colonies to be useful only as exporters of primary materials; processing those materials and using them in manufacturing remained the prerogative of the more developed nations. While the open-door policy allowed cheaper European goods to flood the Syrian market, thereby contributing to the decline of small-scale artisanal production, the lack of interest from French industrialists in setting up factories in the Levant left space for a handful of Syrian entrepreneurs to flourish. In the course of the 1920s and 1930s, pioneering industrialists founded a wave of companies that began to process locally produced materials in mechanized factories and workshops.

The largest ventures were based in the textiles industry, including the Syrian Spinning and Weaving Company of Aleppo, the Spinning and Weaving Company of Damascus, the Industrial Enterprises Company of Aleppo, the Technical Dyeing Company and the al-Shahba Spinning and Weaving Company of Aleppo.

In a departure from previous practice, these firms were organized as modern shareholding companies rather than family-owned enterprises. Nevertheless, company directors and shareholders invariably came from a very narrow section of the population. Historian Geoffrey Schad has estimated that Syria's leading textiles companies were controlled by only a few hundred individuals, many of whom were members of the same elite families of Damascus, Aleppo and Homs.[7] The composition of this new group of industrialists mirrored the character of the urban centres from which they emerged: they were mostly Sunni and Arab, although Christians were also well represented. The Jewish community of Aleppo played a prominent role in the international trade thanks to close ties with their co-religionists in Manchester, Britain's leading city for the textile industry. Provincial Druze and Alawi notables, on the other hand, did not invest in these new industries; factories were clustered in and around Syria's main cities.

Besides textiles, new light industries also sprang up in food processing, cement manufacture and tobacco. Many of the businessmen in these areas pursued political careers alongside their commercial interests. Lutfi al-Haffar, for example, founded the Ain al-Fijch Company that, in 1932, constructed an aqueduct to bring fresh drinking water to Damascus. This display of Syrian entrepreneurship and ingenuity was a source of great prestige to the National Bloc, of which Haffar was a founding member.[8] The National Cement Company, set up in 1930, included among its founders the statesman Faris al-Khouri, a Christian who had established the People's Party alongside Shahbandar, been elected in 1928 and later served twice as speaker of parliament. The director of the National Cement Company was Khalid al-Azm, a young businessman whose combination of commercial and political acumen was later to earn him the nickname the 'Red Millionaire' when he agilely allied himself with the radical left during his tenure as prime minister in the 1950s. Similarly, the Syrian Conserves Company was founded by Shukri al-Quwwatli, a nationalist who had been forced to leave the country during the Great Revolt and only returned to Syria in 1930. Although Quwwatli was so successful that he was known as the 'King of the Apricots' (*malik al-mishmish*), he did not abandon politics and went on to serve as the first president of independent Syria.[9]

Early industrialists such as Haffar, Azm and Quwwatli saw no contradiction between their economic and political aims. As their business interests did not require them to collude with French companies or look to foreign capitalists for investment, their activities could be framed in nationalist terms as serving the greater good of Syria. Looking to the examples of other late industrializing countries such as Germany and Turkey, Syria's nationalist politicians sought to muster whatever private and public resources they could find to build up the country's industrial base: economic development, they felt, would help secure Syria's eventual independence from France.

There are two noteworthy aspects of this economic nationalism of the elite. First, it avoided all mention of social inequality. For all the talk about industrial development, there was silence on the workers who were employed in the new factories, let alone the peasants who lived at barely subsistence levels in much of the country. '*Fuqara' idha iftaraqna wa-aghniya' idha ijtama'na*,' proclaimed the nationalist–entrepreneurs: 'We're poor when we're divided, rich when we're united.' This slogan neatly captured how the leaders of Syria's burgeoning modern private sector felt that their business goals were fully commensurable with the goal of national liberation. Issues of economic inequality were secondary to the question of independence.

The second point of interest is the remarkable alacrity with which the economic nationalism of the business elite came to be defined as a specifically *Syrian* affair. Political leaders in Damascus and Aleppo continued to agitate for the reunification of the State of Syria with the Jabal al-Duruz, the Government of Latakia (the new name given to the State of the Alawites in 1930 as a concession to the nationalists) and the Sanjak of Alexandretta (still attached to Aleppo, but with autonomous status). In contrast, there was less consensus over the prospect of unification with Lebanon. Living in a city that had lost much of its economic hinterland and suffered a blow to its prestige, nationalists in Aleppo were perhaps less inclined to accept colonial lines of partition, but the dominant Damascus wing of the National Bloc gradually came to accept that the territories that now comprised Lebanon would remain separated from Syria proper. Despite occasional rhetorical appeals to reunite Syria with parts of Lebanon such as Tripoli or the Biqaa Valley that were home to large Sunni Muslim populations, Syrian politicians seemed content to leave the fate of Lebanon for Lebanese politicians to decide.

This puzzle deserves deeper consideration. Why was the artificial border between Syria and Lebanon accepted as political reality, albeit begrudgingly, while nationalists bitterly opposed the new borders dividing central Syria from the Jabal al-Duruz and Latakia? The reasons lay partly in politics and partly in the different socio-economic contexts in which Syrian and Lebanese politicians were active. First, France had cultivated powerful constituencies of support for its mandate in Lebanon, especially among the Christian communities. The less militant position of politicians in Beirut had resulted in the country being granted its own constitution in 1926, some four years before Syria. Just as Damascus had gradually become the centre of gravity for political life in Syria, so too had the inhabitants of Lebanon come to turn to Beirut as the natural focus of their attention. The city's population swelled as a result, increasing from 77,820 in 1921 to 161,382 in 1932.[10] An ambitious programme of architectural renewal and rapid urbanization made Beirut look and feel like a capital city. Christian, Druze and Sunni political leaders from across the territories now defined as Lebanon were quickly learning to work within the territorial framework defined by the institutions of the colonial state. For the Lebanese elite, the prospect of reunification with the rest of Syria implied losing their 'national'-level position and becoming little more than minor, provincial politicians on a much larger playing field. Union with Syria would also imply a shift in power from westward-looking Christians to Sunnis facing the Arab world, a move that would upset the delicate balance that had been negotiated between the leaders of Lebanon's communal factions. Few Lebanese politicians had much to gain from advocating a merger with Syria that would inevitably lead to a loss of their own power and prestige.

The second important difference between the two countries was the extent to which coastal Lebanon had been more fully incorporated into the world economy than the Syrian interior.[11] Lebanese commercial and financial interests were by now heavily dependent on maintaining good ties with Europe, an orientation that was anathema to Syria's budding nationalist–entrepreneurs, not only because of their desire for economic independence, but also because the Lebanese preference for free trade stood at odds with the protectionism that Syrian entrepreneurs considered essential to shelter their still-young industrial ventures.[12] By the mid-1930s, Syria's nationalist business community considered the Lebanese to be foreign competitors, not fellow participants in a common project of nation-building. After independence, Syrian politicians would argue incessantly over the merits of unification with Iraq, Jordan and Egypt – but, intriguingly, not Lebanon, despite its much closer similarities in culture and society. Lebanon's divergent politics and economic structure meant that, even after the French withdrawal, there was little real incentive to unite the two countries. Indeed, after independence, successive Syrian and Lebanese governments worked not to reconcile the two states, but to disentangle their common interests and conclude their divorce.[13] In later decades, pragmatism – not principle – would define the parameters of political possibilities in Syria, possibilities with which economic concerns were profoundly intertwined.

From strike to treaty: the rise of popular politics

While French intransigence helped derail the National Bloc's policy of honourable cooperation, the worsening economic situation in the 1930s produced a surge of popular politics that threatened to overtake the relevance of the nationalist political elite. With its currency ties to France and increasing reliance on exporting cash crops such as cotton, Syria could not insulate itself from the worldwide depression initiated by the US financial crash of 1929. Syria's handicraft industry collapsed, unemployment rocketed to 15–20 per cent and exports plummeted by half. The direct effects of the international economic crisis were exacerbated in Syria by the worst drought in decades. The lack of rainfall was especially pronounced in the southern Hawran, from which waves of peasants migrated to Damascus, Beirut and Palestine to escape dying of thirst.[14] The cities were unable to absorb these new migrants, leading to deepening poverty and squalor. Even established notable families felt the pressure: some mortgaged their properties to sustain their lifestyle; others sold parcels of their inherited landholdings to the highest bidder. Rumours that one Damascene family intended to sell land on the Syrian shore of Lake Galilee to the Jewish National Fund caused an outcry in

1934; Damascene merchants organized a grassroots boycott of the Zionist products that were being smuggled into the country (and which often competed with their own goods).

The deep economic downturn made precarious the futures of a whole new generation in Syria. After being depleted by emigration, famine and war in the late Ottoman era, the population had grown steadily during the French Mandate, increasing from some 1.55 million in 1922 to 2.37 million by 1937.[15] This unprecedented bulge in the population gave rise to the entirely new, and very modern, social category of 'youth'. Organizations specifically designed for young people proliferated during the 1930s – and soon acquired a political colouring, once Syrian political leaders grasped that they could use scout troops, youth movements and even schools and universities to rally the next generation to the cause of national independence. Some of this youth mobilization bore a family resemblance to contemporary rightist and paramilitary youth groups in France and Germany, whose discipline and organization appeared impressive. Ironically, these efforts to rally Syrian youth soon produced a generational divide within the nationalist movement. While the National Bloc clung valiantly to its policy of honourable cooperation, a younger generation of nationalists was taking up roles as schoolteachers or scoutmasters; they used these positions as pulpits from which to promote a more hardline approach to achieving independence.

In August 1933, nearly fifty of these younger nationalists from across the region held a secret conference at Qarna'il in Lebanon, where they founded an organization called the League of National Action (LNA – *'Usbat al-'Amal al-Qawmi*). Mostly coming from middle-class families and working in the liberal professions, especially law, the leaders of the LNA held a very different perspective on social and economic affairs to the moneyed elites of National

Bloc – they felt more keenly opposition to Zionists from Europe settling in Palestine and the sense of connection to the Arabic-speaking world beyond Syria. The LNA rallied significant support among Syrian youth in Damascus, Homs and Hama and even as far afield as Deir al-Zour. However, the League maintained an air of exclusivity and did not reach out to workers or peasants. Nevertheless, the popularity of the LNA potentially challenged the National Bloc's virtual monopoly over the Syrian nationalist movement. To stay relevant, the Bloc began to take a more confrontational position towards the French. Frustration with the stalled treaty talks, the appalling economic situation and the new visibility of politicized youth activism, not to mention emerging competition within the nationalist movement itself, all contributed to the first open confrontation between Syrians and French since the Great Revolt a decade earlier.

In January 1936, the mandatory authorities made an ill-advised decision to arrest a number of National Bloc politicians and youth leaders, which prompted the souqs to close and protestors to demonstrate on the streets of Damascus. The police and colonial soldiers met the demonstrators with force: in all six people were killed and 150 arrested. The funerals of the protestors became occasions for mass protest. As many as 20,000 people joined the processions in Damascus, which ended in further deaths and arrests. Protests soon spread to the rest of the country. While the uprisings of the Great Revolt had been transmitted from the Jabal al-Duruz along social networks created by Ottoman education and the economic connections of the grain trade between the Hawran and Damascus, the 1936 protests were disseminated across Syria along the organizational lines provided by youth groups and their branches in different cities. This time, the political elite was marginal to the flow of events. It was young activists, many of them members of the LNA, who were the driving force in rallying public opinion and mobilizing protestors on the streets. By the time the demonstrations and clashes reached Homs, the National Bloc had grown seriously concerned that it had lost control of events on the ground. To regain the initiative, on 27 January, Jamil Mardam declared a general strike that would last until the French freed the imprisoned nationalists and allowed the Bloc's offices to reopen. Mardam's leadership was somewhat undermined by the fact that so many shops, souqs, schools and factories had already closed in the country's main cities: in all but name, a general strike was already under way.

The 1936 strike lasted for thirty-six days. It survived so long owing to the perseverance and commitment of youth leaders, who successfully overturned the elite's attempts to end it or compromise with the French authorities. To break the deadlock, in mid-February High Commissioner de Martel imposed martial law, flooded the streets with troops and arrested nationalist leaders such as Jamil Mardam, Nasib al-Bakri and Sa'dallah al-Jabiri. This move prompted intense criticism by Martel's opponents in France, the pressure of which produced a sudden policy reversal. The High Commission announced that a Syrian delegation was to be allowed to travel to Paris for final treaty negotiations, and the 3,000 people arrested since the start of the strike were to be released. Satisfied by these concessions that promised to take political activity off the streets and back into the parliamentary chamber, the National Bloc announced the end of the general strike and prepared itself for the national independence that now looked to be within its grasp.

Treaty negotiations began in early April. The Syrian delegation to Paris included Jamil Mardam, Hashim al-Atasi, Sa'dallah al-Jabiri, Faris al-Khouri and a host of junior advisors. Talks were interrupted following the French national elections later that month, which resulted in a change of government. When negotiations recommenced in June, the new leftist Popular Front government in France proved receptive to unifying the State of Syria with the Jabal al-Duruz and the Government of Latakia, provided that the rights of 'minorities' be respected. The use of the term 'minority' was itself relatively recent: French colonial officials habitually referred to the population of the Levant in religious rather than numerical terms until the early 1930s. Rather than highlighting France's role as the protector of local Christians, as in the past, French officials now began to echo the talk of minority rights that Britain had deployed to secure its interests during its own treaty negotiations with Iraq.[16] In Syria, the new terminology was to throw up some difficult questions over the next few years. Syria contained such a variety of religious, ethnic and national groups – Sunnis, Christians, Druze, 'Alawis, Shia, Isma'ilis, Kurds, Armenians, Assyrians, Circassians, Bedouin and Turkmen. Which group would qualify as minorities, on what grounds and with what implications?

Despite opening a new set of questions about relationships between social groups, identity and politics, the successful conclusion of a draft treaty that would reunite at least the statelets of Syria, Latakia and Jabal al-Duruz (albeit not all the country) was a major victory for the nationalists. The issue of unification with Lebanon, however, was entirely off the table; France went on to conclude a separate treaty for the Lebanese later that year. Moreover, the unification of Syria came at the cost of one further compromise: much like the Anglo-Iraqi Treaty, the draft Franco-Syrian Treaty guaranteed an alliance between its signatories and provided France with military basing rights in Syria for decades to come. This concession was certainly not to the taste of younger or more radical Syrian nationalists. Nevertheless, Mardam and his team considered the agreement to be a crucial step towards full independence. Once the treaty had been ratified by the French parliament, the period of colonial tutelage would end, and Syria would be accepted into the League of Nations as a sovereign state. For Mardam and his moderates, the treaty represented a major step towards independence.

Tensions of integration

Although the treaty had yet to be ratified, Syrians greeted news of the imminent unification of the statelets of Syria, Jabal al-Duruz and Latakia with four days of celebrations. The National Bloc's treaty success was rewarded with a surge of votes in the general elections of November 1936, which swept it victoriously into government. Jamil Mardam became prime minister and minister of national economy, the Homs notable Hashim al-Atasi was named president, while the presidency was given to the Christian Faris al-Khouri. Mardam and his nationalist cabinet were finally in a position to take over the state, appoint men of their own choosing as regional governors and administrative officials and prepare the country for the independence that the Franco-Syrian Treaty would soon provide.

The prospect of integration into a state dominated by Damascus was not equally welcomed in all parts of the country. As we have seen, the leading families of Jabal al-Duruz had forged an alliance with Damascene nationalists at the time of the Great Revolt and ever since then had maintained a solid commitment to independence from France. Yet Mardam's appointment of a Damascene rather than a Druze to be the Jabal's new governor revived long-standing concerns that national unity would entail a centralization of power in the capital at the expense of local autonomy. Even though the new governor was none other than Nasib al-Bakri – whose longstanding ties with Sultan al-Atrash made him perhaps the best-connected Damascene in the Jabal – a significant number of Druze notables were unconvinced by the Bloc's promises that national unity would deliver infrastructural improvements and employment opportunities. After all, their alliance in the 1920s had been with militant nationalists and men of action such as Shahbandar; the moderate intellectuals and lawyers of the National Bloc were still an unknown quantity.

The Druze notables were by no means unanimous on the issue. In contrast to the Atrash family, who had long guarded the autonomy of Jabal al-Duruz against external intrusion, whether Ottoman, French or Damascene, a younger generation of notables was more inclined to support the cause of national integration. Having received a modern, secular education in Damascus or Beirut, many of this next generation had a political outlook that was closer to that of the National Bloc than their parents. For them, national unity opened up a social and professional world that was larger and more exciting than the limited confines of the Jabal. For similar reasons, lesser Druze notable families such as the Halabis and the 'Amrs, who were subordinate to the Atrash in prestige and status, supported national integration as a way to undermine the dominance of the Atrash family. These Druze unionists were disappointed that the National Bloc eventually compromised and, in February 1938, appointed a governor from the Atrash family as a sign of goodwill. National unity was all very well in principle, but in practice it created a new space in which questions about *how* Syria's regions would relate to the capital were intertwined with questions about *who* would in practice become the regional political elites of the newly constituted state.

Across Latakia, meanwhile, the response to integration was even more mixed than it was in the Jabal al-Duruz. The shackles of colonial administration had already been loosened there in the early 1930s, when the French responded to the National Bloc's arguments for national unity by granting Latakia greater autonomy. The urban elite of the coast was largely unswayed by this concession. Like many of their counterparts in Damascus, Aleppo, Homs and Hama, large landowners of the coast were nationalists who favoured integration with the rest of Syria. However, enough Alawi notables had acquired a stake in the new arrangements introduced by the French that they potentially stood to lose out if the Government of Latakia were integrated into a national state run from and by Damascus. Certain Alawi leaders, the most prominent of whom was Ibrahim al-Kinj, petitioned Paris and the Permanent Mandates Commission at the League of Nations in Geneva against the terms of union proposed by the Franco-Syrian Treaty.

Opposing these separatists was a significant Alawi constituency in favour of union. Much like their Druze counterparts, the opinions of some members of the Alawi elite had slowly converged with those of the National Bloc. This change was a long time coming. But, just as the established upper classes of Damascus and Aleppo had sent their sons to study in missionary schools in the Levant or in universities in Europe, so too had the highest echelon of Alawi society come to recognize the benefits and prestige of modern education. The de facto leader of the pro-union lobby was Munir al-'Abbas, a prominent chief of the Khayyatin tribe who had studied law in Paris. Abbas's modern, secular education had shaped his world view in much the same direction as Syria's urban nationalist elite.

In February 1936, soon after the end of the general strike, 150 Alawi notables, both pro- and anti-union, gathered at a conference organized by Abbas in the coastal town of Tartous. Their agenda was to debate the political future of the region. Given the prior fragmentation of the Alawi population, the fact that such a conference took place at all was quite remarkable. The imminent prospect of a Franco-Syrian Treaty acted as a catalyst for Alawi notables to articulate their interests not in terms of petty personal or family rivalries, as had often been the case in the past, but in terms of alternative political visions that pitted the 'national' (Syrian) against the 'local' (Alawi/provincial). Indeed, the Tartous conference seems to have been the first mass meeting of Alawi notables in recorded history. The deliberations of this unconventional congress were cloaked in secrecy; it was an internal Alawi affair.

Over the following months, however, Alawi activists began to address their communications not just to one another, but to nationalists elsewhere in Syria. A meeting of pro-union religious shaykhs in the mountain village of Qardaha, for example, agreed a manifesto, published in the Damascus press, which asserted that the Alawis were indeed true Arabs and proper Muslims, and rejected any insinuation to the contrary.[17] Unionist Alawis had begun to register themselves as 'Alawi Muslims' for official purposes, playing havoc with the ethnological categories of the French administration, which sought to entrench divisions between Alawis and Muslims. The High Commission swiftly amended the legal system to grant Alawis their own personal status law, on a par with Sunnis, Christians, Druze, Shia and Ismailis, for the very first time.[18] The lives of the impoverished Alawi masses were hardly impacted by such developments, but for the Alawi elite, the Franco-Syrian Treaty opened not simply the pragmatic question of national unity, autonomy or separatism, but also the more profound question of how to define their relationship to the rest of the country in terms of their self-identification not as members of a particular family village, or tribe, but, for the first time, as a distinct *Alawi* community.

Besides, Jabal al-Duruz and Latakia, the unification of Syria under a nationalist government met with unexpected resistance in the Jazira, to the far north-east of the country. Until this point, the politicians of the National Bloc had given little thought to this region, which was so distant that its connections with Aleppo and Damascus were at best tenuous. Fed by streams that wended from the slopes of south-east Turkey down to the Khabour River, which then flowed into the mighty Euphrates, the Jazira held immense and largely untapped agricultural potential. Mostly untouched by the modernizing reforms of the Ottoman Empire that had led to the rise of landowning notable families further west, the Jazira was inhabited by a small population of settled and semi-sedentary tribes of both Kurdish and Arab descent. Even the French occupation came late to the north-east. Military outposts were not established there until 1926 – six years after the conquest of Damascus and Aleppo – and, despite the loosening of colonial control over much of the rest of the country, the local intelligence officers of the *Service des renseignements* stubbornly refused to relax their grip over the Jazira. So far from the gaze of civilization, French officers could indulge their fantasies of colonial power as if they were unfettered by the constraints of the League of Nations. Because of the region's distance from Damascus and Aleppo, as well as its relative under-population, the colonial authorities were able to use the Jazira as the stage for an audacious attempt at social engineering.

Transforming the Jazira from a land of semi-nomadic tribes and scattered farmsteads into a thriving, modern agricultural economy was to be achieved by a method that had been tried and tested in Algeria: colonization. Although it was impossible, given contemporary sensibilities, to import settlers from Europe, it was entirely feasible to channel incoming waves of refugees from Iraq and Turkey to settle in the Jazira. Previous decades had seen an influx into Syria of Armenians, Kurds and Assyrians escaping the repression and genocide that had begun under the Ottoman Empire. By 1927, there were already nearly 10,000 refugees in the Jazira, some 40 per cent of them Christian.[19] This 40 per cent was comprised of a variety of sects, among them Armenian Orthodox, Armenian Catholic, Syriac Catholic, Syriac Orthodox, Chaldeans and Protestants. For the French, the influx of so many Christians presented a superb opportunity to settle the Jazira with a population that was considered both intrinsically loyal and better suited to performing the hard work necessary to cultivate the fruits of civilization than indolent Muslims of either Kurdish or Arab stock.

The French authorities founded a string of new villages – Ras al-'Ayn, Amouda, 'Ain Diwar, Derbassiyya, Derik, Tell Brak, Tell Abyad – and directed refugees to settle in them along homogeneous ethno-religious lines, in keeping with colonial visions of the mosaic society. The French also expanded existing settlements such as Hassakeh, which was transformed from an isolated hamlet into a small town. The crowning glory of this programme of colonization was Qamishli. Founded in 1926 by the local SR officer in a deliberate bid to undercut the market town of Nissibin that lay on the other side of the Turkish border, the new settlement grew rapidly. A French report in 1931 noted that Qamishli 'with its lively souks, solid administrative buildings and electricity station, is today the very picture of a small town. New constructions replace old ones every year; if the current situation continues, then in a few years the town will be surrounded by trees, at the height of its development, dependent on a rationally farmed hinterland and ranking on the second tier of Syria's towns.'[20] By 1937 Qamishli was the sixth largest city in Syria, with over 100,000 inhabitants.

In the space of little more than a decade, the Jazira experienced the establishment of new model towns and the injection of a new population. Village leaders, and, increasingly, the chiefs of tribes such as the Shammar and Tayy, were also granted legal title to agricultural land, turning them into landowners with a vested interest in maintaining the status quo. Initially administered from Deir al-Zour, much further south along the Euphrates, the Jazira was soon upgraded to an independent governorate in its own right. The new-found status and rapid development of the Jazira served to cultivate the beginnings of a new provincial elite in the north-east. When Mardam's nationalist government began to dispatch state officials to the Jazira as part of its programme of centralization, they were surprised to encounter resistance from components of the population that had been until then largely untouched by the demands of national integration.

The autonomist movement in the Jazira coalesced in reaction to the general strike of 1936, which had found only a handful of adherents in the marketplaces of Hassakeh. The autonomists lobbied for devolution of power from the capital and for more local officials under a governor appointed by France, not Damascus. They drew support from the Christians of the towns and Kurdish tribes, but also from Arab Bedouin tribes. The Jazira's pro-unionists were led by Daham al-Hadi, the leading shaykh of the Shammar al-Khursa tribe, who had earlier been elected to parliament on the nationalist list in November 1936. The rapidly changing population and untested political dynamics of the newly colonized Jazira contributed to the outbreak of open hostilities between the two factions.

In February 1937, Mardam's government sent out a new provincial governor, Amir Bahjat al-Shihabi, to assert the capital's control over the governorate. Shihabi decided to achieve this goal by purging autonomists from the local administration, which predictably infuriated the anti-union lobby. By June, tensions had risen to the point that Shihabi deployed additional police on the streets, but his mounting concern for his own safety prompted him to flee back to Damascus. Christians and Kurdish autonomists repeatedly clashed with the men of Daham al-Hadi, first in Hassakeh and then across the region. In August, the violence culminated in a massacre in the small town of Amuda, where Kurdish tribesmen in the pay of Hadi pillaged and burned the Christian quarter before killing two dozen residents. At this point, the French authorities intervened, leading a campaign of aerial bombing against nearby Kurdish villages which killed a further thirty people. Although this show of force dampened any appetite for further violence, the two camps failed to reach a compromise. The autonomists continued to agitate for their cause, going so far as to kidnap the new governor that Mardam's government had sent to replace Shihabi. A third governor arrived in the Jazira in spring 1938 with a more conciliatory approach, but similarly failed to quell the discontent and lasted only a month in the job before also hightailing back to Damascus. The recalcitrant population of the Jazira staged strikes, organized boycotts of local government and threatened to withhold their taxes from Damascus, which was effectively powerless to calm the unrest.

These centrifugal pressures in Syria contributed to a mounting erosion of confidence in the National Bloc government. However, only in one case did these forces reach a critical mass that would allow escape from the orbit of Damascus. The coastal Sanjak of Alexandretta was officially attached to the State of Syria but operated under a special administrative regime that gave it a degree of financial autonomy. Alexandretta was home to a diverse, multicultural population estimated in 1936 by the French authorities to stand at 220,000, of whom 39 per cent were Turks, 28 per cent Alawi, 11 per cent Armenian, 10 per cent Sunni Arab and 8 per cent Greek Orthodox Christian, along with a handful of Kurds, Circassians and Jews.[21] Like much of western Syria, land ownership in Alexandretta was deeply unequal: a minority of wealthy families, mostly Sunni Turks and Arabs, prospered from the labour of peasant sharecroppers, many of whom were Alawi.

French control over the Sanjak had gone uncontested after Turkey renounced its claim to the region in 1921. But in the mid-1930s, Turkish journalists and government officials turned their attention to reclaiming the strategic Mediterranean port town of Alexandretta and its surrounds, for which they invented a new name – Hatay – which alluded to the Bronze Age civilization of the Hittites that once held sway in the region. News of the 1936 Franco-Syrian Treaty prompted a wave of Turkish criticism of French rule in the Sanjak, which they alleged favoured Arabs over ethnic Turks. The Turkish government then raised the issue of Alexandretta's independence from Syria with the French government and the League of Nations.

Opinions were mixed in the Sanjak itself and – perhaps surprisingly – did not cleave predictably along ethnic lines. The inhabitants of Alexandretta fell into four distinct camps: Syrian unionists (who favoured integration into Syria), autonomists (who wanted the continuation of the status quo), separatists (who wanted independence, but with strong ties to Turkey), and Turkish integrationists (who wanted Alexandretta to become Turkey's province of Hatay).

These camps tended to overlap with social and economic class, but were fractured along ethnic lines. Turkish-speaking autonomists were typically powerful landowners who retained the old-fashioned customs and traditions of social deference that Atatürk's republican reforms had abolished in Turkey. Turkish-speaking separatists and integrationists, meanwhile, were members of the aspirational, upwardly mobile middle and lower classes whose participation in Turkish youth groups and schooling had imbued them with the principles of Atatürk's nationalism. This emergent youth movement challenged the positions of both the Turkish elite and the Arabic-speaking population of Alexandretta. The Arabic-speaking Alawi peasantry, along with Armenians (many of whom were solely Turkish-speaking) and Arabic-speaking Greek Christians, typically favoured continuation of the status quo. Arabic-speaking Sunni landowners, on the other hand, believed union with Syria would offer the best chance of retaining their status, while a more radical nationalist strand popular among the young urban intelligentsia, both Sunni and Christian, saw union with Syria as a stepping stone to the reunification of the Arab world more broadly.

In response to Turkey's complaints, in 1937 the League of Nations agreed to revise the mandate to give Ankara more influence in the Sanjak. Alexandretta was to have full autonomy over its internal affairs, with Turkish and Arabic as its two official languages; external affairs would continue to be handled by the State of Syria. The news was rejected by Syria's nationalist government and prompted violent tussles between rival camps of the Sanjak. The League of Nations also stipulated that elections be held, which would allow the balance of public opinion to be gauged. A joint Turkish–French electoral commission decided that voters could register as Turks, Sunnis, Alawis, Armenians, Greek Orthodox or 'other', a mishmash of religious and ethnic categories that were not always mutually distinguishable for many people. The system also pooled pro-Turkey voters while fragmenting the pro-Syria camp. In addition, the electoral commission removed the requirement to document ethnicity or residence, which in time for the election prompted the better-organized pro-Turkey groups to flood the Sanjak with Turks and Turkish-speaking Alawis from Adana (whom Turkish nationalists had reinvented as *Eti Türkleri* or even *Alevi Türkleri* – 'Hittite' Turks? or 'Alawi Turks'). Pro-Turkey landowners even reportedly forced their Arabic-speaking peasants to register as Turks or drove them off their lands. The Syrian government, meanwhile, had been so heavily invested in treaty negotiations with France that it had no presence on the ground to counter these moves, although Alexandretta's radical unionists launched a publicity counter-campaign asserting that Alawis were indeed nothing other than part of the Arab nation.[22]

Even with the collusion of sympathetic French officials in the Sanjak (who often seemed to be acting independently of the High Commission in Beirut), sheer numbers meant that the pro-Turkey campaign failed to register sufficient voters to secure a victory. By this moment, however, street clashes had escalated to the point that French authorities felt they were losing control of the situation, and in May 1937 they hastily signed a friendship treaty with Ankara that allowed Turkish troops to enter the Sanjak to restore calm, which they did two months later. Over the objections of the High Commission, the French foreign minister generously agreed to award no fewer than twenty-two of the forty seats in a new assembly to Turks, thereby giving them a guaranteed majority that rather obviated the need for elections. In its first meeting that September, the Turk-dominated assembly held its discussions in Turkish, and, within the first fifteen minutes, declared the Sanjak an independent 'republic', renaming it Hatay.[23] The French did not formally recognize the region's independence, but acquiesced to the name change and elevated it from a *sanjak* to a state.

In the following months, Arab nationalist campaigners were shut down, and established Turkish notables sidelined. Over the next two years, the so-called 'republic' incrementally adopted Turkish currency, Turkish laws and Turkish administration; customs duties were reimposed on imports from Syria, and free trade allowed with Turkey. In March 1939, the president and first minister of Hatay were accepted as deputies to the Turkish parliament. In June 1939, with rising tensions in Europe, France finally conceded to Ankara's demands to annex the state, if only out of concern that Turkey might otherwise ally with Hitler's Germany. France pulled out its troops and formally renounced its control over the territory. The former Sanjak of Alexandretta was soon thereafter officially incorporated into the Turkish Republic as the province of Hatay.

Turkey's absorption of Alexandretta prompted some 50,000 residents, mainly Armenians and Arabs (Sunni, Alawi and Christian) to abandon their homes and enter Syria as refugees. Members of the National Bloc were publicly outraged that Syrian territory had been truncated, although the ever-pragmatic Prime Minister Jamil Mardam, seemed to grasp in private that the Sanjak was a lost cause. Mardam instead devoted his efforts to securing a French ratification of the treaty with Syria.[24] In this, Mardam was to be sorely disappointed.

With the gradual implosion of the leftist Popular Front government and a fierce campaign against the Franco-Syrian Treaty by the right-wing colonial lobby in France, the French government dragged out negotiations through 1937 and 1938, undermining the position of the National Bloc. Desperate to save the 1936 treaty, Mardam made a series of ill-advised concessions: allowing French officials to remain in the country after independence, granting France oil exploration rights in Syria, maintaining the status of the French language and granting special privileges to French companies. These concessions lost Mardam the support of the Syrian government, which rejected his proposed amendments. The French parliament also refused to ratify the treaty. The recent regional unrest, they felt, only demonstrated that Syria was still a mosaic society, a mishmash of different religions, ethnicities and minorities – not a unified nation. Ironically, the French parliament invoked Syria's lack of national unity to refuse independence to the party most ardently in favour of a unified Syria, the National Bloc.

The Second World War: from invasion to independence

After Jamil Mardam demonstrated himself willing to concede elements of Syrian sovereignty to obtain a treaty that never materialized, he lost the confidence of the National Bloc. Political heavyweights such as Shukri al-Quwwatli and Lutfi al-Haffar resigned from his government. However, Mardam's biggest political challenge came from outside the Bloc. The French authorities had exiled Abd al-Rahman al-Shahbandar from Syria after the Great Revolt, but allowed him to return to Damascus in April 1937 as part of a general amnesty. During this absence, he had developed a cult-like status back home as a principled and honourable nationalist. Upon his return, Shahbandar became a magnet for Mardam's political opponents. Shahbandar and Mardam traded personal insults in the press, and Mardam abused his authority as prime minister to clamp down on pro-Shahbandar organizations, censor critical newspapers and fire Shahbandar supporters from the civil service. When a bomb exploded in Mardam's car, the prime minister had prominent associates of Shahbandar arrested and put on trial.

Faced with the increasing hostility of Syrian politicians, Mardam resigned his position in February 1939. Cleverly, Mardam justified the move as a sign of his refusal to implement a controversial French decree intended to replace religious with civil marriages, which had provoked anger from Syrian Muslims and Christians alike. His immediate successors were no more successful at holding together a nationalist government: now that a treaty was off the table, it became all but impossible to satisfy both the High Commission and the increasingly volatile Syrian public. The new youth movements repeatedly took to the streets in the cities, autonomist movements stirred in the provinces and radical nationalists demonstrated in opposition to the French Mandate *and* the National Bloc government.

Throughout spring 1939, demonstrations, strikes and street violence swept Syria. Soon after, the French high commissioner suspended the constitution, dissolved parliament and placed day-to-day government in the hands of the civil service. Power was devolved to the Jabal al-Duruz and the Government of Latakia; direct military rule was imposed in the Jazira. The clampdown continued when Britain and France declared war against Germany in September 1939, after which the size of the French army in the Levant surged from a meagre 15,000 to a peak of 70,000 the following year. Martial law was declared, strict censorship imposed and smaller, more radical political groups such as the Syrian Communist Party and League of National Action had their activities halted or leadership arrested. Mardam and several other politicians expressed their full loyalty to France's war efforts in the hope of restoring constitutional civilian politics, to no avail. The National Bloc found itself incapacitated by the recent turn of events.

In the interim, Shahbandar became the leading political figure in Syria. To break the political impasse between the French and the nationalists, Shahbandar looked outside the country. During his decade in exile, he had acquired contacts and political awareness that spanned the Arabic-speaking world, where various notions of Arab unification were increasingly being debated. The former monarch of Syria, Faysal, had died in 1933; the Hashemite throne in Iraq was occupied by a regent, as Faysal's grandson was still underage. Shahbandar's vision for a confederation of Arab states led him to turn to the other Hashemite monarch installed by the British, the ambitious Abdullah of Transjordan, whom Shahbandar had rhetorically hailed as 'King of Syria' while visiting Amman in 1939. This Hashemite vision competed with that of the influential prime minister of Iraq, Nuri al-Sa'id, who sought to make Baghdad the centre of a new intra-Arab order. Finally, a new presence on the Arab political scene came from the Kingdom of Saudi Arabia, officially founded in 1933 after religiously inspired Bedouin from the desert conquered the former Ottoman province of the Hijaz and neighbouring regions. The kingdom's ruler, Ibn Sa'ud, was suspicious of Iraqi and Transjordanian designs on the Hijaz, the ancestral home of the Hashemites, claims to which might be strengthened by any union with Syria. Such ruminations had little immediate impact, however, as France voiced its definitive opposition to a Hashemite monarchy in Syria (unsurprisingly, given Hashemite dependency on Britain), which effectively ended the discussion for the rest of the Second World War. In Syria, the impasse remained.

In a shocking twist, in June 1940 Shahbandar was assassinated for reasons that remain to this day unclear. Fourteen individuals, including his political rivals Jamil Mardam and Lutfi al-Haffar, were accused of involvement in his murder, although both men fled the country rather than face trial before a French judge.[25] The movement that had grown up around Shahbandar failed to outlast him, creating a vacuum that was filled by Shukri al-Quwwatli, the 'King of Apricots', whose hardline stance against making concessions to France now propelled him into the leadership of the National Bloc.

Compared to Mardam and even Shahbandar, Quwwatli cut a daring figure. Quwwatli reasoned that the fall of France to Germany in June 1940, and subsequent German and Italian advances against French and British forces in North Africa, would increase pressure on France to hand Syria over to Syrians. He sought to raise that pressure further by building bridges with largely Vichy-supporting mandate officials and took advantage of bread shortages and rising living costs to call for strikes. In response, in February 1941, souqs were closed across Damascus, Aleppo, Homs, Hama and even Deir al-Zour. A new high commissioner, General Dentz, was appointed to Syria and Lebanon by the Vichy regime several months later. By this point, Quwwatli had consolidated his nationalist credentials as the most important voice in the National Bloc.

Quwwatli's calculations of the strategic utility in supporting the Axis powers against the ongoing colonial occupation was shared by the nationalist movement in neighbouring Iraq. Although formally independent, Iraq's sovereignty was deeply compromised, nationalists felt, by the terms of the 1932 Anglo-Iraqi Treaty. In April 1941, radicals led by the former prime minister, Rashid al-Kaylani, seized power from the regent and launched attacks on British airbases in the country. This decisive move caused much excitement among Syrian nationalists. In support of Kaylani's efforts against the British, the High Commission in Syria extended an invitation for Axis powers to make use of its own airbases. At this point, Britain and its allies, the Free French forces led by Charles de Gaulle, launched an invasion to remove the Vichy collaborators from Damascus.

Prior to this second occupation of Syria, the Free French attempted to rally support against the incumbent French administration. Aeroplanes scattered thousands of pamphlets that promised Syrians the new invasion would liberate the country:

> You will become from henceforth a free and sovereign people; you will be able to compose for yourselves separate states or to unite yourselves into a single state. And in either of these

> cases, your independence and sovereignty will be guaranteed in a treaty to make clear the relations between us [. . .] Noble Syrians and Lebanese, you see by this declaration that the Free French forces and the British forces enter your country not to control your freedom but to guarantee it [. . .] We who fight in the name of the freedom of peoples, it is impossible for us to allow the enemy to gradually dominate your country, impose his oversight over you, steal your wealth and enslave you [. . .] With the voices of its sons who are fighting from its life, and for the sake of the world's freedom, France declares your independence.[26]

The promise of independence was made by General Catroux, who had been appointed the senior Free French officer in the Levant on the basis of his experience on the ground in Syria some twenty years earlier, when he had negotiated the first autonomy agreement with the Atrash family of Jabal al-Duruz. Enthused by this prospect, Syrian soldiers in the mandatory power's locally recruited armed forces, the *Troupes spéciales*, defected from the colonial regime. The bulk of the fighting was accomplished by British, Free French, Australian and Indian troops, who benefitted from the absence of Vichy reinforcements or German air support. The Vichy Army of the Levant lost 6,000 soldiers and most of its air force. Within five weeks, the Allies took Damascus and Beirut. An armistice on 14 July allowed Vichy loyalists and armed forces to depart the country.

Despite Catroux's promises, Free France had little intention of ending its control over Syria and Lebanon. In September 1941, Catroux announced the 'independence' of the two countries, a proclamation that no one took seriously when the Syrian presidency was handed to the distinctly non-nationalist and very unpopular Shaykh Taj al-Din al-Hasani. Real power continued to be exercised by the French, although Catroux now found himself in the difficult position of having to liaise with the British, who had appointed a mission led by General Spears to ensure Syria and Lebanon remained stable components of the Allies' military strategy in the eastern Mediterranean.

Britain and France had fundamentally different perspectives on the question of independence. While London assumed the best outcome would be an Iraq-style treaty of alliance, the Free French suspected perfidious Albion of undermining their position to the advantage of Britain's own interests in the region. The remaining years of the war were marked by tension between Catroux and Spears, as much as by tension between Syrian nationalists and the new French occupation. This Franco-British jockeying played a crucial role in securing Syria's independence at the end of the war.

With regard to the Syrian economy, the wartime years in many ways accelerated processes of industrial development that had been under way for the past couple of decades. Under Vichy rule, Syria had been prevented from trading with the outside world by an Allied naval blockade. The ensuing food shortages were exacerbated by a poor harvest in 1941, as well as hoarding and speculation by merchants, which pushed prices even higher. Some local industries, such as cotton production, were able to expand into the gap left by the lack of foreign competition. The Allies attempted to alleviate the food shortages by dumping 80,000 tonnes of wheat on to the market at rock bottom prices in autumn 1941, but Syrian merchants simply bought it up and added it to their grain reservoirs to keep prices elevated. The next year, General Spears formulated an alternative plan: to set up a Wheat Office that would buy grain directly from large landowners for cash, and then redistribute it for sale according to demand. Any reluctance on the part of the landlords to participate in this new state monopoly was reduced by Spears' proposal to maroon them on the island of Kamaran, just off the coast of Yemen, if they did not play their part.[27] The Wheat Office successfully curbed the worst excesses of speculation, while agricultural production increased dramatically in the region of Aleppo and even expanded eastwards into the Jazira.[28] To do its job effectively, the Wheat Office needed an accurate count of the local population, prompting the first thorough census in Syria. To ensure the food supply, the office also took control of a number of mills and bakeries, in what was effectively Syria's first nationalization.[29]

Similar principles of rationing were used to regulate Syria's foreign trade. Since shipping was prioritized for military purposes, commercial imports now required a licence issued by Britain's Middle East Supply Centre in Cairo, which ensured that only essential goods rather than luxury items made it on to supply ships.[30] Syrian businessmen soon found they needed to actively lobby officials for the imported machinery and spare parts they needed to keep their industrial ventures running. Although these wartime measures were intended to prevent Syria and Lebanon from suffering famine, as they did during the previous world war, they had the unintended consequences of stimulating new regulatory powers and giving new institutional capacities to a colonial state best characterized as thin, if not outright skeletal. These restrictions on imports led to several years of increased domestic savings that would fuel an economic boom in Syria after the end of the war.

After the French-selected president, Shaykh Taj al-Din al-Hasani, died in January 1943, the constitution was restored, and elections announced for July. The National Bloc formed a government under Sa'dallah al-Jabiri, while Shukri al-Quwwatli took the presidency. The National Bloc had never regained its unity after the failure of the treaty talks and was still under strain from its various factions. The Bloc also had yet to incorporate any Druze or Alawi notables and had little interest in social or economic reform. In the meantime, new political movements and social organizations – including the Syrian Communist Party, the Muslim Brothers and the Ba'th Party – began to attract support from the next generation and from the traditional, conservative lower middle classes, who had never been entirely at ease with the National Bloc's modern education and easy cosmopolitanism. In the 1943 elections, the first representatives of these emerging political forces were elected to parliament.

Notable among them was the firebrand Akram al-Hawrani, from the conservative town of Hama. A fierce critic of Syria's feudal agricultural system, Hawrani tried repeatedly to raise the issue of peasant rights in parliament but found his démarche blocked by the landowners and bourgeois industrialists of the National Bloc. Hawrani's election was the opening salvo in a social struggle that would take centre stage in Syria after independence.

By 1944, the colonial authorities and the National Bloc were at yet another impasse. Mindful of Mardam's mistakes, the Bloc refused any compromise with France. For their part, the French refused to discuss crucial elements of Syrian sovereignty, such as control of its own armed forces. In May 1945, as the war was ending in Europe, France reinforced its military presence in Syria with new Senegalese troops. The National Bloc government broke off negotiations. Anti-French demonstrations took place not just in the main cities, but also in the Jabal al-Duruz and the coast: a wave of civil disobedience brought turmoil to the streets. On 29 and 30 May, the French authorities made a futile attempt to restore order by shelling and bombing Damascus from the air. The bombardment killed 400 people and – in a crudely symbolic act – the parliament building was all but destroyed.

General Spears' replacement, Terence Shone, reported to British Foreign Secretary Antony Eden:

> The French have instituted nothing short of a reign of terror in Damascus. Apart from indiscriminate shelling, their troops, black and white, are behaving like madmen, spraying the streets with machine-gun fire ... They do not spare vehicles flying the British flag ... even if they had control of their troops they cannot or will not exercise it ... I can only put this to you and implore His Majesty's Government to allow the Commander-in-Chief to intervene without delay.[31]

Concerned that French brutality would upset regional stability, and that inaction might sour its future relations with an independent Syria, Britain – under whose command Allied forces in the Levant still technically fell – ordered French troops back to their barracks and sent in its own forces from Transjordan to re-establish order.[32]

Under the combined weight of protests from Syria, Lebanon, Britain, the Arab League, the United States and the Soviet Union, France agreed to transfer the *Troupes spéciales* to the National Bloc government and to withdraw its remaining forces and personnel from Syria and Lebanon. On 17 April 1946, two days before the League of Nations and its system of mandates was dissolved, the last French troops departed, and Syria declared its independence.

5

Liberalism Implodes, 1946–1949

Syria's independence was greeted with three days of celebration. The streets of Damascus were adorned with national flags, electric lights and portraits of Shukri al-Quwwatli, who remained in office to continue serving as Syria's president. With the national armed forces finally transferred from French to Syrian control, the Syrian army took pride of place in the festivities: tens of thousands of spectators jubilantly watched their soldiers parade through the capital in their uniformed finery. The tank division even decorated a vehicle to look like a crocodile; to the delight of the crowds, the mouth of the crocodile was mechanically rigged to swing open from time to time as it lurched forward.[1] Troops of boy scouts marched after the army parade, while schoolgirls carried placards with slogans praising the struggle against colonialism. The children handed out flowers to the crowds, chanting nationalist rhymes all the while: 'Only our own efforts will help us; our country's life is freedom!'[2]

The central square of al-Merjeh, where in the 1910s Ottoman rulers had hanged Arab nationalists and where in the 1920s the French had gruesomely displayed the corpses of Syrian rebels, now thronged with citizens of an independent republic listening to political speeches and nationalist songs until late at night; men danced the *dabkeh* in celebration and women ululated in sheer elation. Delegations from Egypt, Transjordan and Iraq came to bear witness to Syria's triumph as the first Arab nation to achieve full independence, without any lingering colonial ties or military bases. Overlooking Damascus, on the slopes of Mount Qasyoun, huge letters spelled out phrases that caught the spirit of the moment: 'the army', 'our struggle' and 'independence'. Independence promised to soothe the still-fresh indignities of the colonial past.[3] In front of the Serail – the former seat of French rule – a crowd gathered to proudly hear Quwwatli deliver the first presidential address to liberated Syria.

'This is a day,' began Quwwatli from a second-floor balcony, 'in which the light of freedom shines brightly upon your nation ... a day of great victory and clear conquest.' Quwwatli emphasized that independence had been a collective achievement and that the whole country had made sacrifices. He took care to acknowledge the involvement of every member of the nation: young and old, Christian and Muslim. Besides peasants and workers, Quwwatli also mentioned the role played by teachers ('who spread the glory of nationalism and stirred the spirit of patriotism'), writers ('who defended truth'), merchants ('who left their shops to protest unjust oppression') and women ('who fulfilled their responsibilities with dedication, conviction and patience').

Quwwatli wove into his speech the contributions made by each of Syria's geographical regions. Quwwatli's list of where martyrs fell reads almost like a gazetteer of the Syrian interior: the battles of the Ghuta, the Great Revolt led by Sultan Pasha al-Atrash in the Jabal al-Duruz, the revolt led by Ibrahim Hananu north of Aleppo, the Salih al-Ali revolt in the Alawi Mountains, fighting in the plains of Homs, the valley of Hama, Tall Kalakh, al-Mazra'a, the Hawran, Rashaya and the Qalamoun. All of Syria, the listeners were reminded, had suffered and sacrificed in the name of freedom. 'We are truly one nation,' Quwwatli declared. 'We have no minorities and no majorities.'[4]

Although Quwwatli explicitly rejected the colonial discourse of numerical minorities in favour of a vision of a single united people, the legacies of French rule meant that the central state was in practice weak and could not assert its authority across the whole of the country. The withdrawal of French forces led to renewed tussles over the options of autonomy or integration within a state controlled from Damascus. In Aleppo, Jabal al-Duruz, the coastal mountains and the desert, some sections of the local elites regarded centralization as the best way to access to the wider world, while others looked to neighbouring countries to help them maintain a healthy degree of autonomy from Damascus. The two Hashemite kingdoms – Iraq and Jordan (as Transjordan was officially renamed in 1956) – took advantage of these tensions to forge alliances with opponents of centralization. Although the idea of unifying the states of *Bilad al-Sham* was broadly popular in Syria, especially among younger, more radical political activists (some of whom even aspired to unite the whole Arabic-speaking world), there was little enthusiasm for replacing the republic with a monarchy. King Abdullah of Jordan's aspirations for building a Greater Syria under his leadership thus encountered opposition from the Quwwatli-supporting nationalist bourgeoisie, the rising forces of the Syrian left and the distant, recently founded Kingdom of Saudi Arabia, which had expelled the Hashemites from their ancestral home in the Hijaz and regarded their machinations in the lands of Syria with great suspicion.

Quwwatli himself did little to advance popular support for centralization. Despite his proclamation that he would build up the institutions of the newly independent state, Quwwatli's three years in office were marked by nepotism, corruption and arrogance. In newly independent Syria, old family money spoke the loudest, and politicians were more inclined to intrigue against one another for the spoils of office than to improve the lives of ordinary citizens. This highly unequal, deeply flawed system under Quwwatli was sovereign Syria's first introduction to parliamentary democracy.

The political shortcomings of Quwwatli's rule system would only be exacerbated by the economic and military setbacks that accompanied the early years of independence. The departure of British and French troops meant a sudden end to the foreign military spending that had injected considerable cash into the country during the Second World War. Syria's first three years of independence would be marked by rapid inflation, shortages of basic foodstuffs, frequent strikes and a widespread feeling of crisis. The downward turn was accelerated by Syria's disastrous performance in the 1948 war against the newly declared State of Israel, which army officers blamed on Quwwatli's deliberate failure to invest in the military. Sick of civilian inefficiency and the old elites' internecine squabbling in what was tantamount to a pantomime of parliamentary democracy, in 1949 army officers would overthrow Quwwatli and install a military government. Their coup would be the first of many.

Building a national state

In his first speech as the president of sovereign Syria, Quwwatli declared the start of what he called an 'era of building' to counter fragmentation and ensure stability. Repairing the institutions of government to implement reform programmes, Quwwatli said, would bring about a moral, scientific, economic and social revival that would unleash the true potential of the Syrian people. The proposal to build fully functioning, national institutions was in many ways designed to overcome France's deliberate failure to develop a unified and coherent system of government across Syria's diverse regions. Unfortunately, under Quwwatli little progress was made towards this goal.

Syria's first independent government was characterized by a distinct tolerance for graft. Ministers gave relatives positions for which they were unqualified, civil servants pilfered from government budgets, state property was used for private ends and public appointments were decided on political rather than professional grounds.[5] Journalist Munir al-Rayyis warned that independence had not ushered in a new age of good governance, but simply emboldened ministers and deputies in their outrageous attempts to exploit public office.[6] Even Quwwatli himself was not above this common practice. Muhammad Kurd Ali, a respected intellectual who had founded the Arabic Language Academy in Damascus in 1918, accused the president of filling the ministries with incompetent sycophants whose only qualification was their political loyalty. He alleged that Quwwatli had instructed the Ministry of Public Works to build roads on his family properties at the taxpayers' expense, showered public money on poets and authors who praised his name and corrupted the courts by appointing judges who were biased towards him and his friends. 'His violation of the laws was clear to all who could see,' wrote Kurd Ali in his memoirs. 'Republican government, which was meant to curb tyranny, became capricious rather than legal rule. The form of government was constitutional, but the actual practice was arbitrary.'[7]

Quwwatli's indulgence of the misuse of public office was not merely motivated by a naked desire for self-enrichment. He had inherited substantial family wealth, after all, which he subsequently added to with ventures in agriculture, commerce and industry. Rather Qawwatli used political appointments, sinecures and easy access to state resources to shore up support for himself and his political coterie. Factionalism and petty bickering were rife among Syria's parliamentarians, a fact that Quwwatli skilfully exploited to his advantage. 'It was in the nature of the president to sow the seeds of competition and mutual loathing among the political figures,' observed Khalid al-Azm, who served as Quwwatli's prime minister in 1948, 'so that they would not join forces against him. This meant he alone would always remain in control of the situation.'[8]

In response to the public's growing dissatisfaction with the post-independence government, in early 1947 Quwwatli announced the creation of a new political party – *al-Hizb al-Watani*, the National Party – to contest the elections scheduled for July. Much like its predecessor, the National Bloc, Quwwatli's new organization lacked clear policies, possessed no coherent ideology and had no discipline – none of the features, in other words, that typically characterize a modern political party in the parliamentary tradition. The National Party was yet another loose-knit coalition of essentially the same prominent individuals from prestigious families, who used their deep roots and high social standing in particular neighbourhoods to mobilize the electorate. In return, voters might receive financial largesse or access to public resources, or else ask for political favouritism or mediation to resolve problems with business, the law or the state bureaucracy. The relationship between the elite and the grassroots was mediated by a layer of local neighbourhood strongmen.[9]

From a purely sociological perspective, Quwwatli and the National Party were not so much corrupt as playing their part in what might be called a social pact that allowed the elite to maintain its position at the top of Syrian society in exchange for their patronage of the lower ranks of the population. Of course, the terms of this pact worked to preserve the established, deeply inequitable social hierarchy. 'Before he took office, the president distributed largesse from his own purse,' acknowledged Kurd Ali. 'But when he took office, he dipped deep into the nation's coffers. [...] It has to be admitted that he knew better how to deal with political matters than to rule wisely.'[10]

One of the few figures in the National Party who could check Quwwatli's ambition was his great rival Sa'dallah al-Jabiri, whose death in June 1947 freed Quwwatli to press ahead with his plans to amend the constitution to allow him to stand for a second five-year term as president. This move provoked a backlash from other parliamentarians, who subsequently founded an opposition party named *Hizb al-Sha'b*, the People's Party. The new party included industrialist–politicians such as Rushdi al-Kikhia and Nazim al-Qudsi, most of whom were from Aleppo, in contrast to Quwwatli's Damascus-heavy National Party. Although similar in terms of social background and economic interests, the two parties would spend the next few years locked in political rivalry. However, the most significant challengers to Quwwatli's presidency would come not from the parliamentary elite of Aleppo, but from groups outside the cities that disputed the very idea of being ruled from the capital.

Challenging the central state

In Syria's coastal mountains, Alawi notables had for over a decade regarded the prospect of integration into an independent state run from Damascus with a certain ambivalence. Although many of them had strongly supported the coast being unified with France's State of Syria in the 1930s, after independence several Alawi leaders sought to maintain their autonomy against the steadily expanding authority of the central government in Damascus. During the last years of the Second World War, these leaders had already provoked clashes between Alawis and the Syrian gendarmerie to provide a pretext for France to create an independent Alawi government, albeit without success. In 1945, these Alawi separatists had formed a new political party along with several like-minded Sunni notables, who also rejected the appointment of regional officials sent by the nationalist government in Damascus. A parallel party that supported integration under the National Bloc government included Sunnis and Greek Orthodox Christians, in addition to such prominent Alawi figures as the poet Badawi al-Jabal. Attitudes towards regional autonomy evidently did not fall neatly along ethno-religious lines.

In the course of 1946, the central government tried to clamp down on what it saw as the excesses of a handful of rural Alawi chiefs, who considered it reasonable to appropriate harvests and dispossess peasants from their traditional land rights, in the process accumulating legal title to huge swathes of farmland. Several of them were also bandits who quite literally engaged in highway robbery. The most colourful of these individuals was Sulayman al-Murshid, who had risen to prominence in the early 1920s when, as a young, illiterate shepherd, he had been recognized as an incarnation of the divine by two Alawi religious shaykhs. Murshid's reputation as a miracle-worker spread quickly, and he became the focus of a fast-growing millenarian cult. In 1924, some of Murshid's followers were so zealous in their beliefs that they famously attacked French troops at the village of Alyat armed only with the conviction that the branches in their hands would be miraculously transformed into weaponry. This did not take place, and forty-eight of them, including sixteen women and children, were slaughtered by French machine guns.[11] Nevertheless, his followers, the Murshidin, expanded rapidly: by the late 1930s their number was estimated to have reached as high as 40,000.[12] Murshid was consequently able to parlay his religious status into worldly standing: he became a rich landowner and was elected to parliament in 1936, all the while maintaining quixotic relationships with France and the National Bloc. For figures such as Murshid, the reassertion of government authority implied the end of the unregulated freedom they had become accustomed to enjoying.

In January 1946, the Damascus government dispatched a force of 200 gendarmes and an armoured vehicle to forcibly reopen the road between Masyaf and Safita that had been cut by Alawi autonomists in the coastal hills. Over the next few months, the government pressured some of the local dissident leaders into putting down their arms. In April, the gendarmerie neutralized the forces of Ibrahim al-Kinj, leaving only Murshid in open revolt. Whether Murshid's recalcitrance was fed by the religious sentiments of his supporters or by the immense wealth he had accumulated over the two decades since his divine revelations began is unclear, but over the summer he successfully brought the northern region of the mountains around his home village of Jawbat Burghal under his exclusive suzerainty.

Murshid continued to flout the authority of the central government in the autumn by collecting 'tax' from local farmers in the form of a portion of their harvest. In the capital there was much debate about whether to respond to Murshid with words or rifles. Both President Quwwatli and Sa'dallah al-Jabiri felt that Syria, having enjoyed only a few months of independence, was still too fragile to survive a major episode of internal conflict. If Murshid's followers rose up to support him, local groups in other parts of the country might also exploit the moment to challenge the central state. In an effort to calm the situation, the Damascus-appointed governor of Latakia, Adil al-'Azmeh, ordered that the harvest be held until a legally sanctioned means of tax collection could be agreed. This move unintentionally provoked the ire of Murshid's son Fatih and gave rise to further armed clashes.

The affair came to a dramatic end on the evening of 12 September 1946 when a force of gendarmes marched on Murshid's village and encountered fierce resistance. Exactly what happened next became the subject of some disagreement. The Syrian government maintained that the gendarmes were victorious: after surrounding the village and killing a dozen of his followers, the gendarmes accepted Murshid's surrender but, upon entering his home, found the dead body of his wife, who had apparently been murdered by Murshid's own hand. Other sources suggest that Murshid's wife and son disobeyed his orders and told their supporters to attack the advancing gendarmes.[13] According to these accounts, Murshid killed his wife in a fit of rage upon realizing his men had taken on the forces of the central government so flagrantly. His son Fatih fled the scene and Murshid surrendered.

In the two-month investigation that followed, the gendarmerie arrested 200 individuals who had taken up arms, including Fatih, and confiscated over 1,800 rifles, 700 revolvers and nine machine guns.[14] Gendarmes put to the torch the vast fields of cannabis planted by Murshid, an act that annihilated an important source of his income and symbolized the government's intention to enforce new legislation prohibiting the cultivation of hashish on Syrian territory. On 22 November 1947, fifty-five of those accused were prosecuted in a twelve-day trial. With all eyes on Murshid, his lawyer mounted a spirited and verbose defence. Highlighting both the historical injustices faced by the Alawis and the personal misfortunes of Sulayman al-Murshid, the lawyer argued that the religious shaykhs had cynically exploited the epileptic episodes Murshid had suffered as a child by claiming them to be moments of divine revelation. Furthermore, Murshid was loyal to Syria, as his parliamentary service attested; when Quwwatli had visited the governorate, Murshid had been at the forefront of the welcome delegation. If Murshid had indeed collected taxes or established local courts independently of Damascus, this was not an attempt to create a state within a state; similar practices were tolerated among Syria's Bedouin, for example. The implication of the lawyer's defence was that the military and legal campaign against Murshid was politically motivated – perhaps even the product of clandestine French meddling.

Despite these arguments, the court found Murshid to be guilty on charges of forming an armed gang, robbing the population, taking up arms against and killing gendarmes and murdering his own wife.[15] The court sentenced him to death. In the cold hours before dawn on 16 December 1946, Murshid was hanged at al-Merjeh Square in Damascus, alongside two other members of his entourage.

Contemporary commentators considered the decision to execute Murshid in the capital to be odd. To many, Latakia would have been a more appropriate location in which to warn the troublesome Alawi notables of the dangers of opposing the government. Yet the message did appear to reach its intended recipients: after Murshid's death, never again did an Alawi leader take up arms against the central state. Of course, the Murshid revolt was an extreme case of Alawi dissent. If its leader had fought the longest and the hardest for local autonomy, however, this was not the result of an ideological commitment to a greater Alawi cause, but rather in the interest of preserving the seat of his local power against the encroaching authority of the Syrian state.

Just a decade earlier, for example, Murshid had been quite happy to ally with urban nationalists against the French, when the colonial administration had begun to restrict his freedom of activity. Equally, while political leaders based in Damascus sought to eliminate local challengers to their project of building a centralized state, this did not necessarily entail excluding peripheral communities such as the Alawis from national political life. As part of the joyous celebrations marking Syria's independence, for example, President Quwwatli not only made room in the festivities for a public speech from the venerable Shaykh Salih al-Ali – an Alawi who had led one of the earliest rebel bands against the French occupation in 1919–20 – but explicitly honoured his contribution above and beyond that of other rebels. As historian Joshua Landis points out, Quwwatli consciously bestowed upon Syria's Alawis a 'leading role in the national foundation myth'.[16]

In contrast to Salih al-Ali, the former Druze rebel Sultan al-Atrash was conspicuous in the national celebrations only by his absence. Although the most prominent leader of the Great Revolt against France, Sultan Pasha had refused the invitation to join the festivities in Damascus upon hearing that Quwwatli would not make him guest of honour. This incident was about more than Sultan Pasha's dented ego. During the Great Revolt, Sultan Pasha had allied the Jabal al-Duruz with Abd al-Rahman al-Shahbandar, then leader of the elite nationalists in Damascus, who was later Quwwatli's rival. To weaken Shahbandar, Quwwatli had found it expedient to oppose the Atrash family, creating an enmity that continued after Shahbandar's assassination.

In 1945, the Syrian press reported allegations that, in an unguarded moment, Quwwatli had referred to the Druze as a 'dangerous minority'. In response, Sultan Pasha angrily demanded that Quwwatli publicly withdraw his remarks, or he would attack Damascus with thousands of Druze fighters. Sultan's bluster continued after independence. 'The government has forgotten that it is from and for the people,' Sultan Pasha said in one widely reported speech. 'It does everything other than what is in the best interest of the people. Profiteering reigns everywhere, along with poverty, chaos, and moral corruption. The misdoings of civil servants have spread across all government departments. Patronage has become the basic principle for getting a job.'[17]

More than a mere personal criticism of Quwwatli, Sultan Pasha's words reflected the tensions between Quwwatli's centralizing aspirations and the Atrash family's interest in maintaining the political autonomy of the Jabal al-Duruz. The most prominent member of the family, Hasan al-Atrash, was governor of the Jabal; most government positions, including in the gendarmerie and police, were filled with Atrash loyalists. Upon independence, the Atrash expected not only that they would retain the political autonomy granted under the French, but also that the central government in Damascus would use its resources to improve the economy and infrastructure of the Jabal. The prospect that they might share their monopoly of power with either interlopers from the capital or members of lesser Druze families was if not laughable, then certainly unconscionable for the Atrash.

Quwwatli refused to meet Atrash demands for economic development, even though drought and locusts meant poor harvests in 1946 and 1947. In contrast, Quwwatli consolidated his victory over the rebellious Alawi notables with plans to devote 3.5 million Syrian pounds (S£) to build schools, hospitals and libraries in the governorate of Latakia. Yet even there, the central government was still not confident enough to permit Alawis to occupy positions of authority in the local administration, which were monopolized by Sunnis.[18] Quwwatli thereafter turned his attention to strong-arming the Jabal al-Duruz into the national fold.

During his rivalry with Shahbandar, Quwwatli had fostered cordial ties with several second-tier Druze notable families who shared his goal of diminishing the power of the Atrash. In particular, members of the Asali, the Halabi and the Shufi families had formed a loose-knit political movement called *al-Sha'biyun* – 'the

Populars' – who were in favour of reform. The Populars maintained that the Druze social structure was backward and feudal: they called for a more equitable, egalitarian and democratic distribution of wealth and justice between families from different social classes. The Populars also held that the Jabal was an indivisible part of Syria, supported Syria's constitution as a republic and maintained that the Jabal's local government should derive its authority exclusively from the central government.[19] These aims neatly coincided with Quwwatli's vision for Syria.

With the Populars facing the near-impossible task of defeating the incumbent Atrash in the national elections of July 1947, political tensions between the two groups led to violence. Their clashes were exacerbated by the fact that Quwwatli's money had been used to bring rifles and machine guns into the Jabal. A truce was negotiated by Druze religious shaykhs and the Ministry of the Interior, and elections were finally held in mid-July, two weeks later than originally planned. The voting ended in victory for the Atrash family, who took all five seats. The results met with consternation from both Quwwatli and the Populars. Overruling the Ministry of the Interior official who had declared the elections to be legitimate, Quwwatli announced the results invalid and scheduled a rerun for November. This move only intensified the conflict between the Atrash and the Populars, who had by then seized control of the town of Salkhad – 'in the name of the government', as they put it. The two sides continued fighting until late 1948, when the flows of weapons and arms dried up, and Quwwatli's attention was diverted elsewhere. If the Jabal would not be integrated, Quwwatli reasoned, it could be kept busy with ongoing low-level turmoil.

External challengers: Jordan's Greater Syria project

Although most Syrian politicians were firmly in favour of republicanism, a minority remained attached to the idea of a Hashemite monarchy. After being expelled by the French, Faysal had been granted the throne of Iraq by the British. Upon Faysal's death in 1933, Syrian monarchists had turned to his brother Abdullah, king of Transjordan, as the best alternative. In Damascus, the monarchists were led by the politician Hasan al-Hakim, who had served as a minister in Faysal's short-lived government of 1918–20. A vocal early supporter of the Hashemites, Hakim had won some converts to monarchism among the professional classes of Damascus. In Aleppo, sympathy for Hashemite cause was stronger, although this was as much an expression of dissatisfaction with the inefficiency and corruption of the government in Damascus – as well as the residual rivalry between the two cities – as any genuine preference for monarchical rule. Just three decades earlier, moreover, Aleppo's trade connections with Iraq had been far denser than those with southern Syria. For the elite families of Aleppo, nostalgia for the lost prosperity of Ottoman times also burnished the appeal of unification with Hashemite Iraq.

Of the two Hashemite kingdoms, it was Jordan that most actively pursued the agenda of unification with Syria. Soon after the French withdrawal, King Abdullah announced to the Jordanian parliament his intention to unite Syria and Jordan under his Hashemite monarchy. Abdullah established a new national holiday to commemorate the anniversary of his brother Faysal's confirmation as the last king of Syria. In May 1947, Abdullah went on to publish a white paper justifying the historical grounds for a reunited Syria; a manifesto issued on the Eid al-Fitr holiday advanced an even stronger version of this claim. Abdullah's emissaries contacted Hashemite sympathizers in Aleppo,[20] and made significant campaign donations to monarchists running in the 1947 elections.[21] More importantly, Abdullah also cultivated ties with the disaffected Atrash in the Jabal al-Duruz, who were quick to exploit their longstanding ties with Hashemite Jordan in their ongoing struggle with Quwwatli.

The Atrash family had long enjoyed good personal relations with Abdullah, who had notably given eleven years of haven to Sultan Pasha himself. Sultan Pasha's closest ally, Shahbandar, had also been a staunch pro-Hashemite. The wealth of the Atrash family, essential to maintaining its prestige and dominance over the Jabal, was inextricably intertwined with neighbouring Jordan. Although most of the Jabal was economically dependent on Damascus to provide a market for its agricultural produce, Atrash wealth came from their control of cross-border smuggling operations and the cultivation and supply of hashish.[22] Contemporary observers frequently noted rumours that certain members of the Jordanian royal family were also accumulating considerable private wealth by taking advantage of their diplomatic immunity to smuggle drugs through customs. Such rumours were not entirely without foundation. In April 1942, 200 pounds of hashish had been found travelling with Sultan Pasha's son Nayif in a car belonging to the Queen of Transjordan when the vehicle was stopped near Gaza.[23] The fact that Quwwatli's government had in 1947 outlawed the production of hashish in Syria for the first time added a further resonance to the clashes between the central state and the Atrash administration.

From the perspective of Damascus, the Jabal was an outlying part of the economic periphery; in reality, it was an integral part of a broader transnational economy that thrived on its semi-illicit status.[24] Quwwatli's national project threatened not just to sever these trade connections, but to eliminate the Jabal's autonomy and forcibly reroute its networks along more regular channels, where they could be controlled, regulated and taxed, according to Syrian state law.

During the 1946–47 tensions with Quwwatli, the Atrash turned towards Amman. The governor, Hasan al-Atrash, threatened that the Jabal would secede from Syria and declare itself part of Jordan if his family's demands were not met. Atrash delegations to Amman openly courted the king's support, fuelling Quwwatli's consternation, and even privately asked Abdullah to annex the Jabal al-Duruz – a request that Abdullah and his British advisors considered wiser to decline.[25] When open conflict broke out between the Atrash and the Populars, Quwwatli sent Syria's Desert Force to the border to guard against any military intervention from Jordan. Ever suspicious of King Abdullah's vision for a Hashemite Greater Syria, Quwwatli considered there was a genuine risk that Jordan might seize the Jabal.

Contemporaries observed that Quwwatli's wariness of Jordan gradually intensified into an almost paranoid obsession with King Abdullah and his British-trained army. 'Because of this crisis, our brother Shukri was terrified of Greater Syria,' wrote Quwwatli's confidant Adil Arslan. 'He was always anxious and slept fitfully because he was plagued by nightmares of the Jordanian army sweeping down on Damascus. [. . .] Everyone in the know is aware of how suspicions have overtaken the presidential palace to the extent that the president of the republic has employed an army of spies who paint a picture of the world for him that only further exacerbates his anxieties and delusions. He trembles at the mention of Transjordan, its army, and its king.'[26]

In the steppe and desert, Syria's Bedouin tribes retained their long-standing reticence to be enmeshed by the institutions, regulations and obligations imposed from the cities. They were notably successful at repelling the efforts of Quwwatli's government to abolish the parallel system of tribal law and bring them under the jurisdiction of the Syrian state. Mindful of Damascus's desire to encroach upon their autonomy, tribes of northern Syria such as the Mawali, the Baggara, the Hadidiyyin and the Uqaydat expressed their sympathy for greater ties with Jordan – a move that promised to distract Damascus or even to relocate the centre of political authority to Amman, which lay even further south and even further away from their lands.

Enthusiasm for the Hashemites was notably less pronounced among southern tribes, whose traditional lands lay closer to the Jordanian border. In September 1947, Fawaz ibn Sha'lan, leader of the great Ruwala tribe of southern Syria, presided over a tribal conference at Palmyra which denounced King Abdullah's Greater Syria project. There was a geopolitical dimension to this move. Over previous decades, Ruwala chiefs had cultivated ties with King Abd al-Aziz ibn Sa'ud, founder of Saudi Arabia, who was close to Quwwatli and shared his dislike of the Hashemites. For Syria's southern tribes, the status quo reached with Damascus was preferable to starting from scratch with Amman.

In the region of the Hawran, to the west of the Jabal, residents of the town of Der'a and its surrounding villages maintained close relations with the other side of the Jordanian border. Many Hawranis had kinship ties and business connections in Jordanian towns such as al-Ramtha and Irbid. When the British had entered Syria in 1941, Hawrani notables sent them numerous petitions calling for their region to be annexed to Jordan.[27] Of course, it is difficult to gauge whether the Hawranis would have been content if their petitions to unite the two countries under the Hashemite throne had ever become reality. But faced with the prospect of having their freedom of action curtailed by the steady expansion of state authority emanating from the capital, it is perhaps not surprising that these provincial elites found it useful to play – or to threaten to play – the Hashemite card against would-be state builders in Damascus.

Quwwatli and the armed forces

Of all the nightmares that haunted Quwwatli's sleep, perhaps the most chilling was not the prospect of King Abdullah invading Jabal al-Duruz, but the possibility of the mass defection of the Syrian army to the Hashemite banner.

Quwwatli held little affection for the Syrian armed forces. Under the French, the prototype for the national army, the *Troupes spéciales*, had disproportionately drawn its rank and file from rural communities, in an effort to immunize this force against the anti-colonial sentiments that dominated the cities. As it represented one of the rare avenues for social advancement available to marginalized peasant communities, the army continued to attract a large number of recruits who were Alawi, Ismaili or Druze, in addition to provincial Sunnis from the lower social and economic classes. Men from these backgrounds were often drawn to more radical, populist and leftist political parties. The officers of the *Troupes spéciales*, who were primarily Sunni or Christian, had demonstrated their nationalist credentials by defecting from France at the end of the mandate, yet Quwwatli still considered them compromised by the taint of collaboration. Quwwatli also believed that Hashemite sympathies were particularly rife among senior members of the Syrian officer corps. For those reasons, the army's loyalty to the Republic of Syria could not be assured.

Quwwatli had initially approached Britain, the United States, Sweden and Switzerland for the financial and technical support necessary to upgrade the Syrian army,[28] perhaps intending to use this as an opportunity to extend his networks of patronage into the military institutions of the state. When foreign aid was refused, Quwwatli abandoned his plans to remake the army and turned his attention to the Syrian gendarmerie, which had the responsibility of maintaining law and order in the countryside. At the beginning of the mandate, the French dissolved the existing gendarmerie that had been established by the Ottomans, out of concern that it harboured too many Hashemite loyalists.[29] Ironically, Quwwatli now looked to this same institution to strengthen his hand against pro-Hashemite leanings in the armed forces.

In 1946, the gendarme commander, Hrant Manouliyan, filed a lengthy report which described the Syrian gendarmerie as existing in a state of 'profound decadence and poor organization ... close to anarchy in every area'. The chain of command had deteriorated to the point that many gendarmes did not even know who their commanding officers were, while others had abandoned their stations and gone home, in some cases because the administration had mistakenly stopped paying their salaries. Over the next six months, Manouliyan led a crusade to reform the gendarmerie. He resorted to what he himself described as 'severity and firmness', punishing those who had transgressed official regulations and firing those who seemed unable to live under his new regime.

Manouliyan seemed to share Quwwatli's sentiments about the danger of foreign intervention. For both of them, the gendarmerie was the only reliable force, given that the army lacked the organization, training and equipment to uphold the rule of law inside the country.[30] The rectitude of these convictions seemed to have been confirmed by the salutary performance of the reformed gendarmes against the rebellion of Sulayman al-Murshid. As the then defence minister, Ahmad Sharabati, later recalled, it looked to many as if the gendarmerie, under the control of the Ministry of the Interior, was better equipped for combat than the regular army.[31] Indeed, Quwwatli's overwhelming and increasing irrational fear of a pro-Hashemite coup led him to block reform efforts within the military. This decision was to prove disastrous for Syria's later performance in the 1948 war with Israel.

In December 1947, open conflict broke out in Palestine between Zionist settlers and Palestinians in anticipation of the British withdrawal scheduled for the following May. Syrian public opinion was actively, emphatically opposed to the creation of a Jewish state in Palestine. News that the UN General Assembly had accepted the partition plan proposed by its Special Committee on Palestine was met with mass demonstrations and strikes across Syria. In Damascus, protestors stormed the offices of the US, Belgian and Soviet diplomatic missions, in addition to those of the Communist Party, all of which had supported the plan. In Aleppo, events turned violent: eleven synagogues were set on fire and seventy-six of the city's Jewish population killed by protestors.[32] Syrian newspapers called for government action to assist the Palestinian cause, provoking parliament to impose compulsory military service and raise taxes to support war preparations. Given the parlous state of government finances, campaigns for public donations to support the armed forces were already familiar in Syria: a Civic Association for Donations for Military Aircraft had been founded in June 1946 to raise funds towards creating a Syrian air force. Similar campaigns were launched to elicit donations in support of the Palestinian war effort.

Rather than directing the Syrian armed forces to engage Zionist forces in Palestine, Quwwatli championed the creation of an Arab Liberation Army (ALA), a multinational force of volunteers funded by Syria, Lebanon, Egypt and Saudi Arabia. By January 1948, nearly 4,000 members of the newly formed ALA were undergoing military training inside Syria. The bulk of volunteers came from Syria, Iraq and Palestine, with a small number from Egypt, Jordan and even Yugoslavia. Most of the officers were Syrians who had resigned from their positions in the regular national army to serve in the new force.[33] The commander of the ALA was Fawzi al-Qawuqji, a former Ottoman army officer trained at the War College in Istanbul, who had famously organized the Hama revolt of 1925. Sentenced to death in absentia by the French, Qawuqji had fled to Saudi Arabia, worked for several years as an instructor at the Iraqi military academy in Baghdad, led a series of guerrilla attacks against British and Zionist forces in Palestine in 1936–37, and then supported the anti-British, anti-Hashemite Kaylani coup in Iraq in 1941. Qawuqji's distaste for the Hashemites' cooperation with the colonial powers no doubt made him, in Quwwatli's eyes, an ideal commander for the ALA.

Quwwatli found the Arab Liberation Army useful for several reasons. First, by bringing together several Arab states – but not Jordan – and being stationed in southern Syria, the army would dissuade King Abdullah from any attempt at invading Syria and uniting the two countries militarily. Quwwatli's entire military strategy in the war centred on preventing Abdullah gaining territory in Syria and Palestine, not defeating Israel.[34] Second, the ALA ensured the survival of Quwwatli's republican regime without any need to rely upon the services of the Syrian army, which he believed compromised by pro-Hashemites. Third, the ALA gave Quwwatli the means to thwart King Abdullah's plans to compromise with the Zionists by accepting a Jewish state in exchange for certain Palestinian lands being ceded to Amman. A joint Arab force on the ground would stymie any Hashemite land grab.[35] Fourth, the ALA could fight in Palestine before the official end of the British Mandate in May 1948, which was politically impossible for the regular armies of Syria and the other Arab states. Finally, should the ALA fail in its supposed mission to prevent the establishment of the State of Israel – which Quwwatli admitted was a likely scenario – the inevitable backlash from Syrian public opinion would be dispersed among the various participating Arab states, rather than shouldered by the Syrian government alone. All in all, Quwwatli's support for the ALA appeared to be a sound move.

The ALA failed to make a significant contribution in the 1948 war. Quwwatli refused to order it to defend Haifa and Jerusalem, instead keeping its forces further north – where they were better positioned to defend Syria against the Jordanian army. Even when the British Mandate ended on 14 May, Quwwatli was reluctant to commit the regular Syrian army: contemporary estimates suggested that as few as 2,500 to 4,500 Syrian soldiers were sent into action.[36] Syria's ill-trained, badly equipped army suffered heavy losses from Israeli forces, with 300 casualties in the first few days of hostilities.[37] The Syrian army did manage to seize three tiny pockets of land close to the eastern shore of the Sea of Galilee and the Jordan River, but did not engage in further fighting and made little impact on the course of the war beyond possibly dissuading Jordanian ambitions for northern expansion.

The political conclusion of the 1948 war saw control over Palestinian territories previously under British Mandate consolidated by the newly created State of Israel and by Transjordan, which administered East Jerusalem and the West Bank. Syria's republican regime under Quwwatli survived the crisis. Of the 750,000 Palestinians who were expelled or fled from their homes in 1948, some 100,000 eventually arrived in Syria, where they were directed to settle in camps close to major cities, such as Khan al-Shaykh in Damascus or Nayrab Camp east of Aleppo. Over subsequent decades, successive governments in Syria oversaw the social and economic integration of Palestinians (in contrast to other Arab states, which imposed separation). The refugees and their descendants nevertheless retained their distinct identities and formal legal status as Palestinians – not Syrians – in the hope of one day returning home to Palestine.

Popular discontent with Quwwatli had been running high even before the defeat of 1948 and the arrival of the Palestinian refugees. The earlier preparations for the war had created new opportunities for the endemic corruption of the political class: it was commonly believed that the public's donations to the war effort had been diverted to the personal finances of leading politicians. Prominent finance minister, Wahbah al-Hariri, was notably accused of embezzling funds from the military budget; put on trial in absentia, Hariri was later acquitted for lack of evidence. The public also believed that government officials who were supposed to impose the new income tax to raise funds for the war would commonly reach an 'understanding' with rich individuals, under-assessing their tax liability in return for a sizeable bribe. Government incompetence was almost as common as corruption, although admittedly it was sometimes difficult to discern the difference.

In one example, the Syrian Ministry of National Defence needed nitroglycerine to manufacture explosives during the war. It purchased twenty tons in the United States and transported it from New York, with 'Syrian Ministry of Defence' written on the paperwork, on a cargo ship whose itinerary happened to include the port of Haifa. Here, Israeli officials deduced the nitroglycerine's intended purpose and sent it back to its port of origin.[38] On another occasion, a consignment of weapons worth one million Syrian pounds (S£) was stolen on its way to Syria, and reportedly either ended up in the hands of Greek communists or else was seized by the Greek government that the communists were trying to overthrow.[39] Barely two weeks after war had been declared, Defence Minister Ahmad Sharabati resigned, perhaps because he opposed corruption in the army, his own sideline in selling military supplies for personal profit had been uncovered, or an increasingly volatile Quwwatli was convinced Sharabati was a British spy.[40]

The Syrian public took to the streets in protest at the mishandling of the war. On the one-year anniversary of the reviled UN partition plan, students went on strike and the markets closed. The police and gendarmerie used tear gas to disperse the angry crowds converging on parliament. The indignity of Syria's defeat in the war brought political life to a standstill as the deputies exchanged first bitter recriminations and then physical blows in the chamber. By October, the political elite was paralysed.

Outside parliament, severe economic problems exacerbated the sense of crisis. Oil shortages forced the closure of electricity power plants and the factories that depended on them, while workers came out on strike in protest at the government and the economy. A general strike was declared in November. Four protestors were killed and fifty-seven wounded in riots in Damascus. Unable to navigate the crisis, the prime minister resigned. The opposition People's Party issued a public statement: 'Syria [. . .] is undergoing a national crisis whose causes have long been neglected by the governors, which have brought the country to a plight, which, if not immediately and effectively corrected, will jeopardize both the regime and the state itself.'[41] By this point, the seeds of crisis that had been sown by Quwwatli's strategic tolerance for nepotism and corruption had grown to entangle the whole country.

A state of emergency was declared, and the army imposed a curfew, suspended freedom of assembly and censored the press even more than was usual for Quwwatli's government. Husni al-Za'im, chief of staff of the Syrian armed forces, personally toured Syria to ensure that order was fully restored.

The situation soon calmed. Quwwatli and the new prime minister, Khalid al-Azm, investigated reports that inferior weaponry, ammunitions and provisions had been supplied to the armed forces. When checking the quality of stores at Mezzeh, then a small village on the outskirts of Damascus, Quwwatli reportedly discovered a tin of clarified butter (*samneh*) the contents of which looked black and rotten. Used to fry an egg, the *samneh* gave off a smell so disgusting the president and his prime minister had to cover their faces with their handkerchiefs.[42] The immediate suspicion was that profiteers were procuring foodstuffs of inferior quality for the soldiers, while pocketing the proceeds. The story of the *samneh* incident was later used to symbolize the moral decay and material corruption that critics alleged was afflicting the country's armed forces. 'No self-respecting Arab will cook in anything else,' journalist Patrick Seale observed, 'no Arabic food tastes right without it, and great health-giving qualities are imputed to it. That the heroes at the front should be defrauded of this essential ingredient was a hideous crime.'[43]

Quwwatli consequently ordered the arrest of the quartermaster on charges of corruption. As it turned out, the quartermaster was a childhood friend of Chief of Staff Za'im, who had appointed him to that position only a few months earlier. Instead of following the president's orders, Za'im simply reassigned his associate to an office job in the Ministry of National Defence.

For Za'im and his fellow officers, the *samneh* affair was the latest in a string of insults that had been directed at the Syrian army. They had been sent to war with inferior weaponry, faulty vehicles and inadequate provisions by corrupt civilian politicians, and now those same politicians had the affront to suggest that the quartermaster had exploited his position for personal gain. Even after the ceasefire with Israel, the civilian government had made little effort to remedy the weakness of the armed forces.

Prime Minister Khalid al-Azm instead sought to rein in government spending by further cutting the military budget: austerity savings were made by reducing officer allowances and postponing routine promotions.[44]

Compounding the indignation of the officers, the government set up a special tribunal to investigate the misappropriation of military funds. Captain Fu'ad Mardam, who had negligently lost a shipment of weapons from Italy, was the first to be tried and imprisoned. In the meantime, parliamentarians verbally attacked army officers in the chamber. Particularly egregious were the accusations made by Faysal al-Asali, the fiery, shock-haired member of parliament for Zabadani. After a personal tirade against Za'im on 17 March, the very next day Asali openly accused Za'im and the commander of military police of ordering hand grenades to be hurled at his offices. (As it turned out, the allegations were false, part of a scheme that Asali himself had concocted to discredit the armed forces).[45] At this point, the officers could stomach no further insult.

Za'im convened a secret meeting of his fellow officers in the town of Qunaytra. Although Za'im had entertained the possibility of a coup for some time, the officers decided to send Quwwatli a list of demands to serve as a final act of warning.[46] Their letter called Asali's attacks on the armed forces an unacceptable denigration of the military and demanded that he be arrested and tried in a military court – along with all those politicians who had failed to prepare the army for victory in the 1948 war. The officers also called for an end to civilian oversight of the armed forces: military affairs should no longer be discussed by parliament.[47] Za'im delivered the letter personally but was reportedly rudely rebuffed. Quwwatli refused to read the officers' memorandum, much less act on their demands; he mockingly retorted that officers were now writing petitions as if they were 'village headmen'.[48]

At a second meeting in the Ain al-Kirsh neighbourhood of Damascus, Za'im and thirteen other officers laid down detailed plans for a coup.[49] Just a few days later, on 30 March 1949, Za'im and his co-conspirators successfully overthrew Quwwatli and the regime he had created. Despite his efforts to create a strong, unified Syrian state under his paternalistic leadership, Quwwatli had failed to appreciate one crucial lesson: that controlling or co-opting the military was an essential task for all would-be state builders. Control of the armed forces would repeatedly emerge as a central axis of struggle in Syria over the following two decades.

The first coup: Syria under Husni al-Za'im

Popular stereotypes of military takeovers tend to involve considerable amounts of violence, with civilian institutions being overthrown by the undemocratic workings of a military organization commanded by a ruthless general with pronounced dictatorial tendencies. In contrast, Za'im's coup was a bloodless affair in which not a single shot was fired. In the early hours of 30 March, tanks under Za'im's command advanced through Damascus along streets still wet from a rain shower the previous evening, while his soldiers arrested civilian politicians and seized the police and gendarmerie headquarters. The country's telephone communications were cut, and Radio Damascus stopped its regular broadcast and played nothing but military marches for the next few hours. At 7 a.m., the military music was interrupted for the first communication from Syria's new rulers.

Military Communiqué Number One explained that the poor state of the country had compelled the army to honour its national duty by temporarily assuming power until it could prepare a 'true democratic regime' to replace the current one, which was only spuriously democratic.[50] The communiqué urged the noble people of Syria to remain calm so that the army could fulfil its mission of liberation.

Events immediately following the coup suggest that Za'im originally intended the military's political role to be temporary, lasting only until the excesses of the Quwwatli regime could be corrected. Za'im notably did not employ military force. After his arrest, Quwwatli was first held at the Mezzeh prison in Damascus, but was quickly transferred to a military hospital, as he had been suffering from a stomach ulcer. Za'im then asked him to submit an official letter of resignation. Other important politicians were also arrested, including Prime Minister Khalid al-Azm and Faysal al-Asali, whose outspoken public criticism of military integrity had so angered the conspiring officers. Asali was brought before Za'im in person, who declared he was well within his rights to sentence him to death. Instead, Za'im merely had him imprisoned – but only after ordering his soldiers to shear from Asali's head the luxuriant mane of hair of which he was so proud.[51]

Za'im did not immediately assume the presidency but summoned a number of parliamentarians and invited them to form a civilian government. He even graciously allowed the speaker of parliament, Faris al-Khouri, to visit Quwwatli in hospital. The next day, around half of the deputies voted in favour of a parliamentary motion supporting Za'im's regime, although none agreed to translate their passive support for a fait accompli into an active agreement to serve under him in a coalition government. On 3 April he dissolved parliament, abrogated the constitution and announced that national elections would take place after a new constitution had been promulgated. A few days later, Za'im brandished the official resignations of Quwwatli and Azm, and on 17 April announced the formation of a new government in which he would serve as his own prime minister. By that point,

Syria had completed the transition from civilian to military rule. Za'im's coup was greeted with demonstrations of support in many cities, especially from students who relished every opportunity to march in the streets.

Za'im overcame his initial reluctance to play a prominent political role and soon began to relish the limelight. On 25 June, he was elected as president of Syria in a popular referendum and celebrated his victory by being driven around the streets of Damascus, which were lined with tens of thousands of his supporters. To add further authority to his transition from military interloper to legitimate president, Za'im appointed Muhsin al-Barazi as his prime minister. A member of a wealthy landowning family from the Homs region, Barazi's efforts to dress Za'im's rule in the trappings of legality earned him the mock honorific of the '*mufti* of the Republic'.

Za'im promoted himself to the highest military rank of field marshal and began to compare himself favourably to Emperor Napoleon. He paid great attention to his personal image, sporting a theatrical monocle, and making dramatic costume changes from day to day, which soon became a source of fascination for the local press. He symbolized his new status with a regal-looking and expensive golden sceptre. Despite Za'im's talent for adorning himself with the accoutrements of power, he could not appeal directly to the Syrian people out of fear his voice would break the spell of the spectacle: educated in Turkish and in French, Za'im's command of literary Arabic was so shaky that he refused to deliver his speeches personally and insisted that someone read them out on his behalf.

Za'im did not allow his lack of personal charisma to interfere with his plans for Syria. Combined with his pomposity was a keen awareness that, if his presidential career were to possess longevity, he would need to succeed at the task that Quwwatli had so badly mismanaged. Very soon after becoming president, Za'im began to implement his designs to build stronger, more coherent state institutions.

The first stage of the plan was to curtail the networks of patronage by means of which Quwwatli had cultivated a personal support base. Za'im cut back the state bureaucracy, bloated by nepotism and phantom employees, and ordered civil servants to choose between their private business interests and their public responsibilities. Many civil servants who had been Quwwatli loyalists transferred their allegiance to Za'im rather than resign on a point of principle. Za'im reversed what he considered to be some of the injustices of the former regime and reinstated the quartermaster who had been targeted by Quwwatli for his alleged role in the *samneh* scandal. Za'im also appointed reliable supporters to key positions. His fellow conspirator Adib al-Shishakli was made chief of police and security, while Shishakli's associate, the radical parliamentarian Akram al-Hawrani, was given a position as special advisor at the Ministry of National Defence. New governors, endowed with military as well as civilian authority, were dispatched to the provinces, where their arrival was celebrated with parades. The gendarmerie was taken away from the Ministry of the Interior and reassigned to the Ministry of National Defence.[52] Za'im reversed Quwwatli's policy of neglecting the army by rapidly increasing its size from 5,000 to 27,000 men. Dissolving the military promotions board that had been established in the early 1940s, within two weeks of assuming power, he had promoted half of the entire officer corps, while liberally bestowing commendations for good service and performance in the 1948 war.[53]

To pay for the expansion of the armed forces, Za'im imposed new taxes on income and inheritance, as well as diverting funds from the budgets of other ministries. To raise the prestige of the armed forces in the eyes of the people, he declared that on 9 July each year the nation would celebrate a new national holiday: Army Day. With these reforms, Syria would regain the dignity that had been lost on account of Quwwatli's corruption, bad decision-making and poor planning.

Besides rebuilding Syria's domestic institutions, the further challenges that Za'im faced came from the outside. First was the threat of King Abdullah's dreams of a Greater Syria, against which Za'im sought to defend himself by making external alliances. Understandably, Za'im could not turn to Saudi Arabia for support given that he had just overthrown Quwwatli, who had been King Abd al-Aziz ibn Sa'ud's trusted ally. Instead, Za'im made overtures to the Iraqi branch of the Hashemite monarchy. It was in many ways quite rational for him to favour an alliance with Iraq: a significant section of the Syrian population, including many army officers as well as members of the mainly Aleppo-based People's Party, believed that Syria's national interest lay to the east. Furthermore, a military agreement with Iraq would improve Za'im's hand at the negotiating table during armistice talks with Israel.[54]

In the event, the Iraqi government did not match Za'im's enthusiasm. This provided Egypt with an opportunity to woo Za'im away from Hashemite notions of unification and back towards the Egyptian idea that the Arab world should be comprised of independent, sovereign states within the overall framework of the League of Arab States. Essentially an inter-governmental talking shop, the League of Arab States had been formally established in 1945 and fulfilled the useful function of seeming to respond to the Arab public's aspirations for greater unity without obliging Arab rulers to take any actual steps in that direction. Initially comprised of seven members (Egypt, Syria, Jordan, Lebanon, Iraq, Saudi Arabia and Yemen), the League also provided a way for Egypt to assert a new political role in the region after it had been severed from the Ottoman sphere of influence in the early nineteenth century. Indeed, one of the first questions discussed in the early negotiations was whether Egypt possessed a sufficiently 'Arab' identity to be considered part of the Arab world. When the response was positive, Egypt's King Farouq began to project himself as a potential counterweight to Hashemite ambitions.

In April 1949, Za'im made a secret visit to King Farouq in Cairo to seal their alliance. Upon his return, Za'im underlined his vision of a strong, independent Syria and rejected both Jordan's Greater Syria scheme and Iraq's plan for a 'Fertile Crescent' under the leadership of Baghdad.[55]

In terms of domestic politics, Za'im introduced one important new dimension to the repertoire of Syrian statebuilders: social policy. While previous governments had been content to leave the daily activities of the Syrian people untouched, Za'im was more ambitious and planned to reshape Syrian society in line with his vision of a modern, developed, secular nation. One of Za'im's first moves was to ban Ottoman honorifics such as *bey* and *pasha*, the lingering usage of which served to reinforce the social status of landowning notables. Educated Syrian women were for the first time granted the right to vote. Secular civil law was rolled out to replace Sharia in all areas except personal status (family law, inheritance, etc.) The anachronistic institution of the hereditary *waqf*, a kind of religious trust, was abolished. Modernizing reforms were implemented at the Syrian University, which had been founded in Damascus in 1923.[56]

Not all Za'im's measures were welcomed by the public. His secularizing tendencies met with concern from religious shaykhs and neighbourhood chiefs, over a hundred of whom met at a mosque in Damascus to discuss his proposed laws. The meeting agreed to send twenty-five of their number to persuade Za'im that civil law was contrary to Islam. The delegation was warmly greeted at the president's office. Za'im cut an impressive figure, having donned full dress uniform for the occasion, complete with fresh white gloves and assorted medals and decorations, his expensive baton in hand, and his quirky Prussian monocle in his eye. Before discussion could begin, Za'im received an urgent phone call from Lieutenant Colonel Ibrahim al-Husayni, who was head of the Deuxième Bureau, the internal intelligence service.

In full view – and full earshot – of the visiting delegation, Za'im began to shout down the telephone that he didn't care if the arrested man had not actually fired the revolver he was carrying, he was to be taken from his cell and executed immediately. 'I won't permit it!' he said. 'I won't allow anyone to oppose me!' Hanging up the telephone receiver, Za'im turned to the waiting delegation, whose faces had turned ashen with shock, and calmly explained that he would not allow the people 'to make light of the state and its laws, as Shukri al-Quwwatli taught them. The Quwwatli era was not a time of respect; it was a time of exploitation and chaos! Now,' Za'im added, 'what did you want to discuss?'

The delegation, still pale, awkwardly mumbled they had come to congratulate Za'im on becoming president and beat a hasty retreat. In the meantime, Za'im's private secretary was stifling his giggles with a handkerchief, as he was in on the joke: Za'im had staged the whole scene.[57] His performance was clearly convincing, as the religious leaders were afterwards disinclined to oppose his secularizing reforms.

Za'im entertained bold ideas for future projects. He proposed to impose a ceiling on the ownership of agricultural land and to redistribute state land to the impoverished peasantry, although these plans did not advance. He also planned to invest in major infrastructure programmes, including Syria's first port facilities at Latakia and the draining of the Ghab marshes north-west of Hama; he also ratified a transit pipeline for a US company that would connect Saudi oilfields to a Mediterranean port in Lebanon across Syrian territory. Za'im even mooted that the state should build villages for the Bedouin tribes, so that they would abandon their nomadic ways, and even offered to resettle as many as 300,000 Palestinian refugees expelled by Israel – if accompanied by sufficient financial aid and the eastern half of the Sea of Galilee. He envisaged funnelling these refugees to create an economic boom in Syria's sparsely populated Jazira region.[58]

At a dinner with British diplomats one evening, the new reforms were compared to Turkey's famous banning of the fez in 1925, but Za'im demurred that he did not intend to emulate Atatürk's social revolution. His changes would respect the will of the people and not be imposed from above. The question of abandoning the veil, for example, would not be decided by the state, but would remain a matter of personal choice for Syrian women. Nevertheless, remarked Za'im as an afterthought, he was still going to legislate that the country's men should take more care in their appearance. If they insisted on walking around the city in their nightgowns, then the police would fine them or put them in jail for a month. A British diplomat who attended the dinner noted that, while he concurred with Za'im that wearing nightgowns in public was a disgusting habit, he had thought it better to refrain from suggesting that incarcerating people for wearing their pyjamas would be 'rather dictatorial'.[59]

Za'im imposed numerous other measures that might equally be described as dictatorial. He abolished all political parties, although allowed most of them to operate until June 1949, when he had scheduled a national election to approve of his presidency. (The Communists, whom he hated, were exempt from this provision, and banned outright after one of their publications not only demanded that the army return to the barracks but also described Za'im himself as a 'first-class clown'.)[60] Za'im contested the election unopposed, winning 99.4 per cent of the vote. He cautioned the fractious Syrian press against criticizing the army and gave the military command the power to rescind the licence of any newspaper or journal that published material jeopardizing national security. By mid-April, licences had been withdrawn from seventy-seven of the ninety-four daily periodicals published in Syria.

Za'im deliberately eschewed the cult of personality that would be constructed around later authoritarian regimes. After seeing his image prominently displayed in stores and cafes across Damascus, Za'im banned the printing of more photographs of himself and made himself accessible to requests and petitions from delegations.[61] Radio Damascus reportedly became more objective in its coverage. 'Under the old regime much time was devoted to glorification of President Kuwatli [Quwwatli] who maintained direct control of the station. News from the outside world was presented scantily and subjectively,' noted avid listeners at the British embassy in Damascus. 'Under the present regime broadcasting has been placed under the direction of the Syrian Press Office. News bulletins now give the listener a balanced picture of world affairs.'[62]

While Za'im's short presidency should not be whitewashed, his track record is more mixed than critics allow. Although no benevolent dictator, Za'im's ambitions did at least entail something greater than maintaining himself and his cronies in power: social reform and economic development were central parts of his programme. Za'im's self-importance and grandeur nevertheless isolated him from both the public and the political class. As the summer progressed, Za'im also lost the respect of his fellow officers.

On 1 July, he announced a cabinet reshuffle that made Abdullah Atfah defence minister – the same man who had led the Syrian army to defeat in 1948. Za'im dismissed many officers from the army – including Adib al-Shishakli, who had supported his coup – and in their place relied on officers from Kurdish and Circassian backgrounds. His alliance with Prime Minister Muhsin al-Barazi alienated potential supporters of reform such as Akram al-Hawrani, who was ideologically opposed to the Barazi family's vast landholdings in the Homs region, as well as a good friend of the dismissed Shishakli. Hawrani's influence among the officer corps drove yet another wedge between the president and the army. Many officers felt that Za'im's interests as head of state had diverged from those of the officers who had raised him to that lofty position in the first place.

Za'im's most unfathomable decision took place in early July, when he ordered the extradition of a political activist named Antoun Sa'adah. The Lebanon-born Sa'adah was a radical political thinker who had developed a comprehensive and elaborate – if not quasi-scientific, quasi-metaphysical and rather fascistic – system of ideology based on the premise that the various peoples of *Bilad al-Sham* constituted a nation in itself, united by ties of geography, history and common culture. In 1932, Sa'adah had founded a secret society based on these beliefs; a few years later this society became a fully fledged political party, *al-Hizb al-Qawmi al-Suri* (the 'Syrian Nationalist Party', often known by its French acronym of PPS after mandatory officials mistranslated its name as the *Parti Populaire Syrien*). In the late 1940s, Sa'adah added the word *Ijtima'i* ('Social') to the party name, to distinguish its communitarian politics from those of its socialist rivals. The SSNP built up its own paramilitary force in Lebanon, which was then repressed by the government in Beirut. Sa'adah fled to Damascus, where he befriended and received support from Za'im. Yet on 6 July, the Syrian authorities deported Sa'adah back to Lebanon, where he was tried for high treason and executed.[63]

Za'im's motives for betraying Sa'adah after granting him political asylum are obscure. The resolution of a long-delayed trade dispute between Syria and Lebanon shortly after Sa'adah's extradition perhaps indicates that Za'im bowed to economic pressures. Even those closest to him, such as his private secretary Nadhir Fansah, could not understand his reasoning. When Fansah confronted him, an emotional Za'im reportedly broke down in tears.[64] Whatever his reasoning, the betrayal of Sa'adah was tantamount to political suicide: the SSNP had already acquired a significant support base in the Syrian army. Sa'adah's death made him a martyr, while Za'im was castigated for his role in the affair. Together with his other mistakes – his arrogance and pomp, his alienation from fellow army officers and his attempts to use state power to impose a social revolution – the stage was now set for Za'im's downfall.

Za'im's failures echo those that spurred the removal of Quwwatli. Although early on Za'im had recognized the importance of building effective government institutions, as he came under increasing political pressure, he reverted to the more reassuring loyalties of personal connections. Although Za'im had in mind a more sophisticated architecture for governing Syria than the patrician Quwwatli, in the final analysis he failed sufficiently to reinforce those pillars of the state that would bear the weight of his rule. Za'im's political instincts led him to propose policies that would materially improve the lives of the Syrian people, but at the same time he did so from on high, neglecting the need to cultivate a broader constituency of support among the masses. The accumulated weight of these mistakes would lead disaffected army officers to overthrow him.

Syria's second coup: Sami al-Hinnawi

Syria's second coup was led by one Colonel Sami al-Hinnawi, who lacked not only Za'im's arrogance, but also his ambition, flair and vision. Hinnawi and his fellow putschists were encouraged by Baghdad, which had no interest in seeing Za'im remain in power. The sidelined Akram al-Hawrani was instrumental in winning over new recruits to join the conspiracy.[65] The immediate trigger for Za'im's overthrow came when he moved troops towards the Jabal al-Duruz, whose inhabitants he suspected of collaborating with the Hashemites of Jordan. Unluckily for Za'im, this move alarmed many Druze officers, a large number of whom happened to be sympathizers of the SSNP and were resentful at Za'im's unconscionable betrayal of their martyred leader, Antoun Sa'adah.[66]

On 14 August, the conspirators moved into action. In a repeat of the first coup, they arrested the prime minister and police chiefs, and seized sensitive state institutions and communications headquarters. Za'im's elite Circassian soldiers failed to protect him.[67] In fact, he was seized so quickly that, when news reached Hinnawi and his comrades that their forces were already leaving the presidential palace, they assumed that the coup attempt had failed and set off for Mezzeh airport to make their escape to Iraq, before being told what had happened.[68] However, this second coup involved bloodshed. The conspirators had not intended violence: orders were given to Lieutenant Abu Mansur Fadl Allah only to arrest Za'im and bring him to the army headquarters. In the event, Za'im and his prime minister, Barazi, were executed shortly before dawn.[69] As a supporter of Sa'adah's SSNP, Fadl Allah had no love for Za'im and perhaps believed his stake in this affair merited disobeying orders. Fadl Allah himself maintained that a fellow officer, Isam Muraywid, who also happened to be a member of the SSNP, had incorrectly informed him that Hinnawi had sentenced Za'im and Barazi to death.[70]

Still wearing his pyjamas, with his army uniform shirt hastily pulled over the top, Za'im reportedly spoke his last few words in French in an attempt to calm the nerves of his prime minister: '*N'ayez pas peur, ils ne nous tueront pas. C'est impossible.*'[71]

The morning after Za'im's death, the newly reconstituted Higher Military Council issued a communiqué declaring that the army had saved the nation from tyranny and would now return to the barracks. Indeed, Hinnawi showed no inclination to take power and appointed the respected yet elderly Hashim al-Atasi as president. By September 1949, several of Za'im's restrictions on political life had been repealed. Political parties were permitted to operate once again (apart from the Communists and the Socialist Cooperative Party of Faysal al-Asali, whose attacks on the army in parliament had provoked Za'im's coup in the first place). Universal franchise was granted to all men over eighteen, and now for the first time to adult women who had completed their primary education, although women were still not eligible to run for office.[72]

Both Hinnawi and the Aleppo-based People's Party were known to favour closer ties with Baghdad, which produced a flurry of speculation that Syria might push for political union with Iraq. Even the National Party suddenly reversed its position and backed union.[73] The interim Syrian government, however, refused to commit itself until the November elections. Despite all the fanfare, many Syrians still had serious reservations about replacing their republican system with a monarchy, especially one that was still hamstrung by onerous treaty obligations to Britain, despite its formal independence. These political concerns were particularly acute among army officers, who grew alarmed when the People's Party achieved victory in the November elections. Ominously, the oath used to swear in new members mentioned a commitment to Arab union without reference to safeguarding Syria's republican government. Many army officers became convinced that Syria's parliamentarians were set to sacrifice the country's independence and political system through an ill-considered union with Hashemite Iraq.

On 19 December, Adib al-Shishakli and his coterie of officers launched the third coup of 1949, to overthrow Hinnawi's command of the army as well as the civilian government. While Quwwatli and Za'im had proven unable to elevate the Syrian state from the weak and dysfunctional institutions inherited from French rule, Shishakli would have more success at building a strong central government. In the early 1950s, Shishakli would not only replace Syria's fledgling yet flawed democracy with a consolidated military regime, he would also expand the power and capabilities of state institutions in ways that would reshape the very nature of Syria's society and economy.

6

Military Reform, 1949–1954

Adib al-Shishakli would dominate the political scene for the first half of the 1950s. His coup against Hinnawi followed the same script as the earlier interventions in 1949 and was acted out by largely the same cast of actors who had helped Hinnawi overthrow Za'im only a few months earlier.[1] By this point, a distinct pattern of military intervention in Syrian politics had emerged.

In the early hours of 19 December 1949, tanks and armoured vehicles rolled down the streets of Damascus for the third time that year. Shishakli's forces seized strategic buildings and detained Hinnawi loyalists, but the coup unfolded swiftly and mostly without violence, much like its predecessors.[2] Hinnawi was arrested, along with his brother-in law As'ad Talas, the chief civil servant at the Ministry of Foreign Affairs, whom Shishakli supporters suspected had swayed Hinnawi in favour of union with Iraq.[3] Several senior military officials were also detained, although civilian politicians were left untouched. The traditional Communiqué Number One issued shortly after the coup announced that the army had safeguarded Syria's security and republican government against politicians compromised by foreign interests. Communiqué Number One promised that the army would leave the business of government to the country's legitimate rulers – unless, of course, the security and existence of the country required them to intervene.[4]

Despite this menacing tone, Shishakli did not immediately

assume direct control but called on politicians to form a new civilian government. Over the next two years, there emerged an unsteady tripartite balance of power. The first two groups were the two main civilian parties – the established National Party and the People's Party, which still largely represented the traditional elites of Damascus and Aleppo respectively. Even after Shishakli permitted a civilian government, the two parties continued to exhaust their energies in relentless politicking against one another. The third component of the triangle was the army, which increasingly exercised real power behind the scenes. In November 1951, Shishakli finally ended the charade of civilian rule and installed a military government. Yet even after this bold move, Shishakli still preferred to take a back-seat role and appointed a figurehead, Colonel Fawzi Selu, as both chief of the armed forces and president of the republic. Only in mid-1953 did Shishakli come out into the open: he had a new constitution written, set up a new political party and had himself elected as the self-proclaimed legitimate president of Syria. Despite these efforts to concentrate political power in his own hands, Shishakli's despotism united the opposition against him: in February 1954, Shishakli was himself overthrown by a fourth military coup.

Although Shishakli's regime was relatively brief (albeit longer than those of his immediate predecessors), he was the first Syrian ruler to grasp the importance of institution building. By consolidating the bureaucracy so that the state could start to implement policies capable of reshaping the country's social and economic structure, Shishakli achieved more than a mere military takeover: the early 1950s witnessed a qualitative and quantitative increase in the power of Syrian government. On Shishakli's watch, the Syrian state began unprecedented intervention in a whole range of new activities. It supported industry and agriculture, passed sweeping (although abortive) reforms of land-ownership laws, regulated education, launched new construction projects and approved social justice legislation that benefitted workers and peasants.

The progressive content of Shishakli's reform agenda was inspired by his close associate Akram al-Hawrani, a leading opponent of the Syrian establishment and agitator for peasant rights. Hawrani had played a major role in organizing Shishakli's coup, although Shishakli soon abandoned the leftist politics of his ally in favour of a highly disciplined system of despotism that prioritized social control over popular reform.

Coupled with the economic boom that Syria underwent in the early 1950s, this raft of government planning began to change the country's social and political landscape. While traditional upper-middle-class notables continued to dominate civilian politics, the rising star of the army dislodged their monopoly on power and opened up space for a new generation of political leaders who promised a brighter, more egalitarian future for Syrian peasants and workers. The army consequently became an arena for contestation between new ideological currents, as exemplified by the Ba'thists, Communists and Syrian Social Nationalists.

Like Quwwatli and Za'im before him, Shishakli's vision of building a strong centralized state, with himself at the helm, implied a robust response to centrifugal challenges from provincial elites and projects that sought to merge the Republic of Syria into a larger political territory. The threat from Jordan's Greater Syria project receded when its architect, King Abdullah, died in July 1951; Abdullah's successors King Talal (1951–52) and Hussein (1952–99) harboured few aspirations to bring Syria under their control. The Iraqi branch of the Hashemite dynasty (under its regent, Abd al-Ilah, until 1953, after which Faysal II became king) represented a more serious challenge. When Shishakli used brutal tactics to repress a Druze uprising in 1953, opposition to his regime coalesced and, with support from Baghdad, successfully united to end this experiment in reformist authoritarianism.

The 1950 constitution

Syria's politicians floundered in their efforts to form a civilian government after Shishakli removed Hinnawi from office. The National Party and the People's Party were in a state of confusion as they navigated this new political terrain. The National Party played its hand cautiously and reversed its public commitment to union with Iraq, in recognition of the fact that the army had just overthrown Hinnawi precisely on account of his pro-Baghdad leanings. The more recently founded People's Party was accustomed to playing a secondary role in parliament and lacked the relative cohesion of its rival. Nevertheless, the People's Party had won a majority of seats in the Constituent Assembly elections of November 1949, which had been elected to approve a new constitution. In 1950, there was a rapid succession of prime ministers, who struggled to keep their governments above water.

The first government was led by Khalid al-Azm, who declared his firm allegiance to Syria's republican system of government. His premiership was undermined first by economic difficulties following the unravelling of the Syro-Lebanese customs union and then by criticism spearheaded by Shishakli's truculent advisor, the radical parliamentarian Hawrani. In May, Azm's government fell and was replaced by a cabinet led by Nazim al-Qudsi, who was little more than a caretaker until the new constitution could be approved. The army pressured Qudsi to appoint Colonel Fawzi Selu as the first military defence minister. This novel encroachment of military personnel into the domain of civilian government was an indication of changing times.

The new draft constitution was put before the Constituent Assembly in July 1950. It contained 177 articles, of which several were wildly controversial. Article 3 stated that Syria's official religion was Islam – a radical departure from the compromise first brokered by the 1920 Syrian congress, which specified only the religion of the president, not the state. This novel twist provoked heated debate. In support were the deputies of the Syrian Muslim Brotherhood, a loose-knit local offshoot of a popular religious association founded in Egypt in 1928, as well as many religious scholars and preachers, who rallied a large swathe of public opinion to their side. Against the article stood secular Syrian nationalists such as the late Antoun Sa'adah's Syrian Social Nationalist Party and the Arab nationalist Ba'thists, as well as the Christian churches. As a compromise, the article was amended to declare that Islam would be the religion of the president of the republic and the main source of legislation, but not the country's official religion. Religion was not the only sensitive issue. Article 5 declared the capital of the republic to be Damascus but stipulated that this decision was not irrevocable. This somewhat odd formulation attracted the ire of the Damascus-based National Party, which sniffed a hidden agenda to steal the limelight from the City of Jasmine and spirit away the seat of government northwards to Aleppo. The final text simply stated that Damascus was the capital of the republic, without caveats.

Syria's 1950 Constitution contained two elements that were surprisingly democratic and progressive. First, the new constitution carefully delimited the powers of the president and strengthened the hand of parliament. Although the president was still entitled to appoint the prime minister and confirm the cabinet proposed by the prime minister, the president lost the ability to overrule parliament: he was now obliged to sign legislation within three days or refer it to a special constitutional committee for adjudication. As senior civil servant Abdullah Fikri al-Khani noted in his memoirs: 'This meant that the president of the republic had become a figurehead of government, a powerless symbol. Just like the Queen of England!'[5] Having already watched Quwwatli amend the constitution to further his own political ambitions, the drafting committee prohibited any changes to the ratified document for the next two years. After that time, any proposed modification would require a parliamentary majority to pass. In this way, the new constitution was designed to obstruct any tendency to despotism or personal rule.[6]

The lengthy preamble to the 1950 Constitution inserted a fresh new tone into Syrian political discourse, reflecting the fact that many politicians had come to recognize the urgent need for social reform. The 1950 Constitution enshrined the rights of the citizen at its very heart: citizens were to be freed from 'the woes of poverty, disease, ignorance and fear' by the establishment of a 'correct social and economic regime that would implement social justice, protecting the peasant and the worker, sheltering the weak and the fearful, and giving every citizen access to the benefits of the nation'. Citizens were guaranteed their equality before the law, innocence until proven guilty, freedoms from state torture and mistreatment and the positive freedoms of expression, association and movement.

Even more progressive were the constitution's economic rights. Article 21 specified that property was both public and private in nature. As such, individuals were prohibited from using their private property for purposes that contradicted the public good; the state reserved the right to decide how private property should best serve society. To ensure what it called the 'creation of a just social relationship between citizens', Article 22 stipulated that the state had the authority to appropriate unexploited land, set a ceiling to the amount of land that could be owned by individuals and redistribute land over that amount to the peasantry. The article also called on the state to establish agricultural cooperatives, raise the living standards of peasants and work towards building 'model villages and sanitary housing'. Article 25 obliged the government to implement progressive direct taxation (which, in part due to the difficulties of collection, was so far minimal in Syria). Article 26 announced that employment was 'the right of all citizens'. Work, it said, was not only honourable, but 'the most important basic component of social life'; the state was to provide and even guarantee employment to citizens by 'steering and stimulating the national economy'.[7] The constitution even specified policy targets for future governments, such as the gradual sedentarization of the Bedouin and the abolition of illiteracy within the next ten years.

The 1950 Constitution did not simply codify a set of rules to guarantee the smooth functioning of government, it represented nothing less than a brave new vision of the Syrian social contract. Remarkably, this constitution was approved in September 1950 by an assembly largely comprised of the business-oriented elite rather than leftist radicals. Even the bourgeoisie had to recognize that the suffering of the impoverished peasantry would never allow them to become consumers of the new products manufactured by Syria's budding industrialists.

With the new constitution ratified, the National Party and People's Party then returned to their habitual squabbling and factionalism, under the watchful eye of the army.

Civilian politics, military veto

Although the armed forces had ostensibly returned to the barracks, they soon began to intervene in civilian politics, which they considered had crossed the line of acceptability. In August 1950, for example, an independent, pro-Hashemite deputy named Munir al-Ajlani launched an ill-considered tirade in which he accused the armed forces of interfering with the Ministry of the Interior and the police force, as well as smuggling and spying on members of parliament.[8] The army rewarded Ajlani by issuing a warrant for his arrest and brought him to trial in a military court on charges of conspiring with the Hashemite Kingdom of Jordan against Syrian state security. In October, the army arrested former defence minister Ahmad Sharabati and twenty others, including two serving members of parliament, on charges of conspiring to assassinate Shishakli.[9] Against this violation of parliamentary immunity, Prime Minister Qudsi could only assuage angry elected deputies with the half-hearted defence that immunity did not extend to affairs of national security.[10]

Another indication of growing military power came in January 1951, when the army demanded an increase to the military budget of 4 million Syrian pounds (S£), without offering any explanation of how the funds would be spent. Only two members of the parliamentary budget committee dared voice their dissent. Husni al-Barazi declared that if the government no longer had authority over its expenditure and the army was interfering in politics, the country might as well be under direct military rule.[11] The military did not feel able to silence its most influential critics – Barazi's remarks went unpunished, for example, while Ajlani and Sharabati were eventually acquitted – although many less prominent individuals were imprisoned by the military courts.[12] The reach of the military's power in Syria was nevertheless apparent even to foreign observers. In the eyes of the British embassy in Damascus, it was clear that the army had behaved as an 'inner government' throughout the year.[13]

Throughout 1951, politicians jumped on controversies surrounding Syria's foreign policy to bring down one prime minister after another. When Israeli and Syrian forces clashed over disputed territory in the Hula Valley that April, the prime minister requested urgent military aid. Baghdad was the only capital to respond, sending troops and aeroplanes to buttress Damascus's defences. This display of good faith revived the pro-Iraq lobby: the People's Party attacked the government and prevented it from passing long-awaited legislation authorizing wage increases for civil servants, prompting a strike by state employees. The government standstill paralysed the country and brought down the cabinet.

A new cabinet under the leadership of Hasan al-Hakim did not elicit any objections from the army, despite the fact the elderly Hakim was well known as a pro-Hashemite independent. However, Hakim's sympathies had been personal to the former kings Faysal and Abdullah, as he put it, not the younger generation that had since inherited the thrones of Iraq and Jordan.[14] Hakim's government was also brought to a premature end. When public demonstrations broke out in protest at the US offer that Egypt should join a Western-sponsored Middle East Defence Pact, the People's Party exploited Hakim's pro-Jordanian reputation to portray him as a sympathizer of the West. This allegation was sufficient to lose Hakim the confidence of parliament.[15]

The army remained aloof from these squabbles. Shishakli himself publicly stated that the army would refrain from intervening in politics merely because civilian politicians were having difficulty keeping their governments together. This instability was, Shishakli had said, just a sign of the 'dynamism' of the noble Syrian people.[16] Buoyed by its minor victories, the People's Party chose this moment to test the power wielded by the military: it refused to support the formation of a new government under Ma'rouf al-Dawalibi unless a civilian was placed in charge of the Ministry of National Defence, the 1950 Constitution fully implemented and the gendarmerie returned from military control to the portfolio of the minister of the interior. This ultimatum concerned precisely what the army considered its autonomous domain, where no compromise was possible. The officer corps resorted to a radical solution.

During the night of 28/29 November 1951, government ministers, members of the People's Party and pro-Hashemite independents were arrested in what proved to be the second coup directed by Shishakli. As on previous occasions, Radio Damascus broadcast a military communiqué explaining the army's motivation and asking the people to support the army in ending the 'corrupt elements' that were damaging the independence of the country. Military intervention was needed to preserve national 'honour and glory' and to spread the spirit of 'progressivism' throughout the nation.[17] In contrast to Shishakli's 1949 coup, his 1951 coup abrogated civilian rule and marked a transition from military veto to outright military government. This new intervention freed Shishakli from the constraints imposed by the admittedly limited political pluralism that had existed for the last two years. Now unopposed, Shishakli was able to embark upon the most intensive period of top-down state-building that Syria had witnessed since the French occupation.

Syria under Shishakli

Historians of Syria generally portray the system of government implemented after Shishakli's second coup as an out-and-out military dictatorship.[18] This characterization is not entirely misleading. Soon after the coup, jailed Prime Minister Dawalibi was pressured to resign; Hashim al-Atasi then resigned from the presidency in protest. On 2 December, the new regime announced the dissolution of parliament: power was now exercised by Chief of

Staff Fawzi Selu. Despite Selu being declared Syria's new president, prime minister and defence minister, he was little more than a puppet whose strings were tightly held by Shishakli.[19] Shishakli sought to control society more generally by constricting the space for civil association. In January 1952, the Syrian Muslim Brotherhood was closed down, and civil servants, trade unions, professors, teachers and students were all banned from political activity. Numerous newspapers had their publication licences revoked, and military censorship became commonplace. By April, all of Syria's political parties had been declared illegal, paving the way for Shishakli to launch his own Arab Liberation Movement (*Harakat al-Tahrir al-'Arabi*), in an ambitious and ultimately unsuccessful attempt to establish one-party rule. Such moves have, not unreasonably, earned Shishakli the sobriquet of quintessential military ruler.

However, simply dismissing Shishakli as little more than a tinpot dictator makes it easy to overlook the quite remarkable transformations in the capacity and power of the state that occurred during the years of his rule. The state that independent Syria inherited from the French Mandate comprised weak institutions whose reach barely extended beyond the cities of central Syria. Earlier, Za'im's efforts to use those institutions to impose social reform had been woefully ineffective, provoking a backlash against the somewhat idiosyncratic vision of a new Syria that the field marshal in all his finery had sought to nurture. Shishakli, in contrast, proved more adept at strengthening state institutions and opened up further areas of the country's social and economic life to government regulation for the first time. While Quwwatli had grandiloquently proclaimed the need to crown Syria's independence with a strong state, it was the quietly determined Shishakli who began to realize this lofty vision with characteristic pragmatism and ruthless efficiency.

In his second military communiqué after the overthrow of civilian government, Shishakli denounced the People's Party and blamed their machinations for causing the military to intervene in politics. He accused Qudsi of politicking for personal gain, turning public opinion against the army and 'spreading the seeds of hatred among the nation and its sons, the men of this army'.[20] Shishakli also took concrete measures to curtail foreign influence inside Syria. Government ministries were banned from direct communication with external bodies: all official correspondence with the outside world would henceforth be conducted only through the Ministry of Foreign Affairs. Institutions of higher learning such as the Syrian University and the Arabic Language Academy were also forbidden from contact with institutions abroad. Foreigners inside Syria were placed under surveillance and prohibited from purchasing property. Even Syrians employed in the country by foreign organizations were ordered to submit statements to the authorities outlining their activities and declaring their salaries from foreign sources.[21]

Shishakli's suspicions towards foreigners were not entirely out of kilter with the general mood in the country. Earlier that year, parliamentarians had passed Syria's first raft of nationalizations, which transferred the essential services of electricity, water and transport out of foreign hands and into Syrian public ownership for the first time. After liberating the country from political colonialism, parliamentarians agreed, the time had come to free Syria from foreign corporations.[22] Shishakli took this logic to new extremes. Legislation was passed to regulate foreign-run private schools and to prohibit new missionary schools from being opened in the country. Schools were forbidden from receiving funds from foreign sources without authorization from the Ministry of Education. In March 1952, the British Council, along with French and US cultural institutes, were ordered to halt their activities immediately. Intensive diplomatic lobbying (and, from the British government, hints of the sale of two aircraft to the Syrian Ministry of National Defence) persuaded Shishakli's regime to reverse this decision.[23] The British embassy in Damascus opined that these restrictions were 'part of a planned campaign to bring the minds as well as the bodies of the Syrian people under the army's control'.[24]

As an occupying power, the French authorities had sought to build a state in Syria that was for all intents and purposes defenceless against intrusions from the outside world. Under Shishakli this state of affairs began to be reversed. In an attempt to tighten Syria's relatively porous borders, the government announced it would refuse entry to various categories of person, including beggars and prostitutes, the insane and the criminal, as well as any individual suspected of intending to disrupt public order.[25] Shishakli could not entirely monopolize the country's international connections – this achievement would be left to later rulers – but he asserted the principle that the state had an exclusive right to police its territory against economic, cultural or political incursions from outside. Shishakli sealed his defences with a foreign tour that sought to win support from Egypt, Jordan and Saudi Arabia.

After buttressing Syria's borders against external threats, Shishakli devoted his attention to transforming the domestic environment. He was by no means an original political thinker. Instead, he drew many of the elements of his policy agenda directly from Akram al-Hawrani, the politician and activist who espoused a radically pro-peasant reform agenda and had supported, if not co-orchestrated, all three military coups of 1949. In the course of the 1950s, Hawrani would come to play a leading role in Syrian leftist politics and, even more crucially, in shaping the political fortunes of the Ba'th Party.[26]

Hawrani had been raised in Hama, where the domination of

landowning notables and misery of the peasants were even more pronounced than in the rest of the country. His family had been respectable but not especially wealthy: they were descended from the founders of the Hama branch of the Rifa'i order of Sufis, and Hawrani's father Rashid had raised his position from tradesman to small landowner. Rashid al-Hawrani had himself been critical of social and economic inequality in his hometown and, under the Ottomans prior to the First World War, had been elected to the local Administrative Council. Rashid ambitiously sought to join the Ottoman parliament in Istanbul, but soon discovered his nomination had been blocked by opposition from the established land-owning Hamawi elite, which looked down on upstarts such as the Hawrani family.

As a child, Akram al-Hawrani developed a visceral hatred of the inequitable system of land ownership that made possible the archaic, feudalistic relationships between landlords and peasants that prevailed in the Hama region. He was schooled in Hama and then at the Anbar school in Damascus, a famous hub of activism for nationalist youths. From there, he studied briefly in Beirut, where he was introduced to the Syrian nationalist principles of Sa'adah's SNP. After completing his studies in the College of Law in Damascus, Hawrani founded the first branch of the SNP in Hama, although arguably he was less wedded to the party's quirky brand of quasi-fascism than attracted by its progressive anti-colonial nationalism and its calls for the abolition of feudalism. He soon grew distant from the SNP and concentrated his political energies in developing a small nationalist party called *al-Shabab al-Hamawi* ('Hama Youth'), which had been founded in 1939 by his cousin. Hawrani's commitment to national liberation was not confined to Syria. In 1941, he travelled to Iraq to support the anti-British coup of Kaylani and, in 1948, cemented his nationalist credentials by leading guerrilla bands against Zionist forces in Palestine, an experience that gave him his first taste of what could be achieved by a committed band of brothers united in pursuit of a common cause. By 1950, Hawrani had transformed *al-Shabab al-Hamawi* into the core of a new political party under his leadership, the Arab Socialist Party (*al-Hizb al-'Arabi al-Ishtiraki*).

Hawrani's agenda for the Arab Socialists was not socialist in the orthodox sense, much less communist, but it adopted a radical reform agenda that promised to reverse the deep inequality between peasants and large landowners. The party advocated other left-wing and nationalist policies, such as redistributing land to the poor, emancipating women, free school education, compulsory military service, a national arms industry, new vocational schools, suppressing confessionalism and a republican, parliamentary system of government that would guarantee Syria's national independence.

After being elected to the Syrian parliament in 1943, Hawrani had found that his reform agenda was impossible to implement in the face of entrenched opposition from the notable elites who controlled the assembly. To break this impasse, Hawrani turned to the army. For their part, the elites had disdained the armed forces under both Ottoman and French rule; even after independence, the sons of upper-class families still considered a career in the officer corps to lack social prestige. Their reticence to join the armed forces left a gap that was quickly filled by eager young men from lower-middle-class and poor backgrounds. Hawrani encouraged his party's young supporters to enter the military training academy at Homs and cultivated connections with Husni al-Za'im, Sami al-Hinnawi and Adib al-Shishakli – the latter happened to have been a friend of Hawrani's from their childhood in Hama.

Hawrani's populism won his party immense support in the Hama region, where there was particularly profound and deeply entrenched inequality between four quasi-aristocratic, land-owning families – the Barazis, Azms, Kaylanis and Tayfours – and the impoverished tenant farmers and landless peasants who comprised the majority of the rural population. Hawrani's alliance with Shishakli emboldened him to mobilize the Hama peasantry further than ever before. In summer 1951, the growing anger of the peasants culminated in direct action when they made a stand for the land they cultivated and refused access to the great landowning families and their agents, resulting in violent confrontations. In September, Hawrani capitalized on this movement by organizing an unprecedented three-day 'rally against feudalism' in Aleppo, attended by as many as 40,000 peasants from Hama and the whole country.

The *al-'Ilm* newspaper reported that participants at the Aleppo rally were galvanized by brave new slogans calling for secularism, social reform and peasant rights. 'The worker and the peasant are the bedrock of the nation!' declared one poster. 'No sectarianism, no doctrinalism, no racism! No class discrimination in our future socialist order!' One slogan asserted, 'The People are the root of all strength, and the source of all authority,' voicing a warning that many later rulers would have done well to heed.[27] The popularity of Hawrani's party soon grew to encompass peasants in parts of Idlib, the Qalamoun, Misyaf and even the northern part of Jabal al-Duruz.[28]

While Hawrani had initially encouraged the erratic Za'im to implement elements of his reform agenda after the first coup of 1949, translating these radical ideas into reality became more feasible once his childhood friend Shishakli had consolidated his grip on power. The influence of Hawrani's ideas became transparent when the government launched a new Programme for Workers and Peasants in January 1952, which included an ambitious proposal for land reform. In the event, these reforms proved too far-reaching for the still inexperienced state bureaucracy to implement. The failure of this reform programme did much to persuade Shishakli that the success of his modernizing agenda was contingent on reliable and efficient state institutions. Shishakli was by nature a military man: focused, disciplined and hierarchical. Political debate, as he saw it, was unnecessary: it was simply noise that impeded the smooth running of the state machine, which would do what needed to be done in Syria without any input from politicians. This instinct explains much about Shishakli's methods for reorganizing Syria's political life.

Syria's woefully disorganized civil service would need considerable work before it could be considered a professional, technocratic state bureaucracy. As late as 1949, for example, the Syrian Ministry of Foreign Affairs lacked the skill to translate diplomatic memoranda from English into Arabic.[29] Institutional memory was underdeveloped, if not amnesiac: Syria apparently forgot to declare that it was no longer officially at war with Nazi Germany and Japan until seven years after the end of the Second World War.[30] Under Shishakli, the Ministry of Foreign Affairs was reorganized and the civil service streamlined. State officials were granted higher wages, although national newspapers also announced that civil servants' working hours were non-negotiable: government employees should remain in their offices the whole working day and should not receive visits from friends and family at work. A 1951 article in the *Alif Ba* newspaper explained this new philosophy of public service: 'The fundamental mission of the civil servant is to be the tool of public service with complete impartially. He should serve the public interest without bias towards any particular group or private clique. He must keep his distance from any hint of party politics.'[31] Although Syrian government institutions were still very far from the Weberian ideal of bureaucracy, under Shishakli their administrative effectiveness improved quite substantially.

As the *primus inter pares* of state institutions, the army itself underwent significant changes during the early 1950s. Senior officers who had been recruited under the French were gradually replaced by a younger generation who had received more comprehensive and up-to-date military training in Europe and the United States. At the same time, Shishakli was careful to ensure that no one single officer could accumulate sufficient support in the army to challenge his own position. So confident was Shishakli of his officers that in mid-1953 he even dismissed the civilian governors of Syria's provinces and appointed officers in their place, further effacing the vagaries he believed accompanied civilian rule and replacing them with the disciplined directness of the military chain of command.

A similar logic underpinned Shishakli's political reforms. He wanted to create a system of government to eliminate the waste and ineffectiveness produced by competition between political parties that had served Syria so badly in the past. He instead sought to run the country's affairs through the more efficient mechanism of single-party rule. In August 1952, Shishakli founded a new political organization, the Arab Liberation Movement (ALM), with its headquarters at al-Najmeh Square in Damascus, not far from the parliament. The Arab Liberation Movement was intended to absorb all existing parties and produce a united, and uniform, nation. The first example of a single-party monopoly in the Arab world, the Arab Liberation Movement set a precedent for subsequent autocrats in the region, including Egypt's Gamal Abd al-Nasser, who would create his own single-party monolith, the Arab Socialist Union, nearly a decade later.[32] However, far from representing any ostensibly innate Arab or Middle Eastern tendency to despotism, Shishakli may well have designed his single-party juggernaut on a model that had been pioneered in Europe. According to Abdullah Fikri al-Khani, who served in the secretariats of the president of the republic and Ministry of

Foreign Affairs in the 1940s and 1950s, Shishakli dispatched his foreign minister to Spain on a fact-finding mission to discover how General Franco had consolidated his own regime on the Iberian Peninsula.[33] Shishakli's secular authoritarianism may thus have been partially inspired by the currents of European fascism.

The Arab Liberation Movement announced a thirty-one-point programme that echoed many of the precepts of Hawrani's socialist populism. Yet, to Shishakli's dismay, the ALM was not greeted with anywhere near the same degree of enthusiasm by the general populace, who mostly ignored its existence, as did practically the entire political elite. Even army officers were reluctant to join, although a number of ambitious civil servants did sign up, presumably under the impression that membership in the movement would propel them to the top of the career ladder. Clearly, Shishakli's skills at institutional reform did not extend to building a significant personal following, a task for which he lacked the necessary charisma. Shishakli's failure to cultivate any meaningful personal loyalty became apparent in December 1952, upon his return from a trip to Cairo. He was greeted in Damascus with a list of demands from disgruntled officers who called for the dissolution of the ALM and the restoration of political freedoms. Shishakli cannily agreed to their terms, identified the ringleaders and had them all arrested. In the purge that followed, over two dozen officers were dismissed, while a wave of civilian arrests targeted members of the Ba'th, Arab Socialist and Communist parties, all of which were ostensibly closer than the traditional elites to Shishakli's ideological position.

Hawrani reacted explosively to Shishakli's clampdown. He accused his former comrade of failing to implement the promised social reforms and of betraying the Arab cause by agreeing a deal to allow the United Nations Relief and Works Agency to provide humanitarian aid to Palestinian refugees in Syria. Wary of Shishakli's capacity for ruthlessness, Hawrani fled Syria for Beirut along with the leaders of the Ba'th Party, Michel Aflaq and Salah al-Din al-Bitar, who shared similar left-leaning notions of secularism and social reform. This departure marked the third and final time Hawrani would hastily distance himself from a military officer whom he had helped come to power by means of military coup.

With Hawrani in exile, the social content of Shishakli's policies receded and was soon overtaken by barefaced efforts merely to consolidate his own personal power. On 21 June 1953, Shishakli published the draft of a new constitution that would entail significant changes to Syria's political system. Rather than having the president elected by parliament – and therefore being in principle accountable to members of that parliament – the president would in future be directly elected by public vote. The popularly elected president would be granted far greater powers than ever before, such as possessing the authority to appoint or dismiss ministers. (Until now this power had been vested in the fractious parliament, which had always made approving a new government a precarious affair.)[34] Shishakli explained that his changes were modelled on the constitutional best practice of the United States, which, he pointed out, was well known as a highly efficient system of democratic government. Observers pointed out that the new draft constitution omitted reference to Syria's parliamentary system of government, which they argued revealed Shishakli's plans to transform the country into a dictatorship. Both traditional and radical politicians opposed Shishakli's proposals and argued that only the elected Constituent Assembly had the legal authority to effect constitutional change.

To bypass such arguments, Shishakli announced a referendum for 10 July 1953 to approve the new constitution and elect a new president. This was Shishakli's opportunity to step out of the shadows – where, admittedly, he had been lurking quite visibly for some time, having already promoted himself to brigadier general, minister of the interior and vice president of the republic. Although Shishakli was the only candidate to compete in the presidential election, he still presented voters with his election manifesto so they could make an informed choice about who to vote for. On the airwaves of Radio Damascus, Shishakli painted a curiously paternalistic picture of the new social contract that his election would inaugurate.

'Popular constitutional government is built on trust and confidence between the ruler and his people,' he declared. 'The duties imposed on the ruler are similar to those imposed upon the father by the trust of his sons and by his faith in their future. A happy nation is one harmonious family. Government institutions are useful only inasmuch as they mend the rifts in our family, so that its complete unity can return and the rifts within it can be forgotten. [. . .] The new era will be new in every respect: it will be a clean slate upon which the members of the family can begin a glorious history.'[35]

Shishakli was obsessed with integrating the diverse members of the Syrian family into the framework of a single state that was strong and efficient. If national unity were lacking, Shishakli believed, it could be created by allowing the state to organize the rank and file of the nation and assign everyone to their correct position. Workers and employers were organized into local syndicates overseen by national federations of unions, which were essentially unofficial extensions of the state and operated under tight government control, while even youth groups and scout troops were reorganized by new legislation. The example of Atatürk, who had successfully used the military to build the Turkish nation following the collapse of the Ottoman Empire, was never far from Shishakli's mind.[36] In 1952, the government launched a campaign to construct statues and historical monuments in every governorate and district to commemorate the recent martyrs in the history of the Syrian nation as well as great heroes from the ancient and modern history of the Arabs.[37] Decrees were passed to make Arabic the sole language to be used for public events or official celebrations and to force hotels and restaurants to adopt only Arabic names (rather than names in French, English, Armenian, Syriac or Kurdish, for example). Associations run by and for non-Muslims were ordered to have an equal number of Muslims sitting on their governing bodies, while minority religious leaders were prohibited from speaking in public outside their places of worship. Shishakli's vision of a united, homogeneous national family, organized from above by the state, had little space for anyone who did not identify as both Sunni and Arab.[38]

Shishakli won the July election with 99.6 per cent of the vote. A similarly high proportion also approved the new constitution. Now Shishakli claimed for himself the roles of both president and prime minister, becoming the visible face of power in the country. (As if to confirm his inconsequentiality, the previous incumbent of the presidency, Colonel Fawzi Selu, simply retired from politics and departed Syria for a quiet life in Saudi Arabia.) Shishakli's new cabinet included lawyers, business people and other professionals, but not one member of either the traditional political elite or the new generation of ideological radicals. Perhaps to overcome the unfamiliarity of these new politicians, editors of magazines close to Shishakli even took the unusual step of publishing pictures of the new ministers' faces so that the public might learn to recognize them.[39] Stripped of its overtly political edge by the departure of Hawrani, Shishakli's vision of government was distinctly technocratic.

Parliamentary elections were held in October under a new

law that reduced the number of deputies from 114 to a more manageable (and more docile) eighty-two. The new law also extended the right to vote to women: now, all Syrians over the age of eighteen were eligible to vote, and all Syrians over the age of twenty-five were eligible to run for election. In keeping with Shishakli's corporatist preferences, though, sixty-nine of the parliamentary seats were reserved for Muslims, nine for Christians, and four for Bedouin tribes. Shishakli lifted the prohibition on political parties for the election, and even announced an amnesty to allow Hawrani, Aflaq and Bitar back into the country. Even so, every political party refused to endorse Shishakli's farcical elections with the dignity of participation, with the sole exception of the SSNP, which nevertheless won only a single seat. The Arab Liberation Movement took sixty seats, with a further nine going to tribal leaders and independents. The real turnout was estimated at 8 to 16 per cent, depending on region, which critics argued hardly expressed a vote of confidence in the system.[40]

For all its vaunted efficiency, Shishakli's rule was thin and rigid, and lacked any depth of support among the Syrian people or politicians. The officer corps that provided the backbone of his regime began to feel increasingly distant from Shishakli, whose energies were invested in creating new structures of government rather than cultivating the one constituency that was so vital to his political survival. In the meantime, his ever-tightening grip on power achieved the almost unthinkable result of uniting against him not only the country's squabbling nationalist elite, but also the younger generation of political radicals and the provincial leadership of the Jabal al-Duruz.

Opposition to Shishakli

On 4 July 1953, the opposition held a secret meeting in Homs, the traditional stronghold of the powerful Atasi family, which was effectively shielded against intrusion from Shishakli's prying tentacles. Here, the establishment groupings of the National and the People's parties, radicals such as the Ba'thists and Communists and independents such as Hasan al-Hakim, met under the auspices of former president Hashim al-Atasi and agreed to work together to overthrow Shishakli. Three months after this initial meeting, 143 politicians signed a National Pact that denounced Shishakli's rule and called for the restoration of constitutional government.[41] In December, Hawrani and the Ba'thists staged student demonstrations in Aleppo, which resulted in clashes with the local police. Shopkeepers and lawyers went on strike in support of the students, an unusual display of public protest that provoked Shishakli to make the even more unusual concession of dismissing his head of public security, Colonel Ibrahim al-Husayni, who was renowned for his brutal methods of dealing with regime opponents. The protests and strikes came to an end in Aleppo when troops entered the city, but the demonstrations quickly also spread to Damascus, Homs and Hama. Students and activists across the country distributed leaflets of anti-regime propaganda produced by the Ba'th Party, prompting waves of arrests over the next few weeks.

Most notable among those arrested was Mansour al-Atrash, a Ba'th Party member in his late twenties who had already been briefly arrested the previous May, along with his brother Nasir, for his alleged involvement in an anti-Shishakli bombing campaign. Mansour al-Atrash happened to be the son of no less august a personage than Sultan Pasha; indeed, it was the earlier arrest of his sons that had prompted Sultan Pasha to add his voice to the anti-Shishakli coalition formed at Homs.[42] Historians of Syria have suggested that the arrest of Mansour al-Atrash in Suweida was the cause of an uprising that shook the Jabal al-Duruz in January and February 1954 and paved the way for the overthrow of Shishakli.[43] An alternative account, however, suggests that the uprising began with the regime's heavy-handed and brutal response to the slogans of teenagers in al-Qurayya, the home village of Sultan Pasha, in protest at Mansour al-Atrash's arrest.

In his memoirs, a Druze officer stationed in distant Deir al-Zour at the time of the uprising, Amin Abu Assaf, pieced together the story of what happened in the Jabal soon afterwards from his conversations with Sultan Pasha and other notables in the region.[44] According to Abu Assaf, a group of schoolchildren in al-Qurayya chanted protest slogans as they passed by the village gendarmerie. After allegedly hearing the protestors threaten an armed demonstration the next day, the gendarmes were authorized to use force to apprehend the youths but, when they attempted to make an arrest, the villagers fought back. Several people on each side were killed. The deputy military governor of Jabal al-Duruz, Colonel Fu'ad al-Aswad, declared martial law, and, on the night of 26/27 January 1954, ordered a sizeable military force to surround al-Qurayya. The soldiers met sustained gunfire from the village and were in turn surrounded by reinforcements from neighbouring settlements.[45] The news soon reached Suweida, where Druze shaykhs negotiated with Colonel Aswad to end the impasse and agreed to hand over ten of the eighteen schoolchildren who were allegedly involved in the incident. Aswad's forces withdrew from al-Qurayya and dispersed the following day.

Unfortunately, this was not the end of the story. Abu Assaf tells us that one of Aswad's officers, Lieutenant Colonel Faysal al-Husayni, took matters into his own hands by attacking the nearby village of Nimrah with armoured vehicles. Husayni was said to have personally executed many of those injured, leaving in his wake as many as twenty dead bodies. In Suweida, the shaykhs contained public anger about the deaths and reaffirmed the terms of their agreement with Colonel Aswad, who, they recognized, had kept his word even if his subordinate had not.

Aswad's negotiated settlement was apparently not to the taste of the president. Shishakli ordered Aswad to be replaced by Brigadier General Rasmi al-Qudsi and bestowed upon him wide discretionary powers to deal with the situation. The shaykhs of Suweida met with Qudsi to offer him their cooperation. They emphasized that the Druze had sacrificed much for the nation and did not desire conflict. Qudsi accepted their goodwill with a beneficent smile and thanked them for serving the nation. Two hours later, Qudsi ordered armoured vehicles to open fire indiscriminately on Suweida, starting a battle with townspeople who defended themselves for five hours. Wise to the experience of his predecessor, Qudsi used his artillery to shell the outskirts of the town to prevent reinforcements from reaching the fray.

The attack on Suweida was followed by a sustained campaign of state terror that swept the whole countryside. For the next ten days, Qudsi's rampaging forces destroyed homes, plundered villages and seized hostages across the governorate. 'The battle turned from a punitive campaign into a massacre of killing, plunder, terror and torture, the slaughter of innocent men, women and children,' wrote Abu Assaf, who had actually been an early supporter of Shishakli. 'Many homes and stores were robbed,' he wrote. 'Their doors were burst open by tanks.'[46]

Qudsi's soldiers were reinforced on the eastern fringes of the Jabal by Bedouin tribes who rallied to the campaign at the urging of Captain Salah al-Shishakli, brother of the president and commander of the Syrian Desert Forces. Although tribes such as the

Ghiyath disassociated themselves from this campaign, Salah al-Shishakli armed and equipped many others, strengthening their numbers with soldiers in civilian clothing.[47] Throughout February, these irregular forces attacked numerous villages, destroying houses and arresting the inhabitants, while plundering over a thousand sheep and goats. They stripped homes, built huge bonfires of furniture and personal belongings and torched the lot as the helpless owners watched on.

On Shishakli's orders, the army conducted a campaign of scorched earth in the Jabal al-Duruz. The intention was not simply to intimidate the local population, but to shatter the social structure of the community and destroy the very basis of its livelihood. Druze notables such as Sultan Pasha fled the Jabal for Jordan, as they had so many times in the past; from safety there, they urged restraint upon the young men leading the battle against the rampaging army and irregulars. As Shishakli's forces stood at some 10,000 by this point, the older generation feared annihilation if fighting continued to rage.[48]

Shishakli vanquished the Jabal uprising through a combination of terror tactics, overwhelming military force and widespread political repression. Communications between the Jabal and the rest of the country were severed, leaving even opposition politicians ignorant of the reality of the situation there. The Syrian press was heavily censored, and foreign journalists were banned from setting foot in the country.[49] On the night that Colonel Aswad's forces surrounded al-Qurayya, Shishakli ordered the imprisonment of over twenty prominent politicians, among them Akram al-Hawrani, Sabri al-'Asali, Rushdi al-Kikhia, Michel Aflaq, Salah al-Din al-Bitar, Faydi al-Atasi, Hasan al-Atrash and Munir al-'Ajlani. The venerable Hashim al-Atasi, in contrast, was too powerful for Shishakli to imprison, so was instead placed under house arrest. The jailings provoked protest from the remaining politicians, and from the lawyers' associations of Damascus and Aleppo, but this pressure was insufficient to divert Shishakli from his chosen course of action.

The severity of Shishakli's suppression of the uprising in Jabal al-Duruz can perhaps best be explained by the fact that he believed that the insurrection was inspired by foreign powers. Over the previous two years, Iraqi politicians had reasserted their unionist agenda, going so far as to table a motion at the Arab League that proposed the official federation of Iraq, Syria and Jordan. Iraq had provided safe haven for a number of Syrian dissidents, most notably a former officer, Colonel Muhammad Safa, who had been dismissed by Shishakli for his involvement in the failed coup attempt of December 1952. Since then, Safa had come to head the Free Syrian Forces, which were based in Iraq and represented a direct, if largely symbolic, challenge to the sovereignty and territorial integrity of Shishakli's state-building project. Alarmingly, Shishakli had discovered letters from Colonel Safa in the home of Sultan Pasha that indicated coordination between the Iraq-sponsored dissidents and the Druze, who also happened to possess large quantities of weapons of Iraqi provenance.

Despite his suspicions, if anything Shishakli underestimated the scale and ambition of Iraq's efforts to influence Syrian politics. The Iraqi military attaché in Damascus, Abd al-Mutallib al-Amin, had long been channelling funds to pro-Baghdad Syrian army officers in Beirut, several of whom had been behind the Hinnawi coup of 1949. One of these officers, Isam Muraywid, was apparently responsible for supplying weapons to the Jabal.[50] The Iraqi attaché was also providing funds to some members of domestic political opposition to Shishakli, including Sabri al-Asali, and had, in 1953, even drawn up plans for a possible Iraqi invasion of Syria.[51] Iraqi Prime Minister Fadil al-Jamali, had developed close ties to Michel Aflaq, Salah al-Din al-Bitar and Akram al-Hawrani while they were exiled in Beirut. During the Jabal uprising, Jamali was not only in contact with Hashim al-Atasi, but also accepted Atasi's request to rally international support to the cause of the opposition.[52] Shishakli's suspicion that the Jabal al-Duruz revolt was the first crack in Syria's independence was not entirely without foundation.

Given the recent history of Jordanian aspirations to annex Syria to the territory of the Hashemites, it was also perhaps not unreasonable for Shishakli to be haunted by the spectre of King Hussein's possible involvement in the Jabal uprising. However, the Jordanian government reassured him that their hospitality for Sultan Pasha and his men did not extend to supplying them with weapons. Shishakli similarly accused Israel of exporting arms to the Jabal – a charge for which there is no evidence, although members of Moshe Sharett's cabinet certainly funded several Druze in Syria and debated the merits of arming the insurgents in the Jabal, forging links with Safa's Free Syria movement in Iraq and exploiting the chaos in southern Syria in the hope of capturing new territory in the Golan Heights.[53] The Syrian press fed Shishakli's alarm about foreign conspiracies by attributing the region's disunity to the hidden hand of Britain, which did continue to play an outsized role in Jordan, Iraq and the smaller Trucial States of the Persian Gulf. The Iraqi federation proposal to the Arab League, for example, was described as a 'British plan for colonization' that would transform Syria from an independent, nationalist republic into a vassal of a puppet Iraqi monarchy controlled by London that would join Israel in a Western-sponsored regional defence pact.[54] Interestingly, Shishakli himself seems to have been unconcerned by the suggestion of a British conspiracy, or at least so he intimated in his meeting with the British ambassador several days later:

> [T]he President claimed that he did not consider us directly or indirectly responsible for the Druse disturbances. He said, however, that anti-British feeling was endemic and that the Syrians in general held us responsible for the actions of our ally Iraq. If he announced our innocence the public would for these reasons refuse to believe him, and even consider him mental. [. . .] I got him to promise to curb the Press and to try to insert in his next statement a sentence to the effect that there was no proof whatever of British guilt.[55]

With the uprising in the Jabal repressed, foreign machinations thwarted and civilian politicians arrested, Shishakli seemed to have navigated the crisis of early 1953 without provoking any serious backlash against his authority. Yet, only a few weeks later, he was to be removed from office, just like his predecessors, by a military coup carried out by disaffected officers.

The two men at the heart of the coup were Faysal al-Atasi, chief staff officer in Aleppo and nephew of the politician Hashim al-Atasi, and Amin Abu Assaf, the Druze officer whose memoirs recount the story of the Jabal. Abu Assaf had been a Shishakli loyalist but was reassigned to the garrison at Deir al-Zour when their personal relationship soured. As the US ambassador in Damascus correctly observed, '[b]ecause of its isolated position, Deir-ez-Zour had become something of a place of exile for Army officers, including a disproportionate number of Druzes [. . .]. [B]y allowing a frustrated minority to concentrate in one place, [Shishakli] created a hothouse for the cultivation of rebellious plans.'[56] Indeed, Damascus had so little interest in what happened in far-off Deir al-Zour that, in 1952, it was still possible to find pictures of former ruler Husni al-Za'im adorning the walls of army barracks there.[57] The city provided a safe haven for the conspiracy that would bring Shishakli's rule to an end.

Having agreed on the need to overthrow the president, Atasi and Abu Assaf recruited a coterie of like-minded individuals stationed across the country and developed a plan.[58] On 25 February 1954, Atasi arrested the commander of the northern region, along with Shishakli's top officials in Aleppo, while the rebel forces took control of local government offices and Aleppo's radio station, which was used, in the manner that had by this point become familiar, to broadcast Military Communiqué Number One. As was the case with all the previous coups, the officers promised to withdraw from politics and return to the barracks after they had eliminated 'personal aims' from the 'noble traditions' of the Syrian armed forces; they called on Shishakli to step down from power to avoid any killing.

Over the next few hours, military units around the country announced their defection to the rebels: first Deir al-Zour, then Latakia, Homs and finally the Hawran. The defections were made in a disciplined manner, in the name of each regional force in its entirety rather than in the name of each division's commanding officer. The intention was to convey to Shishakli, and to the Syrian people as a whole, that the insurgency was a coherent, unified movement with a collective leadership. It also served, as Abu Assaf admitted, 'to distance the movement from any connotation of sectarianism' – an evident concern given the prominence of officers from the Jabal al-Duruz in organizing the coup.[59]

Shishakli attempted to rally the troops who remained loyal to him, but many of his forces were committed either to the front with Israel in critical positions from which he refused to withdraw them or had not yet returned from their campaign in the Jabal al-Duruz. Sympathy for the rebels was apparently high across the army as a whole. Some of the forces still in the Jabal refused Shishakli's orders to return to Damascus, while air force pilots reportedly disobeyed instructions to harass Aleppo from the skies.[60] In the meantime, Shishakli's chief of staff, Shawkat Shuqayr, counselled him against recourse to violence that would inevitably tear apart the nation in bloody conflict – the very antithesis of the united and orderly political community that Shishakli had sought to create in Syria.

Seeing each of his options quickly closing before him, Shishakli made the monumental decision to obey the rebels' ultimatum to step down from power and leave the country for Lebanon. Two of Shishakli's ultra-loyalist supporters in Damascus sought to reverse his decision by staging a desperate last stand and insisting that Ma'moun al-Kuzbari, speaker of the parliament, should assume the presidency as per Shishakli's 1953 Constitution. This plan was thwarted by the activism of the public: crowds stormed the parliament building and the headquarters of Radio Damascus in protest at the idea.

Chief of Staff Shuqayr brokered a deal with the rebel officers to restore constitutional government. With the united armed forces closing ranks against them, the few lingering Shishakli loyalists surrendered and fled the country. Shishakli's letter of resignation was delivered to the Syrian parliament, and came to echo down the years as a potential model to be emulated by subsequent dictators desirous of abdication:

> Wishing to avoid shedding the blood of the [Syrian] people whom I love, the army for which I have sacrificed so greatly, and the Arab nation for which I have tried to serve with devotion and integrity, I present my resignation as President of the Republic to my beloved Syrian people, who elected me and bestowed their trust upon me in the hope that my decision will best serve the cause of my nation. I ask God to protect [the nation] from all harm, to unite and empower it and to guide it to glorious heights.

Whether Shishakli's lofty rhetoric rings true when considered alongside the iron-fisted repression of the Druze uprising is a question that his apologists have yet to answer.

Failure of Shishakli

Why did Shishakli's success at laying new foundations for the post-independence Syrian state result in his personal failure as ruler? In many ways, Shishakli's downfall – much like the downfall of both Quwwatli and Za'im before him – can be attributed to the inability of these leaders to perceive the different dimensions in which modern state-building must simultaneously proceed. Unlike Quwwatli, Shishakli intuitively grasped the importance of institutions in bringing order to society. In fact, so much did Shishakli understand the need for institutions that he attempted to organize the entire country into national unions, syndicates and associations to create a perfectly functioning social, economic and political machine under the control of the state, while eradicating any space for independent civil society. While Shishakli's rule did place social issues on the agenda for the first time, this was mainly at the instigation of Hawrani. For his part, Shishakli regarded the common people as the passive object of his technocratic desire for organization, rather than the victims of inequality and oppressive social hierarchy. By devoting all his efforts to building up the institutions of the central state, Shishakli alienated the political and regional elites whose power was directly threatened by his project. Simultaneously, he also neglected the need to cultivate popular legitimacy in the eyes of the people. In consequence, Shishakli's support base was reduced to the army that had brought him to power in the first place. Once Shishakli lost the support of that army, the entire edifice of authority he had constructed was revealed to be as brittle as it was elaborate and easily shattered by the conspiracy of a handful of disaffected officers.

The coup that overthrew Shishakli is often interpreted as a collective revolt of the provinces against the powerful waves of centralization and brutal calls for submission emanating from the capital. One of the main conspirators, Abu Assaf, was a Druze from the Jabal, a region that had suffered disproportionately and horrifically for its transgressions, almost as if Shishakli had wanted to have the chastisement of the Jabal stand as an exemplary lesson to school the rest of the country in the costs of opposition. The other principal conspirator, Faysal al-Atasi, was nephew to the grand old man of the Syrian political elite, Hashim al-Atasi, who at Homs had marshalled the nation's fractious politicians into a common front of dissent. One of the secondary officers, Mustafa Hamdoun, who had led the Aleppo garrison to revolt, was both a political supporter of Shishakli's estranged confidant Akram al-Hawrani and originally a native of Hama. As historian Patrick Seale points out, each of these individuals corresponds to 'an important faction in the coalition which opposed Shishakli'.[61] Even well before his downfall, Shishakli was acutely aware of the regional composition of the loose-knit opposition to his rule. 'My enemies are like a serpent,' Shishakli would growl. 'The head is the Jabal Druze, the stomach Homs and the tail Aleppo. If I crush the head the serpent will die.'

Despite its implied political geography, the anti-Shishakli coup cannot be read as a straightforwardly 'sectarian' movement – or even, for that matter, as a direct expression of the cross-regional coalition that had been formed by the country's political elite. For a start, there is no evidence of planning or coordination between the military conspirators and the politicians. The suggestion of a sectarian motivation for the coup is also difficult to substantiate.

In his memoirs, Abu Assaf focuses his ire on Shishakli's failure to maintain military discipline, blithe toleration of petty corruption and personal self-enrichment, not on his disregard for the Druze community. Indeed, Abu Assaf recounts at length how Shishakli was invited to the Jabal and honourably hosted by local dignitaries, including Sultan Pasha in al-Qurayya. Even once Shishakli's campaign began against the Jabal al-Duruz, the ring of silence drawn around the region meant that even Druze officers, along with the rest of the country, did not hear about the bloody extent of events there until well *after* Shishakli had been ousted. To be sure, Shishakli had little patience for expressions of regional diversity: his political vision aspired to the cultural homogenization of Syrian society. As Shishakli told Druze notables during his 1950 visit, 'After a quarter of a century in which we have combined our efforts and our struggle together, there is no difference between the sons of Damascus and Aleppo, Homs and Hama, Suwayda and Der'a, Latakia and Deir al-Zour, Qamishli and the coast or the mountain.'[62] But this policy of enforced standardization neither involved any explicitly sectarian element nor provoked any explicitly sectarian reaction.

This is not to say that the Jabal al-Duruz was left unscarred by Shishakli's brutal repression. In September 1964, Shishakli was assassinated on the farm in Brazil to which he had eventually fled after leaving Syria. His murderer, Nawas al-Ghazali, was reportedly motivated by revenge for the suffering Shishakli had inflicted on the Jabal all those years earlier. But at the time of Shishakli, the category of 'sect' had not yet acquired political salience in Syria. Sectarian identity gradually became politicized only as a by-product of the profound social and economic changes that swept Syria in the two decades after independence. It is to this post-war economic transformation that the next chapter turns.

الوكلاء
شركة انماء

7

Radicals and Liberals, 1954–1958

After independence, Syria had experienced first inept government by the traditional elite and then the ever-tightening stranglehold of successive military leaders who sought to compensate for the shortcomings of the civilian leadership. Somewhat counter intuitively, this political volatility did not prevent the country from developing a booming new economy that brought with it unprecedented opportunities for social progress. High agricultural profits and a rapid wave of industrial innovation enriched Syria's urban businessmen, but also helped propel workers and peasants into becoming a political force for the first time. The Syrian working classes had already begun shifting their allegiance away from thc political establishment and increasingly supported more radical, leftist parties such as the Ba'thists or the Communists that promised progressive social and economic reform. After Shishakli's downfall in 1954, tensions between the new radicals and the old establishment would be released from the constraints of military rule and quickly escalate to the point of crisis. In the second half of the 1950s, Syria would come to the brink of a civil war that was avoided only by placing the instrument of government beyond the reach of anyone inside the country at all. Ironically, given the long struggle over independence and post-independence state-building, in 1958 the Syrian state would write itself out of existence as a sovereign polity and merge with Egypt.

Syria's union with Egypt was not simply a natural reaction to colonial borders created by Britain and France after the First World War. Although Arab unity was very much part of the political debate in the years after independence, opinions remained intensely divided. Given the variety of political regimes that had been installed in the Arab world in the previous three decades, the question of which country to unite with first raised the question of what kind of political future Syria should look to. Should it be conservative and Westward leaning, like monarchical Iraq and Jordan? Or radical and neutralist, like the new Republic of Egypt that had overthrown its own monarchy in 1952? As Syrians from the rural and lower middle classes became active in politics alongside the established urban bourgeoisie, it was impossible to answer such questions with any consensus. Although many Syrians felt the lingering artificiality of their borders, the union with Egypt was not simply a straightforward rejection of the borders imposed on the region by Britain and France. For the previous thirty years, after all, discussions in Syria about reuniting the Arabic-speaking world had primarily focused on Jordan, Iraq and to a lesser extent Lebanon; Egypt had hardly entered the picture. Syria's lurch into union with Egypt in 1958 was instead the product of a crisis caused by the profound transformations that had begun after independence a decade earlier, and that had accelerated as the largely unintended consequence of policies implemented under military rule.

The new economy, 1946–1954

The peculiar circumstances of the Second World War laid the foundations for Syria's subsequent economic boom. As we have seen, in 1941 the British and Free French invaded Syria and Lebanon to overthrow mandatory authorities that were loyal to the Vichy regime. The size of the occupying army was so great that over the next few years the Allied forces spent an estimated 800 million Syrian pounds (S£) on supplies and local labour.[1] This huge injection of cash provoked rampant inflation in the Syrian economy, which had been left essentially moribund by French colonial policy. While ordinary Syrians found their wages bought less and less, the largest Syrian merchants accepted payment from the Allies in hard currency and thereby protected their profits from being devoured by inflation.

Equally as important as this injection of foreign capital were the wartime measures introduced by Britain to prevent mass famine during the early 1940s. Local speculators took advantage of the cheap wheat redirected to the region by Britain's Middle East Supply Centre in Cairo and learned how to profit from the shortages created by the new rationing system. Even the more scrupulous brokers benefitted indirectly from the shortages as the prices of foodstuffs and basic goods shot sky-high, prompting some traders to hoard grain and stockpile considerable wealth. Wartime trade restrictions had reduced to a trickle the quantity of imports coming into Syria, which meant that merchants and owners of agricultural land had little occasion to fritter away their new-found riches on foreign goods and were forced to save their money for the future. When independence arrived in 1946, the barrage broke and freed these pent-up reservoirs of capital to seek more productive outlets. The subsequent flood of private investment stimulated agricultural production and fuelled the acceleration of modern industry in Syria.

In the late 1940s, agriculture was a naturally attractive field for Syrian investors. The high prices fetched by wheat during the war had for the first time revealed the sheer scale of profit to be made from agriculture, and, although Syria's best land had long been exploited by a small number of established notable families, there remained vast swathes of territory in the north-east of the country that were largely unclaimed and uncultivated. Traversed by tributaries of the Euphrates that rose in the mountains of southern Turkey and flowed south through the desert of *Badiyat al-Sham* and on to Iraq, Syria's north-eastern Jazira region possessed great allure for pioneers from the cities further west. The Jazira was fertile and held the potential for easy irrigation. It was also sparsely populated: unlike other agricultural regions such as Hama, the Jazira lacked a dense social hierarchy with an entrenched landowning elite at its peak. The Jazira therefore provided a space in which new entrepreneurs might make their names and amass great fortunes. Many of these men came from Aleppo, although few were from notable families. In fact, a good number were Armenians who had arrived in Syria in the 1910s and 1920s as refugees from Turkey, bringing with them seed capital and an entrepreneurial mindset.[2]

In the late 1940s and early 1950s, businessmen such as Pierre Mamarbachi, the Asfar and Najjar brothers and Abd al-Massih Asfahan introduced to the Jazira what was tantamount to an agricultural revolution. First, they brought new crops to the region, of which cotton was the most significant. Cotton had been cultivated on a small scale near Aleppo since the eighteenth century, but only in the 1920s did it start to become extensively farmed in Syria. The wisdom of agricultural experimentation in the Jazira was confirmed when global cotton demand soared with the start of the Korean War in 1950, sending prices rocketing. Farmers across the country began to plant more cotton than ever before. The speed of the shift to cotton was staggering. In the years between 1934 and 1938 an annual average of only 30,000 hectares had been devoted to growing cotton across the country. In contrast, in 1950 there were 78,000 hectares of cotton, and in 1951, 217,000 hectares.

Seven times as much land was devoted to cotton in 1951 as it had been in the mid-1930s; the actual quantity of cotton produced increased nearly tenfold during the same period.[3]

These production increases were primarily due to the second component of the agricultural revolution: mechanization. Although rare in Syria before independence, tractors and combine harvesters had become ubiquitous across the Jazira by the mid-1950s and seemed to spark a nationwide trend: agricultural machinery was even spotted in the fields around Homs and Hama, where landowners had traditionally been reluctant to invest in agriculture. Similarly, the expansion in land farmed in the Jazira was made possible only when agricultural entrepreneurs invested in pumps to irrigate dry fields from local rivers. The rational investment of capital into agricultural production, it turned out, could generate greater profit in the long run than the rents that notable landowners would rapaciously extract from peasants on their land.

Foreign observers were astounded at the economic success that the Syrian private sector enjoyed in agriculture. The absence of any real support from the government in Damascus led some observers to argue that the Syrian experience disproved the received wisdom of international development experts, who in the post-war years largely agreed on the crucial need for state intervention to stimulate economic progress. 'It is now fashionable to believe that the economic development of underdeveloped countries needs foreign capital, foreign experts, good public services, long-term planning, agrarian reform, plus, for good measure, a revolution,' wrote economist Doreen Warriner after concluding her field trip to the Jazira in 1955. 'But Syria has none of these things [...] It completely confutes some current doctrines.'[4]

While it was true that entrepreneurial initiative launched Syria's post-war agricultural boom, this early expansion soon encountered a series of obstacles that the private sector proved incapable of overcoming, and to which state intervention in the economy seemed to offer the obvious solution. The growth of state institutions under Shishakli had provided government officials with not only new tools for regulation and investment, but also a new-found confidence that the state could and should provide those elements of economic development that the private sector could not offer.

The first challenge facing agriculture was its heavy dependence on rainfall. Syria's overall lack of irrigation limited the amount of land that could be cultivated and meant harvests were dependent on the extreme variation in precipitation that characterized the local climate. Periodic droughts, such as those that occurred in 1951 and 1955, made precarious not only the well-being of agricultural entrepreneurs and the hundreds of thousands of peasants whose livelihood depended on subsistence farming, but also the viability of the state itself, which derived most of its revenue from taxing agricultural exports. The central government consequently endured profound fiscal unpredictability and had only a limited ability to plan for the future.

To address this problem, the state undertook several irrigation projects as part of a new programme of public works. These included a canal system to distribute water from Lake Homs to the surrounding area, as well as similar schemes at Mazarib in the Hawran, the Khabour River in the Jazira, the Kuwaik River near Aleppo and the Sinn River close to Latakia. These projects were relatively small scale: by the mid-1950s, they serviced only one-eighth of the total area of irrigated agricultural land. More ambitiously, the government also set in motion a plan to double the amount of irrigated territory by reclaiming 35,000 hectares of agricultural land from the Ghab marshes that lay on the Orontes River north-west of Hama. Work on the Ghab project, which also involved the construction of two large reservoirs to irrigate a further 30,000 hectares of agricultural land, began in late 1954. The director general of the Ghab project announced, in language laced with the visionary, high-modernist rhetoric of post-war developmentalism, that the scheme would transform the area from 'unhealthy, brackish swamps that hide all manner of germs that spread deadly diseases' to 'cultivable lands that will be suitable for irrigation and agriculture', thereby helping to 'raise the social and economic level of the nation'.[5]

The state undertook several other major infrastructure projects in the early 1950s. The Ministry of Public Works began the arduous task of building a road network that was adequate for Syria's economic needs, having inherited from the French a system of infrastructure that had been constructed largely according to a colonial logic of military control and occupation. By 1952, Syria had 8,200 kilometres of roads, compared to just 4,500 kilometres in 1939. Over the same period, the number of asphalted roads in the country more than doubled, increasing from 1,500 kilometres to 3,800 kilometres.[6] Even so, the dramatic expansion of agricultural activity in the Jazira rapidly outstripped the speed with which the government could extend the road network to the distant north-east. The cost of transporting cotton and wheat to market was a significant burden for producers in the Jazira, especially during the winter, when many roads became impassable. Even after produce had made its way west from the Jazira breadbasket, agricultural entrepreneurs faced further transport costs to reach the international market, since the newly independent state of Syria lacked its own port. After the First World War, the Syrian interior had been severed, one by one, from the three seaports that had served it during the Ottoman Empire. Haifa was cut off by the borders of first the British Mandate and then, after 1948, the State of Israel; the Syrian coastal town of Alexandretta, accompanied by its entire province, had been ceded to Turkey by France in 1936; then the port in Beirut became no longer economically viable for Syrian exporters after the collapse of the Syro-Lebanese customs union and the mutual imposition of tariffs between the two countries in 1950. At this time, the Syrian government decided to construct new port facilities at Latakia, which were completed four years later.[7] In addition to their practical utility, such feats of state-sponsored civil engineering – reclaiming land from swamps, building new canal systems, extending road networks and constructing a new port – were intended to symbolize Syria's transformation from traumatized post-colonial nation into fully fledged modern state.

Besides irrigation and infrastructure, a third problem facing the development of the country's agricultural sector was the uncertain status of land-ownership rights. Upon independence, Syrian property law, as expressed in the Civil Code of 1949, was an unwieldy, uneven amalgam of the 1858 Ottoman Land Code and French legislation that had been applied in different ways across different parts of the country. Syrian law specified no fewer than five distinct categories of land ownership. The first was *mulk*, in which an individual enjoyed full and unfettered ownership of property. This category corresponded to the Western notion of private property and was the dominant form of land ownership in Syria's cities and towns. The second legal category, prevalent in rural areas, was called *miri*. Here, ownership was conditional rather than absolute: individual rights over *miri* land lasted only as long as the land was being cultivated. If the land were not exploited for five consecutive years, ownership would revert to the state. The logic behind this principle was that rural property owners would be incentivized to have the land worked rather than to leave it idle. The unintended consequence was that this built-in insecurity created a two-tier system of land-ownership rights, in which rural land was deemed inferior to urban property. A third category, *matrouka*, referred to land belonging to the state over which local communities had usufruct: communal pastures, forests and so forth. A fourth category, *matrouka mahmiyya*, comprised state land that was held in trust for the country as a whole: it covered rivers, roads and similar features. Finally, *mawat* – literally 'dead' land – referred to uncultivated land that had not been registered. In principle, *mawat* land belonged to the state, but individuals could obtain *miri* rights if they could prove they had cultivated the land for five or more years.

The smooth operation of this baroque legal system was premised upon the assumption that land had at some point in the past been mapped and registered. Yet in the real word, this was only true for the most populated provinces of western and central Syria. The Jazira and Euphrates regions – which were the main areas of agricultural expansion in the 1950s – along with the Hawran and Jabal al-Duruz in the south, had never been surveyed. Agricultural entrepreneurs in the north-east were not necessarily dissuaded by the uncertainty of land rights, but it did make for some interesting negotiations. For the most part, the entrepreneurs would rent farmland from local tribal shaykhs, to whom legal title had been granted by the Vichy authorities in 1940 and 1941, or they would purchase land directly from the state. But ownership rights were so hazy that sometimes the entrepreneurs would need to hedge their bets by paying state and shaykh simultaneously, because it was not entirely clear who the real owner was.[8]

In addition to this legal confusion, Syria's agricultural potential was severely limited by the inequities of land distribution. A 1945 technical report from the state cadastral mapping service estimated that 52 per cent of land in Syria was the property of large landowners (with 'large' here defined as owning more than 100 hectares of land). In contrast, smallholders with fewer than ten hectares legally owned just 15 per cent of the land. Concentration of land into large estates was most pronounced in the provinces of Homs and especially Hama, where sharecropping was predominant: peasants would farm the land belonging to one of the large families of the area in exchange for a portion of the harvest – usually 50 per cent, but as low as 25 per cent if the landowner provided irrigation or seed. With little investment in the land from the owner and the success of the harvest essentially at the mercy of the climate, the peasant could at best eke out a meagre existence for himself and his family. More often, to survive, the peasant was forced to borrow money from the landowner, at usurious rates of interest, which only entrenched his misery. With most of the peasantry struggling to meet their basic subsistence needs, it was unsurprising that Syria's agriculture had lacked any impetus for modernization. As economist Yousef Helbaoui opined:

> [the Syrian peasant is a] most primitive class that continues to stagnate in an endless cycle of ignorance, poverty and servitude. This has repercussions for his spirit, his mentality, his life and his work skills. It is impossible to overstate the base living standards of this segment of the rural population ... There is no creative impulse. Every new idea, good or bad, is destined to fail. Everything happens the same way year on year, without any innovation or hint of progress.[9]

The Syrian tradition of land ownership was not only deeply inequitable, but also stymied possibilities for economic development.

Politicians and state officials were by this point aware of the need to address rural poverty. The best solution to this problem, it was thought, would be to provide peasants with their own land. This principle had been first expressed in the 1950 Constitution, which, as we have seen, established the state's right to appropriate uncultivated land and limit the size of individual landholdings. The first formal government initiative came in January 1952 in the form of a decree which abrogated the rights of large landowners to unregistered state lands (*mawat*) and undertook to redistribute this land to the peasantry. The decree soon proved unworkable. Not only was the cadastral mapping of the country still not sufficiently advanced to allow the state authorities to know where the *mawat* lands were, but the state had stopped keeping records of *mawat* land that had been taken over by cultivators. This confusion meant there was no real basis upon which to determine the legality of land ownership.

To end this uncertainty, in October 1952, the distinction between registered and unregistered state land was erased: individuals no longer had the right to claim any kind of state land. However, the idea of redistributing land to the poorest peasants was quietly jettisoned by the Shishakli regime after Hawrani and the Ba'thists fell from grace in December 1952. The next month, the government announced that individuals already cultivating land formerly classified as *mawat* would be entitled to purchase the title to that land at a considerable discount.[10] The state's efforts to impose a ceiling on the size of landholdings, on the other hand, were easily outfoxed by wily owners, who could register property in the names of their many relatives. In the meantime, the national land survey recommenced in 1953. However, its slow progress over the following years promised no speedy resolution to the immediate problem of uncertain claims to land rights.

If the state under Shishakli was still too underdeveloped to translate its land reform policy from decree to reality, it proved more effective at building that infrastructure of technical expertise and coordination which the private sector could not provide to Syrian agriculture. The first component of this specialist infrastructure was the Cotton Office, established as part of the Ministry of Agriculture following the disastrous harvest of 1951, caused by a damaging combination of over-cultivation and parasites. The

Cotton Office was intended to prevent the recurrence of such a failed harvest: it supervised the distribution of seed and supplied insecticides, determined the total area to be devoted to cotton, specified the windows for planting and harvesting and regulated cotton exports. This kind of active state intervention in Syrian agriculture was not unprecedented, having been introduced by Britain's Middle East Supply Centre during the Second World War and continued by the post-independence state in the form of a Cereals Office, but a lack of sufficient trained officials meant that the new Cotton Office had to recruit its staff from Egypt, which had longer experience of modern cotton cultivation.[11]

The second component of agricultural infrastructure was provided by the state-run Syrian Agricultural Bank, which responded to the 1951 harvest failure by extending credit to medium as well as large landowners for the first time. The Agricultural Bank was now also tasked with importing and distributing tractors, water pumps and other machinery to stimulate agricultural expansion.[12] Between them, the Cotton Office and the Agricultural Bank helped to prolong the agricultural boom initiated by the immediate post-war flurry of private investment well into the mid-1950s.

In contrast to agriculture, industry had never proven attractive to Syria's notable families. Small artisanal production remained the norm until the early years of independence, when wartime savings began to seek out new economic opportunities opened up by modern industrial technology. With the expansion of cotton production, textiles soon became Syria's leading industry, with food processing (vegetable oils, flour, tobacco) taking second place. Mechanization was materially supported by the expansion of the electricity network, but also depended on the legal and financial infrastructure established by the equally innovative institution of the joint-stock venture, which allowed investors to combine their capital and form what we would now recognize as limited liability companies. The number of industrial joint-stock ventures increased dramatically in the decade following independence. While just five new industrial ventures had been licensed in 1945, fifteen new industrial companies were founded in 1948, twenty in 1949, twenty-four in 1950, twenty-six in 1951 – the number continued to increase throughout the 1950s.[13] Leading national corporations such as the Shahba Spinning and Weaving Company, United Commercial and Industrial Company, Ahliyya Spinning and Weaving Company and United Arab Company for Industry were all founded in these years.

Despite the proliferation of these new ventures, the largest investors came from a remarkably small tranche of society, in which the best-known Syrian notable families were clearly visible. It was often said at the time that the Syrian economy was dominated by just fifty families – an impression which was not entirely groundless. These wealthy investors sought out opportunities for profit wherever they happened to exist: Christians and Muslims from the elites of Damascus and Aleppo frequently established joint-stock ventures together without regard for religion or region.[14] Nevertheless, three-quarters of the new companies founded in the 1950s had their headquarters in Damascus, indicating the extent to which the traditional economic rivalry between the bourgeoisie in the two main cities had been gradually replaced by a pragmatic acceptance of the reality that Damascus was the capital.[15] The emergence of common economic interests between the Damascus and Aleppo elites would provide the core of a national (rather than merely provincial) bourgeoisie in Syria.

Much like the agricultural entrepreneurs, Syria's nascent industrial sector faced significant structural challenges that could not be overcome without state intervention. The first was its sheer fragility and vulnerability to foreign competition. As the experience of the French Mandate had already vividly illustrated, flooding Syrian markets with cheaper, more efficiently produced European goods would drive local producers out of business. Syrian industrialists were therefore convinced that their businesses needed shielding from international competitors and lobbied successive governments to enact protectionist legislation. The industrialists soon discovered that, even under military rule, economic policy remained relatively open to influences from outside government. Well-established networks of chambers of commerce and the newer chambers of industry, along with state-sponsored corporatist institutions such as the Federations of Employers' Syndicates, provided space in which industrialists could advocate policies that favoured their interests.

Over four days in November 1952, for example, Shishakli convened what he called an 'economic parliament' at which representatives of Syria's various commercial, agricultural, industrial, labour and state interests debated economic affairs and submitted lists of policy recommendations that would benefit their sector. On numerous occasions, industrialists influenced policy-making even more directly by taking up official positions in the government themselves. Muhammad Sa'id al-Za'im, vice president of the Aleppo Chamber of Commerce and an important industrialist in his own right, notably served as both foreign minister and acting minister of national economy under the puppet presidency of Fawzi Selu. Ma'moun al-Kuzbari, head lawyer for the powerful Khumasiya industrial collective, was appointed by Shishakli as leader of his new political party, the Arab Liberation Movement.[16] These canny tactics enabled Syria's new industrial capitalists to dominate economic policy-making despite the fundamentally authoritarian nature of Shishakli's regime.

The industrialists' economic agenda dovetailed neatly with Shishakli's concern to prune Syria's excessive links with the outside world.[17] Following the collapse of the customs unions with Lebanon in 1950, the government increased customs duties on imports that competed with locally produced goods such as cloth, canned fruits and vegetables and confectionary from 25 per cent to 40 or 50 per cent. The next year, higher tariffs were imposed on soap, clothing and other goods – up to 70 per cent in the case of glass. Even more substantial support was introduced in September 1952, when industrial companies were granted customs-free imports of machinery, equipment and building materials, and allowed a six-year tax holiday on income from property.[18] The Ministry of Finance in turn supported low-interest bank loans to industry that reached a total of 23 million Syrian pounds (S£) by 1952. For some companies, the provision of these loans meant the difference between a profitable or loss-making venture.

In exchange for these privileges, industrialists were obliged to accept a much more intrusive inspection regime than they had previously encountered: new licensing procedures, standardized book-keeping requirements (to facilitate tax collection), and submitting all kinds of facts and figures to the Ministry of National Economy (to provide data for the production of more meaningful and complete national statistics). While industrialists needed state support, the state also needed their compliance to weave its regulations deep into the fabric of the country's modern industry.

If protectionism allowed modern industry to get off the ground in Syria, manufacturers still faced one further obstacle: who would buy their products? With foreign markets variously awash with cheaper Western goods, placed out of reach by protectionism (as in Turkey), prohibited by politics (as in Palestine), disincentivized by tariffs (as in Lebanon) or lacking a sizeable consumer base (as in Iraq and Jordan), industrialists naturally first looked to sell to the domestic market. However, in its impoverished state, the Syrian peasantry could barely feed itself from the land, much less spend non-existent disposable income on consumer goods and luxury foodstuffs. For this reason, the industrial bourgeoisie lent its support to progressive, social justice causes such as land reform, public health and welfare, which would not only raise living standards for the masses, but in doing so transform the Syrian population from workers and peasants into customers and consumers. Social reform, they believed, would deepen the Syrian market and sustain the economic boom.

The support of business people for social justice explains why it was factory workers, not the vastly more numerous peasants, who first benefitted from the introduction of labour and welfare rights as one of the first acts passed by the newly independent Syrian government in 1946. In that year, Law 269 of 16 June granted workers an eight-hour day, established a minimum wage, stipulated holiday entitlements, banned child labour under twelve years of age and legislated for accident compensation and redundancy. The new labour law also introduced a system of mixed committees to bring together employers, workers and state officials to arbitrate disputes, as well as wage boards in each governorate.[19] So successful was this partnership between workers and management, under the supervision of the Directorate of Labour and Social Welfare established the following year (later upgraded to a fully fledged ministry) – along with Shishakli's policy of purging agitators from labour unions – that industrial strikes all but vanished until after Shishakli's fall from power. In stark contrast to the raft of legislative protections afforded to the relatively small number of industrial workers in Syria, the country's peasants enjoyed zero legal rights or protection from exploitation.

In the late 1940s and early 1950s, there had thus rallied behind the banner of social justice a broad coalition that ranged from bourgeois industrialists and agricultural entrepreneurs to military state builders and leftist radicals. Against this consensus stood only the unreformed notables of the grand families, who interpreted any attempt to address the inequity of land ownership or to uplift the state of the peasantry as an attack on their prestige and position. Nevertheless, the fact that there was such a high degree of consensus between the small yet influential clique of Syrian capitalists, Syria's military rulers and Syria's radical left is quite remarkable. It was not so much that each of the three groups compromised upon its 'real' interests out of purely pragmatic concerns of political strategy, but that capitalists, military rulers and radicals all interpreted the successful achievement of their wider political or economic objectives as depending on the construction of a strong, interventionist state. In working towards this goal, this coalition of convenience inadvertently helped transform the state from simply an instrument to achieve limited objectives into a prize, control over which was an end in its own right. With the restoration of civilian rule following Shishakli's departure from power, the political dynamics of this new reality threatened to tear Syria apart from within.

Elections of September 1954

Syria's return to civilian rule in February 1954 raised the fundamental question of how to deal with the legacies of Shishakli, who had banned political parties, promulgated the authoritarian 1953 Constitution and persecuted the political left. The politicians decided that the best way to counter the aberrations of Shishakli's rule was simply to rewind the clock. The 1953 Constitution was replaced with its more liberal 1950 predecessor, and the National Assembly that had been in place prior to Shishakli's coup reinstated. Although the People's Party had won a majority in the 1949 elections that established this assembly, they now agreed to form a coalition government with the National Party under the leadership of Sabri al-Asali, the Nationals' secretary general. Asali drew his government from across these two parties of the establishment.

The restoration of the 1949 assembly failed to reflect the new popularity of leftist groups that had surged ahead in the intervening years. Akram al-Hawrani's Arab Socialist Party had merged with the Ba'th Party after he fled Shishakli's rule, along with Michel Aflaq and Salah al-Din al-Bitar, to seek haven in Lebanon. The Syrian Communist Party also won much support from peasants and workers, although the appeal of communism was curtailed by its disregard for Arab nationalism and by the Soviet Union's support for the State of Israel. There was little love lost between the radicals and Asali, a bourgeois Damascene lawyer whom they considered tainted by his defence of Syrian feudalism, his close association to former President Quwwatli and his lingering sympathy for the cause of union with the reactionary Hashemite monarchy in Iraq.

Asali's government drew a firm line under the Shishakli years. Five of Shishakli's provincial governors and four ambassadors were replaced, the Supreme Court was dismissed, and a host of lower-ranking civil servants were fired. The government then announced its demand for state officials who had received extraordinary promotions under Shishakli to pay back their salaries from the period of his rule. These punitive measures made enemies of those who had collaborated with the previous regime and provoked the resurrection of Shishakli's Arab Liberation Movement, led by Ma'moun al-Kuzbari, as a focus for political opposition. Asali was in turn accused of stacking the state apparatus with his own supporters. The small size of Syria's administrative elite meant changes at the top rippled through the system along highly personalized lines.

With Shishakli's iron-clad devotion to maintaining Syria's independence now gone, the contentious issue of relations with other Arab states once again surfaced. Asali held a secret meeting in Brumana, Lebanon, with pro-Iraq Syrian MPs and Iraqi Prime Minister Fadil al-Jamali to discuss proposals to bring about union that even went as far as an Iraqi military invasion.[20] Although some members of Asali's National Party, such as Lutfi al-Haffar, had come around to the idea of a Fertile Crescent unity project led by Baghdad, most preferred to maintain the alliance of sovereign states with Egypt and Saudi Arabia that had previously been cultivated by the party's old leader Quwwatli, who had been living in Egypt since the first coup removed him from power in 1949. The rival People's Party had a history of supporting Baghdad but was also keenly aware that the army still considered safeguarding Syria's independent, republican system of government to be its national duty.

The officers who had led the coup against Shishakli initially displayed little interest in further political intervention. As the British embassy observed, 'Even Colonel Faisal Atassi, the ostensible leader of the plot, returned to command the troops in Aleppo without making any further claim for himself and his followers.'[21] Many officers were nevertheless disgruntled when Asali's government allowed soldiers purged by Shishakli to return to their old positions, causing a sudden influx of officers that upset the new status quo. The army was also incensed by the government's decision to take the gendarmerie and police away from the Ministry of National Defence and reassign them to the Ministry of the Interior. A final blow to military autonomy came when the assembly promulgated a law allowing the cabinet to decide unilaterally the termination of military appointments. While such measures might have been intended to prevent the rise through the ranks of another military dictator, they did little to enhance trust between officers and civilian politicians.

Several officers, including Mustafa Hamdoun, Adnan al-Maliki, Abd al-Hamid Sarraj and Muhammad 'Umran, began to discuss the need for intervention. In an incident in June, the prime minister's house was briefly surrounded by soldiers, before the coup attempt was aborted; the officer corps as a whole had no stomach for another foray into politics at this time.[22] Feeling the heat of both military and civilian pressure, on 11 June, Asali announced the resignation of his government.

Asali was replaced by Sa'id al-Ghazzi, a respected lawyer who was careful not to replicate the mistakes of his predecessor. Ghazzi formed an impartial, caretaker cabinet whose job would be simply to oversee new national elections; the government would remain entirely neutral in foreign affairs. In case this were not enough to allay the concerns of the army, Ghazzi appointed Chief of Staff Shawkat Shuqayr as defence minister to reassure the officers there would be no unwelcome political interference in military affairs.

Elections were scheduled for September 1954. Even with the army mollified, the months preceding the vote were far from calm. The removal of Shishakli had reopened space for previously repressed political parties to assert their agenda; it also lifted the constraints on labour activism. A wave of strikes, demonstrations and protests swept the country from Damascus and Aleppo to Homs and Latakia as workers in textiles, cotton, electricity, transport and communications demanded higher wages and better working conditions. State employees followed suit: the police and internal security forces went on strike, demanding wage parity with the gendarmerie, and in late July even judges staged a short-lived strike. The principal party of the left, the now merged Arab Socialist Ba'th Party, was well positioned to take advantage of this groundswell of class discontent. The party organized rallies in the main cities, some of which culminated in violent clashes with anti-left forces, such as the Muslim Brotherhood in Aleppo and the Arab Liberation Movement in Hama. At the same time, the Ba'th increased its already sizeable following in the army. The summer of 1954, and the September elections, were to prove crucial for its rise to power.

The prominence of the Ba'th Party was by no means a forgone conclusion. The party that ran for election in 1954 was produced by a merger between Hawrani's Arab Socialist Party and the Ba'th Party that had been officially founded by Michel Aflaq and Salah al-Din al-Bitar in 1946. Despite their similar vision for social and political reform, the two parties were very different creatures. With its roots in the squalid inequality of the Hama countryside, Hawrani's Arab Socialist Party was vehemently opposed to feudalism; its supporters tended to be motivated by anger and personal experience of poverty. The memoirs of Izz al-Din Diyab, who participated in each party's meetings before their merger during his childhood in Hama, describe the Arab Socialists cultivating a confrontational approach towards the party's rivals that valorized physical bravery. The Ba'thists taught rational thinking, Diyab explains, but 'in the Arab Socialists [. . .] you learned how to duck and weave during demonstrations that clashed with students [of other parties] or the security forces.'[23] Ba'thist gatherings, in contrast, had structure and even reading assignments; perfect for the bookish schoolchild with a love of learning.

The Ba'th Party had an ornate political ideology. Its founders had become close friends while students in Paris in the 1930s, where they read European philosophy, politics and history. Aflaq and Bitar dallied briefly with Marxism yet devoted more time to romantic German nationalists such as Fichte and Herder. What attracted them to these thinkers was their insistence that the nation was the fundamental building block of human society. Contrary to the French idea that people formed nations voluntarily, by deciding to become citizens of a particular civic community, German nationalists argued that people were born into nations that had their own distinct culture and language and that existed independently of the state. In this way, it was possible for them to speak of the existence of the German nation well before the unified state of Germany was founded in 1871.

Aflaq and Bitar found in this argument an obvious parallel with the Arab nation. Although the Arab nation had been fragmented by colonialism into an assortment of states, and although there had never been an independent Arab state in the past, they believed the Arab nation was destined to have a collective independence. The Arab nation was based not on race or biology, they claimed, but on a shared language, a common culture and a glorious history. This understanding of what it meant to be Arab was captured in the famous Ba'thist slogan of 'One Arab nation with an eternal mission' (*Umma 'arabiya wahida dhaata risaala khalida*). While older Syrians did not necessarily consider a shared language to imply much about political identity, young Syrians searching for their place in the world would find the promise of community and future grandeur enticing.

After returning from France to Syria, Aflaq and Bitar obtained teaching positions at the prestigious Tajhiz secondary school in Damascus, where they refined their political programme and developed the nucleus of what was to become a new political party formally registered in 1946 after the end of the French Mandate. The word *ba'th* means 'renaissance' or 'rebirth' and refers to the belief that Arab unity is not simply a political goal, but a catalyst for the social, moral and cultural revitalization of the entire Arab nation. The Ba'thist agenda was thus both politically and socially revolutionary. For Aflaq, revolution was not simply an instrument to implement political ends: it provided a way to wake the Arab nation from the torpor induced by occupation and imperialist division. Arab unity would produce a meaningful freedom for the Arab people, a freedom that would be used to build a just and equal society. To this end, 'unity, freedom and socialism' were the watchwords of the Ba'th Party.

The ideology of the early Ba'thists has been criticized for its romanticism and airy mysticism. Aflaq's writings invoke a renaissance that more resembles a new age spiritual experience than a pragmatic political programme. 'Love, young people, comes before anything else,' says Aflaq in one widely cited passage. 'First comes love, then the definition will follow: [. . .] A tolerant spirituality that will open its heart and will shade with its wings all those who shared with the Arabs their history, who lived for generations in the atmosphere of their language and culture until they became Arab in thought and in sentiment.'[24] While the early Ba'thists were intrigued by the heartfelt nationalism that they believed had empowered Germany and Italy against the then colonial powers of Britain and France prior to the Second World War, their emphasis on national culture led them to neglect the practicalities of building a strong state. Economics, institutions and the mechanics of government are notably absent from their work. For Aflaq and Bitar, Arab unification was first and foremost a cultural imperative.

In the early 1950s, the sheer exuberance of the intellectual and political agenda of the Ba'th Party captured the imagination of a new generation of Syrians, who found the meagre offerings of the personality-based National and People's parties to be conservative, elitist and ideologically vacuous. The Ba'th Party proved popular with teachers, university students, teenaged schoolchildren and educated members of the urban lower middle classes. Its secular commitment to a broad Arab identity, regardless of religion, was attractive to the next generation of Alawis and Druze, especially those sent to school in the cities where they were detached from their communities of origin. Ba'thism thus found a home among lower-middle-class youth from rural and often minoritarian communities: regions such as the Hawran, Suweida and Latakia represented its natural constituencies. Its ideology even attracted a small number of adherents outside the country, notably in Iraq, where a separate but connected branch of the party would later develop.

The cooperation and then merger of Aflaq and Bitar's Ba'th Party with Hawrani's Arab Socialist Party in 1952–53 united two different styles of politics. Hawrani was a man of action, a passionate and powerful public speaker and a legend in his hometown of Hama. In contrast, *The Times* in London observed that Aflaq was 'a saintly figure, once described as "the Ghandi [sic] of Arab nationalism" – a pale, slight man of painful shyness, deep sincerity and debilitatingly frugal habits'. Their description encapsulates the patronizing disregard of many British for anti-colonial movements across their former empire, as well as conveying something of Aflaq's bookish intellectualism.[25] While Aflaq and Bitar were the channels by which new ideas about nationalism filtered into Syrian political life, it was activists, organizers and agitators such as Hawrani who were largely responsible for the meteoric rise of the renamed Arab Socialist Ba'th Party in the decade after Syria's return to civilian politics.

The September 1954 elections were remarkable for three reasons. First, they were the first free and meaningful elections ever held in the Arab world. Not only were they conducted by secret ballot, but the government ordered the gendarmerie officers who oversaw the voting to be reassigned to parts of the country away from their homes.[26] This step was intended to prevent local landowners and notable families from exerting pressure on the gendarmes to turn a blind eye to voting irregularities; it betrayed the social influence that notables could wield in their home communities. Second, the results of these elections marked the first real blow to the political domination of the urban elite that had stretched from the late Ottoman Empire to the post-independence era. The People's Party lost half its seats. While the National Party gained six members of parliament, this increase was negligible given that the assembly had expanded from 114 to 142 members. Not even the triumphant return to Syria of former president Shukri al-Quwwatli could boost the fortunes of the National Party. Rather than dazzling the electorate with his star quality, Quwwatli's homecoming was greeted with protests against his incompetence in the 1948 war, his nepotism and his lack of concern for social reform. Quwwatli's failures were blamed for provoking the army to intervene in politics in the first place.[27]

Most significantly, the 1954 election was marked by a surge of support for the left. The Arab Socialist Ba'th Party took nineteen seats, up from just one in 1949. Hawrani himself achieved a remarkable victory in Hama, where he faced stiff opposition from a party list headed by a scion of the powerful landowning Azm family. Despite their small numbers and the fact their party was still not legally registered, the Communists took their first seat. This was a historic event: Khalid Bakdash became the first communist MP to be elected in the Arab world. Representing the voters of Hayy al-Akrad, the Kurdish quarter in Damascus, Bakdash was a remarkable orator, although his personal influence could not entirely overcome the suspicions of many Syrians that communism would involve Syria becoming a satellite of the Soviet Union. When the elections were over, the question of Syria's relations with the outside world again became the subject of intense debate between the traditional elite parties and Syria's ascendant radical left.

The polarization of politics

Despite its strong election performance, the Arab Socialist Ba'th Party (henceforth referred to simply as the Ba'th Party) did not have enough deputies to form a government. Instead, the National Party and People's Party formed a coalition under the premiership of Faris al-Khuri. A third group in parliament consisted of the Democratic Bloc of thirty-seven independent MPs led by the experienced statesman–businessman Khalid al-Azm, whose successful career as an entrepreneur did not prevent him later making common cause with Syria's progressive left.

Each of these political tendencies had quite different perspectives on Syria's foreign relations. While Shishakli had adopted an alliance with Egypt and Saudi Arabia to counterbalance the unionist threat from Iraq, his removal from power had reopened the whole question of Syria's foreign policy orientation – a question that was becoming even more complex as intra-Arab relations became entangled in the Cold War confrontation between East and West.

The People's Party maintained its longstanding preference for an alliance or even union with Iraq, a position now shared by some of the National Party. Nationals who were supporters of Quwwatli, on the other hand, continued to look towards Egypt and Saudi Arabia. The Ba'th Party, meanwhile, was adamantly opposed to the prospect of unity with Iraq, a country it considered compromised by its conservative, monarchical system of government and its ongoing association with Britain: the Ba'thists accused Baghdad's politicians of being controlled by puppet masters in London. At the same time, the Ba'thists were wary of Egypt's new ruler, Abd al-Nasser, who had come to power in February 1954 after overthrowing the general earlier installed as president after a 1952 military coup that had abolished the monarchy and turned Egypt into a republic. The Ba'thists had favoured the ousted general and suspected that Abd al-Nasser harboured pro-American sympathies. The final centre of power in Syria – the army – still considered itself to be the guardian of Syria's independence and its republican system of government. Many officers nevertheless had political leanings towards the Ba'th Party and shared its suspicions of Iraq.

As if these diverging perspectives on foreign relations were not enough, Syria's political divisions were heightened by the proposal that Iraq should join the Western-sponsored defence agreement signed by Turkey and Pakistan on 2 April 1954 to form a 'northern tier' of states as the frontline against communist expansion into the Middle East. The proposal elicited strong opposition from Egypt's Abd al-Nasser, who insisted instead on a collective Arab defence pact. After spending the summer attempting to navigate this diplomatic impasse, Iraqi Prime Minister Nuri al-Sa'id modified his position (with British approval) and proposed an Iraqi–Turkish accord as the starting point of a pro-Western defence agreement encompassing the Arab states and Turkey. Iraq and Turkey publicly announced their agreement in January 1955, which was formalized in the Baghdad Pact of 25 February.

The declaration of the Baghdad Pact was taken as a serious blow by Abd al-Nasser, whose initially lukewarm attitude towards the West had since given way to the belief that Arab independence was incompatible with supporting the former colonial powers in the Cold War. Intra-Arab relations were now increasingly played out in a field polarized by the mutually antagonistic positions of Iraq and Egypt.

After the election of a new Syrian government, the region looked to see with which country Damascus would side with. The coalition government tried to avoid the question entirely by maintaining its neutrality, but this was difficult given Prime Minister Khouri's pro-Western reputation and the evident divisions in his cabinet. Khouri's government fell in February 1955, when it lost the support of the pro-Egypt wing of the National Party. It was replaced by a coalition of the independents of Khalid al-Azm (who became foreign minister and acting defence minister), the anti-Iraq wing of the National Party now led by Sabri al-Asali (who became prime minister) and the Ba'th Party (with Wahib al-Ghanim appointed acting minister of health). While the Ba'th Party was very much a junior partner in the Asali government, it was able to influence the government's domestic economic and social policy, which essentially reflected the party's reformist agenda, apart from the controversial subject of land redistribution.

This largely pro-Egypt government soon acquiesced to Abd al-Nasser's proposal for an Arab Collective Security Pact that would also include Saudi Arabia.[28] The agreement envisaged a federation between the three countries that would eventually unify their foreign, economic and cultural policies. Although this understanding was largely intended to symbolize the common anti-Iraq position of Egypt, Syria and Saudi Arabia, rather than represent a blueprint for actual unification, it nevertheless broke new rhetorical ground. The Syrian army endorsed the pact and was rumoured to have threatened a coup unless the deal was ratified by the parliament – which it duly was, in the autumn of 1955.

If opposition to the Baghdad Pact opened a new era in Syria's international relations, then the assassination of a prominent Syrian army officer in Damascus the same year had a similarly epoch-shifting impact on the balance of political power inside the country. Just thirty-seven years old when he was murdered, Colonel Adnan al-Malki had already been appointed deputy chief of staff of the Syrian army. A charismatic natural leader who was hugely popular with his fellow officers, Malki had made a name for himself in 1952 when he had personally confronted Shishakli over his autocratic excesses. Typical of many Syrian officers of his generation, Malki was left-leaning and nationalist. Over the previous months he had emerged as one of the army's strongest opponents of Iraq's pro-Western defence plans. Although not a member of the Ba'th, Malki had sympathized with the party's neutralist position.

The young colonel was assassinated in the spectator stand at the Damascus sports stadium on 22 April 1955, twenty minutes into a friendly match between the football teams of the Syrian military police and the Egyptian coastguard. His murderer, a police sergeant named Yunus Abd al-Rahim, then shot himself in the head with a second gun.[29] 'In the confusion,' notes historian Andrew Rathmell, 'the other security men were slow to react, unlike [Chief of Staff] Shuqayr, who "deserted unobtrusively in a private automobile" and the Russian ambassador, who hurdled a four and a half foot fence as he fled the scene.'[30]

Abd al-Rahim was a member of the Syrian Social Nationalist Party, whose supporters Malki had been in the process of purging from the armed forces. The SSNP had a deeply held antagonism towards communism, which led its members to support the pro-Western Baghdad Pact rather than Egypt's policy of neutralism. Idiosyncratically, the SSNP considered the Baghdad Pact as the first step towards the unification of the Levant, which they considered to be more integral to the Syrian nation than any broader Arab identity. The highest-ranking SSNP member who had been expelled from the military, Major Ghassan Jadid, shared an Alawi background and a home village of Safita with Malki's assailant. The spectacular assassination of Malki conveyed to the Syrian public for the first time the intensity of the struggle being waged inside the army to control the political orientation of the officer corps.

After his death, the figure of Malki was lionized by the army: he was mourned as a martyr for the cause of the Arab nation and a symbol of Syria's dignity and nobility. In his eulogy, Chief of Staff Shawkat Shuqayr called Malki a 'hero martyr, the pride of the Syrian army, a model of chivalrous youth, a representative of the army's nationalist spirit [. . .] and its revolt against every foreign constraint'.[31] National newspapers continued the praise. *Al-Nasr* described him as the latest sacrifice for Syrian independence and urged that his blood not be spilled in vain, while *al-Nidal* mourned the loss of one of the greatest supporters of nationalism, devotion and sacrifice, and one of the most brilliant officers in the Syrian army.[32] The official magazine of the Syrian armed forces, *al-Jundi* ('The Soldier'), devoted an entire special issue to Malki's life, career and achievements, which sold out within two hours of hitting the news-stands. Demand was so great that *al-Jundi* went on to print an unprecedented second run.[33]

Despite the instability over the preceding decade, not to mention the numerous military coups that had taken place, Syrian political life had only very rarely witnessed acts of targeted political violence.[34] Malki's shockingly public murder seemed to break all the rules. 'We shall always and forever condemn the tactic of assassination,' declared the *Lisan al-Sha'b* newspaper. 'Resorting to the barrel of a revolver or the sharp edge of a knife – instead of using the force of reason, sound logic or solid argumentation, is a detestable way for a rival to silence his opponent . . . People who adopt this savage tactic in political disputes are primitives governed by the law of the jungle, rather than behaving according to the concepts of human civilization.'[35]

Angered by the loss of their comrade, leftist officers took advantage of the public outrage to eradicate the SSNP not just from the armed forces, but from every aspect of Syrian political life. The SSNP newspaper, *al-Bina'*, ceased publication in

Damascus after its printing press was burned to the ground just a few hours after Malki's death, although the speed with which the act was accomplished led some observers to suggest that the fire may have had less to do with revenge than with party members destroying incriminating documents.[36] Aided by the Ba'th and the Communists, the army launched a fierce political campaign against the SSNP, which was attacked as an instrument of foreign powers intent on undermining Syrian sovereignty. The West, especially the United States, was openly blamed for sponsoring its activities. These allegations further eroded the position of those Syrian politicians who supported the Baghdad Pact and rallied support for the Egyptian-brokered alternative.

Cowed by the pressure, Prime Minister Asali essentially gave free reign to the army in investigating Malki's assassination and punishing those responsible. Hundreds of SSNP supporters were arrested and brought to trial, known SSNP officers were purged from the army and SSNP sympathizers were removed from their jobs in the state bureaucracy. Membership of the party was made illegal under Syrian law. Those arrested were tried in a military court over the summer of 1955: 140 of them were found guilty and variously sentenced to death, hard labour and imprisonment for crimes including conspiracy to murder, unlawful relations with foreign powers, undermining Syria's diplomatic relations and exposing the country to attack.

SSNP leaders fled the country for the relative safety of Lebanon, where they were able to regroup, but by this point the party had ceased to exist as a political force in Syria. The SSNP's implication in the Malki affair so thoroughly sullied the party's reputation that it would remain banned from Syria for the next fifty years. Only in 2005, as part of the so-called liberalizing reforms introduced by then President Bashar al-Assad, was the ban finally lifted.

The aftermath of the Malki affair accelerated the fragmentation of political life in Syria. The purging of the SSNP by leftist army officers, enthusiastically applauded by civilian Ba'thists and Communists, marked the start of frenzied competition for influence between the different parties and factions. This competition directly targeted the state bureaucracy: party loyalists in the civil service overtly appointed fellow members to the best jobs, transferred their rivals to other offices and had political opponents dismissed on spurious grounds. The National Party effectively declared war by displacing the People's Party from local government in Aleppo, its main support base: partisans of the two parties openly clashed in the streets. Both were ideologically divided: the People's Party was split between its pro-Iraq/pro-Western and pro-Egypt/neutralist wings, while Nationals argued incessantly among themselves over the direction of Syrian foreign policy and the wisdom of cooperating with the Syrian left. Amid these disputes, Health Minister Abd al-Wahib al-Ghanim took advantage of his position to turn the entire ministry into a fiefdom of the Ba'th Party, which already held considerable influence in the Ministry of Education and schools across the country. Yet divisions were also emerging between the two wings of the party, the dominant Arab Socialists of Hawrani and the original Ba'th of Aflaq and Bitar, who were concerned that Hawrani's close cooperation with Azm and the Communists could potentially cause Syria to drift too far from its neighbour Iraq, which, they noted, was still a fellow Arab country, despite being under the yoke of imperialism. Non-ideological independents in the parliament formed loose-knit coalitions – the United Constitutional Front and the Independent Liberals – which took their places alongside Azm's Democratic Bloc. For its part, the officer corps was divided between Ba'thist loyalists, leftist nationalists, independent cliques with few ideological convictions and the occasional pocket of reactionary, pro-Hashemite conservatives.

Intrigue between these forces made it an especially convoluted affair to elect a successor to President Atasi, who reached the end of his term in office that summer. The National Party's grand old man, Shukri al-Quwwatli, was hungry to be president, but his candidacy was impeded by his pro-Egypt position, his tarnished reputation and his bourgeois conservatism. The Ba'thists favoured Khalid al-Azm, who had developed a surprisingly strong working relationship with Hawrani. (As already noted, the odd combination of Azm's business interests and political alliance with the left had earned him the nickname 'Red Millionaire'.)

When members of parliament assembled to vote for the new president on 18 August 1955, Quwwatli won the required two-thirds majority – but only after the People's Party decided that they would prefer a National over a putative leftist as president, and several Azm voters reversed their support. Azm resigned his cabinet position in disgust. Quwwatli turned to Sa'id al-Ghazzi to form a new government, although even Ghazzi's safe hands were incapable of preventing the National Assembly and state institutions from being devoured by all these incompatible ideologies and petty personal rivalries.

As if these political shenanigans were not enough, it soon became apparent that Syria's post-war economic miracle had come to an end. In 1954, there had already been unprecedented labour unrest. In 1955, a drought led to the failure of the wheat harvest, and the cotton crop was ruined by locusts and pests. The government took drastic measures. It banned the import of goods competing with Syria products, raised customs tariffs in general and even prohibited Syrians from travelling to Lebanon for weekend shopping trips in a desperate attempt to prevent the country's foreign exchange reserves from being drained. The amicable cooperation with which businessmen, labour officials and state functionaries had previously sought to resolve industrial disputes was rocked by the growing confidence, and political consciousness, of Syrian workers amid worsening conditions. Labour unions became more militant, and the politicization of the government bureaucracy meant that state officials were more sympathetic to the arguments of workers than to those of business owners. By this point, Syria was entering a prolonged – and profound – economic crisis.

External political developments contributed to generalizing this sense of crisis. In September 1955, it was announced Abd al-Nasser had secured a deal for Czechoslovakia to deliver arms shipments to Egypt. This development was interpreted as bringing the neutralist camp closer to political alignment with the Soviet Union. The move was welcomed by the Syrian army and leftist politicians, who promptly went about negotiating a similar agreement for Czechoslovakia to supply Damascus with arms worth 6 million Syrian pounds (S£). This deal marked a rare concrete gain for the Soviet Union, which – despite Western fears – had little real influence in Syria beyond its ability to supply arms. Defence spending continued to be the largest item of Syrian state expenditure – 68 per cent of the national budget in 1955 – a proportion that the military justified with reference to the slow-burning conflict with Israel.[37] In a move symbolic of the rising stock of the Soviet Union, moreover, Syria refused to accept the 25 million Syrian pounds (S£) loan that had been approved by the International Bank of Reconstruction and Development (the World Bank) to upgrade its irrigation and infrastructure.

Abd al-Nasser's apparent swing towards the Soviet camp earned him new-found respect from the Ba'th Party, which sought to draw closer to Egypt to outmanoeuvre the pro-Iraq camp in Damascus. This opened the door for a mutual defence pact to be signed between Egypt and Syria in October 1955. The pact established a joint military command under the ultimate leadership of the Egyptian army chief, Abd al-Hakim Amr. Egypt and Syria wooed Jordan to sign up to the agreement – which would further isolate Iraq and the Baghdad Pact – but Jordanian King Hussein, who had been crowned in 1952, instead devised a compromise designed to placate nationalists within his own army without alienating Britain, Jordan's principal financial and military benefactor. These developments continue to alarm pro-Iraq elements in the Syrian political elite.

In an attempt to contain these tensions, in February 1956, President Quwwatli invoked the threat of Israel to call for a National Pact that would bring détente to the fractious parties. Yet even this failed to prevent further deterioration. Students clashed with police in Damascus, landlords and peasants clashed in Hama, resignations rained down and the Ghazzi government fell. In the new government formed by Asali that June, the Ba'th Party took the two most important positions – foreign minister and minister of national economy – reflecting the new weight of the Syrian left. This development set the stage for a further push towards coordination, perhaps even federation, with Egypt and towards stronger links with the Soviet bloc. Conservative forces rallied in response. 'Red Millionaire' Khalid al-Azm was ousted from his own parliamentary bloc of independents, a new rightist coalition was formed and intrigue in the army blocked the appointment of a leftist chief of staff to replace Shawkat Shuqayr.

By mid-1956, the political unity that had been so striking in Syria at independence had been entirely shattered. Debates about social reform, economic development, Arab relations and the Cold War had become so polarized that rational argument, or even political pragmatism, looked unable to build bridges between the two camps. The fragmentation was complete; the centre could hardly hold. Little over a year later, Syria would cease to exist.

Conspiracies upon conspiracies

Two events especially helped the Syrian left complete its political takeover: the Suez Crisis and the discovery of plans for a pro-Iraq coup. In July 1956, the United States withdrew its offer of aid for Egypt to construct a major dam at Aswan. Abd al-Nasser responded by nationalizing the British- and French-owned Suez Canal, with compensation for the confiscated shares. This act of defiance against the former colonizers consolidated Abd al-Nasser's position as the hero of progressive forces in the Arab world. The Syrian government immediately promised Egypt its full support.

In October 1956, Britain, France and Israel launched a coordinated military attack against Egypt and invaded the Sinai. Syria went on high alert. President Quwwatli flew to Moscow to cement further arms deals and promises of Soviet support, and a few days later Iraq's oil pipeline across Syria was sabotaged, cutting off a vital source of revenue for Baghdad and sending a not-too-subtle message to Iraq's British puppet masters. The Syrian army declared martial law and mobilized its forces in anticipation of invading Israel on 30 November in support of Egypt. In the event, Cairo signalled the Syrians should stand down in anticipation of Egypt's imminent withdrawal from the Sinai as the invasion advanced.

The widespread outrage at the tripartite attack against Egypt heightened anti-Western and anti-Iraq sentiment and moved Syria into even warmer relations with the Soviet Union, following a number of trade agreements, parliamentary visits and cultural exchanges over the previous couple of years. The impact of the Suez Crisis also reverberated across Syria's domestic politics. At the peak of the tension, Syria's chief of military intelligence,

Abd al-Hamid Sarraj, announced the discovery of a far-reaching and elaborate conspiracy to overthrow the Syrian government. Details of the plot became public knowledge when a revolution overthrew the Iraqi monarchy in 1958, revealing the implication of Britain and the United States in the affair, but at the time Iraq was identified as the primary sponsor of the conspiracy. Because pro-Iraq civilian politicians had become so marginalized in Syria, Baghdad had apparently adopted a more direct approach by rallying disgruntled former members of the Syrian armed forces.

The core of the conspiracy was formed of SSNP members such as Ghassan Jadid, who had been forced to flee Syria by the persecution that had followed the Malki affair the previous year, in addition to officers who had revolved too closely in the orbits of former dictators Za'im, Hinnawi and Shishakli to escape unscathed after their fall. The conspirators included Salah al-Shishakli, who persuaded his brother Adib to join their meetings in Lebanon over the summer of 1956. Adib al-Shishakli was repelled by SSNP preparations to assemble hit squads to assassinate prominent Syrian leftists such as Hawrani, Azm and Bakdash: targeted political violence was a step too far even for this deposed military ruler. Beirut was full of political exiles such as these. 'So frequent were the purges in Syria which followed the political upheavals from 1949 to 1955,' historian Patrick Seale observes, 'that there were sometimes said to be more officers outside the Syrian army than inside it.'[38]

The conspirators developed ties with British, American and Iraqi representatives in Lebanon, who coordinated support for their activities through the Iraqi military attaché in Beirut. The group also forged ties with pro-Iraq politicians in Syria, who they intended would lead the government after the coup they were planning. They funnelled Iraqi arms and funds to their supporters inside the country while training an SSNP paramilitary force in Lebanon ready to send into action in Syria.[39]

Syrian military intelligence was tipped off about the plot by a botched arms delivery from Iraq to Syria's Jabal al-Duruz. Details of the conspiracy were announced on Damascus radio, and formal charges brought against forty-seven individuals who had been implicated in the plot. Their number included not only the former officers who had been the ringleaders in Lebanon, but also prominent pro-Iraq notables and politicians inside Syria.[40] The cases against the accused were heard in a military court in Damascus between 8 January and 26 February 1956 and earned the dubious distinction of being the largest political trial that Syria had witnessed.

The atmosphere of the proceedings was dark and repressive. Military police guarded the court with sub-machine guns, while the judge, Colonel Afif al-Bizri, dismissively remarked that the accused would soon hang from the neck in al-Merjeh Square in Damascus.[41] Once the defendants were, almost inevitably, found guilty, the severity of the punishments handed down to them was unprecedented. The death penalty was pronounced against twelve of the accused, while others were sentenced to decades of hard labour. Only Faydi al-Atasi was acquitted of the charges. Adnan al-Atasi – the son of former President Hashim al-Atasi, no less – was one of the twelve facing execution. Adnan al-Atasi's sentence was hugely symbolic: even Shishakli had felt powerless to act against the prestigious and powerful Atasi family during his campaigns of political repression only a few years earlier. Syria's national security machinery was becoming more powerful – and even less beholden to maintaining old social taboos.

Ba'th Party co-founder Michel Aflaq captured the social significance of the executions when he wrote in his party's newspaper that the conspiracy had implicated not just individuals, but an entire 'class driven to treachery in defence of its interests'.[42] At least some of the defendants also recognized the class dimension of the trials. 'There are dark conspiracies afoot in Damascus today,' declared the lawyer Munir al-Ajlani when making a spirited but long-winded case for the defence. 'They seek to purge the elite which until very recently held [Syria's] sound democratic structure safe from collapse.'[43] The conspiracy trials of 1957 not only marked the left's usurpation of the traditional elite from political power, it also sounded the opening salvo in a decade-long campaign to eradicate the upper-class elite from Syrian society.

A cabinet reshuffle spurred by the trials removed conservatives from the government and replaced them with yet more leftists. Shifting diplomatic winds nevertheless revived the fortunes of the pro-Western monarchists. Saudi Arabia had previously stood alongside Egypt in the neutralist camp, but in early 1957 King Ibn Sa'ud seemed to be moving towards the West. This change presented a window of opportunity for anti-left forces to ally themselves with figures such as Quwwatli and Asali, who had felt their earlier cooperation with the left had gone too far.

Working with the chief of staff and a group of right-wing officers, this conservative grouping attempted to transfer nationalist officers to lesser positions in the armed forces, out of concern they might carry out a coup to oppose ongoing efforts to commute the death sentences issued to pro-Iraq politicians in the conspiracy trials. However, the politicization of the army was now so widespread that a sizeable number of officers refused to obey these administrative orders, prompting what was known at the time at the Qatana Mutiny, in reference to the army base outside Damascus where the leftist refuseniks were concentrated.[44]

As Khalid al-Azm had been given control of the Ministry of National Defence in the recent reshuffle, the leftists retaliated with an order dismissing the chief of staff from his position. To prevent a constitutional crisis, President Quwwatli postponed appending his signature to Azm's decree by promptly declaring he had been taken sick. By this point, it became clear that not only had civilian politics become irrevocably polarized, but so had the armed forces. While just a few years earlier the cohesion of the officer corps had been sufficiently tight to support its concerted efforts to rule in the place of civilian politicians, by the late 1950s, the last vestiges of the military chain of command had been eroded. 'The rebellion of the Qatana base and the rejection of direct orders went unpunished by military law,' noted Abu Assaf, military commander of the Damascus region. 'The military bases at Dar'a and Suwaida had declared their support for the chief of staff, but we weren't sure about other bases elsewhere in the country. It was anarchy.'[45] Rampant factionalism had replaced military professionalism.

From the spring of 1957, Syria's political fragmentation was acute. Anti-left and radical forces competed for seats in parliamentary by-elections in a fetid atmosphere of suspicion and mutual distrust. Rumours of conspiracies sponsored by foreign powers were abundant, providing the army with few grounds to rescind the martial law it had imposed in November. Hostilities between rival camps inside the armed forces led to a fresh outbreak of clandestine warfare fought with bureaucratic weapons such as appointments, transfers and unwanted obligatory overseas training missions. Leftist and nationalist elements formed a secret Revolutionary Command Council, modelled on Abd al-Nasser's own organization, intended to steer Syria in the right direction. Conflict in the National Assembly, meanwhile, adopted the form of a bitter contestation over the annual budget, which masked the country's worsening economic situation.

A flurry of developments hinted at the international struggle secretly waged for Syria beneath the surface of everyday life. In July, Damascus announced that a British-embassy-sponsored spy ring had been uncovered. In August, it announced that a US-sponsored coup plot had been foiled, prompting Damascus and Washington to expel one another's diplomats. The Syrian foreign minister, Ba'thist Salah al-Din al-Bitar, attacked the US Eisenhower Doctrine, which sought to keep the Middle East a communist-free zone. Colonel Afif al-Bizri – the officer who had presided over the pro-Iraq conspiracy trials and a noted Communist – was appointed chief of staff. Bizri oversaw a final wave of purges to root out any remaining anti-left officers. Similar purges of the civilian bureaucracy and the police force quickly followed. Because of the prominence of Syrian Communist leader Khalid Bakdash, Khalid al-Azm's vocal attacks on the pro-Western turn of Jordan and Saudi Arabia, and increasing Soviet economic and military aid to Syria, the United States genuinely yet mistakenly feared an imminent communist takeover. From the perspective of policy planners in the Pentagon, Syria looked poised to fall to the wrong side of the Cold War.

Inside Syria, things looked quite different. Admittedly, support for Bakdash's Communist Party had surged during the mid-1950s, but it was not necessarily the case that the crowds who joined its demonstrations were card-carrying members. However, the Communists' growing popularity with the public, not to mention its rising influence in the army, had begun to alarm its ostensible allies in the Ba'th Party. The theoreticians of the party had always kept their distance from Marxist ideology; the party's famous tripartite slogan placed 'socialism' in a position tertiary to the far more important political demands of 'unity' and 'freedom'. Aflaq and Bitar had grown uneasy with Hawrani's energetic cooperation with Azm and the Communists, which threatened to compete with the Ba'th for the support of peasants and workers.

The frenzy of the 1957 US–Syria crisis exacerbated the concerns of the Ba'th co-founders that their party might soon be outshone by the rising star of Bakdash's Communists. These fears focused on the looming prospect of local elections that had originally been scheduled for 18 November, but which the Ba'th successfully fought to postpone after winning tactical support from the conservative National and People's parties. Yet this delay did little to eliminate the Communist threat to the Ba'th Party. Given that there were no other parties in Syria that might be viable political partners, Aflaq and his supporters looked outside Syria to ensure the survival of the party. The only political currents that seemed capable of resisting the allure of Communism at this time were the pro-Western alliance – adherence to which would have betrayed the neutralist and anti-imperialist founding principles of Ba'thism – and the towering figure of Egypt's charismatic hero of the Suez Crisis, Gamal Abd al-Nasser. Only Egypt, it seemed, could save Syria – and the Ba'th – from the alliance of 'Red Millionaire' Khalid al-Azm and the Communist Khalid Bakdash.

On 9 December, Aflaq announced that the Ba'th would table a parliamentary bill for the political federation of Syria and Egypt. Coming after months of tempestuous foreign relations, the idea of union under the strong leadership of Abd al-Nasser, now at the height of his popularity across the Arab world, promised a more secure future for Syria's independence. Conservatives and Communists alike could do little to stem the popular appeal of Aflaq's proposal, which seemed to them just as unrealistic and unlikely to gain traction as previous unfulfilled plans for Arab unity. Yet their analysis reckoned without the input of one further factor: the army.

In early January 1958, the intensity of political factionalism in the army finally reached the point where two senior officers fired their weapons against each other. This incident broke the unspoken taboo against the use of violence within the armed forces, which had remained largely intact despite all the tensions of the previous decade. Sensing that the officer corps was on the brink of collapse, senior army commanders sought to reaffirm the structure of military hierarchy by appealing for arbitration from Abd al-Nasser, who was still – according to the 1955 pact between the two countries – the ultimate commander of the joint Syrian–Egyptian defence force.

On 12 January 1958, a delegation of senior Syrian officers flew to Cairo and met personally with Abd al-Nasser. Taken by surprise at this initiative, Foreign Minister Bitar joined them several days later. Bitar emerged on 21 January and declared that agreement had been reached for a full union between Egypt and Syria. This announcement was unexpected: the Ba'thists had intended a limited federal union, not the merger of two countries into one. Abd al-Nasser, it seemed, had other plans. Back in Damascus, faced with the potential threat of an army coup in favour of union with Egypt, the Syrian government had little choice but to accept this fait accompli as a desperate, last-ditch measure to prevent implosion. On 1 February 1958, the Syrian Republic and the Republic of Egypt ceased to exist: the United Arab Republic was born.

8

Unity, Freedom, Socialism, 1958–1970

Gamal Abd al-Nasser was not the most obvious candidate to be ruler of Syria. To begin with, Egypt had largely been insulated from the Arab nationalist movements that had swept *Bilad al-Sham* in the nineteenth and twentieth centuries. Egyptians were Arabic-speaking, but – much like their Syrian counterparts during the Ottoman Empire – did not necessarily consider themselves as 'Arab', a term historically reserved for those Bedouin tribes who traced their lineage to the Arabian Peninsula. The legacies of Mehmed Ali and the British occupation in 1882, moreover, had set Egypt down a different historical trajectory from a Levant shaped by the experiences of the Tanzimat and the League of Nations' mandates system. The Egyptian struggle for independence had centred on liberating Egypt as a national unit, often identified by Cairo's elites and intellectuals by its unique Pharaonic heritage rather than as part of the wider Arab or Islamic world.[1]

Sociologically too there were considerable differences. Apart from its Coptic Christian minority, Egyptian society lacked the religious and ethnic diversity of the Levant. Naturally, within Egypt there were local distinctions between the various densely populated areas strung along the banks of the Nile and its distributaries through the Delta. But the relative ease of transport afforded by Egypt's great river meant that these communities had not experienced as much isolation as settlements scattered across the valleys, mountains and plains of Syria. In consequence, Egyptian society had not developed the hyper-localized and highly differentiated expressions of identity, culture and sect that characterized *Bilad al-Sham*.[2] The colossal British military presence in Egypt during the Second World War had directly employed more than 200,000 workers at its peak in 1943. After the war ended, Egypt had rapidly built a vast public sector to contain the risk of destabilization posed by such mass unemployment.[3] Egypt was a giant, with some 26 million inhabitants by the late 1950s, compared to just 4 million Syrians. Cairo was already a megacity, three times the size of Damascus and Aleppo combined. Politically, Cairo dominated its hinterland in a way that cities found impossible to replicate in the rebellious rural lands of the Levant. In many respects, Egypt and Syria were worlds apart.

Despite these differences, over the 1940s and 1950s Egypt had come to self-consciously identify itself as an Arab country by virtue of language, history and culture. The foundations for this transition were already in place. The Egyptian popular classes found the Pharaonic pretensions of the elite alien to their own day-to-day experiences, which were mostly grounded in Islam and its reverence for the Classical Arabic language used in religious learning. This sentiment was shared by the emerging professional classes – teachers, doctors, lawyers and engineers – whose growing numbers were driven by a rapid expansion of schooling in the interwar years. Political refugees from the lands of Syria had made their homes in the safety of Cairo and Alexandria since the late Ottoman Empire; in the 1920s and 1930s, Egypt continued to act as a sanctuary for Syrian dissidents who could not stomach the policy of so-called honourable cooperation with their country's French rulers, as well as for radicals who had fled Palestine, Tunisia and other parts of the occupied Arab world. These activists brought news of the wider Arab struggle to a more literate, and increasingly politicized, generation of Egyptian youth. The question of Palestine was crucial in galvanizing Egyptians to reorient themselves towards the Arab world, especially in the wake of the 1936–39 Palestinian revolt and the abysmal failure of the Egyptian monarchy to adequately prepare the country's army for success in the 1948 war with Israel.[4] Throughout the interwar years, business people, intellectuals and students travelled between Egypt and the Levant more frequently than ever before, allowing them to recognize the common features of their shared cultural background.

In the east, intellectuals who rejected the colonial division of the Arab world had, in the 1940s, begun to recognize that Egypt had a special role to play in liberation. One of Syria's most prominent Arab nationalists, Sati' al-Husri, whose work had been a major influence on the founders of the Ba'th Party, explained this line of thinking: 'Nature has endowed Egypt with all the attributes and advantages that behoves it to take on the duty of leadership in reviving Arab nationalism. It is situated in the centre of the Arab world, between its African and Asian parts. It is the biggest of the fragments that the Arab nation has been divided into [. . .] and most exposed to modern global civilization. It has become the most important cultural centre in the Arab world, it is richer than all the Arab countries combined, it is the most seasoned in the structures of the modern state, most powerful in the literary arts and most elevated in eloquence.'[5] As Gamal Abd al-Nasser came to lead the charge against Western hegemony in the Middle East, political progressives in Syria thought the time propitious to bring the two countries into alignment. For his part, Abd al-Nasser came to realize that Egypt's sheer weight could make it a powerful force in regional geopolitics. Yet, as Abd al-Nasser harnessed Egypt's Arab realignment for geopolitical advantage, this very decision drew Egypt into what would be one of its worst foreign policy blunders: the disastrous experiment at union with Syria.

The popularity of Abd al-Nasser

Gamal Abd al-Nasser came to power in 1952 after the Free Officers' coup that abolished the discredited monarchy. His main concern was to liberate Egypt fully from colonialism. Egypt's independence had been gained in 1922 only at the price of an ongoing British military presence and continuous meddling in Egyptian politics – a state of affairs that the new generation of Egyptian nationalists found intolerable. As Abd al-Nasser's drive for independence brought him into open confrontation with the former colonial powers of the region, he turned to the wider Arab world for help. Unlike previous Arab leaders, he appealed directly to the masses. A dynamic, charismatic character, Abd al-Nasser gave dazzling speeches that wove plain words into beguiling tapestries of rhetoric. He proclaimed the greatness of ordinary Egyptians, regaled his listeners with promises to recapture the glories of the past and tempered his grandiloquence with humorous asides in colloquial Arabic. Egyptian peasants had never heard anything like it.

Lebanese academic Ilya Harik described how, during his fieldwork in rural Egypt, villagers would gather around the radio for broadcasts by Abd al-Nasser 'listening as if at a seance. Nasser took them into his confidence, or seemed to do so, by explaining affairs of state in uncomplicated language. He discussed governmental business, how it would affect them, and why. He congratulated himself for what he had done for them, called on their patience for hardships that had to be endured, and lectured them on socialism. The villagers were entertained, moderately enlightened, and above all, flattered by his special consideration of them.'[6] He sounded like a man of the people.

Abd al-Nasser's voice reverberated across the Arab world, amplified by the power of the leading Egyptian radio station, *Sawt al-'Arab* ('Voice of the Arabs'), a giant of the transnational Arab broadcast media unmatched by any other channel. Egypt was already the leading producer of Arab radio, cinema and music:[7] Egyptian film stars and singers were unparalleled in their fame across the region. Abd al-Nasser was quick to harness the potential of this new popular culture. Stars such as Umm Kulthoum and Leila Murad lent their extraordinary voices to patriotic ballads,[8] while composer Muhammad Abd al-Wahhab penned a song with 'O Gamal! O Gamal' as its catchy chorus. By associating his personality with the soft power of Egyptian pop culture, Abd al-Nasser projected his iconic image beyond state borders in a way that no Arab leader had done before. His strategic intention was to rally to his cause publics across the Arab world, who would then exert pressure on their leaders to support his policy of Cold War neutralism rather than taking pro-Western positions. Abd al-Nasser's campaign was, if anything, too successful. The outpouring of popular acclaim that greeted him was so torrential that he could not withstand the pressure to live up to his reputation as a great leader not just of Egypt, but of the Arab nation as a whole. Perhaps against his better judgement – and certainly against the judgement of Egyptian officials and political advisors – he could not reject the Syrian plea for unification.[9] After being assured by the 1958 Syrian delegation to Cairo that their government, military and people were all in favour,[10] he felt he had little choice but to agree to the union of Egypt and Syria.

Abd al-Nasser's acceptance came with conditions: he insisted that both countries should hold a referendum on the question of unification. All party politics should halt, all political parties should disband themselves and all army involvement in politics should cease. The new state would be a presidential republic, meaning that its ministers would be appointed directly by the president rather than by the prime minister. Although taken aback by these demands, Syrian politicians readily agreed. Only Khalid al-Azm voiced any concern, arguing that these changes would undermine Syria's political pluralism and constitutional tradition.[11] Azm's objections were rejected by the officers and other parliamentarians. 'The tide of unity is rising,' observed intelligence chief Abd al-Hamid Sarraj, an ardent enthusiast of union, 'and no one can stop it!' His concerns ignored, Azm bowed to the inevitable.[12]

The United Arab Republic (UAR) was officially born on 1 February 1958: it had one capital, one flag and one president. Later that month, a referendum revealed resounding public support for the union: 99.99 per cent in Egypt; 99.98 per cent in Syria. ('With the army supervising the ballot box,' Azm wryly observed, 'there was only ever going to be one result.')[13] As the Syrian presidency had been abolished along with the Syrian Republic, Shukri al-Quwwatli found himself out of a job. To soothe Quwwatli's offended ego, Abd al-Nasser granted him the honorific title of First Arab Citizen.

'You don't know what you're getting into, Mr President,' Quwwatli told Abd al-Nasser after the unification. 'You have taken on a people who all think themselves politicians, fifty per cent of them think they're leaders, twenty-five per cent of them think they're prophets, and at least ten per cent of them think they're divine. Among this people you've taken on are some who worship God, some who worship fire, some who worship Satan and some who worship *@?*!*!'[14] Abd al-Nasser laughed, and asked Quwwatli why he had not said all that before they signed the treaty.

In celebration of the historic occasion, Abd al-Nasser embarked on a three-week tour of what was now known as the Northern Province of the UAR. It was his first visit to Syria. From Damascus and Aleppo to the villages of Idlib, Latakia and Suwayda, vast crowds excitedly descended to catch a glimpse of their great hero. Abd al-Nasser speeches were received as enthusiastically as they had been in Egypt: even if the president of the UAR occasionally struggled to understand Syrian dialects, the Syrian public loved him.[15] On one day of his visit, Abd al-Nasser's motor vehicle was swarmed by so many joyous supporters that it was forced to slow to a crawl, taking two hours to cover the two miles between Quwwatli's home in the suburb of Mezzeh and the centre of Damascus.

The United Arab Republic introduced major changes to Syrian political life. *Eid al-Jala'*, the public holiday celebrating Syrian independence, was abolished and replaced by an annual holiday commemorating the unity referendum. The Syrian flag was taken down and the UAR flag hoisted in its place: the new flag had three stripes in red, white and black, with twin green stars representing the two constituent provinces of the republic. A new constitution was promulgated that gave sweeping powers to the presidency – a significant change for Syria, where politicians had been careful to curtail the power of the executive after previous episodes with Quwwatli and Shishakli. A central cabinet of ministers was formed to govern such portfolios as foreign affairs, defence and education that affected the whole of the UAR; each of the two regions also had its own sub-cabinet to oversee locally administered functions such as finance, agriculture and justice.

In advance of Abd al-Nasser's deadline, Syria's political parties voluntarily liquidated themselves – apart from the Communists, who went underground. Their leader, Khalid Bakdash, retreated to Moscow for safety. 'Red Millionaire' Khalid al-Azm resigned his position and retired from politics. Chief of Staff Bizri, sympathetic to the Communists, was relieved of his duties, despite having been instrumental in bringing about the union. Abd al-Nasser gave more leeway to the Ba'thists and appointed two of their leaders to high positions: Hawrani was made vice president and Bitar a minister in the central government. The Ba'thists interpreted these appointments as recognition that they would play a leading role in shaping the ideological agenda of the UAR government; the Egyptian leader, they had concluded, was a man of action who lacked a systemic political programme. Ever the teacher, Michel Aflaq thought that Abd al-Nasser would be the front man and that the Ba'thists would school him in ideology behind the scenes. 'Abd al-Nasser's activity did not follow a philosophical principle,' said Aflaq in a surprisingly unguarded newspaper interview soon after the declaration of the union. 'It has drawn strength from the physical forces which support it [...] Abd al-Nasser's activity [...] has responded in short to a movement begun by the Ba'th.'[16] The party clearly believed it would exercise influence in the UAR, like some kind of ideological *éminence grise*.

It soon became clear that Abd al-Nasser had little intention of permitting Syrians, Ba'thist or not, to play a significant role in government. Mere months into the UAR, there was a mounting sense that Syria was being subjected to a policy of involuntary Egyptianization. Mahmud Riyad, the former Egyptian ambassador in Damascus, was appointed the president's special counsellor for the northern region. Speaking as the voice of Abd al-Nasser, Riyad wielded influence in the country that vastly outweighed that of the Syrian regional government. Critics pointed out that French colonialists had also run Syria using 'counsellors', and Riyad was soon sarcastically referred to as Egypt's 'high commissioner'.[17] Syrian ministers found that their official positions conveyed no real authority. Bashir al-Azma, a technocrat appointed minister for health in the central cabinet, relocated to the distant UAR capital to discover he had no responsibilities, no power and no work. He was baffled by the situation. 'After months living in Cairo,' Azma said, 'because of being ignored and kept idle, the central ministers began to whisper and complain. "What do they want from us?" the ministers wondered. "What do they want with us?!"'[18] Azma busied himself with crosswords, bowling and meeting friends at the exclusive Gezira Sporting Club.

Syria's vibrant press was strictly censored, and numerous newspapers closed. The independent Chamber of Agriculture was disbanded and a new more pliable chamber established that was firmly under state control. Syrian army officers were reassigned to Egypt and replaced with Egyptian officers, while Egyptian teachers, civil servants and technical experts were in turn sent to work in the Northern Province.[19] The head of Syrian intelligence, Abd al-Hamid Sarraj, was a staunch supporter of the union and entrusted with command of a newly formed security agency, *al-Maktab al-Khass* (the Special Bureau), attached to the Ministry of the Interior.[20] Sarraj excelled in his job and developed a far-reaching apparatus of political repression that was indispensable to what was becoming a highly authoritarian regime.[21] While Abd al-Nasser himself remained beloved by ordinary people, Syrians chafed under the restrictions of the more centralized – and more ruthlessly authoritarian – style of government imported from Egypt.

As in Egypt, so in Syria: economic unification and its discontents

After adopting an overarching political structure for the two provinces, in autumn 1958 Abd al-Nasser turned his attention towards the economic integration of the UAR. The priority was to restructure the northern region in preparation for full convergence. In September, he announced an ambitious programme of land reform for the Syrian province. The scale of this new endeavour was unprecedented. Decree 161 of 1958 introduced ceilings on individual ownership of agricultural land: a maximum of 80 hectares (equivalent to 198 acres) of irrigated land or 300 hectares (741 acres) of rain-fed land. The law allowed some land in excess of this ceiling to be gifted to wives and children, but no more than 40 hectares (99 acres) of irrigated or 160 hectares (395 acres) of rain-fed land. Any other landholdings above this limit would be expropriated by the state, with compensation issued to the owners in the form of government bonds. Plots of the expropriated land would be distributed to landless peasants, who would receive 8 hectares (20 acres) of irrigated or 30 hectares (74 acres) of rain-fed land. (The land was not given out for free: the peasant was intended to pay compensation to the original owner, plus 10 per cent to cover the government's administrative costs, over the course of forty years.)[22] Almost overnight, the state had effectively issued compulsory purchase orders for over 1.5 million hectares (3.7 million acres) of land that the richest echelons of Syrian society had taken decades to appropriate for themselves.

The new law affected almost 60 per cent of all Syrian agricultural land. Ba'thist Minister of Agriculture Mustafa Hamdoun applied the reforms with great relish, provoking furious accusations that he was using the law to settle old political scores.[23] Many of the country's most established wealthy lineages were among the 3,240 landowners whose holdings were impacted, among them the Mudarris, Rifa'i and Kikhya families of Aleppo; the Barzani, Azm and Kaylani families of Hama; and the Atasi family of Homs. Yet strikingly, the list of those impacted was not confined to the traditional elite. The agricultural expansion in the Jazira meant that entrepreneurs and even tribal shaykhs now featured prominently on the list of Syria's largest landowners. Of the affected landowners, 60 per cent were based in the Euphrates region and the Jazira, where estates were especially large. A thousand landowners – nearly a third of the total – were affected in the governorate of Hassakeh alone,[24] compared to just eleven landowners in Jabal al-Arab, twenty-seven in Der'a and fifty-one in Latakia, where large landholdings were rarer (see Table 1).

TABLE I. DISTRIBUTION OF LAND IN SYRIA BEFORE AGRARIAN REFORM (1955)[25]

REGION	SMALL LANDHOLDINGS (0-10 HECTARES)	MEDIUM LANDHOLDINGS (10-100 HECTARES)	LARGE LANDHOLDINGS (100+ HECTARES)
Damascus	18%	43%	36%
Hawran	46%	45%	6%
Jabal al-Arab	30%	58%	12%
Homs	3%	24%	13%
Hama	1%	27%	35%
Latakia	32%	30%	37%
Aleppo	12%	32%	36%
Euphrates	15%	46%	39%
Jazira	6%	52%	31%

These radical changes to land ownership were intended to bring Syria into harmony with the southern province of the UAR. A similar programme had been implemented there in 1952, successfully disempowering Egypt's old landed elite and rallying popular support for the Free Officers. Indeed, so closely was Syria's Agrarian Reform Law agricultural reform modelled on the Egyptian precedent that it specified identical ceilings for land ownership, without considering the very different climate and conditions in each of the two provinces. Agricultural productivity in the fertile farmlands of the Nile Delta was notably much greater than in Syria: it was possible to grow much more from much less land. In the Syrian Jazira and Euphrates, in contrast, successful agriculture needed intensive investment in machinery and irrigation that proved profitable only when cultivation was undertaken on a large scale. North-east Syria was already suffering from severe drought, but even in normal times the reduced land ceilings would now make it all but impossible to farm there with any profitability. The success of the reforms was further constrained by patterns of population density. The population of north-eastern Syria was so low that there were not even enough landless peasants to take up all the expropriated land, while the more densely inhabited heartlands had so many eligible peasants that there was insufficient land to go around. Landowners and merchants strongly protested the reforms, which they blamed on Ba'thist zeal for class conflict, and sought to evade or sabotage their implementation. Land reform soured any enthusiasm they may have felt for the project of union. In consequence, the success of the reforms was deeply compromised. Although 15,000 peasant families benefitted from the programme, by 1961 the state had distributed a mere 22 per cent of the farmland it had confiscated.[26]

In anticipation of problems that might arise from the removal of large landowners who had previously provided peasants with credit, fertilizer and other inputs, the Agrarian Reform Law created a nationwide system of Agricultural Cooperatives to fill the vacuum and gave the Agricultural Bank a substantial injection of capital, as well as explicit instructions to lend to the cooperatives and small farmers. Another law regulated agricultural labour relations: sharecroppers and tenant farmers were granted greater security in their contracts, and agricultural workers were granted access to wage tribunals and, for the first time, given the same rights to join trade unions as enjoyed by industrial workers.[27] This legislation seriously curtailed the arbitrary power that the great families of landowners had wielded over peasants' lives, and marked a milestone in the struggle for peasants' rights in Syria.[28] In a further strike against the traditional elites, the UAR abolished the law that had exempted the country's tribes from Syrian judicial authority and allowed them to obey their own customary law. Since the power of tribal chiefs was embedded within tribal law, officially bringing the tribes into the legal jurisdiction of the state came as a blow to the shaykhs' status and prestige, at the same time as their recently acquired agricultural estates were being confiscated for redistribution. These measures undermined the power of the shaykhs before they could coalesce into a new rural elite in its own right.

After land reform, the second stage of economic convergence was to introduce free trade, freedom of movement, and a single currency in the two regions of the UAR. For the Syrian business elite, these proposals were extremely worrying. Some were anxious about immigration: the lower population, higher wages and higher standard of living in the Northern Province might provoke a wave of poor migrants from Egypt that Syria would find impossible to absorb. Others were concerned that speculators might move capital between the two regions in search of quick profits, risking imbalances that would compromise economic stability.[29] Syrian liberals were wary that what they considered to be their country's innate spirit of entrepreneurialism would be crushed by the burdensome regulation of the Egyptian model.

'Our people are not sufficiently mature for the harsh discipline needed for a nationalized or state-led economy to succeed, especially in pecuniary affairs,' noted Dr Awad Barakat, one of the architects of Syria's post-independence monetary policy. 'The strength and dynamism of our people principally lies in their spirit of initiative and freedom of action, two qualities that can neither survive nor prosper in a regime of administrative hassles, economic restrictions, regulations and red tape.'[30] The business elite was similarly cautious about a single currency and debated whether such a measure should be implemented in the UAR. One advocate argued that Egypt and Syria could successfully adopt a single currency, just as Germany and Austria had, although an official at the Syrian Central Bank pointed out that this particular instance of monetary unity was the product of Nazi military annexation.[31] The comparison did not bode well for Syria's future.

Disregarding the reservations of the Northern Province's economic elite, Abd al-Nasser forged ahead with plans for convergence. Trade tariffs between the two regions were almost entirely abolished, creating a single market.[32] Plans were announced for a single currency, the Arab dinar, to replace the Syrian and Egyptian pounds. In October 1958, the minister of economy declared that full economic and monetary integration would be achieved within the next nine months.

In response, the Syrian business community panicked. They pulled their capital out of Syria and buried it deep in the vaults of financial institutions in Lebanon, for the most part, which had adopted Swiss-style laws on banking secrecy just two years earlier. The Syrian pound went into freefall, losing 40 per cent of its value. The government accused speculators of manufacturing a currency crisis to make profits, but could do little to prevent capital fleeing the country. The 'current instability . . . in Syria is dominated by a fear psychosis,' opined the business newspaper *Le Commerce du Levant*. 'Nobody seems to have any trust in the methods applied by the UAR government.'[33] Two delegations of Syrian businessmen travelled to Cairo to protest against the land expropriations and economic integration. While Abd al-Nasser refused even to consider rescinding the land reform, the severity of the situation persuaded him to slow the rush to convergence, delay the introduction of a single currency and address some of the business community's concerns.

In November, the government announced a five-year industrial plan for the Northern Province that would create 100,000 new jobs. In January 1959, a three-person Higher Ministerial Committee (with Hawrani its sole Syrian member) was created to accelerate economic development in the Northern Province. In a fanfare of publicity, the committee quickly consulted Syrian officials and interest groups before announcing a series of projects to improve roads, railways, cotton production, construction and irrigation. Many of these projects would have looked suspiciously familiar to anyone who had read the earlier 1955 World Bank report on Syria, which had made similar prescriptions; however, very few of them would be implemented before the collapse of the UAR in 1961. Following the precedent of post-war Egypt, meanwhile, the state continued its expansion into the Syrian economy, imposing further import restrictions, inserting itself into cotton cultivation and even launching new industrial projects.

In addition to responding to concerns of the Syrian business community, the announcement of new projects was also intended to shore up the progressive credentials of the UAR against the challenge of communism, which was unexpectedly on the rise in Iraq. Under King Faysal II, the domestic popularity of the Hashemite Kingdom of Iraq had plummeted owing to its pro-British orientation – even more of a liability after the Suez Crisis – and its failure to deliver material progress. In July 1958, a clique of Iraqi officers led a coup that overthrew the conservative monarchy, leading to public jubilation on the streets of Baghdad. Although Iraqi Ba'thists and Nasserists began to agitate for the country to join the UAR, the considerably more numerous and better organized Iraqi Communist Party opposed a union that would inevitably lead to its disbandment. Iraq's 1958 revolution may have signalled the rising tide of progressive politics in the Middle East, but it also marked the onset of intense competition between communists and Arab leftist-nationalists.

In Syria, the head of the Special Bureau intelligence agency, Abd al-Hamid Sarraj, masterminded a campaign of repression against the underground Communist Party in the Northern Province – a campaign of such ruthlessness that he earned himself the sobriquet of 'Sultan' Abd al-Hamid, a reference to the despotism of the former Ottoman ruler whose iron fist had contributed to the collapse of the empire in the lands of Syria.[34] Communists were mercilessly purged from the military, the bureaucracy and labour unions, leaving a gap that Ba'th Party members were quick to fill. So successful was the campaign of arrests, torture and intimidation against the Communists that the party never recovered from the trauma and permanently lost its grassroots foothold in Syria. Abd al-Nasser came to recognize Sarraj as an indispensable pillar of the UAR regime.

As 1959 progressed, the Syrian business elite continued to evade the new regulations to the best of their ability. In response, Abd al-Nasser tightened the clamps a little, but still gave businessmen room to breathe – a luxury Sarraj had not afforded to the Communists. The lavish remunerations customarily paid to board directors had already been restricted; now, Abd al-Nasser lowered the number of boards that directors could serve on, further disrupting the tight-knit, interwoven family networks that monopolized corporate Syria. In May, Abd al-Nasser reformed the chambers of commerce and ended their input into economic policy-making. In October, he made compliance with economic regulations a matter of national security: economic 'crimes' such as smuggling, hiding or failing to declare profits, or illegally dealing in foreign currency were to be judged by a new system of state security courts, overseen by the military.[35] The same month, he dispatched his right-hand man, Field Marshal Abd al-Hakim 'Amr, to Damascus on a mission to stabilize political and economic life in the Northern Province. Field Marshal Amr was granted full authority to handle Syrian affairs as he saw fit; Syrian ministers were to answer directly to him. After consulting with the businessmen, Amr agreed to relax import restrictions. He also responded positively to the army's representations about pay and transfers, mollified the landowners that the government would take from them any debts associated with expropriated agricultural land and held elections for the National Union that was supposed to represent the Syrian public in the absence of political parties. Despite these conciliatory moves, the physical presence of Field Marshal Amr in Syria did little to quell anxieties over Egyptianization. Amr's critics saw him as an imperial ruler and took to calling him 'the viceroy'.[36] Amr returned to Cairo in December, leaving Syria in what he thought was a more stable condition. It was at that point that the five Ba'thist ministers collectively resigned from the UAR government.

The split between Syrian Ba'thists and Abd al-Nasser was long in the making. The party had failed in its efforts to provide ideological guidance to the president, who was unimpressed by their presumption. Recent concessions to Syria's landed elites and business interests went too far for the Ba'thists. Although they had hoped the National Union might be their road back to greater influence, in the event they fared poorly in its elections: its machinery was designed to exclude Abd al-Nasser's opponents, not give them a means to rally support. After the 1958 coup, the

Ba'thists had initially been optimistic about the prospect of revolutionary Iraq joining the UAR, which might provide a counterbalance to the Jupiter-like political mass of Abd al-Nasser. Yet old tensions between Cairo and Baghdad had flared, causing the prospect of bringing Iraq into the fold to recede beyond the horizon. Given what they saw as the self-evident need to change course, the Syrian Ba'thists decided to stage a collective resignation that would prompt Abd al-Nasser to realize how crucial they were for successful government and invite them to return to the cabinet.

Abd al-Nasser was deeply angered by this coordinated wave of resignations, which he considered a personal betrayal. The divorce became acrimonious.[37] With the Ba'thists sidelined, Abd al-Nasser appointed Sarraj to the position of minister of the interior in addition to his role as intelligence chief. Under Sarraj's leadership, the Special Bureau had already proven to be a brutally effective instrument of repression: torture was so rife in Syrian jails that prisoners would hang themselves or slash their wrists rather than prolong their suffering.[38] Critics accused Sarraj of turning the country into a police state;[39] delivering the Ministry of the Interior to him would simply deliver him another vehicle for his personal control of the Northern Province. As a façade to cover his coercion, Sarraj began to project a public persona: the official media cooed deferentially over his daily activities, and a propaganda film glorified his great qualities as a leader. Sarraj was now by far the most powerful man in Syria.

In early 1960, the UAR adopted dramatic measures to cope with Syria's dire economic situation. For three consecutive years, the Northern Province had experienced severe drought. Rather than exporting grain, Syria was now importing wheat and barley to feed itself; tobacco – an important export – had also suffered. The UAR government blamed the Syrian business community for the failure. It announced that the state would no longer be content to 'guide' a fundamentally incompetent private sector, which had failed to raise living standards; the state itself would now actively intervene in the economy for the good of society.

'Poverty cannot be ended just by redistributing existing wealth,' noted the modified five-year plan. 'The challenge is not just to distribute economic activity across the social and economic body that currently exists, but to *reshape* that body [. . .] The state must control material resources and use them in a way that benefits the general interest and does not concentrate wealth and economic power in the hands of the few.'[40] The UAR proclaimed a new economic paradigm. Breaking from the consensus around a 'guided economy' that had prevailed in Syria during the 1940s and 1950s, the radical objective of government in the 1960s would be to create a Syria that was 'socialist, cooperative and democratic.'

Syria's leading businessmen were alarmed by this new rhetoric. Abd al-Nasser had already nationalized the Egyptian banking sector, which they feared would become a precedent for the state takeover of private businesses in the Northern Province of the UAR. To mitigate this risk, business people began to pull yet more of their money out of Syria into Lebanon, causing the value of the Syrian pound to fall by 10 per cent and prompting the governor of the Syrian Central Bank to tender his resignation. To stem this capital flight, in February 1961 the government froze all foreign currency accounts, banned private foreign exchange and issued compulsory purchase orders for all foreign currency holdings. Imports were restricted yet further. In March, Abd al-Nasser ordered that the state would seize a 35 per cent share of all banks. Syrian businessmen were aghast. With the members of Syria's largest industrial conglomerate, the Khumasiya, leading the charge, they took their grievances directly to the ministers of the Northern Province. Abd al-Nasser, they warned, was intent on seizing private companies and transforming Syria into a fully state-run economy. Of course, the Syrian ministers were powerless to act. Just a few months later, the businessmen's fears became reality.

In July 1961, Abd al-Nasser ordered sweeping nationalization of the UAR's biggest industrial companies, agricultural producers and insurance firms, a measure applied in both Syria and Egypt. The state seized control of seventy-five Syrian companies, including the Khumasiya; a further seventy-nine firms had half their shares confiscated.[41] The shock of the nationalization rippled across Syria; even the normally quiescent grand mufti spoke out against them. A month later, Abd al-Nasser went a step further and abolished the two regional governments in favour of a single body that would meet in Cairo. The new government would have five Egyptian and two Syrian vice presidents, one of whom, Sarraj, was by this point the most unpopular, as well as the most powerful, man in Syria. Sarraj himself understood that his relocation to Cairo was a tactic to break up the autonomous power base that he had built, which had grown too large and too dangerous for Abd al-Nasser's liking. After a month unsuccessfully tussling for power with Field Marshal Amr in Cairo, Sarraj resigned from his position; his departure left his fearful intelligence service effectively paralysed.[42]

Abd al-Nasser's reassertion of control was not well received in Syria. Especially when the seat of government for the Northern Province was relocated to Cairo, many Syrians were left with the impression that the country was being treated like a colony rather than an equal partner in the UAR.[43] This was not the union that Syrians had in mind. Whether businessmen, feudal landowners, traditional politicians, tribal leaders, army officers, Ba'thists or Communists, all had been alienated by the experience of union. Abd al-Nasser's rule had achieved the impossible: it had united the famously fractious Syrian elites. Even so, neither Abd al-Nasser nor Syrians themselves suspected that their experiment in Arab unity was about to meet an abrupt end.[44]

On the brink: the faltering union

On 28 September 1961, Radio Damascus unexpectedly suspended its usual programming to broadcast hours and hours of endless military music – a change that Syrians immediately recognized as the sign of yet another military coup. Led by Colonel Abd al-Karim Nahlawi, head of Field Marshal Amr's office in Syria, and Colonel Haydar al-Kuzbari, commander of the Syrian Desert Forces, a small group of mostly Damascene officers had taken control of the army and seized the capital.

It was clear from the outset that the conspirators wanted to rebalance the United Arab Republic, not to dissolve it. Their Communiqué Number One, broadcast on Radio Damascus in line with Syria's modern tradition of coup-making, pledged to end tyranny and corruption and to return legitimate rights to the people. 'The aim of the movement,' the communiqué clarified, 'is to correct an illegitimate situation.'[45] Although there was no actual evidence, rumours saw the hand of the Khumasiya behind the coup. Colonel Haydar al-Kuzbari was a relative of Ma'moun al-Kuzbari, the son-in-law of one of the conglomerate's five founding members as well as its top lawyer, who was alleged to have funnelled money from the group to the conspirators.[46] Regardless, the officers quickly opened negotiations with Field Marshal Amr. They asked for a reversal of nationalization, a softening of the agricultural reforms, a transition to a federal rather than full union between Syria and Egypt and the removal from the regime of what they euphemistically called 'opportunistic' elements (such as Sarraj). Amr proved conciliatory on all counts.

Radio Damascus triumphantly announced that Field Marshal Amr had understood the genuine motivations of the army and was taking the necessary steps to resolve the issues, 'to the benefit of the union and the strength of the United Arab Republic.'[47] Disaster, it seemed, had been averted.

Abd al-Nasser, on the other hand, had no intention of being outmanoeuvred by a coterie of Syrian officers. He had allowed negotiations to take place only to gain time to plan a military operation: he ordered his naval forces to the Syrian coast and dispatched 140 parachutists to land at the Humaymim Airbase near Latakia, where they were to support army units still loyal to the UAR leadership. However, by the time the Egyptians arrived, the army was fully controlled by the putschists; the parachutists were promptly captured by the Syrians.[48] Sensing that the tide had turned, Abd al-Nasser called off the invasion, and instead launched a full-spectrum propaganda attack in the Egyptian media, which angrily denounced the coup as a crime, a disaster on par with the establishment of the State of Israel. The hostile Egyptian media laid blame on the Khumasiya and even called on Syria's Druze and Alawis to rise up against Damascus, albeit to no effect. In the meantime, Egyptian ministers, teachers and technical experts quietly departed, and Syrian army officers came home from Egypt. Although Egypt would officially cling to the name of the United Arab Republic for another ten years, the union of the two countries would never be successfully rekindled.

Picking up the pieces: the secessionist regime

Between September 1961 and March 1963, a rapid succession of governments wrestled with the economic and political disarray they had inherited upon Syria's secession from the UAR. For four long years – the whole duration of the union with Egypt – Syria had suffered from a painful drought. Repeated crop failures made for the almost total collapse of agricultural exports and – as wheat and barley sales were two of the most important country's sources of hard currency – produced a huge deficit in Syria's balance of payments. To finance the import of essential foodstuffs, Syria had been forced to drain its entire foreign exchange reserves – a figure in excess of US$50 million. At the same time, the UAR government had needed to raise capital to fund its ambitious programme of socialist nationalizations, which it essentially achieved by printing money. By September 1961, the total amount of Syrian currency in circulation had increased by about 40 per cent from the eve of the union.[49] Unusually, this colossal monetary expansion did not result in equally colossal inflation – an indication of the extent to which, incomes had suffered from the collapse of agriculture, which despite the expansion of industry, still provided the livelihood for as much as 75 per cent of the population.

Dealing with this dire economic situation was thc priority for the first government of the secessionist regime. Led by Ma'moun al-Kuzbari (who became prime minister at the invitation of the officers),[50] the business-friendly cabinet was endorsed by the chambers of commerce, agriculture and industry, as well as the professional syndicates. The trade unions, on the other hand, known as bastions of the left, were more lukewarm. At the army's request, a cross-section of Syria's political parties published a National Charter in which they endorsed the secession from the Union;[51] Sultan al-Atrash himself came to Damascus from Jabal al-Arab to convey his support to the new prime minister in person. The Kuzbari government swiftly corrected what it considered the major policy mistakes of the UAR. It abolished the July 1961 nationalization decrees, dissolved the Special Bureau and arrested dozens of intelligence officers – including Sarraj – for their crimes. Mindful of the peasantry's support for land reform, the government did not repeal the 1958 Agrarian Reform Law and reassured the public that they would adopt a moderate economic model, striking a balance between state intervention and private enterprise. In the event, Syrian business people were happy to find that ministers' doors were open to them more than ever before.

To deal with the gaping hole in public finances, the government introduced an austerity programme, devised in autumn 1961 in agreement with the International Monetary Fund (IMF), and repaid public debt to the banks. In return for the implementation of what they described as a 'stabilization programme', the IMF and creditors including the United States and West Germany made available to Syria a stand-by fund of US$41.6 million.[52] This facility allowed the government the following year to relax capital controls and devalue the Syrian pound (by 6.6 per cent) to mitigate the deficit in the balance of payments as well as the decline in Soviet aid that had not survived Syria's divorce from Abd al-Nasser.[53] The government's task was further eased when the drought broke in 1962, producing a bountiful harvest and the resumption of agricultural exports.

The first elections of the secession era, held in November 1961, vindicated the political right wing and punished parties too closely identified with the problems of the UAR regime. One of the two pillars of bourgeois politics, the People's Party, formed the largest bloc in parliament. In the ensuing cabinet reshuffle, Kuzbari was appointed speaker of parliament, Ma'rouf al-Dawalibi, a businessman from Aleppo, was made prime minister and Nazim al-Qudsi became president. The fact that Qudsi's presidency was ultimately secured only with the open endorsement of the army (albeit as their second choice, when Rushdi

Kikhia declined their invitation) illustrates the degree of influence the officers still wielded in civilian politics.[54] The elections also saw the return to parliament of the veteran independent Khalid al-Azm, who had retired from public life during the UAR and, safe from its taint, was re-elected by a landslide. In contrast, the Ba'th Party failed to match its performance in the last round of free elections before the establishment of the UAR. Still reeling from the disharmonious union experiment, Ba'th co-founder Salah al-Din al-Bitar lost his seat in Damascus.

Despite its new direction, the secessionist regime still had to work within the political orthodoxy of Arab unity. Even opponents of the merger with Egypt had to display their ongoing commitment to the idea of unity, even if only rhetorically. The new provisional constitution, for example, promulgated in November 1961, officially renamed the country 'the Syrian *Arab* Republic' – the name it still bears today – and declared it to be 'an independent sovereign state and part of the great Arab fatherland'.[55] The country endlessly debated whether or not Syria and Egypt should repeat the experiment, try a different kind of union or simply leave it for the future; who should be blamed for the collapse of the UAR was the subject of bitter argument and ongoing recrimination. Although the United Arab Republic had ended in failure, the question of future unity remained open for the Syrian Arab Republic.

In January and February 1962, the People's Party government continued to reverse the socialist legacy of the UAR. Many companies, including the Khumasiya, were denationalized, and the Agrarian Reform Law was modified to raise the ceiling on individual land ownership (to 200 hectares of irrigated land and 600 hectares of rainfed land, from 80 and 300 hectares respectively). The government eased import restrictions and business regulations and even started to roll back progressive taxation, although it assured the peasantry that their newly acquired labour rights would be left untouched. All these decisions were designed to dismantle the model of state capitalism that had been set in place during the UAR and to return Syria to the more liberal model of a state-guided economy that had existed prior to 1958. 'The present economic regime,' announced Prime Minister Dawalibi, 'must be based on respect for individual property, on the encouragement of personal initiative [. . .] and on granting to individuals the liberty to exercise their economic, commercial, industrial and agricultural activities, and to pursue their progress with liberty, personal dignity, and economic stability.'[56]

Despite Dawalibi's effusive celebration of new-found freedoms, successive separatist governments did little to relax the restrictions on civil liberties imposed during the UAR. On the contrary, they actively relied on the same repertoire of authoritarian tactics to suppress the fractious political disagreements that were racking the country. Week after week, students demonstrated to demand the return of the UAR; young Ba'thist activists clashed on the streets with religious conservatives; across different sectors – even in the banks – workers went on strike to protest against the government policy of austerity. In the face of such contestation, the separatist government restricted press freedoms, surveilled trade unions, expanded the power of the executive over that of parliament and – most strikingly – refused to lift the ban on political parties dissolved during the UAR. The return of pre-1958 parties, the government argued, would lead Syria back to the chaos that had precipitated the union in the first place.[57] By late March 1962, opposition to these restrictions reached the point that Dawalibi had to resign as prime minister. When President Qudsi refused to hold new elections for a new parliament, Chief of Staff Nahlawi decided that the army would intervene to 'correct' the problems caused by the civilians.

On 28 March 1962, Nahlawi and his conspirators removed Qudsi from power and dissolved parliament. The officers responsible for this intervention against the right-wing government were largely the same that had rebelled against the Egyptianization of the UAR in September 1961, indicating secession did not happen simply on the orders of Syrian big business. Indeed, Nahlawi not only promptly arrested all the government ministers, but, for good measure, also slapped the board members of the Khumasiya – the very people alleged to have bankrolled the coup he had led – into the Mezzeh military prison.[58]

Despite little initial resistance, Nahlawi's coup backfired. Civilian politicians refused to bow to Nahlawi's demand to form a new government; the army itself was deeply divided and the public highly critical. After several days of political vacuum, officers from other factions secretly met with the politicians in Homs and brokered a deal to end the deadlock. Nahlawi and his clique were expelled from the country, the army command reshuffled to bring in more Nasserists, President Qudsi and the civilian politicians instructed to rebalance government policies back to the left and the question of unity with Egypt was put back on the table.[59] Yet even when politics resumed, the agitation continued. On 2 April, after a day of pro-UAR demonstrations in the streets, a coterie of unionist officers – Ba'thists as well as Nasserists – seized control of the Aleppo radio station and garrison, and enthusiastically declared the restoration of the UAR.[60] The conviction proved premature: Abd al-Nasser did not respond to their appeal for reinforcements, and their insurrection was quashed by the rest of the Syrian army after just one day.

A new government was formed under Bashir al-Azma, the physician who had served in Abd al-Nasser's technocratic cabinet in Cairo, and the policy compass swung back towards state intervention. The Khumasiya was nationalized (again), the land-ownership ceiling reduced to its original levels and the banking sector brought back into partial state ownership.[61] At the same time, the Azma government attempted to increase state control over the General Federation of Trade Unions, provoking a wave of strikes and demonstrations in Aleppo, Damascus and Homs that brought thousands of people on to the streets. The police responded with violence, killing several workers and arresting many more. Businessmen and the conservative religious establishment opposed economic policies that they considered socialist, and criticized the ongoing infringements of civil liberties – opportunistically, in some cases, given that the previous right-wing governments they had supported had imposed just the same restrictions.

Under Azma's left-leaning government, the question of relations with Egypt continued to be divisive. In June 1962, Azma announced he would open reunification talks with Abd al-Nasser, but the proposal provoked an instant backlash. Azma was forced to retract his statement. After a series of unexplained explosions in Damascus, Homs and Hama, and the discovery of a plot by Nasserist army officers to smuggle weapons into Syria, the Azma government submitted an official complaint to the Arab League about Egyptian meddling in Syria's domestic affairs. At a special conciliation meeting held by the Arab League in the Lebanese town of Shtaura that August, the two sides met to thrash out their differences. Somewhat provocatively, the Egyptian delegation was led by former ministers, officers and other Abd al-Nasser loyalists from Syria who had chosen to remain in Cairo after the end of the union. The Syrian delegation vehemently attacked Egyptian failings during the UAR and provided detailed documentary evidence of what they denounced as Egyptian plots to destabilize the Syrian government. This fiery confrontation proved impossible to contain: the meeting was adjourned, indefinitely. Despite the rancour between the two sides, the ideal of

Arab unity remained a political orthodoxy so powerful that to deny it outright would – even now – be tantamount to heresy. The balance of pro- and anti-union forces in Syria was so fragile, moreover, that any change in the regional political environment might tilt the scales in one direction or another.

The political elite remained deeply concerned by Egyptian policy towards Syria. In September 1962, the respected Khalid al-Azm took over as prime minister. 'Red Millionaire' Azm quickly lifted the emergency laws, authorized political parties and eased other restrictions on civil liberties. President Qudsi and the army warned Azm that pro-Nasser forces would exploit these freedoms to carry out destructive activities, and advised him to take a harsher stance. 'You don't need a mallet to swat a fly,' Azm retorted.[62]

It was from Iraq, however, that the next challenge emerged. In February 1963, a coup brought the Iraqi branch of the Ba'th Party to power in Baghdad. Inspired by their example, unionists in the Syrian officer corps began to plot their course for a coup just a month later that would once again launch the country down the road to Arab unity.

The Ba'th path to power: 8 March 1963

In the official historiography of the Arab Socialist Ba'th Party, the Glorious Revolution of 8 March 1963 is revered for having brought the party to power in Syria. In reality, this 'Ba'thist revolution' was neither revolutionary – in that it was carried out by a military clique, not the popular masses – nor even particularly Ba'thist. Since the break-up of the UAR, many Ba'thist officers had been imprisoned or involuntarily retired from active service for their political activities.[63] Despite their low number, Ba'thist officers had disproportionate political clout in the armed forces owing to the party's active civilian membership. The party's recent rise to power in Iraq also added to the perception of its political strength, even though its Iraqi branch was geographically, organizationally and to a certain extent socially distinct from the Ba'thist movement in Syria. As vitality began to flow back into Syrian political life after its suppression during the UAR years, civilian Ba'thists were nevertheless faced with the reality that they were unable to resurrect their party in the form in which it had existed in 1958. The experience of the union had produced deep fractures in the movement.

The fault lines dividing the Ba'th in the early 1960s were the consequence of different analyses of who to blame for the failure of the UAR and whether or not to embark on a second attempt at unification. As co-founder and spiritual father, Aflaq occupied a position of special prestige in the party: Aflaq had kept faith in the promise represented by union with Egypt, regardless of its evident practical difficulties. Hawrani, on the other hand, had turned vehemently against the prospect of reaching a new agreement with Abd al-Nasser. When the union ended, both Hawrani and Bitar signed the National Charter in support of secession. As Bitar had played a major role in securing the union with Egypt in the first place, this was a remarkable volte-face. Its audacity was exceeded only by Bitar's next about-turn, in which he moved back into Aflaq's camp in favour of federal union. These political pirouettes earned Bitar a reputation for fickleness, and left the newly re-elected Hawrani as the centre of gravity for Ba'thist parliamentarians.

Outside parliament, differences of position over Abd al-Nasser and the UAR intersected with secondary cleavages, both generational and geographical. In the Syrian provinces, many younger rank-and-file party members resented that they had not been consulted in Aflaq and Bitar's decision to dissolve the party and were unimpressed by how these established urban leaders had navigated the tumult of union and secession. In fact, Ba'thists in Deir al-Zour, Der'a, Latakia and Suwayda had simply disregarded the official orders to disband and continued to meet clandestinely during the UAR, despite the risk of persecution by Sarraj.[64] These second-tier members, who later came to be known as the Regionalists (*Qutriyyun*), had little faith in the traditional leadership that led them into disaster. Of all the Ba'thists, they were most adamantly opposed to reinstating the union with Abd al-Nasser's Egypt. Diametrically opposed to the Regionalists was a cluster called the Socialist Unionists, who remained supportive of Abd al-Nasser, but who were less enthusiastic about the bookish Aflaq. In contrast to these two loose groupings was the better organized yet less visible third network, nicknamed the 'Military Committee', which had been secretly established in 1959 by Syrian army and air force officers in Egypt. The members of the Military Committee were also disillusioned by the experience of the UAR yet had no ties to the party's civilian leadership. A shadowy entity with its own independent agenda, the committee came to form the nucleus of a parallel party network within the armed forces. Its members – just thirteen or fourteen of them at this stage – largely came from rural and minority backgrounds, including Druze, Alawi and Isma'ili officers, as well as provincial Sunnis.[65]

Between the factions of Aflaq, Hawrani, the Regionalists, the Socialist Unionists and the Military Committee – not to mention a host of smaller cliques – the Ba'th had lost any sense of coherent organization. To demonstrate the point, when Aflaq relaunched the Ba'th as an officially registered political party in 1962, many of the other factions simply chose not to join him. Later that year, Hawrani vocally denounced his former ally Abd al-Nasser as a stooge of American imperialism and a traitor to the Palestinian cause, prompting Aflaq to expel him and his supporters from the party. Hawrani never rejoined the Ba'th. While Aflaq and Bitar continued to represent the historical core of the party, it was the younger, peripheral groups – not the traditional leadership – that would radically reshape the Ba'th in the course of the 1960s. The coup of 8 March 1963 was the first indication of the role that these new kinds of Ba'thist were to play.

The civilian party leaders had no involvement in the coup, which was orchestrated by three different groups in the armed forces: the Military Committee (whose members coordinated army officers from behind the scenes), Nasserists (who were included in the new regime despite deciding not to participate actively in the coup at the very last minute) and a group of progressive independent officers led by Colonel Ziyad al-Hariri. The 8 March coup was swift and bloodless, encountering no resistance from civilian politicians or secessionist officers, who either fled the country or did not struggle against being taken into custody.

The 1963 coup marked the decisive end of the bourgeois politicians who had dominated the parliament and the presidency since independence in 1946. Not only were the National Party, the People's Party and the independents of Khalid al-Azm removed from politics, but over the next few years they would witness the relentless destruction of their businesses, property empires and prestige. Although some members of the old elite would cling on to a fragment of their former wealth and position, they never again regained the political prominence they had lost. After 1963, the Syrian bourgeoisie as an organized force in politics was not merely moribund but quite simply dead.

Amid the familiar military refrains, Radio Damascus announced that the newly created National Council for the Revolutionary Command had summoned back into service a number of Ba'thist officers including Muhammad Umran, Salah Jadid and

Hafiz al-Assad – core members of the Military Committee, who now assumed key positions in the army. The National Council for the Revolutionary Command included representatives from all three factions who had supported the coup – independents, Ba'thists and Nasserists – but Ba'thist officers secured most of the positions and ensured that the new government was dominated by their counterparts in the civilian party. Although Bitar himself was made prime minister, the Ba'th Party of Aflaq recognized that their fortune now depended on these military Ba'thists about whose motivations and backgrounds they knew little. Mindful that the centre of political gravity was shifting, the civilian party recognized the Military Committee's autonomous control over the Ba'th's military wing, albeit yet to be formally constituted. The recognition of these men of action acknowledged that Syrian Ba'thism was evolving in a very different direction than that intended by the intellectuals who had been its founders.

Once the 8 March coup had overthrown the secessionist regime, it was only natural for the ruling coalition of Ba'thists, Nasserists and independent progressives to revive hopes for unity by reopening talks with Abd al-Nasser. Although Abd al-Nasser agreed to the negotiations, his confidence in the Ba'th Party had evaporated. The Cairo Unity Talks, convened from mid-March to mid-April 1963 with delegations from Egypt, Syria and Iraq, provided Abd al-Nasser with a perfect opportunity to harangue, lecture and embarrass the Syrian Ba'thists, whom he accused of ideological incoherence, among their many other flaws. Abd al-Nasser had never forgiven the Ba'thists for betraying him. For their part, the Ba'thists pressed on, apparently feeling that abandoning the principle of unity would be more costly than enduring abuse from Abd al-Nasser. A strange double game soon emerged, in which the Ba'thists publicly paid lip service to the ideal of unity with Egypt during the official talks, while simultaneously doing their utmost to undermine the position of Syrian Nasserists at home. Somewhat remarkably, the Cairo negotiations produced a transitional framework for unity to which all parties subscribed: the Syrian national flag was officially replaced with that of the new Egypt–Syria–Iraq union. However, the military Ba'thists knew that, at this particular political moment, power and authority would be controlled by whoever controlled the army.[66]

The Military Committee purged Nasserist officers, prompting Nasserist ministers to threaten to resign unless the changes were reversed. When the news leaked, in Aleppo and Damascus there were large protests in favour of unity, which were repressed with violence. To deal with such demonstrations in future, the Ba'th Party formed a popular militia, the National Guard (*al-Haras al-Qawmi*), specialized in the cruder tactics of street combat. The Military Committee completed their seizure of the armed forces by removing independents from positions of power. Their leader, Ziyad al-Hariri, was surprised to find himself appointed the Syrian military attaché to Washington, D.C., the distance from Damascus intended effectively to neutralize his influence in the officer corps. Hariri refused this redeployment and returned to the capital to rally his supporters, provoking a tense standoff with the Military Committee. Sensing the balance of power shift against him, and wary of breaking the taboo against bloodshed, Hariri accepted his fate, gave up on politics, and lived out the rest of his life in self-imposed exile in France. For their part, the purged Nasserists attempted a comeback by staging a coup on 18 July that broke Syria's longstanding tradition of relatively bloodless putsches. A bout of heavy fighting was followed by the swift court-martialling and execution of over twenty of the participants – death sentences that one critic condemned as the biggest massacre in Syrian history.[67]

Just three days later, Abd al-Nasser denounced Syria's 'fascist regime' in an emotional speech to the Egyptian people. 'There cannot be a joint aim with a system based on treachery and stabbing in the back,' Abd al-Nasser declared. 'The present Ba'th regime in Damascus is an anti-unionist, anti-socialist regime [...] The tripartite unity agreement commits us with Syria, but does not commit us in any way with the existing fascist Ba'thist government in Syria.'[68] By this point, the convergence of interests between Abd al-Nasser and the Ba'thists had well and truly unravelled. When the Iraqi Ba'th Party was removed from power in November 1963, Syrian Ba'thists lost the second pillar of their foreign policy axis. With no external sponsor now available to lend legitimacy to the regime in Syria, the military and civilian wings of the Ba'th Party had to consolidate their control by using only internal forces. This inwards turn brought to the fore latent tensions within the party organization, even as its mission to transform the face of Syria began to provoke indignant resistance from the rest of society.

Shifting tectonics: socialism, sectarianism and state-building

The years following the coup of 8 March 1963 were marked by severe struggles as groups divided by generation, regional background and ideology battled to dominate the new Ba'th regime. Remarkably, these internal struggles did not impair the construction of a coherent and effective set of state institutions that penetrated Syria's society and economy more deeply than ever before. Although the constant jockeying for power caused contortions in the personnel holding top positions, the Ba'th Party was nevertheless able to overcome opposition from businessmen and religious conservatives, and successfully imposed overtly socialist policies that would radically transform the country. The consolidation of the Ba'thist regime in the 1960s is remarkable when considered alongside the many failed attempts of previous decades, where no one state builder or political faction could dominate, much less eliminate, the other elements of Syria's fragmented urban elite or bring the country's fractious rural regions under the control of the central authority.

Several factors help explain the unusual success of the Ba'th. First, the Ba'thists adopted a policy of class warfare against Syria's traditional elites that admitted no space for compromise. To enact this position of no tolerance, the Ba'thists drew on the institutional legacy of the UAR: the new laws, agencies and authoritarian practices introduced under Abd al-Nasser were activated and expanded by the Ba'thists to crush their political opponents. Importantly, rather than relying on patronage or coercive power to conquer the provinces, as Quwwatli and Shishakli had attempted, the Ba'thists incorporated rural populations into the regime at the popular level, giving the masses a stake in the party's revolutionary project. While the upper echelons of the Ba'th Party played an intrigue-filled game of musical chairs for much of the 1960s, they also constructed a stable and unusually durable system for controlling Syrian society.

With Ba'thists firmly in control of the army and parliament, three groups jostled for influence within the party: the traditional core around Aflaq and Bitar, the Military Committee and a younger generation of mainly rural radicals, whose ideology owed more to the materialism of Marx and Lenin than Aflaq's philosophical nationalism. The impact of the radicals was first felt in September 1963 at the Sixth National Congress of the Arab Socialist Ba'th Party, which was attended by party delegates from across the Arab world.

The terminology of this congress deserves further consideration.

In Ba'thist parlance, the word 'national' (*qawmi*) referred to the over-arching Arab nation, not the truncated states created by colonialism. Party branches in Syria, Iraq and other countries were therefore referred to as 'regional' (*qutri*) and were – in theory – secondary to the party's 'national' bodies.

Dominated by militant left-wingers from the grassroots of the party, the Sixth National Congress produced a series of resolutions and reports that reformulated the official ideological position of the Ba'th. Socialism – rather than Arab unity – was now recognized as the most urgent political priority.

Published under the title of 'Some Theoretical Points of Departure' (*Ba'd al-Muntaqalat al-Nazariya*), the new ideology distanced itself from the Ba'th's earlier endorsement of private property – which the leftists blamed on petit bourgeois elements that had infiltrated some party branches – and denounced the Arab bourgeoisie as incapable of delivering social revolution.

Parliamentary democracy was a lie, they argued, a pretext for allowing business and feudal elites to dominate society. Liberal capitalism fostered economic instability and 'turned the state into an apparatus to transfer wealth to the rich and to sustain collaborators with colonialism and parasites on the lifeblood of society, who accumulate money in their pockets while the people live in squalor and backwardness'.[69] The radicals even criticized the party's previous commitment to land redistribution, one of the key tenets of the Ba'thist programme for the last decade. Agrarian reform by itself was insufficient, they maintained; it was also urgently necessary to remove the peasantry from its historical ignorance, elevate its political consciousness and transform the ossified social structures of the countryside into the dynamic relations of modern socialism. Rather than peasants owning land individually, the party instead called for collective farms to be run by the state: peasant participation would be crucial for the success of social revolution.

The new ideology advocated a radically new political architecture for Syria and Iraq as popular democracies, directed by a Ba'thist vanguard for the benefit of the toiling masses. 'Only a socialist regime,' proclaimed the party, 'can mobilize the people and gather its human and material capabilities for progress.'

Although the radical agenda owed much to Marxism–Leninism for its conception of vanguards, nationalization and popular democracy, the militants avoided any explicit mention of Marxist terminology. Doctrinal communism enjoyed only limited appeal in the Arab world, not only for its strident atheism but also for its rejection of Arab nationalism in favour of revolutionary universalism. The radicals were careful to cater to prevailing nationalist sentiments while also differentiating the Ba'th from the political competition: they attacked the Nasserist concept of 'Arab socialism' as petty provincialism, for example, but nevertheless advocated what they called an 'Arab road to socialism'. Replacing the Ba'th's own earlier reformist agenda with a radical call for revolution came as a bitter shock to Aflaq, whose idea of revolution did not go much further than a wave of cultural and spiritual renewal. As left-wing support surged through the party, Aflaq and his faction struggled to keep their seats on the National Command, the body that coordinated party activity across the Arab world. By January 1964, the radicals had mustered sufficient support to expel Salah al-Din al-Bitar himself from the party – albeit only temporarily – following his public criticism of militant Ba'thists in Iraq. The tide within the party was turning.

The third force within the Ba'th, the Military Committee, had quietly and methodically consolidated its control of the army and government over the intervening months. The committee had secured the presidency for General Amin al-Hafiz, who joined its ranks after the 8 March coup; Hafiz further concentrated power in his hands when he also took over Bitar's role of prime minister. Although sharing similar social backgrounds and political concerns with the radicals, the Military Committee was more pragmatic about the pace of social transformation and suspicious of the independent centres of power that the leftists were developing within the party. In hastily convened meetings of the Syrian Regional Congress and the National Congress, in February 1964, the Military Committee joined forces with Aflaq's faction to remove the leading radicals from their positions, and ejected them from the party membership. Although the Military Committee now dominated the party, with the greatly weakened group of Aflaq on the margins, it nevertheless retained the language, policies and ideological imprint of socialism that it had inherited from the expelled left-wingers.

The leftward lurch of the Ba'th Party in many ways reflected the palpable shift in its membership after the end of the UAR. Aflaq and Bitar had in the past concentrated their energy on a small elite of intellectual pioneers and been uninterested in grass-roots recruitment. However, after the coup of 8 March 1963, the Military Committee flung open the doors to all manner of newcomers. Over the following year, party membership swelled to five times its previous size, as the regime sought to replenish the ranks of an army hollowed out by successive purges of Nasserists and independents.[70] Drawing on friends and family, Ba'thist officers predominantly recruited new members from the towns and villages where they had grown up. The preponderance of minorities in the army and party meant that much of this influx was comprised of Druze, Alawis and Isma'ilis, some of whom were enthusiastic about radically rebalancing relations between city and countryside, while others were committed less to the ideological cause of the Arab road to socialism than to their own cause of getting a job.

Critics accused the Military Committee of deliberately staffing the army with recruits from their home communities. The leftist philosopher Muta' Safadi, who broke with the regime in July 1963, notably alleged that these 'sectarian pseudo-Ba'thists' were assigned military positions after receiving little more than a uniform and rudimentary training. The Ba'thists, Safadi alleged, had deliberately purged Sunnis from the officer corps and banned them from entering the War College.[71] While there is little evidence of deliberate discrimination, it was certainly the case that, in an officer corps that was politically fragmented and riddled with plots and conspiracies, it was easier to build trust among individuals who shared a common social or regional background. Given the dense geographical concentration of minorities in places such as Jabal al-Arab and Jabal al-Ansariya, these networks of trust inevitably overlapped with communal groups such as the Druze and Alawis. The congruence of recruitment patterns, communal identities and rapid expansion meant that some army units had high concentrations of specific minority groups. Considered more trustworthy by members of the Military Committee, who were themselves from disproportionately rural and minority backgrounds, these minority-dominated units were typically stationed closer to Damascus, while Sunni-majority units were positioned further afield.[72] Even if not conscious, this 'strategic sectarianism', as Safadi called it, was a potential vulnerability for a Ba'th regime that wielded power in the name of Arab socialism, unity and freedom, not in the name of minority empowerment.

Despite this structural sectarianism, power cliques at the highest levels were based on personalities and political preferences rather than communal identities: alliances and betrayals often traversed sectarian lines. The (Sunni) officer Mustafa Tlass, for example, famously abandoned his (Sunni) ally Amin al-Hafiz when Hafiz threatened to discipline him for getting into a fight in a nightclub. Tlass switched to (the Alawi) Salah Jadid to defend his position.[73]

In contrast, Military Committee member Muhammad Umran, an Alawi, was accused of deliberately invoking sectarian language in an attempt to mobilize supporters in his struggle for power with Amin al-Hafiz. 'The Fatimiyya [i.e. the Druze, Alawis and Isma'ilis],' Umran allegedly said, 'must have their day!' Breaking the taboo of sectarianism earned Umran a stern response: he was expelled from the Military Committee, the Ba'th Party and the country.[74] At the same time, though, there was a lingering suspicion that the accusation of sectarianism served to cover up what were actually ideological differences. Not only was Umran substantially more sympathetic to Abd al-Nasser than the rest of his colleagues on the Military Committee, he had also built bridges to the Aflaq faction to secure their support against Hafiz. As Safadi insightfully noted, accusing Umran of inflaming sectarianism was, somewhat ironically, a convenient way to derail his unionist agenda.[75] Disentangling where political differences ended and sectarian divisions began was in practice a difficult task: conflating them for instrumental purposes was much easier.

Although the Military Committee was engrossed in a struggle for power internally as well as with the faction of Michel Aflaq, the regime was nevertheless able to drive through reforms to expand the reach and capabilities of the Syrian state. Although the Ba'thists had a general sense that the state should play a much more prominent role in controlling rather than simply guiding Syrian society and the economy, the direction of the reforms evolved gradually as a series of responses to minor crises that accumulated over the course of several years to bring about a fundamental transformation of Syrian state power. In this, the logic of state expansion from 1963 to 1970 had much in common with the earlier phase of state-building in the early 1950s, which also proceeded gradually and yet still resulted in the steady expansion of state institutions.[76] The Ba'thist state-building project pursued three distinct avenues, simultaneously targeting the state bureaucracy, civil society and the economy.[77]

Soon after the coup of 8 March 1963, the government attacked collusion between the civil service and big business under the secessionist regime: it dismissed large numbers of senior government officials and expanded its lower ranks to admit thousands of new bureaucrats. In 1960, Syria had some 34,000 employees in government and the public sector. By 1971, this number had swelled to a staggering 198,000. Many of these new government employees came from the countryside and were believed to possess a better 'understanding of the legislation required by the socialist transformation stage' than their urban counterparts.[78] Coupled with an influx of peasants who abandoned their villages in search of a better life in the city, the expansion of state employment launched a new phase of rural–urban migration.

The population of Damascus, for example, increased from around 530,000 inhabitants in 1960 to nearly 837,000 in 1970. Peasants had often fled to cities to escape the hardship of the countryside – the village of Jaramana, originally outside Damascus but soon absorbed into the expanding city limits, had long been home to Druze families from the Jabal, for example. But the new wave of the 1960s for the first time included large numbers of Alawis who moved from the coast to Damascus, Aleppo and other beacons of government employment. Critics of the Ba'th were quick to attack the influx of Alawis whose rural customs and accents were markers of difference in urban settings. 'From the moment the party appeared on the stage,' wrote a disenchanted former Ba'thist, 'caravans of villagers began to descend on Damascus from the plains and mountains, and the perturbing letter *qaf* [a characteristic of the Alawi peasant accent] soon dominated its streets, coffeehouses and the waiting rooms in government offices.'[79]

As the 1960s wore on, expelled Ba'thists drew ever more attention to the allegedly pernicious effects of Alawi domination on Syria's social fabric. 'Alawi supremacy has pervaded all levels to such a degree that you see Alawi women act without restrictions as if they were the authorities,' said one non-Alawi officer after he had been purged from the army. 'The neighbours of all houses inhabited by Alawis can see clearly how they dominate in the name of the authorities and the party. Every Alawi, big or small, knows what developments, transfers and arrests, will happen, even earlier than some high officials!'[80] The urban middle classes were alarmed by the rural and minoritarian composition of the Ba'th regime as much as by its lurch towards socialism.

The second component of Ba'thist state-building involved organizing society into structures that supported the new political system. The Syrian labour movement was purged of its Nasserist elements, and the General Federation of Trade Unions brought under state control. A new body, the General Peasants' Union, was established in December 1964 to organize the sector of society that the Ba'thists considered most desperately in need of elevated political consciousness. The Peasants' Union was rolled out across the country and, by 1970, counted some 120,000 members. The new Agrarian Reform Law that had been promulgated in June 1963 stipulated that confiscated land could only be distributed to members of the state's Agricultural Cooperatives. This acted as a great incentive for peasants to sign up as members. In just a few years, membership of the Agricultural Co-ops increased dramatically: in the governorate of Raqqa, for example, membership jumped from just 343 individuals in 1962 to 2,069 in 1966.[81] The responsibilities of the Co-ops rapidly expanded, making them an indispensable resource for smaller farmers and inserting the tendrils of state intervention ever deeper into the countryside. Other state-controlled unions were founded for women, university students and schoolchildren,[82] and the professional syndicates for doctors, lawyers and teachers were subjected to enhanced levels of state surveillance and intervention.

This unionizing strategy aimed to organize the different sectors of the population and formally incorporate them into the regime. In principle, it would produce a harmonious unity of state and society whose energies could be directed by the Ba'th Party in its role of revolutionary vanguard. 'Can workers and peasants rule directly at the current time?' asked the authors of 'Some Theoretical Points of Departure'. 'Do they possess the capabilities?'[83] Until such time as workers and peasants could achieve the necessary level of political education, the party would exercise the function of leadership on their behalf. In practice, these 'popular organizations' (*munazzamat sha'biyya*) channelled peasants and workers into spaces created and controlled by party and state. So effective for the smooth reproduction of the Ba'th regime were these various unions and syndicates that they would remain in place, unchallenged and substantially unchanged, for over forty years.

The third element of Ba'thist state-building was the extension of direct state control over large swathes of the economy. Soon after the 8 March coup, the regime announced that Syrian capitalists would not be permitted to undermine the government. The banks were renationalized and their directors replaced, controls on foreign exchange were re-established, the ceiling on land ownership was lowered again and prominent businessmen were arrested – with great publicity – when they were caught trying to ghost their wealth out of the country. Regime officials attacked Syrian business people with unprecedentedly hostile language. 'The bourgeoisie is incapable of playing any positive role on the economic front,' the 1963 Sixth National Congress declared. 'Its opportunism makes it an ally of neo-colonialism.'[84] Not only France and Britain, but also the United States and Israel, were frequently accused of harbouring designs on Syria's independence.

Despite some recognition that Syria was not quite ready to transition to an economy without big business, the Ba'th regime was unwilling to betray its ideological position by making concessions. Businesses halted their investment in Syria and adroitly evaded currency restrictions to pull out illegally whatever money they had left in the country. By early 1964, the economy was in crisis. The government cut spending again, raised tariffs to protect foreign currency reserves and introduced a rationing system for basic foods. The atmosphere of growing discontent emboldened the regime's opponents. The Damascus Chamber of Commerce openly criticized the government's economic policy, while Islamic conservatives and Nasserists mobilized their supporters for direct action. This opposition culminated in the first major challenge to the new regime.

Between February and April 1964, student groups, business associations and religious networks based in mosques began demonstrations, strikes and mobilization to protest the radical policies of the Ba'th. As clashes took place first in the coastal town of Baniyas, then in Homs, Latakia and Aleppo, the government blamed the unrest on 'a group determined on sowing sectarian dissent', with support from counter-revolutionary politicians and tribal leaders.[85]

In Hama, a relatively minor incident escalated into a major armed confrontation, when in April a high-school student was arrested after erasing a Ba'thist slogan that his teacher had written on the blackboard.[86] Students took to the streets in protest, preachers denounced the Ba'th in their Friday sermons and shopkeepers closed the markets in support. While the governor of Hama, Abd al-Halim Khaddam, advocated resolving the problem by negotiations with local religious leaders, the commander of the National Guard adamantly opposed any measure that would reinforce the authority of traditional figures.[87] The security forces attempted to break up the demonstrations, clashing with protestors with such severity that it provoked a major uprising.

A local commander, Hamad 'Ubayd, cordoned off the city and called in tanks to quell the unrest. The tanks shelled the central Sultan Mosque, which collapsed on top of protestors who had sought refuge there from government forces. At least fifty people were killed or wounded; others were arrested and later given death sentences by state security courts. This show of strength ensured that no further unrest hit the streets, but left the Ba'th vulnerable to criticism. In addition to the violence, opponents were quick to portray the bloody episode as further evidence of the regime's sectarian bias. As Hamad 'Ubayd was Druze, critics alleged that his brutality in Hama came in revenge for the town being the birthplace of dictator Adib al-Shishakli, who had visited such destruction upon Jabal al-Arab just a decade earlier.[88]

With the uprising repressed, the Ba'th regime felt confident to continue its assault on the private sector. In 1965, the government passed the Ramadan Socialist Decrees that nationalized most of Syria's industry, took over the cotton trade and removed the private sector from the import-export trade in essential foods and machinery needed for agriculture and industry. This time, the regime squashed any sign of protest as soon as it began, even passing death sentences on eleven men accused of orchestrating strikes. The regime had also brought the religious establishment into line: a new, more biddable grand mufti, Shaykh Ahmad Kaftaro, had been appointed, who led a delegation of religious leaders to express their support for the government. Big business had little room for manoeuvre: its political leadership had been crushed or exiled, its major assets nationalized and its capital movement restricted. Civil society had been incorporated into the architecture of state-controlled organizations and counter-revolutionary forces violently suppressed. Collectively, these steps taken by the Ba'th – even in the midst of its own internal strife – would lay the foundations of its rule for decades to come. Remarkably, the most radical years of the Ba'th Party had produced a winning formula for a durable regime.

Ba'thism 2.0

By the mid-1960s, political competition within the Ba'th Party revolved around two basic axes: on the one hand, the tension between Aflaq's wing and the Military Committee and, on the other, conflict within the Military Committee. The Hama uprising of April 1964 had prompted a rebalancing of power within the party. Faced with internal criticism for its handling of the affair, the Military Committee allowed the moderate wing of the party to regain some positions. With the return of Salah al-Din al-Bitar to take over the role of prime minister from Amin al-Hafiz, the government abandoned the language of class conflict and instead called for a peaceful social revolution. Bitar reinstated the commitment to individual land redistribution and gave building the public sector priority over nationalizing the private sector. Arrested demonstrators were released from jail, and some members of the National Guard were chastised for their brutal tactics during the revolt.

These measures did little to weaken the Military Committee. On the contrary, its members took advantage of the respite in internal hostilities to extend party membership to a large influx of Regionalists (*Qutriyyun*), those provincial Ba'thists hostile to Aflaq and Bitar who had secretly continued their activities during the UAR and were only now formally rejoining the organization. In September 1964, the Regional [Syrian] Command of the Ba'th Party, controlled by the Military Committee and their Regionalist allies, withdrew support for Bitar's cabinet and reappointed President Amin al-Hafiz as premier, paving the way for a wave of nationalization and state-building. While Aflaq and Bitar still held sway in the National Command of the party, they had effectively lost all real influence in the organization inside Syria. As Ba'thists from across the Arab world gathered for the Eighth National Congress in April 1965, Aflaq was faced with his impotence in controlling the party he had created. He refused to be re-elected as its secretary general, a role he had held since 1947. Echoes of the conflict reverberated through the official publications of the Ba'th Party: its *al-Thawra* newspaper carried the voice of the Syrian Regional Command, while *al-Ba'th* spoke for the National Command dominated by Aflaq.

For its part, the staunchly Ba'thist officer corps was a fermenting cauldron of personal rivalries. Although General Amin al-Hafiz was both president and prime minister of the Syrian Arab Republic, he by no means monopolized power. His principal rival was Salah Jadid, whose shrewd planning and political calculations had allowed him to insert his supporters into key positions throughout the armed forces. The structural logic of strategic sectarianism endowed their conflict with a communal character. As the most powerful Alawi officer, Jadid naturally inherited the Alawi following of Umran, who had earlier been expelled from the army for his allegedly sectarian impulses. Hafiz counterbalanced Jadid's support by drawing on urban Sunni officers, and by summer 1965 reached out to the civilian wing of Aflaq and Bitar for additional leverage. In doing so, Hafiz effectively threw a lifeline to their imperilled faction. The Hafiz–Aflaq coalition of convenience even mooted rehabilitating the disgraced Muhammad

Umran and giving him a seat on the National Command – which would position him as a prospective power broker to fragment Jadid's Alawi bloc. In the event, they did not need to recruit Umran for the job: a crisis in the military chain of command abruptly moved events in a different direction.

On 19 December 1965, Jadid supporter Mustafa Tlass arrested two senior officers in his brigade in Homs – a breach of military discipline so brazen that there was uproar across the armed forces. Riding the crest of this wave of disapproval, the National Command decreed that the Regional Command should immediately hand over all its powers and disband. Remarkably, so great was the disapproval from the officer corps that the Regional Command obeyed these instructions. With the unexpected blow to Jadid and the officer corps, Aflaq's resurgent civilian wing attempted to regain control of the army and party membership. Bitar again became prime minister and, in January 1966, recalled Muhammad Umran from Spain to serve as defence minister. Bitar's cabinet also included a number of non-Ba'thists, as well as a couple of unionists sympathetic to Abd al-Nasser. Finally, Bitar ordered the dismissal of several high-ranking officers close to Jadid whose political volatility he did not trust. Any one of these factors would have antagonized the officer corps; together, they were a pointed provocation to the party's military organization in general, and to Jadid in particular. On 23 February 1966, Jadid rallied his officers and responded to this challenge with force.

Although successful, Jadid's coup was not bloodless: it entailed open fighting between Ba'thist army units in Damascus, Homs and Qunaytra, close to the front line with Israel. Bitar, Hafiz and Umran were placed under arrest; Aflaq simply fled. Radio Damascus paused its military music to announce that the commander of the air force, Major General Hafiz al-Assad, had been appointed acting defence minister. A few days later, Nur al-Din al-Atasi was appointed president of the Syrian Arab Republic and Yusuf Zu'ayyin prime minister. The two men came from very different backgrounds: the new president had thrown off his class origins in the great landowning Atasi family of Homs to become a devoted nationalist and card-carrying Ba'thist; the new prime minister was a radical Regionalist from the Euphrates town of Albu Kamal, close to the border with Iraq.

Significant changes were made to the party as well as the government. In March, the dissolved Regional [Syrian] Command of the Ba'th Party was reconstituted. Official procedures were meticulously followed to terminate the party membership of Michel Aflaq, Salah al-Din al-Bitar and their supporters. As a contemporary observer noted, '[Jadid's] coup completed the metamorphosis of the party in Syria. Sloughing off the skin of the old Ba'th, the neo-Ba'th proper emerged into the light of day.'[89] While the first half of the 1960s had witnessed ideological innovation, generational change and an upheaval in party personnel, it was Jadid's coup of February 1966 that marked the reboot of the Ba'th. The party of Aflaq no longer existed in Syria: this was Ba'thism 2.0.

Radical agendas: sliding into war

With Salah Jadid as its strongman, the new Ba'th regime came to be known for two characteristics: its distinctly Alawi character and its decidedly radical politics. The former was a consequence of numerous rounds of strategic sectarianism, the fact that coups and conspiracies were communicated along networks of trust that tended to overlap with communal ties of region and sect. Jadid's coup was followed by a purge of the supporters of Amin al-Hafiz, who were predominantly Sunni, thus further enhancing the preponderance of minorities at the top of the regime. Hafiz's ousted allies attempted to stage a comeback with the help of Hamad 'Ubayd, the officer from Jabal al-Arab who had been responsible for the suppression of the 1964 Hama uprising, and who felt slighted when Hafiz al-Assad was given the job of defence minister that he had long coveted. 'Ubayd's plans for a coup were foiled, however, and he and his supporters arrested by Jadid loyalists.

A more serious challenge was posed by a second Druze officer, Salim Hatum, who, in 1966, began to establish a secret organization of primarily Druze officers from the Jabal and at least one Sunni from the neighbouring region of the Hawran.[90] Hatum also felt slighted by the Jadid regime's failure to promote him, even though he had actively participated in the February coup that brought it to power. Hatum made common cause with a faction of Druze Marxists who had broken from the Ba'th the year after it came to power. After a separate, largely Druze plot was uncovered by Jadid, Hatum's clique openly criticized the regime for arresting so many alleged conspirators when, miraculously, there was not a single Alawi among them. Hatum's critique hit its mark, and he won over to his side the Suwayda branch of the civilian Ba'th Party, which threatened to reject the authority of the Regional Command if the Druze purges continued.

In response to this burst of Druze autonomy, the Regional Command sent a high-level delegation to Suwayda to calm the waters, among them President Atasi and Jadid himself. Hatum promptly captured the delegation and held them hostage while he negotiated with Defence Minister Hafiz al-Assad back in Damascus. Assad refused to cave to Hatum's demands to purge Jadid's supporters and readmit the Druze Marxists. Instead, he sent a rocket battalion to Suwayda and threatened to level the city. Hatum and his supporters wisely reassessed their options and, drawing from the Druze playbook since the time of the mandate, hopped over the border to seek asylum in Jordan.[91] The Jadid regime purged Hatum's sympathizers, several of whom received death sentences from military courts.

The suppression of the two plots by 'Ubayd and Hatum broke up the remaining networks of trust that relied on Druze officers, leaving the army almost entirely in the hands of networks dominated by Alawis. Opponents of the Syrian Ba'th in general, and the Jadid regime in particular, were quick to frame the situation in terms of a deliberate power grab by the Alawis. Hatum took advantage of the safety of Jordan to rail against the 'shameful' tribal and sectarian loyalties he accused the regime of fostering. 'Powerful places in the state and its institutions are reserved for a specific segment of the Syrian population,' Hatum told a press conference in Amman. 'The Alawis in the army have attained a ratio of five to one of all other religious communities.'[92]

This perception was enhanced when a last network of challengers, centred on Chief of Staff Ahmad Suwaydani and a group of officers from the Hawran region, was discovered and purged over the next couple of years. Nevertheless, the emergence of Alawis as a force to be reckoned with in the state, public sector and military was less the product of a sect-wide conspiracy than the convergence of several separate factors: the expansion of government, the drive to escape rural poverty and the effectiveness of strategic sectarianism in an officer corps dominated by factionalism, suspicion and justifiable paranoia. Between 1963, when the Ba'th Party came to power, and the eve of the June 1967 war, some 700 officers – more than a third of the entire corps – had been purged from the army.[93] While many officers from Jabal al-Arab, the Hawran, Damascus and Aleppo continued their military careers, they did so as individuals, not as members of region-based power blocs. In the brutally competitive political environment of the 1960s, Alawis and their networks were the last men standing.

Jadid's regime swiftly acquired a reputation for being even more radical than its predecessors. The government accelerated the redistribution of agricultural land to peasants and launched large state-run farms in the Jazira. It relaxed the prohibition on the Communists, allowing Khalid Bakdash to return to Syria, and appointed a Communist to the cabinet, although the party was still officially banned. It negotiated a deal with the Soviet Union to complete a major infrastructural project: the construction of a vast dam on the Euphrates River that had originally been planned with aid from West Germany. It made agreements with firms from China, Poland, Czechoslovakia and the Soviet Union to construct modern factories for steel, fertilizer and textiles, consolidated many smaller nationalized manufacturing companies into fewer, larger ventures and expanded state control over imports and exports. The government decreed that any violation of its economic regulations would be punished with up to fifteen years in jail. In the first five months of 1967, food prices rose by a third. Syrian shopkeepers chafed under the new restrictions, amid simmering discontent with the Jadid regime's radicalism. As in the previous uprising in 1964, three years later it was similarly a coalition of urban merchants and Islamic conservatives that was able to mobilize this discontent into action.

On 25 April 1967, the official magazine of the Syrian armed forces, *Jaysh al-Sha'b* ('The People's Army') published an article by party ideologue Ibrahim Khalas entitled 'The Road to Create our New Arab Person'. Although the publication had limited reach – it was only distributed to soldiers serving in the armed forces – the article had a devastating impact on public opinion and almost provoked a full-scale insurrection. Imbued with the spirit of existentialist philosophy then fashionable in the literary and cultural circles of the Arab avant-garde, the article declared the need for revolutionary socialist values to replace the tired and obsolete ideals of Islam and Christianity.

'The only way to build a new Arab civilization and society,' the author proclaimed, 'is to create a new Arab socialist person who believes that God, religions, feudalism, capitalism, and the super-rich – all the values that dominated previous societies – are nothing but mummified relics in the museum of history [. . .] We have no need for a person who prays devoutly, kneeling humbly to ask for mercy and forgiveness.' Heaven and hell did not exist, said the article; instead of the promise of an afterlife, it offered the bleak materialism of physical decay: 'death and nothing but death'.[94] The new socialist revolutionary believed that man was an absolute truth unto himself.

The reaction to this attack on religion was led by Shaykh Hasan Habannaka, a respected Islamic scholar from the Maydan neighbourhood of Damascus, who angrily condemned the article in his sermon on the first Friday in May.[95] Streaming from the mosques, thousands of prayer goers took to the streets. The protests spread from Damascus to Aleppo, Homs and Hama, and were joined by Christians as well as Muslims. The regime used surprisingly little violence to disperse the demonstrations, but that evening arrested dozens of preachers. The next day, the markets closed their shutters as protestors took to the streets once more. This time, the regime responded with force but, with so many simultaneous protests in so many cities, struggled to quell the unrest. A hastily convened military court found the author and the entire *Jaysh al-Sha'b* editorial team guilty of attempting to instigate religious sedition. Those responsible were expelled from the army and sentenced to heavy labour. Although the streets emptied, the Jadid regime was evidently pushing the limits of its control.

The new radicalism was also reflected in Syria's foreign policy.

While conflict on the border with Israel had flared repeatedly over the previous two decades, Syrian governments were generally too embroiled in the country's own internal affairs to risk confronting or provoking their neighbour. This situation changed under Jadid. Adopting the doctrine of popular liberation that swept Africa, Asia and Latin America in the 1960s, Jadid funnelled aid and ammunition to the new Palestinian organizations that had felt frustrated by the failings of Arab governments and now sought to achieve national liberation through guerrilla warfare. Jadid used money to keep his Palestinian nationalists on a tight leash: they were allowed to train in Syria but could only launch attacks against Israel from Jordanian territory. The one time this rule was breached, in May 1966, Defence Minister Hafiz al-Assad responded by incarcerating the leaders of the main Palestinian faction, Fatah, including none other than Yasser Arafat.

The Syrian media warned that Israel was on the brink of attacking Syria, a threat that Jadid cannily exploited, with Soviet support, to engineer a rapprochement with Abd al-Nasser in 1966. Cairo even signed a treaty of mutual defence with Damascus that November. Jadid encouraged more guerrilla attacks against Israel, exploiting the threat of regional instability in an attempt to offset the opposition to his regime's radical economic policies at home.

In April 1967, tensions between Syria and Israel reached such a point that an exchange of fire on the front line escalated into an aerial dogfight. As it happened, Jadid's concerns that the national air force might be used in an internal coup against his regime meant that the Syrian planes involved in the clash had deliberately been left unarmed. Unprepared for a serious confrontation, seven aircraft were lost. Despite its belligerent rhetoric, the Jadid regime did not expect war just a few months later.

June 1967: the aftermath of defeat

By the summer of 1967, turbulence was not limited to Jadid's Syria but rippled across the region. Over nearly two decades, successive Israeli governments had expanded their borders towards the north-east by pushing beyond the 1949 armistice line to absorb parts of the demilitarized zones that separated them from Syria. Like Syria, and the vast majority of new states in the 1950s and 1960s, Israel had adopted a policy of state-led economic development. Unlike in Syria, however, Israeli leaders did not have to contend with deeply entrenched social divisions, political polarization, or rampant factionalism. The Israeli armed forces were well disciplined, efficient and professional. In May 1967, Soviet and Syrian intelligence reported – incorrectly – that Israel was preparing to attack Syria for its ongoing support of Palestinian guerrillas. From Cairo, Abd al-Nasser watched on with alarm as a younger generation of Syrian and Palestinian radicals seemed to flirt recklessly with starting a conflict they could not hope to win. To regain the initiative, Abd al-Nasser asked the UN observer force to withdraw from positions on Egypt's border with Israel, sent Egyptian troops into the Sinai and closed the Straits of Tiran to ships bound for the Israeli port of Eilat. While Abd al-Nasser intended such measures as an act of brinkmanship that would prompt intervention from the United States and Soviet Union, Israeli generals interpreted these moves as signs of aggression that justified a pre-emptive strike. With Nasser riding high on a wave of popular support, Arab leaders scrambled to join his cause: Jordan and then Iraq rapidly agreed mutual defence treaties with Egypt.

On the morning of 5 June 1967, the Israeli air force bombed Egyptian bases and runways, destroying nearly 70 per cent of

Egypt's military aircraft. Exploiting the element of surprise, Israel went on to wreck the Jordanian and Syrian air forces, as well as a couple of squadrons of Iraqi planes in Jordan. Israeli land forces poured over the borders, swiftly pushing back Egyptian forces to take control of Gaza and the Sinai Peninsula and Jordanian forces to take the West Bank and East Jerusalem.

For several days, taken aback by the loss of its airfleet, the Syrian regime did not respond. Then on 9 June – almost as an afterthought – Israeli Defence Minister Moshe Dayan ordered his troops over the Syrian border and into the region of the Golan, the fertile western fringe of the Hawran plain. Syrian troops defended against the invasion with surprising tenacity, destroying 160 Israeli tanks, but were ordered to fall back to the regional capital of Qunaytra. On 10 June, Radio Damascus falsely broadcast the news that Qunaytra had fallen. Syrian soldiers fled for their lives, leaving the way open for Israeli troops to take the city. The Soviet Union brokered a ceasefire, leading to cessation of hostilities a day later, although Israel nevertheless seized a Syrian station on Mt Hermon, which later became a key listening post for intercepting Syrian radio communications.[96]

In addition to the deaths of some 15,000 people, the Six Day War led to massive displacement, as families sought to escape the fighting. Over 300,000 Palestinians fled the Israeli occupation for Jordan. An estimated 80,000 to 100,000 Syrians also fled the Israeli-occupied Golan; only three small towns inhabited by Syrian Druze remained. Those who fled, known as the *Nazihin* ('Displaced'), scattered across Syria, but were to cling on to their distinctive local customs and accents for generations. The *Nazihin* received no support or assistance from the government in replacing their lost homes and farms or rebuilding their lives. As an unwelcome lasting reminder of Syria's national defeat, they were virtually ignored by the authorities.

Syria's defeat would haunt Defence Minister Hafiz al-Assad, who only narrowly avoided being ousted from his position. A careful and methodical character, Assad blamed the failure on Jadid's hot-headed support for Palestinian guerrillas and his ardent pursuit of radical policies at home, which had distracted and divided the nation at a time of crisis. For Assad, 'unity' trumped 'socialism' in the Ba'thist triad of values. Assad argued that the priority was to build Syria's military capabilities in preparation for the next confrontation with Israel. To that end, he advocated closer coordination with the other Arab states, even for a rapprochement with the rival Aflaq wing of the Ba'th Party, which would come to power in Iraq in July 1968, and for a less doctrinaire, more pragmatic approach to the private sector. Jadid and his clique were adamant that they would not halt their socialist revolution, which, if anything, needed to be accelerated as a prerequisite for a stronger nation. Antagonisms between the two camps were thus reflected in their preferences for economic policy.

The intense conflict between Jadid and Assad saw each of them consolidate control over key institutions. Skilfully using his powers of appointment, transfer and promotion, Assad single-handedly took control of the armed forces. Jadid monopolized the civilian wing of the Ba'th Party and forbade its members from having any contact with the party's organization in the armed forces.

Assad made his first move against Jadid in February 1969, when he decided to bring the Latakia branch of the Ba'th into his own sphere of influence. He arrested the branch's pro-Jadid leaders and the provincial governor, replacing them with his own loyalists. Assad then stationed tanks around the capital, seized control of Radio Damascus and replaced the editors of the *al-Ba'th* and *al-Thawra* newspapers, which would subsequently become sympathetic to his cause. Led by Assad's younger brother, the impetuous Rif'at al-Assad, troops surrounded the headquarters of Abd al-Karim al-Jundi, intelligence chief and founding member of the Military Committee; several of Jundi's supporters were arrested. Feeling desperately isolated and powerless, Jundi shot himself in the head. Assad did not attend the funeral. Jundi's suicide deprived Jadid of a key ally at the helm of the internal security and surveillance system.

With Jundi's death, Assad had effectively obtained the upper hand, although the two camps reached an uneasy equilibrium and jointly formed a new political bureau within the Ba'th Party to run the country. Détente survived until the following year. Two factors broke the fragile peace. The first came when Assad again engaged his ministerial powers of appointment to transfer, demote or dismiss Jadid's supporters in the armed forces. The second came from the changing geopolitical environment. Palestinian guerrillas had become bolder in their attacks on Israel, buoyed by Abd al-Nasser's pursuit of a war of attrition to regain control of the Sinai, occupied by Israel in 1967, and by Fatah leader Yasser Arafat's election as chairman of the Palestinian Liberation Organization, transforming it from a talking shop into a coordination body for Palestinian militant factions. Assad was sceptical of the anarchistic guerrilla movement, whose attacks on Israel risked provoking reprisals against neighbouring states with scant regard for *raison d'état*.

Assad's concerns seemed to be justified when, in September 1970, a radical faction named the Popular Front for the Liberation of Palestine (PFLP) hijacked four foreign aeroplanes in Jordan and took hundreds of hostages. Jordan's King Hussein ordered his troops to move against the militants, in the process inflicting heavy casualties and serious damage to several Palestinian refugee settlements. This infamous episode of overt intra-Arab conflict – which was for some tantamount to civil war – became known as Black September.

Assad initially responded to Palestinian requests for support during the crisis with weapons. He then issued orders to dispatch Syrian tanks across the Jordanian border to Irbid, with the aim of pressuring King Hussein to relent the onslaught and allow the Palestinians space to negotiate. These limited objectives were reflected in Assad's refusal to order the Syrian air force to support the expedition, against the wishes of Jadid and his radicals. Jordan showed little restraint in sending both tanks and aeroplanes to engage the Syrian force, which sustained heavy losses. Uncertain of the Syrian regime's intentions, King Hussein then conveyed to the United States that he would not oppose any Israeli airstrike on Syria. With the United States and Israel conspicuously signalling their intentions with troop movements in Syria's general direction, Assad ordered his troops back across the border rather than provoke a wider conflict for which his country was at the time ill prepared. Jadid's supporters were furious with what they saw as Assad's half-hearted approach to Palestine. Just a week after the incident, the death of Abd al-Nasser seemed to deliver a further blow to the radicals' vision of Arab nationalism, prompting them to action.

In one last bid to regain control, the Jadid faction called for an emergency National Congress, which began on 30 October 1970. Over the next few days, they eventually pushed through resolutions that Hafiz al-Assad and his right-hand man, Mustafa Tlass, should be relieved of their military responsibilities. Assad responded with decision. On 13 November, the day after the congress ended, Assad ordered the army and security forces to move against the Jadid camp. Assad gave the chief of Air Force Intelligence, Muhammad al-Khuli, eight hours to round up Jadid and his supporters in the party and state bureaucracy. Khuli reportedly boasted to Assad that he trapped them 'like rabbits in their beds'.[97] In fact, so smooth and swift were the arrests and Assad's seizure of power that they provoked no resistance and shed no blood; so silent was it that everyday life in the cities, towns and villages continued without interruption. Reportedly rejecting Assad's offer of exile, Jadid was jailed in the infamous Mezzeh prison of Damascus until he died there in 1993. Extended imprisonment soon came to be one of Assad's preferred methods of dealing with political opponents from within the system.

Much like the instigators of previous coups, Assad liked to maintain he had been obliged to act in order to correct the country's errant political direction. Subsequently, 13 November 1970 was celebrated in the regime's official hagiography as the Corrective Movement (*al-Haraka al-Tashihiya*). In truth, this intervention was not merely a coup like so many before: Assad had carried out what would be the country's last successful military takeover. The leadership of Hafiz al-Assad would last for the next three decades: under his rule, Syria would be transformed.

9

Building Assad's Syria, 1970–1982

For many observers, the key to understanding late twentieth-century Syria can be found in the inscrutable cipher of just one man: Hafiz al-Assad. Aptly named the 'sphinx of Damascus' by one of his many biographers,[1] even Assad's closest allies found him difficult to read. 'I could easily write twenty pages on the heroism, leadership and struggle of Hafiz al-Assad,' noted his childhood companion Mustafa Tlass, the long-serving defence minister who owed his entire career to Assad, 'yet I would have taken barely a step into the real depth of this great man.'[2] Assad was cautious yet ruthless, a dogged fighter and shrewd tactician who played the longest of long games. An ardent Ba'thist, Assad united the party and expanded its ranks yet diluted its ideology for the sake of expediency and turned radical activists into career bureaucrats. He endowed the Syrian state with the most powerful institutions it had ever possessed, yet undercut those institutions by riddling them with cliques based on family, region and sect. He crushed the opposition and eradicated all space for politics yet entrusted to his loyal followers a surprising degree of autonomy. He watched Syrian citizens chant his name, pledge oaths of love and allegiance and hang his image in offices, schools and shops across the country, yet he had no personal charisma: his speeches were dry and tedious, his rhetoric formal, heavy and humourless. None of this mattered. Hafiz al-Assad was a workhorse, a meticulous planner and a master coalition builder, not to mention an implacable and pitiless despot. Assad's singular longevity as ruler meant that, for his supporters, his name became all but synonymous with Syria itself.

Although Assad's absolute and fundamental centrality to the new political order cannot be denied, one man by himself cannot hold together a regime. As a whole line of aspiring authoritarian rulers had discovered to their cost, the diversity and complexity of the lands of Syria could not easily be governed from a single source of power. Mehmed Ali, Cemal Pasha, Shukri al-Quwwatli, Adib al-Shishakli, Abd al-Hamid Sarraj, Gamal Abd al-Nasser, Salah Jadid – each of them had relied too heavily on one social group, one mode of repression or one particular institution in their attempts to stay in power. Assad did not make these mistakes. He intuitively realized that Syria could only be governed through multiple, uneven sources of power: parallel institutions, competing circles, contradictory strategies. By working on several fronts simultaneously, the Assad regime could gradually permeate the country, reaching peasants and businessmen, students and workers, tribes and sects in ways that not only responded to the highly localized variations in Syrian society, but also lashed that social and regional diversity to the central core of power. Rather than simply using the state to crush society, Assad's Syria was built upon a complex architecture of institutions, enticements and intimidation, which, even when the cracks began to show, still proved remarkably resilient. It was during the first twelve years of Assad's rule that the foundations were laid not only for the long-lived dictatorship of Hafiz himself, but also for the regime of his son Bashar that would follow.

Formative influences: from al-Qardaha to the October War

Hafiz al-Assad was born in 1930 in the village of al-Qardaha, high in Syria's coastal mountains. His grandfather, Sulayman, had gained standing in the village for his physical strength, which earned him the nickname of 'the Beast' (*al-wahsh*). His father, Ali Sulayman, fought the French alongside Salih al-Ali and adopted the nobler-sounding surname of al-Assad ('the lion') in the 1920s. Despite the rising social status of the Assad family, they were just as desperately poor as the other Alawi villagers in the hills. Ali Sulayman secured for his son Hafiz one of the few places at the newly opened primary school in al-Qardaha, which was followed by secondary school in Latakia – a difficult transition for Assad, given that he was not only away from his family for the first time, but also one of very few Alawis in a city that was predominantly Sunni and Christian. 'In those days the thirty kilometers from Qurdaha to Latakia seemed almost as great as thc distance today between Damascus and London,' Assad told his biographer Patrick Seale in the 1980s.[3] Although Assad's family was respected in his home village, like all Alawis in the city he faced judgement for his rural mannerisms, distinctive accent and sectarian background. In the highly politicized school environment of the late 1930s and 1940s, it is perhaps not surprising that Assad joined the nascent Ba'th movement, whose first principles he was taught by the itinerant physician Wahib al-Ghanim, a former student of the nationalist thinker Zaki al-Arsuzi, an Alawi from Alexandretta. Assad became a frontline local activist and was elected head of the Union of Syrian Students, a national body that gave him his first taste of political organization. Upon graduation, the limited options for Alawis led him to sign up for the army before being accepted for training as one of the first pilots in the newly created Syrian air force. From there, Assad was relocated to Cairo during the UAR period, where – as we have seen – he joined the secret Military Committee and quietly rose to prominence in the Ba'th Party. After surviving successive rounds of conspiracies, purges and intrigue, by 1970 Assad was the last man standing.

After the chaos of the 1960s, Assad was keen to establish a new tone for politics. He initially appointed himself prime minister, but assumed the presidency in February 1971 and had his position confirmed by a national referendum the following month. Rather than arresting or purging the remaining followers of former opponents such as Salah Jadid or Michel Aflaq, Assad allowed them to remain in the party and even offered them government positions on condition they created no trouble. Assad eased tensions with the remnants of the country's other political forces by declaring that the Ba'th would not govern alone. He ordered the formation of a political coalition named the National Progressive Front – much to the surprise of the Regional Command of the Ba'th, to whom any notion of power-sharing was quite alien.[4] Established in 1972, the Front included Communists, Nasserists and the lingering vestiges of other progressive movements. These parties were granted legal recognition and a place in politics alongside the Ba'th, but this was largely a formality. In reality, they enjoyed only limited autonomy, and their space to organize or mobilize political support was highly restricted.

No mercy was offered to political figures who declined Assad's invitation. Jadid himself was detained at the Mezzeh prison, where he was held for twenty-three years until he died of a heart attack at the age of sixty-three. When the exiled Muhammad Umran openly announced he intended to return to Syria in 1972, he was preemptively murdered in Lebanon – likely an ominous indication of the expanding reach of the Syrian intelligence services. Aflaq and other Ba'thists who had defected to the rival Iraqi branch of the party were sentenced to death *in absentia*. Assad's intolerance of political disunity was evident from the very beginning. To balance against Iraq and maintain his legitimacy as an Arab nationalist, Assad announced that Syria would join the ongoing unity talks alongside Egypt, Sudan and Libya. The talks resulted in the declaration of a new Federation of Arab Republics in 1971, but Egypt's new president, Anwar Sadat, had as little interest as Assad in revisiting the problems posed by political and economic unification. From this time onwards, Arab nationalism could at best be considered a goal to be pursued by cooperation between Arab states that retained their independence; at worst it was a lost cause to which Arab leaders paid little more than lip service. In much the same way, Assad announced to Ba'thists at the Eleventh National Congress in 1971 that he had carried out a 'Corrective Movement' to bring the party back to its true ideological mission, but in practice the new regime suspended exporting the Ba'th revolution to the rest of the Arab world. Deepening the Ba'thist regime inside Syria was the priority.

On the domestic front, Assad sought to end the hostility between the Ba'th and the Syrian private sector. Restrictions were eased on imports of goods and inbound capital transfers, punishments for economic crimes were suspended and a new agency was established to encourage investment in Syria's free zones, which would be exempted from the country's strict regulations on trade. Articles in the new constitution, promulgated in 1973, specifically guaranteed the right of private property, although it also iterated a commitment to a 'planned socialist economy' that would end all forms of exploitation. The 1973 Constitution also promised citizens equality before the law as well wide-ranging freedoms of assembly, expression and protest. However, the ongoing state of emergency that had been in force since 1963 meant that these rights were suspended – ostensibly on a temporary basis, although the emergency laws remained in force until April 2011, nearly fifty years on. What was left of the Syrian business community welcomed Assad's more conciliatory approach, but they understood that the new regime was capable of policing their activities just as harshly as its predecessors. Assad saw political utility in relaxing the restrictions on business, for he believed that most Syrian citizens were uninterested in politics as long as their basic economic needs were met. Only a small proportion of individuals were politically active, Assad once told a colleague, 'and it is for them that the Mezzeh prison was originally intended'.[5]

These political and economic overtures were not simply an instrument to expand Assad's base against threats from potential rivals. They were also part of a broader strategy to rehabilitate Syria after the traumatic experience of the Six Day War with Israel. The defeat of 1967 had been disastrous for Assad personally as well as for Syria and the Arabs generally. As defence minister at the time, Assad had a measure of responsibility for the loss, while Syrians were horrified that yet another slice of territory had been carved from the country by an outside power. For many Arab intellectuals, the *Naksa* ('Setback') of 1967 meant much more than the loss of the Golan or a mere military defeat. The year 1967 stood as an indictment of the parlous state of nothing less than Arab civilization itself. The most damning analysis came from Syrian philosopher Sadiq al-Azm, whose 1968 book *Self-Criticism After the Defeat* identified the loss as symptomatic of an underlying social, political and intellectual crisis in the Arab world. Even self-proclaimed Arab revolutionaries clung to conservative values, claimed Azm: Arab society was dominated by traditionalism and tribalism, rigidity and magical thinking. The existing elites had failed: the struggle for Palestine could be won only if the masses seized power and reshaped society with a genuine revolution. The 1967 defeat similarly compelled Damascene poet Nizar Qabbani, renowned for addressing lyrical affairs of love and romance, to turn his pen to politics. 'My grieved country,' Qabbani mused in his *Marginalia in the Book of the Defeat*, 'in a flash / You changed me from a poet who wrote love poems / To a poet who writes with a knife [. . .] Our enemies did not cross the border / They crept through our weakness like ants [. . .] We are a nation of crooks and jugglers.'[6] The iconoclasm of writers like Azm and Qabbani sounded like a clarion call for Arabs dissatisfied with the status quo, who concurred that the defeat had been caused not simply by the forces of Zionism and Western imperialism, but by a crisis internal to Arab society and culture.

Much as an earlier generation had turned against those held responsible for the Arab defeat in 1948, so did the new rulers of Syria and Egypt seek to right the ignominious wrongs of 1967. After opening a new, post-Abd al-Nasser chapter in diplomatic relations by making Syria part of the proposed federation that included Egypt, Assad set about cultivating ties with the Soviet Union – in his view the only source of military technology and diplomatic support that had even a hope of balancing US support for Israel. Coordination between Egypt and Syria progressed to the point where the two countries were prepared to launch a surprise strike on Israel. Israel and the United States simply did not see it coming, convinced that it would be foolhardy for the Arab countries to launch a war given the military inferiority they had demonstrated in 1967.[7] Assad and Sadat took advantage of being underestimated and ordered the attack to commence on two fronts simultaneously.

On 6 October 1973, 100,000 Egyptian troops and 1,000 tanks crossed the Suez Canal into the Israeli-occupied Sinai, while a force of 35,000 Syrian soldiers and 800 tanks burst into the Israeli-held

Golan. The element of surprise – given that the war commenced on the Jewish holiday of Yom Kippur – gave Egyptian and Syrian troops an early taste of jubilant success, until the Egyptian forces stopped advancing and dug in before they had taken back the entire Sinai. Sadat, it seemed, did not share Assad's goal of liberating the territory captured in 1967. Instead, he wanted to use the war as a catalyst to relaunch peace negotiations with Israel on a sounder footing – a message he communicated to US Secretary of State Henry Kissinger, who advised as much to Israel.

Over the next three days, the Israeli air force paused attacks on the Egyptian front to concentrate fire on the Syrian troops, subjecting them to intense bombardment that effectively stopped them in their tracks. Israeli planes struck targets deep inside Syria – the outskirts of Damascus, the Homs oil refinery, electricity plants and port facilities. By this point, the tide of war had turned: even a belated advance from the Egyptian forces came as too little, too late. On 16 October, much to the surprise of Assad, Sadat gave a speech calling for a ceasefire and for peace negotiations to be sponsored by the United Nations. Meanwhile, Kissinger agreed with his Russian counterpart the text of a ceasefire agreement that did nothing to resolve the aftermath of the 1967 war, but rather left the question of the occupied Syrian and Egyptian territories, as well as the fate of Palestine, to a later date. Faced with the double-dealing of Sadat and ongoing Israeli advances – including the recapture of an observation point on Mount Hermon, overlooking the Golan – Assad reached out to the leaders of other Arab states for assistance, but was met with silence. With few remaining options, an isolated Assad had little option but to accept the ceasefire.

The experience of 1973 confirmed for Assad the validity of adopting a 'Syria-first' policy. Admittedly, the petroleum-producing Arab countries had indirectly supported the war efforts by imposing an oil embargo on the United States and other supporters of Israel, but the ill-fated coordination with Egypt once again underscored the many obstacles to unity of purpose that stood between the Arabs. In the months and years that followed, Egypt was prised away even further from the cause of Arab nationalism, culminating in Sadat's signing of the US-brokered Camp David peace deal with Israel in 1978. For his part, Assad engaged in protracted negotiations with Kissinger, where he put to good use the stamina acquired from sitting through many hours of interminable meetings on the finer principles of Ba'thist ideology.[8] In the end, Israel withdrew from the Syrian territories it had seized in 1973 and ceded a small amount of land taken in 1967, including the abandoned town of Qunaytra.

In Syria, this outcome was feted as a great success. The Syrian army had demonstrated its ability to use modern military technology, maintain professional discipline and land a serious blow on a State of Israel that had begun to give the impression of being invulnerable. In official Syrian discourse the 1973 conflict became known as the Glorious October War of Liberation. Two years later, the historic victory was further commemorated when a new state newspaper was founded with the name *Tishrin* ('October'). The ruined town of Qunaytra was not rebuilt, but kept in a battle-scarred state of quasi-demolition, a permanent ghost town to remind Syrians of what had been lost at the hands of Israel – and what had been regained at the hands of President Assad. Every spring on Independence Day, carloads of displaced Golanis and Syrians from the rest of the country would descend on Qunaytra to grill meat, drink tea and watch their children play in the lush green fields that surrounded this abandoned urban mausoleum. In the meantime, the Israeli government encouraged settlers to move into the occupied Golan, which was placed under military administration, until it was effectively annexed as an integral part of the State of Israel in 1981. For decades to follow, as first Egypt and then Jordan made their separate peace, Syrians were repeatedly reminded that Assad was the only Arab statesman who remained principled and steadfast in the ongoing struggle with Zionism.

Elites, economics and institutions after 1973

After the October War, the new regime sought to consolidate its position by expanding key Syrian institutions more rapidly than ever before. The armed forces swelled and the state bureaucracy ballooned, overlaid by the parallel structures of the Ba'th Party hierarchy that now opened its doors to newcomers as never before. The popular organizations that had been founded in the 1960s, such as the Peasants' Union and the Women's Union, served to insert different sectors of society firmly into the fabric of the regime, while the first national elections since the 1963 Ba'th coup produced a People's Assembly crammed with party members, National Progressive Front loyalists and compliant 'independents'. The economic radicalism of the 1960s was replaced with a pragmatic restraint of hostility towards the private sector, while the state built new industrial factories, hospitals, schools and power plants to connect Syrian towns and villages to the modern world. The state was by far the leading provider of employment, public goods and infrastructure; its reach became more extensive, and more difficult to avoid, than ever before.

For these reasons, the 1970s are often portrayed as the decade in which the Syrian state finally acquired the capabilities to govern successfully at the national level. The years of the Ottoman Empire, French Mandate and early independence had produced only thin and ineffective structures of administration. That had begun to change in the 1950s, owing to the efforts of aspiring military rulers of one hue or another, but the ideological radicalism and internecine factional disputes of the Ba'th Party in the 1960s had limited the extent to which the Syrian population as a whole had been drawn into the emerging system of state governance. It was under Assad that the Syrian state was ultimately transformed from a fragmented archipelago into a coherent national body. His state sought to produce – and control – a unified national population. However, the underlying social and economic unevenness within the Syrian population still meant that the state had little choice but to embed itself in micro-dynamics that were often surprisingly local in character. The very project of building a national Syrian state also depended on the smooth flow of aid from the Soviet Union and the Gulf Arab states, supportive of Syria's stance against Israel. This aid allowed Syria to form a bubble that was insulated from the global economic downturn of the 1970s. In this way, the state built by Assad did not exist at the purely 'national' scale but was wedded to myriad forces that were also both international and local in character.

At the core of the Assad regime were a handful of individuals whose personal loyalty to the president was beyond doubt. Many of them were Assad's relatives or shared his Alawi background, although this was less a sign of overt sectarianism than a consequence of the fact that the only officer cliques to have survived the purges of the 1960s had happened to be predominantly Alawi. Assad's younger brother, Rif'at, was head of an elite military unit, the Defence Companies (*Saraya al-Difa'*). Originally established with the limited aim of securing Syria's airfields, the Defence Companies had been under Assad's direct control since his days as commander of the air force. Assad similarly built up Air Force Intelligence as the most prominent (and most feared) of Syria's security agencies, commanded by the reliable Muhammad al-Khuli. A relative, Adnan al-Assad, was head of a second elite unit, the Struggle Companies (*Saraya al-Sira'*), responsible for safeguarding the capital against coup attempts and invasion. Adnan Makhlouf, a cousin of Hafiz al-Assad's mother, was entrusted with command of the Republican Guard (*al-Haras al-Jumhuri*), founded in 1976 as the third pillar of Assad's praetorian guard. Although the highest echelons of Syria's military and security establishment were disproportionately comprised of Alawis, a number of Sunnis, Christians, Druze, Ismailis and other minorities could also be found among their ranks.[9] Assad's old associate from military training, Mustafa Tlass, a Sunni from the town of Rastan near Homs, was appointed as Assad's defence minister in 1972 and notably held this post for over thirty years. The former governor of Hama, Abd al-Halim Khaddam – a Sunni from the coastal town of Baniyas – served as foreign minister from 1970 to 1984, and as vice president from 1984 to 2005. However, non-Alawis rarely if ever held any autonomous power in their own right. Even in the military and security forces, commanding officers inevitably found themselves under the watchful eye of a second in command who was Alawi. This unspoken distribution of power was acknowledged among the Syrian population as a whole, who might speak the name of intelligence chiefs such as Muhammad al-Khuli or Ali Douba only in private – and even then in hushed tones – but could roll their eyes comically at the mention of Defence Minister Mustafa Tlass, whose reputation as a womanizer preceded him.[10]

With this inner circle secured, following the October War, Assad dramatically expanded the Syrian army, which increased from 93,250 soldiers in 1970 up to a staggering 257,000 in 1980.[11] This build-up of military might was not necessarily intended to strengthen Syria in anticipation of a renewed conflict with Israel – Assad was too much of realist for that – but certainly held symbolic value for Syria's political standing in the region. A larger army also decreased the likelihood of any potential coup attempt. Ten or twenty years earlier, a small number of rebel officers could quickly seize key positions for themselves; now the sheer size and complexity of the armed forces would necessitate many more conspirators scattered around the country to coordinate their plans without a breach in secrecy, thereby increasing the likelihood of the plot being compromised. Syria's military expenditures soared from around 10 per cent of GDP before 1973 to an average of 15 per cent of GDP for over a decade after the war. Much of this spending was covered by aid from the Gulf states to support Syria's frontline position in the Arab–Israeli conflict or by soft loans from the Soviet Union, which meant that Syria's military was less a drain on state resources than an investment of time and energy that paid back a useful 'war dividend'.[12] While officers had been the principal source of contestation to challenge Syrian regimes prior to 1970, that changed decisively under Hafiz al-Assad. The officer corps effectively ceased to exist as a body with any autonomy from the political regime; for all intents and purposes, the armed forces were an integral part of the regime itself.

The Ba'th Party launched a major recruitment drive which which led to its membership expanding from 100,000 in the early 1970s to 375,000 by 1980. While some of these new members were no doubt believers in the party's philosophical principles, most of them joined for more expedient reasons. The Ba'th Party provided opportunities for Syrian workers and peasants to rise through its ranks and even potentially reach dizzying heights of power at the national level; good standing as a party member was also helpful, to say the least, for teachers, bureaucrats and low-level government employees seeking promotion. Parallel to the civilian organization, a separate party apparatus was maintained in the armed forces. As in the past, provinces with large rural minorities, such as

Latakia, Tartous and Suwayda, were over-represented in the party membership, as were Der'a and Hama, where the largely Sunni peasant communities had most benefitted from land reform.[13] Despite Assad's efforts to appoint Damascenes, especially, to prominent positions in the regime, neither the capital city nor Aleppo ever became redoubts of overwhelming support for the Ba'th. As time wore on, the desiccated ideology of Ba'thism became a set of empty, endlessly repeated slogans, and the party apparatus a vehicle for careerism and patronage rather than political activism.

Despite the erosion of its principles, the Ba'th Party nevertheless retained a degree of institutional autonomy from the upper echelons of the regime. The party's Peasant Bureau played an especially important role in formulating and implementing agrarian policy, in cooperation with the Ministry of Agriculture and Peasants' Union. Successful candidates in internal elections often brought their own agenda to the next level of the party hierarchy, providing a way to articulate local promises and problems within the system. Pressure from the grassroots could even help bring down party members whose corruption became too egregious or excessive. As a towering bureaucracy, moreover, the party was large enough to sustain its own norms, values and institutional culture that could on occasion lead it to diverge from the policy preferences of leading officials. Resolutions passed by the 1975 Regional Congress, the party's highest representative body in Syria, resolutely supported state control of the economy, and were quite out of tune with Assad's shift towards a more liberal approach. Over the years, party members regularly continued to resist the expansion of market forces and call for enhanced state intervention. While the party could never oppose President Assad, it could certainly express its collective position on specific policies and programmes of government ministers.

Assad's economic strategy in the 1970s contained two principal strands. The first was the continued easing of restrictions on the private sector, which was now called upon to contribute to the national interest by developing its activities in light industry, construction and imports. (In contrast, heavy industry, banking and oil were considered strategic sectors in which only the state could operate.) The private sector grew over the decade, and, in 1977, the government even permitted private companies to take on projects in Syria's nascent tourism industry, albeit in formal partnerships with the state. As this new 'mixed' sector was legally shielded from market competitors, the policy sanctioned the creation of what were effectively quasi-monopolies in certain areas. The profitability of obtaining one of these concessions opened up new opportunities for collusion – and corruption – between government officials and the country's top businessmen. Although liberalization did entice some members of the pre-1963 bourgeoisie to trickle back into the country, the millionaires who acquired wealth from these partnerships with the state in the 1970s were mostly newcomers to the economic elite. Their number included such characters such Sa'ib Nahhas, a Shia from Damascus, who founded a tourism business named Transtour in 1978. Transtour was granted exclusive rights to the car rental business across the whole country; it monopolized the taxi trade at Damascus international airport and ran extensive coach services both nationally and internationally (including for the lucrative pilgrimage routes from Iran to Shia shrines in Damascus and in Syria). Syrians began to refer to Nahhas and other super-rich entrepreneurs as the 'new class' – neither the old bourgeoisie nor the state elite.[14] The name was not intended as a compliment.

The second dimension of Assad's economic policy was a sustained programme of state-led industrialization and infrastructural expansion. New factories were built for fertilizers, cement, sugar, cotton and a whole range of goods from tyres and ceramics to tinned foods and pharmaceuticals. These industrial projects were intended not so much to create employment – they were mostly capital-intensive rather than requiring a large labour force – but to replace imported goods with products manufactured domestically. Self-sufficiency, it was believed, would enhance Syria's national independence by reducing its reliance on the outside world. The basic philosophy of Assad's industrial policy was not unique: much of Latin America and other developing countries had adopted similar policies of import-substituting industrialization (ISI) after the Second World War, in many cases inspired by the work of Argentine economist Raúl Prebisch. Yet the Syrian case retained several characteristics that distinguished it from global ISI norms: whereas many Latin American states had opened their doors to the domestic private sector and foreign investment, the Syrian Arab Republic remained firmly closed to international private capital and tightly controlled the opportunities it made available to Syrian businessmen. The state now unleashed a wave of industrialization that swept the country on an unprecedented scale, but its zeal for modernization meant that many of these projects were haphazard and poorly planned. Costs went unchecked, construction materials were in short supply and decisions about where to locate factories were made on the basis of corruption and patronage politics rather than economic rationality. Despite these inefficiencies, state-owned industries expanded dramatically. By 1985, the public sector came to employ 140,000 workers – some 40 per cent of the industrial labour force.

Syria's flurry of industrialization was in many ways a legacy of the 1973 war with Israel. The hike in oil prices had turned the Arab oil states into serious players in regional politics, ready to show their support for the Palestinian cause with loans and grants to such frontline countries as Syria. In 1972, the oil-producing

Arab states – foremost among them Saudi Arabia and Kuwait – had given Syria grants worth some US$45 million. In 1977, that figure increased to US$1,141 million. Although much of this was channelled into military and arms purchases, the influx of Gulf money also freed up the Syrian budget for industrial investment, and even contributed to the establishment of 'mixed' public–private ventures such as the Syrian–Saudi Company for Industrial and Agricultural Investments (1976), which produced one of the most popular domestic yoghurt brands in the country, among other products. Syria had begun to produce, refine and export oil in the late 1960s, although its importance was limited owing to the relatively small quantity involved and the fact that it took four years to repair the Homs oil refinery and other petroleum infrastructure that had been targeted by Israel in 1973.[15] Additionally, Damascus earned transit revenues from Iraq, whose oil was piped through Syria via the port of Tartous, and also Tripoli in Lebanon. Meanwhile, tens of thousands of Syrian workers travelled to work in the oil-fuelled construction boom then sweeping the Gulf. They were especially drawn to Saudi Arabia and Kuwait, where salaries could be as much as four to seven times higher than they were at home.[16] By the end of the 1970s, these migrant workers were sending $600–900 million to their families back in Syria each year.[17]

Directly and indirectly, oil wealth helped insulate Syria from the combination of decreasing profits and stagflation that had begun to chill the world economy in the 1970s, marking an end to three decades of unprecedented economic improvement enjoyed in Western Europe and North America. However, the colossal increases in government spending and the relaxation of restrictions on imports contributed to several years of painful inflation, which had climbed to 18–20 per cent by the late 1970s. In 1977, Syrian government agencies calculated that the consumer price index had doubled in the space of just five years.[18] The government relied on subsidies to ensure that rice, tea, sugar, flour and other basic foodstuffs remained affordable, rather than raising public sector salaries, which remained stubbornly where they had been earlier in the decade. Even among constituencies loyal to the Ba'th, the difficulties of day-to-day living provoked a widespread groundswell of discontent.

The party cannily allowed some such frustrations to be released in the official media. The *al-Ba'th* newspaper published a plaintive open letter from one Syrian university professor who petitioned Prime Minister Khulayfawi to solve his accommodation problem by allowing him to pitch a tent on campus, as his monthly rent was now higher than his entire salary. An editorial in the state-run *al-Thawra* newspaper, no less, attacked those who 'profited from the leadership and nation being absorbed in essential matters [i.e. foreign policy] [. . .] to busy themselves with making money at the expense of the country, spreading a feeling of hopelessness and the seeds of irresponsibility in people's hearts'. *Al-Thawra* also published satirical caricatures by a young cartoonist named 'Ali Farzat, whose work targeted private sector speculators, wasteful bureaucracy and the super-rich elite of the 'new class'.[19]

Such criticisms were kept strictly within the red lines determined by the regime. Generic complaints about businessmen, bureaucrats or even government ministers may have been tolerated, but Assad himself, high on his pedestal, was beyond reproach. Nevertheless such rumblings hinted at deeper ambivalence about the rapidity of the changes introduced in Syria during the 1970s. As Assad was to discover, his policies of pragmatic yet accelerated industrialization would prove to be a double-edged sword.

Cities, roads and resettlements: remaking Syria's regions

The Assad regime's commitment to its rural constituents was reflected in the distribution of the new economic ventures it created in the 1970s. Many of the new factories were located not in Damascus and Aleppo, where they had historically been concentrated, but in secondary cities such as Homs, Tartous and Latakia, and in smaller towns along the coast. This dispersed industrialization was underpinned by a new ripple of infrastructure building across the regions. When Assad came to power in 1970, only 218 of Syria's thousands of villages had been electrified. By 1980, the electricity network now brought power to nearly 2,000 villages. Over the same period, about half of all rural villages and almost every urban home obtained access to clean piped drinking water.[20] New roads were built to connect the major cities with previously isolated hamlets in regions such as the Jazira and coastal mountains, opening the way for the reliable transport of agricultural products from the countryside to the cities. New primary and secondary schools, clinics and hospitals were built to service Syria's growing population, improving literacy rates and public health and providing concrete expressions of what were claimed as the glorious achievements of the Ba'th Party. Syria's population grew from 6.3 million in 1970 to 9 million in 1981.

The transformation of rural life during the 1970s is vividly captured by a new wave of Syrian film-makers, whose work provides rare glimpses behind the curtain of Ba'thist political conformity. Scenes in Ossama Mohammed's 1978 film, *Khutwa Khutwa* ('Step by Step'), show the poverty endemic to one village in the coastal hills, where young children play barefoot in mud, men perform back-breaking labour for ten hours a day and frustrated teenagers punctuate the monotony of daily life by throwing stones at the cattle they are driving.[21] Yet even here, in this isolated hamlet, the next generation can discern the promise of a better life. A commercial aeroplane flies over the village, hinting at possibilities of travel and technology; the newly constructed rural schools are crammed with children memorizing texts and songs. 'Either you study or go to the fields,' one old man tells his son. With no jobs in the countryside, village men with even a basic level of schooling flock to the city to work in construction or the armed forces, where they quickly learn to navigate a more complex and dangerous world than that of the village they have left behind. At one point in the film, the narrator asks a recruit what he would do if he were ordered to turn his tank against his family because they were enemies of the state. 'I'd go to my family and say this is what's going to happen,' the soldier says. 'But I couldn't refuse an order. I'd tell them I was coming now to demolish their home.' Another man cheerfully tells the camera that if his brother admitted to damaging national security – or 'cursing the Party or cursing the leadership' – he would personally 'go and put a gun in his ear'. The recruits have quickly internalized the idea that loyalty to the government trumped loyalty to the village.

Despite the improvements to rural living, migration from the countryside to the cities continued to accelerate. In 1960, 63 per cent of Syrians lived in rural areas; by 1978, the proportion had fallen to 51.2 per cent. Unlike in countries such as Iraq, Jordan and Egypt, where internal migration was primarily concentrated on movement to the capital cities, in Syria population flows were more evenly distributed among the major cities of each governorate. Not only Damascus and Aleppo, but also towns such as Homs, Hassakeh and Latakia, expanded rapidly.

The population of Damascus grew from 530,000 in 1960 to an estimated 1.14 million in 1978. The old orchards and agricultural plots of the Ghouta oasis were replaced with new streets of concrete apartment buildings; outlying villages such as Kafr Sousseh, Qadam, Berzeh and Mezzeh were now incorporated into Damascus as urban neighbourhoods. The expansion was guided by a master plan developed in 1968 by French urbanist Michel Écochard (who had ironically also been the planner for developing Damascus under the French Mandate), but the scale of the population increase led to building on areas that the master plan had intended to remain green. Entirely new developments, often built on neatly ordered grid patterns, were built in the mid-1970s some way outside the city, at locations such as Mashrou' Dummar and al-Dimas.[22] These new neighbourhoods were typically intended for state employees or officers, in which case they were likely to have been constructed by the gargantuan army-owned building company, Milihouse, which provided army officers with another source of graft.

As if to reaffirm the political centrality of Damascus, in 1970 the capital was separated from its surroundings for the purposes of local government and elevated to a governorate in its own right. The remainder of the area, the new governorate of Rif Dimashq ('Rural Damascus'), stretched from Qatana, to the south-west of the city, as far as Yabroud, halfway to Homs. Although many of the Ghouta suburbs were now attached to the governorate of Damascus, the quarter known as Yarmouk Camp (mainly home to Palestinian refugees who had fled to Syria in 1948) was administratively detached from the capital to become part of Rural Damascus. The decision to create distinct administrative bodies to govern central Damascus and its surrounding suburbs was ostensibly driven by rationalization, given the size of the capital, but inevitably produced problems of coordination and even a degree of rivalry between the two adjacent governorates.

The city of Aleppo also welcomed huge numbers of rural migrants, although it grew more slowly than Damascus. By 1978, Aleppo had around 900,000 inhabitants, but nearly 40 per cent of them were recent migrants from the countryside. Aleppo's business community had taken advantage of the Assad regime's opening to build new luxury apartments for the middle classes, leading to a speculative boom at the high end of the property market. The municipal government lacked the capacity to build affordable housing to accommodate the rapid influx of newcomers, which meant that rural migrants were largely left to their own devices: they consequently built their own homes informally, and often somewhat haphazardly.

'In the more recent quarters,' wrote French geographer Jean-Claude David, who worked as a consultant urban planner at the municipality of Aleppo in the late 1960s and 1970s, 'the roads are just adjoining spaces left empty between buildings, totally impassable by cars – and sometimes pedestrians – that become muddy potholes in winter and dusty potholes in summer, interspersed with limestone ridges and hollows.'[23] The slum-like conditions endured by rural migrants in Aleppo and Damascus, concurrent with the frenzied construction of expensive modern housing, served as a stark reminder of the deep social inequality that still shaped Syrian geography.

Smaller cities also felt the impact of rural migration. In central Syria, the new factories built at Homs made the city an especially attractive destination for newcomers, as did its location at the hub of Syria's rapidly expanding road infrastructure. In 1981, the population of Homs reached 346,871. It thus overtook the 177,208 inhabitants of neighbouring Hama, where the economy remained heavily based on agriculture and artisanal industry. Hama had hardly any rural migrants: its average annual population growth from 1970 to 1981 stood at just 2.33 per cent, compared to 4.44 per cent for Homs,[24] and 4.2 per cent and 5.3 per cent for the coastal cities of Latakia and Tartous – the latter had been promoted to the capital of its own governorate in 1967. In the south, Der'a increased from around 27,000 to over 49,000. In contrast, the tight-knit Druze community in Suwayda proved less enticing to non-Druze rural migrants and consequently grew much more slowly, at about half the speed of the other cities. In the north, the town of Idlib was elevated to the status of provincial capital by the creation of another new governorate of the same name, thus chipping away at the influence Aleppo had historically exerted over this marginal area to its west. A second tier of smaller coastal towns, such as Dreykish, Sheikh Bader and Assad's home village of al-Qardaha, also grew significantly, owing to the provision of new state jobs in bureaucracy and industry, even though these towns still lacked a significant local private sector.

The extension of state bureaucracy, industry and infrastructure into the countryside had goals that were as much political as developmental. Such projects were intended to weaken the old urban elites, create a constituency of grateful supplicants, and transform the peasantry into new Syrians, imbued with loyalty to the Assad regime. State employees charged with executing this mission nevertheless often found a gap between these lofty modernizing aspirations and the harsh reality of limited resources and resistance to government interference in local affairs. A 1974 documentary titled *Everyday Life in a Syrian Village* (*al-Hayat al-Yawmiya fi Qarya Suriya*), directed by the famed Omar Amiralay, reports the trials and tribulations of government officials and local residents in the Euphrates region. 'Here it is written "take a bath three times a week",' a schoolteacher reads his pupils from the official textbook. 'But we don't have any baths. Or any taps. Or any water that's very hot. What can we do? We can't wash three times a week. Once a week, on a Friday, is quite sufficient.' In another scene, a uniformed official sitting behind an imposing desk reminisces about when he first arrived in the village. 'I was very surprised by this region,' he says. 'People don't understand very much. Most of the results we're seeing show that they don't have much awareness ... A guy hits his cousin for something trivial then it escalates, harshly.'[25] For their part, the villagers initially shared much of this incomprehension at the state's intrusion into their daily lives, but swiftly found ways to navigate the rules and regulations of the Ba'th's socialist programme.

One of the finest illustrations of the dance between the aspirations of the central state authorities and the realities of daily life could be found to the north-west of Hama, where state irrigation projects had drained the impassable swamps of the Ghab, seven or eight miles wide and nearly forty miles long, and replaced it with fertile farmland. The promise of receiving a parcel of this reclaimed land had attracted peasants from the hills of the coast, Idlib and Salamiya – including Sunnis, Alawis, Christians and Ismailis. Agricultural production was to follow the instructions of the General Administration for the Development of the Ghab, a state body established in 1969. Each year the General Administration would devise a production plan for the Ghab to contribute to meeting national targets: the plan specified which crops to plant, determined which seed types and quantities of fertilizer to use and calculated how much credit to give the farmers. The state would also unilaterally fix the prices at which farmers could sell their crops. This set-up was intended to run as a smoothly functioning machine, rationally and efficiently, with good Ba'thist peasants as its engine.

In practice, enterprising peasants quickly learned to work the system. In between the successive crops of the wheat, cotton or sugar beet mandated by the General Administration, they would sow fast-growing crops such as melons, onions or cucumbers – off the record – and then sell them privately at market. Peasant families with excess manpower might grow extra cucumbers by secretly renting land from families that lacked labour, clandestinely siphoning off water from state-controlled irrigation channels to support their side hustle. Peasants who owned agricultural machinery could make extra money by renting it out to other families, or nominating one member of the family to operate the machinery for money while his brothers covered his labour on the farm. Other families opened repair shops for this machinery using technical skills that sons or nephews had acquired in the army. Meanwhile, some sought to obtain salaried jobs in ministries, schools or the General Administration for their children.[26] These collective, family-based strategies allowed peasants not only to diversify the sources of their income, but also to gain a foothold within state institutions as insurance against discovery or sanctions. Whereas the state had intended to remake local society in its own image, the peasants were beginning to subvert its energies for their own purposes.

A second irrigation project – even more massive and impactful than the draining of the Ghab – came to fruition in 1973 with the completion of the vast Euphrates Dam. Nearly three miles long, the Euphrates Dam was built between Aleppo and Raqqa with Soviet financial and technical aid. Not only was this dam intended to unleash new potential for irrigation and hydroelectricity, it also stood as the physical embodiment of the technical know-how, engineering skill and modernity to which the Syrian state laid claim. The Euphrates Dam thus represented for Syria everything that the mighty Aswan Dam had represented for Egypt; indeed, many of the Soviet engineers came to Syria fresh from finishing the Aswan Dam in 1970. To celebrate the regime's success, the new reservoir that formed on the Euphrates was given the name Lake Assad, while a new town, al-Thawra (meaning literally 'Revolution'), was founded to accommodate the 12,000 Syrian workers needed to build the dam. By 1974, the population of this new town had reached 40,000.[27] The concrete austerity of its geometric planning and identical characterless apartment buildings stood as a testimony to the regime's commitment to technocratic egalitarianism. Just as in the Ghab, the town of al-Thawra was projected to be a new space in which a mélange of new migrants from across the country would form the basis of a new Syrian society: not divided by class, sect and region, but united as Arab, Ba'thist and socialist. Syrians never took to the Soviet-style urban planning: al-Thawra remained a soulless dormitory town.

Behind the bright new future promised by the Euphrates Dam was cast a dark shadow of violence. Villages that had been home to 60,000 people – members of the Weldeh tribe, for the most part – were flooded as the water level rose steadily behind the dam. To help encourage them to leave, the government had sent in the army to blow up schools and irrigation channels before the flood waters reached their homes. Nevertheless, many villagers had refused to believe that the water would reach them and stayed on their land until the last possible moment. The government announced they would be resettled in the north-east, along the Turkish border, but many villagers were distrustful of a scheme that would parachute them into territory that was not only unfamiliar, but also largely inhabited by Kurds. Many of those displaced instead relocated to higher ground or migrated to Raqqa, which was now becoming a boom town. Nevertheless, around 4,600 households participated in the official resettlement programme and settled in one of the forty-one new villages built along the border on land that had been confiscated from the old elites. All but nine of the new settlements deliberately mixed families from different villages, breaking up old social solidarities and replacing them with a new set of tensions and neighbourhood disputes.[28] There was no integration between the Weldeh newcomers (nicknamed *al-Maghmourin*, 'the flooded') and the region's pre-existing Kurdish inhabitants, whose relations with the central government had already been under severe strain for well over a decade.

The contemporary roots of tensions between north-eastern Kurds and Damascus go back to the right-wing governments that were in power in Syria between 1961 and 1963. These secessionist governments were sympathetic to rolling back the gains made by peasants and workers during the union with Egypt. One of the largest landowners in Qamishli, the parliamentarian Abd al-Baqi Nizam al-Din, protested to the government that his confiscated lands should be returned to him on the grounds they had allegedly been redistributed to Kurdish peasants who were recent migrants from Turkey, not Syrian citizens. The government sided with his argument, and the peasants were forcibly removed from the lands (despite reportedly putting up a fight with sticks, rifles and Molotov cocktails).[29] The incident brought renewed attention to the mixed population of the Jazira region. The simultaneous outbreak of hostilities between Kurds and central government in neighbouring Iraq highlighted to Damascus the latent risk that any spread of Kurdish nationalism might pose to the newly proclaimed 'Arab' character of the Syrian Arab Republic.

In 1962, the government held an exceptional census in the governorate of al-Hassakeh to determine the number of non-Syrian Kurds living in the region, many of whom they claimed had only recently entered the country from Turkey. The census was carried out by the governor of al-Hassakeh, Sa'id al-Sayyid, originally from Deir al-Zour, who was well-known for taking his

Arab nationalism to the point of chauvinism. Sayyid's brother, Jalal, had notably been one of the early founders of the Ba'th, but had split with the party when it began confiscations from large landowners of the Arab tribes. Sayyid's census defined as Syrian any individual whose name appeared in the civil registry code no later than 1945. This date excluded anyone who had arrived in the Jazira from Iraq or Turkey to meet the desperate labour shortage that needed filling to launch the region's agricultural boom after the Second World War. The criteria also excluded anyone who had lost, or never obtained, the correct paperwork – not an uncommon situation given the absence of state bureaucracy in the north-east until relatively recently. Suspicious of the motives of the state authorities, many residents deliberately avoided the census-takers, who had mostly been brought in from Aleppo rather than recruited from the local community. Although the census was held on just one day, its arbitrary and inconsistent classifications would deprive thousands of Kurds of the right of citizenship for generations.[30]

The census recorded 85,000 'foreigners' (*ajanib*) who lacked the necessary paperwork to prove their status, even though many had lived in Syria for decades. By the stroke of a pen, they lost any claim to a nationality and were turned into immigrants. These 'foreigners' were not deported, but were denied the right to own property, benefit from state employment, receive a passport or even own a car. Individuals who missed the census – known in Arabic as the *maktoumin*, or 'unregistered' – were like ghosts: from the perspective of the state, they simply did not exist. Their lack of official documentation sentenced *maktoumin* to a life in legal limbo: even entering primary school was difficult for the unregistered. Male 'foreigners' and *maktoumin* could not marry Syrian citizens. Their legal status was automatically passed on to their children, which would subsequently produce further new generations of stateless Kurds in Syria. Inconsistencies in how the 1962 census was administered meant that members of the same family – even brothers and sisters – could be assigned differing legal status. Although rural and poor Kurds were disproportionately affected by the census, some of Syria's most prominent figures were shocked to discover they had also been swept into statelessness. Their number included several former members of parliament and one former chief of staff. In an ironic twist, among their ranks was Abd al-Baqi Nizam al-Din himself, whose complaints about 'Turkish' Kurds had been the catalyst for the census in the first place.

Beyond the Jazira and Euphrates, Syria's Kurdish population was clustered in the region of Kurd Dagh (known in Arabic as Jabal al-Akrad, 'Mountain of the Kurds'), north-west of Aleppo, as well as specific neighbourhoods of cities such as Damascus. The dispersed nature of the Kurdish community make it challenging to determine its size. In 1945, French officials estimated that 8.5 per cent of the Syrian population spoke Kurdish, although of course language was not the sole indication of Kurdish identity, especially in cities where Kurdish families had undergone varying degrees of cultural Arabization. It was nevertheless from these urban neighbourhoods that Kurds with modern, secular educations first began to articulate the principles of Kurdish political activism. In 1957, they founded the Kurdish Democratic Party in Syria (KDPS), the first of its kind in the country.

In 1968, the KDPS revealed that it had obtained a copy of a secret Ba'th Party report arguing that Syria should be purged of its Kurdish minority.[31] The report had been written in November 1963 by Muhammad Talab Hilal, chief of political intelligence in al-Hassakeh under the title *A Study of the Governorate of the Jazira: Some Political, Social and Nationalist Aspects*.[32] Hilal's report is a study in sheer racism. It denies the existence of a Kurdish people or nation, unfavourably compares their political imagination to that of Zionists and refers to the nascent Kurdish movement as a 'malignant tumorous growth' that needs to be excised from the body of the Arab nation.[33] He outlines a twelve-point plan for displacing Syria's Kurds and replacing them with loyal Arab citizens (ideally from the Shammar tribe, he suggests, who have the advantage of being both ardent Arab nationalists and land poor). His plan further proposes the creation of a militarized ethnic security cordon the length of Syria's borders, guarded by state-run agricultural colonies of settlers with military training ('exactly like the Jewish colonies on [Israel's] border', as he put it).[34]

When the Assad regime resettled the Weldeh villagers along the Turkish border, Kurdish political activists accused the government of implementing Hilal's 'Arab Belt' agenda. As if to confirm their suspicions, the Syrian government decreed that many Kurdish villages in the area would now be known by new Arabic names.[35] The government also continued to enforce the ban on publishing or broadcasting in the Kurdish language. However, there is no historical evidence that the Hilal report was influential in shaping these policies. In fact, when the report was submitted to the Ba'th Regional Congress of 1963, the presidency of the congress dismissed it as crude and refused to discuss its contents: the left-leaning congress at the time saw the Kurds in terms of class, rather than ethnicity. At the same time, the strident Arab nationalism of the Ba'th Party meant there was no place for Kurdish cultural or political expression. Despite ongoing regime brutality and the socio-economic marginalization of Kurdish-majority areas, there was no overt attempt at ethnic cleansing, destruction of Kurdish villages or expulsions of the Kurdish population. Kurds who were content to operate within the cultural and linguistic context of Arabic could sometimes find their way to high office: Shaykh Ahmad Kaftaro held the position of grand mufti of the republic for forty years, for example, while Hikmat al-Shihabi was Assad's first head of military intelligence before being appointed chief of staff of the Syrian armed forces from 1974 to 1998. Many Kurds were also recruited into elite military units, such as the Defence Companies commanded by Rif'at al-Assad. The attempted Arabization of Kurdish place names in the Jazira was successful only on paper; on the ground, the old names continued to be used, even by the Arab *maghmourin* newcomers, who were themselves not especially sympathetic to political programmes announced by high-handed and distant government authorities. At some point, official publications also stopped using some of the new designations; for example, the grandiloquent name Madinat al-'Uruba – literally 'the City of Arabism' – was ditched in favour of plain old Afrin again.[36] As the regime discovered, there were limits to how far top-down social engineering could reach.

The years from 1973 to 1976 were pivotal in weaving Syria's regions into a new pattern that the regime believed would sustain its survival. Buoyed by the influx of oil wealth from the Gulf, Syria's infrastructure, institutions and economy went through a period of accelerated development that Assad and his supporters harnessed to maintain themselves in power. At the same time, such rapid changes soon provoked objections from those who had been left behind or excluded from the new status quo. Along with mounting economic pressures, cracks quickly began to appear in the regime's façade of control. The first of these fractures was caused not by what the Assad regime was doing to Syria, but in its recent undertakings in neighbouring Lebanon.

Violence as a tool of government

Contrary to Syria's pattern of political development, Lebanon had acquired neither strong state institutions nor a strongman dictator. The forces of the Lebanese left had never risen up on behalf of the peasantry (as the Ba'thists across the border characterized their mission). Lebanon's ruling class was effectively a coalition of traditional elites who distributed economic and political power along sectarian lines. Despite the dominance of financial and commercial interests who were committed to laissez-faire capitalism, Lebanon could not entirely escape the leftward tendencies that had swept the region since the 1960s: strikes, demonstrations and agitation against the country's sclerotic political system continued to bubble up throughout the 1970s. To this already potentially volatile situation was added the Palestine Liberation Organization (PLO), which had moved its base of operations to Lebanon after being violently expelled from Jordan in the aftermath of 1970's Black September conflict. From the neglected Palestinian refugee camps of south Lebanon, the guerrillas continued their cross-border military operations in Israel – activities to which Israel responded by demolishing homes and villages in the south of the country, or by bombing Lebanese infrastructure. Lebanon's Christian elites were horrified at the prospect of being dragged into a conflict with Israel that would shatter the delicate sectarian balance that had been more or less maintained since independence. In contrast, Sunni and Druze elites were more sympathetic to the secular, left-wing nationalism of the PLO and advocated that the Lebanese army should defend Palestinians on Lebanese soil from Israeli attacks. Throughout 1975, these assorted tensions spilled over into first street shootings and abductions, then orchestrated attacks by local militias and finally open warfare in residential neighbourhoods of Beirut between right-wing Christian forces and Palestinian militants and their Muslim allies. By the end of the year, Lebanon had descended into fully fledged civil war.

In Damascus, Hafiz al-Assad had been intently following these events, concerned to prevent Israel from building a relationship with the Maronite Christians, who were hostile to Arab nationalism in general, and to Palestinian nationalists in particular, creating an opportunity for Israel to extend its influence in Lebanon.[37] When his efforts to encourage a political solution failed, Assad considered more direct means of intervention. However, the United States had warned him that Israel would consider Syrian troops entering Lebanon to be a declaration of war – a risk that Assad was unwilling to run. This uneasy stalemate lasted until a sudden volte-face from Israel, which had been persuaded by US Secretary of State Henry Kissinger of the strategic advantages of leaving Syria to weigh in on the conflict and rein in the Palestinians. Israel conveyed its red lines for Syrian military intervention in Lebanon, which included a limited ground presence south of the Beirut–Damascus highway. In spring 1976, this change of policy gave a green light to Assad's plans. That April, after an official request from Lebanon's (Maronite Christian) President Franjiyeh, the first Syrian forces began to move into Lebanon. The Syrian regime, after all, did not consider Lebanon merely to be its strategic backyard. 'Syria and Lebanon are one people in two states,' as the official discourse would have it.[38]

The convoluted politics of Syria's intervention in the Lebanese civil war – in support of Maronite Christian militias against Palestinians and left-leaning Arab nationalists – sent shockwaves across the Arab world. Egypt severed diplomatic relations, Iraq moved troops to the Syrian border and Palestinian radicals called for war against Damascus. The Gulf states restricted the flow of aid money to Syria, while the Soviet Union was so thoroughly displeased Assad had sided against progressives in Lebanon that Moscow delayed the next wave of arms shipments. The repercussions of Assad's decision were also felt at home. Opposition within the army corps led to dozens of officers being arrested. Palestinian militants seized a hotel in Damascus and took its guests hostage in protest at Assad's position. The militants were ultimately unsuccessful – and were publicly executed – but in the following months there was a wave of attacks across Syria. Bombs targeted the officers' club, air force headquarters and a police station in Damascus during the summers of 1976 and 1977. Leading regime officials and Alawi professionals were assassinated, including the rector of the University of Damascus, the commander of the missile corps and commander of the Hama garrison. In December 1977, Syrian Foreign Minister Abd al-Halim Khaddam – a key figure in Syria's operations in Lebanon – narrowly escaped an attempt on his life. The security forces were taken off balance by the attacks, which went unclaimed but could have conceivably been the work of Palestinian radicals, Islamist militants or the Lebanese opposition. The Syrian parliament passed anti-terrorism legislation that gave the security forces greater powers than ever before. Hundreds of army officers were transferred out of sensitive positions, and hundreds more Ba'thists arrested and purged from the party. In March 1978, Assad even fired his intelligence chief, Naji Jamil, who had not only failed to halt the violence and clashed with Rif'at al-Assad over tactics, but was also reported to have questioned Assad's own leadership.

The ongoing erosion of the rule of law and the encroachment of anti-terrorism legislation on to what remained of civil liberties provoked a backlash from middle-class professionals, who were already suffering from declining living standards. As one of the last bastions of autonomy from the Ba'th regime, members of the Syrian lawyers' syndicate spearheaded the peaceful liberal opposition, joined by intellectuals, artists, cinematographers and university students. They signed petitions against the intervention in Lebanon, passed resolutions demanding the end of the state of emergency and called for the release of prisoners and the end of arbitrary detention and torture. In December 1978, the lawyers' syndicate held a one-day strike to protest the beating of a Damascene lawyer and his wife by members of Rif'at al-Assad's Defence Companies (*Saraya al-Difa'*), whose brutality was now infamous. Emblematic of this widespread discontent, Ba'th Party candidates unexpectedly lost elections for the leadership of several syndicates and trade unions, which fell to critics of the regime.[39] Workers went on strike over pay and working conditions in the Rmeilan oilfield; workers in several state-owned factories even tried to follow suit. The regime did not deviate from its course and continued its clampdown regardless of these developments.

On 16 June 1979, the boldest, bloodiest act of defiance against the Ba'th regime took place, when trainee officers at the Aleppo Artillery School were massacred in cold blood. Reports suggested between thirty and eighty cadets were killed, many of them Alawis. Especially shocking to the regime was the fact that one of the key perpetrators, Captain Ibrahim al-Yusuf, was himself an army officer and a member of the Ba'th Party. Yusuf had secretly forged links with an extremist jihadi network known as the Fighting Vanguard of the Mujahidin (*al-Tali'a al-Muqatila li'l-Mujahidin*), which had masterminded the entire operation. The following year, Yusuf was apprehended by the regime in a raid on Aleppo: his dead body was paraded before the incoming class at the Artillery School. So enraged were the cadets that Defence Minister Mustafa Tlass later recalled that they 'almost tore his corpse apart with their teeth'.[40]

The Fighting Vanguard had its origins in the April 1964

insurrection in Hama, when the regime had shelled the mosque sheltering a hard core of opponents led by a man named Marwan Hadid. Hadid became a key figure in transmitting radical Islamist ideas into Syria. He was strongly influenced by the architect of modern jihadism, the Egyptian Sayyid Qutb, who openly called for Muslims to take up arms against the ungodly regimes of Abd al-Nasser and other impious leaders. For Hadid, the sectarian as well as secular foundations of Syria's Ba'thist regime made its violent overthrow an urgent duty. After undergoing military training with Palestinian guerrillas in Jordan in the late 1960s, he and his devoted followers returned to Syria to wage jihad against the Assad regime. Hadid himself had been captured by Syrian security forces in 1976 and died in jail a year later – the regime claimed this was the result of a hunger strike, although his followers believed he had been deliberately poisoned or tortured to death. Either way, Hadid posthumously became an icon for the jihadi cause. Zealous new members flocked to the ranks of the Fighting Vanguard, which was then able to expand and accelerate its campaign of violence.

In the wake of the Artillery School massacre, the regime launched an unprecedented wave of repression. Thousands of people were detained and hundreds of officers pre-emptively dismissed from duty. In a trial of fifteen imprisoned Islamists that was broadcast on Syrian state television, the judge of the State Security Court asked why the militants had targeted the Artillery School. 'Because you made the army sectarian,' came the response. The judge pressed on, asking why they had resorted to the tactics of murder given that Syrians could use parliament and political parties to express their positions. 'The Ba'th Party is a skeleton of bones, and parliament is a theatre performance that doesn't go anywhere,' said the jihadi. 'Murder is the only language in which we can converse with the state.'[41] The judge ordered the execution of all fifteen prisoners.

By late 1979, the level of repression was so extreme that concerns about the cost and effectiveness of escalation began to be expressed in some circles of the regime, who conceded the need for a change in approach. In September, the Ba'th and other parties in the National Progressive Front published a collective statement that, while careful to blame the ongoing violence as part of an 'imperialist–Zionist–Sadatist plot', also declared there had been 'unjustified dereliction' in implementing President Assad's political programme. The statement called for a number of reforms, notably restricting the jurisdiction of the powerful state security courts, respecting legal verdicts, simplifying trial proceedings, punishing officials who failed to do their duty and tackling the housing crisis.[42] It also called for the government to act against smuggling, opportunities for which had grown exponentially with Syria's ongoing military presence in Lebanon. Smuggling was a particularly sensitive issue because army officers and senior regime officials, including the president's brother Rif'at, were heavily involved in illegal cross-border trade and narcotics production.

The Ba'th Party established a special commission to investigate the crisis and held a closed-door meeting at the University of Damascus with important intellectuals and writers, who boldly used the opportunity to voice criticism and call for fundamental changes and reform. The proceedings of the seven-hour meeting were secretly tape-recorded by participants, and cassettes of the discussion soon found their way into general circulation. Even more significantly, the regime released tens of political prisoners and, in January 1980, a new prime minister, Abd al-Ra'uf Kasm, was appointed and launched a clampdown on corruption. That Kasm happened to be not only a Damascene, but also the son of a respectable religious scholar, seemed to hint that the regime was serious about changing its approach.

The hopes of the reformists were dashed at the Seventh

Regional Congress of the Ba'th Party, which met twice, in late December 1979 and early January 1980. The resurgence of the hardliners was driven by Rif'at al-Assad himself, who delivered a powerful speech that outlined a harsh, uncompromising response to the ongoing violence. Rif'at denounced the extremism of the Muslim Brotherhood, which he blamed for causing the crisis to defend economic interests opposed to the Ba'th revolution. Rif'at ominously called for a Law of National Cleansing (*Qanun al-Tazhir al-Watani*) to rid Syria of anyone who harmed national security or denied nationalist thought. Training camps in the desert, he proposed, would re-educate these 'ideological deviants' in the political doctrines of Ba'thism, as well as teaching them artisanal skills so they could make a useful economic contribution when they returned to society. (Internees at the camps would also undertake agricultural work to green the desert, Rif'at noted, which would effect a positive change to the Syrian climate.) After leaving the camp cured of their illness, they could return home so long as they passed annual examinations to prove they were still 'clean'.[43] Rif'at's speech left little room for compromise.

After the Artillery School massacre, the regime took to describing the violence as the work of the Muslim Brotherhood, not simply the radical fringe movement of the Fighting Vanguard. This apparent lapse was entirely strategic. The Muslim Brotherhood in Syria had been founded by Islamic scholars inspired by the Egyptian organization initiated by Hasan al-Banna, which they had encountered during their studies in Cairo in the 1930s. The Egyptian Muslim Brotherhood (*al-Ikhwan al-Muslimun*) believed that Islam did not merely govern religious activity but provided a comprehensive approach in conformity with which all of life – from education and family to science and technology – needed to be consciously restructured. Rather than traditional Islamic scholars, this message appealed to Egypt's educated middle-class professionals – engineers, doctors and teachers – who were enthused by its promise of an apparently authentic, non-Western modernity.

While the Egyptian Muslim Brotherhood was built as a brand-new organization that was centralized, rationally structured and separate from the traditional religious hierarchy, its Syrian counterpart had to accommodate a much wider variety of pre-existing groups in different parts of the country. Upon independence from French rule, a wide variety of Islamic charities and youth groups in Syria announced they were now part of a nationwide movement, the Muslim Brotherhood, which nevertheless continued to reflect the strong regional differences between Damascus, Aleppo, Hama and Latakia. From the outset, the Syrian Muslim Brotherhood was less dogmatic than its Egyptian parent, a consequence of the country's religious diversity as well as the enduring influence of Sufism, the mystical movement of Islam, upon Syria's religious scholars. Candidates from the Syrian Muslim Brotherhood had run for and been elected to parliament from the late 1940s until 1963, when the Ba'th came to power, at which point the organization was driven underground or into exile. Nevertheless, the leaders of the Syrian Muslim Brotherhood refused to endorse violence and maintained that the founder of the Fighting Vanguard, Marwan Hadid, had been expelled from the organization on account of his extremism. The position of the Brotherhood began to change in the mid-1970s: with many of the organization's moderates having fled the country, the space was clear for the ascendancy of radicals such as Sa'id Hawwa, a thinker noted for his explicitly anti-Alawi theology, and Adnan Sa'd al-Din, who became the movement's leader. Both men came from the conservative city of Hama. In October 1979, after months of extreme persecution from the Syrian regime, the Brotherhood decided the situation had reached the point where violence was unavoidable: they would establish a military wing and form an alliance with the Fighting Vanguard.

Jihadi attacks continued into early 1980 and were now met with the unremitting force advocated by Rif'at al-Assad. Local militias were set up and armed by the Ba'th Party to seek out regime opponents, a duty they typically discharged capriciously, without reference to due process or rule of law. The professional associations again protested against these measures and called for the state of emergency to be repealed. In March, shopkeepers in Aleppo, Hama, Homs, Idlib, Deir al-Zour and al-Hassakeh protested by closing their stores; the Damascus souq remained open only through the intercession of Badr al-Din Shallah, head of the Chamber of Commerce, who lobbied his fellow merchants in support of the regime. Strikes and demonstrations across the country edged closer to violence. Local police had to flee the town of Jisr al-Shughur, in the governorate of Idlib, when protestors burned down the local headquarters of the Ba'th Party and seized ammunition from the army barracks. The regime responded swiftly and sent in units from the Special Forces, who imposed order by killing two hundred people and destroying some seventy buildings. In nearby Ma'arrat al-Nu'man and Idlib, security forces opened fire on protestors, killing dozens more. In Deir al-Zour, thirty-eight teenage demonstrators disappeared after being taken into custody, and were never heard from again. When the professional associations spoke out once more, the government disbanded them and arrested their leaders, many of whom were tortured or executed. New associations, with more pliant bodies, were planted in their stead. Clashes in the streets of Aleppo grew so serious that the regime dispatched tanks, armoured vehicles and 30,000 soldiers to quash the insurrection. In operations that lasted a month, they combed the city neighbourhood by neighbourhood to flush out the opposition. They brutally retaliated against subsequent attacks by collectively punishing civilians, on one occasion randomly rounding up hundreds of males over the age of fifteen and firing on them with machine guns. Summary mass executions were now part of the regime's standard repertoire of counter-insurgency tactics. 'Violence is no longer just a tool to "correct" the political system,' observed French sociologist Michel Seurat. 'Violence is the way in which the system now works.'[44]

The words of Seurat, a close observer of Syria at the time, repeatedly rang true as the regime plumbed new depths of brutality in its attempt to repress what had begun as terrorism and insurgency and now looked set to transition into a popular uprising. By this point, Hafiz al-Assad himself had taken to directly addressing the Syrian people. Breaking from his reputation as an unimpressive public speaker, Assad began to give speeches that were passionate and angry, even electrifying, in their tone and delivery. In doing so, he made himself an even more attractive target for the militant opposition. On 16 June 1980, Assad only narrowly escaped assassination through the intervention of his bodyguard, who jumped on to a hand grenade that had been hurled at the president. The regime's retaliation for this ultimate transgression was swift. At 3 a.m. the following morning, units from Rif'at al-Assad's Defence Companies and other elite units were flown by helicopter to the desert town of Palmyra, where hundreds of Islamists were incarcerated. Sweeping into the jail, the soldiers opened fire on the prisoners in a frenzy of bloody killing. Although over five hundred people were massacred in just thirty minutes, the atrocity was shrouded in silence until the following year, when one of the perpetrators confessed what had happened, after being arrested in Jordan for his role in a Syrian plot to assassinate the Jordanian prime minister. With the benefit of hindsight, it was clear that Rif'at's declaration that Syria would 'fight a hundred battles, destroy a thousand citadels and sacrifice a million martyrs' was not hyperbole. In July 1980, the Syrian government passed Law 49 that made membership of the Muslim Brotherhood punishable by death. The regime continued to clamp down on the secular opposition. Later that year, political dissidents such as the Communist Riyad al-Turk, the intellectual Michel Kilo and the respected nationalist Jamal al-Atasi were also imprisoned. Regime hardliners had been successful in their drive to radicalize the government's response to the uprising.

From guerrilla warfare to urban insurrection: the 1982 Hama uprising

The regime's mass executions and massacres after 1979 had the unintended consequence of narrowing the distance between the more moderate Syrian Muslim Brotherhood and the uncompromising Fighting Vanguard. Members of the Brotherhood from Hama had been instrumental in driving this shift, against the reservations of their peers from Aleppo. The Fighting Vanguard was now dominated by the charismatic and volatile figure of Adnan Uqla – who had earlier orchestrated the slaughter of cadets at the Artillery School and advocated relentless violence to overthrow the regime. The Vanguard and Brotherhood announced they had formed a common 'Islamic Front in Syria', with a joint command to direct the pursuit of jihad. The Front published a political manifesto, the Declaration of the Islamic Revolution, secretly circulated alongside the Muslim Brotherhood's *al-Nadhir* newsletter, which gave the faithful regular updates on the ongoing struggle. Among their criticisms of the Assad regime, these pamphlets denounced the sectarianization of the armed forces, which they claimed were monopolized by Nusayris – a pejorative name for

Alawis. Nevertheless, Brotherhood publications largely eschewed overt sectarianism and instead promised to respect the religious rights of all Syria's minorities, even invoking the country's long history of coexistence to urge the Alawi community itself to turn against the Assad regime.[45]

Rather than focusing on theology, the pages of *al-Nadhir* contained frequent diatribes against the Assads' economic crimes. It accused Hafiz, his brothers and his wife's family, the Makhloufs, of plundering state finances, handing the public sector to thieves and awarding lucrative government contracts on the basis of sizeable bribes.[46] One article denounced the regime's crude attempt to buy loyalty by increasing the salaries of government workers – a rise that it said was 'much less of the nation's bounty and wealth than [the people] deserve [. . .] We know from the past that unless higher salaries are accompanied by increases in production and goods distributed to the people, they will fuel inflation, raise prices and lower buying power.'[47] Rather than calling for the Ba'th regime to be replaced by a caliphate, the Declaration called for democratic elections and a separation of power between the executive, legislative and judiciary bodies that seemed to draw inspiration from the republican constitutions of France or the United States more than the classical traditions of Islam.

The conciliatory tone of this rhetoric largely reflected the Muslim Brotherhood's endorsement of a pluralist society which safeguarded the rights of religious minorities. In the eyes of the Fighting Vanguard, this vision was shockingly liberal. Adnan Uqla was dismissive of the Brotherhood's pontification and its belated conversion to the cause of armed conflict. Without coordinating with the leadership of the Brotherhood, in December 1981, Uqla returned to Hama and began to plan a full-scale popular uprising. If the whole of Hama rose up against the regime, Uqla reasoned, the wall of fear would be broken, and other cities would soon follow. In February 1982, Uqla gave the signal. A hard core of several hundred jihadis led the charge, distributing weapons to the residents of Hama and launching attacks on government outposts across the city.[48] Within days, thousands of Hamawis had joined the jihadis and seized control of the city.

The regime response was decisive. It surrounded the city with units from Rif'at al-Assad's Defence Companies, as well as the Special Forces and the Third Armoured Division that had brutalized Aleppo two years earlier. After sealing the exits, these forces began to comb every shop, mosque and home to hunt down the radicals. They killed hundreds of people in mass executions, often arbitrarily, and demolished whole buildings full of people with their inhabitants trapped inside.[49] The killing was indiscriminate: even Ba'th Party members were not spared punishment. For days on end, artillery and tanks relentlessly attacked the city, flattening entire neighbourhoods, in an orgy of death and destruction.

The leadership of the Muslim Brotherhood, disconnected from events on the ground, could only appeal to Syrians to rise up against the Ba'th, as they once had against the French. 'They fought [then] as one close unit, Christians side by side with Alawis side by side with Sunnis. There was no narrow clannishness [*'asabiyya*], regionalism, or sectarianism. The revolutionary masses were led in the war of independence by men who belonged to the entire people [. . .] O sons of the Alawi sect among our citizens, [. . .] this government is doing the work of the enemy by dividing the nation, spreading the seed of division among the people and feeding the spirit of sectarianism.'[50] The Brotherhood's appeal went unheeded, and the other cities watched Hama's massacre unfold in silence. It was impossible to count how many people were killed that February: guesses range from 5,000 to as high as 30,000. After the city was crushed, the faltering alliance between the Muslim Brotherhood and the Fighting

Vanguard finally shattered. Adnan Uqla was caught, and presumably killed, by Syrian security later that year; his fellow combatants dispersed, some leaving the fight, others taking their jihad to fight Russian atheists and communists in Afghanistan. Among their number was a man known as Abu Mus'ab al-Suri, who later became an associate of Osama bin Laden and a prominent ideologue for al-Qaeda after 9/11.

The sheer devastation visited upon Hama was a blow from which popular resistance to the regime of Hafiz al-Assad would never recover. Professional associations were disbanded, intellectuals imprisoned, Islamists slaughtered or expelled and corpses buried beneath the reconstructed city centre. The story of Hama became a tragedy, a warning and a taboo – a symbol of how far the regime would go to maintain its grip on power. Fear of repeating these events would chill opponents of the regime for the next thirty years. When the next uprising began in 2011, the regime would look back to the Hama massacre of 1982 as a model for its brutality.

10

Seasons of Discontent, 1982–2003

The Hama uprising was repressed with such ruthless brutality that it was enshrined in the annals of the Muslim Brotherhood as the tragedy of their age.[1] The Brotherhood's organization inside Syria had been shattered, secular dissidents imprisoned and the urban middle classes cowed. With the backbone of opposition crushed, the regime systematically annihilated any hope of resurrecting resistance. Syrian society was now thoroughly penetrated by intelligence agents and informers. These networks of constant surveillance were anchored in political prisons across the country where barbaric acts of torture scarred those inmates who managed to survive incarceration. Even Syrians outside the prisons found themselves encaged within a rigid set of rules governing what could and could not be said. Any transgression of the regime's unwritten yet fiercely policed red lines was met with swift retribution against the perpetrator – and often the perpetrator's family, if denunciation of the guilty relative was too slow or unconvincing. There was little attempt to disguise the arbitrary arrests, extortion, physical abuse and murders routinely carried out by Syria's multiple and overlapping security services, the *mukhabarat*: a climate of fear and paralysis was deliberately fostered to dissuade opposition or complaint. The experience of the 1979–82 uprisings was decisive in shaping not just an entire generation of the Syrian public – which for over thirty years feared to stage an open revolt – but also a whole generation of the regime elite, which now had no compunction about retaining power through extreme violence.

On the economic front, in the years after 1982, there was a series of missed opportunities to reform the system. The collapse of world oil prices in the mid-1980s hit Syria hard. The country experienced not only the rapid decline in financial aid from governments in the Gulf, but also plummeting private remittances from Syrian migrant workers there, who now found themselves unemployed. The drop in these oil-financed income streams from the Gulf challenged the tenuous stability that the Assad regime had built on the back of fear and loathing, pushing it to relax some of the long-standing restrictions that it had imposed on the Syrian business elite. The regime calculated that Syrian businessmen would sell their political loyalty in exchange for greater access to economic opportunity. It balanced the urgent imperative for economic reform against its obsessive compulsion to eliminate any sign of independent organization and to monopolize power at all costs; as a result, the reforms were begrudging and cosmetic. Ever the pragmatist, Assad himself saw little need for fundamental change. Even after the end of the Cold War, the collapse of communism and the global rise of neoliberal doctrines of free markets, the Syrian Arab Republic clung to an economic model that had scarcely been modified since Assad came to power in 1970 – and which would survive his death thirty years later. A brief window of opportunity for political change appeared when Assad's son Bashar ascended to the presidency in the year 2000, but was once again slammed shut by regime hardliners to ensure their political survival. A domestic policy of prisons and patronage, in tandem with a foreign policy of war preparation and steadfast stubbornness, maintained the status quo despite the momentous changes that unfolded across the Middle East, and around the world, by the start of the new millennium.

A society of prisons

The locations of the largest prisons and detention centres were common knowledge in Syria. The prison at Mezzeh, a suburb of Damascus, had been used to house political prisoners since the early days of independence and continued to hold Salah Jadid and other leading Ba'thists that Assad had deposed in his bid for power. Another major facility was located at Adra, and a women's prison could be found at Qatana, both just outside the capital. The ancient citadel of Damascus was itself used as a jail until 1984, when it was rehabilitated with a view to becoming a tourist attraction. A new jail near the Christian town of Saydnaya, between Damascus and Homs, was constructed to replace it and quickly developed its own notorious reputation. Some of the worst torture was carried out at interrogation centres located in the dank basements of intelligence headquarters and branches across the country. This network extended beyond Syria's borders: the town of Anjar became the de facto headquarters of Syrian intelligence in Lebanon, where hundreds of Lebanese citizens were detained and tortured for political reasons. But it was the site at Palmyra, deep in the Syrian desert, where Rif'at al-Assad's men had embarked on a killing spree of Islamist prisoners in 1980, that was the bloodiest stain on this dark map of inhumanity.

Prisoners typically faced physical and mental abuse as soon as they began to be interrogated by the security services. Beatings were common: fists, truncheons, iron rods, electric cables and leather straps would target every vulnerable part of the body – the feet, the back, the belly, the face, the genitals. Prisoners were stripped naked, deprived of sleep and food. Their bodies, scarred from burning cigarettes, would grow thin and weak from cold and disease. Guards would force prisoners' heads and torsos into rubber car tires, then hit the exposed soles of their feet hundreds of times with sticks or whips. They would tie inmates to a horizontal metal bar, strung up like a rotisserie chicken, and then beat them within an inch of their lives. They would remove prisoners' fingernails with pliers, insert white-hot metal skewers into their rectums and administer electric shocks to all parts of the body. In addition to the constant insults, humiliation and psychological cruelty, guards would devise cruel and unusual ways to dehumanize their victims yet further, forcing them to bark like dogs, to bray like donkeys or to swallow dead mice.[2]

Prisoners were often held in collective cells known as dormitories, which could be crammed with so many bodies that inmates had to take turns lying on the floor to sleep. Periodically prisoners would be allowed outside to enjoy short bursts of daylight, a practice known as allowing them a 'breath'. Each time, inmates knew that this breath could be their last. Some prisoners were kept isolated from their peers for long stretches of time: Communist dissident Riyad al-Turk spent eighteen years in almost continuous solitary confinement. Such lengthy sentences were not at all unusual. Another Communist, a medical student at Aleppo University named Yasin al-Hajj Salih, was arrested in 1980 'as a precaution', as the authorities put it at the time. Hajj Salih faced trial twelve years later and was eventually released in 1996 – sixteen years after his arrest. 'By virtue of its chronological length and sociological breadth,' Hajj Salih would later muse, 'prison has become the quintessential national experience.'[3]

Even outside the walls of Palmyra and Saydnaya, ordinary Syrians found themselves trapped in an invisible cage that restricted their speech and restrained their actions. Passive compliance with instructions from the authorities was no longer enough: they were required to actively express their loyalty to the regime by parroting official slogans and hyperbolic rhetoric about the president. In the 1980s, Assad's lionization reached new heights. He was hailed as the 'leader for eternity' and 'saviour of Lebanon', the 'father' of the nation, a 'knight of war' and a 'man of peace'. State media celebrated his 'steadfastness' and 'sacrifice' in the face of the ongoing threat said to be posed by neighbouring Israel. Images of President Assad, his face stern yet benevolent, proliferated across public spaces from government offices to schools, shopfronts to taxi windscreens. Tellingly, the regime did not need to rely on government officials to paper the walls with these pictures. Often it was private citizens who displayed these images voluntarily, whether to demonstrate their support for the president, to proclaim their compliance with the regime or to ward off the unwelcome attention of the intelligence services – or perhaps all three. The government was mainly responsible for the many monuments to Assad erected around the country: statues and busts of him went up in parks and museums, alongside highways and above town squares. The president's fixed gaze was an unsubtle reminder that Syrians were constantly being watched. Citizens came to demonstrate their loyalty to Assad by pledging the *bay'a*, a religious term that historically referred to a Muslim's oath to the caliph that was now appropriated by the regime for its own political purposes, despite the Ba'th Party's claim to secularism. Assad's personality cult was in full sway.

Foreign observers had for years noted the increasingly hollow rigidity of Ba'thist political language. In his valedictory dispatch upon leaving Damascus in 1979, outgoing British Ambassador James Craig had noted – somewhat witheringly – that the Ba'thist leaders 'have an attachment to a sententious ideology in which few of them sincerely or comprehendingly believe. They speak in slogans which permit of private cynicism but never of public doubt [. . .] They prefer to say nothing unless the need to speak is plainly inevitable; and when they do speak, their words are bland or guarded or superficial.'[4] Syrians quickly became fluent in the new regime's rhetoric, which provided them with clear guidelines for permissible public speech.

By the early 1980s, this guarded blandness had come to permeate public conversations among both party members and private citizens. Proficiency in the permitted language did not take long to attain because, as a former government employee once explained, 'since 1970, there have been only 50–60 sentences. It is a very impoverished discourse.'[5] The more that officially permitted statements fixated on the person of President Assad, the more important it was to volunteer expressions of personal loyalty, the absence of which might prompt an informant in the neighbourhood or the workplace – or your own family – to write a 'report' outlining your suspicious behaviour and to submit their observation to the *mukhabarat*.

'From the 1970s this epidemic [of report-writing] spread everywhere under the influence of fear and ambition,' wrote Hajj Salih, who returned to opposition politics after eventually being released from jail. 'Fear that if you didn't write a report on an event you had seen, someone else might write one about you to say you were a witness, putting you at risk of grave consequences for covering up the matter; and ambition for advancement and reward for the sincerity of your ambition. Loyalty was always wedded to fear, and to personal gain at the expense of others.'[6]

The skeins of fear and self-interest were held taut thanks to the state's still-growing array of institutions, which organized the population more thoroughly and pervasively than ever before. The ideological refrains of Assad's emaciated Ba'thism were chanted in primary and secondary schools and reinforced by obligatory lessons in what the regime called 'national culture'.

Largely reviled by young Syrian men, military service provided a further opportunity for them to be drilled in the slogans of the state as much as in army discipline and combat manoeuvres. National festivities were dominated by Ba'thist holidays such as the anniversary of the 8 March 1963 'Revolution' and the Corrective Movement that brought Assad to power in 1970, celebration of which dwarfed 17 April, the date on which Syria had liberated itself from French colonial rule. Violence, torture, fear and self-interest left no space for free political expression. 'There is only one politician and only one architect of policies,' noted Hajj Salih, 'and that is Hafiz al-Assad. No political parties, no public political discussions, no political debates in the parliament or newspapers or universities, no free opinion, no independent voluntary association, no public protest or collective manifestation of the word "no". As far as politics is concerned, all Syrians but one are either slaves or corpses.'[7]

Despite the aspirations of Assad's regime, Syrians proved difficult to indoctrinate into genuine acquiescence. For the most part, the regime was forced to accept the population behaving 'as if' they believed the empty phrases that kept them safe from harm.[8] The mechanical rehearsal of true belief was more important than the sincerity of the performance. This strategy proved so remarkably effective in silencing the Syrian population that the next threat to Hafiz al-Assad came from an unexpected source: the bosom of his own family.

Fighting for the family business

The clash between Hafiz al-Assad and his brother Rif'at in the early 1980s had all the elements of an epic family drama: an ambitious younger sibling in the shadow of his high-achieving elder brother, a fraternal schism that divides their mutual friends, and a stern matriarch who is later credited with solving the impasse by bashing the boys' heads together (and thereby saving the country from civil war). However, while it is difficult to deny these dimensions of family politics, it would be wrong to reduce their conflict to a mere episode of sibling rivalry.

Hafiz and Rif'at were not only competing for the central position of power in Syria, they were competing for the only position that afforded the ability to determine the country's strategic direction in terms of both foreign policy and economic philosophy. Each brother represented a different orientation to crucial issues of the day: the question of Israel and Palestine, the defection of Egypt from the ranks of Arab unity, the upheavals of the Iranian Revolution in 1979, the ongoing rivalry with Saddam Hussein in Iraq and the relative desirability of state socialism and free-market enterprise. More than just a 'war of brothers',[9] the tensions between Hafiz and Rif'at al-Assad expressed a recurrent struggle over competing political visions for Syria's future. As in previous generations, this struggle was at its clearest when it came to the country's foreign policy. Yet different positions towards regional geopolitics were also inextricably caught up with different domestic priorities – especially as far as the economy was concerned.

By the early 1980s, Hafiz al-Assad's assessment of Syria's international environment was dominated by one looming concern: Israel. The lingering impact of the defeat of 1967 had not been erased by the relative gains of the 1973 October War: Syria's Golan territories remained under occupation and were unilaterally annexed by the Israeli Knesset in 1981. (This move was rejected by the United Nations, which passed Security Council Resolution 497 declaring the extension of Israeli domestic law to the Golan to be null, void and without legal effect.)[10] Concern over Israel's increasing military advantage – and the potentially disastrous consequences of a full-scale conflict for which the Arab states were ill prepared – had led Assad to make several foreign policy decisions that were surprising to many observers. In 1976, most notably, he had sent the Syrian armed forces to intervene in the Lebanese Civil War, siding with the right-wing Maronite Christian parties over the leftist Palestinian factions, whose militancy towards Israel, he believed, would otherwise unwisely provoke a wider confrontation before its time. His subsequent relationship with Yasser Arafat – leader of Fatah, the most mainstream of the Palestinian factions – was highly fraught. Assad declined to commit his forces to help defend the umbrella Palestine Liberation Organization from Israeli attack in Lebanon, and in 1983 declared Arafat persona non grata in Syria. A war with the 'Zionist entity', as Syria's official media called Israel, could not in Assad's assessment be won by guerrilla warfare, but only by conventional forces collectively fielded by Arab states that were, first and foremost, unified and powered by an engine built from modern technology, an educated population and a strong economy. As a pragmatic Ba'thist, Assad believed that social and economic development within the Arab world as a whole was a necessary precondition for the successful military liberation of Palestine.

For that reason, Assad was especially wounded that Egypt had broken ranks with its Arab brothers both in what he believed was its premature abandonment of the 1973 War and in its wayward eagerness to negotiate a separate peace deal with Israel, signed at Camp David in 1978. Assad interpreted this development as an attempt to divide and conquer the Arabs, orchestrated by Israel's new right-wing Likud government (elected for the first time in 1977, after decades of left-wing leadership) and duplicitous US Secretary of State Henry Kissinger. Assad signalled his displeasure with the United States by declining to condemn the Soviet invasion of Afghanistan in 1979 and then signing a cooperation treaty with Moscow, although the Soviet Union was never even remotely successful at reducing Syria to the status of a client state. Around this time, Syria also renewed its associations with such radical, ostentatiously anti-American states as Cuba, South Yemen and Libya, largely for symbolic purposes. Syria's relationship with Iran, in contrast, served Assad's geopolitical objectives more directly.

The alliance between the Syrian Arab Republic and the Islamic Republic of Iran is at first glance baffling. What could bring together a secular Arab nationalist regime with a quasi-theocratic, majority-Persian regime that sought to export a revolutionary religious ideology? Yet from Assad's perspective, Iran's recent political history perhaps seemed somewhat familiar. The 1979 Revolution had overthrown the Western-friendly, pro-Israel, bourgeois regime of the Shah, much as the Ba'thist 'Revolution' of 8 March 1963 had overthrown the reactionary forces of Syria's old bourgeois elite. The explicitly Shia religious characteristics of the Iranian Revolution would not necessarily have been a cause of consternation for Assad, given his familiarity with the Shia communities of Lebanon, who, in the 1970s, were for the most part still marginalized peasants living in rural communities in the Biqaa Valley and the south; their relative social status was not altogether different from that of Alawis in the village communities of Assad's youth. Prior to the 1979 Revolution, Assad's links to Shiism had primarily been channelled through religious scholars such as the Imam Musa al-Sadr, who had been the inspirational leader of a movement to improve Shia living conditions in Lebanon and who had sought to connect Alawi communities to his endeavours by issuing a religious opinion that Alawis were definitively part of the brotherhood of Islam. Although some analysts like to explain the Damascus–Tehran alliance as a consequence of common religious identity – the expression of a 'Shia crescent' across the Middle East – this is a misconception. The Syrian architect of this policy, Hafiz al-Assad, conceptualized the identities of Alawi and Shia in terms of ethnicity and class, rather than theology. To the extent that Assad had a doctrine, it was one of Arab nationalism and geopolitical pragmatism, not religious communitarianism.

Turning to Iran had two distinct advantages, Assad calculated. First, it would counterbalance the loss of Egypt from the coalition against Israel; Iran's antagonism to the United States would also bolster the cause of anti-Zionism in the region. 'This [Islamic] Revolution introduced important changes in the strategic balance,' Assad said. 'From a regional and global point of view it supports the Arabs, without hesitation, in actions for the sake of liberating our land ... How can we lose a country like Iran of the Islamic Revolution ... with all its human, military, economic potential?'[11] Second, an alliance with Iran would help offset the troublesome issue of Saddam Hussein, whose Ba'thist coterie had consolidated their control of Iraq in 1979 after executing some fifty fellow party members for alleged involvement in a plot to benefit Damascus. Saddam Hussein loudly blamed Syria for instigating sedition and betraying the cause of Ba'thism, to which he believed himself to be the sole legitimate heir. In 1980, he declared war on Iran, embroiling Iraq in what Assad considered to be an unnecessary venture that would distract Arab attention and divert Arab resources better channelled to the struggle against Israel. Relations further deteriorated when Iraqi forces stormed the Syrian embassy in Baghdad, and claimed to find weapons and ammunition there that was brandished as evidence of scheming in Damascus. The two 'brotherly' Ba'thist regimes severed formal diplomatic connections in October 1980. Assad's support for Iran was predicated on the assumption that the Iraqi regime would not last long, and that a united political front against Zionism and imperialism could then be rebuilt. For Hafiz al-Assad, the conflict with Israel took priority over all other geopolitical struggles.

Relative to the sober rationality of his brother Hafiz, Rif'at al-Assad cut a more colourful, quixotic figure. Despite being a vocal advocate of brutality against opponents of the regime, Rif'at was also identified with more conciliatory positions towards both the private sector and Syria's geopolitical rivals. He had personally taken advantage of Syria's limited opening to business in the 1970s to involve himself in a range of commercial ventures, both licit and illicit, which he used to reward his supporters and enrich himself. The periodic anti-corruption campaigns orchestrated by the regime, critics noted, strangely avoided infringing on Rif'at's own shadowy business interests. Rif'at also cleverly positioned himself as a charismatic leader of Syrian youth. He established a League of Higher Graduates for young professionals interested in computers and foreign languages, which provided a space for its soon thousands of members to discuss public affairs outside the formal structures of the state or the Ba'th Party. He established parachute training as a way to inculcate patriotism in the next generation, an activity which many young Syrians took up with enthusiasm, not least because of the extra credit they were awarded at high school in gratitude for their service. Rif'at sponsored a youth magazine, *al-Fursan* ('The Knights'), which was also the name given to a housing development reserved for his supporters in the Damascus suburb of Mezzeh. As commander of the elite Defence Companies, which by this point stood over 50,000 strong, Rif'at ensured that his men received pay and conditions that were superior to the regular armed forces. Rif'at was equally strategic in his private life as he was in his public affairs: several of the children from his four well-positioned, inter-sectarian marriages in turn married into the families of senior figures in the military, intelligence and business, cementing his centrality in the regime's criss-crossing networks of kin-based support.

Rif'at's interest in modernizing Syria's economy drew him towards disagreement with Hafiz on the relative importance of strategic competition with Israel, which he believed had the potential to burn up resources better employed elsewhere. An over-reliance on Soviet support also placed Syria on what Rif'at saw as an unnecessary collision course with the West. 'If favourable circumstances arose,' Rif'at was reported to have told the Americans privately, 'I could not only rid the armed forces of ... pro-Soviet officers, but also call for the withdrawal of all Soviet troops from Syria.'[12] Rif'at's instinctive distrust of mixing religion and politics – illustrated by his oversight of the violent atrocities during Syria's uprising in the late 1970s and early 1980s – extended to Syria's foreign policy, which he thought to be unwisely close to that of the Islamic Republic of Iran. This distrust did not, on the other hand, extend to the Kingdom of Saudi Arabia, to whose crown prince he was related through one of his wives. Taken to its logical conclusion, Rif'at's approach implied abandonment of Syria's claim to the mantle of nationalist leadership in the Arab world: it would leave Lebanon to the Lebanese, Palestine to the Palestinians and Syria to the Assad regime – with the pick of the spoils of office reserved for Rif'at and his own inner circle of allies.

Differences between the brothers' approaches came to the fore in November 1983, when Hafiz al-Assad suffered what seemed to be a heart irregularity induced by stress. On doctor's orders, he withdrew to a coastal villa to recuperate, and in his absence left the smooth running of the country in the hands of a six-person committee, which included Foreign Minister Khaddam, Defence Minister Tlass, Chief of Staff Shihabi and Assistant Secretary of the Regional Command Mashariqa – but, significantly, not Rif'at. Nervous that the president's ill health might presage a new struggle for power, Rif'at and his supporters agitated to assert their influence. His network was strong enough to convene a meeting of the Regional Command, which then voted to take over for itself the responsibilities of the six-person committee. Rif'at saw this change as his opportunity to move the regime in a new direction. He pushed for changes in the cabinet, raised his public profile and rallied his supporters in the armed forces.

In February 1984, the conflict between the pro-Rif'at and pro-Hafiz camps reached a critical juncture. Military units from the opposing sides were deployed in Damascus, and a tense stand-off ensued, which was temporarily defused a few weeks later with the announcement that the Syrian Arab Republic would now have three vice presidents: Rif'at, Khaddam and Mashariqa. Hafiz used the lull to transfer several of Rif'at's allies out of sensitive command positions. Feeling the tide turn, at the end of March, Rif'at ordered his Defence Companies to move on the capital: tanks and infantry took to the streets, surrounding key military and party installations and important landmarks like the Sheraton and Méridien Hotels.[13] Damascus was on tenterhooks. For the first time in nearly fifteen years, it looked as if a coup was about to overthrow the regime.

Perhaps mindful that open military confrontation with his brother would ruin his hard-earned reputation for bringing stability to Syria, Hafiz al-Assad played a different card. He brought the family matriarch, their mother Na'isa, to Damascus and sent her to stay at Rif'at's home. Cannily assessing that Na'isa's presence would restrain his impetuous younger brother, Hafiz went in person to confront Rif'at at home. 'You want to overthrow the regime?' Hafiz reportedly asked. 'Here I am. I am the regime.'[14] Faced with the stark choice of fomenting family discord as well as civil strife, Rif'at backed down and accepted Hafiz's offer of reconciliation. His troops withdrew, and calm returned to the capital.

Had he known what would follow, Rif'at might have made a different decision. A few weeks later, after his League of Higher Graduates was forbidden from holding a public rally, he gave an impassioned speech to an assembly of Syrian high society in which he protested his loyalty and his patriotism. To avoid further loss of face, he accepted the leadership of a diplomatic mission to Moscow, accompanied by many of his most important supporters as well as many of his most prominent adversaries in the regime. Several weeks later, Hafiz allowed his loyalists to return to Syria, while Rif'at took up residence in Switzerland. In his absence, the Defence Companies were reduced to less than half their former strength. Rif'at's remaining supporters in the military and security forces were sacked, encouraged to resign or sidelined from positions of authority. Without his patronage, the League of Higher Graduates shrivelled into irrelevance, and his parachutists had their high-school credit revoked. Rif'at himself retained the official title of vice president and returned to Syria in time to watch his brother reconsolidate control over the Ba'th Party at its Eighth Regional Congress in January 1985. A month later, a referendum confirmed Hafiz al-Assad's presidency of the Syrian Arab Republic with 99.97 per cent of the vote. Rif'at removed himself to France, where he established a new life in uneasy, quasi-official exile.

With Rif'at out of the picture, there remained no credible internal challenger for the presidency. Hafiz al-Assad's person and strategic vision now came to be almost synonymous with the Syrian state itself – or at least that version of the state that was being stamped on Syrian society. Yet for all his pragmatism and steadfastness in the realm of geopolitics, Assad had little interest in the detail of other areas of policy. So long as Syria's military expenditure was being met – mostly on the basis of Soviet support – then the wider national economy merited little attention. Yet in the mid-1980s, plummeting world oil prices began to wreak havoc on the cost of living in Syria and forced the regime to reassess its approach.

Economic crisis, 1986–1991

The early 1980s had all the warning signs. Ordinary Syrians perhaps felt the winds of the coming crisis first as inflation reached 30 per cent and their cost of living soared. The political leadership would have noted that the once-plentiful financial-aid flows from brotherly Arab states began to slow after 1983 as the Gulf states grew weary of Syria's alliance with Iran.[15] Engineers and managers in Syria's state-owned factories would have had first-hand experience of the problem, as old machinery broke down and imported spare parts disappeared from the marketplace, leading to slowdowns and stoppages. Production at the vast iron and steel factory at Hama ground to a halt and took two years to start up again. In Syria's breadbasket, the north-east, farmers would have observed the slowing pace of mechanization and land being brought into cultivation: two years of low rainfall in 1984 and 1985 hit agricultural production hard.[16] Shopkeepers could no longer supply their regular customers with basic foodstuffs such as vegetable oil and sugar, even tea and coffee. Long queues formed outside bakeries and butchers' shops. Cotton, toilet paper and even *samneh* (that same clarified butter whose poor quality in 1949 was said to have contributed to the first coup in Syria) were in short supply. In the chambers of commerce, businessmen were so worried about fluctuations in the exchange rate that they shared their concerns about the state of the world economy in a three-hour meeting with President Assad himself, who promised to have words with the finance minister.[17]

Statistical data from the 1980s confirms popular impressions of a darkening sky. Syria had begun to produce a very modest amount of oil in the late 1960s, with Assad's government introducing profit-sharing agreements allowing foreign companies (among them Shell and Petro-Canada) to drill further. After a period of expansion, Syria became a net exporter of oil in the late 1970s, but then a net importer from 1981 to 1985. An economic growth rate of 1 per cent from 1982 to 1985 was quickly outpaced by population growth as high as 3.4 per cent. Expatriate remittances from Syrians working overseas, especially in the Gulf states, began to dry up as the world price of oil fell in the early 1980s and then collapsed to under $10 a barrel in 1986. By 1987, Syria faced a budget deficit of 40 per cent, a collapse of its foreign exchange reserves and inflation that the government itself admitted had reached 60 per cent. (Unofficial estimates suggested it was, in fact, over 100 per cent.)[18] By this point, the crisis was undeniable – and, for most Syrians, unbearable.

Like most economic crises, there were multiple factors that produced this particular calamity in Syria, which was a consequence of sudden exogenous shocks meeting longstanding structural problems the regime had failed to remedy. While proximate causes could be found in the collapse of world oil prices and cuts in Arab aid, there was a long list of domestic policy shortcomings to which blame could also be apportioned. Lagging agricultural production, industrial bottlenecks, bureaucratic rigidity and grassroots subversion of the state-planning process were the most obvious factors, but widespread smuggling, rampant corruption among the elite, and excessive military spending all played their role.

The gradual accumulation of problems meant that the regime was initially slow to grasp the full-blown nature of the crisis. Its first response in the early 1980s was to introduce what was effectively an austerity programme. Under euphemisms such as 'self-reliance' (*al-i'timad 'ala al-dhat*) and 'guiding consumption' (*tarshid al-istihlak*), the government attempted to rein in public spending. Public sector salaries were allowed to fall behind inflation; new hires in most of the public sector were slowed, then frozen; and investments in new projects that had been scheduled to take place in the next five years were indefinitely postponed. The government devalued the currency: between 1985 and 1989 the Syrian pound lost nearly 80 per cent of its value against the US dollar.[19] Harsh new penalties were imposed on Syrians caught illicitly changing foreign currency or smuggling their wealth out of the country. 'What do you get for the dollar?' ran the new joke that circulated behind closed doors. 'Twenty years!' came the bitter punchline. The Syrian government explained its policy in terms of belt-tightening after a period of over-spending, but its measures were not enough for the economy to regain balance. More radical steps seemed required.

One of the chief obstacles to building a path out of the crisis was the near bankruptcy of economic thinking among the upper echelons of the Assad regime. While Assad famously maintained tight personal control over questions of foreign policy, his grasp of the finer points of economic policy was at best tenuous. (According to one US diplomat who met him, Assad once presented the fact that so many Damascene taxi drivers had medical degrees as an indication of his government's economic success.)[20] Government officials who had received formal training in economics were few and far between; most of them had studied in the Soviet Union or Eastern Europe, which naturally inclined them towards looking for solutions that came from the state. Government bureaucracies and popular organizations were also largely vested in maintaining the statist status quo. One 1987 report from Syria's General Federation of Trade Unions, for example, advocated more central planning, a larger public sector and stricter government control over exports, foreign exchange and private sector competition.[21] Despite these ideological preferences, the apparent inability of 'self-reliance' and austerity to prevent the slide into economic decline led the regime to look to the private sector, albeit in a gradual, piecemeal fashion.

The first indication of this shift came in January 1985, at the Eighth Regional Congress of the Syrian Arab Socialist Ba'th Party. Over the course of two weeks, nearly 800 high-ranking party members gathered to approve new policies and decide who would serve on the elite committees that dominated party life. Delegates debated – and defeated – several motions that called for greater state control of the economy and issued a final statement criticizing the shortcomings of the public sector and calling for greater support for private investment.[22] This move was not altogether surprising: Assad had already presided over an earlier rapprochement with the private sector in the 1970s and, even at the level of the peasantry, the regime had long tolerated a certain degree of entrepreneurialism. This time, tolerance gave way to active encouragement.

Just two months later, a new government was formed with Muhammad al-Imadi as minister of economy and foreign trade. With a PhD in Economics from New York University, Imadi had previously occupied the same role in the 1970s and was widely regarded as the architect of the earlier wave of liberalization. Imadi was a technocrat who – significantly – had never become a member of the Ba'th Party. The ability of the regime to adopt this new direction was no doubt facilitated by the fall from grace of Rif'at al-Assad, who could no longer either represent the pro-business faction within the party or protect his former associates, who were unceremoniously removed from their positions at the same congress. (Some of Rif'at's former partisans tried to avoid the purge by humbly confessing their transgressions to the congress in the hope of leniency.) With Rif'at's influence dismantled, Hafiz al-Assad's regime could adopt policies that favoured the private sector without losing ground to challengers from within.

Tellingly, the government began to address the business community with persuasion, rather than coercion. In a speech at the Central Bank to an audience that included the heads of the chambers of commerce and industry, Prime Minister Abd al-Ra'uf Kasm openly called upon national capital (*al-ra'smal al-watani*) to prove its credibility by helping to rebuild Syria's productive economy.[23] This kind of language seemed to hark back to the economic nationalism of the 1950s, not Ba'th-era socialism. Before long, this approach came to be described as the new *infitah* (liberalization). In another indication of the changing political climate, this term was borrowed from the transition out of socialism that had taken place in Egypt following the death of Abd al-Nasser.

The government passed several pieces of legislation in the late 1980s to entice private capital to invest in the Syrian economy. The laws typically granted private investors special privileges for getting involved in new projects. Legislative Decree 10 of 1985, for example, allowed for the creation of joint agricultural ventures between the public and private sectors: land would be supplied by the Ministry of Agriculture in exchange for a 25 per cent stake in the business as a sleeping partner. In exchange for investing capital, its private co-owners would receive the remaining 75 per cent and actively manage the venture. These joint ventures were granted special exemptions from customs and import duties and Syrian employment law; they were allowed to transfer hard currency at any time and had guarantees against nationalization by the government. New investments in tourism were similarly granted tax holidays and customs exemptions. While numerous companies were formed under the auspices of Decree 10, only a handful became active; they largely produced profits because of their special financial status, rather than their skill or efficiency in agriculture.

In 1991, a major piece of legislation was passed in the form of Law No. 10, which allowed Syrian and non-Syrian investment in private or public–private joint ventures in practically any field of the economy, subject to a minimum threshold of US$240,000 and approval from the newly formed Higher Council for Investments, headed by the prime minister. These projects were granted tax exemptions on profits and imports for up to seven years, and were allowed to take their profits out of Syria if the business failed.[24] Separately, new laws lowered the tax on business profits from what was previously a rate of 90 per cent. Collectively, these measures were interpreted as heralding a real change in fortunes for the Syrian bourgeoisie, which had been cowed by successive Ba'th regimes for almost three decades.

These signs of change were confirmed by President Assad himself, whose speech marking the twenty-seventh anniversary of the 1963 Ba'thist revolution underlined the productive economic role played by the public, private and 'mixed' sectors in Syria.[25] Assad captured this ideological revisionism by introducing a new slogan into the regime's restrictive political lexicon: *ta'addudiyya iqtisadiyya*, or 'economic pluralism'. Just a few months later, in May 1990, national parliamentary elections took place. As usual, the elections were tightly controlled by the regime. But this time – for the first time – five of the thirteen seats allocated to Damascus were won by businessmen running as independents outside the Ba'th-dominated National Progressive Front, whose automatic share of parliamentary seats was now reduced to just two-thirds.

Two of the newly elected deputies, Badi Fallaha and Baha al-Din Hasan, were respectable members of the city's Chamber of Commerce; the other three – Ahmad Haydar, Ma'moun al-Homsi and Ihsan Sanqar – were part of a younger generation of entrepreneurs. None of these new private sector parliamentarians came from the super-rich elite who had made their fortunes in the first *infitah* of the 1970s. Those older giants had certainly not ignored the new business opportunities of the late 1980s and 1990s – no less a figure than Sa'ib Nahhas was the principal shareholder in Ghadaq, one of the three largest agro-companies created under the new laws, for example.[26] But for the first-wave nouveau-riche businessmen, a parliamentary career was of limited interest, given their already powerful connections in the regime. In contrast, for representatives of the bourgeoisie who had survived the Ba'th Party's socialist purges, or for those aspiring to upward mobility, a parliamentary seat promised social status, an opportunity to increase their access to patronage resources and, perhaps, a certain recognition by the regime that businessmen could be part of the establishment – as long as they remained inside the indicated red lines.

For a while, it seemed as if Syria might travel further down the path of economic liberalization. State newspapers openly discussed poor performance and corruption in the public sector, consultants were commissioned to provide ministries with policy recommendations and would-be reformers tried to spread the notion that the private sector was not by nature parasitic or unproductive.[27] '"Public sector" is not a magic word that can solve all society's problems!' warned an expert writing for the bulletin of the Damascus Chamber of Commerce in 1990. 'Privatization is a change of priorities, not a defeat in a battle between two sides!'[28]

Despite these shifting tides, in the 1990s there was no further economic reform. The much-touted pragmatism of the Assad regime cut two ways: when necessary the regime could embrace change, but it saw no reason to do so for the sake of ideological consistency. As the domestic crisis eased and Assad's attention fixated once again on foreign policy, questions of economic reform receded into the background.

Syrian society after the Cold War

In the late 1980s, a wave of revolutions swept away the communist regimes of Eastern Europe, leading to the fall of the Berlin Wall, the formal termination of the Cold War between the United States and the Soviet Union and, in December 1991, the dissolution of the Soviet Union itself. Without the material and symbolic support of the Soviets, lingering communist governments soon found themselves unable to maintain power in countries from Afghanistan to Angola, South Yemen to Somalia. While the Syrian regime had remained steadfastly Ba'thist – never communist – the demise of the Soviet Union nevertheless deprived Assad of a leading source of arms and aid as well as a prime example of a hitherto apparently successful state monopoly over politics and society. Assad was swift to distance Syria from the changes taking place in Eastern Europe, highlighting that the recent introduction of 'pluralism' in both the economy and parliament signalled an adaptation of the official ideology, not its repudiation.

An October 1991 editorial in the state-run *Tishrin* newspaper clarified the government's position: 'The collapse of the regimes that used to call themselves socialist in eastern Europe does not mean the end of socialism and socialist thinking. Rather, it signals the collapse of a pattern of socialist practice that will be rightly judged and assessed by history [. . .] [Assad's 1970 Corrective] Movement advanced the principle of political and economic pluralism almost two decades ago. It also devised methods for political and social development that proved capable of withstanding the toughest foreign pressures.'[29] This line may have been overt revisionism, but it signalled a conviction that Syria had its own path to follow.

As a further indication of this new pluralism, in 1991 and 1992, the regime released nearly 3,000 political prisoners – many of them Islamists – and transferred the jurisdiction over certain economic crimes from the security forces to civilian courts. Advocates of greater economic liberalization failed to be mollified. 'The prevailing political style is one of caution, along with complacency,' later noted Nabil Sukkar, a Syrian economic consultant who had authored reports for the government. '[E]conomic reform is being delayed because Syria has not yet reconciled its outdated economic ideology with current global economic thought.' While there might be growing consensus on the gaps in the old system, Sukkar wrote, there remained 'doubt about the virtues of the free market and deep bewilderment over how to reconcile marketization and globalization with the cherished concept of economic self-reliance.'[30]

Naturally, President Assad himself demonstrated little such doubt and instead orchestrated a constitutional amendment to enable him to run for a fourth consecutive term in office. His candidacy was duly confirmed by the parliament and approved by a public referendum held on 2 December 1991, which Assad won with 99.98 per cent of the vote. Large-scale celebrations were held across the country to celebrate this very predictable outcome. While foreign political observers mused that the Middle East in the 1990s might soon follow the waves of democratization that had recently swept South America and Eastern Europe, Assad's tight grip on power made this outcome unlikely in Syria.

While the regime allowed little space for the independent non-governmental organizations or professional associations that might be heralded as green shoots of democracy, in the 1990s it did deliberately loosen its control over one sector of society: organized religion. Following the repression of the Hama uprising, the regime calculated that rather than expand the government institutions that oversaw religious affairs – a strategy that might backfire by creating space for a pro-Islamic camp to grow within the state itself – it would instead allow respected yet reliable Muslim figures to guide how religion was practised in the country. Two institutes in Damascus – the Abu al-Nur Islamic Centre, run by the venerable Shaykh Ahmad Kaftaru (grand mufti of Syria from 1964 to 2004), and Shaykh Salih al-Farfour's al-Fath Institute – were allowed to take on more students, award more certifications and assume responsibility for Friday sermons in mosques across the capital. In Aleppo, the local religious hierarchy was more rural in origin and less tightly connected to respected urban families, prompting more direct intervention from the city's *mukhabarat* to keep the clerics in check. Several of Aleppo's religious shaykhs took advantage of the parliamentary opening in the early 1990s to have themselves or their family members elected as independent deputies. Notably, for example, Shaykh Ahmad Badr al-Din Hassoun used this opportunity to build ties with the regime: he was later appointed mufti of Aleppo (1999) and then grand mufti of Syria (2005). Arguably the most prominent of these loyalist shaykhs was Sa'id Ramadan al-Buti, who had famously condemned the violence of the late 1970s and early 1980s, while seeming to maintain his political independence from the regime. Buti reputedly enjoyed long audiences with Assad himself and had actively lobbied for leniency for Islamist prisoners.[31] In the meantime, visible signs of religiosity slowly reappeared in public spaces: mosques once again became active between prayer times, and even the wives of government ministers felt able to wear headscarves without fear of censure. While any threat from radical Islamists could not be tolerated by the regime, Ba'thist secularism found it impossible to displace social practices of religion that were deeply woven into Syria's Sunni Muslim communities. Perhaps nowhere was the regime's ideological volte-face more visible than in the many new branches of the so-called Hafiz al-Assad Institute for the Memorization of the Qur'an that had proliferated across the country since the 1980s.

In much the same way, the necessity of tolerating other social forces that existed autonomously from the regime also became apparent in the 1990s. Family connections of tribe and sect continued to play an important role, sometimes perceptibly so. Alongside the religious shaykhs newly elected to the 1990 parliament sat independents who came from the major tribes in the governorates of Deir al-Zour (mostly the Baggara), Homs and rural Aleppo. In the governorate of Suweida, a non-Ba'thist member of the prominent Atrash family won a seat. In the coastal city of Latakia, the elections had to be rerun after the president's brother, Jamil al-Assad, won a parliamentary seat with more votes than had been cast at the ballot box.

One of the most visible signs of change in the 1990s was the illegal proliferation of satellite dishes on rooftops across the country. The regime initially considered clamping down on households receiving satellite broadcasts that were by definition outside its control, but chose not to do so. Syrians pondered whether this laxity reflected Assad's new pluralism, recognition of the sheer difficulty of policing millions of private homes or pressure from those well-connected individuals who had smuggled satellite dishes into Syria in the first place.[32] In the event, satellite television became a tolerated part of the media landscape. The slow erosion of the regime's ability to control the flow of news prompted it to launch its own satellite channel in 1995, as a slightly more glamorous and youthful face for its propaganda than that provided by the dour terrestrial television run by the state. During the same decade, the trickle of independent television production companies in Syria turned into a torrent, owing to injections of cash from investors in the Gulf. More than simply soap operas, the miniseries (*musalsalat*) produced by these companies engaged with contemporary social problems (especially family and gender politics), criticized government bureaucracy and satirized the absurdities of daily life under authoritarian rule. The writing and acting in *musalsalat* were often of a high standard: plots were adapted from literary Arabic novels, poets were employed as scriptwriters and stories set in the time of the late Ottoman Empire or the French Mandate. Despite often being owned by individuals with deep connections to the regime (including the son of Syrian Vice President Abd al-Halim Khaddam, former governor of Hama and foreign minister), 1990s *musalsalat* continued to offer a surprising space for political criticism.

One such *musalsal*, titled *Al-Dughri* ('The Honest Man', 1991), tells the story of a duplicitous local village politician who cynically takes bribes, manipulates his neighbours and blackmails his colleagues as he climbs his way to the top. The show proved hugely popular. Although the story had been adapted from a Turkish novel originally published thirty years earlier, rumours quickly identified the lead character as based on the career of Vice President Khaddam.[33] Despite this sensitivity, not only was *Al-Dughri* broadcast without interference from the authorities, but its director met with no trouble and continued to work in television.

While *Al-Dughri* was not the only miniseries to engage in

such limited and often coded criticism, this new wave of television drama of the 1990s was not a sign of political liberalization. Viewers no doubt watched some storylines with baited breath, hardly believing how close the *musalsalat* were veering towards the unspeakable. Yet the red lines of Syrian political discourse remained very much in place: censorship – or worse – could be reimposed at any moment, often seemingly arbitrarily. Syrians also understood that these miniseries could be a safety valve to allow audiences to release their political frustrations harmlessly, without expressing them in more explosive ways. Even so, this chance to 'breathe out' (*tanfīs*), as it was called, could not be taken for granted. Syrians were aware that the regime's grip around their necks had been only slightly relaxed.

Regional politics after the Cold War

In the 1990s, Syria's internal stasis was not matched by its foreign policy. Rapid changes in Syria's international standing – especially in its relationship with the United States – in many respects provided a bulwark against domestic pressures for reform. The thaw with Washington had already been set in motion because of Syria's détente with Egypt, which Damascus had previously attacked for its acceptance of a defeatist, US-brokered peace treaty with Israel long after other Arab states had sought to end Cairo's isolation within the Arab world. But by 1989, Assad too had reached an understanding with his Egyptian counterpart, Hosni Mubarak, which culminated in the Syrian president visiting Cairo the following July. In turn, this rapprochement opened the door for new overtures from Egypt's sponsor, the United States.

In early 1990, delegations of US senators and then senior US officials visited Syria, as did former US president Jimmy Carter, followed by direct telephone conversations between presidents Hafiz al-Assad and George Bush That August, Iraq's invasion of Kuwait provided the opportunity for diplomatic breakthrough. Assad swiftly decided to support the military expulsion of Iraqi forces from Kuwait, a move that, along with the support of Egypt and Saudi Arabia, was crucial in lending an essentially Western initiative the appearance of a global coalition. In September, US Secretary of State James Baker flew to Damascus to meet with Assad; in November, presidents Assad and Bush themselves met in person in Geneva. Diplomatic relations between Syria and Britain were restored after having been broken off three years earlier.[34] Even under the auspices of UN resolutions, siding with the West against Saddam Hussein would no doubt be unpopular with the Syrian people: the Iraqi leader was riding high on a regional popularity wave after emerging seemingly victorious from his eight-year war with Iran. Assad defended his position in an open address to Saddam, delivered on Radio Damascus, in which he assured Syria's friendship and support if Iraq would withdraw from Kuwait. Assad nevertheless calculated the cost of repressing any domestic discontent would pale into insignificance compared to the strategic gains that Syria might make from backing the winning side in the Gulf War. His gamble paid off. Iraq's invasion of Kuwait met with disapprobation from the Arab Gulf states, allowing Syria to reconcile with Saudi Arabia and other countries that had disapproved of Damascus siding with Tehran during the Iran–Iraq War. In the years following Iraq's withdrawal from Kuwait, Syria was rewarded by the Gulf states with aid worth more than US$2 billion. This sum was sufficient to postpone the need for any further economic liberalization in Syria for the rest of the century. Syria also retained its strategic alliance with Iran.

Syria's political payback for siding with the West came in two forms. The first was the de facto recognition of Damascus's hegemony over Lebanon. As the world's attention was riveted on Kuwait, Syrian forces in Beirut militarily defeated the last outpost of opposition to the 1989 peace agreement hammered out at Taif, Saudi Arabia, by the parties to the civil war. The Taif Accord established a new formula for power-sharing in Lebanon along sectarian lines and established a special 'peacekeeping' role for Syria in the country. This arrangement was formalized in May 1991 with the signing of the so-called Treaty of Brotherhood, Cooperation and Coordination between the two countries, followed by the Defence and Security Agreement in September the same year. Even as it sought to remove Iraq's occupying forces from Kuwait, the international community turned a blind eye to what would effectively be the occupation of Lebanon by over 30,000 Syrian troops for the next fifteen years.

For Assad, maintaining a Syrian force in Lebanon made sound strategic sense in view of Israel's ongoing occupation of the south of the country. It was the Syrian presence that ensured the Lebanese militias obeyed the political terms of the Taif Accord and were disarmed – with the notable exception of Hizbullah, which was exempted on the grounds it was a resistance movement fighting the Israeli occupation of south Lebanon, not a militia. To Assad, supporting Hizbullah represented a means to remain relevant in the ongoing struggle against Israel while also keeping the Syrian frontline quiet. Given that the Shia Hizbullah had originally been inspired by the Islamic Revolution in Iran, which continued to support its activities financially and materially as well as spiritually, it was here that the strategic interests of Damascus and Tehran clearly converged. Syria maintained tight control over Lebanese politics through its network of intelligence operatives based in the town of Anjar in the Biqaa Valley. Syria controlled the outcome of elections, the composition of the Lebanese cabinet of ministers and even the incumbent of the presidency. In 1995, 1998 and again in 2004, Damascus was unwilling to endorse any of the candidates eligible to be president and so forced through constitutional amendments to allow its preferred client–politician to take the job. At all levels of the political system, only candidates that supported or reconciled themselves to the inevitability of the Syrian presence in Lebanon found themselves able to advance their careers. Throughout the 1990s, Lebanon experienced a distorted political stability under the heavy hand of Syria, but nothing approaching actual democracy. Lebanese critics of the Syrian presence would darkly compare the role of Ghazi Kan'an, Assad's intelligence chief in Lebanon from 1982 to 2002, to that of the French commissioner during the French Mandate, or even to that of Ayatollah Khomeini, the 'spiritual guide' of the Iranian Revolution.[35]

While opportunities for self-enrichment in Syria were relatively limited owing to the glacial pace of liberalization, the Syrian state elite found that Lebanon offered a feast of options for illicit payoffs, crooked backroom deals and general corruption in the context of the fast pace of post-war reconstruction. Spearheaded by the tycoon Rafiq al-Hariri, who made his fortune from construction in Saudi Arabia and with Syrian blessing became prime minister of Lebanon in 1992, Lebanese politicians channelled major government contracts to businesses from which they, their families and their supporters typically stood to make sizeable profits.[36] Hariri's own stake in Solidere, the company that reconstructed Beirut's central district with luxury apartments and designer clothing stores, is perhaps the best-known example of these grey transfers of public goods into private hands. In Lebanon it was the private sector, not the state, that played the most significant role in rebuilding the country after nearly fifteen years of civil war.

High-ranking Syrian military and intelligence officials were quick to get in on the action. The sons of intelligence maestro Ghazi Kan'an and Syrian Chief of Staff Hikmat al-Shihabi were both shareholders in Lebanon's lucrative telecommunications sector, for example, while control of the Syrian–Lebanese border granted the Syrian security apparatus de facto control over illicit trade. By the 1990s, smuggling had expanded from simple consumer goods, cigarettes and petrol to such sizeable items as luxury automobiles. The opportunities to make money on the side were so enticing that Syrian officers now competed to land themselves prime postings in Lebanon. Syrian conscripts who completed their military service in Lebanon often later crossed the border once again to join the ranks of the tens – if not hundreds – of thousands of Syrian workers who provided the bulk of labour for Lebanese construction and agriculture. Syrian businessmen themselves used family and personal connections to take their money out of Syria and funnel it into the greater safety of investments in Lebanon. In this way, Lebanon during the 1990s effectively functioned as a gigantic free trade zone for the Syrian economy, providing a safety valve for economic pressures that might otherwise have forced the Assad regime's hand in accelerating the liberalization process back home.

Besides tacitly being given a free hand in Lebanon, Syria's second reward for joining the coalition against Saddam Hussein was its participation in a round of US-sponsored talks with Israel. US Secretary of State James Baker had the arduous task of securing terms for the talks that were agreeable to both Israeli Prime Minister Yitzhak Shamir and President Assad. The latter required long, involved discussions with the Syrian president in Damascus – including one particularly gruelling meeting that lasted an epic twelve hours (famously not including a bathroom break) and entailed Assad lecturing Baker on Syrian history, starting with the evils of the Sykes–Picot Accord. Once the terms of the talks were finally agreed, Syrian, Israeli, Lebanese and Jordanian–Palestinian delegations met in Madrid for a peace conference in November 1991.

From the outset, the Syrians maintained that full Israeli withdrawal from all territories occupied in 1967 was a prerequisite for peace. For their part, the Israelis argued that their withdrawal from Egypt's Sinai between 1979 and 1982 had already fulfilled the conditions for peace with Arab states laid down in UN Security Council Resolution 242. Talks soon broke down. The Israeli premier attacked Syrian support for the Palestinians as state-sponsored terrorism, while Syrian Foreign Minister Farouq al-Shara' brandished an old photo of Shamir which declared him 'WANTED' for his role in the 1948 assassination of Volke Bernadotte, the UN mediator in the first Arab–Israeli conflict. Although the Madrid conference produced no immediate results beyond this robust exchange of views over who should call whom a terrorist, it did give rise to a back channel between Damascus and Tel Aviv. This secret line of communication became more important after Shamir lost the next elections and Yitzhak Rabin of the Labour Party became Israel's new prime minister.

Syria had always advocated that the Arab states which had lost territory in the 1967 war should negotiate collectively with Israel. This approach had been undercut by Egypt's separate peace agreement in 1979; it was further undermined by Rabin's bilateral deals with the Palestinian Liberation Organization at Oslo in 1992 and the Hashemite Kingdom of Jordan in 1994. Syria and Lebanon were left alone to fight for what Assad saw as the only deal that was just and comprehensive: Israel's full withdrawal from the Golan and south Lebanon to the borders that existed the day prior to the 1967 war. Shortly before news of the secret Oslo agreement hit the headlines, Assad believed he had received such an offer from Rabin – albeit with significant and, for Assad, unacceptable conditions attached. Relays of messages between Damascus and Tel Aviv, conveyed through US diplomats, failed to deliver progress or even clarification that Israel was prepared to withdraw to the border of 4 June 1967.[37]

In November 1995, Rabin was assassinated by an Israeli nationalist who opposed the Oslo Accords. Rabin's successor, Shimon Peres, reportedly endorsed what Assad referred to as the 'Rabin deposit' but placed new emphasis on water rights and regional economic development, including joint Syrian–Israeli commercial ventures on the Golan. For Assad, peace was one thing, and normalization another: Israeli economic activity on Syrian territory was not welcome. Discussions were further slowed by Peres's decision to assassinate a Hamas bomb-maker, which prompted a wave of suicide attacks in Israel in early 1996, followed in April that year by an Israeli seventeen-day military operation in occupied south Lebanon. Launched as retaliation against Hizbullah's ongoing rocket attacks in northern Israel, Operation Grapes of Wrath caused the displacement of 400,000 civilians and the deaths of many more, including 105 civilians killed in an Israeli attack on the Lebanese village of Qana. Peres' difficulties in Lebanon contributed to his losing the May 1996 election to the right-wing Benjamin Netanyahu, who had no interest in continuing discussions with Syria. In December 1999 and January 2000, US President Clinton oversaw a meeting between Syrian Foreign Minister Shara' and newly elected Israeli Prime Minister Ehud Barak, which fizzled out after details of the talks were leaked to the Israeli press.[38] Clinton himself met Assad in Geneva in March 2000 in an effort to relaunch the peace process, and, in May, Barak finally withdrew Israeli forces from south Lebanon. By this point, it was Assad's ill health that made further movement unlikely. Assad's death from natural causes in June 2000 not only ended this round of talks, but also effectively laid down the red lines for his successor to follow.

In contrast to the different positions taken by what must have seemed to Assad a revolving door of Israeli politicians through the 1990s, Assad placed unwavering insistence on Israel's full withdrawal to the borders of 4 June 1967 as an essential precondition for any further discussion. He explained his position clearly to his domestic audience in a speech to the annual congress of the Syrian General Federation of Trade Unions in December 1992:

> Peace is not something that can be sold or bought; it is an issue of rights and commitments – rights which should return completely to their owners without any relinquishment [. . .] We will continue the peace process, since we have already started it, but not indefinitely [. . .] Despite our definite desire for peace, it will never be at the expense of the territory, because the Arabs – with the Syrian people in the forefront – will not relinquish their territory, no matter how many years, decades or generations it takes; because territory is the dearest; it is dignity, it is the homeland.[39]

The clarity of Assad's position left little room for ambiguity. It would certainly make it difficult for his eventual successor to accept anything less than Israel's full withdrawal from the Golan. However, in the event, Syria's negotiating position with Israel was not tested again. Despite much talk in the 1990s of how a settlement with Israel would generate a 'peace dividend' for the whole Middle East, talks between Israel and Syria were not relaunched after Assad died. For the last ten years of his life, Assad had focused on foreign affairs while his apparatus of repression quietly and ruthlessly removed any dissent. His declining health increasingly removed him from the routine business of government, which was consequently cautious, defensive and repetitive. Stasis, not innovation, became the rule of thumb. By the time of Assad's death, even regime loyalists recognized the need for change.

Y2K: Bashar al-Assad

In hindsight, the uneventful transition of power from Hafiz to Bashar appears both improbable and inevitable. In the late 1980s, it was Hafiz's eldest son, Basil, who had appeared in regime propaganda as Syria's dashing new hero and heir apparent. When Basil died in a car accident in 1994, Hafiz recalled Bashar from his job as an eye doctor in London and groomed him for the succession. At first, this slightly awkward advocate of computing and the music of Phil Collins appeared to be cut from a different cloth than the horse-racing army officer Basil. But Bashar undertook intensive military training, took a command in the Republican Guard and, fast-tracked for promotion, by 1999 had climbed to the rank of colonel. Besides his position as chair of the Syrian Computing Society, which sought to bring the internet to the country, Bashar played a senior role in maintaining Syrian interests in Lebanon, gradually sidelining Vice President Abd al-Halim Khaddam from the job.

As a precursor of the generational change that was to come, a handful of other high-ranking officers 'retired' from their careers in the military and intelligence, and were replaced with supporters of Bashar, including his brother-in-law, Assef Shawkat. Bashar was careful to cultivate ties with Arab leaders by, for example, visiting King Abdullah of Jordan (three years his senior) to pay his condolences for the death of his father Hussein in 1999. While visiting Saudi Arabia the same year, Bashar also took the opportunity to go to the holy city of Mecca, perhaps taking a card from his father's playbook in reminding any potential Sunni critics that Alawis were indeed members of the Muslim community. Although the late president had never openly named Bashar as successor, an article in the *al-Thawra* newspaper had made the case: 'In a short time, Bashar has proven that he is a branch of the blessed tree. This branch has rapidly grown into a solid trunk that answers the call of his brethren of the homeland to fulfil Basil's mission and protect the legacy of the great leader on the path to the third millennium.'[40] In the eerily quiet days following Hafiz al-Assad's death on 10 June 2000, a more prosaic refrain was quietly muttered around the country: *ma fi ghayru*. 'There is no one else.'

The ranks of the regime seemed to close behind the figure of Bashar. On the day Hafiz's death was announced, the Syrian parliament speedily amended the constitution to lower the age requirement for president from forty to thirty-four, the age of Bashar. A week later, Bashar was appointed general secretary of the Ba'th Party, just a few days after meeting US Secretary of State Madeleine Albright in Damascus, who reported that Bashar was eager to restart the peace process. At the end of June, the Syrian parliament unanimously selected Bashar as president of the Syrian Arab Republic. The decision was endorsed in the national referendum of 10 July, with 97.29 per cent of the vote. Suggestions that the slight opening of space to discuss reform in the months leading up to Hafiz's death were seemingly confirmed by Bashar's first presidential speech to the Syrian parliament. In this, Bashar outlined a veiled critique of economic policy-making on his father's watch:

> Performance in the economic field, in particular, went through sharp fluctuations as a result of changing circumstances that in turn were the subject of sharp changes, particularly as our

economy moved from an economy that has open markets to an economy that has to be competitive. This point was addressed through issuing laws and decrees which were sometimes experimental, sometimes impulsive, sometimes a reaction to a certain state of affairs.

Very rarely was this point addressed effectively by taking the initiative to precede events. The reason was that there was no clear strategy to bring about certain legislation; rather the economic strategy came as a result of all this legislation. Hence, it came out weak with many loopholes and was partially to blame for many of the difficulties from which we suffer today. This means that today we need economic, social and scientific strategies that may serve both development and steadfastness. Such strategies are not available as ready recipes; rather they need deepened studies [. . .]

Figures do not, lie and therefore they are genuine and transparent. Dealing with figures requires honesty and transparency. The term 'transparency' has been frequently used and discussed lately in dialogues and essays and in other places as well. Some used to call for a transparent economy and others called for transparent media while some others called for a transparent mentality in other domains [. . .]

I would like to reiterate here that finding solutions is the responsibility of all of us in order to make these solutions complete and effective. You should not rely solely on the state nor should you let the state rely solely on you. Let us work together as one team.[41]

What is striking about these passages is not simply Bashar's advocacy of modernization for Syria: even within the Ba'th Party, the need for change was largely recognized, if only to accommodate the needs of a new generation rising to power. But, for Syrians who had for so long heard little but the hollow reverberations of Ba'thist ideological slogans, Bashar's introduction of such notions as transparency, individual initiative and evidence-based policy must have sounded more like the language of a management consultant than the traditionally bombastic Arab nationalism to which they were accustomed. Although Bashar was no more charismatic in his delivery than his father, the different tone confirmed the impression that discussion of reform was no longer anathema to the regime.

Hints of this change had already been apparent in Syria in the months prior to Bashar's becoming president. An anti-corruption drive spearheaded by Bashar resulted in long-standing Prime Minister Mahmoud al-Zu'bi and two more ministers expelled from the Ba'th Party and prosecuted for illegally profiting from the purchase of six Airbus passenger planes for Syrian Arab Airlines. (Zu'bi was found dead in his home, allegedly killed by his own hand, just a few months later.) The new government appointed in March 2000 included as minister of planning Isam al-Za'im, a reform-minded technocrat thought to represent the preferred policy direction of Bashar, alongside the other legacy Ba'thists in the cabinet. Around the same time, reports suggested that the regime intended later that year to hold the first Regional Congress of the Ba'th Party since 1985, at which Bashar's status as heir apparent would presumably be consolidated.

Interpreting these events as an indication of changing times, Syrian intellectuals and political opponents inside the country slowly began to organize gatherings to discuss the way forward. The first of these meetings took place in late May 2000. Although held in private homes, the content of these discussion groups crossed both political and legal red lines, in that the numbers of people attending rapidly expanded beyond the strict controls on freedom of assembly in place under Syria's nearly forty-year-old emergency laws. From these first few tentative steps in Damascus came an avalanche of salons, debating groups and rejuvenated political discourse, which soon picked up pace around the country. Within six months, each of these meetings could attract two or three hundred participants, if not more. The 'Damascus Spring' – as it was soon called – had begun.

The core of this movement came from the same kind of secular intellectuals and activists who had opposed the regime back in the late 1970s and early 1980s. Indeed, some of the individuals involved had themselves been active at that time. Michel Kilo, a Christian from Latakia, for example, was one of those arrested then; similarly, the Communist Riyad al-Turk, who had only recently been released from eighteen years in prison, was an outspoken critic of Bashar inheriting the republic. One of the most prominent organizers was Riyad Seif, an industrialist turned politician, who had been elected to the Syrian parliament in 1992, and subsequently used his position to attack government corruption. After taking part in the earliest salons in Damascus, Seif sought to obtain a licence for future meetings and approached no less august a personage than Abd al-Halim Khaddam, the country's vice president and long-standing pillar of the Hafiz regime. When Khaddam advised him to wait, Seif decided to carry on regardless and established the National Dialogue Forum (*Muntada al-Hiwar al-Watani*), which held its first meeting at Seif's home on 13 September 2000. Each week, throngs of eager participants gathered for a one-hour lecture followed by a two-hour debate on topics relating to civil society in Syria. News of Seif's meetings spread quickly, in part owing to coverage by the transnational Qatar-based satellite television station Al Jazeera. Similar meetings soon sprang up in Aleppo, Latakia, Tartous, Suwayda, Hassakeh and other towns. 'By January [2001] it was like a fashion,' Seif told a

British interviewer. 'Every week you heard an announcement of the opening of a new forum.'[42]

The salons' diagnosis of the problems facing Syria at the turn of the millennium – and their critique of the Assad regime of the father and the son – was built upon lines of thought that were laid down by the country's secular opposition in the late 1970s and early 1980s, and had continued, clandestinely, during the 1990s.[43] The best way to liberate the people from the violence and repression of the state, it emerged in these debates, was to revive – or to create – civil society in Syria. For Kilo, Seif, Turk and other intellectuals, the free association of individuals in an organized civic life of associations, political parties and public debate was needed to counter both the state's despotism and the tendency of society to resort to the ties of kinship, sect, religion and ethnicity. Civil society represented a way to overcome these fractures and bring about an overarching national unity, in which secularism would be the guarantor of social freedoms. The kind of 'civil society' Syrian leftists envisaged was not the liberal variety advocated by Western campaigns to promote democracy in the Middle East during the 1990s.[44] Inspired by Gramsci rather than Tocqueville, Syrian intellectuals sought to use the cultural space of civil society to regroup and recuperate at a time of political weakness.

In the six months from September 2000 to February 2001, this strategy seemed to be working. Ninety-nine leading Syrian intellectuals signed a petition calling for an end to the emergency laws, the release of political prisoners, the establishment of state of law and the return of individual and collective liberties.[45] Published in the transnational *al-Hayat* newspaper on 27 September, this 'Statement of the 99' was carefully phrased to minimize confrontation. Encouragingly, the regime implemented several small yet not inconsequential reforms. Six hundred political prisoners were released, and the closure of the infamous Mezzeh prison was announced, while restrictions on the media were gently relaxed and licences granted to publish the first private magazines. Two Syrian human rights organizations and several citizen-led popular committees – variously organizing campaigns to rally support for the second Palestinian intifada, for a consumer boycott of US goods or against the international sanctions on Iraq – were permitted by the regime to operate unhindered. The newly installed editor of the government's *al-Thawra* newspaper, Mahmud Salamah, opened up its pages to surprisingly candid (in Syrian terms) essays on civil society, reform and progress. In January 2001, fifty-five prominent lawyers added their voices to the call for change.[46] A second statement – this time appended with the signatures of 1,000 Syrian intellectuals collected by Michel Kilo's Committees for the Revival of Civil Society – was published in the Lebanese *al-Safir* newspaper.[47] This intervention was more direct in its articulation of the need for fundamental reforms than the earlier 'Statement of the 99'. Kilo tried to ensure a soft landing by recognizing in a press statement just how central President Bashar al-Assad was to the success of reform in Syria.[48]

Kilo's conciliatory approach was founded on the conviction that the limited freedoms currently granted to the civil society movement were conditional on not challenging the incumbent regime directly and on not maintaining connections to foreign powers. In contrast to Kilo's cautious approach, the parliamentarian Riyad Seif calculated that the regime's plans for reform would soon provide more space for manoeuvre.[49] In anticipation of a new law that would allow the creation of new political parties to widen participation in the regime's own parliamentary coalition, the National Progressive Front, in February 2001, Seif began to prepare his political salon for transition into a fully fledged political party. Kilo and others in the civil society movement feared that Seif's step was too confrontational. The regime seemed to share their concerns.

In February 2001, President Bashar al-Assad gave an interview to the transnational *al-Sharq al-Awsat* newspaper in which he described Syrian intellectuals as an isolated minority who only represented themselves. If their actions adversely affected national security, Assad stated, they might well be foreign agents.[50] Regime conservatives rallied behind Assad's interview. The following week, Vice President Khaddam delivered a crushing speech at the University of Damascus in which he railed against the civil society movement. 'Democracy is not an off-the-peg ensemble that we can buy from the market or borrow from another country,' Khaddam declared to an auditorium of Ba'thists.[51] Britain and France began their journeys to democracy centuries ago, Khaddam pointed out, but only became fully democratic when they took into account the needs of their citizens. For Syria, improving the economy and creating employment was a greater priority than opening up to the kind of political pluralism that in the 1990s had proven disastrous for Yugoslavia and Algeria, he pointedly warned. Although a notable exception was made for the Jamal al-Atasi Forum (associated with a loose-knit grouping of venerable leftist political factions, the National Democratic Gathering, which had been tolerated since the 1980s and which the regime seemed to believe might yet be integrated into the status quo), the regime ordered all other salons to be immediately shuttered until further notice.

Civil society activists would later debate the causes of what came to be known as the 'February Crisis'. Had the movement progressed too quickly? Was the regime rattled by Seif's plans to create a new political party? Did the explicit reference to Syria's ethnic and religious diversity in one of Seif's founding documents sound alarm bells in breaking a long-standing taboo?[52]

To what extent did geopolitical factors – such as hardliner Ariel Sharon becoming the Israeli prime minister in the same month – also play a role?

Initially, there was optimism that the salon closures were only a temporary setback. Kilo released a political statement distancing the movement from radical demands and emphasizing its rejection of ethnic and sectarian differences in favour of national unity. Salameh, the reformist head of *al-Thawra* newspaper, wrote an editorial in which he declared the Damascus Spring to be 'in its beginning, not its end'.[53] In May, Salameh was relieved of his position. Undaunted, Seif used his parliamentary position to launch a blistering attack on the government's awarding of new mobile phone licences to Assad's cousin, businessman Rami Makhlouf, on preferential terms that Seif alleged would cost the public US$8 billion in lost earnings over fifteen years.[54] The civil society movement tentatively explored new ways forward, such as founding a new human rights organization in Syria. Outside the country, the remnants of the shattered Syrian Muslim Brotherhood announced from London that it would work within a pluralistic opposition movement in the future.[55] The regime soon took decisive action to repress the nascent lobby for political reform.

The 'August Crisis' of 2001 began with the arrest of leading figures of the Damascus Spring, including Ma'moun al-Homsi (who went on hunger strike to protest against Syria's ongoing emergency laws) and Riyad al-Turk (who had publicly characterized the regime as a dictatorship on Al Jazeera television). Civil society activists responded with indignation and called for their immediate release. In the meantime, Seif relaunched his political salon without official permission, starting with a talk by the France-based Syrian sociologist Burhan Ghalyoun, which attracted hundreds of participants. The following day, Seif was arrested and taken to the Adra prison. Seven more opposition intellectuals were also arrested. In a departure from tradition, Seif and Homsi were granted public trials in October and November 2001, partially in genuflection to their status as members of the Syrian parliament, but also in keeping with the regime's announcement earlier that year that the emergency laws were to be 'frozen' – albeit in practice a freezing that was arbitrarily implemented.[56] The cases dragged on, some for over a year, hinting at uncharacteristic uncertainty within the regime over the extent to which an example should be made of the activists.

The regime's ambivalence over how, and whether, to proceed with reform was no doubt exacerbated by geopolitical changes in the Middle East after the September 11 attacks on the United States in 2001. At first, the regime was able to exploit the aftermath of 9/11 to deflect attention from its domestic repression. The first hearing of Seif's case took place the same day as the Damascus press conference of British Prime Minister Tony Blair, who had come to Syria to cement Assad's support for the emerging international alliance against al-Qaeda, the transnational Islamist network responsible for the attacks. Assad pledged Syria's full support for the US-led war on al-Qaeda. The US State Department notably credited Syria with supplying intelligence that foiled an al-Qaeda attack on the US Fifth Fleet in Bahrain in 2002. Syrian intelligence was also responsible for torturing at least one wrongly accused al-Qaeda operative – a Syrian–Canadian dual national whom the US authorities expelled and clandestinely rendered to Syria for interrogation.[57]

Despite this cooperation, certain influential figures in the Washington, D.C., policy establishment sought to include Syria as a target within the ever-widening remit of what they described as a global war on terror. In May 2002, US Under Secretary of State for Arms Control and International Security John Bolton described Syria – alongside Libya and Cuba – as 'rogue states' for their alleged pursuit of weapons of mass destruction (WMDs). Bolton further noted that these states were only one step removed from President George W. Bush's 'axis of evil', comprising Iraq, Iran and North Korea. Support grew in the US Congress for sanctioning Syria for its putative WMD programme, its ongoing military occupation of Lebanon and the aid it supplied to Palestinian armed groups and the Lebanese Hizbullah. Syria did lend its support to the UN Security Council Resolution 1441 of 8 November 2002, which called on Iraq to allow international weapons inspectors to resume their work inside the country and implied 'serious consequences' in the event of non-compliance. In the event, what Damascus described as this 'Syrian diplomatic victory' in the United Nations was insufficient either to force Saddam Hussein to cooperate with the inspectors or to dissuade US policy-makers from declaring war on Iraq just a few months later.

The March 2003 invasion of Iraq by 130,000 US, 45,000 British and 2,000 Australian soldiers – with additional support from dozens of other countries – led to rapid deterioration in relations between Washington and Damascus. Syria's long-standing enmity with Iraq had already begun to recede after Bashar al-Assad became president. Since late 2000, Iraq had been exporting as much as 200,000 barrels of cheap oil per day to Syria via the Kirkuk–Baniyas pipeline, in contravention of UN sanctions. In April 2003, US Secretary of Defence Donald Rumsfeld accused Syria of supplying the regime of Saddam Hussein with night-vision binoculars. Syria was also accused of harbouring senior Iraqi officials who had fled the country and of developing its own chemical weapons programme. In May 2004, the United States began to impose sanctions on the Syrian banking sector as stipulated in the Syria Accountability and Lebanese Sovereignty Restoration Act of December 2003. Although US policy-makers' appetite for further military involvement began to weaken as an insurgency against the occupation picked up pace in Iraq, Syria now faced a concerted campaign of diplomatic pressure that seemed to put Bashar al-Assad on the back foot. If there had been any voices in his regime in favour of reviving the space for civil society in Syria, they fell silent in the aftermath of the Iraq invasion. Regime security had trumped political reform.

11

From Social Market to Civil War, 2003–2014

In the early years of the twenty-first century, political manoeuvring inside the regime revolved around the struggle between President Bashar al-Assad's reform-minded 'new guard' and the obstinate 'old guard' that clung to the legacies of Assad's late father Hafiz.

Bashar al-Assad himself minimized the importance of intergenerational tensions. 'You have young people who didn't work with my father and who have the same mentality,' he said in a 2003 interview he gave to *The New York Times* at the age of thirty-eight. 'It is not a matter of old guards or new guards ... Some of this generation whom you call 'old guard' are more enthusiastic about reform than me!'[1] He reframed the question as a difference of what he called mentalities. Different mentalities within the Syrian government, state institutions, Ba'th Party and even the private sector had different preferences for stability and change, Assad explained. Reform could not be imposed from above but had to be slow, steady and incremental to win the support of Syrians who would be impacted by the changes. 'I am not a dictator!' he declared.

Coming so soon after Assad had clamped down on public debate and jailed key figures of the 2000–01 Damascus Spring, the president's words already rang hollow. Yet even if the political opposition was in no position to challenge his plans, Assad recognized, the impetus for reform could easily be derailed by resistance within the system itself. To deliver his vision, he had to replace powerful insiders appointed by his father with individuals who supported his new project of reform for the state, society and economy. By 2005, this peaceable transition in personnel would be virtually complete.

As if to signal the success of Assad's efforts, the 2005 Regional Congress of the Ba'th Party would triumphantly declare that Syria was to undergo a historic transition from central planning to a new kind of economic model it hailed as the Social Market Economy. This shift would rebalance economic activity away from the state in favour of the private sector. For Assad's modernization project to be successful, this shift implied the need to cultivate new constituencies of support outside the party and the state – especially in business and non-governmental organizations. For wealthy, urban Syrians, the Social Market Economy would usher in a new era of consumerism: fine restaurants, imported cars, personal computers, mobile phones, English language classes and expensive clothes. It was poor and rural Syrians who would ultimately bear the cost of these refinements.

Assad's decision to shelter the security services from the imperatives of reform meant that the old habits of torture, brutality and coercion would never be eradicated from the system. Throughout the decade of the 2000s, the *mukhabarat* continued to operate as the dark shadow cast by Assad's social market liberalism. The older generation that had lived through the bloody repression of the 1970s and 1980s remained wary of what the future might hold. Syrian sociologist Burhan Ghalyoun had once warned that should the 'wall of fear' protecting the regime ever tumble, the regime's erosion of all forms of social justice, equality and solidarity would produce not a democratic transition, but violence and the collapse of the rule of law at the hands of people who had been 'stripped of their humanity and who harboured despair'.[2] When the wall of fear collapsed and Syria was ripped apart by conflict in 2011, Ghalyoun's words seemed less like pessimism and more like fateful prediction.

Preparing for reform

Soon after Bashar al-Assad came to power, a number of older intelligence chiefs were quietly edged into retirement, although giants of the Hafiz al-Assad era, such as Tlass and Khaddam, initially retained their respective positions as defence minister and vice president. The new president now concentrated his efforts on introducing change to the ministerial bureaucracy and the stagnant ranks of the Ba'th Party. In March 2002, he lowered the retirement age to sixty, in one fell swoop removing 80,000 ageing officials from the senior ranks of the civil service. This purge created space to hire new recruits and promote mid-career bureaucrats whose path to advancement had been blocked by the old incumbents. The same year, the lowest levels of the Ba'th Party were renewed by elections. In July 2003, it was announced that Ba'th Party members would no longer be given preferential treatment in appointments to the government or public sector. Eligibility criteria were also raised. From 2003 onwards, candidates for parliament would need at least an undergraduate degree (or for those running for seats reserved for 'peasants and workers', a high school diploma). These changes admitted new faces into the system but changed little about how the system operated.

When the Ba'th Party in neighbouring Iraq was disbanded following the US-led invasion in 2003, pressure increased to rejuvenate Syria's ossified command structures. Parliamentary elections that year resulted in 178 newcomers joining the 250-strong chamber. Bashar al-Assad replaced the prime minister appointed in his father's last days with a reformist, former governor of Homs Naji al-'Utri, who proposed the intriguing novelty of a cabinet comprised of liberals and technocrats in which Ba'thists would be a minority. This prospect was quickly vetoed by the Ba'th's Regional Command, which argued that it would be unwise to step back from power given the instability that followed the invasion in Iraq.

The old guard tried to strengthen their position by reasserting their role in regional geopolitics after the long-serving Hafiz loyalist Tlass was finally replaced as defence minister in 2004. Their attempt to achieve this goal by assassinating Lebanon's anti-Syrian prime minister, Rafiq al-Hariri, proved a spectacular miscalculation. Hariri's killing on Valentine's Day 2005, prompted an international outcry, as well as mass protests in Lebanon that led to Syria ending its thirty-year military presence in the country. Syria's former intelligence chief in Lebanon, Ghazi Kan'an – who was largely believed to have masterminded the assassination – gave evidence to the UN team set up to probe Hariri's death and then died apparently by suicide. By the end of the year, Vice President Khaddam – another old-guard stalwart to whom Kan'an had been close – had speedily fled the country for the safety of France after denouncing Assad's policy in Lebanon and defecting from the regime. By this point, the old guard had lost the initiative.[3]

In his speech to the Tenth Regional Congress of the Ba'th Party in June 2005, Bashar al-Assad struck an uneasy balance between his reform agenda and the familiarly strident tones of populist nationalism. Syria would maintain its principled resistance to Israel and to Western intervention in the Middle East, he declared. It was true that Syria's geopolitical position had been left fragile from the defeat of Saddam Hussein's rival – albeit still

Ba'thist – regime in Iraq. Now, the United States also sought to isolate Damascus for its roles in supporting the Iraqi insurgency and the Hariri assassination. These pressures perhaps discouraged Assad from embarking upon the more significant restructuring of domestic politics that reform advocates had hoped he would announce at the Regional Congress. A much-mooted law authorizing the creation of new political parties never saw the light of day, although the formerly prohibited Syrian Social Nationalist Party (SSNP) was admitted to the official ruling coalition in parliament. The Ba'th retained its constitutionally enshrined position as Syria's leading party in state and society. Although change to Syria's foreign policy and domestic politics was effectively frozen, the country's economy was a different story.

The Social Market Economy

When the Tenth Regional Congress declared, in June 2005, that Syria would adopt the Social Market Economy (*iqtisad al-suq al-ijtima'i*), the decision did not come out of the blue. Steps in this direction had been taken since Bashar al-Assad came to power in 2000: teams of Syrian economists had been tasked with writing reports on how to reform the economy, including several with input from French experts. Although their recommendations had not been implemented, the mere fact that the authorities had invited such discussions allowed advocates of reform to marshal their arguments and rally support for their cause.

On the domestic front, Syria had passed legislation in 2001 allowing private banks to operate for the first time since 1963. The government's tight control of the Syrian Central Bank was relaxed, and foundations were laid for the development of commercial insurance services. Private sector involvement in education and the media was permitted, plans for a stock market were announced and restrictions on rental contracts and property eased to facilitate investment from business interests in Syria and overseas, notably companies based in the Gulf.[4] Encouragingly for the liberals, Syria had signed free trade agreements with other states in the region, notably Iraq, Jordan and Saudi Arabia, soon to be followed by Turkey. In 2001, Syria had even requested membership of the World Trade Organization, although its accession had been effectively torpedoed by political opposition from the United States and Israel. In 2005, a technocrat, Abdullah al-Dardari, often credited with being the architect of the Social Market Economy, was elevated to the position of deputy prime minister for economic affairs. The official adoption of the Social Market Economy by the Regional Congress later the same year nevertheless signalled the end of policy discussions with experts.[5] Decisions over the direction, content and pace of reform were no longer up for debate, but were firmly in the hands of the regime.

What exactly government officials meant when they spoke of the Social Market Economy was never entirely clear. There was indeed a sense that the regime wanted to introduce economic reforms without abandoning its traditional commitments to workers and peasants – a concern that ostensibly distinguished Syria's approach from both the kind of free-market radicalism that had followed hot on the heels of the collapse of communism in Russia and Eastern Europe and the plundering of Egypt's public assets for private interests in the 1990s. Beyond those distinctions, there was no methodical, considered or even coherent expression of what Syria's new economic model would entail.[6] The Syrian state would somehow be responsible for instigating a historic shift from central planning to the private sector, abolishing market-distorting subsidies and maintaining fiscal discipline, while simultaneously guaranteeing welfare protections and the 'sound distribution of economic resources [...] according to the principles of social justice'.[7] Exactly which policies or even which institutions should be tasked with managing these contradictions remained a mystery. Sceptics wondered whether the Social Market Economy was a solution genuinely capable of tackling Syria's economic problems, or simply an assortment of ad hoc policies to woo the private sector and recruit businessmen to the ranks of the regime.[8]

For their part, wealthy Syrians quickly took advantage of the new markets created by the regime in sectors from telecommunications and tourism to education and construction. Foremost among them were individuals with close family connections to regime insiders. Assad's first cousins on his mother's side, Rami and Ihab Makhlouf, were already in a strong position to take over large swathes of the Syrian economy. Decades earlier, the Makhloufs' father had amassed wealth by using family ties to secure sinecures at the head of several state-owned companies. In the 2000s, his sons targeted lucrative opportunities in the new private sector, from mobile phones to duty-free shopping, banking and property. Damascus Spring activists of 2000–01 had criticized corruption in obtaining exclusivity and tax-free holidays for Syriatel, the country's largest mobile phone network, which the Makhloufs controlled. By 2005, the combination of regime complicity, bullying tactics and connections to the security services allowed the Makhlouf brothers to accumulate wealth estimated at an astounding US$3 billion.[9] Other members of the Assad family built strategic partnerships with businessmen whose careers were underpinned by this high-level patronage. The support of Assad's brother Maher, for example, allowed one Muhammad Hamsho to acquire extensive business interests in sectors from information technology to tourism. Hamsho bolstered his nouveau-riche status by getting himself elected to parliament as a deputy for

Damascus, supported by the patronage of Maher. While businessmen had been allowed to take advantage of the limited economic openings in Syria in previous decades, the sheer scale of the accumulated wealth – and the ruthlessness with which regime cronies exploited and secured their interests – now dwarfed anything seen in the past.

Alongside the new class of super-rich business tycoons with family connections to the Assads, Syria's merely very rich businessmen also sought to find their place in the Social Market Economy. They did so by means of a financial innovation newly introduced to Syria: the holding company. In 2007, Rami Makhlouf founded the al-Cham holding company, which soon attracted over seventy members; it initially aimed to amass a modest US$200 million for investment, but proved so popular that its working capital soon reached US$350 million. Makhlouf himself estimated that al-Cham Holding accounted for 60 per cent of all economic activity in Syria.[10] Businessmen wary of joining the team of Makhlouf (who had a reputation for using coercive tactics to acquire the assets of junior partners as well as rivals) could join the rival Souria holding company launched by the Latakia-based Joud family, which attracted a slightly younger group of investors. A good proportion of the members of the al-Cham and Souria holdings came from the old Sunni and Christian urban elite. Among them were members of such prominent families as the Kuzbaris, the Attars and the Atasis, from which the backbone of high society in Damascus and Aleppo had long been drawn, and who now benefitted from Bashar al-Assad's more tolerant disposition towards private wealth. Nevertheless, one analysis calculated that even after excluding the Makhloufs and other close relatives of high-ranking regime insiders, an estimated three-quarters of the top 100 richest members of the Syrian business elite were still the sons of other regime figures, their close partners or individuals closely tied to the security services. Their ranks were also heavily skewed towards Syria's western provinces, especially Damascus, Aleppo and Latakia, The eastern governorates were barely represented, and Druze, Kurds and Ismailis were entirely absent from this list of business power brokers.[11] Proximity to power granted access to wealth.

Members of the new elite rarely engaged in entrepreneurial risk-taking but instead sought out monopolies or quasi-monopolies where they were shielded from competition. A new arrangement pioneered in Syria at this time was the 'build–operate–transfer' (BOT) model, whereby public authorities granted private companies long-term leases over the profits generated from new infrastructure projects in return for raising the capital to build them. Cham Holding, for example, was given a forty-year lease to turn the historic Hijaz Railway Station in Damascus into a luxury shopping mall. Souria Holding reportedly paid US$6 million in 2009 for a seventy-five-year lease to construct two forty-storey skyscrapers (complete with a five-star hotel, restaurants and parking for 2,500 cars) to replace the capital's chaotic bus station at Baramkeh. Companies often entered into these public–private partnerships with city councils, a move that opened up further opportunities for under-the-table inducements to ensure the paperwork was smoothly processed along the way.[12] Often in partnership with investors from the Gulf states, the Syrian business elite was primarily interested in opportunities for enrichment through state-sanctioned speculation.[13] 'Trade and transit come first, followed by tourism and services, and then agriculture,' said Haytham Joud, when asked what Syria's economic priorities should be.[14] Productive investment was far less appealing.

Assad's reform agenda redistributed responsibility for social welfare from the state to non-governmental organizations, which were tasked with putting the 'social' into the Social Market Economy.

The regime therefore relaxed some of its draconian restrictions on associational life. Between 2000 and 2010, 605 new non-profits and charities were founded in Syria – more than had been established during the previous four decades combined.[15] Most of these new initiatives were set up around the time the Social Market Economy was first launched. As most of Syria's NGOs were small-scale charities, the country's civic landscape was quickly dominated by behemoths which benefitted from the patronage of Assad's wife, the British-Syrian Asma al-Akhras. Part of a well-established and respectable Sunni family from Homs, Asma was born and raised in London, where she studied computer science and worked in investment banking before meeting Bashar, whom she married in December 2000.

Asma al-Akhras brought a touch of cosmopolitan glamour to the reform project. She toured the country, listened to the people and founded several important new charities. In 2007, these were brought under the umbrella of the Syria Trust for Development (*al-Amana al-Suriya li'l-Tanmiya*), of which she was patron.[16] Each organization in the Syria Trust had a specific remit, such as rural development, youth, children and culture, although they shared a tendency to use training and education to spread an ethos of entrepreneurship, self-improvement and liberalism that ran contrary to traditional Ba'thist commitments. The Syria Trust and its operations proved wildly popular with foreign donors as well as with a new generation of reform-minded, educated, young professionals, who found Akhras's projects warmly welcomed their skills and contributions to the modernization project. Outside the Syria Trust, elite organizations such as the Junior Chamber International and Syrian Young Entrepreneurs provided opportunities for well-educated liberals of the next generation to volunteer their free time, network with their peers and enact their belief in the president's promises of reform.[17] Syrians whose worlds were still defined by the old, seemingly anachronistic institutions of the state – the Peasants' Union, the Ba'th Party, the *mukhabarat* – were often suspicious of the new mindset and jargon of the Syria Trust, despite its *bona fide* position within the regime.

Outside the rhetoric of the government and the Syria Trust, the closest that most people came to the new Social Market Economy was when they encountered the rising price of consumables. In keeping with the new economic orthodoxy of the free market, the Syrian government repealed its decades-long policy of consumer subsidies.[18] Advocates of reform, such as Deputy Prime Minister Dardari, had calculated that increasing the cost of fuel to its international price alone would save Syria some US$3.5 billion, effectively solving its budget deficit. On 1 May 2008, the government announced the end of fuel subsidies. The cost of diesel – which provided the most common form of heating in homes during Syria's often bitter winters – shot up overnight from S£7–20 (14 to 50 US cents).[19] Meanwhile, the price of a canister of cooking gas rocketed from 145 to 250 Syrian pounds (US$2.90 to $5), and prices at the petrol pump doubled. The cost of bread went up by 50 per cent, and even the price of vegetables rose 20 per cent.

The Social Market Economy might have brought new opportunities for the rich, but ordinary Syrians soon felt cast adrift. In the late 2000s, the gap between the 'haves' and 'have-nots' was widening to the point that it began to resemble the old inequalities between feudal landowners and rural peasantry that had become so starkly entrenched in the late nineteenth and early twentieth centuries. Ironically, it was this very imbalance that had motivated the Ba'th Party's original commitment to wealth redistribution. Nearly fifty years after the Ba'th had seized power, the inequalities and contradictions engendered by Bashar al-Assad's deeply compromised project of reform meant that Syria was once again about to reach a critical, if not revolutionary, historical juncture.

Fractures: inequality, regionalism, coercion

For sixty years before Bashar al-Assad came to power, the driving force of state-building in Syria had been the imperative to integrate the country's diverse regions, communities and economies into a single centralized system. In principle, at least, during this time it was the state that built infrastructure, directed investment and allocated resources After 2000, this top-down guiding logic was abandoned. The owners of capital were granted free rein to invest or disinvest in different cities, neighbourhoods and regions as they saw fit, with little government direction. This shift exacerbated pre-existing inequalities – and created new inequities – between different parts of the country, in ways that became increasingly visible as the decade progressed.

In cities such as Damascus, Aleppo and Latakia, the wealthy and upper middle classes enjoyed a cultural and culinary renaissance. Businessmen launched new cafes, restaurants and bars, offering everything from the cappuccinos and sushi of contemporary globalization to Levantine fine dining inspired by reimagined Ottoman traditions. Struggling residents of the once neglected Old City of Damascus sold their crumbling courtyard homes only to see them restored into boutique hotels for discerning foreign tourists. By 2008, there were almost a hundred restaurants and sixty-five hotels in the inner streets of the Old City, which ten years earlier had been sleepy, relatively unvisited and mostly residential.[20] The new Four Seasons Hotel in Damascus, constructed in 2006, brought a touch of Dubai-style bling to the heart of the capital.

Tourism to Syria increased significantly after 2008 following the end of the country's diplomatic isolation by the West and its lifting of visa restrictions on Turkish and Iranian citizens. Syria also continued to be a popular destination for tourists from Saudi Arabia, Jordan, Lebanon and Iraq. In 2010, a total of 8.5 million tourists visited – an increase of 40 per cent from the previous year. While tourism accounted for 14 per cent of the Syrian economy that year, its benefits were concentrated in the urban or coastal areas and scarcely touched the north-east. For their part, middle-class Syrians were quick to take advantage of the free trade agreement with Turkey, implemented in 2007, which afforded new opportunities for visa-free retail tourism. The southern Turkish city of Gaziantep became a desirable destination for weekend shopping trips from the north: the local Chamber of Commerce estimated that, by 2010, 60,000 Syrians were visiting Gaziantep every month. After decades of cool relations with Syria, Turkey's new ruling party, the religious AKP, saw commerce as a vehicle for reorientating the country towards its Middle Eastern neighbours.

Syrian investors proposed a series of large-scale, aspirational construction projects to redevelop urban centres, although such plans were largely slow to get off the ground in well-heeled neighbourhoods.[21] More successful were initiatives that started from scratch, on the edge of the cities, such as the luxury villas and gated communities in the distant Ya'four exurb of Damascus, off the highway to Beirut, or the construction of the new palatial home for the Ministry of Foreign Affairs in the previous market gardens of the capital's Kafr Susseh neighbourhood. Newly built shopping facilities, from Cham City Center in Damascus to the Shahba Mall in Aleppo, provided for those with a taste for the globalized retail experience that had become popular by the early twenty-first century.

Despite their glamour, such bubbles of consumerism were ultimately sustained only by Syria's richest businessmen and their partners in the Gulf, who sought attractive opportunities for investment, speculation and capital appreciation. Beyond the bright lights of Syria's western cities, on their suburban and rural fringes – and especially in the north and north-east of the country – there were very few illusions about the difficulties of making ends meet.

Although Syria's poverty rate had decreased to 30.1 per cent of the population (equivalent to 5.1 million people) by 2003–4, it rose to 33.6 per cent (6.7 million people) by 2007. These national figures concealed some important regional variations. Hardship was most pronounced in rural Syria, especially in the northern and eastern governorates of Idlib, Aleppo, Raqqa, Deir al-Zour and Hassakeh, which were by then home to 23.1 per cent of the population but no less than 37 per cent of those in abject poverty. The coastal provinces held the lowest proportion of the poor overall, but the cities of the south – including Damascus and Der'a – saw poverty almost double between 2003–4 and 2007.[22]

These regional variations are partly explained by the severe drought that adversely impacted north and eastern Syria from 2006. The two easternmost provinces of Deir al-Zour and Hassakeh received less than two-thirds of the average rainfall in 2007–8, ruining crop yields and forcing Syria to import wheat to meet domestic consumption needs for the first time since the early 1990s. An estimated 1.3 million people were directly affected by multiple years of drought. Farmers in the north-east were forced to exhaust their seed supply and slaughter their herds due to the rising cost of fodder, just to keep their families afloat. By 2009, an estimated 60–70 per cent of villages in Hassakeh and Deir al-Zour had been abandoned. At least 300,000 people – not just single unemployed men, as had happened in the past, but this time entire families – fled the dust-bowl conditions of the east.[23]

These migrants tended to congregate in tents on the margins of Damascus, Aleppo and Der'a (which had recovered more quickly from less protracted drought in the south). Others reached Syria's coastal cities or crossed the border to neighbouring Lebanon in search of work.

While climate patterns in the Jazira had produced periodic crises in the past, the impact of the 2006–10 drought was exacerbated by the government's agricultural policy. The perceived need to ensure Syria's self-sufficiency in food production had, since the 1990s, encouraged the state to relax its regulations on agricultural irrigation. The Jazira landscape was increasingly pockmarked with wells – the number rose from around 135,000 in 1999 to over 213,000 in 2007 – that served to irrigate fields of wheat and cotton. Mechanical pumps relentlessly drained the groundwater to the extent that the Balikh and Khabour rivers, historic tributaries of the Euphrates, ran dry, making water an increasingly scarce – and correspondingly expensive – commodity in the north-east.

The provisions of the Social Market Economy also played a part. The deregulation of rental contracts, in force from December 2007, gave landlords unlimited rights to expel tenants from their land. This reform prompted a wave of rural evictions as large landowners removed long-term tenants and sold their properties to capitalize on rising real estate values, especially on the outskirts of urban centres. In addition, large swathes of state-owned farmland were rather chaotically redistributed between former owners and current workers in parts of Raqqa and rural Aleppo governorates. As in previous episodes of land reform, this conflict-ridden process resulted in land ownership being concentrated in the hands of local elites, especially from the major tribes of the north-east and the urban middle classes of Raqqa.[24] The north-east was hit hard by the removal of fuel subsidies in May 2008, which affected not only the principal source of domestic heating, but also the diesel that fuelled the water pumps irrigating Syria's most important grain-producing region.

While liberalization had opened the floodgates to investment in urban real estate and luxury service provision, very little of this funding was channelled into sectors that produced jobs for Syria's growing population. By 2010, unemployment was conservatively estimated to stand at around 15–20 per cent; among the young, the jobless estimate was closer to 50 per cent.[25] The influx of cheap imports, especially from Turkey after the bilateral trade deal came into effect in 2007, forced dozens of small workshops to close on the industrial fringes of Damascus, Aleppo and other cities.[26] Prices rose across the board as producers struggled to absorb the costs of subsidy cuts. Between 2000 and 2008, the price of basic foodstuffs increased by an astonishing 56 per cent. Inflation was rampant: 10 per cent in 2006 and 15.5 per cent in 2008.[27] Although Syria's relative insulation from international markets meant that the global financial crisis of 2008–09 did not immediately impact its economy, the worldwide crash did slow the breakneck pace of foreign investment into the country. The crash also meant that international demand for exports – notably for Syrian agricultural products in countries such as Iraq, Germany, France, Italy and Saudi Arabia – declined in the following two years, dealing yet another blow to producers.

The high levels of outside investment into Syria in the mid-2000s drove a speculative boom in property that placed home ownership – and often even renting – beyond the reach of many Syrians. Across the country, the cost of housing increased by an average of 300 per cent between 2004 and 2006; in the most desirable districts, land prices reportedly increased by as much as 3,000 per cent.[28] The restrictions and prohibitive costs of construction and obtaining legal permits meant that poorer Syrians had long sought their own solution to affordable housing by building homes informally – without official authorization or planning permission – on the outskirts of major cities in neighbourhoods known as *mukhalafat*: areas in collective violation of government regulations. Although many of these settlements were slums, the better ones were constructed from cinder blocks (to varying degrees of sophistication and stability) and benefitted from infrastructure provision such as electricity and water (however inadequate). With some dexterity in handling the relevant legal and administrative processes, these dwellings even could be contractually purchased, sold, inherited and even taxed by the government – somewhat miraculously given that they did not officially exist in government records.[29] Rural migrants to the cities had long made their homes in *mukhalafat* alongside their families, friends and neighbours: rather than being assimilated into urban life, they reproduced village life inside the city. While the distinction between city dwellers from rural and urban backgrounds had been apparent since the 1970s, the rapid inflation of property prices in the 2000s heightened the competition for scarce affordable homes and accelerated the expansion of *mukhalafat* neighbourhoods.

In consequence, housing became a lightning rod for tensions between migrants, gentrifiers and established residents. In Homs, for example, the local governorate and the Qatari Al-Diyar company signed a contract to commence the 'Homs Dream' project in 2007 to regenerate a section of the city centre. The project was opposed by the mainly Sunni inhabitants of old Homs, who saw it as part of the push to drive out their community that they believed had brought so many rural Alawi migrants to the city. In reality, internal Sunni migration to Homs was greater than that of the Alawis, albeit less perceptible to old Homs residents.[30] After the invasion of Iraq, over a million migrants who had fled violence there came to settle primarily in Damascus, especially at the peak of sectarian killings in 2005–06. They clustered in neighbourhoods such as Jaramana (formerly home to a mixed Druze and Christian community), Qudsaya and Sayyida Zaynab, where the main thoroughfare was named 'Iraqi Street'.[31] As Iraqi businesses, eateries and social practices began to visibly transform parts of the capital, struggling Damascenes could easily believe that demand from these new arrivals was driving the crippling increases in rental costs.

Elsewhere in the country, underlying social tensions became manifest in isolated episodes of communal conflict. Druze and Bedouin tribes clashed in Suweida in November 2000, Isma'ilis and Alawis in the coastal mountain town of Qadmous in July 2005, the Shammar and Jabbour tribes in Hassakeh in August 2005 and Kurdish and Arab football supporters in Qamishli in March 2004. This latter incident escalated into major clashes between Kurds and pro-government forces across northern Hassakeh province; connected protests were also led by Kurdish residents of Damascus and Aleppo.

Faced with this potential for unrest, alongside the Social Market Economy the Assad regime unfurled a three-part strategy for social control. First, to mitigate the worst of the hardships created by the reforms, the regime made some minor concessions. When fuel price controls were lifted, for example, the government announced that each family would be granted 1,000 litres of heavily subsidized heating diesel in the first year, then a small cash lump sum in the second year to ease the transition to higher prices. In 2008, drivers of minibuses – a crucial means of local transport – organized an informal strike in Damascus to protest against risings costs, which was broken up by the security forces, but was also accompanied by the authorization to increase fares. In 2010, a second wildcat strike by protesting drivers prompted the Ministry of Transport to rethink plans to replace the independent minibuses with regular modern bus services run by private investors. On several occasions after the 2004 Qamishli uprising, senior regime figures, including the president and the defence minister, publicly discussed the need to extend citizenship to some of the 120,000–150,000 Kurds who had been registered as foreigners – and consequently denied nationality papers – in the 1962 census. Nothing of substance immediately came from these musings, although the last 300 prisoners arrested during the Qamishli uprising were granted amnesty and released in March 2005.

Second, to compensate for the declining importance of the Ba'th Party to channel local frustrations, the regime created space for various social elites to neutralize potential discontent. This tactic was arguably most successful with the religious leadership. Regime connections allowed Muslim shaykhs to secure election to parliament or appointment to positions of prominence within the state's religious bureaucracy. Shaykh Ahmad Badr al-Din Hassoun, for example, was elected as an independent parliamentarian in 1990, and in 2005 received Bashar al-Assad's personal approval to be elevated to the lofty position of grand mufti of the republic. Hassoun's appointment came as part of a wider relaxation of controls over what the Muslim religious establishment could say in their public statements. The regime also dramatically expanded the number of Sharia-focused high schools, opened a new Faculty of Islamic Law in Aleppo and gave mosque workers a 50 per cent salary increase. A quasi-underground women's religious network, the Qubaysiyat, popular among the respectable urban middle class, was granted permission to conduct their activities in mosques, and a representative council of (male) religious scholars was re-established in 2006, after having been disbanded forty years earlier by the more fiercely radical Ba'thists of the 1960s.[32] A radical preacher in Aleppo known as Abu al-Qa'qa was even permitted to recruit militants to join the jihad against the US occupation in Iraq, with collusion from the *mukhabarat*. This apparent leniency emboldened some of the leading religious shaykhs to express more vocally their opinions on controversial topics of the day such as mooted legal changes to improve women's rights, government broadcasting policy on religious sermons and the recurrent spectre of Iran-sponsored Shia proselytism in Syria. Some preachers even began to criticize those government ministers whom they considered overly enamoured with secularism. As if to symbolize how much the regime's attitude to religion had changed, the phrase 'God protect Syria!' found its way into the acceptable political lexicon after featuring in a speech delivered by President Assad himself. Syria's Christian denominations also benefitted from this relaxation of constraints on religious expression and felt more confident in publicly celebrating their festivals and displaying symbols of their faith than in the past.

Religious charities enjoyed the resurgence, as they also benefitted from the more general revival of associational life in the 2000s. Such initiatives offered several advantages for the regime. By collecting donations from pious Muslims, including wealthy business people, the charities tapped into capital reserves that the regime itself found difficult to mobilize and channelled that support to the poorest members of society. The largest religious charities, such as those associated with the Zayd movement in Damascus, regularly provided thousands of people with meals and clothing, paid medical bills, staged public celebrations on religious holidays, subsidized the cost of weddings, offered educational instruction and even constructed hospitals.[33] In doing so, they eased pressure on those hit hardest by the economic reforms in many of the same urban communities from which the Islamist opposition had appeared in the 1970s and early 1980s. Muslim and Christian charities were also allocated the operation of several orphanages, schools for the blind and deaf and other facilities for which the government had previously borne full responsibility. Some of these welfare arrangements bore a family resemblance to the public–private partnerships pioneered in the private sector. *Jam'iyyat al-Bustan al-Khayri* (The Garden Charitable Association), founded by the regime's favoured businessman Rami Makhlouf, signed several agreements with the Ministry of Health to take over a number of health facilities in Latakia previously operated by the government.[34]

Regime personnel did much to cultivate this revival of associational life. NGOs were encouraged to register with the Ministry for Social Affairs and Labour, which gave the authorities control and oversight of their activities. They were tolerant, however, towards several well-established, often Christian groups, which were allowed to continue their charitable work without legal incorporation.[35] Favoured organizations were allowed to purchase state-owned land for heavily discounted or nominal sums. Official visits to the various associations by government ministers were dutifully covered by state newspapers and news broadcasts, although it was always visits from Asma al-Akhras, Assad's wife, that attracted the most fanfare.

The regime's cultivation of the religious establishment, non-profit and young technocrats revealed its essentially urban orientation at this time. The increasingly dire situation in the countryside, especially in the north-east, meant the regime struggled to develop a coherent rural strategy. While it had some success deploying economic incentives to co-opt leading figures of some of the smaller tribes, especially in the area of Raqqa and rural Aleppo,[36] the sheer devastation wrought by drought and environmental mismanagement made it difficult to win over the leadership of the larger, more powerful tribes of eastern Syria. For example, in 2005, a leading shaykh of the Baggara tribe of Deir al-Zour even added his voice to the mounting opposition calls for political reform. For the eastern Arab tribes, conditions in the steppe and Jazira more closely resembled those of shattered Iraq – from which they were separated only by a porous border – than they did the more developed and more urban western Syria.

In Suweida, the leading Druze families continued to act as intermediaries for the regime and helped restore calm after violent clashes with neighbouring Bedouin tribes in 2000. The most prominent family of religious shaykhs, the Jarbou', burnished its reputation during this time. Excluded from the ranks of the regime's crony capitalists and from their speculative activities in Damascus, Aleppo and Latakia, local investment in Suweida was largely the work of Druze emigrants who had made money overseas: continuing Druze emigration to South America was so commonplace that the capital city of Jabal al-Arab was jokingly referred to as 'Venez-suweida'. Although often channelled into private industrial ventures that sustained some local employment, this injection of new money was nevertheless insufficient to spark urban development or to challenge the leading Druze families. Farmers in Suweida remained as reliant on traders in Damascus to market their produce as their grandfathers had been in the 1920s.[37] With the elite families dominating the local administration, emigration from this tight-knit community offered the only viable alternative to the status quo.

In Hassakeh governorate, the regime continued to prohibit Kurdish political parties but clandestinely permitted many of them to operate under the strict oversight of the *mukhabarat*. These disorganized, highly factionalized parties walked a careful line between colluding with the Syrian regime and maintaining public support. They displayed a rare show of unity in calming the north-east and rallying to the regime after the 2004 Kurdish uprising in Qamishli, for example, a rerun of which they had calculated would cross the red lines laid down by the regime and bring about bloody repression of a kind not seen since Hama in 1982. The ageing leadership of these small political factions consequently found themselves out of step with the younger generation, which for inspiration instead looked to the radical Kurdish movement of Turkey (the PKK) and its Syrian offshoot, the *Partîya Yekîtî ya Dêmokrat* (PYD, the Democratic Unionist Party), founded in 2003.[38] The anarcho-leftist activism of the PYD proved especially popular among Kurds north of Aleppo, in areas such as Afrin and Kobanî (Ayn al-Arab), where the tribal structure had already been eroded by decades of proletarianization. The PYD found it more challenging to penetrate Hassakeh province, where Kurdish clans and their hierarchies were more firmly entrenched.

While the regime's ability to incorporate or co-opt different sectors of Syrian society was strained by the introduction of the Social Market Economy, the deterioration of regime capabilities did not extend to its security apparatus. After the 2004 Qamishli uprising was quelled by the elite Republican Guard and Ba'thist militias, the *mukhabarat* arrested and punished 2,000 participants with the same array of torture techniques it had been using for decades in its filthy, lice-infested jails. Practices such as beating naked prisoners with cables, administering electric shocks to genitals and staging fake executions were routine components of this repertoire, the horrific features of which were by now so well rooted in the public imagination that some protestors were even said to have removed their own fingernails prior to arrest, to prevent the *mukhabarat* ripping them out in prison. Torture was also used against children. Amnesty International documented more than twenty cases of torture against children as young as twelve after the Qamishli uprising. Legal proceedings were undertaken against some of the arrested adults, who faced charges in the State Security Court that included accusations of attempting to cede Syrian territory to a foreign state, membership of organizations seeking to weaken the nation, and inciting civil war and interethnic conflict. Others languished in the prisons while awaiting a specially created military tribunal before finally being granted amnesty a year later.[39]

Mukhabarat abuse also targeted a prominent Kurdish Sufi shaykh, Muhammad Mashuk al-Khaznawi, who, on a visit to Europe, had expressed criticism of the Syrian regime and even met the head of the banned Syrian Muslim Brotherhood, which had been eradicated from the country twenty years earlier.[40] Khaznawi's previous history of cooperation with the regime did not prevent him going missing in May 2005. A month later, his corpse was found, bearing obvious signs of torture.

Such high-profile incidents revealed the tight grip that the security forces continued to hold on the north-east after the Qamishli uprising and illustrated to the local population the likely cost of further protest. Kurds were also disproportionately affected when the government issued Decree 49 of 2008, which tightened up the legal requirement for all property sales close to Syria's borders to obtain prior authorization from the relevant authorities, ostensibly for reasons of national security. The extent of Syria's border zones was liberally interpreted to encompass the whole of Hassakeh province.[41] Decree 49 inserted yet another layer of surveillance, intrusion and control into the mundane workings of ordinary life, not to mention the need for more rounds of bribes to obtain the necessary authorization from the security services, which was often denied to Kurds. Further concern was created by a second legislative decree in 2008, which gave the authorities the right to demolish illegally constructed buildings, such as those in the informal *mukhalafat* neighbourhoods of the cities that housed thousands of migrants from the north-east, including many Kurds.

In an additional burst of authoritarianism, the Ba'th Party's powerful National Security Bureau abruptly ended the entente with the religious establishment and reasserted the state's direct control over spiritual affairs. In September 2008, the regime accused a Lebanese jihadi group of planting a car bomb that claimed seventeen lives in Damascus, and used the event to justify further clampdowns on the activities and funding of private religious institutions. Several prominent religious figures were detained or arrested for corruption. In 2010, the veil was banned from Syrian universities and over a thousand veiled schoolteachers transferred out of the classroom. The authorities said the decisions were intended to ensure that education remained secular, although the moves were generally seen as an effort to curb the sway of the popular Qubaysiyat women's movement and prompted complaints from even pro-regime shaykhs.[42] It seemed that the hardline, authoritarian camp within the regime had rolled back some of the freedoms earlier granted during Bashar al-Assad's reformist push. Some members of the religious community bristled at the change in tone. The opening of a new casino near Damascus Airport in December 2010 by Khalid Hububati, a businessman well connected to the regime, was interpreted as an affront to public morals by the religious leaders, who had ensured gambling remained prohibited in Syria since they had forced Hubabati's father's operations to close down in the late 1970s. Muhammad Habash, a religious scholar and member of the People's Assembly, now announced he would use parliamentary procedure to force the casino to close again. Murmurs of discontent with the regime's clampdown on the religious sector became louder.

The secular intellectuals who had been pioneers in the quashed Damascus Spring of 2000–01 continued to advocate constitutional reform and political liberalization, although their single remaining 'civil society' forum was closed down in 2005, when one of its members read out the exiled Muslim Brotherhood's declaration that it had renounced violence and embraced democracy. After the 2005 Ba'th Regional Congress failed to open the system to new political parties, the opposition issued the Damascus Declaration for Democratic National Change, which called for an end to the *mukhbabarat* state in Syria and the instauration of civil, democratic rule. In addition to leftist and nationalist groups, the list of signatories to the Damascus Declaration included – surprisingly – the Muslim Brotherhood and the Kurdish parties, the latter in recognition of their ability to mobilize protestors, as had been demonstrated in the Qamishli uprising. This was the first occasion on which Syria's fragmented political opposition was able to agree on a common statement of their shared demands. The issues of religion versus secularism and Kurdish/Arab nationalism nevertheless remained controversial and hotly contested.

A novel twist to the story of the political opposition occurred when, in 2006, defected former Vice President Khaddam joined forces with the regime's nemesis, the Muslim Brotherhood, in a coalition called the National Salvation Front. The Front's potential capacity to appeal to both disaffected Muslims and disgruntled Ba'thists no doubt caused consternation for the regime, but it also struck a sour note for the opposition, many of whom found it distasteful – to say the least – to ally themselves with a senior regime insider who had been responsible for ending the Damascus Spring.

That year the opposition called for the normalization of relations between Syria and Lebanon, and the regime rolled out a new wave of arrests, detentions and show trials.[43] By 2008, prospects for the civil society opposition were bleak: its leaders had been neutralized, its supporters blocked and its ability to rally support from the masses pre-emptively annihilated.

The curtailed space for secular debate contrasted sharply with the regime's relative relaxation of controls on the religious sector. Even among Islamists, discussion seemed to be flourishing more freely. Some members of the secular opposition believed this difference to be deliberate on the part of the regime. 'When you repress the parties,' noted Yasin al-Hajj Salih in 2005, 'for all practical purposes you are imprisoning the people in a framework of traditional or family-centric relationships [. . .] The crushing of independent, free political life in Syria has fostered a rebirth of sectarianism and has created this crisis.'[44] In 2011, the disastrous implications of inequality, institutional atrophy and continued repression quickly became apparent.

The outbreak of the 2011 uprising

On 17 December 2010, a young Tunisian man named Muhammad Bouazizi set fire to himself in protest at the harassment and humiliation he had suffered at the hands of the state. Protests quickly spread from Bouazizi's small town to the whole of Tunisia, defying the Tunisian regime's heavy-handed response and rejecting its paltry offers of reform. After the army refused to move against the protestors, on 14 January 2011 President Ben Ali stepped down from office after over two decades in power. This historic display of popular sovereignty sent ripples across the Arab world. In neighbouring Egypt, calls for protests against the thirty-year regime of Hosni Mubarak led tens of thousands of demonstrators to occupy Cairo's central Tahrir Square on 25 January, launching an occupation that grew in strength with each passing day. Hundreds of thousands of people protested across Egypt; street fights against regime forces broke out in Cairo, Alexandria and other major urban centres. As had been the case in Tunisia, the army refused to turn its weapons against the protestors in Tahrir. By 11 February, Mubarak had also stepped down. Broadcast across the Arabic-speaking world by the Al Jazeera satellite television channel, the previously unimaginable scale of the uprisings in Tunisia and Egypt caught both ordinary people and regimes by surprise. Inspired by these events, protestors began to gather in countries as distant as Algeria and Jordan.

While following these developments closely, Damascus initially seemed to believe that Syrians would not follow suit. Unlike the old regimes in Egypt and Tunisia, after all, Assad was already spearheading reforms on behalf of the next generation. Syria's incremental yet proactive approach to reform was reaffirmed by Assad in a 31 January interview with the *Wall Street Journal*, in which he announced forthcoming plans to reorganize local government and issue new laws for civil society and political parties (the latter had been on ice since 2005).

Geopolitics too, it was thought, strengthened Syria's position. By early 2011, Syrian steadfastness seemed to have successfully weathered the US-led campaign of international isolation, which had gradually lost momentum when a new US president took office in 2009. Barack Obama's opposition to the Iraq war promised the impending withdrawal of US forces and implied a different approach to Syria. In January 2011, a US ambassador returned to Syria after a six-year hiatus. British Foreign Secretary William Hague visited Damascus and met Assad in person the same month. Syria's principled opposition to Israel and imperialism, Assad reasoned, had insulated his regime from the criticisms of collaboration that had been levelled against Mubarak and Ben Ali. 'We have more difficult circumstances than most of the Arab countries but in spite of that Syria is stable. Why?' asked Assad. 'Because you have to be very closely linked to the beliefs of the people. This is the core issue.'[45] Unlike the flailing gerontocracies in Egypt and Tunisia, Assad implied, his regime enjoyed popular legitimacy.

Advocates of the reform project at the time foresaw no adverse consequences from the economic transformation that had created such acute dislocations in Syria. 'By January 2011 I was satisfied that the macro-economic fundamentals were very very strong,' later reflected Dardari, the architect of the Social Market Economy.[46] Reformists believed that Assad's leadership put Syria in a different category from the regimes that had been overthrown in Egypt and Tunisia.

This confidence initially appeared well placed: in early February, the first online appeals for popular protests in Syria generated no measurable response. The regime even lifted its long-standing – and easily skirted – prohibition of websites such as Facebook and YouTube, although lifting this ban of course also facilitated the surveillance of potential dissenters. Then, on 19 February, a crowd of people intervened against a traffic policeman's ill treatment of a young man in the old Damascene neighbourhood of Hariqa next to the Souq al-Hamidiya. Chanting 'The Syrian people shall not be humiliated,' and 'There is no God but God,' the crowd persisted until the minister of the interior himself arrived on the scene, whereupon he was met with the regime slogan 'With blood and with soul, we sacrifice for you Bashar!' as if the crowd were invoking the name of the president himself for protection against regime forces. Three policemen were disciplined for their role in provoking the crowd, which dispersed without further incident. After consulting with its interlocutors across the country, the regime announced a limited general amnesty for prisoners accused of petty crimes, as well as the elderly, although political prisoners were pointedly excluded.[47]

A core of younger, better-organized Syrian activists undertook several peaceful actions around this time. A small protest in support of the January revolution in Egypt was followed in February by several hundred protestors gathering in front of the Libyan embassy in the upmarket Damascene neighbourhood of Abu Rummaneh, where they expressed opposition to the Gaddafi regime's violent repression of protests in Tripoli. 'He who kills his own people is a traitor,' appeared among their slogans. A small gathering in front of the Ummayyad Mosque on 15 March chanted, 'God, Syria and freedom – that's enough!' This assembly was easily dispersed by the security apparatus. The next day, relatives of political prisoners held a sit-in protest in front of the Ministry of the Interior; dozens of participants were arrested.

Despite the impetus provided by events in Tunisia, Egypt and Libya, it was local developments in the Syrian city of Der'a that prompted the spread of mass protests across the country. As many as seventy adolescent boys were initially detained by political security in Der'a, reportedly on suspicion of writing anti-regime graffiti on the walls of a school. By early March, over a dozen boys, mostly between the ages of twelve and fifteen, were still in detention. The efforts of their families and local elites to obtain their release met with scorn from regional security officials. One version of events held that Atif Najib, the heavy-handed head of political security in Der'a (and the son of Assad's maternal aunt), told local notables to forget about their missing children. If they could not, Najib was rumoured to have said, his men could give their wives some new ones. In response, the notables called for a day of community solidarity to be held on Friday 18 March. Residents marched to the centre of Der'a calling for the return of the children and the resignation of both Najib and the provincial governor. Regime forces shot into the crowd, killing two; their funerals the following day turned into full-scale protests attracting thousands of people, who were dispersed by tear gas and helicopter units. Renewed protests on 20 March burned down buildings belonging to the government and Syriatel, the mobile phone provider owned by Rami Makhlouf.

At first, the regime turned to its tried-and-tested tactics of using local elites to control the streets. A series of high-ranking officials were dispatched from Damascus (including Foreign Minister Faysal Miqdad, who was originally from the Hawran region) to discuss concessions in exchange for the return of calm. Besides the removal of Najib, the release of the children, an official apology and a visit with President Bashar, the dignitaries asked for several wider social, economic and political measures, including the abrogation of the country's emergency laws, cheaper fuel prices, the return to the classroom of female teachers who wore the headscarf and the cancellation of Decree 49, which had subjected property sales in border areas to approval by the security apparatus.[48] The regime's early attempts at negotiation in Der'a alongside a controlled show of force was not surprising, given that the agricultural Hawran region had historically been a reliable source of support for the Ba'th Party. The large, clan-like families that made up the social fabric of Der'a also seemed to offer an efficient mechanism for restoring calm, if leading voices in the clans could be successfully mollified with relatively low-cost concessions.

In the event, when news of Najib's impending removal failed to disperse the protestors with sufficient speed, security forces again shot into the crowds, who re-formed to stage a sit-in at the al-Umari Mosque, which they turned into a makeshift hospital. The protestors then created organizing committees to manage the occupation, inspired more by the direct action of activists at Cairo's Tahrir Square than the traditional tactics of mediation preferred by Der'a's community elders. This younger generation of protestors quickly became brazen in its refusal to submit. Sporadic violence, such as the sniper fire that killed eighteen people on 8 April, only emboldened the protestors to stage more demonstrations, festoon public space with images of the fallen martyrs and even to return fire at the security forces, which largely kept their distance as if uncertain how to respond to such a volatile situation in what should have been a regime stronghold. The stand-off ended in late April, when security forces and the Syrian armed forces encircled and severed contact between Der'a and the outside world – no electricity, no internet, no phone lines, no food. For three long weeks, there was ominous silence from the city. The policy of starvation and shooting residents who left their homes allowed the government to declare order restored by mid-May. By this point, though, protests had begun to spread uncontrollably to smaller towns across the south-west.

Similar patterns of political opposition and local grievance, targeted violence and aggrieved protest began to develop elsewhere in Syria as March and April progressed. Regime snipers dispersing a small political demonstration in Homs killed a sixteen-year-old girl, prompting thousands to descend on the city's Clock Square on Friday 25 March. More protests gave rise to more deaths, more funeral processions to more protests, culminating in tens of thousands of people occupying the central plaza of Homs on 18 April. For several hours, crowds called for the removal of the governor of Homs, considered the architect of the Homs Dream urban development project, as well as the fall of the regime, until the security forces dispersed them with heavy gunfire, killing dozens. Once again, the regime attempted to mobilize local notables to calm the situation, but the mounting number of deaths soon left dignitaries powerless to quell the discontent. Comparable dynamics unfolded in the coastal towns of Latakia, Baniyas and Jableh, as well as the smaller towns around Damascus.[49]

The regime's determination to prevent a Tahrir-style occupation in Damascus and Aleppo translated into relatively less brutal tactics against the small-scale, often ephemeral organized protests there. Damascus did see grassroots protests after Friday prayers, notably centred on the Rifa'i Mosque in Kfar Sousseh and the Hasan Mosque in Midan, where the sway of the religious establishment was at least sufficient to persuade the security apparatus to resort to beatings and detentions rather than gunfire to disperse the crowds. On Good Friday 2011, protestors from the suburbs of Damascus attempted to march on Abbasiyin Square. The sheer number of those streaming into the city prompted the security forces to open fire, thereby giving rise to a new burst of protests the following Friday – and the one after that, and the one after that. Demonstrations rippled across the poorer outskirts of the capital. Other cities and towns soon followed suit. Time and time again, initially small-scale protests were galvanized by killings at the hands of the security forces; by June, surges of tens of thousands of demonstrators were effectively seizing control in towns such as Hama, Rastan, Deir al-Zour, Ma'arrat al-Numan, Saraqib and Jisr al-Shughur.[50] Activists seeking to mobilize mass protests in central Damascus and Aleppo looked on with amazement as cities they had previously regarded as backwaters – and even some towns the names of which they had never heard before – boldly came out in open opposition to the regime. As one urban activist admitted, 'The revolution has taught us the map of Syria.'[51]

After the first few weeks of demonstrations, the announcement of an important speech by Bashar al-Assad raised hopes that the president would launch a comprehensive package of political, economic and legal reforms in response to popular demand. In his address to the nation on 30 March, Assad dismissed the protests as a conspiracy instigated from the outside, invoking the word 'sedition' (*fitna*) no fewer than seventeen times and dismissing the sacrifice of those who had been killed by describing them as 'victims' rather than 'martyrs'. Assad promised a continuation – in due course – of the same political reforms that the regime had kept stalling since he had come to power over a decade earlier.[52] The presidential address was disappointing. 'As Assad was delivering his speech, the only thing you could hear in Damascus was the cooing of doves as they flew from one balcony to the next in the Old City [. . .],' wrote a commentator for the Lebanese *al-Akhbar* newspaper. 'And after his speech, Damascus seemed as noisy, and as lonely, as ever. Many did not understand, and many understood but wished they had not.'[53]

Two weeks later, in an address to his newly reshuffled government, Assad sounded more conciliatory. He acknowledged a gap had opened between the state and its citizens, referred to all those who had died as 'martyrs' and expressed his intent to support the public sector, small and medium-sized businesses and rural Syria. As well as his ongoing commitment to the familiar list of stalled political reforms (including liberalizing the creation of new political parties and reorganizing local government), Assad voiced frustration with the bureaucratic inertia that impeded presidential decrees from being implemented on the ground.[54] His proposed solutions – computerization and devolved administrative responsibility – seemed out of step with the pace of events around the country.

The regime did, it is true, make several concessions. After a round of consultations with notables, public-sector workers received a pay increase, citizenship rights were granted to tens of thousands of Syrian-born Kurds previously registered as foreigners, resignations were accepted from several regime officials in the provinces and official investigations were launched into what had gone wrong on the ground. In June and July 2011, the regime even allowed some of its old political opponents from the Damascus Spring to organize a small forum in the capital and participate in a regime-sponsored National Dialogue conference led by Vice President Farouq al-Shara', which publicly recommended that excesses by the security forces be curtailed.

To many, such concessions indicated a certain schizophrenia, especially given that regime snipers and security forces were killing and maiming hundreds of participants in largely peaceful protests at this time. Assad himself bounced backwards and forwards between hardline and more conciliatory responses, issuing orders not to open fire on the demonstrations while also empowering the *mukhabarat* chiefs to establish a Central Crisis Management Cell (CCMC) tasked with monitoring and reacting to the uprisings. Assad had nothing that resembled his father's ruthless, single-handed control of the Syrian security apparatus. His regime had effectively devolved into a network of quasi-autonomous fiefdoms dominated by powerful figures who had little patience for the niceties of the president's vision of reform. Prominent among them were Bashar's hot-tempered younger brother Maher and Deputy Defence Minister Assef Shawkat, who was married to Bashar's older sister. Whether Assad's hesitation to adopt a 'security solution' to the crisis was genuine or feigned, the heads of the security forces felt unconstrained in adopting increasingly brutal tactics, especially towards those protestors taken into custody by the *mukhabarat*. 'The time of tolerance and meeting demands is over,' stated minutes from a CCMC meeting on 18 April later smuggled out of Syria by defectors. Two days later, the CCMC removed the remaining constraints and authorized the full use of force against protestors to 'demonstrate the power and capacity of the State'.[55]

The CCMC initially ordered local security branches to 'do what was necessary' with detainees. When that leeway did not prove effective at quelling the protests, a stricter policy was enacted.

In August 2011, the CCMC launched a coordinated nationwide campaign of arrests that targeted lists of tens of thousands of individuals, including women, children and the elderly, who were suspected of taking part in protests, criticizing the regime or even simply circulating video clips or news stories said to be injurious to national unity. Those arrested were interrogated by the security services so they would reveal more names to add to the list. Prisoners were even passed backwards and forwards between different agencies, although this policy could be counterproductive. One agency reporting to the CCMC apologetically noted that they had been unable to 'thoroughly interrogate some of the detainees due to their poor medical condition caused by severe beating which, in some cases, has led to permanent disability while being prolongedly detained at some security agencies before they were handed over to us.'[56]

The sheer scale of the industrial torture practised by the Assad regime was exposed to the outside world in August 2013, when a military photographer, code-named 'Caesar', fled the country with more than 53,000 photographs of nearly 7,000 dead bodies that he had been tasked with documenting while working at two military hospitals in Syria since May 2011. The images showed horrific signs of torture from beating, whipping, strangulation, starvation and mutilation.[57] The extent of regime repression meant that the existing infrastructure of incarceration was insufficient to accommodate the vast numbers of detainees arrested after the uprising broke out. Schools, government buildings, youth camps and even mosques were commandeered as short-term detention facilities. As the regime response to protestors became more militarized, both elite units and loyalist paramilitaries set up their own secret prisons in parallel with those of the *mukhabarat*.[58] Yet despite the expanded use of torture since the uprising began, it would be a mistake to think of 2011 as a radical departure. In the recesses of the Syrian system, killing had long been a routine mechanism of regime maintenance.

Civil opposition, sectarianism, militarization

Over the first few weeks of the unrest, protests rooted in highly localized grievances adopted the characteristics of a nationwide uprising. Three initiatives to coordinate the originally disconnected elements of the uprising quickly appeared. The first was that of grassroots activists on the ground, who formed loose-knit networks often referred to as Local Coordination Committees (*Tansiqiyat*), although in truth this was the name of just one of several umbrella groups intended to provide national-level organization.[59] The *Tansiqiyat* worked to spread the word about protests, developed strategies to escape arrest, oversaw online communications and provided support to individuals and communities facing repression by the regime. *Tansiqiyat* activists were generally younger educated professionals or students; they were often based in urban areas and oriented towards secular politics, whether liberal or progressive. A significant proportion, moreover, were women. Although targeted and hunted down by the regime, the non-hierarchical, amorphous organization of the *Tansiqiyat* meant their activities could survive the arrest of individual members. Since arrested *Tansiqiyat* activists typically knew little about their peers other than their shared commitment to the revolution, regime torture was less successful at eliciting the names of their fellows in the network.

While the *Tansiqiyat* developed organically from within the Syrian uprising itself, the second initiative claimed to speak for the revolt from outside the country. In October 2011, several political currents met in Istanbul to establish the Syrian National

Council (SNC), which brought together secular intellectuals from the Damascus Spring (including sociologist Burhan Ghalyoun, who became its first president) with the exiled Syrian Muslim Brotherhood, Syrian Kurdish parties and even somewhat sceptical representatives of the *Tansiqiyat*. The SNC benefitted from considerable international support, especially from Turkey and Qatar; it rapidly became the main interlocutor for Western countries who hoped to cultivate an alternative government in the event that the Assad regime did not survive the upheavals. Although intended to be politically inclusive, the SNC was increasingly dominated by the Muslim Brotherhood; by November 2012, the *Tansiqiyat* had disaffiliated from it. A replacement body, the National Coalition, similarly floundered over internal divisions and its inability to create meaningful connections with Syrians inside the country.

The third coordinating element, the Free Syrian Army (FSA), focused on conscripts and officers who decided to defect from the Syrian army rather than obey orders to shoot at civilian protestors. Much like its civilian counterpart the *Tansiqiyat*, the FSA was intended as an umbrella to coordinate the activities of the relatively autonomous armed groups of defected soldiers and neighbourhood rebels that had sprung up across the country. Its origins can be traced to June 2011, when regime forces fired on a demonstration in the town of Jisr al-Shughur in Idlib governorate. This time, the protestors fought back, likely aided by soldiers who refused to follow orders. The rebels killed as many as 120 regime loyalists and seized control of the town. When the Syrian army was sent to regain control, Lieutenant Colonel Hussein Harmoush recorded a YouTube video announcing that he and his men had defected from the regime on the grounds that the army was supposed to protect civilians, not target them. While the regime soon regained control of Jisr al-Shughur, albeit by forcing the rebels and local civilians alike to flee into neighbouring Turkey, Harmoush's defection provided a model followed by numerous dissenting officers over the coming months. At the end of July, another defected officer, Colonel Riyad al-As'ad, announced the creation of the Free Syrian Army (FSA) from a refugee camp in Turkey. The relocation of the FSA leadership outside the country limited the extent of its control and made it vulnerable to criticism from rebels still fighting on the frontline.

The focus of the armed conflict shifted several times after Jisr al-Shughur. The FSA's Khalid ibn Walid Brigade seized the central town of Rastan in September 2011 before withdrawing under intense pressure from the Syrian army. The Farouq Battalion, commanded by Abd al-Razzaq Tlass – a relative of old guard defence minister and Rastan native Mustafa Tlass – proved more resilient in defending the Homs neighbourhood of Baba Amr until February 2012, when the regime began to use indiscriminate artillery fire against the besieged, starving city before ground troops went in to remove the rebels. American journalist Marie Colvin was killed in the bombardment, along with Commander Tlass and hundreds of FSA fighters and civilians. Baba Amr was reduced to a ghost town. In consequence, numerous European and Gulf states withdrew their ambassadors from Damascus in protest at the disregard for civilian life. From the regime's perspective, this cost was irrelevant. Homs was successfully cleared of insurgents, albeit that most of the civilian population had fled the city in the process.

In the southern Hawran, the FSA Omari Battalion used guerrilla tactics against regime forces stationed throughout the outlying villages around Der'a. FSA-affiliated units also attacked regime positions in the eastern Damascene suburbs of the Ghouta, the mountain town of Zabadani and the Jabal al-Zawiya region of Idlib, centring on Ma'arrat al-Nu'man. These military activities relied on not only weapons that had been taken by defecting soldiers – of whom there were an estimated 60,000 by early 2012 – but also those that had been smuggled into the country from Iraq and northern Lebanon.

The regime's militarized response was rooted in its conceptualization of the revolt as the product of vast international conspiracies, which were multiplying 'like germs' in Syria, as Assad said in his third speech delivered after the outbreak of the uprising. He went on to blame the violence on criminals, outlaws and Islamic extremists whose ideology 'kills in the name of religion, destroys in the name of reform, and spreads chaos in the name of freedom'. Assad accused foreign interests of fomenting unrest and provoking sectarian enmity. 'All this,' he added, 'under the heavy shadow of a media campaign launched through satellite TV stations and in cyberspace that has made it difficult to distinguish what is real from what is illusory and what is genuine from what is fake.'[60]

The Syrian media certainly did their best to amplify the uncertainty and confusion that surrounded unfolding events. Government newspapers and television channels quickly picked up the narratives of Islamic extremism, sectarianism and foreign sabotage. Civilian deaths were blamed on armed rebels, confessions of conspiratorial involvement broadcast to the nation and implausible counter-narratives circulated to defend and legitimize the regime response. Recurrent fears of foreign 'infiltrators' lurking inside the frontlines were useful in enabling the regime to empower loyalist thugs to police their own local communities on its behalf.

These thugs were generically known as *shabbiha*, a term first used on the Syrian coast in the 1980s and 1990s to refer to elements of the Alawi underworld that engaged in smuggling, extortion and other criminal activities. Folk etymologies variously trace the origins of the word *shabbiha* to the word for 'ghost' (an allusion to the way the thugs were said to disappear in the night); or the once preferred mode of transport of high-ranking officers, the Mercedes with tinted windows, nicknamed 'the ghost' (a reference to the invisibility of those within); or a slang term meaning 'quick' or 'daring' in the vernacular of the coast; or a phrase used by torturers in Syrian jails meaning 'string him up by his hands'; or the notion of 'stretching' of authority to the point of abuse and bullying.[61] *Shabbiha* would use respectful terms such as 'teacher' and 'uncle' to refer to their bosses, who were often connected to local regime personnel by ties of family or friendship.

In the region of Latakia, these bosses included established minor mafiosi members of the extended Assad family. In other areas, new groups of *shabbiha* vigilantes sprang up autonomously: in Homs, for example, they adopted the name of Popular Committees. Elsewhere, *shabbiha* could be drawn from groups based on pre-existing tribal solidarity (such as that of the Birri clan of Aleppo), or created from the top down by intelligence officials or regime financiers such as the president's cousin Rami Makhlouf.[62] Over time, these groups became the backbone of a variety of locally organized, pro-government militias; their rank-and-file members typically reflected the social composition of their towns and villages of origin, whether Alawi, Shia, Christian, Druze or Sunni.

Although *shabbiha* were paid for turning out to repress the regular Friday protests, they also looted opposition neighbourhoods so heavily that they set up special markets to sell their haul. Despite these material benefits, their relationship to the regime was not purely transactional. Deployed as the muscle to assault protestors, *shabbiha* came to bond ever more tightly with their 'brothers': such familial loyalty was soon transposed to the figure of Bashar al-Assad, to whom they declared their fervent loyalty. This cultish devotion fuelled animosities between different sectarian communities. When protests took place in mixed areas, *shabbiha* violence disproportionately targeted Sunni districts, which they associated with the demonstrators. *Shabbiha* elements would accompany the regular armed forces to reassert control over fractious neighbourhoods, giving them ample opportunity to take matters in their own hands with tactics that included rapes, kidnappings and summary executions.[63]

In one extreme incident that took place in al-Hula, on the eastern edge of the coastal mountains, in May 2012, *shabbiha* were accused of slitting the throats of 108 residents, among them nearly fifty children. The targeted killings of entire families and the decimation of entire neighbourhoods led the opposition to accuse the regime of ethnic cleansing. The Syrian government did not deny events, but time and time again blamed the deaths on armed jihadists and terrorists. Despite the best efforts of the *Tansiqiyat*, the Syrian National Council and many protestors to stage a civic uprising against the regime that appealed to Syrians of all sects and ethnicities, such acts of orchestrated brutality fuelled a similarly violent trend of sectarian retaliation among opposition militants.

Ripples of insecurity swept regime-held territories even away from the frontline of violence. In December 2011, two car bombs struck Syrian military intelligence buildings in Damascus, in an explosion that killed forty-four people and was heard throughout the city. This attack launched a year-long series of bombings in the major cities. In July 2012, one such bombing took place inside a *mukhabarat* headquarters in Damascus, killing senior members of the regime's Central Crisis Management Cell (including the defence minister, the vice president and Assad's brother-in-law Deputy Defence Minister Assef Shawkat). Swirling tales of jihadi militants, foreign conspiracies, *shabbiha* brutalities and detained civilians made it difficult for many Syrians to discern the border between truth and propaganda, fear and distrust.[64] Reams of gruesome images and video footage were circulated in private and in public, by virtue of coverage from Arabic satellite television channels such as Al Jazeera, which sometimes failed to check the veracity of claims it broadcast. The regime could consequently counterclaim that the world was lying about what was happening in the country: it alleged that fake footage was being recorded in vast film sets built in the Gulf states to mimic the architecture of Syrian towns and villages. Syria's domestic news channels staged their own scenes of rebel attacks and tried to pass them off as documentary footage, albeit with only varying degrees of success.

Thousands of government officials and public sector workers were regularly instructed to take to the streets in 'spontaneous' demonstrations to profess support and even love for the Assad regime. 'We love you!' (*Mnhibbak!*) had been popularized as a political slogan in a song that Rami Makhlouf's mobile telephone network SyriaTel had sponsored for Assad's presidential campaign in 2007, and the overstated emotions in which regime supporters expressed their loyalty since the uprising soon earned them the sarcastic sobriquet of *mnhibbakji*s ('the "we love you" crew') from the opposition. Meanwhile, the opposition also began to refer to the regime in general as *shabbiha*, language which regime supporters proudly reclaimed for their own ends. The president's appearance at one official rally in January 2012 was greeted with chants of '*Shabbiha* forever for your sake [*min ajl uyunak*], O Assad!!'[65]

In June 2012, Assad admitted that Syria faced a state of internal war.[66] To ensure its survival, his regime would prove itself prepared to reduce the Syrian nation to ashes. By that summer, it had adopted a scorched-earth strategy: artillery and, increasingly, aerial bombardment of rebel-held towns to displace the population was followed by the demolition of their homes to prevent the possibility of return. Barrel bombs filled with nails, screws and shrapnel were first dropped during this time in Aleppo. The practice soon spread to other cities. In early 2013, dwindling airpower resources were replenished with ballistic missiles that had originally been acquired to use in any possible future conflict with Israel. Now the regime used them against its own people. Collectively, these tactics were intended to convey to Syrian civilians the dangers of siding with the opposition and to dissuade rebels from entering new territories lest they provoke terrible retribution. Another slogan of the time, 'Assad or we burn the country,' had at first seemed to convey a stylistically exaggerated degree of blind allegiance to the regime, but soon, it became clear, was intended as a cold-blooded promise.

Managing the chaos: new political projects

Wars between sovereign states tend to encourage the strengthening of existing institutions, the better to channel a nation's resources into the war effort. Wars *within* sovereign states, in contrast, often have the opposite effect, as the power, reach and capability of the central state are whittled away by armed insurgency, lawlessness and unpredictability. In Syria, the retreat of the central state from towns and regions in which it could no longer maintain control did not inevitably give rise to anarchy. Instead, civilians, armed factions, regime militias and opportunistic combatants from outside Syria began to experiment with new forms of governance, even as destruction raged all around.

Since the regime was unable to respond to all FSA advances simultaneously, from 2012 onwards, many towns found themselves effectively autonomous, as the regime concentrated resources on securing its core territories, notably the western cities and the coast. By 2013, the more autonomous 'liberated' zones had grown to encompass large swathes of rural Deir al-Zour, Raqqa, Hassaka, Idlib and Aleppo, as well as urban neighbourhoods on the outskirts of Damascus. The sudden severance from central government obliged residents to develop their own institutions to deal with such everyday concerns as collecting rubbish, running schools, supplying bread, repairing power lines, tracking property transactions and recording deaths, marriages and births in the civil register. Around the country, ad hoc Local Administrative Councils were therefore created to oversee civilian affairs.

Initially, former activists from the *Tansiqiyat* were instrumental in launching these experiments in self-government, although membership of the Local Administrative Councils varied: some were democratically elected, others were co-opted from important local families or tribes and yet others emerged following agreements between community leaders and commanders of nearby armed groups. The rural, conservative milieu of the liberated towns meant that virtually no women participated in council decision-making. Many of the councils supported the Syrian National Coalition, the official voice of opposition outside the country, which, from late 2012, began to redistribute funding from foreign supporters, including Qatar, France, Germany, Britain and the United States.[67] Not all these hundreds of initiatives were successful. Some councils floundered because of infighting, insufficient finances or a low level of technical ability; others were formed in the hope of attracting external funding and dissolved when that promise was unmet. Yet especially in northern provinces such as Idlib and Aleppo, Local Administrative Councils provided a relatively effective and capable mechanism of governance amid the ongoing violence.[68]

Despite the fact that these local councils were outside the control of the Assad regime – and were even affiliated to the incipient administrative structures of the new 'Syrian Interim Government' tentatively established by the external opposition in 2013 – in many cases they did not break completely from the government in Damascus. The central state continued to pay for teachers' salaries and rubbish collection, or provided support for bakeries in some towns, even as its troops targeted civilians waiting in line for bread elsewhere. From the regime's perspective, these services threw a lifeline to potential sympathizers, who would be needed once Damascus had reasserted its authority; they also potentially offered a basis to negotiate future truces with or surrenders of the 'liberated' zones.[69] Even in opposition-held towns subjected to intense military assaults and brutal sieges that forced residents to flee or face starvation, the regime still permitted local intermediaries to smuggle some essential supplies over the frontline (albeit on a hefty commission).[70] The line dividing government- and rebel-controlled territories was more often blurred than tightly sealed.

As the conflict continued, armed opposition to the Assad regime increasingly assumed an Islamist tone. There were several reasons for this shift. First, the competition for funding and supplies from wealthy backers and private supporters in the Gulf (especially Kuwait, Qatar and Saudi Arabia) meant that even secular and nationalist battalions of the Free Syrian Army began to grow beards and adopt the outward trappings of religion, to match the expectations of donors. 'Every time you try to raise money, the first question you're asked is, "Where do you situate itself within Islam?" or "Will you give your brigade an Islamic name?"' complained one FSA fighter from the Ghouta. 'That's why, in the videos made by our brigade, we like to recite verses from the [Qur'an] and to include Islamic symbols in the background. We are all salesmen, in a way: we must bend in any direction to fit our potential donors, whatever our actual beliefs, and the donor is always right.' As another FSA fighter commented acerbically, 'If our donors want us to rename our brigade to the "Syrian soldiers for Madonna, we'd do it!"'[71]

Second, the Assad regime decided to release hundreds of jihadis from its prisons in 2011. This move reinvigorated Syria's radical Islamist current with a new flux of experienced – not to mention brutalized – militants. Several of these amnestied prisoners went on to assume senior leadership roles among the Islamist militias that rapidly proliferated during the early years of the uprising, among them such groups as Ahrar al-Sham and Suqur al-Sham in Idlib and Liwa al-Islam in Douma.[72] By late 2012, these groups had coalesced into two loose-knit coalitions. The first was the Syrian Islamic Liberation Front, a primarily military organization which maintained ties with the FSA and the secular leadership outside the country. The second was the more radical Syrian Islamic Front, which, in addition to overthrowing the Assad regime, aspired to purify the mores of Syrian society.

The third factor contributing to the Islamization of the uprising was the export into Syria of a peculiar Iraqi vector of instability. In the anarchy that followed the 2003 invasion, in Iraq the brand of al-Qaeda had been creatively reinvented to justify outright savagery against other Muslims. Whereas Osama bin Laden and the previous generation of al-Qaeda's international leadership had prioritized attacks against the United States (which they referred to as the 'far enemy'), the leader of al-Qaeda's Iraq chapter, Abu Musab al-Zarqawi, directed his anger against 'near' enemies: both Shia Muslims, whom he accused of heresy, and Sunni Muslims who cooperated with the occupation or simply opposed al-Qaeda's sheer brutality. On Zarqawi's orders, by 2005–06, al-Qaeda had targeted mosques with suicide bombers, broadcast beheadings online and burned prisoners alive to stoke conflict and push Iraq into civil war.

Al-Qaeda's new, second-generation strategy found its intellectual justification in ostensibly theological tracts circulating online such as *Idarat al-Tawahhush* ('The Management of Savagery'), which argued that acts of extreme brutality that ripped apart a terrified society could catalyse the construction of a 'pure' Islamic project amid the chaos. Although Zarqawi was killed by the Americans in 2006, and al-Qaeda in Iraq had alienated even its erstwhile supporters by such bloodthirsty extremism, its embattled successor leadership thought that Syria's unravelling presented an ideal opportunity to continue its mission.

Now operating under the name of Islamic State of Iraq (ISI), in 2011, the organization dispatched to Syria an operative known as Abu Muhammad al-Jolani, who quietly oversaw an escalating campaign of bombs against the regime and ingratiated himself with the Syrian opposition.[73] Jolani's newly formed group, *Jabhat al-Nusra* (the Victory Front), declared its existence in January 2012. At first hiding its affiliation to the Islamic State of Iraq, Nusra presented itself as a Syria-focused militant group. Benefitting from the training of its cadres in Iraq, by 2013, it had emerged as a highly militarily effective, well-funded and powerful element in the Islamist opposition. It attracted recruits trying to escape the crushing poverty of Syria's conflict-ridden periphery, especially in the rural northern and eastern provinces of Deir al-Zour, Raqqa, Idlib and Aleppo. Rather than simply executing military operations, Nusra also provided public services and set up religious courts, often in collaboration with other Islamist militias, which helped identify the group to Syrians as a supporter of law and order.

Although Nusra continued to deny its connection to Islamic State in Iraq, in April 2013, the ISI leader publicly announced that Jolani's organization was a subordinate affiliate that would henceforth be dissolved and merged with his organization into a new body, the Islamic State of Iraq and Syria (ISIS: *al-Dawla al-Islamiya fi al-'Iraq wa'l-Sham*). Jolani rejected this unilateral declaration as a hostile acquisition, putting Nusra on a collision course with ISIS. Under the command of an Iraqi, Abu Bakr al-Baghdadi, who had been radicalized in US detention camps after the 2003 invasion, ISIS refused the type of compromise that had made Nusra so effective in Syria. ISIS strategy maximized brutality, alienated entire communities and aimed to eliminate all competitors, whether spiritual or worldly. Baghdadi therefore determined his first target in Syria to be Jabhat al-Nusra itself.

In May 2013, ISIS forces wrested control of the city of Raqqa from Nusra and Ahrar al-Sham, which had collectively seized control there earlier in the year. Nusra subsequently redoubled its efforts further west. By summer 2014, ISIS also controlled Deir al-Zour and many of its nearby oilfields, allowing its leadership to finance a massive burst of recruitment. The success of ISIS in Syria provided a springboard for its subsequent expansion back in Iraq: in June 2014, it took control of the Iraqi city of Mosul and large tracts of the provinces of Anbar and Nineveh. That summer, ISIS theatrically bulldozed what it declared to be the 'Sykes–Picot' border between Syria and Iraq, broadcasting its efforts for the world to see, and declared the establishment of an Islamic caliphate.[74] Henceforth, it announced, ISIS would simply be known as Islamic State' in allusion to its rejection of existing national state borders and its universal aspirations.

The demands of governing a body of population that stretched from Raqqa in the west to Mosul in the east obliged Islamic State to curb its maximalist approach to violence. Instead, it began to adopt a more managerial attitude towards the instigation of savagery. It developed a series of offices and institutions to provide residents with bread, water, electricity and other basic services – which, despite its vocal renunciation of the Western-imposed state system, for all intents and purposes resembled the bureaucracy of any other modern state. Perhaps learning from its mistakes – or from the successes of Nusra – Islamic State also adopted a more nuanced policy towards Syria's powerful tribes, whose cooperation it initially sought to entice rather than coerce.[75] At the same time, it established a strict system of behavioural control monitored by a religious police force called the Hisbah. Children were indoctrinated into its crude, radical theological world view and trained to fight; gender segregation and enforced marriage were imposed; and infractions of various laws could be punished with beatings, prison, torture or public execution.[76] On its territorial periphery, Islamic State engaged in unrestrained brutality against Yezidi inhabitants of Sinjar, Iraq, whom it deemed to be infidels. Thousands of Yezidis were killed, and over 10,000 Yezidi women and young girls captured, trafficked and forced into servitude and marriage with ISIS fighters, in which they were physically, mentally and sexually abused. Islamic State's genocide against the Yezidis was met by the first US and British airstrikes in August 2014. In Syria, the several thousand ideologically committed foreign fighters among its cadres, not to mention its ambivalence towards the cause of the fight against Assad, distinguished Islamic State from other Salafi (puritanical) opposition elements in Syria, with which it continued to clash.

Alongside local councils, Salafi Sharia courts and the reborn caliphate, one further novel political project was launched. Although Syria's famously fragmented Kurdish political parties had managed to set aside their differences and for the first time form an umbrella organization, the Kurdish National Congress (KNC), in October 2011, it was the more radical *Partiya Yekîtiya Demokrat* (PYD) that quickly became the dominant force in the far north-east as well as the Kurdish areas north of Aleppo. PYD militants took control of Kurdish towns as regime forces withdrew from the north-east in summer 2012, to defend against rebel incursions in Damascus and Aleppo. The PYD maintained a policy of studied neutrality towards, if not de facto collusion with, the Assad regime. It also sought to marginalize potential competitors such as local *Tansiqiyat* chapters and its rivals in the KNC, despite occasional movements towards reconciliation. In November 2013, the PYD felt sufficiently in control to declare the establishment of a new transitional administration in what it called Rojava (literally the West' in reference to the compass of an imagined homeland of Kurdistan), divided into the three cantons of Afrin (north-west of Aleppo), Kobanî (after the town also known as Ayn al-Arab, north-east of Aleppo) and Cezire (north of Hassakeh).

Based on a quasi-anarchist notion of democratic autonomy, the Rojava project eschewed centralized political authority and established loose-knit structures for political representation. In practice, though, decision-making was dominated by the PYD.[77] Its militia, the People's Protection Units (YPG: *Yekîneyên Parastina Gel*), was responsible for external security; internal stability was assured by the Asayish security agency, while a system of so-called people's courts was set up to dispense justice, often to the detriment of those who were less than enthusiastic about a PYD political monopoly.

While the YPG militia had initially clashed with units of the Free Syrian Army and Jabhat al-Nusra as it consolidated control, the emergence of Islamic State saw increased coordination to fight this common enemy. In autumn 2014, the YPG, FSA and the Islamist militia Liwa al-Tahwid began to defend the besieged town of Kobanî against Islamic State. Alongside the YPG's support in rescuing Iraq's Yezidi community from Islamic State brutality earlier that year, external backers – notably the United States – began to recognize the strategic utility of Rojava's armed forces in what had become a broader international coalition against Baghdadi's horrific extremism. US airstrikes in support of YPG advances were instrumental in turning the tide of the battle and liberating Kobanî from Islamic State.

This remarkable achievement produced a ripple of enthusiasm for the YPG. The United States underwrote the creation of the Syrian Democratic Forces (SDF) as an umbrella under which to include both YPG fighters and new recruits from the Arab tribes of the north-east.[78] Although opposed to Islamic State, these tribal volunteers found the political ideology of the PYD to be rather less motivational than the prospect of a regular salary. By the end of 2015, the SDF had become the primary recipient of US military aid in Syria.

For its part, the Assad regime did not embark upon substantive reform or a new political project during the war, but its survival was contingent on a major reconfiguration. By mid-2012, the black-or-white absolutism of 'Assad or we burn the country' had driven away its reformist wing, as evidenced by a string of high-level defections, including a prime minister. While the regime weathered these civilian losses with relative equanimity, the declining number of officers and soldiers in the Syrian Arab Army risked undermining its survival. Casualties and political attrition meant that the size of the Syrian armed forces shrank from 325,000 to an estimated 178,000 within the first two years of the uprising. Faced with increasingly serious challenges to its control, the regime now took decisive action. In late 2012, the first reports emerged of the use of chemical weapons in Syria, in what seemed to be an initially tentative challenge to President Obama's warning about the red lines for US military intervention. The regime tested these lines more assertively in August 2013, when it killed nearly 1,500 people in a chemical attack in the rebel-held

Ghouta towns of Zamalka, Ain Tirma and Mu'adamiya, just days after the arrival of a UN investigations team.

Obama did not follow through on his warning about disregard for standards censuring the use of chemical weapons. Faced with ongoing opposition from Russia, wavering support from allies such as Britain and an acute awareness of lessons on the limitations of military intervention learned from Iraq in 2003 and Libya in 2011, the White House let Assad's tactics pass without a military response. Russia took advantage of US hesitancy to broker its own deal with the regime, which supposedly culminated in the destruction of Syria's chemical weapons stockpile. Damascus obfuscated the extent of its programmes, failed to comply in full and continued to use some chemical weapons – notably chlorine gas and sarin – against rebel-held areas.[79]

As the war progressed, the regime revealed itself to be simultaneously dismissive of international opinion, barbarous in its scorched-earth strategy against its own population and desperate to survive the onslaught of multiple local insurgencies. Nevertheless, by 2015, the ongoing attrition of its increasingly brittle armed forces meant that its continued existence looked seriously threatened. The Assad regime found itself forced to look to allies outside the country to secure its survival.

12

New Divisions, New Beginnings: An Overview, 2015–2025

The territorial divisions of Syria in 2015 bore little resemblance to the stress lines that had shaped the country in previous generations. In the nineteenth century, local elites had tussled over the merits of integration or autonomy within aspirational political projects launched from Cairo and Istanbul. Categories of identity such as Syrian and Arab acquired manifestly new meanings at this time. The unravelling of imperial Ottoman order during the First World War was later the catalyst for further redefinitions of political community and regional order. From the 1920s to the 1960s, there was more jostling over questions of integration and autonomy. Centralizing state builders clashed with provincial autonomists seeking to maintain their distance from Damascus, as well as with political challengers whose ideological commitments led them to look beyond the borders of the republic for leverage. In the 1970s, these transnational ties were severed by the pragmatism of Hafiz al-Assad, who prioritized the interests of the Syrian state at the expense of both Arab nationalism and liberal pluralism. The first phase of the civil war in the early 2010s brought about a decisive rupture with these historical dynamics. The territorial integrity of the Syrian state had been shattered by rebel incursions, its urban fabric torn apart by regime bombardments.

By 2015, the country's fragmentation was so great that the continued existence of the Assad regime – if not the Syrian state itself – now appeared questionable. Appealing to foreign powers for help was the regime's last, best hope for survival.

Prior to the Russian intervention in 2015, Syria had become divided into five zones of control. The regime held what journalists would sometimes refer to as 'rump' or 'useful' Syria (in continuation of the colonial notion of *la Syrie utile* that had originated with the French): the strip from Damascus to western Aleppo, including the cities of Homs and Hama, along with the cities of the coast. Several pockets in the north-east were still also controlled by the regime. A large part of Syria's north was held by the brutal jihadis of Islamic State, including its so-called capital at Raqqa, and extending to the desert town of Palmyra, where the organization's destruction of archaeological monuments received worldwide condemnation after its capture in May 2015. At around the same time, Islamic State had extended its control to the Iraqi city of Ramadi, giving it a transnational territorial reach. A third zone – comprising the areas of Afrin and Kobanî, north-west and north-east of Aleppo, and Qamishli in the Jazira – was held by the Kurdish Democratic Union Party, which received US support in its campaign against Islamic State. In April 2015, the PYD's armed forces seized the city of Hassakeh, followed by the town of Tell Abyad two months later. The fourth zone, centred on Idlib and parts of Latakia governorates, had fallen under the control of Islamist rebels who were opposed to Islamic State. Foremost among them was Jabhat al-Nusra, which had, in March 2015, formed a military coalition with another major jihadi faction, Ahrar al-Sham, and successfully captured the city of Idlib. Finally, in 2014, secular units affiliated with the Free Syrian Army had also formed a new coalition, the Southern Front; they now controlled much of the south-western Hawran region, although the regime continued to hold the city of Der'a, the symbolic cradle of the revolution.

Far from being static frontlines, borders between these five regions could shift quite rapidly. Towns changed hands, competing rebel factions launched rival operations and smuggling networks trafficked food, weapons, medical supplies and even people across checkpoints and chokeholds, if they paid off the right people at the right moments. In areas held by the Assad regime, the institutions of the central state often held little sway. An array of loyalist militias was instead empowered by the regime to maintain control, freeing up the regular armed forces for assaults on the rebels. These loyalist militias were rarely restrained from thuggery, extortion and criminality. The entirety of eastern Aleppo was in the hands of rebels, as were the capital's eastern suburbs, the Ghouta, which the regime had been starving by a punishing and brutal siege since 2013. In April 2015, jihadis seized the devastated Damascus neighbourhood of Yarmouk, primarily inhabited by Palestinians before the war, and turned it into a satellite of Islamic State. By summer 2015, the regime held on to only 20–30 per cent of Syria's territory (see Map 5).

This string of losses revealed quite how eviscerated the regime's military and economic resources had become. The fear and frustration of many Syrians living even in supposedly secure regime-held zones reached the point that Assad had to rally support in a televised public address in which he explicitly acknowledged popular concerns over the regime's shortcomings.

'Are we abandoning certain areas? Why are we losing others? Where is the army in some areas, why doesn't it come?' Assad asked rhetorically in July 2015. 'Every inch of Syria is precious, invaluable and unrelinquishable. Demographically and geographically, every place is equally important,' he noted. 'There is no discrimination.' He acknowledged it was nevertheless impossible to win all battles on all fronts simultaneously: priorities therefore had to be established on tactical and strategic grounds. All the nation's resources had to be mobilized – an end that excused the army commandeering private property for the war effort.

'War is not the war of the armed forces, but the whole homeland,' Assad declared. 'This is the war of all society [. . .] Syria's victory in its war will not only mean defeating terrorism, but also mean that the region will regain its stability. The future of our region will determine and shape its features based on the future of Syria.'[1]

Assad's optimism was neither particularly inspiring nor universally shared. Even his most ardent supporters at home saw him principally as a symbol of the regime, not the regime itself. From outside the country, Saudis, Kuwaitis and Qataris continued to fund Syrian Islamist rebel factions. Turkey strategically aided both secular and Islamist rebels against the Kurdish PYD, which was – inconveniently for Ankara – backed by its NATO ally, the United States, as a provider of effective fighters against Islamic State. By mid-2015, even the Assad regime's own external supporters were reassessing its likelihood of survival. President Vladimir Putin of Russia reportedly shared in conversation with his US counterpart, Barack Obama, 'a sense that the Assad regime [was] losing a grip over greater and greater swaths of territory inside of Syria and that the prospects for [an Islamist] takeover or rout of the Syrian regime [was] not imminent but [was becoming] a greater and greater threat by the day'.[2] With the regime on the brink of collapse, Moscow's decision to intervene militarily on its behalf would mark a turning point in the war.

Changing fortunes: Russian intervention

The 2015–16 Russian intervention was not an automatic consequence of the historical legacies of Moscow's foreign policy in the Middle East. During the Cold War, the Soviet Union had supported Bashar al-Assad's father, Hafiz, but supplies of Russian military equipment, training and ammunition had failed to transform Syria into a full Soviet client. After the collapse of the Soviet Union in 1991, Moscow had been too preoccupied with affairs closer to home to project its influence in the Middle East. By the time the Arab uprisings began two decades later, ties with Syria were no longer strong. Russia's old naval facility at Tartous had dwindled to a staff of barely fifty; Bashar al-Assad visited Moscow only once during his presidency. 'When I hear that Russia has some special interests [in Syria],' Putin had said at a 2012 press conference in Paris, 'this is an absolute delusion.'[3] When the uprising began, Russian expert opinion differed from the Western diplomatic orthodoxy that Assad's days were numbered.[4] Moscow argued that the principle of state sovereignty meant Assad should remain in power. Russia had already accused the United States and its allies of breaching state sovereignty on two previous occasions: in Iraq in 2003 and in Libya in 2011, where Russia believed a UN resolution to protect civilians had been little more than a cover for regime change. Putin warned the West not to repeat the 'Libya scenario' in Syria and continued to supply Damascus with arms.[5]

By 2015, Assad's rapid territorial losses to Islamic State, Nusra and other rebel factions seemed to herald the fall of his regime. Since an estimated 7,000 of the 30,000 foreign fighters in Syria were Islamists from Russia and other post-Soviet states, Moscow was concerned that victory for Islamic State might see it spread conflict to Muslim populations in the Caucasus in search of a new frontline for jihad.[6] Shoring up the Assad regime offered Putin a convenient opportunity to contain the transnational Islamist threat and assert Russia as a geopolitical power of comparable weight to the United States in shaping international order.[7]

In August 2015, Damascus signed an agreement for Russia to use its airbase at Hmaymim, near Latakia. A month later, Assad made a formal request for Russian military intervention. Despite putative concerns about Islamic State, some 80 per cent of Russian airstrikes targeted secular, Nusra and other Islamist rebels in the first few months, inflicting losses that allowed the regime to regain control of rural Latakia and parts of the central provinces. Russian ground troops were largely committed to defending the Hmaymim Airbase, although Moscow did deploy military advisors to train the Syrian armed forces. Private Russian military companies such as the Wagner Group also fought in key locations. In the first nine months, the Russian air force carried out 11,000 aerial sorties; by the end of the first three years of the intervention, Moscow would estimate that over 63,000 Russian military personnel had fought in Syria in some capacity.[8] The sheer scale of Russia's intervention quickly turned the tide of the war.

Russia's bombing campaign needed to be coordinated not only with Damascus, but also with the second principal backer of the regime, Iran. Tehran had been helping to organize and train Assadist militias in Syria and channelling Shia foreign fighters from Iraq, Afghanistan and Pakistan to fight alongside them on behalf of the Syrian regime. Another Iran-backed Shia militia, Lebanon's Hizbullah, had notably captured border areas near the town of Qusayr for the regime in 2013. At the start of the Russian intervention, Iran amplified its presence in Syria and reportedly doubled the size of its Republic Guards deployment in the country to 3,000. Russia and Iran shared tactical interests in the Syrian regime: each of them wanted to challenge the international system defined by the West, but they differed on strategic issues such as Iran's nuclear programme and its enmity towards Israel and Saudi Arabia, as well as Tehran's preferences for using militias over conventional armed forces. Putin's vision of political power was more state-centric than that of the Islamic Republic's Revolutionary Guard.

Russia's new-found importance in the conflict helped it revive the previously largely ineffective international peace negotiations over Syria. Several previous rounds of talks, sponsored by the United Nations, had failed owing to the irreconcilable positions of all parties involved. Taking advantage of softening positions in the West, Moscow successfully pressed for Iranian involvement in the talks for the first time. Excluded from these new discussions were Islamic State, Nusra and (at Turkey's insistence) the PYD. Territories held by these groups were therefore excluded from the subsequent ceasefire agreed under Russian sponsorship in late February 2016. Even if it was halting and incomplete, the Russian ceasefire was successfully sustained for several weeks, partly thanks to the leverage that Moscow exerted over the Assad regime. In sponsoring this deal, Moscow's intention seems to have been to drive a wedge between Islamic State, Nusra and other irreconcilable regime opponents on the one hand, and those elements potentially amenable to some form of settlement on the other. The Assad regime did not share Russia's vision. The regime consistently signalled its total refusal to talk to terrorists – which in the regime's definition covered *all* the rebels, whether civilians or militants – and insisted on regaining every inch of lost Syrian territory. The regime engaged in the talks only with the aim of dragging out deliberations interminably while its military advances created new facts on the ground.

Irked by Assad's obstinacy, Moscow suddenly announced that it would withdraw its forces from Syria. Yet just ten days later,

Russian airpower supported regime armed forces in recapturing the town of Palmyra from Islamic State: talk of withdrawal was simply a tactic to attempt to compel the regime to take the talks more seriously. The bad faith of the regime, along with the fact that secular rebels, Islamists, jihadis and civilians were intermingled on the ground, meant that the terms of the ceasefire were quickly strained. An upsurge of fighting – including regime airstrikes in Idlib that led to the death of thirty-seven civilians in a marketplace – prompted the opposition to withdraw from the negotiations. Open hostilities soon recommenced.

Once the Syrian regime had successfully diverted Russia's push towards a negotiated settlement, Russian analysts muttered that the tail had begun to wag the dog.[9] Yet by 2016, Russia had invested so much diplomatic and military energy – and had acquired such considerable military assets and economic interests – that abandoning Syria seemed unappealing, despite Assad's obduracy. Assad pressed his advantage, declaring as part of his Victory Day salutations to Putin that Aleppo was Syria's equivalent to Stalingrad.[10] In late May, Russia recommenced airstrikes on rebel-held eastern Aleppo. Turkey agreed to suspend aid to rebel holdouts in Aleppo in exchange for Russia allowing its forces to enter northern Syria. Russia then stepped up its air campaign in support of an onslaught of Shia militias and regime forces against Syria's second city. By mid-December, eastern Aleppo was back in Assad's hands. Under a deal enforced by Russia and Turkey, around 10,000 remaining rebels and their families were bussed out to Idlib (supporters of Islamic State were instead expelled to Palmyra, which the group had recently reclaimed from the regime). By the end of 2016, the fortunes of the Assad regime had quite remarkably reversed.

Building on these territorial gains, in January 2017 Russia organized a new round of talks, this time co-sponsored by Iran and Turkey. Although the United Nations Special Envoy for Syria, Staffan de Mistura, did attend, the talks held at Astana were distinct from the previous UN negotiations. This time they excluded not only Nusra, Islamic State and the PYD, but also representatives of the civilian Syrian opposition, whose political relevance had long been eclipsed by fighters on the ground. Despite this concession to its hardline stance, the Assad regime still refused to compromise. As if to mark its independence from Russian diplomacy, in April, regime forces orchestrated a chemical weapons attack at Khan Shaykhoun in Idlib that seemed to make a mockery of Moscow's claim to have successfully overseen the end of Syria's chemical arsenal. When newly elected US President Donald Trump punished the chemical attack by launching Tomahawk missile attacks against a Syrian airbase, skilfully avoiding Russian air defences, Moscow's muted response was interpreted as a sign of its ongoing irritation with Assad.

The Astana talks produced a tentative agreement for localized de-escalation zones in four areas: the eastern Ghouta, Idlib province, Rastan north of Homs and parts of the Hawran to the south. In early May 2017, temporary ceasefires were implemented in these areas. While Russia envisaged imposing a settlement on the warring parties in Syria, the Assad regime relentlessly pursued its own maximalist vision. The loyalist slogan 'Assad or we burn the country' still seemed to capture the spirit of the regime and its disregard for the people living in the carnage of the conflict.

Raqqa and after: new dynamics, 2017–2019

After a steady stream of advances in the war against Islamic State, by the end of 2016, the United States was ready to make its move on Raqqa, the group's self-proclaimed capital. The dominant

Kurdish party in Syria, the PYD – along with its YPG militia and the affiliated Syrian Defence Forces (SDF) – continued to act as Washington's proxies in the campaign. Keen to secure a landmark victory by liberating Raqqa, in early 2017, President Trump authorized the direct arming of the YPG for the first time. US special forces in Syria increased to several hundred, although they were far less significant than the broad-based SDF, which had undergone a massive recruitment drive: its ranks now included some 50,000 Syrian Arab tribesmen, Kurds and even Yezidi volunteers from Iraq, whose community had suffered appalling brutality at the hands of Islamic State. These ground forces were supported by an intensification of US airpower when Trump loosened the safeguards that the previous administration had put in place to limit civilian deaths. In the first six months of the Trump presidency, reportedly twice as many civilians were killed as in two and a half years under Obama.[11]

Following the liberation of the Iraqi city of Mosul from Islamic State in July, the Syrian campaign began with the encirclement of Raqqa and lasted four months. The capture of Raqqa came at the cost of great devastation. The bombardment forced 270,000 residents to flee, destroyed as many as 11,000 buildings, reduced five square kilometres of the city centre entirely to rubble and obliterated Raqqa's health, education and water systems. In October, the estimated three hundred IS fighters who had survived were granted safe passage out of the devastated city, along with several thousand of their family members, in an act of clemency considered appropriate by the Arab proxy forces. After the loss of Mosul and Raqqa in quick succession, Islamic State retreated to a string of smaller towns along the Euphrates in eastern Syria, from which it was finally dislodged a year later. The campaign against Islamic State left behind it a trail of devastation from which local communities would find it impossible to recover on their own.

Yet the United States made little headway in rebuilding Raqqa, and in March 2018, President Trump suspended all recovery aid to Syria. Trump defined American interest narrowly, in terms of the defeat of Islamic State, not reconstruction or intervention in Syria's civil war.

The defeat of Islamic State seemed to confirm the rising star of the leftist PYD, which sought autonomy in the primarily Kurdish north-eastern parts of Syria. Yet alongside its successes, the party struggled with unresolved tensions over its ideology, identity and leadership. Many PYD military commanders had originally been trained in isolated camps in Iraq's Qandil Mountains, where they had been indoctrinated in the ideology of the party's Turkish parent organization, the PKK, which had for decades waged an on-and-off guerrilla campaign against Ankara in south-eastern Turkey. For these trained cadres, the Syrian PYD story was largely a side quest to the original PKK mission in Turkey. For the PYD's civilian leaders, in contrast, the challenges of local governance rapidly became the main focus, as they captured large swathes of territory from Islamic State in north-eastern Syria.

Although the PYD had a political vision that was multi-ethnic, in practice its political dominance – and its authoritarian tendencies – meant that the incipient administration it set up in northern and eastern Syria tended to be identified as a Kurdish project. The new name adopted by this administration in March 2016 – the Democratic Federation of Rojava: Northern Syria – did little to assuage concerns of ethnocentrism: in Kurmancî Kurdish, Rojava referred to the West of a Kurdistan that stretched from Syria and Turkey across to northern Iraq and Iran. In a concession to critics, Rojava was dropped from the official name by the end of the year. In September 2018, the name changed again, this time to the Autonomous Administration of North and East Syria (AANES), encompassing Raqqa, Deir al-Zour and other areas regained from Islamic State, in addition to the three cantons of Qamishli, Afrin and Kobanî already held. Many Western observers would nevertheless often use the name of Rojava as shorthand for the experiment in grassroots-led democratic activism that the PYD claimed to be leading in Syria. Supporters of Kurdish parties other than the PYD notably reported political repression, human rights abuses and the heavy handedness of PKK-trained guerrilla cadres, who monopolized decision-making behind the façade of gender equality, pluralism and the slogan of 'democratic autonomy'.

Washington had assessed that the Syrian PYD was organizationally distinct from the PKK, but the history of the two groups was so entangled that the United States needed to tread carefully for fear of alienating Turkey, which recognized no such distinction. For Turkey, PYD-governed territories in Syria simply gave the PKK a launching pad for attacks across the border. The campaign against Islamic State could therefore not be entrusted to Washington's preferred proxies. In August 2016, Turkey seized the Syrian border town of Jarablus from Islamic State – ostensibly as part of an effort to clear the group from lands adjacent to Turkey, but also to interrupt PYD aspirations to bridge their three geographically disconnected cantons across northern Syria. In a second operation, from January to March 2018, Turkey invaded and conquered the PYD-held canton of Afrin, despite fierce resistance from the Kurdish militia. This show of strength against what Ankara maintained to be a terrorist organization bolstered nationalist support for President Erdoğan's increasingly authoritarian agenda at home. Turkish-occupied territories in Syria were reinforced by remnants of the old Free Syrian Army, now regrouped as a new organization, the Syrian National Army, which had become largely a proxy force armed and equipped by Ankara. Turkey's intrusion into Syria under an increasingly assertive Erdoğan represented a potential existential threat for the PYD, whose security was ultimately assured only as long as the small contingent of US special forces remained in Syria to eradicate Islamic State from its last remaining holdouts.

While international attention was focused on Islamic State, the Assad regime was steadily regaining control of rebel-held pockets in the west of the country. By besieging, bombarding and starving areas outside its control, the regime had forced insurgents to accept what were euphemistically called local reconciliation agreements. These fragile truces were advertised to the outside world as a method to de-escalate the violence between the two sides and to reintegrate rebel enclaves into government-held territory. In reality, the regime offered fighters and the civilian population a stark choice between submission and expulsion. Tens or even hundreds of thousands of inhabitants had already fled the fighting in these areas; of the thousands who remained, those who declined the offer of reconciliation were evacuated by bus to the rebel-held Idlib province. Residents who remained were required to clarify their individual status with the authorities. After checking that their names did not appear on lists of wanted 'terrorists', men who had not completed their military service were obliged to enlist in loyalist militias, regime paramilitaries or the national armed forces. For their part, local community leaders would often petition the regime to provide food and economic aid, public services and information on individuals who had disappeared at the hands of the security forces. The regime rarely proved responsive to such requests. The government bureaucracy lacked the capacity or resources to support citizens in staunchly loyalist areas, much less in recently reconciled towns that had been devastated by conflict; the regime tightly controlled UN-provided aid, which was typically funnelled to its most stalwart supporters – or its most corrupt operatives. Tens of thousands of detainees remained in regime custody, where brutalization, torture and murder remained routine. These reconciliation agreements were initially welcomed by some international observers: with track-one negotiations at an impasse, it seemed as if local truces might offer the building blocks of a lasting bottom-up peace. But for the Assad regime, reconciliation was simply a euphemism for surrender.

While the regime had used negotiations to regain territory earlier in the conflict – albeit partially and inconsistently – it was only after the Russian intervention that these gains came to be consolidated across large areas of west-central Syria. In 2017, a series of agreements sponsored by Russia reduced hostilities around the remaining rebel-held territories in Idlib, north-central Homs, the Ghouta east of Damascus and the Hawran in the south-west. The uneasy détente lasted until the following year. Supported by Russian airpower, regime forces began to advance on the Ghouta. Fighting concluded in April 2018, when the regime launched a chemical weapons attack against the remaining pockets of rebellion; some four thousand hardline Islamist fighters were escorted out to Idlib from the now largely abandoned Ghouta, which had been devastated by five years of siege warfare. The United States, Britain and France responded to this repeat deployment of chemical weapons with limited air-strikes that served as little more than a slap on the wrist. Just a few days later, the regime retook the final neighbourhood of Damascus, the largely Palestinian Yarmouk Camp, which had been controlled by Islamic State for the previous three years.

In May, after several weeks of intense fighting, the rebel-held towns of Rastan and Talbiseh, in Homs governorate, concluded their own agreement with the regime. Nearly 3,000 militants and their families were again escorted to Idlib. The south-western Hawran region bordering the Israeli-occupied Golan Heights was retaken in July, following an understanding reached between Russia and Israel that no Iranian forces would be deployed in the process. The city of Der'a and the all-important border crossing to Jordan – across which support for the rebels had previously been supplied – were soon back in the hands of the regime. Several thousand rebel fighters and their families were yet again bussed to Idlib, the only surviving de-escalation zone.

Of the three million people living in Idlib and rebel-held parts of its neighbouring governorates, almost half had been internally displaced – often multiple times, from different parts of Syria, and within Idlib itself, as they fled aerial bombardment or shelling by Russian and regime forces. Conditions were so difficult that, in 2018, the United Nations reported that over two million of Idlib's inhabitants needed humanitarian aid.[12] As Idlib was the principal recipient of Islamist rebels expelled from territories that had been 'reconciled' to the regime, it became home to an assortment of jihadi groups with a wide yet sometimes quite nuanced assortment of ideological, theological and strategic differences of opinion. Over time, ongoing conflict between these various groups had whittled down their number. The al-Qaeda affiliated Jabhat al-Nusra notably eliminated several rivals to benefit its own position, but its international connections came to be seen as a hindrance in making the most of its improving support. After the 2015 Russian intervention, many Idlib rebels felt that their movement needed greater unity in order to survive. However, since 'Syria-first' Islamists prioritized national liberation before the liberation of the wider Muslim community, they distrusted Nusra's connections to the al-Qaeda network, whose commander, the Egyptian-born Ayman al-Zawahiri, was based in Afghanistan. In July 2016, Nusra removed this obstacle by formally breaking its ties with al-Qaeda and adopting a new name. After a steady stream of mergers and outright military confrontations with other

Islamist groups – including its main challenger, Ahrar al-Sham, 2017 saw the consolidation of a new body, *Hay'at Tahrir al-Sham* (HTS: Organization for the Liberation of Syria), which continued to be led by the politically agile Abu Muhammad al-Jolani.

HTS rapidly became the leading authority in Idlib. From 2017, it embarked on a wave of institution building, establishing a political bureau, distinct from its military wing, to enable dialogue with the international community and donors, and a relatively autonomous bureaucracy of technocrats, the Syrian Salvation Government, to take charge of public works and day-to-day governance.[13] Despite the trappings of civilian rule, HTS nevertheless exercised ultimate control in Idlib.

HTS now presented itself as part of the Syrian tradition of revolution against the regime, not as part of the global jihadi struggle. Jolani was personally involved in a series of public events that included meeting civilian community leaders, visiting the troops, distributing gifts at children's parties and appearing in the selfies of internally displaced people. He even gave a speech at the opening ceremony for an important new road. 'Freedom comes from military strength,' he said, 'and dignity comes from economic and investment projects, through which the people and the citizens live a dignified life that befits Muslims.'[14] Although Idlib under HTS did not pretend to be democratic, Jolani's was a campaign of public diplomacy worthy of any politician seeking election.

HTS efficiently eliminated or expelled more radical elements who opposed its split with global jihad, including cells of Islamic State supporters who had trickled into Idlib after the territorial collapse of the caliphate, although the ongoing population displacement, disorder and violence meant its control of the region was never absolute. Islamic State's self-declared caliph, Abu Bakr al-Baghdadi, was killed in Idlib in an operation by US special forces in October 2019. Although HTS maintained that Baghdadi had been in hiding and evaded its surveillance, sceptics asked whether the group's break with hardline radicalism was as clean as it claimed. Despite making conciliatory noises towards non-Muslims and Syria's minority communities, HTS members were responsible for confiscations from Christian and Druze property owners in Idlib. Critics of the organization could be arrested, subjected to a one-sided legal process, tortured or even summarily executed. Such reports made it difficult to converge on a common understanding of the true nature of HTS: suspicions about this would hang over Jolani for many years.

One final stretch of territory exchanged hands before the frontlines of control stabilized. After President Trump announced that the mission of defeating Islamic State had been successfully completed, in October 2019, Turkey launched a major attack on the northern Syrian towns of Tell Abyad and Ras al-Ayn, both controlled by the SDF. Operation Peace Spring essentially moved into the gap left by the withdrawal of US forces from the north-east. Turkey and Russia agreed a ceasefire that required the SDF to pull back from the Syria–Turkey border everywhere except Qamishli; Turkey would continue to occupy a buffer zone from Tell Abyad to Ras al-Ayn. In the meantime, a change of heart from Trump meant the United States maintained a military presence in eastern Syria, ostensibly to guard against an Islamic State revival.

Just two months later, a regime offensive supported by Russia and Iranian militia made significant inroads into Idlib. Thousands of Syrians fleeing the fighting massed at the border, prompting Erdoğan to dispatch Syrian National Army proxies and 5,000 Turkish troops to help regain lost territory, although the initiative lost momentum once a clash with Russian forces looked likely. A ceasefire in March 2020 consolidated the regime's gains in northern Syria, which amounted to half of the 2017 de-escalation zone. With the onset of the global pandemic in spring 2020, Syria's four zones of de facto control were brought into a state of uneasy equilibrium (see Map 6).

From normalization to collapse: 2020–2024

After nearly a decade of conflict, the territory of Syria was divided, but the country had not experienced the outright collapse of government that often accompanied civil wars around the world in the twentieth and early twenty-first centuries.[15] The state that had inherited the mantle of sovereignty continued to preside from Damascus, however atrophied its capabilities and truncated its power. The Assad regime of the early 2020s was riddled with contradictions. Its claims to sovereignty were supported by the pillar of a national army, but that army's ranks were filled by enforced young conscripts who were starved and terrified. At the local level, security had been subcontracted to a decentralized array of loyalist militias, whose thuggery, corruption and criminality the regime was reluctant or powerless to curtail. Yet the regime was fearless in chastising, disciplining and even removing those kingpins whose ongoing support seemed vital for its own well-being. No less a figure than Rami Makhlouf – the cousin of Bashar al-Assad whose towering business interests had dominated the Syrian economy for nearly two decades – was notably stripped of all his assets in 2020, providing a cautionary tale to the new wave of Syrian entrepreneurs and profiteers that had risen to prominence during the civil war. Whole towns and neighbourhoods across the country had been reduced to rubble, and millions of people displaced from their homes. In place of reconstruction, however, the regime proposed plans for luxury living and aspirational apartment buildings in exclusive developments built on land repossessed from the original owners. The regime, its personnel and its associated commercial instruments had been placed under stringent sanctions by the United States, European Union and other countries, only to see the emergence of a state-sanctioned drugs trade centred on Syria that produced a stimulant known as Captagon and exported it to the Gulf and the Mediterranean.[16] While the existential guarantees of the Assad regime had ultimately been underwritten by Russian and, to a lesser extent, Iranian military resources, it had been forced to eviscerate and cannibalize its own internal organs in the aim of self-preservation.

From the outside, it was difficult to discern the degree of the regime's degradation. If anything, its sheer tenacity in withstanding over a decade of isolation lent weight to arguments for reconsidering positions towards Syria. With meaningful reform or rehabilitation looking impossible for the Assad regime, accepting the status quo seemed to some countries to offer better prospects for their policy goals. Delivering such outcomes as the return of refugees to Syria, stemming the supply of Captagon or even securing cut-price deals for future reconstruction would be impossible in the near term without the partnership of Assad's Syria, regardless of its record of brutality. In 2023, Syria was readmitted to the Arab League after Jordan and Saudi Arabia opened the path for regional normalization.

Domestically, the logic of normalization could also be seen at work in the rival political projects set up in Syria beyond the reach of the Assad regime. In the north-east and the north-west, the PYD and HTS each found that the pragmatic demands of day-to-day governance – not to mention the exigences of managing international relations – often required a certain softening, if not moderation, of their core ideological principles. Life under the Autonomous Administration of North-East Syria faced continuing security challenges, including periodic attacks from Turkish forces and clandestine operatives with allegiance to Islamic State. In the opposition stronghold of Idlib, HTS entrenched its position and deepened its connections to the local population during the post-pandemic years. Even the suffering inflicted by the aftermath of a calamitous 7.8 magnitude earthquake centred on Idlib and south-west Turkey in February 2023 – and the difficulty of delivering international aid to Idlib when it was run by an organization under strict international sanctions – was insufficient to dislodge HTS from its position. Syria seemed to be becoming a fragile, divided and continuously violent country, despite its relative stability in overall terms.

The 'new normal' emerging in Syria was shattered in late 2024. In an astonishing, unexpected move, on 27 November, the armed forces of HTS and its allied Islamists successfully attacked the frontline, burst out of Idlib and headed east for Aleppo, which they conquered in just three days. They then turned south, sweeping into the central cities of Hama and Homs. At the opposite end of the country, local rebels seized control of Der'a. The Syrian armed forces mounted a half-hearted resistance, fled or pulled back in the face of rebel advances, effectively abandoning less strategic cities such as Suweida, Qunaytra and Deir al-Zour to concentrate on defending the capital. The regime's main foreign backer, Russia, was too mired in its own conflict in Ukraine to offer any significant military or diplomatic support. Iran and Hizbullah, for their part, had recently suffered serious setbacks at the hands of Israel and were also in no position to assist. These geopolitical shifts in international relations left the Assad regime newly vulnerable. Bashar al-Assad boarded a plane and abandoned the country to go into hiding in Russia; his brother Maher reportedly fled to Iran. On 8 December, rebel forces streamed into the heart of Damascus and jubilantly declared the end of fifty-three years of Assad rule. A new era had begun.

Postscript: the nation belongs to all

The sudden overthrow of the Assad regime no doubt surprised HTS as much as it did Bashar al-Assad. Within scarcely two weeks, a regime that had seemed solid, albeit corrupt and emaciated, had all but melted away. The leader of HTS – who now found himself effectively the new leader of Syria – marked the end of the popular revolution by abandoning his *nom de guerre*, Abu Muhammad al-Jolani; henceforth he would be known by his given name, Ahmad al-Shara'.

The family name of Shara' immediately identified the previously mysterious figure of Jolani as originating from south-western Syria. In fact, his family were *nazihin* – inhabitants of the Golan Heights forced to flee when their lands were seized by Israel in 1967. Shara' himself had been born in Riyadh in 1982, to a father who in his own political trajectory moved from young Nasserist in the 1960s to career oil economist, taking up employment in the Gulf before returning to Syria to serve as a government consultant. After leaving the public sector, Shara's father supported his family by running a supermarket and real estate brokerage in the affluent Damascene suburb of Mezzeh. Perhaps in rebellion against the expectations of his secular, professional father, Shara' found himself drawn to jihadism. Following the 2003 war in Iraq, Shara' travelled to Iraq (apparently with the connivance of Abu Qa'qa, the regime-sponsored militant cleric of Aleppo) and joined the ranks of al-Qaeda. Imprisoned for six years at the US military detention centre of Bucca, whose inmates offered him an accelerated immersion course in jihadi leadership skills, Shara' quickly climbed the ranks of the Islamic State in Iraq before returning to Syria during the early uprising. Instead of identifying him with the radical alienation typical of al-Qaeda operatives, the life history of Shara' locates him squarely within the political and social context of contemporary Syria. It also perhaps explains why Shara' placed such emphasis on winning the hearts and minds of the local community to implement the political project of HTS, rather than simply using brute force to break and remake Syria in its own image.

In the immediate aftermath of regime change, HTS issued statements intended to reassure Syrians and the international community that it would respect the rights of all Syrians, including minorities, and that it would refrain from imposing measures that did not reflect the will of the people. Shara' entertained a rapid succession of foreign dignitaries, who attempted to assess the new leader and his political vision. Was his conciliatory tone simply a ruse to persuade Western diplomats to remove HTS from their list of prohibited terrorist organizations, lift sanctions and open the door to reconstruction funds? Or did it express the lessons of political moderation that HTS had genuinely taken to heart over the previous seven years of governing Idlib? Shara's proposal that a national dialogue be convened to draft a constitution within three years, and that national elections be held within four years, was subject to a similar interrogation. Was this timetable realistic given the chaos affecting the country, or was it a delaying tactic to allow HTS to consolidate an authoritarian regime of its own making in Syria?

While Syrians were rightfully concerned about the answers to such questions, whichever group came to power would have immediately faced the same set of problems. The war had destroyed a vast amount of infrastructure. There was a lack of housing, electricity shortages and insufficient jobs; tens of thousands of people were injured, traumatized or missing; millions had become refugees or been internally displaced. There was a very real possibility of revenge killings against supporters of the Assads, or those accused of supporting the regime, as well as of attacks by regime remnants who had few prospects in the new political climate and very little to lose. HTS offered a general amnesty for those who worked for the former regime: Ba'th Party members, army officers, policemen, even Assadist militiamen and intelligence officials, flocked to have their names checked, obtain new civilian identity cards and surrender their weapons. While the rebels now controlled both Idlib and the territories of the former regime, the depth of that control remained untested. Turkish forces still occupied northern Syria, Israel still occupied the Golan, the PYD still held the north-east and Islamic State cells were still active in the desert and the east. At the outbreak of the uprising, regime supporters had issued their ultimatum: 'Assad or we burn the country.' In the wake of their departure, the Assads had left the nation in ashes.

Whatever was to follow, December 2024 ushered in one of those exceptional, critical moments in which Syria's political future seemed genuinely undetermined. For the first time in over half a century, there was space in which political questions could at least be posed without the answers necessarily being imposed from above. Despite the historical rupture delivered by the astonishing implosion of the Assad regime, in many ways the debates in Syria of the 2020s resonated with the same set of challenges that earlier generations of Syrians had also faced.

The first was, on the one hand, the tension between previous rulers' desire to monopolize power, centralize authority and impose their own vision on society and, on the other, the existence of powerful centrifugal forces throughout the regions of Syria agitating for their own local autonomy. The second challenge was the temptation to resolve this tension by recourse to violence. As Syria had experienced so often in its history, not only did violence beget further violence, but it also created chains of complicity with violence that entangled ethnic loyalties and sectarian identities to disastrous effect. The third challenge was that of what Syrians might call social justice. The entrenched inequalities that had characterized the country since the late Ottoman Empire were not simply the outcome of poor economic planning or suboptimal policies that could be modified by foreign direct investment, business-friendly legislation or the creation of free markets. More significantly, they arose from the sheer unevenness of economic development to which Syria had been exposed for nearly two centuries. Time and time again, connections between and among the cities, villages and fields of the lands of Syria were twisted, torn and transformed into new configurations by the seismic forces that shaped the global economy. Even as those who struggled for power in Syria reshaped the world around them, they did so on a terrain not of their own making but one equally shaped by international forces, transnational currents and global crises. While the destruction visited upon Syria was extreme, its experience of making and remaking was by no means exceptional in the modern world. In this respect – and in so many others – we have much to learn from the history of Syria, this nation that 'belongs to All'.

Notes

EPIGRAPH

1. Yāsīn al-Ḥājj Ṣāliḥ, *al-Thawra al-Mustaḥīla: al-Thawra, al-Ḥarb al-Ahlīya, wa'l-Ḥarb al-'Āmma fī Sūrīya* [The Impossible Revolution: Revolution, Civil War and Generalized War in Syria] (Beirut: al-Mu'assasa al-'Arabīya li'l-Dirāsāt wa'l-Nashr, 2017), 37–38.

1. OF PEASANTS AND GRAND FAMILIES: THE LANDS OF SYRIA, 1800S–1860S

1. M. Şükrü Hanioğlu, *A Brief History of the Late Ottoman Empire* (Princeton: Princeton University Press, 2010), 6–41.
2. Martin Van Bruinessen, 'The Ethnic Identity of the Kurds in Turkey', in *Ethnic Groups in the Republic of Turkey*, ed. Peter A. Andrews and Rüdiger Benninghaus (Wiesbaden: Reichert, 1989).
3. Philip S. Khoury, *Urban Notables and Arab Nationalism: The Politics of Damascus 1860–1920* (Cambridge: Cambridge University Press, 1983), 18.
4. Molly Greene, 'The Ottoman Experience', *Daedalus* 134, no. 2 (2005): 88–99; Daniel Neep, '"What Have the Ottomans Ever Done for Us?" Why History Matters for Politics in the Arab Middle East', *International Affairs* 97, no. 6 (2021): 1825–41.
5. 'Iraq' was commonly used in Arabic to refer to the inhabited region along the lower Euphrates and Tigris well before the creation of the new state given the same name after the First World War. Reidar Visser, 'Proto-Political Conceptions of Iraq in Late Ottoman Times', *International Journal of Contemporary Iraqi Studies* 3, no. 2 (2009): 143–54, https://doi.org/10.1386/ijcis.3.2.143/1; Muḥammad Jamāl Bārūt, *al-Takawwun al-Tārīkhī al-Ḥadīth li'l-Jazīra al-Sūrīya: As'ila wa-Ishkālīyāt al-Taḥawwul min al-Badwana ilā al-'Umrān al-Ḥaḍarī* [The Historical

Formation of Modern Syrian Jazīra: Questions and Problematiques of the Transition from Nomadism to Sedentarism] (Beirut: al-Markaz al-'Arabī li'l-Abḥāth wa-Dirāsat al-Siyāsāt, 2013), 41–50.

6. The Jazira mostly fell into the provinces of Diyarbekir and Raqqa. Despite the name, Raqqa province was governed from Urfa (al-Ruha), since Raqqa town had been abandoned.
7. Fruma Zachs, *The Making of a Syrian Identity: Intellectuals and Merchants in Nineteenth-Century Beirut* (Leiden: Brill, 2005), 18–23.
8. Mikhā'īl Mishāqa, *Kitāb Mashhad al-'Ayān bi-Ḥawādith Sūriyā wa-Lubnān* [Book of Eyewitnesses to the Events in Syria and Lebanon] (Cairo: n.p., 1908), 133.
9. J. B. Fourier, 'Preface historique' in *Description de l'Egypte* (Paris: Imprimerie Imperiale, 1809), v–vi, cited in Anne Godlewska, 'Map, Text and Image. The Mentality of Enlightened Conquerors: A New Look at the *Description de l'Egypte*', *Transactions of the Institute of British Geographers* 20, no. 1 (1995): 5–28.
10. 'Abd al-Raḥmān al-Jabartī, *Al-Jabartī's Chronicle of the First Seven Months of the French Occupation of Egypt, 15 June–December 1798*, trans. Shmuel Moreh (Leiden: Brill, 1975), 40–43.
11. Khaled Fahmy, *All the Pasha's Men: Mehmed Ali, His Army, and the Making of Modern Egypt* (Cairo: AUC Press, 2002).
12. Stanford J. Shaw, 'The Origins of Ottoman Military Reform: The Nizam-I Cedid Army of Sultan Selim III', *Journal of Modern History* 37, no. 3 (1965): 291–306.
13. Roger Owen, *The Middle East in the World Economy, 1800–1914* (London and New York: I.B. Tauris, 1981), 64–73.
14. Norman N. Lewis, *Nomads and Settlers in Syria and Jordan, 1800–1980* (Cambridge: Cambridge University Press, 1987), 39.
15. Qustantin al-Basha, *Mudhakkirāt Tārīkhīya* (Lebanon, n.d.), 77, cited in Moshe Ma'oz, *Ottoman Reform in Syria and Palestine, 1840–1861: The Impact of the Tanzimat on Politics and Society* (Oxford: Clarendon Press, 1968), 18.
16. Dick Douwes, *The Ottomans in Syria: A History of Justice and Oppression* (London: I.B. Tauris, 2000), 207.
17. Bruce Masters, *The Arabs of the Ottoman Empire, 1516–1918: A Social and Cultural History* (Cambridge: Cambridge University Press, 2013), 151.

18. ʻAbd Allāh Ḥannā, *al-ʻĀmmīya wa'l-Intifāḍāt al-Fallāḥīya, 1850–1918, fī Jabal Ḥawrān* [The 'Ammiyya and Peasant Revolts in Jabal Hawran, 1850–1918] (Damascus: al-Ahālī li'l-Ṭibā'a wa'l-Nashr wa'l-Tawzī', 1990), 55; Bīrjīt Shīblīr, *Intifāḍāt Jabal al-Durūz-Ḥawrān min al-ʻAhd al-ʻUthmānī ilā Dawlat al-Istiqlāl, 1850–1949: Dirāsa Antrubulūjīya-Tārikhīya* [The Uprisings of the Hawran Jabal al-Duruz from the Ottoman Period to Independence, 1850–1949: A Historical-Anthropological Study]. Arabic translation of Birgit Schaebler, *Aufstande im Drusenbergland: Ethnizitat und Integration einer landlichen Gesellschaft Syriens vom Osmanischen Reich bis zur staatlichen Unabhangigkeit 1850–1949* (Beirut: Dār al-Nahār bi'l-Ta'āwun ma' al-Ma'had al-Almānī li'l-Abḥāth al-Sharqīya, 2003), 28–29.
19. Kamal S. Salibi, *The Modern History of Lebanon* (Delmar, N.Y.: Caravan Books, 1977), 40–42.
20. Cited in Afaf Lutfi Sayyid-Marsot, *Egypt in the Reign of Muhammad Ali* (Cambridge: Cambridge University Press, 1984), 240.
21. Ian S. Lustick, 'The Absence of Middle Eastern Great Powers: Political "Backwardness" in Historical Perspective', *International Organization* 51, no. 04 (1997): 653–83, https://doi.org/10.1162/002081897550483.
22. Rifā'at Rāfi' al-Ṭahṭāwī, *Kitāb Takhlīṣ al-Ibrīz ilā Talkhīṣ Bārīz: Aw, al-Dīwān al-Nafīs bi-Īwān Bārīs* [The Book of Producing Gold in the Summarization of Paris] (Cairo: Dār al-Taqaddum, 1905), 7.
23. Eugen Weber, *Peasants into Frenchmen: Modernization of Rural France, 1870–1914* (Stanford: Stanford University Press, 1976), 14.
24. Selim Deringil, *The Well-Protected Domains: Ideology and the Legitimation of Power in the Ottoman Empire, 1876–1909* (London: I.B. Tauris, 1999), 41.
25. Selim Deringil, '"They Live in a State of Nomadism and Savagery": The Late Ottoman Empire and the Post-Colonial Debate', *Comparative Studies in Society and History* 45, no. 2 (2003): 311–42.
26. Joel S. Migdal, *Strong Societies and Weak States: State–Society Relations and State Capabilities in the Third World* (Princeton: Princeton University Press, 1988), 57.
27. Bruce Masters, 'The Political Economy of Aleppo in an Age of Ottoman Reform', *Journal of the Economic and Social History of the Orient* 53, no. 1–2 (2010): 290–316.

28. Owen, *The Middle East in the World Economy, 1800–1914*, 169.
29. Khoury, *Urban Notables and Arab Nationalism*, 23.
30. Jacques Weulersse, *Paysans de Syrie et Du Proche Orient* (Paris: Gallimard, 1946), 99–112.
31. 'Abd Allāh Ḥannā, *Al-Qaḍīya al-Zirā'īya wa'l-Ḥaraka al-Fallāḥīya fī Sūrīya wa-Lubnān, 1920–1945* [The Agricultural Question and the Peasant Movement in Syria and Lebanon, 1920–1945], vol. 2 (Damascus: Dār al-Farābī, 1978), 51–72.
32. Gertude Bell, *Syria: The Desert and the Sown* (New York: Arno Press, 1973), 223–27.
33. Hanna Batatu, *Syria's Peasantry, the Descendants of Its Lesser Rural Notables, and Their Politics* (Princeton: Princeton University Press, 1999), 100–101.
34. Ussama Makdisi, *The Culture of Sectarianism: Community, History, and Violence in Nineteenth-Century Ottoman Lebanon* (Berkeley: University of California Press, 2000), 114–45.
35. Samir Khalaf, *Civil and Uncivil Violence in Lebanon: A History of the Internationalization of Communal Conflict* (New York: Columbia University Press, 2003), 273–303.
36. Makdisi, *The Culture of Sectarianism*; Owen, *The Middle East in the World Economy, 1800–1914*, 160–65.
37. Haim Gerber, *The Social Origins of the Modern Middle East* (Boulder: Lynne Rienner Publishers, 1987), 176–77.
38. Ḥannā, *al-'Āmmīya wa'l-Intifāḍāt al-Fallāḥīya*, 124–46.
39. The term *falīta* today carries negative connotations, but was current in the Jabal at the time. Ḥannā, 158.
40. Linda Schatkowski Schilcher, *Families in Politics: Damascene Factions and Estates of the 18th and 19th Centuries* (Stuttgart: Franz Steiner Verlag Wiesbaden, 1985), 47, 77–78.
41. Haytham al-'Awdāt, *Intifāḍat al-'Āmmīya al-Fallāḥīya fī Jabal al-'Arab* [The Peasant Commoners' Revolt in Jabal al-Arab] ([Damascus]: al-'Awdāt, 1976), 32–33.
42. Ḥannā, *al-'Āmmīya wa'l-Intifāḍāt al-Fallāḥīya*, 182–83.
43. Shīblīr, *Intifāḍāt Jabal al-Durūz*, 112, 120–23; Ḥannā, *al-'Āmmīya wa'l-Intifāḍāt al-Fallāḥīya*, 160–61.
44. Ḥannā, *al-'Āmmīya wa'l-Intifāḍāt al-Fallāḥīya*, 188–89.

45. Max L. Gross, 'Ottoman Rule in the Province of Damascus 1860–1909' (PhD, Georgetown University, 1979), 441; Birgit Schaebler, 'State(s) Power and the Druzes: Integration and the Struggle for Social Control (1838–1949)', in *The Syrian Land: Processes of Integration and Fragmentation: Bilād al-Shām from the 18th to the 20th Century*, ed. Thomas Philipp and Birgit Schaebler (Stuttgart: Franz Steiner Verlag, 1998), 339.
46. Ḥannā, *al-'Āmmīya wa'l-Intifāḍāt al-Fallāḥīya*, 190–92.
47. For the text of the Declaration of Majdal al-Shur, see Ḥannā, 194–96; 'Awdāt, *Intifāḍat al-'Āmmīya al-Fallāḥīya fī Jabal al-'Arab* [The Peasant Commoners' Revolt in Jabal al-Arab], 55–58.
48. Ḥannā, *al-'Āmmīya wa'l-Intifāḍāt al-Fallāḥīya*, 213–21.
49. Stefan Winter, 'The Alawis in the Ottoman Period', in *The 'Alawis of Syria: War, Faith and Politics in the Levant*, ed. Michael Kerr and Craig Larkin (Oxford: Oxford University Press, 2015), 58–59.
50. Samuel Lyde, *The Asian Mystery Illustrated in the History, Religion, and Present State of the Ansaireeh or Nusairis of Syria* (London: Longman, Green, Longman, and Roberts, 1860), 199.
51. Winter, 'The Alawis in the Ottoman Period'.
52. Stefan Winter, *A History of the 'Alawis: From Medieval Aleppo to the Turkish Republic* (Princeton: Princeton University Press, 2016), 161–81.
53. Winter, 178–79, 182.
54. Yvette Talhamy, 'The Nusayri Leader Isma'il Khayr Bey and the Ottomans (1854–58)', *Middle Eastern Studies* 44, no. 6 (2008): 895–908, https://doi.org/10.1080/00263200802426013.
55. Hanna Batatu, 'Some Observations on the Social Roots of Syria's Ruling, Military Group and the Causes for Its Dominance', *Middle East Journal* 35, no. 3 (1981): 331–44.
56. Kurt Lee Mendenhall, 'Class, Cult and Tribe: The Politics of 'Alawi Separatism in French Mandate Syria' (PhD Austin, University of Texas at Austin, 1991), 135–59.
57. Lewis, *Nomads and Settlers in Syria and Jordan, 1800–1980*, 3–12.
58. Mark Sykes, *The Caliphs' Last Heritage: A Short History of the Turkish Empire* (London: Garnet, 1915), 300–301.
59. Sykes, 315–16.

2. REFORMS AND REGIONALISM: THE LATE OTTOMAN EMPIRE, 1860s–1920

1. Ma'oz, *Ottoman Reform in Syria and Palestine, 1840–1861: The Impact of the Tanzimat on Politics and Society*, 31–32.
2. Jens Hanssen, 'Practices of Integration: Center-Periphery Relations in the Ottoman Empire', in *The Empire in the City: Arab Provincial Capitals in the Late Ottoman Empire*, eds Jens Hanssen, Thomas Philipp and Stefan Weber (Würzburg: Ergon in Kommission, 2002), 49–74.
3. 'Abd al-'Azīz Muḥammad 'Awaḍ, *al-Idāra al-'Uthmānīya fī Wilāyat Sūrīya, 1864–1914* [Ottoman Administration in the Province of Syria] (Egypt: Dār al-Ma'ārif, 1969), 70–77.
4. Hasan Kayali, *Arabs and Young Turks: Ottomanism, Arabism, and Islamism in the Ottoman Empire, 1908–1918* (Berkeley: University of California Press, 1997), 25–28.
5. Deringil, *The Well-Protected Domains*, 22–30.
6. Eric Hobsbawm and Terence Ranger, *The Invention of Tradition* (Cambridge: Cambridge University Press, 1992).
7. Deringil, *The Well-Protected Domains*, 44–92. Bedouin tribes were generally considered lax in religious affairs, with the notable exception of adherents to Arabia's Wahhabi movement, which had not yet made few inroads further north.
8. Benjamin C. Fortna, *Imperial Classroom: Islam, the State, and Education in the Late Ottoman Empire* (Oxford: Oxford University Press, 2002).
9. Michael Provence, 'Ottoman Modernity, Colonialism, and Insurgency in the Interwar Arab East', *International Journal of Middle East Studies* 43, no. 2 (2011): 205–25, https://doi.org/10.1017/S0020743811000031.
10. Eugene L. Rogan, 'Asiret Mektebi: Abdulhamid II's School for Tribes (1892–1907)', *International Journal of Middle East Studies* 28, no. 1 (1996): 83–107.
11. Ruth Roded, 'Social Patterns Among the Urban Elite During the Late Ottoman Period (1876–1916)', in *Palestine in the Late Ottoman Period: Political, Social, and Economic Transformation*, ed. David Kushner (Leiden: Brill, 1986).
12. Eugene L. Rogan, 'Instant Communication: The Impact of the Telegraph in Ottoman Syria', in *The Syrian Land: Processes of Integration and Fragmentation. Bilad al-Sham from the 18th to the 20th Century*, ed.

Thomas Philipp and Birgit Schaebler (Stuttgart: Franz Steiner Verlag, 1998), 113–28, http://www.indiebound.org/book/9783515073097.

13. Linda S. Schilcher, 'Railways in the Political Economy of Southern Syria, 1890–1925', in *The Syrian Land: Processes of Integration and Fragmentation: Bilād al-Shām from the 18th to the 20th Century*, ed. Thomas Philipp and Birgit Schäbler (Franz Steiner Verlag, 1998).
14. Eric J. Hobsbawm, *The Age of Capital, 1848–1875* (London: Abacus, 2003), 49.
15. John Gallagher and Ronald Robinson, 'The Imperialism of Free Trade', *The Economic History Review* 6, no. 1 (1953): 1–15, https://doi.org/10.2307/2591017.
16. Muhammad Sa'īd al-Qāsīmī and Jamal al-Dīn al-Qāsimī, *Qāmūs al-Sinā'āt al-Shāmīya* [The Dictionary of Damascene Industries], ed. Zafir al-Qāsimī (Paris: Mouton, 1960), 55–57.
17. Ṣulṭān al-Aṭrash, *Aḥdāth al-Thawra al-Sūrīya al-Kubrā ka-mā Saradahā Qā'iduhā al-'Āmm Ṣulṭān Bāshā al-Aṭrash, 1925–1927* [The Events of the Great Syrian Revolt of 1925–1927, as Narrated by its General Commander Sultan Pasha al-Atrash] (Damascus: Dār 'Alā al-Dīn, 2004), 42; Michael Provence, *The Great Syrian Revolt and the Rise of Arab Nationalism* (Austin: University of Texas Press, 2009), 36.
18. Owen, *The Middle East in the World Economy, 1800–1914*, 249.
19. Owen, 171.
20. Andreas Resch and Dieter Stiefel, 'Vienna: The Eventful History of a Financial Center', in *Global Austria*, ed. Günter Bischof et al. (New Orleans: University of New Orleans Press, 2011), 20.
21. Scott Mixon, 'The Crisis of 1873: Perspectives from Multiple Asset Classes', *The Journal of Economic History* 68, no. 3 (2008): 722–57; Scott Reynolds Nelson, 'A Storm of Cheap Goods: New American Commodities and the Panic of 1873', *The Journal of the Gilded Age and Progressive Era* 10, no. 4 (2011): 447–53, https://doi.org/10.2307/23045123.
22. Barry Eichengreen, *Globalizing Capital: A History of the International Monetary System*, 2nd ed. (Princeton: Princeton University Press, 2008), 14–19.
23. Kevin H. O'Rourke, 'The European Grain Invasion, 1870–1913', *The Journal of Economic History* 57, no. 4 (1997): 775–801, https://doi.org/10.2307/2951160.

24. Owen, *The Middle East in the World Economy, 1800–1914*, 100–110.
25. In parallel, Egypt had also turned to debt-fuelled development after the veto imposed on Mehmed Ali's strategy of indigenous industrialization four decades earlier: in 1882 Britain occupied Egypt, ostensibly to secure the scheduled repayment of public debt. As the second occupation of Egypt highlighted, the economic reforms were essential to raise funds to keep British and French bankers from further infringements of Ottoman sovereignty – and to prevent their governments from invading the Ottoman Empire to guarantee its debt repayments. Roger Owen, 'Egypt and Europe: From French Expedition to British Occupation', in *Studies in the Theory of Imperialism*, ed. Roger Owen and Bob Sutcliffe (London: Longman, 1972).
26. Charles Issawi, *An Economic History of the Middle East and North Africa* (London: Routledge, 2006), 64–65.
27. Owen, *The Middle East in the World Economy, 1800–1914*, 104.
28. In 1881 the empire also participated in the global shift from bimetallism to the gold standard, albeit that in practice it lacked the infrastructural power to enforce the withdrawal of silver currency in many of its territories. Sevket Pamuk, *A Monetary History of the Ottoman Empire* (Cambridge: Cambridge University Press, 2000), 217.
29. L. Schatkowski Schilcher, 'The Hauran Conflicts of the 1860s: A Chapter in the Rural History of Modern Syria', *International Journal of Middle East Studies* 13, no. 2 (1981): 175.
30. *Thamarat al-Funūn* 25, 1181 (1898), cited in Linda Schatkowski Schilcher, 'Violence in Rural Syria in the 1880s and 1890s: State Centralization, Rural Integration, and the World Market', in *Peasants and Politics in the Modern Middle East*, ed. Farhad Kazemi and John Waterbury (Gainesville: University Press of Florida, 1991), 54.
31. Jamāl al-Dīn al-Qāsimī and Muḥammad Sa'īd al-Qāsimī, *Qāmūs al-Sinā'āt al-Shāmīya* [The Dictionary of Damascene Industries], ed. Ẓāfir al-Qāsimī (Paris: Mouton, 1960), 55–57.
32. al-Qāsimī and al-Qāsimī, 88.
33. Owen, *The Middle East in the World Economy, 1800–1914*, 260–61.
34. Yoav Di-Capua, 'Nahda: The Arab Project of Enlightenment', in *The Cambridge Companion to Modern Arab Culture*, ed. Dwight F. Reynolds (Cambridge: Cambridge University Press, 2015); Jens Hanssen and Max

Weiss, eds, *Arabic Thought Beyond the Liberal Age: Towards an Intellectual History of the Nahda* (Cambridge: Cambridge University Press, 2016); Albert Hourani, *Arabic Thought in the Liberal Age 1798–1939* (Cambridge: Cambridge University Press, 1983); Elizabeth Suzanne Kassab, *Contemporary Arab Thought: Cultural Critique in Comparative Perspective* (New York: Columbia University Press, 2010).

35. Zachs, *The Making of a Syrian Identity*, 36.
36. Ahmad Faris al-Shidyaq, *Leg Over Leg*, ed. and trans. Humphrey Davies, 4 vols. (New York: NYU Press, 2013).
37. Fawwaz Traboulsi, 'Ahmad Faris al-Shidyaq (1804–87): The Quest for Another Modernity', in *Arabic Thought Beyond the Liberal Age: Towards an Intellectual History of the Nahda*, ed. Jens Hanssen and Max Weiss (Cambridge: Cambridge University Press, 2016).
38. Rebecca C. Johnson, 'Foreword', in *Leg Over Leg*, by Ahmad Faris al-Shidyaq, ed. and trans. Humphrey Davies, vol. 1 (New York: NYU Press, 2013), xxiv.
39. Buṭrus al-Bustānī, *Nafīr Sūrīyā* [The Clarion of Syria] (Beirut: Dār al-Fikr, 1990 [1861]), *Waṭanīya* V, 27–28, cited and translated in Stephen Sheehi, 'Butrus al-Bustani: Syria's Ideologue of the Age', in *The Origins of Syrian Nationhood: Histories, Pioneers and Identity*, ed. Adel Beshara (Abingdon: Routledge, 2011), 72.
40. *Ḥadīqat al-Akhbār*, 29 May 1866, cited and translated in Zachs, *The Making of a Syrian Identity*, 166.
41. Ami Ayalon, *The Press in the Arab Middle East: A History* (Oxford: Oxford University Press, 1995), 31–39; Ami Ayalon, 'The Syrian Educated Elite and the Literary Nahda', in *Ottoman Reform and Muslim Regeneration*, ed. Buṭ rus Abū Mannah and Itzchak Weismann (London: I.B. Tauris, 2005).
42. Marwa Elshakry, *Reading Darwin in Arabic, 1860–1950* (Chicago: University of Chicago Press, 2014); Fruma Zachs and Sharon Halevi, *Gendering Culture in Greater Syria: Intellectuals and Ideology in the Late Ottoman Period* (London: I.B. Tauris, 2014).
43. Hourani, *Arabic Thought in the Liberal Age 1798–1939*, 103–92.
44. Although the term Salafi was coined to describe this modernizing current (in reference to turning back to the origins of Islam) in the early twentieth century, within a few decades Salafism had largely come to be identified with more puritanical movements in Islam

such as Wahhabism. Henri Lauzière, *The Making of Salafism: Islamic Reform in the Twentieth Century* (New York: Columbia University Press, 2015).

45. Kayali, *Arabs and Young Turks*, 41–45.
46. ʿAbd al-Raḥmān al-Kawākibī, *Umm al-Qurā: wa-huwa ḍabṭ Mufāwaḍ āṭ wa-Muqarrarāt Muʾtamar al-Nahḍa al-Islāmīya al-munʿaqid fī Makka al-Mukarrama Sanat 1316* [The Mother of Villages: Proceedings of the First Conference on the Islamic Awakening Held in Holy Mecca in the year 1316] (Beirut: Dār al-Rāʾid al-ʿArabī, 1982).
47. Birgit Schaebler, 'From Urban Notables to "Noble Arabs": Shifting Discourses in the Emergence of Nationalism in the Arab East, 1910–1916', in *From the Syrian Land to the States of Syria and Lebanon*, ed. Thomas Philipp and Christoph Schumann (Würzburg: Ergon Verlag, 2004).
48. Ayalon, *The Press in the Arab Middle East*, 65.
49. Rashid Khalidi, *Palestinian Identity: The Construction of Modern National Consciousness* (New York: Columbia University Press, 2010), 80–82.
50. For an overview, see Kayali, *Arabs and Young Turks*, 82–96.
51. Kayali, 109–10.
52. Schaebler, 'From Urban Notables to "Noble Arabs"', 193.
53. ʿAbd al-Ghani al-ʾUraysi, cited in Asʿad Khalīl Dāghir, *Thawrat al-ʿArab: Muqaddimātuhā, Asbābuhā, Natāʾijuhā: al-Mulk fī al-ʿArab* [The Precursors, Causes and Results of the Arab Revolt: Sovereignty Among the Arabs] (Egypt: Maṭbaʿat al-Muqaṭṭam, 1916), 115.
54. Mustafa Aksakal, *The Ottoman Road to War in 1914: The Ottoman Empire and the First World War* (Cambridge: Cambridge University Press, 2008).
55. Letter from Cemal Pasha to Talat, Damascus, 7 August 1915, cited in M. Talha Çiçek, *War and State Formation in Syria: Cemal Pasha's Governorate During World War I, 1914–1917* (London: Routledge, 2014), 44, ft.24.
56. Çiçek, 51.
57. For an illustrative discussion of how the martyrs' hangings impacted previously loyal Ottoman citizens, see Khālid al-ʿAẓm, *Mudhakkirāt Khālid al-ʿAẓm* [The Memoirs of Khālid al-ʿAẓm], vol. 1 (Beirut: al-Dār al-Muttaḥida li'l-Nashr, 1973), 67–79.

58. Leila Tarazi Fawaz, *A Land of Aching Hearts: The Middle East in the Great War* (Cambridge: Harvard University Press, 2014), 243–50; Fruma Zachs, 'Transformations of a Memory of Tyranny in Syria: From Jamal Pasha to 'Id al-Shuhada', 1914–2000', *Middle Eastern Studies* 48, no. 1 (1 January 2012): 73–88.
59. One observer noted that more people fled than were conscripted into the army. al-'Aẓm, *Mudhakkirāt Khālid al-'Aẓm*, 1973, 1:75.
60. Fawaz, *A Land of Aching Hearts*, 81–120; Najwa al-Qattan, 'Safarbarlik: Ottoman Syria and the Great War', in *From the Syrian Land to the States of Syria and Lebanon*, ed. Thomas Philipp and Christoph Schumann (Würzburg: Ergon Verlag., 2004).
61. Tariq Tell, 'Guns, Gold, and Grain: War and Food Supply in the Making of Transjordan', in *War, Institutions, and Social Change in the Middle East*, ed. Steven Heydemann (Berkeley: University of California Press, 2000), 33–58.
62. William Ochsenwald, 'Ironic Origins: Arab Nationalism in the Hijaz, 1882–1914', in *The Origins of Arab Nationalism*, ed. Rashid Khalidi et al. (New York: Columbia University Press, 1991).
63. Eliezer Tauber, *The Arab Movements in World War I* (Abingdon: Frank Cass, 1993).
64. L. Schatkowski Schilcher, 'The Famine of 1915–1918 in Greater Syria', in *Problems of the Modern Middle East in Historical Perspective: Essays in Honour of Albert Hourani*, ed. John Spagnolo (Reading: Ithaca Press, 1996).
65. Khayrīya Qāsimīya, *Al-Ḥukūma al-'Arabīya fī Dimashq Bayna 1918–1920* [The Arab Government in Damascus] (Egypt: Dār al-Ma'ārif, 1971).
66. Qāsimīya, 62.
67. Michael Provence, *The Last Ottoman Generation and the Making of the Modern Middle East* (Cambridge: Cambridge University Press, 2017), 104.
68. Malcolm B. Russell, *The First Modern Arab State: Syria under Faysal, 1918–1920* (Minneapolis: Bibliotheca Islamica, 1985), 60–65.
69. Elizabeth F. Thompson, *How the West Stole Democracy from the Arabs: The Syrian Arab Congress of 1920 and the Destruction of its Historic Liberal-Islamic Alliance* (New York: Grove Press, 2020), 107–29.
70. Interview with *al-Fatat* member 'Izzat Darwaza, cited in Qāsimīya, *Al-Ḥukūma al-'Arabīya fī Dimashq*, 144.

71. James L. Gelvin, *Divided Loyalties: Nationalism and Mass Politics in Syria at the Close of Empire* (Berkeley: University of California Press, 1999), 86–137.
72. Eliezer Tauber, 'The Struggle for Dayr al-Zur: The Determination of Borders between Syria and Iraq', *International Journal of Middle East Studies* 23, no. 3 (1991): 361–85.
73. Papers of Muḥibb al-Khaṭīb, cited in Qāsimīya, *al-Ḥukūma al-'Arabīya fī Dimashq*, 165.
74. The precise boundaries of these territories were not demarcated. The congress included at least one representative from the northern coastal town of Antakya, although not from Cilicia proper.

3. FROM KINGDOM TO COLONIALISM, 1920–1927

1. Ḥasan al-Ḥakīm, *al-Wathā'iq al-Tārīkhīya al-Mu'alliqa bi'l-Qaḍīya al-Sūrīya fī al-'Ahdayn al-'Arabī al-Fayṣalī wa'l-Intidābī al-Faransī 1915–1946* [Historical Documents Related to the Syrian Question in the Faysal-Arab and French Mandate Eras] (Beirut: Dār Ṣādir, 1974), 194–213; Russell, *The First Modern Arab State*, 149; Elizabeth F. Thompson, 'Rashid Rida and the 1920 Syrian-Arab Constitution: How the French Undermined Islamic Liberalism', in *The Routledge Handbook of the History of the Middle East Mandates*, ed. Cyrus Schayegh and Andrew Arsan (Abingdon: Routledge, 2015).
2. Qāsimīya, *Al-Ḥukūma al-'Arabīya fī Dimashq*, 231–32.
3. Gelvin, *Divided Loyalties*; Russell, *The First Modern Arab State*, 142–47.
4. Gelvin, *Divided Loyalties*, 134.
5. Stefan Winter, *A History of the 'Alawis: From Medieval Aleppo to the Turkish Republic* (Princeton: Princeton University Press, 2016), 248.
6. Shīblīr, *Intifādāt Jabal al-Durūz*, 187–88.
7. Leland Barrows, 'The Impact of Empire on the French Armed Forces, 1830–1920', in *Double Impact: France and Africa in the Age of Imperialism*, ed. G. Wesley Johnson (Westport, Greenwood Press, 1985); Benjamin Claude Brower, *A Desert Named Peace: The Violence of France's Empire in the Algerian Sahara, 1844–1902* (Columbia University Press, 2011).
8. Jean Gottmann, 'Bugeaud, Galliéni, Lyautey: The Development of French Colonial Warfare', in *Makers of Modern Strategy: Military Thought*

from Machiavelli to Hitler, ed. Edward Mead Earle (Princeton: Princeton University Press, 1943).

9. Edmund Burke III, *The Ethnographic State: France and the Invention of Moroccan Islam* (Oakland: University of California Press, 2014).
10. Janet L. Abu-Lughod, *Rabat: Urban Apartheid in Morocco* (Princeton: Princeton University Press, 1980); Gwendolyn Wright, *The Politics of Design in French Colonial Urbanism* (Chicago: University of Chicago Press, 1991).
11. Edmund Burke III, 'A Comparative View of French Native Policy in Morocco and Syria, 1912–1925', *Middle Eastern Studies* 9, no. 2 (1973): 179.
12. Henri Gouraud, *La France en Syrie* ([Corbeil]: [Imp. Crété], 1922).
13. Abel Jean Ernest Clément-Grandcourt, *Au Levant: histoires de brigands, histoires vraies* (Paris: Attinger, 1936), 30.
14. Georges Catroux, *Deux missions en Moyen-Orient* (Paris: Plon, 1958), 44–50; al-Aṭrash, *Aḥdāth al-Thawra al-Sūrīya al-Kubrā*, 59–60.
15. Victor Müller, *En Syrie avec les Bédouins: les tribus du désert* (Paris: Libraire Ernest Leroux, 1931).
16. Centre des Archives Diplomatiques, Nantes, versement 1 (henceforth CADN) 552, 'Note au sujet de la Politique Bédouine', 3 April 1925.
17. CADN 1536, 'Note au sujet de la question bédouine dans les Etats sous Mandats français', n.d. (c.1930).
18. Philip S. Khoury, *Syria and the French Mandate: The Politics of Arab Nationalism, 1920–1945* (Princeton: Princeton University Press, 1987), 127–39.
19. Roger Owen, *State, Power and Politics in the Making of the Modern Middle East*, 3rd ed. (London: Routledge, 2004), 10–11.
20. Jean-David Mizrahi, *Genèse de l'État mandataire: service des renseignements et bandes armées en Syrie et au Liban dans les années 1920* (Paris: Publications de la Sorbonne, 2003).
21. Munīr al-Rayyis, *Al-Kitāb al-Dhahabī li'l-Thawrāt al-Waṭanīya fi al-Mashriq al-'Arabī* [The Golden Book of National Revolutions in the Arab East], vol. 2 (Damascus: Matabi' Alif Bā', 1969), 74.
22. al-Aṭrash, *Aḥdāth al-Thawra al-Sūrīya al-Kubrā*, 73–74; MAE 237, 'Rapport Daclin', 7 September 1926, 234.
23. Weber, *Peasants into Frenchmen*.
24. MAE 234, Carbillet's evidence to the Daclin inquiry, cited in Lenka Bokova, 'La Révolution Française Dans le Discours de l'insurrection

Syrienne Contre le Mandat Français (1925–1927)', *Revue du Monde Musulman et de la Méditerrannée* 51–53 (1989): 207–17.

25. Provence describes the idea of Druze feudalism as 'a mirage, a convincing and durable fake, invented to justify and render coherent a colonial project of domination'. Provence, *The Great Syrian Revolt and the Rise of Arab Nationalism*, 29.
26. MAE 237, 'Rapport Daclin'; MAE 239, 'French Translation of Druze Petition', 27 June 1925; al-Aṭrash, *Aḥdāth al-Thawra al-Sūrīya al-Kubrā*, 78; 'Abd al-Raḥmān Shahbandar, *al-Thawra al-Sūrīya al-Waṭanīya: Mudhakkirāt* [The Patriotic Syrian Revolt: Memoirs] (Damascus: Wizārat al-Thaqāfa, 1993).
27. Gabriel Carbillet, *Au Djebel Druse: choses vues et vécues* (Paris: Éditions Argo, 1929), 77–78.
28. Ḥannā Abī Rāshid, *Jabal al-Durūz* [The Druze Mountain] (Cairo: n.p., 1925), 252 cited in Provence, *The Great Syrian Revolt*, 52–53.
29. Charles de Gaulle et al., *Histoire des troupes du Levant* (Paris: Impr. nationale, 1931), 23–24; al-Rayyis, *Al-Kitāb al-Dhahabī*, 1969, 2:151–65; Charles Joseph Édouard Andréa, *La Révolte Druze et l'Insurrection de Damas, 1925–1926.* (Paris: Payot, 1937), 53.
30. Provence, *The Great Syrian Revolt and the Rise of Arab Nationalism*, 70–71.
31. Numerous former military officers joined the ranks of the rebels: Sultan Pasha recalls the names of 23 of them in his memoirs. al-Aṭrash, *Aḥdāth al-Thawra al-Sūrīya al-Kubrā*, 95.
32. For a wealth of fascinating detail about these social connections, see Provence, *The Great Syrian Revolt and the Rise of Arab Nationalism*, 42.
33. Munīr al-Rayyis, *Al-Kitāb al-Dhahabī li'l-Thawrāt al-Waṭanīya fī al-Mashriq al-'Arabī* [The Golden Book of National Revolutions in the Arab East], vol. 3 (Damascus: Matabi' Alif Bā', 1977), 251–66.
34. al-Lajna al-Tanfīdhīya li'l-Mu'tamar al-Sūrī al-Falasṭīnī, *Al-Qadīya al-Surīya: Maẓālim al-Faransīyīn wa Fadā'i'uhum* [The Syrian Question: French Oppression and Atrocities] (Cairo: al-Matba'a al-'Arabīya bi-Miṣr, 1926).
35. Fawzi al-Qāwuqjī, *Mudhakkirāt Fawzī al-Qāwuqjī, 1912–1932* (Beirut: Dār al-Quds, 1975), 82–92.
36. Alice Poulleau, *À Damas sous les bombes: journal d'une Française pendant la révolte syrienne (1924–1926)* (Yvetot: Bretteville, 1926), 76.

37. CADN 1816, 'Compte rendu de la journée du 14 octobre 1925', Damascus.
38. SHAT 4H151, 'Compte rendu des opérations aériennes', 19–21 October 1925.
39. Khoury, *Syria and the French Mandate*, 178.
40. CADN 2389, Gamelin to High Commissioner, May 1926.
41. Da'd al-Ḥakīm, ed., *Ṣafaḥāt min Ḥayāt Nazīh Mu'ayyad al-'Aẓm* [Pages from the Life of Nazīh Mu'ayyad al-'Aẓm] (Damascus: Wizārat al-Thaqāfa, 2006), 45; 'Adnān 'Aṭṭār, *Thawrat al-Ḥurrīya fī al-Minṭaqa al-Sādisa bi-Dimashq, 1925–1926: Wādī Baradā wa'l-Muhājirīn wa'l-Ṣaliḥīya bi-Qiyādat Sa'īd 'Akkāsh* [The Freedom Revolt in the Sixth Region of Damascus, 1925–26] (Damascus: Dār Sa'd al-Dīn, 1991), 19–21.
42. al-Rayyis, *Al-Kitāb al-Dhahabī*, 1969, 2:218–19.
43. Muḥammad Sa'īd al-' Āṣ, *Al-Tajārib al-Ḥarbīya fī Ḥurūb al-Thawra al-Sūrīya* [Military Experience in the Wars of the Syrian Revolt] (Beirut: Dār al-Fikr, 1990).
44. MAE281, Gamelin to Ministère de la Guerre, Beirut, 10 February 1926.
45. CADN 1704, Bulletins de Renseignements 250–252, 14–16 December 1925; al-Rayyis, *Al-Kitāb al-Dhahabī*, 1969, 2:328–29.
46. al-Rayyis, 2:286–87; Muḥammad Sa'īd al-'Āṣ, *Ṣafḥa min al-Ayyām al-Ḥamrā': Kitāb Yabḥath 'an al-Thawra al-Sūrīya wa-Tatawwurātihā. al-Waqā'i' al-Mustaqilla* [A Page from the Days of Blood: A Book on the Syrian Revolt and its Development: The Independent Facts] (Cairo: n.p., 1930), 40–41; al-Ḥakīm, *Ṣafaḥāt*, 34.
47. al-'As, *Ṣafḥa min al-Ayyām al-Hamra'*, 83; see also al-Aṭrash, *Aḥdāth al-Thawra al-Sūrīya al-Kubrā*, 212–13; Ẓāfir al-Qāsimī, *Wathā'iq Jadīda 'an al-Thawra al-Sūrīya al-Kubrā, 1925–1927* (Beirut: Dār al-Kitāb al-Jadīd, 1965), 259–62.
48. For a full discussion, see Daniel Neep, *Occupying Syria Under the French Mandate: Insurgency, Space and State Formation* (Cambridge: Cambridge University Press, 2012), 81–86.
49. 'Āṣ, *Ṣafḥa min al-Ayyām al-Ḥamrā'*, 146–47.
50. Neep, *Occupying Syria Under the French Mandate*, 117–29.
51. Andréa, *La Révolte Druze*, 82–84.
52. SHAT 4H157, Commandant le Génie des Troupes de Syrie to Capitaine Chef du Génie de Damas, Beirut, 11 February 1926.
53. Khoury, *Syria and the French Mandate*, 237.

4. LIBERAL NATIONALISM AND POPULAR POLITICS, 1927–1946

1. Edmond Rabbath, *Courte Histoire du Mandat en Syrie et au Liban* (n.p., n.d), 53, cited in Khoury, 248.
2. For a detailed discussion of the National Bloc membership, see Khoury, 248–62.
3. Khoury, 339.
4. The concept of *mise en valeur* was best articulated in a book by the former governor of Indochina and minister for the colonies during the first four years of the mandate: Albert Sarraut, *La Mise en Valeur des Colonies Françaises* (Paris: Payot, 1923).
5. James Long Whitaker, 'The Union of Demeter with Zeus: Agriculture and Politics in Modern Syria' (PhD University of Durham, 1996).
6. Youssef Helbaoui, *La Syrie: Mise en Valeur d'un Pays Sous-Developpé* (Paris: Librairie générale de droit et de jurisprudence, 1956), 62–65.
7. Geoffrey D. Schad, 'Colonialists, Industrialists, and Politicians: The Political Economy of Industrialization in Syria, 1920–1954' (PhD, Pennsylvania, University of Pennsylvania, 2001), 46–54.
8. Luṭfī al-Ḥaffār, *Dhikrayāt: Muntakhabāt min Khuṭab wa-Aḥādīth wa-Maqālāt* [Memoires: Selected Speeches, Anecdotes and Essays] (Damascus: Maṭābiʿ Ibn Zaydūn, 1954).
9. Khoury, *Syria and the French Mandate*, 282.
10. Meir Zamir, *Lebanon's Quest: The Search for a National Identity, 1926–39* (London: I.B. Tauris, 2000), 41.
11. Carolyn Gates, *Merchant Republic of Lebanon: Rise of an Open Economy* (London: I.B. Tauris, 1998).
12. Frank Peter, 'Dismemberment of Empire and Reconstitution of Regional Space: The Emergence of "National" Industries in Damascus between 1918 and 1946', in *The British and French Mandates in Comparative Perspectives*, ed. Nadine Méouchy and Peter Sluglett (Leiden: Brill, 2004).
13. For a definitive account, see Youssef Chaitani, *Post-Colonial Syria and Lebanon: The Decline of Arab Nationalism and the Triumph of the State* (London: I.B. Tauris, 2007).
14. Khoury, *Syria and the French Mandate*, 397–400.

15. Batatu, *Syria's Peasantry*, 6.
16. Benjamin Thomas White, *The Emergence of Minorities in the Middle East: The Politics of Community in French Mandate Syria* (Edinburgh: Edinburgh University Press, 2011), 131–43.
17. Munīr Sharīf, *al-Muslimūn al-'Alawīyūn: man hum wa-ayna hum* [The Alawi Muslims: Who and Where They Are] (Beirut: Mu'assasat al-Balāgh, 1994).
18. Giffe Yaffe-Schatzmann, 'Alawi Separatists and Unionists: The Events of 25 February 1936', *Middle Eastern Studies* 31, no. 1 (1995): 28–38.
19. CADN 571, 'Rapport sur la situation des Réfugiés en Haute Jézireh en Octobre 1927', 6 January 1928.
20. CADN 550, Lt Dilleman, 'Etude du développement économique du bassin supérieur du Djagh-Djagh depuis l'occupation française 1926–1931', al-Qamisli, October 1931.
21. Khoury, *Syria and the French Mandate*, 495.
22. Keith D. Watenpaugh, '"Creating Phantoms": Zaki al-Arsuzi, the Alexandretta Crisis, and the Formation of Modern Arab Nationalism in Syria', *International Journal of Middle East Studies* 28, no. 3 (1996): 363–89.
23. Majid Khadduri, 'The Alexandretta Dispute', *The American Journal of International Law* 39, no. 3 (1945): 406–25, https://doi.org/10.2307/2193522.
24. Khoury, *Syria and the French Mandate*, 506.
25. Khoury, 588–89.
26. Markaz al-Wathā'iq al-Tārīkhīya [Centre for Historical Documentation] (henceforth MWT), Damascus; 'Events' 17: Declaration from General Catroux in the name of General de Gaulle, n.d. (in Arabic). Dropped over al-Nabak by a British aeroplane at 1800 hours on 8 June 1941, along with a pamphlet with a statement from the British ambassador in Cairo.
27. A. B. Gaunson, *The Anglo-French Clash in Lebanon and Syria, 1940–45* (New York: St. Martin's Press, 1987), 90.
28. Sir Alexander Gibb, *The Economic Development of Syria* (London: Knapp, Drewett and Sons, 1947), 28.
29. Robert Vitalis and Steven Heydemann, 'War, Keynesianism, and Colonialism: Explaining State-Market Relations in the Postwar Middle East', in *War, Institutions, and Social Change in the Middle East*, ed.

Steven Heydemann (Berkeley: University of California Press, 2000), 120–24.

30. Martin W. Wilmington, *The Middle East Supply Centre*, 1st ed. (Albany: State University of New York Press, 1971).
31. FO371/45566/E3490, 45568/E3626 and FO954/xv.4, Shone to Eden, 30 May 1945, cited in Gaunson, *The Anglo-French Clash in Lebanon and Syria, 1940–45*, 174.
32. Meir Zamir, *The Secret Anglo-French War in the Middle East: Intelligence and Decolonization, 1940–1948* (London: Routledge, 2014), 127–28.

5. LIBERALISM IMPLODES, 1946–1949

1. Naṣūḥ Bābīl, *Ṣiḥāfa wa-Siyāsa: Sūrīya fi'l-Qarn al-'Ishrīn* [Press and Politics: Syria in the 20th Century] (London: Riyad El-Rayyis, 1987), 248.
2. 'Mā rāḥ yufīdna illā ijtihadnā, hiya al-ḥurrīya ḥayāt bilādna!' Bābīl, 249.
3. al-Rayyis, *Al-Kitāb al-Dhahabī*, 1977, 3:405.
4. The full text of the speech can be found in Shukrī al-Quwwatlī, *Shukrī al-Quwwatlī yukhāṭib Ummatahu: Mukhtarāt min Khuṭabihi wa Bayānātihi* [Shukrī al-Quwwatlī Addresses His Nation: Selections from His Speeches and Declarations] (Damascus: Maṭba'at al-Fujayra al-Waṭanīya wa-Maktabātiha, 2001), 98–118.
5. *Al-Barada*, 5–6 June 1946.
6. al-Rayyis, *Al-Kitāb al-Dhahabī*, 1977, 3:405.
7. Muḥammad Kurd 'Alī, *al-Mudhakkirāt* [Memoirs], vol. 4 (Damascus: Maṭba'at al-Taraqqī, 1951), 906–9.
8. Khālid al-'Aẓm, *Mudhakkirāt Khālid al-'Aẓm* [The Memoirs of Khālid al-'Aẓm], vol. 2 (Beirut: al-Dār al-Muttaḥida li'l-Nashr, 1973), 185.
9. Quwwatli frequently received his clients in the presidential palace, where they would lobby the president to use his position to grant export licences or influence decisions over government regulation to their advantage. al-Rayyis, *Al-Kitāb al-Dhahabī*, 1977, 3:482–83.
10. Kurd 'Alī, *al-Mudhakkirāt*, 4:906–9.
11. CADN 1703, Bulletin de Renseignement 67, 30 April 1925.
12. Weulersse, *Paysans de Syrie et Du Proche Orient*, 278.
13. Muḥammad Ma'rūf, *Ayyām 'Ishtuhā, 1949–1969: al-Inqilābāt al-'Askarīya wa-Asrāruhā fi Sūrīya* [Days I Lived: 1949–1969: Military Coups and

Their Secrets in Syria] (Beirut: Riyāḍ al-Rayyis li'l-Kutub wa'l-Nashr, 2003), 63–67; See also Hāshim 'Uthmān, *al-Maḥākamāt al-Siyāsīya fī Sūrīya* [Political Trials in Syria] (Beirut: Riyāḍ al-Rayyis li'l-Kutub wa' l-Nashr, 2004), 137–42; Joshua M. Landis, 'Nationalism and the Politics of Za'ama: The Collapse of Republican Syria, 1945–1949' (PhD, Princeton University, 1997), 162–63.

14. *Al-Jundi* 6 (5 November 1946), 8.
15. 'Uthmān, *al-Maḥākamāt al-siyāsīya*, 117–35.
16. Landis, 'Nationalism and the Politics of Za'ama', 157.
17. Bābīl, *Ṣiḥāfa wa-Siyāsa: Sūrīya fī'l-Qarn al-'Ishrīn* [Press and Politics: Syria in the 20th Century], 256.
18. 'Syria Weekly Summary No. 5', 4 February 1947, UK Foreign Office 501/1.
19. Bābīl, *Ṣiḥāfa wa-Siyāsa: Sūrīya fī'l-Qarn al-'Ishrīn* [Press and Politics: Syria in the 20th Century], 283.
20. Foreign Office Research Department, 'The Greater Syria Movement', 10 January 1948, 9–12, FO501/2.
21. Mary Christina Wilson, *King Abdullah, Britain and the Making of Jordan* (Cambridge: Cambridge University Press, 1987), 157.
22. US National Archive (USNA), Memminger (Damascus) 890D/8-2047 (20 August 1947) and USNA 809D.114 (3 Sept 1947), cited in Landis, 'Nationalism and the Politics of Za'ama', 79–80.
23. FO 371/52867 and FO 371/62202, cited in Wilson, *King Abdullah, Britain and the Making of Jordan*, 158, ft.29.
24. On the drugs economy of the interwar Levant, see Cyrus Schayegh, 'The Many Worlds of 'Abud Yasin; or, What Narcotics Trafficking in the Interwar Middle East Can Tell Us About Territorialization', *The American Historical Review* 116, no. 2 (1 April 2011): 273–306.
25. FO371/68403/E300, cited in Landis, 'Nationalism and the Politics of Za'ama', 86.
26. 'Ādil Arslān, *Mudhakkirāt al-Amīr 'Ādil Arslān: al-Mustadrak, 1948* [The Memoirs of Amīr Ādil Arslān: The 1948 Appendix], ed. Yūsuf Ībish (Beirut: al-Dār al-Taqaddumīya, 1994), 115, 121–22.
27. 'The Greater Syria Movement', 10 January 1948, 12, FO501/2.
28. Joshua Landis, 'Syria and the Palestine War: Fighting King 'Abdullah's "Greater Syria Plan"', in *The War for Palestine: Rewriting the History of*

1948, ed. Eugene Rogan (Cambridge: Cambridge University Press, 2001), 181.

29. Ibrahīm Ghāzī, *Nash'at al-Shurṭa wa-Tārīkhuha fī Surīya* [The Evolution of the Police and Its History in Syria] (Damascus: Dār al-'Ilm al-Ḥadīth, 1999).
30. MWT, State Documents: Gendarmerie 54/45/16, Harant Mānūlīyān, 'Al-Hāla al-Rūḥīya wa'l-Inḍibāt wa'l-Tanẓīm 1945' [The State of Morale, Discipline and Organization], Damascus, 5 July 1946.
31. Interview with Ahmad Sharabati, Beirut, 1 June 1970, cited in Michael Van Dusen, 'Intra- and Inter-Generational Conflict in the Syrian Army' (PhD, Johns Hopkins University, 1971), 44, ft.3.
32. Gordon Torrey, *Syrian Politics and the Military, 1945–1958* (Columbus: Ohio State University Press, 1964), 104.
33. Ma'rūf, *Ayyām 'Ishtuhā, 1949–1969: al-Inqilābāt al-'Askarīya wa-Asrāruhā fī Sūrīya* [Days I Lived: 1949–1969: Military Coups and Their Secrets in Syria], 79.
34. Landis, 'Syria and the Palestine War: Fighting King 'Abdullah's "Greater Syria Plan"', 194.
35. Avi Shlaim, *Collusion Across the Jordan: King Abdullah, the Zionist Movement and the Partition of Palestine* (Oxford: Clarendon Press, 1988).
36. An estimated 2,500 to 4,500 Syrian troops entered Palestine in May 1948: Landis, 'Syria and the Palestine War: Fighting King 'Abdullah's "Greater Syria Plan"', 198.
37. Quwwatli's right-hand man Adil Arslan reported several instances of lax discipline, mechanical failure, and corruption in the Syrian army. See, for example, Arslān, *Mudhakkirāt al-Amīr 'Ādil Arslān 1948*, 126–27, 148.
38. Arslān, 206.
39. Arslān, 218.
40. Torrey notes, 'While the exact cause [of Sharabati's] resignation has never been divulged, there is reason to believe that his resignation arose out of differences of military policy and in protest to corruption in army procurement.' Torrey, *Syrian Politics and the Military, 1945–1958*, 106; Arslān, on the other hand, notes that Sharabati was said to have purchased twice as many Egyptian blankets as were needed by the army at a low price, imported them into Syria without paying customs duties and then sold the surplus on the free market. Sharabati

also allegedly authorized American cigarettes to be imported for the Syrian army for nearly double their regular price. Arslān also reports that he had been told by Nazih al-Azmah, a prominent member of the National Party, that Quwwatli had warned him against speaking openly in front of Sharabati, who was an 'English spy'. Arslān, *Mudhakkirāt al-Amīr 'Ādil Arslān 1948*, 125, 163.

41. Torrey, *Syrian Politics and the Military, 1945–1958*, 110.
42. Many of the weapons and supplies had been procured from a Syrian company called al-Khumasiya al-Sughra. al-'Aẓm, *Mudhakkirāt Khālid al-'Aẓm*, 1973, 2:182.
43. Patrick Seale, *The Struggle for Syria: A Study of Post-War Arab Politics, 1945–1958* (London: I.B. Tauris, 1986), 42.
44. Nadhīr Fanṣah, *Ayyām Ḥusnī al-Za'īm: 137 Yawman Hazzat Sūriyā [The Times of Husni al-Za'im: 137 Days That Shook Syria]* (Beirut: Dār al-Āfāq al-Jadīda, 1982), 17–22.
45. Fanṣah, 16; al-'Aẓm, *Mudhakkirāt Khālid al-'Aẓm*, 1973, 2:184.
46. Za'im had discussed his plans for a coup in considerable detail with a member of the US Legation in Damascus on several occasions and had mentioned his plans obliquely to both the British and the French. There are no grounds to suggest, contrary to popular belief, that this coup was financed or inspired by the US, although Za'im was certainly encouraged by his American interlocutor. For a detailed discussion of the historical evidence, see Itamar Rabinovich, *The View from Damascus: State, Political Community and Foreign Relations in Twentieth-Century Syria* (Berkeley: University of California Press, 2008), 201–8; Andrew Rathmell, *Secret War in the Middle East: The Covert Struggle for Syria, 1949–1961*, 2nd ed. (London: I.B. Tauris, 2013), 36–44.
47. al-'Aẓm, *Mudhakkirāt Khālid al-'Aẓm*, 1973, 2:186–87; News of Asali's speeches played a key role in rallying lower-ranking officers to the cause of the coup, even among those who were not keen supporters of Za'im personally. Ma'rūf, *Ayyām 'Ishtuhā, 1949–1969: al-Inqilābāt al-'Askarīya wa-Asrāruhā fī Sūrīya* [Days I Lived: 1949–1969: Military Coups and Their Secrets in Syria], 86.
48. Fanṣah, *Ayyām Ḥusnī al-Za'īm*, 22; Torrey, *Syrian Politics and the Military, 1945–1958*, 122; Prime Minister Khalid al-Azm, who was present at the meeting, recalls that Quwwatli responded to Za'im's demands

coolly, but without mocking him. al-'Aẓm, *Mudhakkirāt Khālid al-'Aẓm*, 1973, 2:189.

49. Fanṣah, *Ayyām Ḥusnī al-Za'īm*, 21.
50. The full text of the communiqué, Balāgh Raqm 1, can be found in Fanṣah, 8.
51. Fanṣah, 33.
52. The unification was decreed by Legislative Order 11 of 11 April 1949. Lt Akram Shaykhū, 'Al-Darak wa'l-Jaysh Silāḥān li-yuttahidā bi'l-Salām' [The Gendarmerie and the Army Are Two Weapons to Be United in Peace], *al-Jundī* 56, 15 July 1949.
53. Van Dusen, 'Intra- and Inter-Generational Conflict in the Syrian Army', 123–24.
54. Za'im proved remarkably pragmatic when negotiating with Israel, going as far as offering to meet face-to-face with President David Ben-Gurion, which would have implied Syrian recognition of Israel. Za'im also expressed willingness to compromise over territory taken in the 1948 war and to resettle as many as a quarter of a million Palestinian refugees inside Syria. Za'im's quid pro quo was significant military assistance and development aid from the USA. In the event, Ben-Gurion refused to meet Za'im, while Syrian Foreign Minister Adil Arslan (along with most of the officer corps) was resolutely opposed to any hint of normalization with Israel.
55. For detailed accounts of these diplomatic manoeuvres, see Seale, *The Struggle for Syria*, 46–57; Rathmell, *Secret War in the Middle East*, 26–30.
56. The Syrian University was renamed the University of Damascus in 1958, when the country's second university was founded in Aleppo.
57. Fanṣah, *Ayyām Ḥusnī al-Za'īm*, 60–63.
58. Rabinovich, *The View from Damascus*, 187–225; Avi Shlaim, 'Husni Za'im and the Plan to Resettle Palestinian Refugees in Syria', *Journal of Palestine Studies* 15, no. 4 (1986): 68–80.
59. Broadmead to Bevin, 'Conversation with Colonel Za'im', Damascus, 23 May 1949, FO501/3.
60. The publication said that Za'im could only be a '*bahlawān min alttirāz al-awwal*', or a foreign agent, or a dupe. Fanṣah, *Ayyām Ḥusnī al-Za'īm*, 44.

61. Broadmead to Bevin, 'New Regime in Syria', Damascus, 25 April 1949. FO501/3.
62. Broadmead to Bevin, 'Syrian Press and Radio: Changes following Colonel Za'im's "Coup d'Éxtat"', 18 April 1949. FO501/3.
63. Seale, *The Struggle for Syria*, 64–72.
64. Fanṣah, *Ayyām Ḥusnī al-Za'īm*, 82.
65. Ma'rūf, *Ayyām 'Ishtuhā, 1949–1969: al-Inqilābāt al-'Askarīya wa-Asrāruhā fī Sūrīya* [Days I Lived: 1949–1969: Military Coups and Their Secrets in Syria], 119–21.
66. Za'im's government had been pursuing the SSNP across Syria and had investigated Druze villages near Jabal al-Shaykh on suspicion of harbouring party members. al-'Aẓm, *Mudhakkirāt Khālid al-'Aẓm*, 1973, 2:859.
67. Ma'rūf, *Ayyām 'Ishtuhā, 1949–1969: al-Inqilābāt al-'Askarīya wa-Asrāruhā fī Sūrīya* [Days I Lived: 1949-1969: Military Coups and their Secrets in Syria], 122; however, another of the conspirators, Fadl Allah, asserts in his memoirs that the loyalty of Za'im's Circassian guard was obtained through bribery. Abū Manṣūr Faḍl Allāh, *A'āṣīr: Mudhakkirāt 'an Khafāyā al-Inqilābāt al-Sūrīya al-Arba'a, Katabahā Shāhid 'Iyān Ashama fī Takhṭīṭ al-A'māl al-Inqilābīya wa-fī Tanfīdhihā: Ḥaqā'iq wa-Wathā'iq wa-Asrār Lam Tunshar Ba'd* [Storms: Memoirs of the Background to the Four Syrian Coups, Written by an Eye Witness Who Participated in Planning and Implementing the Putsch Action: Facts, Documents and Secrets That Have Not yet Been Published] (Beirut?; n.p., 1959).
68. This was despite an initial agreement among the conspirators that they would retreat to the safety of the Jabal al-Duruz if the coup failed, as Hinnawi had reportedly agreed with Hasan al-Atrash Faḍl Allāh, *A'āṣīr*, 81–82.
69. Abū 'Assāf Amīn, *Dhikrayātī* [My Memories] ([Damascus]: al-Dār al-Waṭanīya al-Jadīda, 1996), 240–43; Ma'rūf, *Ayyām 'Ishtuhā, 1949–1969: al-Inqilābāt al-'Askarīya wa-Asrāruhā fī Sūrīya* [Days I Lived: 1949–1969: Military Coups and Their Secrets in Syria], 126–27.
70. Faḍl Allāh, *A'āṣīr*, 76.
71. 'Don't be afraid, they won't kill us. It just isn't possible.' Faḍl Allāh, 76.

72. Ma'rūf, *Ayyām 'Ishtuhā, 1949–1969: al-Inqilābāt al-'Askarīya wa-Asrāruhā fī Sūrīya* [Days I Lived: 1949–1969: Military Coups and Their Secrets in Syria], 135.
73. al-'Aẓm, *Mudhakkirāt Khālid al-'Aẓm*, 1973, 2:897.

6. MILITARY REFORM, 1949–1954

1. Faḍl Allāh, *A'āṣīr*, 99–105; Amīn, *Dhikrayātī* [My Memories], 286–87.
2. Two military policemen were reportedly killed during the coup. Ma'rūf, *Ayyām 'Ishtuhā, 1949–1969: al-Inqilābāt al-'Askarīya wa-Asrāruhā fī Sūrīya* [Days I Lived: 1949–1969: Military Coups and Their Secrets in Syria], 184.
3. Hinnawi was imprisoned for 11 months and then exiled to Lebanon. Ma'rūf, 190.
4. Bābīl, *Ṣiḥāfa wa-Siyāsa: Sūrīya fī'l-Qarn al-'Ishrīn* [Press and Politics: Syria in the 20th Century], 386.
5. 'Abd Allāh Fikrī al-Khānī, *Sūrīya bayna al-Dīmuqrāṭīya wa'l-Ḥukm al-Fardī: 'Ashr Sanawāt fī'l-Amāna al-'Āmma li-Ri'āsat al-Jumhūrīya, 1948–1958* [Syria between Democracy and Despotism: Ten Years in the General Secretariat of the Presidency of the Republic] (Beirut: Dār al-Nafā'is, 2004), 93.
6. Majid Khadduri, 'Constitutional Development in Syria: With Emphasis on the Constitution of 1950', *Middle East Journal* 5, no. 4 (1951): 137–60.
7. The full text of the 1950 Constitution can be found in Yūsuf Quzmakhūrī, *Al-Dasātīr fī al-'Ālam al-'Arabī: Nuṣūṣ wa-Ta'dīlāt: 1839–1987* [Constitutions in the Arab World: Texts and Amendments] (Beirut: Dār al-Ḥamrā', 1989), 259–71.
8. Ajlani's accusation of army involvement in smuggling was made even more sensitive given allegations that Shishakli's brother Salah, an officer in the Desert Force, was implicated in smuggling hashish and other contraband from Turkey through Syria to Jordan, where it allegedly found its way into the hands of King Abdullah's son Nayif. Even if Ajlani were not aware of these rumours, Shishakli himself certainly was. Amīn, *Dhikrayātī* [My Memories], 305.
9. Yezid Sayigh, *Armed Struggle and the Search for State: The Palestinian National Movement, 1949–1993* (Oxford: Oxford University Press, 1997);

for an account of the trial of Ajlani and the other alleged conspirators, see 'Uthmān, *al-Maḥākamāt al-siyāsīya*, 177–94.

10. Torrey, *Syrian Politics and the Military, 1945–1958*, 185; a parliamentary committee convened to investigate the legality of the trial concluded that, as Ajlani had been arrested during a recess of the Chamber of Deputies, parliamentary immunity did not apply. 'Uthmān, *al-Maḥākamāt al-siyāsīya*, 161.
11. Barazi also criticized cabinet ministers for simply implementing the will of the army, disparaging them as paid civil servants rather than elected members of the government. Bābīl, *Ṣiḥāfa wa-Siyāsa: Sūrīya fī'l-Qarn al-'Ishrīn* [Press and Politics: Syria in the 20th Century], 419.
12. Amīn, *Dhikrayātī* [My Memories], 317.
13. FO501/5, 'Annual Political Review of Syria, 1950', 4.
14. Interview with Hasan al-Hakim, 10 November 1960, cited in Seale, *The Struggle for Syria*, 310.
15. For a full account, see Seale, 111–15.
16. Bābīl, *Ṣiḥāfa wa-Siyāsa: Sūrīya fī'l-Qarn al-'Ishrīn* [Press and Politics: Syria in the 20th Century], 421.
17. *Alif Bā'*, 30 November 1951, 2.
18. E.g. Sami M. Moubayed, *Damascus Between Democracy and Dictatorship* (Lanham: University Press of America, 2000).
19. Amīn, *Dhikrayātī* [My Memories], 367; *Alif Bā'*, 5 December 1951.
20. *Alif Bā'*, 30 November 1951.
21. *Al-Ayyām*, 11 December 1951, 2.
22. *Alif Bā'*, 31 January 1951, 1.
23. FO501/6, Montagu-Pollack to Eden, 10 March 1952, 6; FO501/6, Eden to Montagu-Pollack, 3 April 1952, 11.
24. FO501/6, Montagu-Pollack to Eden, 21 March 1952, 8.
25. Seale, *The Struggle for Syria*, 121.
26. For Hawrani's biography and political career, Akram al-Ḥawrānī, *Mudhakkirāt Akram al-Ḥawrānī* [The Memoirs of Akram al-Hawrani], 4 vols. (Cairo: Maktabat Madbūlī, 1999); Batatu, *Syria's Peasantry*, 124–30; 'Izz al-Dīn Diyāb, *Akram al-Ḥawrānī Kamā A'rifuhi* [Akram al-Hawrani as I Know Him] (Beirut: Bīsān, 1998); Hānī Khayyir, *Akram al-Ḥawrānī bayna al-Tanaqqulāt al-Siyāsīya wa'l-Inqilābāt al-'Askarīya* [Akram al-Ḥawrānī between Political Positions and Military Coups]

(Damascus: Tawzī' Maktabat al-Sharq al-Jadīd, 1996); Ḥamdān Ḥamdān, *Akram al-Ḥawrānī: Rajul li'l-Tārīkh* [Akram al-Hawrani: A Man for History] (Beirut: Baysān li'l-Nashr wa-al-Tawzī', 1996); Jonathan P. Owen, 'Akram Al-Hourani: A Study of Syrian Politics, 1943–1954' (PhD, Johns Hopkins University, 1992).

27. Al-'Ilm, 18 September 1951, cited in Khayyir, *Akram al-Ḥawrānī*, 63.
28. Batatu, *Syria's Peasantry*, 128.
29. al-Khānī, *Sūrīya bayna al-Dīmuqrāṭīya w'al-Ḥukm al-Fard*, 91.
30. MWT, Wizārat al-Difā', Legislative Decree 46, 6 January 1952.
31. *Alif Bā'*, 14 December 1951, 2.
32. Iliya Harik, 'The Single Party as a Subordinate Movement: The Case of Egypt', *World Politics* 26, no. 1 (1973): 80–105.
33. al-Khānī, *Sūrīya bayna al-Dīmuqrāṭīya w'al-Ḥukm al-Fard*, 103.
34. For the full text of the 1953 Constitution, see Quzmakhūrī, *Al-Dasātīr fī al-'Ālam al-'Arabī*, 259–71; an English translation can be found in Mary Louise Manley, 'The Syrian Constitution of 1953', *Middle East Journal* 7, no. 4 (1953): 520–21.
35. Hānī Khayyir, *Adīb al-Shīshaklī: Ṣāḥib al-Inqilāb al-Thālith fī Sūrīyā: al-Bidāya wa'l-Nihāya* [Adīb al-Shīshaklī, Leader of the Third Coup in Syria: The Beginning and the End] (Damascus: Maktab al-Fayhā', 1994), 90.
36. Torrey, *Syrian Politics and the Military, 1945–1958*, 218.
37. MWT, Wizārat al-Difā' 55, Legislative Decree 62, 14 January 1952.
38. Seale, *The Struggle for Syria*, 135.
39. *Al-Shurṭa wa'l-Amn al-'Āmm*, August 1953, 6–7.
40. Al-Sūrī al-Jadīd, 5 July 1930, cited in Torrey, *Syrian Politics and the Military, 1945–1958*, 230.
41. Seale, *The Struggle for Syria*, 133–34.
42. Joshua Landis, 'Shishakli and the Druzes: Integration and Intransigeance', in *The Syrian Land: Processes of Integration and Fragmentation*, ed. Thomas Philipp and Birgit Schäbler (Stuttgart: Franz Steiner Verlag, 1998), 369–96.
43. Torrey, *Syrian Politics and the Military, 1945–1958*, 234; Landis, 'Shishakli and the Druzes'; Rathmell, *Secret War in the Middle East*, 85.
44. This narrative account draws on Abu Assaf, whose account is the only source that discusses these events in detail. Amīn, *Dhikrayātī*

[My Memories]; see also Faḍl Allāh, *A'āṣīr*, 110–11; Landis, 'Shishakli and the Druzes'.

45. FO501/8, Gardener to Eden, 'The Recent Disturbances in Syria and Their Effect upon the Position of the Present Regime', 9 February 1954.
46. Amīn, *Dhikrayātī* [My Memories], 355.
47. Amīn, 458–63; see also Ma'rūf, *Ayyām 'Ishtuhā, 1949–1969: Al-Inqilābāt al-'Askarīya wa-Asrāruhā fī Sūrīya* [Days I Lived: 1949–1969: Military Coups and Their Secrets in Syria], 202.
48. Faḍl Allāh, *A'āṣīr*, 110–11.
49. Amīn, *Dhikrayātī* [My Memories], 402.
50. Ma'rūf, *Ayyām 'Ishtuhā, 1949–1969: Al-Inqilābāt al-'Askarīya wa-Asrāruhā fī Sūrīya* [Days I Lived: 1949–1969: Military Coups and Their Secrets in Syria], 191, 203.
51. Seale, *The Struggle for Syria*, 137–38.
52. Ma'rūf, *Ayyām 'Ishtuhā, 1949–1969: Al-Inqilābāt al-'Askarīya wa-Asrāruhā fī Sūrīya* [Days I Lived: 1949–1969: Military Coups and Their Secrets in Syria], 199–201.
53. Rathmell, *Secret War in the Middle East*, 85–86.
54. FO501/8, Gardener to Eden, 'Political Situation', 3 February 1954.
55. FO501/8, Gardener to Eden, 'Presidents' Comments on the Druse [*sic*] Disturbances', 11 February 1954.
56. USNA, Moose to Dept of State, 'Inception and Execution in Aleppo of the February 25 Coup', 11 March 1954, cited in Landis, 'Shishakli and the Druzes'.
57. Amīn, *Dhikrayātī* [My Memories], 379.
58. Notably Kazim Zaytouni, chief staff officer in Latakia, Colonel Mahmoud Shawkat in Homs and Captain Mustafa Hamdoun in Aleppo. Amīn, 402–6.
59. In Abu Assaf's words, '*li-kay nub'id al-ḥaraka 'an al-ṣibgha al-ṭā'ifīya.*' Amīn, *Dhikrayātī* [My Memories].
60. Amīn, 429–30; Rathmell, *Secret War in the Middle East*, 198 ft.203.
61. Seale, *The Struggle for Syria*, 132.
62. Amīn, *Dhikrayātī* [My Memories], 325.

7. RADICALS AND LIBERALS, 1954–1958

1. Helbaoui, *French Syrie: Mise En Valeur d'un Pays Sous-Developpé*, 72.
2. A. J. Meyer, *Middle Eastern Capitalism. Nine Essays.* (Cambridge: Harvard University Press, 1959), 37.
3. Doreen Warriner, *Land Reform and Development in the Middle East* (Oxford: Oxford University Press, 1962), 71–72.
4. Warriner, 74.
5. 'Abd al-Basīṭ al-Khaṭīb, 'Al-Mashārī' al-Inshā'īya fī al-Ghāb' [Construction Projects in the Ghab] in *Majallat al-Shurṭa wa'l-Amn al-'Amm*, 2 February 1953, 24–25.
6. International Bank for Reconstruction and Development, *The Economic Development of Syria* (Baltimore: Johns Hopkins Press, 1955), 133.
7. Matthieu Rey, 'L'extension du Port de Lattaquié (1950–1955), Étude sur les Premiers Temps de la Fabrique du Développement en Syrie', in *Développer en Syrie : Retour sur une Expérience Historique*, ed. Cyril Roussel and Élisabeth Longuenesse, Cahiers de l'Ifpo (Beirut: Presses de l'Ifpo, 2014), 59–82.
8. Warriner, *Land Reform and Development in the Middle East*, 90–91.
9. Helbaoui, *La Syrie: Mise en Valeur d'un Pays Sous-Developpé*, 92–93.
10. Fawzī Silū, *Al-Bayān al-Awwal min Dawlat al-Za'īm Fawzī Silū Ilā al-Sha'b al-Sūrī 'an A'māl al-'Ahd al-Jadīd khilāl Thalāthat Ashhur Kanūn al-Awwāl – Adhār 1951–52* [The First Statement from the Government of Brigadier Fawzi Silu to the Syrian People about the Achievements of the New Era During the Three Months from December 1951 to March 1952] (Damascus: Maṭba'at al-Jumhūrīya al-Sūrīya, 1952), 5–52.
11. Silū, 27–30; See also Bū 'Alī Yāsīn, *al-Quṭn wa-Ẓāhirat al-Intāj al-Aḥādī fī al-Iqtiṣād al-Sūrī* [Cotton and the Appearance of Monoculture Production in the Syrian Economy] (Beirut: Dār al-Ṭalī'a, 1974).
12. Silū, *Al-Bayān al-Awwal*, 33; Yahya Sadowski, 'Political Power and Economic Organization in Syria: The Course of State Intervention, 1946–1958' (PhD, University of California, Los Angeles, 1984), 219–21.
13. Wizārat al-Iqtiṣād al-Waṭanī, *Al-Majmū'a al-Iḥṣā'īya al-Sūrīya 1961* [Syrian Statistical Abstract] (Damascus: Government Press, 1962), table 8.

14. Steven Heydemann, *Authoritarianism in Syria: Institutions and Social Conflict, 1946–70* (Ithaca: Cornell University Press, 1999), 42.
15. Heydemann, 34.
16. Schad, 'Colonialists, Industrialists, and Politicians', 365–68.
17. Yaḥyā 'Arūdkī, *al-Iqtiṣād al-Sūrī al-Ḥadīth* [The Modern Syrian Economy], vol. 2 (Damascus: Wizārat al-Thaqāfa wa-al-Irshād al-Qawmī, 1972), 97–107.
18. Yaḥyā 'Arūdkī, *al-Iqtiṣād al-Sūrī al-Ḥadīth* [The Modern Syrian Economy], vol. 1 (Damascus: Wizārat al-Thaqāfa wa-al-Irshād al-Qawmī, 1972), 312–14.
19. 'Abd Allāh Ḥannā, *al-Ḥaraka al-'Ummālīya fī Sūrīya wa-Lubnān, 1900–1945* [The Workers' Movement in Syria and Lebanon, 1900–1945] (Damascus: Dār Dimashq, 1973), 493–500.
20. Seale, *The Struggle for Syria*, 169–70.
21. FO 501/9, Gardener to Eden, Damascus, 8 March 1954, 16.
22. FO 501/9, Gardener to Eden, 21 June 1953, 21.
23. Diyāb, *Akram Al-Ḥawrānī Kamā A'rifuhu* [Akram al-Hawrani as I Know Him], 70–71.
24. Mīshīl 'Aflaq, *Fī Sabīl al-Ba'th* [On the Path to Rebirth], 4th ed. (Beirut: Dār al-Ṭalī'a, 1970), 118.
25. *The Times*, 8 July 1959, cited in Seale, *The Struggle for Syria*, 158.
26. Seale, 171–73.
27. Bābīl, *Ṣiḥāfa wa-Siyāsa: Sūrīya fī'l-Qarn al-'Ishrīn* [Press and Politics: Syria in the 20th Century], 448.
28. Bābīl, 457.
29. Amīn, *Dhikrayātī* [My Memories], 493.
30. Rathmell, *Secret War in the Middle East*, 98.
31. *Al-Mālikī: Rajul wa Qadīya* [al-Malki: The Man, the Affair] (Damascus: Manshūrāt al-Far' al-Thaqāfī al-'Askarī, 1956), 12.
32. Cited in 'Hadhā mā Qālat al-Ṣuḥuf 'an Istishād al-'Aqīd al-Rukn al-Majāz 'Adnān al-Mālikī' [This is What the Papers Say about the Martyrdom of Colonel Adnan al-Malki', in *al-Jundī* 205, 5 May 1955, 7–8.
33. *Al-Jundī* 205, 5 May 1955.
34. The notable exception was the execution of Husni al-Za'im and Muhsin al-Barazi during the 1949 Hinnawi coup. Quwwatli and Shishakli both ordered the coercive apparatus of the state, whether the gendarmerie

or the armed forces, to take up arms against rebellious populations in the country's peripheries, but neither one used violence targeted at particular individuals with social or political standing, much less in so public a venue as a football stadium.

35. Cited in *Al-Jundī* 205, 5 May 1955.
36. FCO 501/10, Gardener to Eden, 27 April 1955, 9.
37. Torrey, *Syrian Politics and the Military, 1945–1958*, 298.
38. Seale, *The Struggle for Syria*, 269.
39. The only account of the plot from one of those involved is Ma'rūf, *Ayyām 'Ishtuhā, 1949–1969: al-Inqilābāt al-'Askarīya wa-Asrāruhā fī Sūrīya* [Days I Lived: 1949–1969: Military Coups and Their Secrets in Syria], 227–50. Ma'ruf details his various meetings with Ghassan Jadid in Beirut, with Nuri Sa'id and the Regent Abd ul-Ilah in Baghdad, and with Adib al-Shishakli over a glass of Ricard in a Parisian cafe.
40. They included names such as Mikhail Ilyan, Faydi al-Atasi, Faysal al-Asali, Munir al-Ajlani, Sami Kabbara, Fadallah Jarbu', Hasan al-Atrash and Shaykh Ha'il al-Surur.
41. Torrey, *Syrian Politics and the Military, 1945–1958*, 329.
42. *Al-Ba'th*, 18 Jan 1957, cited in Seale, *The Struggle for Syria*, 281–82.
43. *Difā' al-Duktūr Mūnīr al-'Ajlānī amām al-Maḥkama al-'Askarīya bi-Dimashq* [The Defence of Dr Munir al-Ajlani before the Military Court in Damascus] (n.p.: n.p., 1957), 3.
44. The leaders of the Qatana Mutiny included Abd al-Hamid Sarraj, Amin al-Nafouri, Mustafa Hamdoun, and Afif al-Bizri. All but Bizri had recently received orders transferring them to posts outside Syria.
45. Amīn, *Dhikrayātī* [My Memories], 543.

8. UNITY, FREEDOM, SOCIALISM, 1958–1970

1. A. I. Dawisha, *Arab Nationalism in the Twentieth Century: From Triumph to Despair* (Princeton: Princeton University Press, 2003), 98–106.
2. A Syrian minister in the UAR government in Cairo, Bashir al-Azma, was surprised at how much Egyptians had in common with one another compared to Syrians, where regional differences were pronounced. 'Damascenes', Azma noted, 'could recognize people from other parts of the country before they even opened their mouth!'

Bashīr al-'Aẓma, *Jīl al-Hazīma min al-Dhākira* [Generation of Defeat: Memoires], 2nd ed. (Beirut: al-Mu'assasa al-'Arabīya li'l-Dirāsāt wa' l-Nashr, 1998), 192–94.

3. Vitalis and Heydemann, 'War, Keynesianism, and Colonialism'.
4. Israel Gershoni and James P. Jankowski, *Redefining the Egyptian Nation, 1930–1945* (Cambridge: Cambridge University Press, 1995), 7–31.
5. Abū Khaldūn Sāṭi' al-Ḥuṣrī, *Abḥāth Mukhtāra fī al-Qawmīya al-'Arabīya* [Selected Studies in Arab Nationalism], 2nd ed. (Beirut: Markaz Dirāsāt al-Waḥda al-'Arabīya, 1985), 105.
6. Iliya F. Harik, *The Political Mobilization of Peasants: A Study of an Egyptian Community* (Bloomington: Indiana University Press, 1974), 141.
7. By 1960, Egypt was the sixth largest producer of radio broadcasts on the planet. Dawisha, *Arab Nationalism in the Twentieth Century*, 147–50.
8. Hanan Hammad, *Unknown Past: Layla Murad, the Jewish-Muslim Star of Egypt* (Stanford: Stanford University Press, 2022).
9. James P. Jankowski, *Nasser's Egypt, Arab Nationalism, and the United Arab Republic* (Boulder: Lynne Rienner Publishers, 2002), 108–11.
10. Muḥammad Ḥasanayn Haykal, *Mā alladhī Jarā fī Sūriyā* [What Happened in Syria] (Cairo: al-Dār al-Qawmīya li'l-Ṭibā'a wa'l-Nashr, 1962), 36.
11. Khālid al-'Aẓm, *Mudhakkirāt Khālid al-'Aẓm* [The Memoirs of Khālid al-'Aẓm], vol. 3 (Beirut: al-Dār al-Muttaḥida li'l-Nashr, 1973), 136.
12. Azm signed the declaration of the UAR along with representatives of all Syria's political parties and parliamentary blocs apart from the Communists: Khalid Bakdash alone refused.
13. Azm was suspicious of the result, pointing out that the referendums staged by Quwwatli in 1949 and Shishakli in 1953 to confirm their positions had turnouts of 15 per cent and 5 per cent respectively. This time, he estimated the turnout to be no more than 5 per cent; in some districts there were more votes cast than there were registered voters. al-'Aẓm, *Mudhakkirāt Khālid al-'Aẓm*, 1973, 3:164.
14. Unfortunately, Abd al-Nasser's close advisor, Muhammad Hasanayn al-Haykal, did not preserve the precise obscenity for posterity. Haykal, *Mā alladhī Jarā fī Sūriyā*, 40.
15. al-'Aẓma, *Jīl al-Hazīma*, 184.

16. L'Orient, 25 February 1958, cited in John F. Devlin, *The Ba'th Party: A History from the Origins to 1966* (Stanford: Hoover Institution Press, 1976), 132.
17. Aḥmad 'Abd al-Karīm, *Aḍwā' 'alā Tajribat al-Waḥda* [Insights into the Unity Experiment] (Damascus: al-Ahālī li'l-Ṭibā'a wa'l-Nashr wa'l-Tawzī', 1991), 126–27.
18. al-'Aẓma, *Jīl al-Hazīma*, 196.
19. The influx of so many Egyptians, accustomed to living in a more liberal environment than the socially conservative Syrian interior, provoked a wave of consternation about inappropriate behaviour towards Syrian women. See, for example, Fawzī Shu'aybī, *Shāhid Min al-Mukhābarāt al-Sūrīyya Min 'Āmm 1955–1968* [A Witness from Syrian Intelligence] (Beirut: Bīsān li'l-Nashr wa'l-Tawzī', 2018), 72; however, the number of Egyptians sent to Syria was often exaggerated: the number was actually only a few hundred. Jankowski, *Nasser's Egypt, Arab Nationalism, and the United Arab Republic*, 131.
20. Shu'aybī, *Shāhid min al-Mukhābarāt al-Sūrīya*, 69.
21. 'Abd al-Karīm, *Aḍwā' 'alā Tajribat al-Waḥda*, 131, 139, 157–58, 197–98.
22. The government forgave 50 per cent of outstanding peasant debt in July 1961. As Bu Ali Yasin points out, when the state paid owners compensation in the form of forty-year government bonds bearing a 1.5 per cent interest rate, it meant that the UAR was essentially taking on long-term debt to finance its purchase of these lands. Bū 'Alī Yāsīn, *Ḥikāyat al-Arḍ wa'l-Fallāḥ al-Sūrī, 1858–1979* [The History of the Land and the Syrian Peasantry] ([Beirut]: Dār al-Ḥaqā'iq, 1979), 49–51.
23. In response to the complaints, implementing the reforms was subsequently delegated to a five-member committee. Haykal, *Mā alladhī Jarā fī Sūriyā*, 97–98.
24. Yāsīn, *Ḥikāyat al-Arḍ*, 51–52.
25. The figures for each region are incomplete: the missing percentage of land is accounted for by the category of *amlak al-dawla*, state-owned land. Yāsīn, 35, based on data from United Nations Economic and Social Office in Beirut, *Studies on Development Problems in Selected Countries of the Middle East* (New York: United Nations Economic and Social Office in Beirut, 1971), 6.

26. Ziad Keilany, 'Land Reform in Syria', *Middle Eastern Studies* 16, no. 3 (1980): 212.
27. As Nasser never authorized the creation of agricultural trade unions in the UAR, these rights existed mainly in principle rather than practice. Elie Podeh, *The Decline of Arab Unity: The Rise and Fall of the United Arab Republic* (Eastbourne: Sussex Academic Press, 1999), 76.
28. Yāsīn, *Ḥikāyat al-Arḍ*, 61–64. The rights granted to peasants did not include the right to strike or to protest.
29. Chafic Akhras, 'Reflexions Sur Certains Aspects de l'Union Économique Entre La Syrie et l'Egypte', in *Union Économique et Monétaire Dans La RAU: Opinions* (Damascus: Centre d'Études et de Documentations économiques, financières et sociales, 1959).
30. Awad Barakat, 'Reflexions à Propos de l'union Monétaire Entre Les Deux Régions de La République Arabe Unie', in *Union Économique et Monétaire Dans La RAU: Opinions* (Damascus: Centre d'Études et de Documentations économiques, financières et sociales, 1959).
31. Kamal Ghali, 'La Durée de La Phase Transitoire de l'Union Économique Totale: L'Union Monétaire', in *Union Économique et Monétaire Dans La RAU: Opinions* (Damascus: Centre d'Études et de Documentations économiques, financières et sociales, 1959); Yassar Bitar, 'De l'Union Monétaire Entre La Syrie et l'Egypte', in *Union Économique et Monétaire Dans La RAU: Opinions* (Damascus: Centre d'Études et de Documentations économiques, financières et sociales, 1959).
32. Tariffs of 50 per cent or 100 per cent remained in place for nine key commodities, including tobacco, sugar, salt, and shoes.
33. Cited in Podeh, *The Decline of Arab Unity*, 81.
34. 'Abd al-Laṭīf al-Baghdādī, *Mudhakkirāt 'Abd al-Laṭīf al-Baghdādī*, vol. 2 (Cairo: al-Maktab al-Miṣrī al-Ḥadīth, 1977), 57 cited in Jankowski, *Nasser's Egypt*, 120.
35. Heydemann, *Authoritarianism in Syria*, 99.
36. Haykal, *Mā alladhī Jarā fī Sūriyā*, 76.
37. For a detailed discussion, see Podeh, *The Decline of Arab Unity*, 101–5.
38. Deaths in custody included Farajallah al-Hilu, a senior member of the Syrian and Lebanese Communist Party. Muṭī' al-Sammān, *Waṭ an wa-'Askar: Qabla an Tudfana al-Ḥaqīqa fī al-Turāb. Mudhakkirāt 28*

Aylūl 1961–8 Ādhār 1963 [Nation and Soldiers: Before the Truth is Buried in Dust. Memoires from 28 September 1961 to 8 March 1963] (Beirut: Bīsān li'l-Tawzī' wa'l-Nashr, 1995), 22.

39. 'Abd al-Karīm, *Aḍwā' 'alā Tajribat al-Waḥda*, 197.
40. Wizārat al-Takhṭīṭ [Ministry of Planning], *Mashrū' al-Tanmiya al-Iqtiṣādīya wa'l-Ijtimā'īya li'l-Sanawāt al-Khamīs 1960–1 1964–5* [The Five-Year Social and Economic Development Plan for 1960–1 to 1964–5] (Damascus: al-Maṭba'a al-Jadīda, 1960), 7.
41. Podeh, *The Decline of Arab Unity*, 143.
42. Shu'aybī, *Shāhid Min al-Mukhābarāt al-Sūrīya*, 94–96.
43. Podeh, *The Decline of Arab Unity*, 145.
44. An intelligence officer based in Suwayda claimed to have discovered evidence of the plot, but his Egyptian superiors dismissed his claim as some kind of tactic to keep Sarraj in Syria. Shu'aybī, *Shāhid min al-Mukhābarāt al-Sūrīya*, 85–88, 102.
45. al-Sammān, *Waṭan wa-'Askar*, 27.
46. The allegations were made in Egyptian and Lebanese newspapers. Podeh, *The Decline of Arab Unity*, 149; Egyptian propaganda also emphasized the likely role of the recently nationalized Khumasiya. Haykal, *Mā alladhī Jarā fī Sūriyā*, 120–25; however, Kuzbari's own memoirs do not indicate he had any involvement or advance knowledge of the coup. Ma'mūn al-Kuzbarī, 'Mudhakkirāt [Memoirs]', (unpublished). I am grateful to the Kuzbari family for access to these documents.
47. al-Sammān, *Waṭan wa-'Askar*, 31–32.
48. The parachutists were transferred to military facilities in Homs. The local commander observed the parachutist seemed unprepared for a serious mission: they lacked sufficient arms, ammunition and funds. al-Sammān, 43–44.
49. International Bank for Reconstruction and Development, 'The Economy of the Syrian Arab Republic', 31 October 1963, 10.
50. al-Kuzbarī, 'Mudhakkirāt'.
51. al-'Aẓm, *Mudhakkirāt Khālid al-'Aẓm*, 1973, 3:207.
52. International Bank for Reconstruction and Development, 'The Economy of the Syrian Arab Republic', 11–13.
53. Rami Ginat, 'The Soviet Union and the Syrian Ba'th Regime: From Hesitation to Rapprochement', *Middle Eastern Studies* 36, no. 2 (2000): 156.

54. al-Sammān, *Waṭan wa-'Askar*, 106.
55. Emphasis added. Podeh, *The Decline of Arab Unity*, 160.
56. 'Déclaration ministerielle du gouvernement Dawalibi devant la chamber,' *L'Economie et les finances de la Syrie et des pays arabes* 61 (January 1961): 116–128, cited in Heydemann, *Authoritarianism in Syria*, 146.
57. Heydemann, 151.
58. al-Kuzbarī, 'Mudhakkirāt'.
59. al-Sammān, *Waṭan wa-'Askar*, 129.
60. Itamar Rabinovich, *Syria under the Ba'th, 1963–66: The Army–Party Symbiosis* (New York: Halsted Press, 1972), 30–35; Devlin, *The Ba'th Party*, 199; al-Sammān, *Waṭan wa-'Askar*, 130.
61. al-'Aẓma, *Jīl al-Hazīma*, 213–15.
62. al-'Aẓm, *Mudhakkirāt Khālid al-'Aẓm*, 1973, 3:331–32.
63. Muḥammad 'Umrān, *Tajribatī fī al-Thawra* [My Experience in the Revolution] (Damascus: n.p., 1970), 21.
64. In some regions, Ba'thists were so well connected to local elites that the security apparatus sometimes hesitated to move against them. In Suwayda, for example, the most prominent Ba'thist was Mansour al-Atrash, son of Sultan Pasha himself. The intelligence officer for Suwayda protested to Sarraj that the 'tribal nature' of the Jabal meant that the Druze Ba'thists merited less harsh treatment than party members in the rest of the country. Shu'aybī, *Shāhid Min al-Mukhābarāt al Sūrīya*, 84 85; see also Manṣūr Sulṭān al Aṭrash, *al Jīl al-Mudān: Sīrah Dhātīyah, min Awrāq Manṣūr Sulṭān al-Aṭrash* [The Accursed Generation: An Autobiography from the Papers of Manṣūr Sulṭān al-Aṭrash], ed. Rīm Manṣūr Aṭrash (Beirut: Riyāḍ al-Rayyis li'l-Kutub wa'l-Nashr, 2008), 292–93.
65. Muṭā' Ṣafadī, *Ḥizb al-Ba'th: Ma'sāt al-Mawlid, Ma'sāt al-Nihāya* [The Ba'th Party: The Tragedy of Its Birth, the Tragedy of Its Demise] (Beirut: Dār al-Ādāb, 1964), 301; 'Umrān, *Tajribatī fī al-Thawra* [My Experience in the Revolution], 18.
66. Munīf al-Razzāz, *Al-Tajriba al-Murra* [The Bitter Experience] ([Beirut?]: Dār Ghandūr li'l-Tibā'a wa'l-Nashr, 1967), 97.
67. Ṣafadī, *Ḥizb al-Ba'th*, 314.
68. Cairo Radio, 22 July 1963, cited in Devlin, *The Ba'th Party*, 250.

69. Ḥizb al-Ba'th al-'Arabī al-Ishtirākī, 'Ba'ḍ al-Munṭalaqāt al-Naẓarīya [Some Theoretical Points of Departure]', in *Niḍāl al-Ba'th* [The Struggle of the Ba'th], vol. 4 (Beirut: Dār al-Ṭalī'a li'l-Ṭibā'a wa'l-Nashr, 1976), 208.
70. al-Razzāz, *Al-Tajriba al-Murra* [The Bitter Experience], 110.
71. Ṣafadī, *Ḥizb al-Ba'th*, 339–40.
72. Nikolaos Van Dam, *The Struggle for Power in Syria: Politics and Society under Asad and the Ba'th Party*, 4th ed (I.B. Tauris, 2011), 36.
73. Van Dam, 38–39; see also Tlass, 626–34.
74. According to Hafiz's supporters, the root of Umran's hatred of Hafiz was the fact he was a Sunni in a senior leadership position. al-Razzāz, *Al-Tajriba al-Murra* [The Bitter Experience], 341; Van Dam, *The Struggle for Power in Syria*, 340.
75. Ṣafadī, *Ḥizb al-Ba'th*, 342. Umran was thereafter appointed ambassador to Spain.
76. Daniel Neep, 'Narrating Crisis, Constructing Policy: Economic Ideas, Institutional Change, and Statism in Syria', *New Political Economy* 23, no. 4 (2018): 495–511.
77. Heydemann, *Authoritarianism in Syria*.
78. US National Archives, Aleppo to Department of State, 4 June 1965, no. A-598, RG59/2684, cited in Heydemann, 174.
79. Sāmī al-Jundī, *Al-Ba'th* (Beirut: Dar al-Nahār li'l-Nashr, 1969), 136–37.
80. Cited in Van Dam, *The Struggle for Power in Syria*, 57.
81. Syrian Arab Republic, Wizārat al-Takhṭīṭ, Mudīrīyat al-Iḥṣā', *Al-Majmū'a al-Iḥṣā'īya al-Sūrīya 1960–68* [Syrian Statistical Abstract] (Damascus: Government Press, 1968).
82. For a superb study of the Women's Union, see Esther Meininghaus, *Creating Consent in Ba'thist Syria: Women and Welfare in a Totalitarian State* (London: I.B. Tauris, 2016).
83. Ḥizb al-Ba'th al-'Arabī al-Ishtirākī, 'Ba'ḍ al-Munṭalaqāt al-Naẓarīya', 1976, 216.
84. Ḥizb al-Ba'th al-'Arabī al-Ishtirākī, 'Qirārāt al-Mu'tamar al-Qawmī al-Sādis, 1963', in *Niḍāl al-Ba'th*, vol. 4 (Beirut: Dār al-Ṭalī'a li'l-Ṭibā'a wa'l-Nashr, 1976), 162.
85. Radio Damascus, 17 February 1964, 7.15pm, cited in Rabinovich, *Syria Under the Ba'th, 1963–66*, 110.

86. In a 2011 interview, the then governor of Hama, Abd al-Halim Khaddam, later recalled that the incident began with local opposition to the transfer to Deir al-Zour of three teachers accused of imparting anti-Ba'th messages to their students. Raphaël Lefèvre, *Ashes of Hama: The Muslim Brotherhood in Syria* (Oxford: Oxford University Press, 2013), 45.
87. Muḥammad Ibrāhīm al-ʿAlī, *Ḥayātī wa'l-Iʿdām* [My Life and Execution], vol. 2 (Damascus: n.p., 2005), 325–26.
88. Ṣafadī, *Ḥizb al-Baʿth*, 341.
89. Avraham Ben-Tzur, 'The Neo-Ba'th Party of Syria', *Journal of Contemporary History* 3, no. 3 (1968): 180.
90. Van Dam, *The Struggle for Power in Syria*, 48–56.
91. When war broke out with Israel in June 1967, Hatum returned to Syria to serve in the conflict. Before the end of the month, the Jadid regime had arrested Hatum, tried him in a special military court and executed him.
92. Cited in Van Dam, *The Struggle for Power in Syria*, 56–57.
93. Batatu, *Syria's Peasantry*, 157.
94. *Jaysh al-Sha'b* no. 794, 25 April 1967, reprinted in ʿUthmān, *al-Maḥākamāt al-siyāsīya*, 307–10.
95. Habannaka had long been a critic of Ba'thist socialism. Although the favourite of religious scholars for the position of grand mufti, he had lost out to the Ba'th's preferred candidate, Shaykh Ahmad Kaftaro. Thomas Pierret, *Religion and State in Syria: The Sunni Ulama from Coup to Revolution* (Cambridge: Cambridge University Press, 2013), 44–46.
96. The literature on the 1967 War is voluminous. For the most recent insights, see Guy Laron, *The Six Day War: The Breaking of the Middle East* (New Haven: Yale University Press, 2017); Wm Roger Louis and Avi Shlaim, eds, *The 1967 Arab–Israeli War: Origins and Consequences* (Cambridge: Cambridge University Press, 2012).
97. Patrick Seale, *Asad: The Struggle for the Middle East* (Berkeley: University of California Press, 1990), 164.

9. BUILDING ASSAD'S SYRIA, 1970–1982

1. Moshe Maʿoz, *Asad: The Sphinx of Damascus. A Political Biography* (Grove Weidenfeld, 1988).

2. Hānī Khalīl, *Ḥāfiẓ al-Asad: al-Aydiyūlūjiyā al-Thawrīya wa'l-Fikr al-Siyāsī* [Hafiz al-Assad: Revolutionary Ideology and Political Thought] (Damascus: Ṭalās li'l-Dirāsāt wa'l-Tarjama wa'l-Nashr, 1987), 11–12.
3. Seale, *Asad*, 11.
4. Muṣṭafā Ṭalās, *Mir'āt Ḥayātī, 1968–1978: al-Zilzāl* [The Mirror of My Life, 1968–1978: The Earthquake], vol. 3 part 1 (Damascus: Dār Ṭalās, 2003), 468–69.
5. Conversation with Hamud al-Shufi, cited in Batatu, *Syria's Peasantry*, 205–6.
6. Nizār Qabbānī, *Hawāmish 'alā Daftar al-Naksa: Qaṣīda Ṭawīla* [Marginalia in the Notebook of Defeat: A Long Ode] (Beirut: Manshūrāt Nizār Qabbānī, 1970).
7. Moshe Ma'oz, *Syria and Israel: From War to Peacemaking* (Oxford: Clarendon Press, 1995), 119–30.
8. For a detailed account, see Seale, *Asad*, 226–66.
9. Batatu's comprehensive indexing found Alawis comprised no less than 61.3 per cent of the elite military and security apparatus. For details, see Batatu, *Syria's Peasantry*, 218–24.
10. Tlass himself seems to confirm his reputation at several points in his epic five-volume memoirs, which include remarks such as 'nothing in nature is more perfect than a naked woman'. Muṣṭafā Ṭalās, *Mir'āt Ḥayātī: al-'Aqd al-Awwal, 1948–1958: al-Niḍāl* [The Mirror of My Life: The First Decade, 1948–1958: The Struggle], vol. 1 (Damascus: Dār Ṭalās, 1991), 48.
11. Malik Mufti, *Sovereign Creations: Pan-Arabism and Political Order in Syria and Iraq* (Ithaca: Cornell University Press, 1996), 236.
12. Volker Perthes, 'Si Vis Stabilitatem, Para Bellum: State Building, National Security, and War Preparation in Syria', in *War, Institutions, and Social Change in the Middle East*, ed. Steven Heydemann (University of California Press, 2000).
13. Raymond A. Hinnebusch, *Authoritarian Power and State Formation in Ba'thist Syria: Army, Party, and Peasant* (Boulder: Westview Press, 1990), 177–85.
14. 'Syria: Significance of the Revival of Interest of the Private Sector', *Arab Economist*, July 1972, 42 edition; Volker Perthes, 'A Look at Syria's

Upper Class: The Bourgeoisie and the Ba'th', *Middle East Report*, no. 170 (1991): 31–37.

15. Elisabeth Longuenesse, 'L'industrialisation et Sa Signification Sociale', in *La Syrie d'aujourd'hui*, ed. André Raymond (Paris: Éditions du Centre national de la recherche scientifique, 1980), 335–36.
16. Onn Winckler, 'Syrian Migration to the Arab Oil-Producing Countries', *Middle Eastern Studies* 33, no. 1 (1 January 1997): 107–18.
17. Volker Perthes, *The Political Economy of Syria under Asad* (London: I.B. Tauris, 1997), 33.
18. US Department of Agriculture in cooperation with the US Agency for International Development and the State Planning Commission, Syrian Arab Republic, *Syria: Agricultural Sector Assessment. Volume 4: Agricultural Marketing Annex*, 1980, 11.
19. Michel Seurat, 'Les Populations, l'état et La Société', in *La Syrie d'aujourd'hui*, ed. André Raymond (Paris: Éditions du Centre national de la recherche scientifique, 1980), 127–29.
20. Batatu, *Syria's Peasantry*, 66.
21. *Khuṭwa Khuṭwa* [Step by Step], 1978, https://www.youtube.com/watch?v=Zs9rsF2LUxo.
22. Eric Verdeil, 'Michel Écochard in Lebanon and Syria (1956–1968). The Spread of Modernism, the Building of the Independent States and the Rise of Local Professionals of Planning', *Planning Perspectives* 27, no. 2 (1 April 2012): 249–66.
23. Jean-Claude David, 'Alep', in *La Syrie d'aujourd'hui*, ed. André Raymond (Paris: Editions du CNRS, 1980), 400.
24. Mohamed al-Dbiyat, *Homs et Hama en Syrie centrale: concurrence urbaine et développement régional* (Damas: Institut français de Damas, 1995), 83.
25. *Al-Ḥayāt al-Yawmīya fī Qarya Sūrīya* [Everyday Life in a Syrian Village], 1974, https://www.youtube.com/watch?v=OQWJs4lWxqY.
26. Françoise Métral, 'State and Peasants in Syria: A Local View of a Government Irrigation Project', *Peasant Studies* 11, no. 2 (1984): 69–89.
27. André Bourgey, 'Le barrage de Tabqa et l'aménagement du bassin de l'Euphrate en Syrie', *Géocarrefour* 49, no. 4 (1974): 343–54.
28. Gunter Meyer, 'Rural Development and Migration in Northeast Syria', in *Anthropology and Development in North Africa and the Middle East*,

ed. Muneera Salem-Murdock, Michael M. Horowitz and Monica Sella (Boulder: Westview Press, 1990).

29. Bārūt, *al-Takawwun al-Tārīkhī al-Ḥadīth li'l-Jazīra al-Sūrīya*, 717.
30. Inconsistencies in how the 1962 census was administered meant that members of the same family – even brothers and sisters – could be assigned differing legal statuses. Harriet Allsopp, *The Kurds of Syria: Political Parties and Identity in the Middle East* (London: I.B. Tauris, 2015).
31. Ismet Charif Vanly, 'The Kurds of Syria and Lebanon', in *The Kurds: A Contemporary Overview*, ed. Philip G. Kreyenbroek and Stefan Sperl (London: Routledge, 1992).
32. 26/08/2024 14:16:00
33. Muḥammad Ṭalab Hilāl, *Dirāsa 'an Muḥāfaẓat al-Jazīra: Min al-Nawāḥī al-Qawmīya wa'l-Ijtimā'īya wa'l-Siyāsīya* [A Study of the Governorate of al-Jazira: Some Political, Social, and Nationalist Aspects] (Irbil: Kāwā li'l-Nashr wa'l-Tawzī', 2001), 16.
34. Hilāl, 59–60.
35. The Arabization campaign was overseen by Zuhayr Masharqa, previously governor of Aleppo, whose loyalty to Assad earned him appointments first as of education and then vice president of the republic. Masharqa held the latter position from 1984 until 2006. Bārūt, *al-Takawwun al-Tārīkhī al-Ḥadīth li'l-Jazīra al-Sūrīya*, 747.
36. Middle East Watch, *Syria Unmasked: The Suppression of Human Rights by the Asad Regime* (New Haven: Yale University Press, 1991), 186 ft.20.
37. Muṣṭafā Ṭalās, *Mir'āt Ḥayātī, 1968–1978: al-Zilzāl* [The Mirror of My Life, 1968–1978: The Earthquake], vol. 3 part 2 (Damascus: Dār Ṭalās, 2003), 1158.
38. Ṭalās, 3 part 2:1119.
39. Elisabeth Longuenesse, 'État et Syndicalisme En Syrie: Discours et Pratiques', *Sou'al*, no. 8 (1988): 104–5.
40. Muṣṭafā Ṭalās, *Mir'āt Ḥayātī*, vol. 4 (Damascus: Dār Ṭalās, 2003), 84, ft.1.
41. *Al-Nadhīr*, 1 February 1980, 9–13.
42. Statement of the National Progressive Front Central Command, 26 September 1979, transl. Foreign Broadcast Information Service, Middle East and North Africa Daily Report (FBIS-MEA-79-190), 28 September 1979.

43. 'Adnān Sa'd al-Dīn, *Al-Ikhwān al-Muslimūn fī Sūrīya: Mudhakkirāt wa Dhikrayāt. Sanawāt al-Majāzir al-Mur'iba. Min 'Āmm 1977 wa-Ḥattā 'Āmm 1983* [The Muslim Brotherhood in Syria: Memoires and Memories. The Years of Terrible Massacres (1977 to 1983)] (Cairo: Maktabat Madbūlī, 2010), 115–35.
44. Michel Seurat, *Syrie, l'État de barbarie* (Paris: Presses Universitaires de France, 2015), 37.
45. Sa'd al-Dīn, *Sanawāt al-Majāzir al-Mur'iba*, 225.
46. *Al-Nadhīr*, 31 May 1980, 9.
47. *Al-Nadhīr*, 21 February 1980, 18.
48. Lefèvre, *Ashes of Hama*, 125–28.
49. For accounts from the perspective of the Muslim Brotherhood, see Sa'd al-Dīn, *Sanawāt al-Majāzir al-Mur'iba*, 329–431; and *al-Nadhīr*, 27 February 1982.
50. *Al-Nadhīr*, 27 February 1982, 25.

10. SEASONS OF DISCONTENT, 1982–2003

1. Jam'īyat al-Ikhwān al-Muslimīn, al-Maktab al-I'lāmī, *Ḥamāh Ma'sāt al-'Aṣr* [Hama: Tragedy of the Age] ([Beirut]: Min Manshurāt al-Taḥāluf al-Waṭanī li-Tahrīr Sūrīya, 1983).
2. This section draws on accounts of life in Syrian prisons during the 1980s and 1990s from sources including Faraj Bayraqdār, *Khiyānāt al-Lugha wa'l-Ṣamt: Taghrībatī fī Sujūn al-Mukhābarāt al-Sūrīya* [The Betrayals of Speech and Silence: My Disappearance in the Prisons of Syrian Intelligence] (Beirut: al-Jadīd, 2006); Luṭfī Ḥaddād, *Riyāḍ al-Turk: Māndīllā Sūriya* [Riyad al-Turk: Syria's Mandela] (Newburgh: Mu'assasat Judhūr al-Thaqāfiya, 2005), 61–65; Muṣṭafā Khalīfa, *al-Qawqa'a: Yawmiyyāt Mutalaṣṣiṣ* [The Shell: The Diary of a Voyeur] (Beirut: Dār al-Ādāb, 2008); Middle East Watch, *Syria Unmasked*.
3. Yāsīn al-Ḥājj Ṣāliḥ, *Bi'l-Khalāṣ yā Shabāb: 16 'Āmman fī al-Sujūn al-Sūrīya* (Beirut: Dar al-Sāqī, 2012), 29–30.
4. Craig further opined that the Ba'thists '[l]ike all Arabs, say one thing and mean another.' With a classically Orientalist, philological flourish to his racism, Craig went on to accuse the Arabic language itself of

producing 'cant, hypocrisy, bombast, and self-deceit'. FCO 93/2255, Craig, Valedictory Despatch, 18 September 1979.

5. Quoted from an original interview in Lisa Wedeen, *Ambiguities of Domination: Politics, Rhetoric, and Symbols in Contemporary Syria* (Chicago: University of Chicago Press, 1999), 46.
6. Yāsīn al-Ḥājj Ṣāliḥ, 'Al-Ṣultān al-Ḥadīth: al-Manābi' al-Siyāsī wa'l-Ijtimā'ī li'l-Ṭā'ifiya fī Sūriya' [The New Sultan: The Political and Social Origins of Sectarianism in Syria], *al-Jumhūriya*, 26 January 2015.
7. al-Ḥājj Ṣāliḥ.
8. Wedeen, *Ambiguities of Domination*.
9. Seale, *Asad*, Chapter 24 'The Brothers' War' (revised 1995), 421–40.
10. The USA was the first country to recognize Israel's declaration of sovereignty over the Syrian Golan, by virtue of a presidential proclamation by Trump, nearly forty years later. Donald J. Trump, 'Proclamation on Recognizing the Golan Heights as Part of the State of Israel', 25 March 2019, https://trumpwhitehouse.archives.gov/presidential-actions/proclamation-recognizing-golan-heights-part-state-israel/.
11. Cited in Ma'oz, *Syria and Israel*, 187.
12. *Afrique-Asie*, 13 August 1984, cited in Haim Shaked and Daniel Dishon, eds, *Middle East Contemporary Survey Vol. 8 (1983–1984)* (Boulder: Westview Press, 1984), 680.
13. For the fullest account of this episode – albeit one which reflects the position of the pro-Hafiz camp – see Seale, *Asad*, 421–40.
14. Seale, 435.
15. Arab aid transfers were US$1.8 billion in 1981. By 1986–88, this amount had fallen to $500 million. Raymond A. Hinnebusch, 'The Political Economy of Economic Liberalization in Syria', *International Journal of Middle East Studies* 27, no. 3 (1995): 312.
16. Volker Perthes, 'The Syrian Economy in the 1980s', *Middle East Journal* 46, no. 1 (1992): 37–58.
17. *Al-Nashra al-Iqtisādīya li-Ghurfat Tijārat Dimashq* no. 2 (1982), 2.
18. Nabil Sukkar, 'The Crisis of 1986 and Syria's Plan for Reform', in *Contemporary Syria: Liberalization Between Cold War and Cold Peace*, ed. Eberhard Kienle (London: British Academic Press, 1994).
19. Samir Seifan, *The Road to Economic Reform in Syria* (Centre for Syrian Studies, University of St Andrews, 2011).

20. Flynt Leverett, *Inheriting Syria: Bashar's Trial by Fire* (Washington, D.C.: Brookings Institution, 2005), 32.
21. General Federation of Trade Unions, al-Taqrīr al-'Āmm li-Mu'tamar al-Ibdā' al-Waṭanī wa'l-I'timād 'alā al-Dhāt [The General Report from the Conference on National Innovation and Self-Reliance] (Damascus, 1987), cited in Sukkar, 'The Crisis of 1986 and Syria's Plan for Reform', 30–31.
22. Yahya M. Sadowski, 'Cadres, Guns and Money: The Eighth Regional Congress of the Syrian B'ath' 134 (1985): 3–8.
23. *Al-Nashra al-Iqtisādīya lī Ghurfat Tijārat Dimashq* (1986), no. 1–2: 3–4.
24. Linda Matar, *The Political Economy of Investment in Syria* (Houndmills: Palgrave Macmillan, 2016), 102–5.
25. The text of the speech can be found in *Al-Nashra al-Iqtisādīya li-Ghurfat Tijārat Dimashq* (1990), no. 1: 4.
26. Joseph Bahout, *Les entrepreneurs syriens: Économie, affaires et politique* (Beirut: Presses de l'Ifpo, 1994).
27. Nabil Sukkar et al, *Naḥwa Iqtisād Ishtirākī Mutatawwar fi'l-Qutr al-'Arabī al-Sūrī* [Towards an Advanced Socialist Economy in the Syrian Arab Region] (1987), cited in Sukkar, 'The Crisis of 1986 and Syria's Plan for Reform', ft.2.
28. Muḥammad Riyād al-Abrash, 'Al-Takhsīs Marra Ukhrā [Privatization, One More Time]', *Al-Nashra al-Iqtisādīya li-Ghurfat Tijārat Dimashq* 4 (1990): 50–62.
29. Cited in Ami Ayalon, ed., *Middle East Contemporary Survey*, vol. 15 (Boulder: Westview Press, 1991): 670.
30. Nabil Sukkar, 'Syria: Strategic Economic Issues', in *Economic Challenges Facing Middle Eastern and North African Countries: Alternative Futures*, ed. Nemat Shafik (Houndmills: Macmillan Press, 1998), 154.
31. Thomas Pierret, *Baas et Islam en Syrie: La dynastie Assad face aux Oulémas* (Presses Universitaires de France, 2011).
32. Yāsīn al-Ḥājj Ṣāliḥ, *Al-Sayr 'alā Qadam Wāḥida:* [Walking on One Leg] (Beirut: Dār al-Ādāb, 2012), 140.
33. Rebecca Joubin, *The Politics of Love: Sexuality, Gender, and Marriage in Syrian Television Drama* (Lanham: Lexington Books, 2013), 126–32.
34. Britain had severed diplomatic relations in 1987 because of Syria's role in an (unsuccessful) plot to bomb an Israeli flight from Tel Aviv to London by Jordanian national Nizar al-Hindawi.

35. Salīm al-Ḥuṣṣ, *Li'l-Ḥaqīqa wa'l-Tārīkh: Tajārib al-Ḥukm mā Bayna 1998 wa-2000* [For Truth and History: Experiences of Government between 1998 and 2000] (Beirut: Sharikat al-Maṭbū'āt li'l-Tawzī' wa'l-Nashr, 2001), 61. Despite serving as prime minister of Lebanon three times between the late 1970s and 2000, Hoss considered himself to be an ally of Syria, not its client.
36. Hannes Baumann, *Citizen Hariri: Lebanon's Neo-Liberal Reconstruction* (Oxford: Oxford University Press, 2017); Rola El-Husseini, *Pax Syriana: Elite Politics in Postwar Lebanon* (Syracuse: Syracuse University Press, 2012); Reinoud Leenders, *Spoils of Truce: Corruption and State-Building in Post-War Lebanon* (Ithaca: Cornell University Press, 2012).
37. Syrian and Israeli accounts differ on the status and veracity of the various stages of the negotiations. See, for example, Itamar Rabinovich, *The Brink of Peace: The Israeli–Syrian Negotiations* (Princeton: Princeton University Press, 1998); Patrick Seale, 'The Syria-Israel Negotiations: Who Is Telling the Truth?', *Journal of Palestine Studies* 29, no. 2 (2000): 65–77; Bouthaina Shaaban, *Damascus Diary: An Inside Account of Hafez Al-Assad's Peace Diplomacy, 1990–2000* (Boulder: Lynne Rienner Publishers, 2013); Fārūq al-Shara', *Al-Riwāya al-Mafqūda* [The Missing Account] (Beirut: al-Markaz al-'Arabī li'l-Abḥāth wa-Dirāsāt al-Siyāsāt, 2015).
38. Shaaban, *Damascus Diary*, 185.
39. Foreign Broadcast Information Service, Daily Report Near East & South Asia (FBIS-NES-92-242), 46.
40. *Al-Thawra*, 19 January 1997. The author, Bahjat Sulayman, later became chief of Syrian General Intelligence and subsequently ambassador to Jordan.
41. 'Kalimat al-Sayyid al-Ra'īs Bashshār al-Asad amām Majlis al-Sha'b ba'd Udā'ihi al-Qism Ra'īsan li'l-Jumhūrīya [The Address of President Bashar al-Assad before Parliament]', YouTube, 17 July 2000, https://www.youtube.com/watch?v=dsNwHs9B6RI.
42. Alan George, *Syria: Neither Bread nor Freedom* (London: Zed Books, 2003), 37.
43. In the 1990s, Syrian opposition criticism was either reframed as a general critique of 'Arab' society, often in the Arab press, or transformed into

literary discourse. See Miriam Cooke, *Dissident Syria: Making Oppositional Arts Official* (Durham: Duke University Press, 2007); Elizabeth Suzanne Kassab, *Enlightenment on the Eve of Revolution: The Egyptian and Syrian Debates* (New York: Columbia University Press, 2019), 83–125.

44. Muḥammad Jamāl Bārūt and Kīlānī Shams al-Dīn, 'Muqaddima [Introduction]', in *Sūrīya bayna 'Ahdayn: Qaḍāyā al-Marḥala al-Intiqālīya* [Syria between Two Eras: Issues for the Transition Period], eds Muḥ ammad Jamāl Bārūt and Kīlānī Shams al-Dīn ('Amman: Dār Sindbād li'l-Nashr, 2003), 37.
45. For a translation of the text, see George, *Syria*, 178–81.
46. Muḥammad Jamāl Bārūt and Kīlānī Shams al-Dīn, eds, *Sūrīya bayna 'Ahdayn: Qaḍāyā al-Marḥala al-Intiqālīya* [Syria between Two Eras: Issues for the Transition Period] ('Amman: Dār Sindbād li'l-Nashr, 2003), 123–25.
47. Translation in George, *Syria*, 182–88.
48. Bārūt and Shams al-Dīn, 'Sūrīya bayna 'Ahdayn', 2003, 48.
49. Yūsuf al-Bujayramī, *Ḥiwārāt al-Iṣlaḥ wa'l-Infitāḥ fi Sūriyā* [Dialogues of Reform and Liberalization in Syria] (Damascus: Dār al-Ḥawrān li'l-Tibā'a wa'l-Nashr, 2001), 173–80.
50. 'Interview with Bashar al-Asad', *al-Sharq al-Awsat*, 8 February 2001, English translation at https://al-bab.com/documents-section/interview-president-bashar-al-assad edition.
51. 'Abd al-Ḥalīm Khaddām, 'Muḥāḍarat Nā'ib al-Ra'īs 'Abd al-Ḥalīm Khaddām [Lecture by Vice President Khaddam], University of Damascus, 16 February 2001', in *Sūrīya bayna 'Ahdayn: Qaḍāyā al-Marḥala al-Intiqālīya* [Syria between Two Eras: Issues for the Transition Period], ed. Muḥ ammad Jamāl Bārūt and Kīlānī Shams al-Dīn ('Amman: Dār Sindbād li'l-Nashr, 2003), 140.
52. The text of one of the group's documents, published in a Lebanese newspaper, mentions Syria's 'beautiful mosaic canvas'. Radwān Ziyāda, ed., 'Ḥarakat al-Silm al-Ijtimā'ī: Mabādi' Awwaliya li'l-Ḥiwār [The Social Peace Movement: First Principles for Dialogue], al-Safir, 2 February 2002', in *al-Muthaqqaf Ḍidda al-Sulṭa: Ḥiwārat al-Mujtama' al-Madanī fi Sūrīya* [The Intellectual against Authority: Civil Society Dialogues in Syria] (Cairo: Markaz al-Qāhira li'l-Dirāsāt Ḥuqūq al-Insān, 2003), 129. Seif later stated that at the time he was unaware that the idea of

Syria's 'mosaic' society came from French colonial strategies of divide-and-rule in the country. 'Introduction' in Bārūt and Shams al-Dīn, eds, *Sūriya bayna al-'Ahdayn*, 52–53.

53. Bārūt and Shams al-Dīn, *Sūrīya bayna 'Ahdayn*, 2003, 149–152, 302–304.
54. Violetter Daguerre, ed., *Démocratie et Droits Humains En Syrie*, trans. Ahmed Manai and Hakim Arabdiou (Paris: Editions Eurabe, 2002), 453–56.
55. Bārūt and Shams al-Dīn, eds, *Sūrīya bayna 'Ahdayn*, 2003, 167–75.
56. Reinoud Leenders, 'Prosecuting Political Dissent: Courts and the Resilience of Authoritarianism in Syria', in *Middle East Authoritarianisms: Governance, Contestation, and Regime Resilience in Syria and Iran*, eds Steven Heydemann and Reinoud Leenders (Stanford: Stanford University Press, 2012), 178.
57. *Commission of Inquiry into Actions of Canadian Officials in Relation to Maher Arar* (Ontario: Public Works and Government Services Canada, 2006), www.therenditionproject.org.uk.

11. FROM SOCIAL MARKET TO CIVIL WAR, 2003–2014

1. Interview transcript, *The New York Times*, 1 December 2003.
2. Burhān Ghalyūn, *Bayān min ajl al-Dīmuqrāṭīya* [Manifesto for Democracy], 5th ed. (Morocco: al-Markaz al-Thaqāfī al-'Arabī, 1986), 13–14.
3. Raymond Hinnebusch, 'The Ba'th Party in Post-Ba'thist Syria: President, Party and the Struggle for "Reform"', *Middle East Critique* 20, no. 2 (2011): 109–25.
4. Samir Seifan, *Syria on the Path to Economic Reform* (Centre for Syrian Studies, University of St Andrews, 2010).
5. Muḥammad Jamāl Bārūt, *Al-'Aqd al-Akhīr fī Tārīkh Sūrīya: Jadalīyat al-Jumūd wa'l-Iṣlāḥ* [The Last Decade in the History of Syria: The Dialectic of Stagnation and Reform] (Doha: al-Markaz al-'Arabī li'l-Abḥāth wa-Dirāsat al-Siyāsāt, 2012), 49–51.
6. Samer Abboud, 'Locating the "Social" in the Social Market Economy', in *Syria from Reform to Revolt: Political Economy and International Relations*, ed. Raymond A. Hinnebusch and Tina Zintl (Syracuse: Syracuse University Press, 2014).

7. 'Al-Khiṭṭa al-Khamsīya al-'Āshira fī Sūrīya 2006–2010' [The Tenth Five-Year Plan for Syria] (Damascus: Syrian Arab Republic, 2005), 3.
8. Akram al-Bunnī, 'Iqtisād al-Sūq al-Ijtimā'i [The Social Market Economy]', Al Jazeera.net, 13 January 2006, https://www.aljazeera.net/opinions/2006/1/13/اقتصاد-السوق-الاجتماعي-ماله-وما-عليه.
9. Leverett, *Inheriting Syria*, 84.
10. Bārūt, *Al-'Aqd al-Akhīr*, 73.
11. Samīr Sa'īfān, 'Siyāsāt Tawzī' al-Dakhl wa-Dawrihā fī al-Infijār al-Ijtimā'ī fī Sūrīya [The Politics of Distributing Income and Its Role in the Social Explosion in Syria]', in *Khalfiyyāt al-Thawra al-Sūrīya: Dirāsāt Sūrīya [Backdrop to the Syrian Revolution: Syrian Studies]*, ed. 'Azmī Bishāra (Doha: Arab Center For Research and Policy Studies, 2013), 112–13.
12. Corruption was notably common (or perhaps notably apprehended) in the city of Aleppo. Bārūt, *al-'Aqd al-Akhīr*, 82.
13. Gulf investment in Syria increased by 3.5 times between 2004 and 2005 alone. Bārūt, 70.
14. 'Hiwār al-Iqtisādī al-Kāmil ma' Rajul al-A'māl Haytham Jūd [The Full al-Iqtisādī Interview with Haytham Joud]', *al-Iqtisādī*, July 2011.
15. Bārūt, *al-'Aqd al-Akhīr*, 150–51.
16. Salam Kawakibi, 'The Paradox of Government-Organized Civil Activism in Syria', in *Civil Society in Syria and Iran: Activism in Authoritarian Contexts*, ed. Paul Aarts and Francesco Cavatorta (Boulder: Lynne Rienner Publishers, 2013).
17. For insight into these unique social spaces, see Mandy Terc, '"To Promote Volunteerism among School Children": Volunteer Campaigns and Social Stratification in Contemporary Syria', in *Syria from Reform to Revolt: Political Economy and International Relations*, ed. Raymond A. Hinnebusch and Tina Zintl (Syracuse: Syracuse University Press, 2014).
18. Nabīl Marzūq, 'Al-Tanmīya al-Mafqūda fī Sūrīya [Lost Development in Syria]', in *Khalfiyāt al-Thawra al-Sūrīya: Dirāsāt Sūrīya* [Backdrop to the Syrian Revolution: Syrian Studies], ed. 'Azmī Bishāra (Doha: Arab Center for Research and Policy Studies, 2013).
19. Sa'īfān, 'Siyāsāt Tawzī' al-Dakhl', 134.
20. Yannick Sudermann, 'When Authoritarianism Embraces Gentrification: The Case of Old Damascus, Syria', in *Global Gentrifications: Uneven*

Development and Displacement, ed. Loretta Lees, Hyun Bang Shin and Ernest López-Morales (Bristol: Bristol University Press, 2015).

21. Leïla Vignal, 'Dubai on Barada? The Making of "Globalized Damascus" in Times of Urban Crisis', in *Under Construction: Logics of Urbanism in the Gulf Region*, ed. Steffen Wippel, Katrin Bromber, and Birgit Krawietz (London: Routledge, 2014).
22. Khalid Abu-Ismail, Ali Abdel-Gadir and Heba El-Laithy, 'Poverty and Inequality in Syria (1997–2007)', Arab Development Challenges Report Background Paper 2011/15 (Cairo and New York: UNDP, 2011).
23. Francesca de Châtel, 'The Role of Drought and Climate Change in the Syrian Uprising: Untangling the Triggers of the Revolution', *Middle Eastern Studies* 50, no. 4 (2014): 521–35.
24. Myriam Ababsa, 'The End of a World: Drought and Agrarian Transformation in Northeast Syria (2007–2010)', in *Syria from Reform to Revolt: Political Economy and International Relations*, ed. Raymond A. Hinnebusch and Tina Zintl (Syracuse: Syracuse University Press, 2014).
25. Saʿīfān, 'Siyāsāt Tawzīʿ al-Dakhl', 127.
26. Fred H. Lawson, 'Revisiting the Political Economy of the Syrian Uprising', in *The Syrian Uprising: Domestic Origins and Early Trajectory*, ed. Raymond Hinnebusch and Omar Imady (Abingdon: Routledge, 2018).
27. Bārūt, *Al-ʿAqd al-Akhīr*, 98.
28. Robert Goulden, 'Housing, Inequality, and Economic Change in Syria', *British Journal of Middle Eastern Studies* 38, no. 2 (2011): 187–202.
29. Baudouin Dupret, Myriam Ababsa and Eric Denis, eds, *Popular Housing and Urban Land Tenure in the Middle East: Case Studies from Egypt, Syria, Jordan, Lebanon, and Turkey* (Cairo: American University in Cairo Press, 2012).
30. ʿAzmī Bishāra, *Sūrīya: Darb al-Ālām Naḥwa al-Ḥurrīya: Muḥāwala fī al-Tārīkh al-Rāhin* [Syria: The Painful Path to Freedom: An Essay in Contemporary History] (Beirut: al-Markaz al-ʿArabī li'l-Abḥāth wa-Dirāsat al-Siyāsāt, 2013), 69.
31. Sophia Hoffmann, *Iraqi Migrants in Syria: The Crisis before the Storm* (Syracuse: Syracuse University Press, 2016).
32. Pierret, *Religion and State in Syria*.

33. Thomas Pierret and Kjetil Selvik, 'The Limits of "Authoritarian Upgrading" in Syria: Private Welfare, Islamic Charities, and the Rise of the Zayd Movement', *International Journal of Middle East Studies* 41, 4 (2009): 595–614.
34. Laura Ruiz de Elvira, 'State-Charities Relations in Syria: Between Reinforcement, Control and Coercion', in *Civil Society and the State in Syria: The Outsourcing of Civil Responsibility*, ed. Tina Zintl and Laura Ruiz de Elvira (St Andrews: University of St Andrews Centre for Syrian Studies, 2012), 7–31.
35. Laura Ruiz de Elvira, 'Christian Charities and the Ba'thist Regime in Bashar al-Asad's Syria', in *Syria from Reform to Revolt: Culture, Society, and Religion*, ed. Leif Stenberg and Christa Salamandra (Syracuse: Syracuse University Press, 2015).
36. Haian Dukhan, *State and Tribes in Syria: Informal Alliances and Conflict Patterns* (London: Routledge, 2019), 102–5.
37. Cyril Roussel, 'Les grandes familles druzes entre local et national', *Revue des mondes musulmans et de la Méditerranée*, no. 115–16 (31 December 2006): 135–53, https://doi.org/10.4000/remmm.3024.
38. Allsopp, *The Kurds of Syria*, 176–94.
39. Amnesty International, 'Les Kurdes de la République Arabe Syrienne un an après les événements de Mars 2004' (MDE 24/002/2005, 2005).
40. Jordi Tejel, *Syria's Kurds: History, Politics and Society* (London: Routledge, 2009), 101–2.
41. Bishāra, *Sūrīya: Darb al-Ālām*, 66.
42. Hamza Muṣṭafa al-Mustafā, *Al-Majāl al-ʿĀmm al-Iftirādī fī al-Thawra al-Sūrīya: al-Khasā'is, al-Ittijāhāt, Āliyāt Ṣanʿ al-Ra'ī al-ʿĀmm* [Virtual Public Space in the Syrian Revolution: Specificities, Directions and the Tools of Manufacturing Public Opinion] (Doha: al-Markaz al-ʿArabī li'l-Abḥāth wa-Dirāsat al-Siyāsāt, 2012), 98–99; Bishāra, *Sūrīya: Darb al-Ālām*, 72–73; Thomas Pierret, 'The State Management of Religion in Syria: The End of "Indirect Rule"?', in *Middle East Authoritarianisms: Governance, Contestation, and Regime Resilience in Syria and Iran*, ed. Steven Heydemann and Reinoud Leenders (Stanford: Stanford University Press, 2012).
43. Najib Ghadbian, 'Contesting Authoritarianism: Opposition Activism under Bashar al-Asad, 2000–2010', in *Syria from Reform to Revolt: Political*

Economy and International Relations, ed. Raymond A. Hinnebusch and Tina Zintl (Syracuse: Syracuse University Press, 2014).

44. Joshua M. Landis and Joe Pace, 'The Syrian Opposition', *The Washington Quarterly* 30, no. 1 (Winter 2006): 62.
45. 'Interview With Syrian President Bashar Al-Assad', *Wall Street Journal (Online)*, 31 January 2011.
46. Interview cited in Alan George, 'Patronage and Clientelism in Bashar's Social Market Economy', in *The 'Alawis of Syria: War, Faith and Politics in the Levant*, ed. Michael Kerr and Craig Larkin (New York: Oxford University Press, 2015), 178.
47. Bārūt, *Al-'Aqd al-Akhīr*, 189–90.
48. 'Interview with Shaykh Ahmad al-Sayāsana, Imam of the Umari Mosque in Dera'a', *al-Arabiya TV*, 22 March 2011, https://www.youtube.com/watch?v=lVNzMMdA43g.
49. For a granular account of these developments, see the magisterial work by Kevin Mazur, *Revolution in Syria: Identity, Networks, and Repression* (Cambridge: Cambridge University Press, 2021).
50. Bishāra, *Sūrīya: Darb al-Ālām*, 108–66.
51. Author's interview with activist, Damascus, June 2011.
52. 'Al-Ra'īs al-Asad amam Majlis al-Sha'b' [President Assad Before the People's Assembly], *SANA*, 1 April 2011, https://web.archive.org/web/20110819072639/http://sana.sy/ara/2/2011/03/30/339278.htm.
53. Ghassān Sa'ūd, 'Bashar al-Asad on Today's Issue: Fighting "Sedition", Then Reform' [Bashshār al-Asad fī al-Amr al-Yawm: Muwājahat 'al-Fitna' Thumma al-Islāh], *al-Akhbār*, 31 March 2011, https://al-akhbar.com/Politics/85961.
54. 'Al-Ra'īs al-Asad li'l-Ḥukūma al-Jadīda' [President Assad to the New Government], *SANA*, 17 April 2011, https://web.archive.org/web/20110818171502/https://sana.sy/ara/2/2011/04/17/341921.htm.
55. Syria Justice and Accountability Centre, 'Walls Have Ears: An Analysis of Classified Syrian Security Sector Documents', 2019, 17–19, https://syriaaccountability.org/content/files/2022/04/Walls-Have-Ears-English.pdf.
56. Head of the Joint Investigative Committee in Hama to the Military and Security Chief, cited in Commission for International Justice and Accountability, 'Behind the Curtain: Unravelling the Bureaucracy of Syria's Machinery of Death', 2023, https://cijaonline.org/news/2023/12/19/

behind-the-curtain-unravelling-the-bureaucracy-of-syrias-machinery-of-death.

57. Garance Le Caisne, *Operation Caesar: At the Heart of the Syrian Death Machine*, trans. David Watson (Cambridge: Polity Press, 2018); Human Rights Watch, 'If the Dead Could Speak: Mass Deaths and Torture in Syria's Detention Facilities', December 2015, https://www.hrw.org/report/2015/12/16/if-dead-could-speak/mass-deaths-and-torture-syrias-detention-facilities.
58. Jaber Baker and Uğur Ümit Üngör, *Syrian Gulag: Inside Assad's Prison System* (London: Bloomsbury Publishing, 2023), 285–206.
59. 'Āṣī Abū Najm, 'Al-Tansīqīyāt: Mawlūd min taḥt al-Arḍ [the *Tansiqiyat*: Born from Underground]', *al-Akhbar*, 29 September 2011, https://al-akhbar.com/Arab/95305.
60. 'Speech of Syrian President Bashar al-Assad at Damascus University on June 20, 2011', *Syria Report*, 21 June 2011, https://syria-report-com.proxy.library.georgetown.edu/speech-of-syrian-president-bashar-al-assad-at-damascus-university-on-june-20-2011/.
61. Mamdūḥ 'Adwān, *Ḥaywanat al-Insān: Dirāsa* [The Bestialization of Man: A Study], 6th ed. (Damascus: Dār Mamdūḥ 'Adwān li'l-Nashr wa'l-Tawzī', 2016), 155–58; al-Ḥājj Ṣāliḥ, *al-Thawra al-Mustaḥīla*, 46.
62. Aron Lund, 'Chasing Ghosts: The Shabiha Phenomenon', in *The 'Alawis of Syria: War, Faith and Politics in the Levant*, ed. Michael Kerr and Craig Larkin (New York: Oxford University Press, USA, 2015).
63. For details on early *shabbiha* massacres in Karam al-Zaytun, Homs see Uğur Ümit Üngör, 'Shabbiha: Paramilitary Groups, Mass Violence and Social Polarization in Homs', *Violence: An International Journal* 1, no. 1 (2020): 59–79, https://doi.org/10.1177/2633002420907771; for an indicative list of massacres from 2011 to 2013, see Syrian Center for Political and Strategic Studies and Syrian Expert House, *Syria Transition Roadmap* (Washington, D.C.: SCPSS, 2013), 163–65, https://web.archive.org/web/20160712181733/http://syrianexperthouse.org/download/813/.
64. Lisa Wedeen, *Authoritarian Apprehensions: Ideology, Judgment, and Mourning in Syria* (Chicago: University of Chicago Press, 2019).
65. Lund, 'Chasing Ghosts: The Shabiha Phenomenon', 213.
66. Syria News Press, 'Bashar al-Assad Speech, 3 June 2012', 3 June 2012, https://www.youtube.com/watch?v=5pOod4bamfc.

67. The level of donor interest can be gauged by the number of sponsored research projects on local councils during this time. See, for example, the informative analyses in Centre for Humanitarian Dialogue, 'Local Administration Structures in Opposition-Held Areas in Syria', 2014, https://www.google.com/url?sa=t&source=web&rct=j&opi=89978449&url=https://um.dk/en/-/media/websites/umen/danida/partnerships/research/local-administration-structures-syria.ashx&ved=2ahUKEwifiLzy60OGAxUeEVkFHXwcBZcQFnoECBQQAQ&usg=AOvVaw10B_O3ZVxInhi9vg9_4hsL; Institute for War and Peace Reporting, 'Local Governance Inside Syria', 9 April 2014, https://iwpr.net/global-voices/print-publications/local-governance-inside-syria; Doreen Khoury, 'Losing the Syrian Grassroots: Local Governance Structures Urgently Need Support', SWP Comments (Stiftung Wissenschaft Politik, 2013); Local Administration Councils Unit, 'The Indicator of Needs for the Local Councils of Syria', 2014, https://www.peacefare.net/wp-content/uploads/2015/10/Needs-for-the-Local-Councils-of-Syria-Public-Policy-Report.pdf; Swiss Peace, 'Perceptions of Governance: The Experience of Local Administrative Councils in Opposition-Held Syria', 2017, http://www.swisspeace.ch/fileadmin/ user_upload/pdf/Mediation/WOTRO_Report_The_Experience_of_Local_Administrative_ Councils_in_Opposition-held_Syria.pdf.
68. Ṣabr Darwīsh, *Sūrīya: Tajribat al-Mudun al-Muḥarrara* [The Experience of Liberated Towns in Syria] (Beirut: Riyāḍ al-Rayyis li'l-Kutub wa'l-Nashr, 2015); Dipali Mukhopadhyay and Kimberly Howe, *Good Rebel Governance: Revolutionary Politics and Western Intervention in Syria* (Cambridge: Cambridge University Press, 2023).
69. Rim Turkmani et al., 'Hungry for Peace: Positives and Pitfalls of Local Truces and Ceasefires in Syria' (London: London School of Economics and Political Science, 2014).
70. Will Todman, 'Sieges in Syria: Profiteering from Misery', Policy Focus (Middle East Institute, 2016), https://www.mei.edu/sites/default/files/publications/PF14_Todman_sieges_web_0.pdf.
71. '"Islamist Posturing" Is a Strategy to Raise Funds, Says Syrian Rebel', *France 24*, 21 November 2013, https://observers.france24.com/en/20131121-islamist-posturing-funds-syrian-rebel.

72. Charles R. Lister, *The Syrian Jihad: Al-Qaeda, the Islamic State and the Evolution of an Insurgency* (Oxford University Press, 2016).
73. Fawaz A. Gerges, *ISIS: A History* (Princeton: Princeton University Press, 2016); Lister, *The Syrian Jihad*; Michael Weiss and Hassan Hassan, *ISIS: Inside the Army of Terror (Updated Edition)* (New York: Regan Arts, 2016).
74. Lister, *The Syrian Jihad*, 236–40; for remarkable contemporary video footage, see *VICE News*, 'Bulldozing the Border Between Iraq and Syria: The Islamic State', 13 August 2014, https://www.youtube.com/watch?v=TxX_THjtXOw.
75. Weiss and Hassan, *ISIS*, 186–93.
76. Ariel I. Ahram, 'Sexual Violence, Competitive State Building, and Islamic State in Iraq and Syria', *Journal of Intervention and Statebuilding* 13, no. 2 (2019): 180–96; Charles C. Caris and Samuel Reynolds, 'ISIS Governance in Syria', Middle East Security Report (Institute for the Study of War, 2014), https://www.understandingwar.org/sites/default/files/ISIS_Governance.pdf; Mara Redlich Revkin, 'What Explains Taxation by Resource-Rich Rebels? Evidence from the Islamic State in Syria', *Journal of Politics* 82, no. 2 (April 2020): 757–64.
77. Harriet Allsopp and Wladimir van Wilgenburg, *The Kurds of Northern Syria: Governance, Diversity and Conflicts* (London: Bloomsbury Academic, 2019).
78. Holmes, Amy Austin, *Statelet of Survivors: The Making of a Semi Autonomous Region in Northeast Syria* (Oxford: Oxford University Press, 2023), 36–70; Michael Knights and Wladimir van Wilgenburg, *Accidental Allies: The US–Syrian Democratic Forces Partnership Against the Islamic State* (London: Bloomsbury Publishing, 2021), 38–85.
79. Christopher Phillips, *The Battle for Syria: International Rivalry in the New Middle East* (New Haven: Yale University Press, 2016), 168–81; Joby Warrick, *Red Line: The Unraveling of Syria and America's Race to Destroy the Most Dangerous Arsenal in the World* (New York: Doubleday, 2020).

12. NEW DIVISIONS, NEW BEGINNINGS: AN OVERVIEW, 2015–2025

1. 'al-Ra'īs al-Asad: al-Ma'raka Ma'rakat Miḥwar Mutakāmil yumaththil Manhaj min al-Istiqlālīya wa'l-Karāma [President Asad: The Battle Is an Integrated Approach for Independence and Dignity]', *SANA*, 26 July 2015, https://sana.sy/?p=245771.
2. Thomas L. Friedman, 'Obama Makes His Case on Iran Nuclear Deal', *The New York Times*, 14 July 2015, https://www.nytimes.com/2015/07/15/opinion/thomas-friedman-obama-makes-his-case-on-iran-nuclear-deal.html.
3. 'Russia Does Not Have Special Interests in Syria – Putin', *Interfax*, 2 June 2012, https://interfax.com/newsroom/top-stories/56227/.
4. Dmitri Trenin, *What Is Russia Up To in the Middle East?* (Cambridge: Polity Press, 2018), 57.
5. 'Putin Warns West Against Repeating Libyan Scenario in Syria', *TASS*, 3 December 2012, https://tass.com/russia/686367.
6. John W. Parker, *Putin's Syrian Gambit: Sharper Elbows, Bigger Footprint, Stickier Wicket*, Institute for National Strategic Studies Strategic Perspectives 25 (Washington, D.C.: National Defense University Press, 2017), 5.
7. For a global perspective of Russian foreign policy, see Trenin, *What Is Russia Up To in the Middle East?*, 34–50; Phillips, *The Battle for Syria*, 219–23.
8. Trenin, *What Is Russia Up To in the Middle East?* 70; 'Russia Says Tens of Thousands of Its Troops Fought in Syria', *AP News*, 22 August 2018, https://apnews.com/article/----f787223e4fee4946be853662505e95c4.
9. Parker, *Putin's Syrian Gambit*, 32.
10. 'President Al-Assad Congratulates Putin on Victory Day: Syrians Will Not Be Satisfied Until Defeating the Enemy', *SANA*, 5 May 2016, sec. Presidency of Syrian Arab Republic, http://sana.sy/en/?p=76435.
11. Samuel Oakford, 'Trump's Air War Has Already Killed More Than 2,000 Civilians', *The Daily Beast*, 17 July 2017, sec. world, https://www.thedailybeast.com/president-trumps-air-war-kills-12-civilians-per-day.
12. United Nations Office for the Coordination of Humanitarian Affairs, 'Syria: Recent Developments in North-West Syria',

12 September 2018, https://reliefweb.int/report/syrian-arab-republic/syria-recent-developments-north-west-syria-12-sep-2018.

13. Ahmad Abazeid and Thomas Pierret, 'Les Rebelles syriens d'Ahrar al-Sham: ressorts contextuels et organisationnels d'une déradicalisation en temps de guerre civile', *Critique internationale* 78, no. 1 (2018): 63–84, https://doi.org/10.3917/crii.078.0063; Jerome Drevon, *From Jihad to Politics: How Syrian Jihadis Embraced Politics* (Oxford: Oxford University Press, 2024); International Crisis Group, *Containing Transnational Jihadists in Syria's North West*, Middle East Report 239 (Brussels: ICG, 2023).
14. Abu Muhammad al-Jolani, 'Speech at the Opening Event of the Aleppo–Bab al-Hawa Road', Amjad Foundation for Media Production, 8 January 2022, https://bit.ly/3wYIEed, cited in Aaron Y. Zelin, *The Age of Political Jihadism: A Study of Hayat Tahrir al-Sham* (Lanham: Rowman & Littlefield, 2023), 30.
15. I. William Zartman, ed., *Collapsed States: The Disintegration and Restoration of Legitimate Authority* (Boulder: Lynne Rienner Publishers, 1995).
16. Dr Karam Shaar and Caroline Rose, 'From 2015–2023: The Captagon Trade's Trends, Trajectory, and Policy Implications' (New Lines Institute for Strategy and Policy, May 2024).

Bibliography

Ababsa, Myriam. 'The End of a World: Drought and Agrarian Transformation in Northeast Syria (2007–2010)'. In *Syria from Reform to Revolt: Political Economy and International Relations*, edited by Raymond A. Hinnebusch and Tina Zintl. Syracuse: Syracuse University Press, 2014.

Abazeid, Ahmad, and Thomas Pierret. 'Les Rebelles syriens d'Ahrar al-Sham: ressorts contextuels et organisationnels d'une déradicalisation en temps de guerre civile'. *Critique internationale* 78, no. 1 (2018): 63–84. https://doi.org/10.3917/crii.078.0063.

'Abd al-Karīm, Aḥmad. *Aḍwā' 'alā Tajribat al-Waḥda* [Insights into the Unity Experiment]. Damascus: al-Ahālī li'l-Ṭibā'a wa'l-Nashr wa'l-Tawzī', 1991.

Abboud, Samer. 'Locating the "Social" in the Social Market Economy'. In *Syria from Reform to Revolt: Political Economy and International Relations*, edited by Raymond A. Hinnebusch and Tina Zintl. Syracuse: Syracuse University Press, 2014.

Abī Rāshid, Ḥannā. *Jabal al-Durūz* [The Druze Mountain]. Cairo: n.p., 1925.

Abrash, Muḥammad Riyād al-. 'Al-Takhsīs Marra Ukhrā' [Privatization, One More Time]. *Al-Nashra al-Iqtisādīya Li-Ghurfat Tijārat Dimashq* 4 (1990): 50–62.

Abū Najm, 'Āṣī. 'Al-Tansīqīyāt: Mawlūd Min Taḥt al-Arḍ' [The Tansiqiyat: Born from Underground]. *al-Akhbar*, 29 September 2011. https://al-akhbar.com/Arab/95305.

Abu-Ismail, Khalid, Ali Abdel-Gadir and Heba El-Laithy. 'Poverty and Inequality in Syria (1997–2007)'. *Arab Development Challenges Report Background Paper 2011/15*. Cairo and New York: UNDP, 2011.

Abu-Lughod, Janet L. *Rabat: Urban Apartheid in Morocco*. Princeton: Princeton University Press, 1980.

'Adwān, Mamdūḥ. *Ḥaywanat al-Insān: Dirāsa* [The Bestialization of Man: A Study]. 6th ed. Damascus: Dār Mamdūḥ 'Adwān li'l-Nashr wa'l-Tawzī', 2016.

'Aflaq, Mīshīl. *Fī Sabīl al-Ba'th* [On the Path to Rebirth]. 4th ed. Beirut: Dār al-Ṭalī'a, 1970.

Ahram, Ariel I. 'Sexual Violence, Competitive State Building, and Islamic State in Iraq and Syria'. *Journal of Intervention and Statebuilding* 13, no. 2 (2019): 180–96.

Akhras, Chafic. 'Reflexions sur certains aspects de l'union économique entre la Syrie et l'Egypte'. In *Union économique et monétaire dans la RAU: opinions*. Damascus: Centre d'études et de documentations économiques, financières et sociales, 1959.

Aksakal, Mustafa. *The Ottoman Road to War in 1914: The Ottoman Empire and the First World War*. Cambridge: Cambridge University Press, 2008.

Al-'Arabiya TV. 'Interview with Shaykh Ahmad al-Sayāsana, Imam of the Umari Mosque in Dera'a'. 22 March 2011. https://www.youtube.com/watch?v=lVNzMMdA43g.

Al-Ḥayāt al-Yawmīya fī Qarya Sūrīya [Everyday Life in a Syrian Village], 1974. https://www.youtube.com/watch?v=OQWJs4lWxqY.

Alī, Muḥammad Ibrāhīm al-'. *Ḥayātī wa'l-I'dām* [My Life and Execution]. Vol. 2. 3 vols. Damascus: n.p. 2005.

Al-Iqtisādī. 'Hiwār al-Iqtisādī al-Kāmil Ma' Rajul al-A'māl Haytham Jūd' [The Full al-Iqtisādī Interview with Haytham Joud]. July 2011.

'Al-Khiṭṭa al-Khamsīya al-'Āshira fī Sūrīya 2006–2010' [The Tenth Five-Year Plan for Syria]. Damascus: Syrian Arab Republic, 2005.

al-Lajna al-Tanfīdhīya li'l-Mu'tamar al-Sūrī al-Falasṭīnī. *Al-Qadīya al-Surīya: Maẓālim al-Faransīyīn wa Fadā'i'uhum* [The Syrian Question: French Oppression and Atrocities]. Cairo: al-Matba'a al-'Arabīya bi-Miṣr, 1926.

Allsopp, Harriet. *The Kurds of Syria: Political Parties and Identity in the Middle East*. London: I.B. Tauris, 2015.

Allsopp, Harriet, and Wladimir van Wilgenburg. *The Kurds of Northern Syria: Governance, Diversity and Conflicts*. London: Bloomsbury Academic, 2019.

Al-Mālikī: Rajul wa Qadīya [al-Malki: The Man, the Affair]. Damascus: Manshūrāt al-Far' al-Thaqāfī al-'Askarī, 1956.

Al-Sharq al-Awsat. 'Interview with Bashar al-Asad'. 8 February 2001, English translation at https://al-bab.com/documents-section/interview-president-bashar-al-assad edition.

Amīn, Abū 'Assāf. *Dhikrayātī* [My Memories]. [Damascus]: al-Dār al-Waṭanīya al-Jadīda, 1996.

Amnesty International. 'Les Kurdes de La République Arabe Syrienne Un an Après Les Événements de Mars 2004'. MDE 24/002/2005, 2005.

Andréa, Charles Joseph Édouard. *La Révolte Druze et l'Insurrection de Damas, 1925–1926*. Paris: Payot, 1937.

AP News. 'Russia Says Tens of Thousands of Its Troops Fought in Syria'. 22 August 2018. https://apnews.com/article/----f787223e4fee4946be853662505e95c4.

Arab Economist. 'Syria: Significance of the Revival of Interest of the Private Sector'. July 1972, 42 edition.

Arslān, 'Ādil. *Mudhakkirāt al-Amīr 'Ādil Arslān: al-Mustadrak, 1948* [The Memoirs of Amīr Ādil Arslān: The 1948 Appendix], edited by Yūsuf Ībish. Beirut: al-Dār al-Taqaddumīya, 1994.

'Arūdkī, Yaḥyā. *al-Iqtiṣād al-Sūrī al-Ḥadīth* [The Modern Syrian Economy]. Vol. 1. 2 vols. Damascus: Wizārat al-Thaqāfah wa-al-Irshād al-Qawmī, 1972.

———. *al-Iqtiṣād al-Sūrī al-Ḥadīth* [The Modern Syrian Economy]. Vol. 2. 2 vols. Damascus: Wizārat al-Thaqāfah wa-al-Irshād al-Qawmī, 1972.

'Āṣ, Muḥammad Sa'īd al-. *Ṣafḥa min al-Ayyām al-Ḥamrā': Kitāb Yabḥath 'an al-Thawra al-Sūrīya wa-Tatawwurātihā. al-Waqā'i' al-Mustaqilla* [A Page from the Days of Blood: A Book on the Syrian Revolt and its Development: The Independent Facts]. Cairo: n.p., 1930.

'Āṣ, Muḥammad Sa'īd al-. *Al-Tajārib al-Ḥarbīya fī Ḥurūb al-Thawra al-Sūrīya* [Military Experience in the Wars of the Syrian Revolt]. Beirut: Dār al-Fikr, 1990.

Aṭrash, Manṣūr Sulṭān al-. *al-Jīl al-Mudān: Sīra Dhātīya, min Awrāq Manṣūr Sulṭān al-Aṭrash* [The Accursed Generation: An Autobiography from the Papers of Manṣūr Sulṭān al-Aṭrash], edited by Rīm Manṣūr al-Aṭrash. Beirut: Riyāḍ al-Rayyis li'l-Kutub wa'l-Nashr, 2008.

Aṭrash, Ṣulṭān al-. *Aḥdāth al-Thawra al-Sūrīya al-Kubrā ka-mā Saradahā*

Qā'iduhā al-'Āmm Ṣulṭān Bāshā al-Aṭrash, 1925–1927 [The Events of the Great Syrian Revolt of 1925–1927, as Narrated by its General Commander Sultan Pasha al-Atrash]. Damascus: Dār 'Alā al-Dīn, 2004.

'Aṭṭār, 'Adnān. *Thawrat al-Ḥurrīya fī al-Minṭaqa al-Sādisa bi-Dimashq, 1925–1926: Wādī Baradā wa'l-Muhājirīn wa'l-Ṣaliḥīya bi-Qiyādat Sa'īd 'Akkāsh* [The Freedom Revolt in the Sixth Region of Damascus, 1925–26]. Damascus: Dār Sa'd al-Dīn, 1991.

'Awaḍ, 'Abd al-'Azīz Muḥammad. *al-Idāra al-'Uthmānīya fī Wilāyat Sūrīya, 1864–1914* [Ottoman Administration in the Province of Syria]. Egypt: Dār al-Ma'ārif, 1969.

'Awdāt, Haytham al-. *Intifāḍat al-'Āmmīya al-Fallāḥīya fī Jabal al-'Arab* [The Peasant Commoners' Revolt in Jabal al-Arab]. [Damascus]: al-'Awdāt, 1976.

Ayalon, Ami, ed. *Middle East Contemporary Survey*. Vol. 15. Boulder: Westview Press, 1991.

———. *The Press in the Arab Middle East: A History*. Oxford: Oxford University Press, 1995.

———. 'The Syrian Educated Elite and the Literary Nahda'. In *Ottoman Reform and Muslim Regeneration*, edited by Buṭrus Abū Mannah and Itzchak Weismann. London: I.B. Tauris, 2005.

'Aẓm, Khālid al-. *Mudhakkirāt Khālid al-'Aẓm* [The Memoirs of Khālid al-'Aẓm]. Vol. 1. 3 vols. Beirut: al-Dār al-Muttaḥida li'l-Nashr, 1973.

———. *Mudhakkirāt Khālid al-'Aẓm* [The Memoirs of Khālid al-'Aẓm]. Vol. 2. 3 vols. Beirut: al-Dār al-Muttaḥida li'l-Nashr, 1973.

———. *Mudhakkirāt Khālid al-'Aẓm* [The Memoirs of Khālid al-'Aẓm]. Vol. 3. 3 vols. Beirut: al-Dār al-Muttaḥida li'l-Nashr, 1973.

'Aẓma, Bashīr al-. *Jīl al-Hazīma min al-Dhākira* [Generation of Defeat: Memoires]. 2nd ed. Beirut: al-Mu'assasa al-'Arabīya li'l-Dirāsāt wa'l-Nashr, 1998.

Bābīl, Naṣūḥ. *Ṣiḥāfa wa-Siyāsa: Sūrīya fī'l-Qarn al-'Ishrīn* [Press and Politics: Syria in the 20th Century]. London: Riyad El-Rayyis, 1987.

Baghdādī, 'Abd al-Laṭīf al-. *Mudhakkirāt 'Abd al-Laṭīf al-Baghdādī*. Vol. 2. Cairo: al-Maktab al-Miṣrī al-Ḥadīth, 1977.

Bahout, Joseph. *Les Entrepreneurs syriens: Économie, affaires et politique*. Beirut: Presses de l'Ifpo, 1994.

Baker, Jaber, and Uğur Ümit Üngör. *Syrian Gulag: Inside Assad's Prison System*. London: Bloomsbury Publishing, 2023.

Barakat, Awad. 'Reflexions à Propos de l'union Monétaire Entre Les Deux Régions de La République Arabe Unie'. In *Union Économique et Monétaire Dans La RAU: Opinions*. Damascus: Centre d'Études et de Documentations économiques, financières et sociales, 1959.

Barrows, Leland. 'The Impact of Empire on the French Armed Forces, 1830–1920'. In *Double Impact: France and Africa in the Age of Imperialism*, edited by G. Wesley Johnson. Westport, Conn.: Greenwood Press, 1985.

Bārūt, Muḥammad Jamāl. *Al-'Aqd al-Akhīr fī Tārīkh Sūrīya: Jadalīyat al-Jumūd wa'l-Iṣlāḥ* [The Last Decade in the History of Syria: The Dialectic of Stagnation and Reform]. Doha: al-Markaz al-'Arabī li'l-Abḥāth wa-Dirāsat al-Siyāsāt, 2012.

———. *al-Takawwun al-Tārīkhī al-Ḥadīth li'l-Jazīra al-Sūrīya: As'ila wa-Ishkālīyāt al-Taḥawwul min al-Badwana ilā al-'Umrān al-Ḥaḍarī* [The Historical Formation of Modern Syrian Jazīra: Questions and Problematiques of the Transition from Nomadism to Sedentarism]. Beirut: al-Markaz al-'Arabī lil-Abḥāth wa-Dirāsat al-Siyāsāt, 2013.

Bārūt, Muḥammad Jamāl, and Kīlānī Shams al-Dīn. 'Muqaddima' [Introduction]. In *Sūrīya bayna 'Ahdayn: Qaḍāyā al-Marḥala al-Intiqālīya* [Syria Between Two Eras: Issues for the Transition Period], edited by Muḥammad Jamāl Bārūt and Kīlānī Shams al-Dīn, 17–65. 'Amman: Dār Sindbād li'l-Nashr, 2003.

———, eds. *Sūrīya bayna 'Ahdayn: Qaḍāyā al-Marḥala al-Intiqālīya* [Syria between Two Eras: Issues for the Transition Period]. 'Amman: Dār Sindbād li'l-Nashr, 2003.

Batatu, Hanna. *Syria's Peasantry, the Descendants of Its Lesser Rural Notables, and Their Politics*. Princeton: Princeton University Press, 1999.

———. 'Some Observations on the Social Roots of Syria's Ruling, Military Group and the Causes for Its Dominance'. *Middle East Journal* 35, no. 3 (1981): 331–44.

Baumann, Hannes. *Citizen Hariri: Lebanon's Neo-Liberal Reconstruction*. Oxford: Oxford University Press, 2017.

Bayraqdār, Faraj. *Khiyānāt al-Lugha wa'l-Ṣamt: Taghrībatī fī Sujūn al-Mukhābarāt al-Sūrīya* [The Betrayals of Speech and Silence: My Disappearance in the Prisons of Syrian Intelligence]. Beirut: al-Jadīd, 2006.

Bell, Gertude. *Syria: The Desert and the Sown*. New York: Arno Press, 1973.

Ben-Tzur, Avraham. 'The Neo-Ba'th Party of Syria'. *Journal of Contemporary History* 3, no. 3 (1968): 161–81.

Bishāra, 'Azmī. *Sūrīya: Darb al-Ālām Naḥwa al-Ḥurrīya: Muḥāwala fī al-Tārīkh al-Rāhin* [Syria: The Painful Path to Freedom: An Essay in Contemporary History]. Beirut: al-Markaz al-'Arabī li'l-Abḥāth wa-Dirāsat al-Siyāsāt, 2013.

Bitar, Yassar. 'De l'Union Monétaire Entre La Syrie et l'Egypte'. In *Union Économique et Monétaire Dans La RAU: Opinions*. Damascus: Centre d'Études et de Documentations économiques, financières et sociales, 1959.

Bokova, Lenka. 'La Révolution Française Dans Le Discours de l'insurrection Syrienne Contre Le Mandat Français (1925–1927)'. *Revue Du Monde Musulman et de La Méditerrannée* 51–53 (1989): 207–17.

Bourgey, André. 'Le barrage de Tabqa et l'aménagement du bassin de l'Euphrate en Syrie'. *Géocarrefour* 49, no. 4 (1974): 343–54.

Brower, Benjamin Claude. *A Desert Named Peace: The Violence of France's Empire in the Algerian Sahara, 1844–1902*. New York: Columbia University Press, 2011.

Bujayramī, Yūsuf al-. *Ḥiwārāt al-Iṣlaḥ wa'l-Infitāḥ fī Sūriyā* [Dialogues of Reform and Liberalization in Syria]. Damascus: Dār al-Ḥawrān li'l-Tibā'a wa'l-Nashr, 2001.

Bunnī, Akram al-. 'Iqtisād al-Sūq al-Ijtimā'i' [The Social Market Economy]. Al Jazeera.net, 13 January 2006. https://www.aljazeera.net/opinions/2006/1/13/اقتصاد-السوق-الاجتماعي-ماله-وما-عليه.

Burke III, Edmund. *The Ethnographic State: France and the Invention of Moroccan Islam*. Oakland: University of California Press, 2014.

———. 'A Comparative View of French Native Policy in Morocco and Syria, 1912–1925'. *Middle Eastern Studies* 9, no. 2 (1973): 175–86.

Caisne, Garance Le. *Operation Caesar: At the Heart of the Syrian Death Machine*. Translated by David Watson. Cambridge: Polity Press, 2018.

Carbillet, Gabriel. *Au Djebel Druse: choses vues et vécues*. Paris: Éditions Argo, 1929.

Caris, Charles C., and Samuel Reynolds. 'ISIS Governance in Syria'. Middle East Security Report. Institute for the Study of War, 2014. https://www.understandingwar.org/sites/default/files/ISIS_Governance.pdf.

Catroux, Georges. *Deux missions en Moyen-Orient*. Paris: Plon, 1958.

Centre for Humanitarian Dialogue. 'Local Administration Structures in Opposition-Held Areas in Syria', 2014. https://www.google.com/url?sa=t&source=web&rct=j&opi=89978449&url=https://um.dk/en/-/media/websites/umen/danida/partnerships/research/local-administration-structures-syria.ashx&ved=2ahUKEwifiLzy60OGAxUeEVkFHXwcBZcQFnoECBQQAQ&usg=AOvVaw10B_O3ZVxInhi9vg9_4hsL.

Chaitani, Youssef. *Post-Colonial Syria and Lebanon: The Decline of Arab Nationalism and the Triumph of the State*. London: I.B. Tauris, 2007.

Châtel, Francesca de. 'The Role of Drought and Climate Change in the Syrian Uprising: Untangling the Triggers of the Revolution'. *Middle Eastern Studies* 50, no. 4 (2014): 521–35.

Çiçek, M. Talha. *War and State Formation in Syria: Cemal Pasha's Governorate During World War I, 1914–1917*. London: Routledge, 2014.

Clément-Grandcourt, Abel Jean Ernest. *Au Levant: histoires de brigands, histoires vraies*. Paris: Attinger, 1936.

Commission for International Justice and Accountability. 'Behind the Curtain: Unravelling the Bureaucracy of Syria's Machinery of Death', 2023. https://cijaonline.org/news/2023/12/19/behind-the-curtain-unravelling-the-bureaucracy-of-syrias-machinery-of-death.

Commission of Inquiry into Actions of Canadian Officials in Relation to Maher Arar. Ontario: Public Works and Government Services Canada, 2006. www.therenditionproject.org.uk.

Cooke, Miriam. *Dissident Syria: Making Oppositional Arts Official*. Durham N.C.: Duke University Press, 2007.

Dāghir, As'ad Khalīl. *Thawrat al-'Arab: Muqaddimātuhā, Asbābuhā, Natā'ijuhā: al-Mulk fī al-'Arab* [The Precursors, Causes and Results of the Arab Revolt: Sovereignty among the Arabs]. Egypt: Maṭba'at al-Muqaṭṭam, 1916.

Daguerre, Violetter, ed. *Démocratie et Droits Humains En Syrie*. Translated by Ahmed Manai and Hakim Arabdiou. Paris: Editions Eurabe, 2002.

Darwīsh, Ṣabr. *Sūrīya: Tajribat al-Mudun al-Muḥarrara* [The Experience of Liberated Towns in Syria]. Beirut: Riyāḍ al-Rayyis li'l-Kutub wa'l-Nashr, 2015.

David, Jean-Claude. 'Alep'. In *La Syrie d'aujourd'hui*, edited by André Raymond. Paris: Editions du CNRS, 1980.

Dawisha, A. I. *Arab Nationalism in the Twentieth Century: From Triumph to Despair*. Princeton: Princeton University Press, 2003.

Dbiyat, Mohamed al-. *Homs et Hama en Syrie centrale: concurrence urbaine et développement régional*. Damascus Institut français de Damas, 1995.

Deringil, Selim. *The Well-Protected Domains: Ideology and the Legitimation of Power in the Ottoman Empire, 1876–1909*. London: I.B. Tauris, 1999.

———. '"They Live in a State of Nomadism and Savagery": The Late Ottoman Empire and the Post-Colonial Debate'. *Comparative Studies in Society and History* 45, no. 2 (2003): 311–42.

Devlin, John F. *The Ba'th Party: A History from the Origins to 1966*. Stanford: Hoover Institution Press, 1976.

Di-Capua, Yoav. 'Nahda: The Arab Project of Enlightenment'. In *The Cambridge Companion to Modern Arab Culture*, edited by Dwight F. Reynolds. Cambridge: Cambridge University Press, 2015.

Difāʿ al-Duktūr Mūnīr al-ʿAjlānī Amām al-Maḥkama al-ʿAskarīya Bi-Dimashq [The Defence of Dr Munir al-Ajlani before the Military Court in Damascus]. n.p.: n.p., 1957.

Diyāb, ʿIzz al-Dīn. *Akram al-Ḥawrānī Kamā A'rifuhi* [Akram al-Hawrani as I Know Him]. Beirut: Bīsān, 1998.

Douwes, Dick. *The Ottomans in Syria: A History of Justice and Oppression*. London: I.B. Tauris, 2000.

Drevon, Jerome. *From Jihad to Politics: How Syrian Jihadis Embraced Politics*. Oxford: Oxford University Press, 2024.

Dukhan, Haian. *State and Tribes in Syria: Informal Alliances and Conflict Patterns*. London: Routledge, 2019.

Dupret, Baudouin, Myriam Ababsa and Eric Denis, eds. *Popular Housing and Urban Land Tenure in the Middle East: Case Studies from Egypt,*

Syria, Jordan, Lebanon, and Turkey. Cairo: American University in Cairo Press, 2012.

Eichengreen, Barry. *Globalizing Capital: A History of the International Monetary System, Second Edition*. 2nd ed. Princeton: Princeton University Press, 2008.

El-Husseini, Rola. *Pax Syriana: Elite Politics in Postwar Lebanon*. Syracuse: Syracuse University Press, 2012.

Elshakry, Marwa. *Reading Darwin in Arabic, 1860–1950*. Chicago: University of Chicago Press, 2014.

Elvira, Laura Ruiz de. 'Christian Charities and the Ba'thist Regime in Bashar al-Asad's Syria'. In *Syria from Reform to Revolt: Culture, Society, and Religion*, edited by Leif Stenberg and Christa Salamandra. Syracuse: Syracuse University Press, 2015.

———. 'State-Charities Relations in Syria: Between Reinforcement, Control and Coercion'. In *Civil Society and the State in Syria: The Outsourcing of Civil Responsibility*, edited by Tina Zintl and Laura Ruiz de Elvira, 7–31. St Andrews: University of St Andrews Centre for Syrian Studies, 2012.

Faḍl Allāh, Abū Manṣūr. *A'āṣīr: Mudhakkirāt 'an Khafāyā al-Inqilābāt al-Sūrīya al-Arba'a, Katabahā Shāhid 'Iyān Ashama fī Takhṭīṭ al-A'māl al-Inqilābīya wa-fī Tanfīdhihā: Ḥaqā'iq wa-Wathā'iq wa-Asrār Lam Tunshar Ba'd* [Storms: Memoirs of the Background to the Four Syrian Coups, Written by an Eye Witness Who Participated in Planning and Implementing the Putsch Action: Facts, Documents and Secrets That Have Not Yet Been Published]. Beirut? n.p., 1959.

Fahmy, Khaled. *All the Pasha's Men: Mehmed Ali, His Army and the Making of Modern Egypt*. Cairo: AUC Press, 2002.

Fanṣah, Nadhīr. *Ayyām Ḥusnī al-Za'īm: 137 Yawman Hazzat Sūriyā* [The Times of Husni al-Za'im: 137 Days That Shook Syria]. Beirut: Dār al-Āfāq al-Jadīdah, 1982.

Fawaz, Leila Tarazi. *A Land of Aching Hearts: The Middle East in the Great War*. Cambridge: Harvard University Press, 2014.

Fortna, Benjamin C. *Imperial Classroom: Islam, the State, and Education in the Late Ottoman Empire*. Oxford: Oxford University Press, 2002.

France 24. '"Islamist Posturing" Is a Strategy to Raise Funds, Says Syrian

Rebel'. 21 November 2013. https://observers.france24.com/en/20131121-islamist-posturing-funds-syrian-rebel.

Friedman, Thomas L. 'Obama Makes His Case on Iran Nuclear Deal'. *The New York Times*, 14 July 2015. https://www.nytimes.com/2015/07/15/opinion/thomas-friedman-obama-makes-his-case-on-iran-nuclear-deal.html.

Gallagher, John, and Ronald Robinson. 'The Imperialism of Free Trade'. *The Economic History Review* 6, no. 1 (1953): 1–15. https://doi.org/10.2307/2591017.

Gates, Carolyn. *Merchant Republic of Lebanon: Rise of an Open Economy*. London: I.B. Tauris, 1998.

Gaulle, Charles de, Louis Pierre Jean Yvon, Jean Martin Gallevier de Mierry and Exposition coloniale. *Histoire des troupes du Levant*. Paris: Imprimerie nationale, 1931.

Gaunson, A. B. *The Anglo-French Clash in Lebanon and Syria, 1940–45*. New York: St. Martin's Press, 1987.

Gelvin, James L. *Divided Loyalties: Nationalism and Mass Politics in Syria at the Close of Empire*. Berkeley: University of California Press, 1999.

George, Alan. *Syria: Neither Bread nor Freedom*. London: Zed Books, 2003.

———. 'Patronage and Clientelism in Bashar's Social Market Economy'. In *The 'Alawis of Syria: War, Faith and Politics in the Levant*, edited by Michael Kerr and Craig Larkin. New York: Oxford University Press, 2015.

Gerber, Haim. *The Social Origins of the Modern Middle East*. Boulder: Lynne Rienner Publishers, 1987.

Gerges, Fawaz A. *ISIS: A History*. Princeton: Princeton University Press, 2016.

Gershoni, Israel, and James P. Jankowski. *Redefining the Egyptian Nation, 1930–1945*. Cambridge: Cambridge University Press, 1995.

Ghadbian, Najib. 'Contesting Authoritarianism: Opposition Activism under Bashar al-Asad, 2000–2010'. In *Syria from Reform to Revolt: Political Economy and International Relations*, edited by Raymond A. Hinnebusch and Tina Zintl. Syracuse: Syracuse University Press, 2014.

Ghali, Kamal. 'La Durée de La Phase Transitoire de l'Union Économique Totale: L'Union Monétaire'. In *Union Économique et*

Monétaire Dans La RAU: Opinions. Damascus: Centre d'Études et de Documentations économiques, financières et sociales, 1959.

Ghalyūn, Burhān. *Bayān Min Ajl al-Dīmuqrāṭīya* [Manifesto for Democracy]. 5th ed. Morocco: al-Markaz al-Thaqāfī al-'Arabī, 1986.

Ghāzī, Ibrahīm. *Nash'at al-Shurṭa wa-Tārīkhuha fī Surīya* [The Evolution of the Police and Its History in Syria]. Damascus: Dār al-'Ilm al-Ḥadīth, 1999.

Gibb, Sir Alexander. *The Economic Development of Syria*. London: Knapp, Drewett and Sons, 1947.

Ginat, Rami. 'The Soviet Union and the Syrian Ba'th Regime: From Hesitation to Rapprochement'. *Middle Eastern Studies* 36, no. 2 (2000): 150–71.

Godlewska, Anne. 'Map, Text and Image. The Mentality of Enlightened Conquerors: A New Look at the Description de l'Egypte'. *Transactions of the Institute of British Geographers* 20, no. 1 (1995): 5–28.

Gottmann, Jean. 'Bugeaud, Galliéni, Lyautey: The Development of French Colonial Warfare'. In *Makers of Modern Strategy: Military Thought from Machiavelli to Hitler*, edited by Edward Mead Earle. Princeton: Princeton University Press, 1943.

Goulden, Robert. 'Housing, Inequality, and Economic Change in Syria'. *British Journal of Middle Eastern Studies* 38, no. 2 (2011): 187–202.

Gouraud, Henri. *La France en Syrie*. [Corbeil]: [Imp. Crété], 1922.

Greene, Molly. 'The Ottoman Experience'. *Daedalus* 134, no. 2 (2005): 88–99.

Gross, Max L. 'Ottoman Rule in the Province of Damascus 1860–1909'. PhD, Georgetown University, 1979.

Ḥaddād, Luṭfī. *Riyāḍ al-Turk: Māndīllā Sūrīya* [Riyad al-Turk: Syria's Mandela]. Newburgh: Mu'assasat Judhūr al-Thaqāfīya, 2005.

Ḥaffār, Luṭfī al-. *Dhikrayāt: Muntakhabāt min Khuṭab wa-Aḥādīth wa-Maqālāt* [Memoires: Selected Speeches, Anecdotes, and Essays]. Damascus: Maṭābi' Ibn Zaydūn, 1954.

Ḥakīm, Da'd al-, ed. *Ṣafaḥāt min Ḥayāt Nazīh Mu'ayyad al-'Aẓm* [Pages from the Life of Nazīh Mu'ayyad al-'Aẓm]. Damascus: Wizārat al-Thaqāfa, 2006.

Ḥakīm, Ḥasan al-. *al-Wathā'iq al-Tārīkhīya al-Mu'alliqa bi'l-Qaḍīya al-Sūrīya fī al-'Ahdayn al-'Arabī al-Fayṣalī wa'l-Intidābī al-Faransī*

1915–1946 [Historical Documents Related to the Syrian Question in the Faysal-Arab and French Mandate Eras]. Beirut: Dār Ṣādir, 1974.

Ḥamdān, Ḥamdān. *Akram al-Ḥawrānī: Rajul li'l-Tārīkh* [Akram al-Hawrani: A Man for History]. Beirut: Baysān lil-Nashr wa-al-Tawzī', 1996.

Hammad, Hanan. *Unknown Past: Layla Murad, the Jewish-Muslim Star of Egypt*. Stanford: Stanford University Press, 2022.

Hanioğlu, M. Şükrü. *A Brief History of the Late Ottoman Empire*. Princeton: Princeton University Press, 2010.

Ḥannā, 'Abd Allāh. *al-Ḥaraka al-'Ummālīya fī Sūrīya wa-Lubnān, 1900–1945* [The Workers' Movement in Syria and Lebanon, 1900–1945]. Damascus: Dār Dimashq, 1973.

———. *al-'Āmmīya wa'l-Intifāḍāt al-Fallāḥīya, 1850–1918, fī Jabal Ḥawrān* [The Ammiyah and Peasant Revolts in Jabal Hawran, 1850–1918]. Damascus: al-Ahālī lil-Ṭibā'a wa'l-Nashr wa'l-Tawzī', 1990.

———. *Al-Qaḍīya al-Zirā'īya wa'l-Ḥaraka al-Fallāḥīya fī Sūrīya wa-Lubnān, 1920–1945* [The Agricultural Question and the Peasant Movement in Syria and Lebanon, 1920–1945]. Vol. 2. Damascus: Dār al-Farābī, 1978.

Hanssen, Jens. 'Practices of Integration: Center-Periphery Relations in the Ottoman Empire'. In *The Empire in the City: Arab Provincial Capitals in the Late Ottoman Empire*, edited by Jens Hanssen, Thomas Philipp and Stefan Weber. Würzburg: Ergon in Kommission, 2002.

Hanssen, Jens, and Max Weiss, eds. *Arabic Thought Beyond the Liberal Age: Towards an Intellectual History of the Nahda*. Cambridge: Cambridge University Press, 2016.

Harik, Iliya. 'The Single Party as a Subordinate Movement: The Case of Egypt'. *World Politics* 26, no. 1 (1973): 80–105.

Harik, Iliya F. *The Political Mobilization of Peasants: A Study of an Egyptian Community*. Bloomington: Indiana University Press, 1974.

Ḥawrānī, Akram al-. *Mudhakkirāt Akram al-Ḥawrānī* [The Memoirs of Akram al-Hawrani]. 4 vols. Cairo: Maktabat Madbūlī, 1999.

Haykal, Muḥammad Ḥasanayn. *Mā alladhī Jarā fī Sūriyā* [What Happened in Syria]. Cairo: al-Dār al-Qawmīya li'l-Ṭibā'a wa'l-Nashr, 1962.

Helbaoui, Youssef. *La Syrie: Mise En Valeur d'un Pays Sous-Developpé*. Paris: Librairie générale de droit et de jurisprudence, 1956.

Heydemann, Steven. *Authoritarianism in Syria: Institutions and Social Conflict, 1946–70*. Ithaca: Cornell University Press, 1999.

Hilāl, Muḥammad Ṭalab. *Dirāsa ʿan Muḥāfaẓat al-Jazīra: Min al-Nawāḥī al-Qawmīya wa'l-Ijtimāʿīya wa'l-Siyāsīya* [A Study of the Governorate of al-Jazira: Some Political, Social and Nationalist Aspects]. Irbil: Kāwā li'l-Nashr wa'l-Tawzīʿ, 2001.

Hinnebusch, Raymond. 'The Ba'th Party in Post-Ba'thist Syria: President, Party and the Struggle for "Reform"'. *Middle East Critique* 20, no. 2 (2011): 109–25.

Hinnebusch, Raymond A. *Authoritarian Power and State Formation in Ba'thist Syria: Army, Party, and Peasant*. Boulder: Westview Press, 1990.

———. 'The Political Economy of Economic Liberalization in Syria'. *International Journal of Middle East Studies* 27, no. 3 (1995): 305–20.

Ḥizb al-Baʿth al-ʿArabī al-Ishtirākī. 'Baʿḍ al-Munṭalaqāt al-Naẓarīya' [Some Theoretical Points of Departure]. In *Niḍāl al-Baʿth* [The Struggle of the Ba'th], Vol. 4. Beirut: Dār al-Ṭalīʿa li'l-Ṭibāʿa wa'l-Nashr, 1976.

———. 'Qirārāt al-Mu'tamar al-Qawmī al-Sādis, 1963'. In *Niḍāl al-Baʿth*, Vol. 4. Beirut: Dār al-Ṭalīʿa li'l-Ṭibāʿa wa'l-Nashr, 1976.

Hobsbawm, Eric J. *The Age of Capital, 1848–1875*. London: Abacus, 2003.

Hobsbawm, Eric, and Terence Ranger. *The Invention of Tradition*. Cambridge: Cambridge University Press, 1992.

Hoffmann, Sophia. *Iraqi Migrants in Syria: The Crisis before the Storm*. Syracuse: Syracuse University Press, 2016.

Holmes, Amy Austin. *Statelet of Survivors: The Making of a Semi-Autonomous Region in Northeast Syria*. Oxford: Oxford University Press, 2023.

Hourani, Albert. *Arabic Thought in the Liberal Age 1798–1939*. Cambridge: Cambridge University Press, 1983.

Human Rights Watch. 'If the Dead Could Speak: Mass Deaths and Torture in Syria's Detention Facilities', December 2015. https://www.hrw.org/report/2015/12/16/if-dead-could-speak/mass-deaths-and-torture-syrias-detention-facilities.

Ḥuṣrī, Abū Khaldūn Sāṭiʿ al-. *Abḥāth Mukhtāra fī al-Qawmīya al-ʿArabīya*

[Selected Studies in Arab Nationalism]. 2nd ed. Beirut: Markaz Dirāsāt al-Waḥda al-ʿArabīya, 1985.

Ḥuṣṣ, Salīm al-. *Li'l-Ḥaqīqa wa'l-Tārīkh: Tajārib al-Ḥukm Mā Bayna 1998 wa-2000* [For Truth and History: Experiences of Government between 1998 and 2000]. Beirut: Sharikat al-Maṭbūʿāt li'l-Tawzīʿ wa'l-Nashr, 2001.

Institute for War and Peace Reporting. 'Local Governance Inside Syria', 9 April 2014. https://iwpr.net/global-voices/print-publications/local-governance-inside-syria.

Interfax. 'Russia Does Not Have Special Interests in Syria – Putin'. 2 June 2012. https://interfax.com/newsroom/top-stories/56227/.

International Bank for Reconstruction and Development. 'The Economy of the Syrian Arab Republic', 31 October 1963.

International Bank for Reconstruction and Development. *The Economic Development of Syria*. Baltimore: Johns Hopkins Press, 1955.

International Crisis Group. *Containing Transnational Jihadists in Syria's North West*. Middle East Report 239. Brussels: ICG, 2023.

Issawi, Charles. *An Economic History of the Middle East and North Africa*. London: Routledge, 2006.

Jabartī, ʿAbd al-Raḥmān al-. *Al-Jabartī's Chronicle of the First Seven Months of the French Occupation of Egypt, 15 June–December 1798*. Translated by Shmuel Moreh. Leiden: Brill, 1975.

Jamʿīyat al-Ikhwān al-Muslimīn, al-Maktab al-Iʿlāmī. *Ḥamāh Ma'sāt al-ʿAṣr* [Hama: Tragedy of the Age]. [Beirut]: Min Manshurāt al-Taḥāluf al-Waṭanī li-Tahrīr Sūrīya, 1983.

Jankowski, James P. *Nasser's Egypt, Arab Nationalism, and the United Arab Republic*. Boulder: Lynne Rienner Publishers, 2002.

Johnson, Rebecca C. 'Foreword'. In *Leg Over Leg*, by Ahmad Faris al-Shidyaq, edited by Humphrey Davies, Vol. 1. New York: NYU Press, 2013.

Joubin, Rebecca. *The Politics of Love: Sexuality, Gender, and Marriage in Syrian Television Drama*. Lanham: Lexington Books, 2013.

Jundī, Sāmī al-. *Al-Baʿth*. Beirut: Dar al-Nahār li'l-Nashr, 1969.

Kassab, Elizabeth Suzanne. *Contemporary Arab Thought: Cultural Critique in Comparative Perspective*. New York: Columbia University Press, 2010.

———. *Enlightenment on the Eve of Revolution: The Egyptian and Syrian Debates*. New York: Columbia University Press, 2019.
Kawākibī, 'Abd al-Raḥmān al-. *Umm al-Qurā: wa-huwa ḍabṭ mufāwaḍ āṭ wa-Muqarrarāt Mu'tamar al-Nahḍa al-Islāmīya al-mun'aqid fī Makka al-Mukarrama Sanat 1316* [The Mother of Villages: Proceedings of the First Conference on the Islamic Awakening Held in Holy Mecca in the year 1316]. Beirut: Dār al-Rā'id al-'Arabī, 1982.
Kawakibi, Salam. 'The Paradox of Government-Organized Civil Activism in Syria'. In *Civil Society in Syria and Iran: Activism in Authoritarian Contexts*, edited by Paul Aarts and Francesco Cavatorta. Boulder: Lynne Rienner Publishers, 2013.
Kayali, Hasan. *Arabs and Young Turks: Ottomanism, Arabism, and Islamism in the Ottoman Empire, 1908–1918*. Berkeley: University of California Press, 1997.
Keilany, Ziad. 'Land Reform in Syria'. *Middle Eastern Studies* 16, no. 3 (1980): 209–24.
Khaddām, 'Abd al-Ḥalīm. 'Muḥāḍarat Nā'ib al-Ra'īs 'Abd al-Ḥalīm Khaddām' [Lecture by Vice President Khaddam], University of Damascus, 16 February 2001. In *Sūrīya bayna 'Ahdayn: Qaḍāyā al-Marḥala al-Intiqālīya* [Syria Between Two Eras: Issues for the Transition Period], edited by Muḥammad Jamāl Bārūt and Kīlānī Shams al-Dīn, 149–145. Amman: Dār Sindbād li'l-Nashr, 2003.
Khadduri, Majid. 'The Alexandretta Dispute'. *The American Journal of International Law* 39, no. 3 (1945): 406–25. https://doi.org/10.2307/2193522.
———. 'Constitutional Development in Syria: With Emphasis on the Constitution of 1950'. *Middle East Journal* 5, no. 4 (1951): 137–60.
Khalaf, Samir. *Civil and Uncivil Violence in Lebanon: A History of the Internationalization of Communal Conflict*. New York: Columbia University Press, 2003.
Khalidi, Rashid. *Palestinian Identity: The Construction of Modern National Consciousness*. New York: Columbia University Press, 2010.
Khalīfa, Muṣṭafā. *al-Qawqa'a: Yawmiyyāt Mutalaṣṣiṣ* [The Shell: The Diary of a Voyeur]. Beirut: Dār al-Ādāb, 2008.
Khalīl, Hānī. *Ḥāfiẓ al-Asad: al-Aydiyūlūjiyā al-Thawrīya wa'l-Fikr al-Siyāsī*

[Hafiz al-Asad: Revolutionary Ideology and Political Thought]. Damascus: Ṭalās li'l-Dirāsāt wa'l-Tarjama wa'l-Nashr, 1987.

Khānī, 'Abd Allāh Fikrī al-. *Sūrīya bayna al-Dīmuqrāṭīya wa'l-Ḥukm al-Fardī: 'Ashr Sanawāt fī'l-Amāna al-'Āmma li-Ri'āsat al-Jumhūrīya, 1948–1958* [Syria Between Democracy and Despotism: Ten Years in the General Secretariat of the Presidency of the Republic]. Beirut: Dār al-Nafā'is, 2004.

Khayyir, Hānī. *Adīb al-Shīshaklī: Ṣāḥib al-Inqilāb al-Thālith fī Sūriyā: al-Bidāya wa'l-Nihāya* [Adīb al-Shīshaklī, Leader of the Third Coup in Syria: The Beginning and the End]. Damascus: Maktab al-Fayhā', 1994.

———. *Akram al-Ḥawrānī bayna al-Tanaqqulāt al-Siyāsīya wa'l-Inqilābāt al-'Askarīya* [Akram al-Ḥawrānī Between Political Positions and Military Coups]. Damascus: Tawzī' Maktabat al-Sharq al-Jadīd, 1996.

Khoury, Doreen. 'Losing the Syrian Grassroots: Local Governance Structures Urgently Need Support'. SWP Comments. Stiftung Wissenschaft Politik, 2013.

Khoury, Philip S. *Syria and the French Mandate: The Politics of Arab Nationalism, 1920–1945*. Princeton: Princeton University Press, 1987.

———. *Urban Notables and Arab Nationalism: The Politics of Damascus 1860–1920*. Cambridge: Cambridge University Press, 1983.

Khuṭwa Khuṭwa [Step by Step], dir. Ossama Muhammad, 1978. https://www.youtube.com/watch?v=Zs9rsF2LUxo.

Knights, Michael, and Wladimir van Wilgenburg. *Accidental Allies: The US–Syrian Democratic Forces Partnership Against the Islamic State*. London: Bloomsbury Publishing, 2021.

Kurd 'Alī, Muḥammad. *al-Mudhakkirāt* [Memoirs]. Vol. 4. Damascus: Maṭba'at al-Taraqqī, 1951.

Kuzbarī, Ma'mūn al-. 'Mudhakkirāt' [Memoirs] (unpublished).

Landis, Joshua. 'Shishakli and the Druzes: Integration and Intransigeance'. In *The Syrian Land: Processes of Integration and Fragmentation*, edited by Thomas Philipp and Birgit Schäbler, 369–96. Stuttgart: Franz Steiner Verlag, 1998.

———. 'Syria and the Palestine War: Fighting King 'Abdullah's "Greater Syria Plan"'. In *The War for Palestine: Rewriting the History of 1948*, edited by Eugene Rogan. Cambridge: Cambridge University Press, 2001.

Landis, Joshua M. 'Nationalism and the Politics of Za'ama: The Collapse of Republican Syria, 1945–1949'. PhD, Princeton University, 1997.

Landis, Joshua M., and Joe Pace. 'The Syrian Opposition'. *The Washington Quarterly* 30, no. 1 (Winter 2006): 45–68.

Laron, Guy. *The Six Day War: The Breaking of the Middle East*. New Haven: Yale University Press, 2017.

Lauzière, Henri. *The Making of Salafism: Islamic Reform in the Twentieth Century*. New York: Columbia University Press, 2015.

Lawson, Fred H. 'Revisiting the Political Economy of the Syrian Uprising'. In *The Syrian Uprising: Domestic Origins and Early Trajectory*, edited by Raymond Hinnebusch and Omar Imady. Abingdon: Routledge, 2018.

Leenders, Reinoud. *Spoils of Truce: Corruption and State-Building in Post-War Lebanon*. Ithaca: Cornell University Press, 2012.

———. 'Prosecuting Political Dissent: Courts and the Resilience of Authoritarianism in Syria'. In *Middle East Authoritarianisms: Governance, Contestation, and Regime Resilience in Syria and Iran*, edited by Steven Heydemann and Reinoud Leenders. Stanford: Stanford University Press, 2012.

Lefèvre, Raphaël. *Ashes of Hama: The Muslim Brotherhood in Syria*. Oxford: Oxford University Press, 2013.

Leverett, Flynt. *Inheriting Syria: Bashar's Trial by Fire*. Washington, D.C.: Brookings Institution, 2005.

Lewis, Norman N. *Nomads and Settlers in Syria and Jordan, 1800–1980*. Cambridge: Cambridge University Press, 1987.

Lister, Charles R. *The Syrian Jihad: Al-Qaeda, the Islamic State and the Evolution of an Insurgency*. Oxford University Press, 2016.

Local Administration Councils Unit. 'The Indicator of Needs for the Local Councils of Syria', 2014. https://www.peacefare.net/wp-content/uploads/2015/10/Needs-for-the-Local-Councils-of-Syria-Public-Policy-Report.pdf.

Longuenesse, Elisabeth. 'État et Syndicalisme En Syrie: Discours et Pratiques'. *Sou'al*, no. 8 (1988): 97–130.

———. 'L'industrialisation et Sa Signification Sociale'. In *La Syrie d'aujourd'hui*, edited by André Raymond. Paris: Éditions du Centre national de la recherche scientifique, 1980.

Louis, Wm Roger, and Avi Shlaim, eds. *The 1967 Arab–Israeli War: Origins and Consequences*. Cambridge: Cambridge University Press, 2012.

Lund, Aron. 'Chasing Ghosts: The Shabiha Phenomenon'. In *The 'Alawis of Syria: War, Faith and Politics in the Levant*, edited by Michael Kerr and Craig Larkin. New York: Oxford University Press, 2015.

Lustick, Ian S. 'The Absence of Middle Eastern Great Powers: Political "Backwardness" in Historical Perspective'. *International Organization* 51, no. 04 (1997): 653–83. https://doi.org/10.1162/002081897550483.

Lyde, Samuel. *The Asian Mystery Illustrated in the History, Religion, and Present State of the Ansaireeh or Nusairis of Syria*. London: Longman, Green, Longman, and Roberts, 1860.

MAE 237. 'Rapport Daclin', 7 September 1926. 234.

MAE 239. 'French Translation of Druze Petition', 27 June 1925.

Ma'oz, Moshe. *Asad: The Sphinx of Damascus. A Political Biography*. Grove Weidenfeld, 1988.

———. *Ottoman Reform in Syria and Palestine, 1840–1861: The Impact of the Tanzimat on Politics and Society*. Oxford: Clarendon Press, 1968.

Ma'rūf, Muḥammad. *Ayyām 'Ishtuhā, 1949–1969: al-Inqilābāt al-'Askarīya wa-Asrāruhā fī Sūrīya* [Days I Lived: 1949–1969: Military Coups and Their Secrets in Syria]. Beirut: Riyāḍ al-Rayyis li'l-Kutub wa'l-Nashr, 2003.

Makdisi, Ussama. *The Culture of Sectarianism: Community, History, and Violence in Nineteenth-Century Ottoman Lebanon*. Berkeley: University of California Press, 2000.

Manley, Mary Louise. 'The Syrian Constitution of 1953'. *Middle East Journal* 7, no. 4 (1953): 520–21.

Ma'oz, Moshe. *Syria and Israel: From War to Peacemaking*. Oxford: Clarendon Press, 1995.

Marzūq, Nabīl. 'Al-Tanmīya al-Mafqūda fī Sūrīya' [Lost Development in Syria]. In *Khalfīyāt al-Thawra al-Sūrīya: Dirāsāt Sūrīya* [Backdrop to the Syrian Revolution: Syrian Studies], edited by 'Azmī Bishāra. Doha: Arab Center for Research and Policy Studies, 2013.

Masters, Bruce. *The Arabs of the Ottoman Empire, 1516–1918: A Social and Cultural History*. Cambridge: Cambridge University Press, 2013.

———. 'The Political Economy of Aleppo in an Age of Ottoman Reform'. *Journal of the Economic and Social History of the Orient* 53, no. 1–2 (2010): 290–316.

Matar, Linda. *The Political Economy of Investment in Syria*. Houndmills: Palgrave Macmillan, 2016.

Mazur, Kevin. *Revolution in Syria: Identity, Networks, and Repression*. Cambridge: Cambridge University Press, 2021.

Meininghaus, Esther. *Creating Consent in Ba'thist Syria: Women and Welfare in a Totalitarian State*. London: I.B. Tauris, 2016.

Mendenhall, Kurt Lee. 'Class, Cult and Tribe: The Politics of 'Alawi Separatism in French Mandate Syria'. PhD dissertation, University of Texas at Austin, 1991.

Métral, Françoise. 'State and Peasants in Syria: A Local View of a Government Irrigation Project'. *Peasant Studies* 11, no. 2 (1984): 69–89.

Meyer, A. J. *Middle Eastern Capitalism. Nine Essays*. Cambridge: Harvard University Press, 1959.

Meyer, Gunter. 'Rural Development and Migration in Northeast Syria'. In *Anthropology and Development in North Africa and the Middle East*, edited by Muneera Salem-Murdock, Michael M. Horowitz and Monica Sella. Boulder: Westview Press, 1990.

Middle East Watch. *Syria Unmasked: The Suppression of Human Rights by the Asad Regime*. New Haven: Yale University Press, 1991.

Migdal, Joel S. *Strong Societies and Weak States: State–Society Relations and State Capabilities in the Third World*. Princeton: Princeton University Press, 1988.

Mishāqa, Mikhā'īl. *Kitāb Mashhad al-'Ayān Bi-Ḥawādith Sūriyā wa-Lubnān* [Book of Eyewitnesses to the Events in Syria and Lebanon]. Cairo: n.p., 1908.

Mixon, Scott. 'The Crisis of 1873: Perspectives from Multiple Asset Classes'. *The Journal of Economic History* 68, no. 3 (2008): 722–57.

Mizrahi, Jean-David. *Genèse de l'État mandataire: service des renseignements et bandes armées en Syrie et au Liban dans les années 1920*. Paris: Publications de la Sorbonne, 2003.

Moubayed, Sami M. *Damascus Between Democracy and Dictatorship*. Lanham: University Press of America, 2000.

Mufti, Malik. *Sovereign Creations: Pan-Arabism and Political Order in Syria and Iraq*. Ithaca: Cornell University Press, 1996.

Mukhopadhyay, Dipali, and Kimberly Howe. *Good Rebel Governance: Revolutionary Politics and Western Intervention in Syria*. Cambridge: Cambridge University Press, 2023.

Müller, Victor. *En Syrie avec les Bédouins: les tribus du désert*. Paris: Libraire Ernest Leroux, 1931.

Musṭafā, Hamza Muṣṭafa al-. *Al-Majāl al-ʿĀmm al-Iftirāḍī fī al-Thawra al-Sūrīya: al-Khasāʾis, al-Ittijāhāt, Āliyāt Ṣanʿ al-Raʾī al-ʿĀmm* [Virtual Public Space in the Syrian Revolution: Specificities, Directions, and the Tools of Manufacturing Public Opinion]. Doha: al-Markaz al-ʿArabī li'l-Abḥāth wa-Dirāsat al-Siyāsāt, 2012.

Neep, Daniel. *Occupying Syria under the French Mandate: Insurgency, Space and State Formation*. Cambridge: Cambridge University Press, 2012.

———. 'Narrating Crisis, Constructing Policy: Economic Ideas, Institutional Change, and Statism in Syria'. *New Political Economy* 23, no. 4 (2018): 495–511.

———. '"What Have the Ottomans Ever Done for Us?" Why History Matters for Politics in the Arab Middle East'. *International Affairs* 97, no. 6 (2021): 1825–41.

Nelson, Scott Reynolds. 'A Storm of Cheap Goods: New American Commodities and the Panic of 1873'. *The Journal of the Gilded Age and Progressive Era* 10, no. 4 (2011): 447–53. https://doi.org/10.2307/23045123.

Oakford, Samuel. 'Trump's Air War Has Already Killed More than 2,000 Civilians'. *The Daily Beast*, 17 July 2017, sec. world. https://www.thedailybeast.com/president-trumps-air-war-kills-12-civilians-per-day.

Ochsenwald, William. 'Ironic Origins: Arab Nationalism in the Hijaz, 1882–1914'. In *The Origins of Arab Nationalism*, edited by Rashid Khalidi, Lisa Anderson, Muhammad Muslih and Reeva S. Simon. New York: Columbia University Press, 1991.

O'Rourke, Kevin H. 'The European Grain Invasion, 1870–1913'. *The Journal of Economic History* 57, no. 4 (1997): 775–801. https://doi.org/10.2307/2951160.

Owen, Jonathan P. 'Akram al-Hourani: A Study of Syrian Politics, 1943–1954'. PhD, Johns Hopkins University, 1992.
Owen, Roger. *The Middle East in the World Economy, 1800–1914*. London & New York: I.B. Tauris, 1981.
———. *State, Power and Politics in the Making of the Modern Middle East*. 3rd ed. London: Routledge, 2004.
———. 'Egypt and Europe: From French Expedition to British Occupation'. In *Studies in the Theory of Imperialism*, edited by Roger Owen and Bob Sutcliffe. London: Longman, 1972.
Pamuk, Sevket. *A Monetary History of the Ottoman Empire*. Cambridge: Cambridge University Press, 2000.
Parker, John W. *Putin's Syrian Gambit: Sharper Elbows, Bigger Footprint, Stickier Wicket*. Institute for National Strategic Studies Strategic Perspectives 25. Washington, D.C.: National Defense University Press, 2017.
Perthes, Volker. *The Political Economy of Syria under Asad*. London: I.B. Tauris, 1997.
———. 'A Look at Syria's Upper Class: The Bourgeoisie and the Ba'th'. *Middle East Report*, no. 170 (1991): 31–37.
———. 'Si Vis Stabilitatem, Para Bellum: State Building, National Security, and War Preparation in Syria'. In *War, Institutions, and Social Change in the Middle East*, edited by Steven Heydemann. University of California Press, 2000.
———. 'The Syrian Economy in the 1980s'. *Middle East Journal* 46, no. 1 (1992): 37–58.
Peter, Frank. 'Dismemberment of Empire and Reconstitution of Regional Space: The Emergence of "National" Industries in Damascus between 1918 and 1946'. In *The British and French Mandates in Comparative Perspectives*, edited by Nadine Méouchy and Peter Sluglett. Leiden: Brill, 2004.
Phillips, Christopher. *The Battle for Syria: International Rivalry in the New Middle East*. New Haven: Yale University Press, 2016.
Pierret, Thomas. *Baas et Islam en Syrie: La dynastie Assad face aux Oulémas*. Presses Universitaires de France, 2011.
———. *Religion and State in Syria: The Sunni Ulama from Coup to Revolution*. Cambridge: Cambridge University Press, 2013.
———. 'The State Management of Religion in Syria: The End of "Indirect

Rule"?' In *Middle East Authoritarianisms: Governance, Contestation, and Regime Resilience in Syria and Iran*, edited by Steven Heydemann and Reinoud Leenders. Stanford: Stanford University Press, 2012.

Pierret, Thomas, and Kjetil Selvik. 'The Limits of "Authoritarian Upgrading" in Syria: Private Welfare, Islamic Charities, and the Rise of the Zayd Movement'. *International Journal of Middle East Studies* 41, no. 4 (2009): 595–614.

Podeh, Elie. *The Decline of Arab Unity: The Rise and Fall of the United Arab Republic*. Eastbourne: Sussex Academic Press, 1999.

Poulleau, Alice. *A Damas sous les bombes: journal d'une Française pendant la révolte syrienne (1924–1926)*. Yvetot: Bretteville, 1926.

Provence, Michael. *The Great Syrian Revolt and the Rise of Arab Nationalism*. Austin: University of Texas Press, 2009.

———. *The Last Ottoman Generation and the Making of the Modern Middle East*. Cambridge: Cambridge University Press, 2017.

———. 'Ottoman Modernity, Colonialism, and Insurgency in the Interwar Arab East'. *International Journal of Middle East Studies* 43, no. 2 (2011): 205–25. https://doi.org/10.1017/S0020743811000031.

Qabbānī, Nizār. *Hawāmish 'alā Daftar al-Naksa: Qaṣīda Ṭawīla* [Marginalia in the Notebook of Defeat: A Long Ode]. Beirut: Manshūrāt Nizār Qabbānī, 1970.

Qāsimī, Jamāl al-Dīn al-, and Muḥammad Sa'īd al-Qāsimī. *Qāmūs al-Sinā'āt al-Shāmīya* [The Dictionary of Damascene Industries], edited by Ẓāfir al-Qāsimī. Paris: Mouton, 1960.

al-Qāsimī, Ẓāfir al-. *Wathā'iq Jadīda 'an al-Thawra al-Sūrīya al-Kubrā, 1925–1927* [New Documents on the Great Syrian Revolt]. Beirut: Dār al-Kitāb al-Jadīd, 1965.

Qāsimīya, Khayrīya. *Al-Ḥukūma al-'Arabīya fī Dimashq Bayna 1918–1920* [The Arab Government in Damascus]. Egypt: Dār al-Ma'ārif, 1971.

Qattan, Najwa al-. 'Safarbarlik: Ottoman Syria and the Great War'. In *From the Syrian Land to the States of Syria and Lebanon*, edited by Thomas Philipp and Christoph Schumann. Würzburg: Ergon Verlag, 2004.

Qāwuqjī, Fawzi al-. *Mudhakkirāt Fawzī al-Qāwuqjī, 1912–1932*. Beirut: Dār al-Quds, 1975.

Quwwatlī, Shukrī al-. *Shukrī al-Quwwatlī Yukhāṭib Ummatahu:*

Mukhtarāt Min Khuṭabihi wa-Bayānātihi [Shukrī al-Quwwatlī Addresses His Nation: Selections from His Speeches and Declarations]. Damascus: Maṭba'at al-Fujayra al-Waṭanīya wa Maktabātiha, 2001.

Quzmakhūrī, Yūsuf. *Al-Dasātīr fī al-'Ālam al-'Arabī: Nuṣūṣ wa-Ta'dīlāt: 1839–1987* [Constitutions in the Arab World: Texts and Amendments]. Beirut: Dār al-Ḥamrā', 1989.

Rabinovich, Itamar. *The Brink of Peace: The Israeli–Syrian Negotiations*. Princeton: Princeton University Press, 1998.

———. *Syria under the Ba'th, 1963–66: The Army–Party Symbiosis*. New York: Halsted Press, 1972.

———. *The View from Damascus: State, Political Community and Foreign Relations in Twentieth-Century Syria*. Berkeley: University of California Press, 2008.

Rathmell, Andrew. *Secret War in the Middle East: The Covert Struggle for Syria, 1949–1961*. 2nd ed. London: I.B. Tauris, 2013.

Rayyis, Munīr al-. *Al-Kitāb al-Dhahabī Li'l-Thawrāt al-Waṭanīya fī al-Mashriq al-'Arabī* [The Golden Book of National Revolutions in the Arab East]. Vol. 2. Damascus: Matābi' Alif Bā', 1969.

———. *Al-Kitāb al-Dhahabī Li'l-Thawrāt al-Waṭanīya fī al-Mashriq al-'Arabī* [The Golden Book of National Revolutions in the Arab East]. Vol. 3. Damascus: Matābi' Alif Bā', 1977.

Razzāz, Munīf al-. *Al-Tajriba al-Murra* [The Bitter Experience]. [Beirut?]: Dār Ghandūr li'l Tibā'a wa'l-Nashr, 1967.

Resch, Andreas, and Dieter Stiefel. 'Vienna: The Eventful History of a Financial Center'. In *Global Austria*, edited by Günter Bischof, Fritz Plasser, Anton Pelinka and Alexander Smith, 117–46. New Orleans: University of New Orleans Press, 2011.

Revkin, Mara Redlich. 'What Explains Taxation by Resource-Rich Rebels? Evidence from the Islamic State in Syria'. *Journal of Politics* 82, no. 2 (April 2020): 757–64.

Rey, Matthieu. 'L'extension Du Port de Lattaquié (1950–1955), Étude Sur Les Premiers Temps de La Fabrique Du Développement En Syrie'. In *Développer En Syrie : Retour Sur Une Expérience Historique*, edited by Cyril Roussel and Élisabeth Longuenesse, 59–82. Cahiers de l'Ifpo. Beirut: Presses de l'Ifpo, 2014.

Roded, Ruth. 'Social Patterns among the Urban Elite during the Late Ottoman Period (1876–1916)'. In *Palestine in the Late Ottoman Period: Political, Social, and Economic Transformation*, edited by David Kushner. Leiden: Brill, 1986.

Rogan, Eugene L. 'Asiret Mektebi: Abdulhamid II's School for Tribes (1892–1907)'. *International Journal of Middle East Studies* 28, no. 1 (1996): 83–107.

———. 'Instant Communication: The Impact of the Telegraph in Ottoman Syria'. In *The Syrian Land: Processes of Integration and Fragmentation. Bilad al-Sham from the 18th to the 20th Century*, edited by Thomas Philipp and Birgit Schaebler, 113–28. Stuttgart: Franz Steiner Verlag, 1998. http://www.indiebound.org/book/9783515073097.

Roussel, Cyril. 'Les grandes familles druzes entre local et national'. *Revue des mondes musulmans et de la Méditerranée*, no. 115–116 (31 December 2006): 135–53. https://doi.org/10.4000/remmm.3024.

Russell, Malcolm B. *The First Modern Arab State: Syria under Faysal, 1918–1920*. Minneapolis: Bibliotheca Islamica, 1985.

Sadowski, Yahya. 'Political Power and Economic Organization in Syria: The Course of State Intervention, 1946–1958'. PhD dissertation, University of California, Los Angeles, 1984.

Sadowski, Yahya M. 'Cadres, Guns and Money: The Eighth Regional Congress of the Syrian B'ath' 134 (1985): 3–8.

Ṣafadī, Muṭā'. *Ḥizb al-Ba'th: Ma'sāt al-Mawlid, Ma'sāt al-Nihāya* [The Ba'th Party: The Tragedy of Its Birth, the Tragedy of Its Demise]. Beirut: Dār al-Ādāb, 1964.

Sa'd al-Dīn, 'Adnān. *al-Ikhwān al-Muslimūn fī Sūrīya: Mudhakkirāt wa Dhikrayāt. Sanawāt al-Majāzir al-Mur'iba. Min 'Āmm 1977 wa-Ḥattā 'Āmm 1983* [The Muslim Brotherhood in Syria: Memoires and Memories. The Years of Terrible Massacres, 1977 to 1983]. Cairo: Maktabat Madbūlī, 2010.

Sa'īfān, Samīr. 'Siyāsāt Tawzī' al-Dakhl wa-Dawrihā fī al-Infijār al-Ijtimā'ī fī Sūrīya' [The Politics of Distributing Income and Its Role in the Social Explosion in Syria]. In *Khalfiyāt al-Thawra al-Sūrīya: Dirāsāt Sūrīya* [Backdrop to the Syrian Revolution: Syrian Studies],

edited by ʿAzmī Bishāra. Doha: Arab Center for Research and Policy Studies, 2013.
Salibi, Kamal S. *The Modern History of Lebanon*. Delmar: Caravan Books, 1977.
Ṣāliḥ, Yāsīn al-Ḥājj. *Al-Sayr ʿalā Qadam Wāḥida* [Walking on One Leg]. Beirut: Dār al-Ādāb, 2012.
———. ʻal-Ṣultān al-Ḥadīth: al-Manābiʿ al-Siyāsī wa'l-Ijtimāʿī Li'l-Ṭā'ifīya fī Sūriyā' [The New Sultan: The Political and Social Origins of Sectarianism in Syria]. *al-Jumhūriya*, 26 January 2015.
———. *al-Thawra al-Mustaḥīla: al-Thawra, al-Ḥarb al-Ahlīya, wa'l-Ḥarb al-ʿĀmma fī Sūrīya* [The Impossible Revolution: Revolution, Civil War and Generalized War in Syria]. Beirut: al-Mu'assasa al-ʿArabīya li'l-Dirāsāt wa'l-Nashr, 2017.
———. *Bi'l-Khalāṣ yā Shabāb: 16 ʿĀmman fī al-Sujūn al-Sūrīya*. Beirut: Dar al-Sāqī, 2012.
Sammān, Muṭīʿ al-. *Waṭan wa-ʿAskar: Qabla an Tudfana al-Ḥaqīqa fī al-Turāb. Mudhakkirāt 28 Aylūl 1961–8 Ādhār 1963* [Nation and Soldiers: Before the Truth Is Buried in Dust. Memoires from 28 September 1961 to 8 March 1963]. Beirut: Bīsān li'l-Tawzīʿ wa'l-Nashr, 1995.
SANA. ʻal-Ra'īs al-Asad: al-Maʿraka Maʿrakat Miḥwar Mutakāmil yumaththil Manhaj min al-Istiqlālīya wa'l-Karāma' [President Assad: The Battle is an Integrated Approach for Independence and Dignity]. 26 July 2015. https://sana.sy/?p=245771.
SANA. ʻal-Ra'īs al-Asad Amām Majlis al-Shaʿb' [President Assad before the People's Assembly]. 1 April 2011. https://web.archive.org/web/20110819072639/http://sana.sy/ara/2/2011/03/30/339278.htm.
SANA. ʻal-Ra'īs al-Asad Li'l-Ḥukūma al-Jadīda' [President Assad to the New Government]. 17 April 2011. https://web.archive.org/web/20110818171502/https://sana.sy/ara/2/2011/04/17/341921.htm.
SANA. 'President al-Assad Congratulates Putin on Victory Day: Syrians Will Not Be Satisfied until Defeating the Enemy'. 5 May 2016, sec. Presidency of Syrian Arab Republic. http://sana.sy/en/?p=76435.

Sarraut, Albert. *La Mise En Valeur Des Colonies Françaises*. Paris: Payot, 1923.

Sa'ūd, Ghassān. 'Bashshār al-Asad fī al-Amr al-Yawm: Muwājahat 'al-Fitna' Thumma al-Islāḥ' [Bashar al-Asad on Today's Issue: Fighting "Sedition", Then Reform]. *al-Akhbār*, 31 March 2011. https://al-akhbar.com/Politics/85961.

Sayigh, Yezid. *Armed Struggle and the Search for State: The Palestinian National Movement, 1949–1993*. Oxford: Oxford University Press, 1997.

Sayyid-Marsot, Afaf Lutfi. *Egypt in the Reign of Muhammad Ali*. Cambridge: Cambridge University Press, 1984.

Schad, Geoffrey D. 'Colonialists, Industrialists, and Politicians: The Political Economy of Industrialization in Syria, 1920–1954'. PhD, University of Pennsylvania, 2001.

Schaebler, Birgit. 'From Urban Notables to "Noble Arabs": Shifting Discourses in the Emergence of Nationalism in the Arab East, 1910–1916'. In *From the Syrian Land to the States of Syria and Lebanon*, edited by Thomas Philipp and Christoph Schumann. Würzburg: Ergon Verlag, 2004.

———. 'State(s) Power and the Druzes: Integration and the Struggle for Social Control (1838–1949)'. In *The Syrian Land: Processes of Integration and Fragmentation: Bilād al-Shām from the 18th to the 20th Century*, edited by Thomas Philipp and Birgit Schaebler. Stuttgart: Franz Steiner Verlag, 1998.

Schatkowski Schilcher, L. 'The Famine of 1915–1918 in Greater Syria'. In *Problems of the Modern Middle East in Historical Perspective: Essays in Honour of Albert Hourani*, edited by John Spagnolo. Reading: Ithaca Press, 1996.

Schatkowski Schilcher, Linda. *Families in Politics: Damascene Factions and Estates of the 18th and 19th Centuries*. Stuttgart: Franz Steiner Verlag Wiesbaden, 1985.

———. 'Violence in Rural Syria in the 1880s and 1890s: State Centralization, Rural Integration, and the World Market'. In *Peasants and Politics in the Modern Middle East*, edited by Farhad Kazemi and John Waterbury, 50–84. Gainesville: University Press of Florida, 1991.

Schayegh, Cyrus. 'The Many Worlds of 'Abud Yasin; or, What Narcotics Trafficking in the Interwar Middle East Can Tell Us About Territorialization'. *The American Historical Review* 116, no. 2 (1 April 2011): 273–306.

Schilcher, L. Schatkowski. 'The Hauran Conflicts of the 1860s: A Chapter in the Rural History of Modern Syria'. *International Journal of Middle East Studies* 13, no. 2 (1981): 159–79.

Schilcher, Linda S. 'Railways in the Political Economy of Southern Syria, 1890–1925'. In *The Syrian Land: Processes of Integration and Fragmentation: Bilād al-Shām from the 18th to the 20th Century*, edited by Thomas Philipp and Birgit Schäbler. Franz Steiner Verlag, 1998.

Seale, Patrick. *Asad: The Struggle for the Middle East*. Berkeley: University of California Press, 1990.

———. *The Struggle for Syria: A Study of Post-War Arab Politics, 1945–1958*. London: I.B. Tauris, 1986.

———. 'The Syria–Israel Negotiations: Who Is Telling the Truth?' *Journal of Palestine Studies* 29, no. 2 (2000): 65–77.

Seifan, Samir. *The Road to Economic Reform in Syria*. Centre for Syrian Studies, University of St Andrews, 2011

———. *Syria on the Path to Economic Reform*. Centre for Syrian Studies, University of St Andrews, 2010.

Seurat, Michel. *Syrie, l'État de barbarie*. Paris: Presses Universitaires de France, 2015.

———. 'Les Populations, l'état et La Société'. In *La Syrie d'aujourd'hui*, edited by André Raymond. Paris: Éditions du Centre national de la recherche scientifique, 1980.

Shaaban, Bouthaina. *Damascus Diary: An Inside Account of Hafez al-Assad's Peace Diplomacy, 1990–2000*. Boulder: Lynne Rienner Publishers, 2013.

Shaar, Dr Karam, and Caroline Rose. 'From 2015–2023: The Captagon Trade's Trends, Trajectory, and Policy Implications'. New Lines Institute for Strategy and Policy, May 2024.

Shahbandar, 'Abd al-Raḥmān. *al-Thawra al-Sūrīya al-Waṭanīya: Mudhakkirāt* [The Patriotic Syrian Revolt: Memoirs]. Damascus: Wizārat al-Thaqāfa, 1993.

Shaked, Haim, and Daniel Dishon, eds. *Middle East Contemporary Survey Vol. 8 (1983–1984)*. Boulder: Westview Press, 1984.

Shara', Fārūq al-. *Al-Riwāya al-Mafqūda* [The Missing Account]. Beirut: al-Markaz al-'Arabī li'l-Abḥāth wa-Dirāsāt al-Siyāsāt, 2015.

Sharīf, Munīr. *al-Muslimūn al-'Alawīyūn: man hum wa-ayna hum* [The Alawi Muslims: Who and Where They Are]. Beirut: Mu'assasat al-Balāgh, 1994.

Shaw, Stanford J. 'The Origins of Ottoman Military Reform: The Nizam-I Cedid Army of Sultan Selim III'. *Journal of Modern History* 37, no. 3 (1965): 291–306.

Sheehi, Stephen. 'Butrus al-Bustani: Syria's Ideologue of the Age'. In *The Origins of Syrian Nationhood: Histories, Pioneers and Identity*, edited by Adel Beshara, 57–78. Abingdon: Routledge, 2011.

Shīblīr, Bīrjīt. *Intifādāt Jabal al-Durūz-Hawrān min al-'Ahd al-'Uthmāni ilā Dawlat al-Istiqlāl, 1850–1949: Dirāsa Antrubulūjīya-Tārikhīya* [The Uprisings of the Hawran Jabal al-Duruz from the Ottoman Period to Independence, 1850–1949: A Historical-Anthropological Study]. Arabic translation of Birgit Schaebler, *Aufstande im Drusenbergland: Ethnizitat und Integration einer landlichen Gesellschaft Syriens vom Osmanischen Reich bis zur staatlichen Unabhangigkeit 1850–1949*. Beirut: Dār al-Nahār bi'l-Ta'āwun ma' al-Ma'had al-Almānī li'l-Abḥāth al-Sharqīya, 2003.

Shidyaq, Ahmad Faris al-. *Leg Over Leg*. Translated by Humphrey Davies. 4 vols. New York: NYU Press, 2013.

Shlaim, Avi. *Collusion Across the Jordan: King Abdullah, the Zionist Movement and the Partition of Palestine*. Oxford: Clarendon Press, 1988.

———. 'Husni Za'im and the Plan to Resettle Palestinian Refugees in Syria'. *Journal of Palestine Studies* 15, no. 4 (1986): 68–80.

Shu'aybī, Fawzī. *Shāhid Min al-Mukhābarāt al-Sūrīya Min 'Āmm 1955–1968* [A Witness from Syrian Intelligence 1955–1968]. Beirut: Bīsān li'l-Nashr wa'l-Tawzī', 2018.

Silū, Fawzī. *Al-Bayān al-Awwal Min Dawlat al-Za'īm Fawzī Silū Ilā al-Sha'b al-Sūrī 'an A'māl al-'Ahd al-Jadīd khilāl Thalāthat Ashhur Kanūn al-Awwāl – Adhār 1951–52* [The First Statement from the Government of Brigadier Fawzi Silu to the Syrian People About the Achievements of the New Era During the Three Months from

December 1951 to March 1952]. Damascus: Maṭbaʿat al-Jumhūrīya al-Sūrīya, 1952.

Sudermann, Yannick. 'When Authoritarianism Embraces Gentrification: The Case of Old Damascus, Syria'. In *Global Gentrifications: Uneven Development and Displacement*, edited by Loretta Lees, Hyun Bang Shin and Ernest López-Morales. Bristol: Bristol University Press, 2015.

Sukkar, Nabil. 'The Crisis of 1986 and Syria's Plan for Reform'. In *Contemporary Syria: Liberalization Between Cold War and Cold Peace*, edited by Eberhard Kienle. London: British Academic Press, 1994.

———. 'Syria: Strategic Economic Issues'. In *Economic Challenges Facing Middle Eastern and North African Countries: Alternative Futures*, edited by Nemat Shafik. Houndmills: Macmillan Press, 1998.

Swiss Peace. 'Perceptions of Governance: The Experience of Local Administrative Councils in Opposition-Held Syria', 2017. http://www.swisspeace.ch/fileadmin/ user_upload/pdf/Mediation/WOTRO_Report_The_Experience_of_Local_Administrative_Councils_in_Oppositionheld_Syria.pdf.

Sykes, Mark. *The Caliphs' Last Heritage: A Short History of the Turkish Empire*. London: Garnet, 1915.

Syria Justice and Accountability Centre. 'Walls Have Ears: An Analysis of Classified Syrian Security Sector Documents', 2019. https://syriaaccountability.org/content/files/2022/04/Walls-Have-Ears-English.pdf.

Syria News Press. 'Bashar al-Assad Speech, 3 June 2012', 3 June 2012. https://www.youtube.com/watch?v=5pOod4bamfc.

Syria Report. 'Speech of Syrian President Bashar al-Assad at Damascus University on June 20, 2011'. 21 June 2011. https://syria-report-com.proxy.library.georgetown.edu/speech-of-syrian-president-bashar-al-assad-at-damascus-university-on-june-20-2011/.

Syrian Arab Republic, Wizārat al-Takhṭīṭ, Mudīrīyat al-Iḥṣāʾ. *Al-Majmūʿa al-Iḥṣāʾīya al-Sūrīya 1960–68* [Syrian Statistical Abstract]. Damascus: Government Press, 1968.

Syrian Center for Political and Strategic Studies and Syrian Expert House. *Syria Transition Roadmap*. Washington, D.C.: SCPSS, 2013.

https://web.archive.org/web/20160712181733/http://syrianexperthouse.org/download/813/.

Ṭahṭāwī, Rifāʿat Rāfiʿ al-. *Kitāb Takhlīṣ al-Ibrīz Ilā Talkhīṣ Bārīz: Aw, al-Dīwān al-Nafīs Bi-Īwān Bārīs* [The Book of Producing Gold in the Summarization of Paris]. Cairo: Dār al-Taqaddum, 1905.

Ṭalās, Muṣṭafā. *Mirʾāt Ḥayātī: al-ʿAqd al-Awwal, 1948–1958: al-Niḍāl* [The Mirror of My Life: The First Decade, 1948–1958: The Struggle]. Vol. 1. 5 vols. Damascus: Dār Ṭalās, 1991.

———. *Mirʾāt Ḥayātī, 1968–1978: al-Zilzāl* [The Mirror of My Life, 1968–1978: The Earthquake]. Vol. 3 part 1. 5 vols. Damascus: Dār Ṭalās, 2003.

———. *Mirʾāt Ḥayātī, 1968–1978: al-Zilzāl* [The Mirror of My Life, 1968–1978: The Earthquake]. Vol. 3 part 2. 5 vols. Damascus: Dār Ṭalās, 2003.

———. *Mirʾāt Ḥayātī*. Vol. 4. 5 vols. Damascus: Dār Ṭalās, 2003.

*al-al-al-al-*Talhamy, Yvette. 'The Nusayri Leader Isma'il Khayr Bey and the Ottomans (1854–58)'. *Middle Eastern Studies* 44, no. 6 (2008): 895–908. https://doi.org/10.1080/00263200802426013.

TASS. 'Putin Warns West Against Repeating Libyan Scenario in Syria'. 3 December 2012. https://tass.com/russia/686367.

Tauber, Eliezer. *The Arab Movements in World War I*. Abingdon: Frank Cass, 1993.

———. 'The Struggle for Dayr al-Zur: The Determination of Borders Between Syria and Iraq'. *International Journal of Middle East Studies* 23, no. 3 (1991): 361–85.

Tejel, Jordi. *Syria's Kurds: History, Politics and Society*. London: Routledge, 2009.

Tell, Tariq. 'Guns, Gold, and Grain: War and Food Supply in the Making of Transjordan'. In *War, Institutions, and Social Change in the Middle East*, edited by Steven Heydemann, 33–58. Berkeley: University of California Press, 2000.

Terc, Mandy. '"To Promote Volunteerism among School Children": Volunteer Campaigns and Social Stratification in Contemporary Syria'. In *Syria from Reform to Revolt: Political Economy and International Relations*, edited by Raymond A. Hinnebusch and Tina Zintl. Syracuse: Syracuse University Press, 2014.

Thompson, Elizabeth F. *How the West Stole Democracy from the Arabs: The Syrian Arab Congress of 1920 and the Destruction of Its Historic Liberal–Islamic Alliance*. New York: Grove Press, 2020.

———. 'Rashid Rida and the 1920 Syrian-Arab Constitution: How the French Undermined Islamic Liberalism'. In *The Routledge Handbook of the History of the Middle East Mandates*, edited by Cyrus Schayegh and Andrew Arsan. Abingdon: Routledge, 2015.

Todman, Will. 'Sieges in Syria: Profiteering from Misery'. Policy Focus. Middle East Institute, 2016. https://www.mei.edu/sites/default/files/publications/PF14_Todman_sieges_web_0.pdf.

Torrey, Gordon. *Syrian Politics and the Military, 1945–1958*. Columbus: Ohio State University Press, 1964.

Traboulsi, Fawwaz. 'Ahmad Faris al-Shidyaq (1804–87): The Quest for Another Modernity'. In *Arabic Thought Beyond the Liberal Age: Towards an Intellectual History of the Nahda*, edited by Jens Hanssen and Max Weiss. Cambridge: Cambridge University Press, 2016.

Trenin, Dmitri. *What Is Russia Up To in the Middle East?* Cambridge: Polity Press, 2018.

Trump, Donald J. 'Proclamation on Recognizing the Golan Heights as Part of the State of Israel', 25 March 2019. https://trumpwhitehouse.archives.gov/presidential-actions/proclamation-recognizing-golan-heights-part-state-israel/.

Turkmani, Rim, Mary Kaldor, Wisam Elhamwi, Joan Ayo and Nael Hariri. 'Hungry for Peace: Positives and Pitfalls of Local Truces and Ceasefires in Syria'. London: London School of Economics and Political Science, 2014.

'Umrān, Muḥammad. *Tajribatī fī al-Thawra* [My Experience in the Revolution]. Damascus: n.p., 1970.

Üngör, Uğur Ümit. 'Shabbiha: Paramilitary Groups, Mass Violence and Social Polarization in Homs'. *Violence: An International Journal* 1, no. 1 (2020): 59–79. https://doi.org/10.1177/2633002420907771.

United Nations Economic and Social Office in Beirut. *Studies on Development Problems in Selected Countries of the Middle East*. New York: United Nations Economic and Social Office in Beirut, 1971.

United Nations Office for the Coordination of Humanitarian Affairs. 'Syria: Recent Developments in North-West Syria', 12 September 2018. https://reliefweb.int/report/syrian-arab-republic/syria-recent-developments-north-west-syria-12-sep-2018.

US Department of Agriculture in cooperation with the US Agency for International Development and the State Planning Commission, Syrian Arab Republic. *Syria: Agricultural Sector Assessment. Volume 4: Agricultural Marketing Annex*, 1980.

'Uthmān, Hāshim. *al-Maḥākamāt al-Siyāsīya fī Sūrīya* [Political Trials in Syria]. Beirut: Riyāḍ al-Rayyis li'l-Kutub wa'l-Nashr, 2004.

Van Bruinessen, Martin. 'The Ethnic Identity of the Kurds in Turkey'. In *Ethnic Groups in the Republic of Turkey*, edited by Peter A. Andrews and Rüdiger Benninghaus. Wiesbaden: Reichert, 1989.

Van Dam, Nikolaos. *The Struggle for Power in Syria: Politics and Society Under Asad and the Ba'th Party*. 4th ed. I.B. Tauris, 2011.

Van Dusen, Michael. 'Intra- and Inter-Generational Conflict in the Syrian Army'. PhD, Johns Hopkins University, 1971.

Vanly, Ismet Charif. 'The Kurds of Syria and Lebanon'. In *The Kurds: A Contemporary Overview*, edited by Philip G. Kreyenbroek and Stefan Sperl. London: Routledge, 1992.

Verdeil, Eric. 'Michel Écochard in Lebanon and Syria (1956–1968). The Spread of Modernism, the Building of the Independent States and the Rise of Local Professionals of Planning'. *Planning Perspectives* 27, no. 2 (1 April 2012): 249–66.

VICE News. 'Bulldozing the Border Between Iraq and Syria: The Islamic State', 13 August 2014. https://www.youtube.com/watch?v=TxX_THjtXOw.

Vignal, Leïla. 'Dubai on Barada? The Making of "Globalized Damascus" in Times of Urban Crisis'. In *Under Construction: Logics of Urbanism in the Gulf Region*, edited by Steffen Wippel, Katrin Bromber and Birgit Krawietz. London: Routledge, 2014.

Visser, Reidar. 'Proto-Political Conceptions of Iraq in Late Ottoman Times'. *International Journal of Contemporary Iraqi Studies* 3, no. 2 (2009): 143–54. https://doi.org/10.1386/ijcis.3.2.143/1.

Vitalis, Robert, and Steven Heydemann. 'War, Keynesianism, and Colonialism: Explaining State-Market Relations in the Postwar

Middle East'. In *War, Institutions, and Social Change in the Middle East*, edited by Steven Heydemann. Berkeley: University of California Press, 2000.

Wall Street Journal (Online). 'Interview with Syrian President Bashar al-Assad'. 31 January 2011.

Warrick, Joby. *Red Line: The Unraveling of Syria and America's Race to Destroy the Most Dangerous Arsenal in the World*. New York: Doubleday, 2020.

Warriner, Doreen. *Land Reform and Development in the Middle East*. Oxford: Oxford University Press, 1962.

Watenpaugh, Keith D. '"Creating Phantoms": Zaki al-Arsuzi, the Alexandretta Crisis, and the Formation of Modern Arab Nationalism in Syria'. *International Journal of Middle East Studies* 28, no. 3 (1996): 363–89.

Weber, Eugen. *Peasants into Frenchmen: The Modernization of Rural France, 1870–1914*. Stanford: Stanford University Press, 1976.

Wedeen, Lisa. *Ambiguities of Domination: Politics, Rhetoric, and Symbols in Contemporary Syria*. Chicago: University of Chicago Press, 1999.

———. *Authoritarian Apprehensions: Ideology, Judgment, and Mourning in Syria*. Chicago: University of Chicago Press, 2019.

Weiss, Michael, and Hassan Hassan. *ISIS: Inside the Army of Terror* (Updated Edition). New York: Regan Arts, 2016.

Weulersse, Jacques. *Paysans de Syrie et Du Proche Orient*. Paris: Gallimard, 1946.

Whitaker, James Long. 'The Union of Demeter with Zeus: Agriculture and Politics in Modern Syria'. PhD University of Durham, 1996.

White, Benjamin Thomas. *The Emergence of Minorities in the Middle East: The Politics of Community in French Mandate Syria*. Edinburgh: Edinburgh University Press, 2011.

Wilmington, Martin W. *The Middle East Supply Centre*. 1st ed. Albany: State University of New York Press, 1971.

Wilson, Mary Christina. *King Abdullah, Britain and the Making of Jordan*. Cambridge: Cambridge University Press, 1987.

Winckler, Onn. 'Syrian Migration to the Arab Oil-Producing Countries'. *Middle Eastern Studies* 33, no. 1 (1 January 1997): 107–18.

Winter, Stefan. *A History of the 'Alawis: From Medieval Aleppo to the Turkish Republic*. Princeton: Princeton University Press, 2016.

———. 'The Alawis in the Ottoman Period'. In *The 'Alawis of Syria: War, Faith and Politics in the Levant*, edited by Michael Kerr and Craig Larkin. Oxford: Oxford University Press, 2015.

Wizārat al-Iqtiṣād al-Waṭanī. *Al-Majmū'a al-Iḥṣā'īya al-Sūrīya 1961* [Syrian Statistical Abstract]. Damascus: Government Press, 1962.

Wizārat al-Takhṭīṭ [Ministry of Planning]. *Mashrū' al-Tanmiya al-Iqtiṣādīya wa'l-Ijtimā'īya Li'l-Sanawāt al-Khamīs 1960–1 1964–5* [The Five-Year Social and Economic Development Plan for 1960–1 to 1964–5]. Damascus: al-Maṭba'a al-Jadīda, 1960.

Wright, Gwendolyn. *The Politics of Design in French Colonial Urbanism*. Chicago: University of Chicago Press, 1991.

Yaffe-Schatzmann, Giffe. 'Alawi Separatists and Unionists: The Events of 25 February 1936'. *Middle Eastern Studies* 31, no. 1 (1995): 28–38.

Yāsīn, Bū 'Alī. *al-Quṭn wa Ẓāhirat al-Intāj al-Aḥādī fī al-Iqtiṣād al-Sūrī* [Cotton and the Appearance of Monoculture Production in the Syrian Economy]. Beirut: Dār al-Ṭalī'a, 1974.

———. *Ḥikāyat al-Arḍ wa'l-Fallāḥ al-Sūrī, 1858–1979* [The History of the Land and the Syrian Peasantry]. [Beirut]: Dār al-Ḥaqā'iq, 1979.

YouTube. 'Kalimat al-Sayyid al-Ra'īs Bashshār al-Asad Amām Majlis al-Sha'b Ba'd Udā'ihi al-Qism Ra'īsan Li'l-Jumhūrīya' [The Address of President Bashar al-Assad before Parliament], 17 July 2000. https://www.youtube.com/watch?v=dsNwHs9B6RI.

Zachs, Fruma. *The Making of a Syrian Identity: Intellectuals and Merchants in Nineteenth-Century Beirut*. Leiden: Brill, 2005.

———. 'Transformations of a Memory of Tyranny in Syria: From Jamal Pasha to "Id al-Shuhada", 1914–2000'. *Middle Eastern Studies* 48, no. 1 (1 January 2012): 73–88.

Zachs, Fruma, and Sharon Halevi. *Gendering Culture in Greater Syria: Intellectuals and Ideology in the Late Ottoman Period*. London: I.B. Tauris, 2014.

Zamir, Meir. *Lebanon's Quest: The Search for a National Identity, 1926–39*. London: I.B. Tauris, 2000.

———. *The Secret Anglo-French War in the Middle East: Intelligence and Decolonization, 1940–1948*. London: Routledge, 2014.

Zartman, I. William, ed. *Collapsed States: The Disintegration and Restoration of Legitimate Authority*. Boulder: Lynne Rienner Publishers, 1995.

Zelin, Aaron Y. *The Age of Political Jihadism: A Study of Hayat Tahrir al-Sham*. Lanham: Rowman & Littlefield, 2023.

Ziyāda, Radwān. 'Ḥarakat al-Silm al-Ijtimā'ī: Mabādi' Awwalīya Li' l-Ḥiwār, al-Safīr [The Social Peace Movement: First Principles for Dialogue], 2 February 2002'. In *al-Muthaqqaf Ḍidda al-Sulṭa: Ḥiwārat al-Mujtama' al-Madanī fī Sūrīya* [The Intellectual Against Authority: Civil Society Dialogues in Syria]. Cairo: Markaz al-Qāhira li'l-Dirāsāt Ḥuqūq al-Insān, 2003.

Index

'Abbas family 47
al-'Abbas, Munir 154
Abduh, Muhammad 75
Abdulhamid, Sultan 22
Abdulhamid II, Sultan
  imposition of personal control 57–8, 60–61, 74
  opposition to 75, 76, 77–8, 79
Abdullah, King of Jordan 440
Abdullah, king of Transjordan 107, 166, 196, 219
  vision of Greater Syria 177, 189–90, 191
Abdülmecid I, Sultan 17
'Abid family 63
Abu al-Nur Islamic Centre 429
Abu Assaf, Amin 241–2, 250, 251
  coup against Shishakli 246, 247
Adra, prison 407
Adwan tribe 50
al-Afghani, Jamal al-Din 75
Afghanistan, Soviet invasion 413–14
Aflaq, Michel 236, 239, 243, 245, 270, 363
  and 1956 coup plot 290–91
  and Ba'th Party 274–5, 276, 326, 327, 334, 337, 354
  and Hafiz 344–5
  and United Arab Republic 294–5, 304
Afrin region 503, 508
Agrarian Reform Law (1958) 308, 321
Agricultural Bank 308–9
Agricultural Reform Law (1963) 339
agriculture 11, 36–42, 49, 382–3
  and 2006-2010 drought 466–7
  collapse (1961) 319
  collective farms 333
  cooperatives 223, 262, 308–9, 339
  falling production 420, 421
  French policy 140–42
  irrigation 141–2, 257, 258–9, 467
  and land ownership rights 260–64
  musha' communal system 28–9
  Ottoman land reform (1858) 19–20
  post-war expansion 255–9
  private investment 257, 424
  state-run farms 349
  and UAR land reforms 308–9
al-'Ahd society 81, 87, 90
al-Ahram, Egyptian newspaper 74

Ahrar al-Sham, Islamist group 499, 508
Ain al-Fijeh Company 143
Air Force Intelligence 369–70
'Ajlani family 32
al-Ajlani, Munir 224, 243, 291
al-Akhbar Lebanese newspaper 486
al-Akhras, Asma, wife of Bashar Assad 462–3, 473
Akkash family 126–7
Al Jazeera satellite television station 444, 480, 495
Al-Diyar company 469
Al-Dughri miniseries 431
al-Qaeda
  and al-Nusra 500, 521–2
  and Syrian civil war 499–500
  US-led war on 449
  see also Islamic State of Iraq (ISI)
al-Qardaha 361, 381
al-Qurayya village 241, 251
al-Thawra new town 384
Alawis xvii, 1, 441
  Assad and 361–2, 369–70, 414–15
  and Ba'th Party 276, 335, 346–9
  conflict with Isma'ilis 470
  in Damascus 338–9
  ethno-religious identity 45, 110–111, 155
  French 'Territory of the Alawites' 99, 110–111, 114, 138
  Jabal al-Ansariya 43–7
  opposition to Quwwatli's government 181–8
  relations with Ottoman government 46, 58, 59
  support for unification 154–5
Albright, Madeleine, US Secretary of State 441
Aleppo 6, 24–5, 79, 99
  civil war 509, 514
  economy 139, 466
  Faculty of Islamic Law 471
  and French occupation 102, 107, 108, 114
  National Bloc in 137
  opposition parties 181
  protests 232, 240–41, 398–9
  religious hierarchy 429
  rural migrants in 380
  support for unification with Iraq 189
  taken by HTS (2024) xi, 526
Aleppo Artillery School, massacre (1979) 393–4
Alexandretta, port of 259
Alexandretta, Sanjak of 107, 114
  ethnic divisions 160–61
  reaction to reunification 159–63
  to Turkey 160–63
  see also Hatay
Alexandria, naval yard 11
Algeria, French colonialism 156
al-Ali, Salih, Alawi rebel leader 93, 99, 110, 186
Alif Ba newspaper 233
Allenby, General 87
American University of Beirut 59
al-Amin, Abd al-Mutallib 244
'Amir family, Jabal al-Duruz 80

Amiralay, Omar, *Everyday Life in a Syrian Village* (film) 381–2
'Ammiyya Revolt (1888) 41–2, 67
Amnesty International 475
'Amr family 153
'Amr, Field Marshal Abd al-Hakim 287, 313, 316–17
Anaza tribe 48, 50
Anbar province, ISIS in 501
Anglo-Turkish Commercial Convention (1838) 17
Anjar, Lebanon, Syrian intelligence headquarters 407, 434
anti-terrorism legislation 392–3
anti-Zionism 147–8, 149
Aqaba 86
Arab Collective Security Pact, proposed 280
Arab League 244, 324–5, 525
Arab Liberation Army (ALA), for 1948 War 195–7
Arab Liberation Movement (*Harakat al-Tahrir al-'Arabi*) (ALM) 227, 234, 235, 239, 266, 270
  and 1954 elections 273
Arab nationalism xv, 299, 363, 364
  Assad and 415
  Ba'th Party and 274, 385, 388–9
  French view of 106–7, 108
Arab Renaissance (*Nahda*) 70–75, 76
Arab Revolt (1916-18) 85–7, 89
Arab Socialist Party (*al-Hizb al-'Arabi al-Ishtiraki*) 231
  merger with Ba'th Party 270, 273, 276
  see also Ba'th Party
Arab unity movement 165–6, 254
Arab uprisings (Arab Spring 2011) xii, 479–80
Arabian Peninsula 77, 78–9
Arabic language 2, 238
  revival of 70, 71–2, 77
Arabic Language Academy 228
Arabism (*al-'uruba*) 81
  Cemal Pasha's persecution of 82–3
Arab–Israeli War (1948) 178, 195–9
Arafat, Yasser 351, 355, 413
Archard, Edouard 140–41
Armée du Levant 113, 165, 168
  Troupes spéciales 113–14, 168, 172
Armenians xvii, 1, 84, 256
Arslan, Adil 191
Arslan, Amin 76
Arsuzi family 47
al-Arsuzi, Zaki 361
al-'As, Sa'id 129
al-As'ad, Colonel Riyad 491
Asali family 187
al-Asali, Faysal 201, 203, 214
al-'Asali, Sabri 243, 244, 270–72, 280
al-'Asali, Shukri 79
Asfahan, Abd al-Massih 256
Asfar brothers 256
al-Assad, Bashar
  on 2011 protests 485–6
  and 'Damascus Spring' 447, 453–4

al-Assad, Bashar – *cont.*
flight to Russia (2024) xi, 526
as heir to Hafiz 440–42
loyalist militias 493–4, 495
and modernization 442–3, 453–4
and peace negotiations 513–14
and Putin 514
reaction to Arab Spring 480
and Saudi Arabia 440–41
and social control strategy 470–71
and Social Market Economy xvi, xx, 454–5
see also Assad regime
al-Assad, Basil 440
al-Assad, Hafiz xv–xvi, xx, 329, 362, 372, 428
and Arafat 413
character 359–60
clash with Rif'at 411–20
conflict with Israel 365–7, 391, 416, 436–8, 439
death 438–41
defeat of Jadid 354, 356–7
as defence minister 345–6, 351, 354
economic policies 363, 372–5, 421–2
foreign policy 411–16, 419–20, 439
formative influences 361–3
and George Bush 433
illness 417–18
inner circle 369–70
intervention in Lebanese civil war 391, 413
intuition of Syrian complexity 360
and Iran 414–16
and Iraq 415–16
and Mubarak 432
and October War 365–7
personality cult 409
rise to power 354–7
and Soviet Union 365, 414, 427–8, 511
see also Assad regime
al-Assad, Jamil 430
al-Assad, Maher 459, 487, 526
al-Assad, Na'isa (mother) 418–19
al-Assad, Rif'at 355, 395, 416–17
call for Law of National Cleansing 396
Defence Companies 369, 389, 416
economic modernization ideas 416, 417
fall of 418–19, 423–4
League of Higher Graduates 416, 419
repression of jihadi terrorism 396, 398–400
rivalry with Hafiz 411–20
Assad regime
amnesty for supporters 529
and Arab uprisings xii, xvi, 480, 485–6, 492
erratic response to ceasefire (2020-24) 524–6
fall of (2024) xi
forced conformity 408–411
and Kurds 385–9

and loss of territory (2015) 509–510, 511
loyalist militias 493–4, 495
overthrown (2024) 526
and peace negotiations 513–14
protests against 376, 392–6, 398–400
see also civil war
Astana, peace talks (2017) 515
al-Aswad, Colonel Fu'ad 241–2
Atasi family 32, 240, 306, 460
al-Atasi, Adnan 290
al-Atasi, Faydi 243, 290
al-Atasi, Faysal 250
coup against Shishakli 246, 247, 271
al-Atasi, Hashim 135, 150, 152, 240, 243–4
as president 214, 226, 285
al-Atasi, Jamal 400
al-Atasi, Nur al-Din, president 345–6
Atatürk (Kemal Mustafa) 93, 110, 237
Atfar, Abdullah 211
Atrash family 38–42, 80, 153, 430
and French Mandate 109–110, 120
and Greater Syria project 190–91
and Quwwatli 186–8
and Syrian Arab Kingdom 99–100
al-Atrash, Ali 122
al-Atrash, Hasan 187, 191, 243
al-Atrash, Ibrahim 39–40
al-Atrash, Ismail 38, 39
al-Atrash, Mansour 240–41
al-Atrash, Najm 40
al-Atrash, Nayif 190
al-Atrash, Salim 109, 117
al-Atrash, Shibli 41
al-Atrash, Sultan 99, 110, 119, 120, 121–3, 152–3, 240–41, 243, 319
and nationalist movement 134, 186–7, 190
Attar family 460
'August Crisis' (2001) 448–9
Autonomous Administration of North and East Syria (AANES) 517–18, 525–6
Ayalon, Ami 79
Azm family 4–5, 6, 32, 232, 306
Azm, As'ad Pasha 4
al-Azm, Khalid 143–4, 203, 280, 285, 291–2
'Democratic Bloc' 278, 284
as prime minister 180, 200, 220, 321, 325
resignation and retirement 302, 303–4
al-Azm, Sadiq, *Self Criticism after the Defeat* 364
al-Azma, Bashir 304–5, 323–5
al-Azma, Yusuf 102
al-'Azmeh, Adil, governor of Latakia 183

Baba Amr, Homs 491
Baggara tribe 50, 192, 430, 473
Baghdad Pact (1955) 279, 280
al-Baghdadi, Abu Bakr, ISIS 501, 522–3
Bakdash, Khalid 277, 293, 303

Baker, James, US Secretary of State 433, 436–7
al-Bakri, Nasib 121–2, 124, 125, 150, 152–3
Balfour Declaration (1917) 88, 92
Balkans, Ottoman army revolt (1908) 79
Baniyas 43
al-Banna, Hasan 396
Barak, Ehud, Israeli prime minister 438
Barazi family 32, 124, 232
al-Barazi, Husni 135, 224
al-Barazi, Muhsin 204, 211, 213–14
Barbar Mustafa, governor of Tripoli 46
al-Baroudi, Fakhri 79
Barudi family 32
Barzani family 306
Bashir II, Emir, Mount Lebanon 7–8, 14, 17, 34, 70
al-Ba'th newspaper 344, 354, 376
Ba'th Party (Arab Ba'th Socialist Party) xiii, 171, 221, 280
  and 1954 elections 272–6, 277
  1963 coup 325–31
  Alawi domination 346–9
  antipathy to Kurds 387–8
  and Asali government (1956) 287
  and civil service 284, 338
  and class conflict 308, 332, 333–4
  and Communists 293–4
  divisions within 326–8, 332–5, 343–6
  and Egypt 294–5
  and HTS administration 529
  ideology 273–5, 333–4, 343–4, 346–51, 409–411
  increased membership 335, 368, 371–2
  influence in army 325–6
  merger with Arab Socialist Party 270, 273, 276
  Military Committee 327–8, 329, 334–8, 343–4, 362
  National Congresses 332–4, 335, 340–41, 344, 363
  National Security Bureau 477
  and need for modernization 442–3
  opposition to union with Iraq 278
  Peasant Bureau 372
  Regional Command 343–4, 346, 418, 456
  Regional Congresses 372, 388, 396, 423, 443, 454, 456, 457
  and religious establishment 342, 350
  social controls 339–40, 342–3
  and Social Market Economy 464
  socialist policies 331–4, 335, 349–51, 372
  split from Nasser 313–14
  state building (from 1963) 331–43
  structural sectarianism 335–6
  and UAR 304, 314, 321
Bedouin tribes 3, 5, 13–14, 27, 48, 209
  conflict with Druze 470, 474
  cultural significance 78
  and education system 59

French relations with 111–12
and Great Syrian Revolt 120
and Greater Syria project 191–2
and Jabal al-Duruz uprising 242–3
Jabal Hawran 36
rebellion against 1910-11 census 80–81
sedentarization 223
Beirut 17, 56, 74, 145–6
and French Greater Lebanon 107–8
port development 60, 259
Syrian forces in 434
Bell, Gertrude 32
Ben Ali, Tunisian president 479
Bernardotte, Volke 437
Bilad al-Sham ('lands of Damascus') xiv, 4–6, 24–6
effect of Tanzimat reforms 19–20
reforms of Ibrahim Pasha 13–16
see also Syria
Bin Laden, Osama 499
al-Bina newspaper 282–3
Biqaa Valley 89, 93–4, 99, 414
Birri clan, Aleppo 493
al-Bitar, Salah al-Din 236, 239, 243, 245, 270
and Ba'th Party 274, 321, 326, 334
and Eisenhower Doctrine 293
as prime minister 345, 346
and UAR 295, 304
al-Bizri, Colonel Afif 290, 293, 304
Black September 355–6
Blair, Tony, British prime minister 449
Bolton, John, US Under Secretary of State 449–50
bombing
ballistic missiles 496
barrel bombs 496
car bombs, Damascus 494
French aerial (1944) 171–2
Great Syrian Revolt 123–4, 125–6
Homs 491
Raqqa 516–17
regime scorched earth (2012) 495–6
Russian campaign 512, 514
borders
French mandated territories 139
geographical xiv, 73
with Iraq 474
security measures 476
Shishakli and 229
Sykes-Picot xvii
with Turkey 107
Bouazizi, Muhammad 479
British Council 228–9
Bush, George, US President 450
business elites 142–5, 256, 264–6, 268
and 1990 elections 425–6
and Ba'th regime 341, 406
capital flight 310, 315, 341
connections to Bashar Assad 460–61
and corruption 435
and Lebanon 435–6
and Nasser's nationalizations 315–16

business elites – *cont.*
opposition to UAR policies 310–311, 312–13, 315–16
rich entrepreneurs 373, 426
urban redevelopment 465
and wealth from Social Market Economy 459–61, 464–5
al-Bustani, Butrus 72–3
al-Buti, Sa'id Ramadan 429–30
buwaykis, grain merchants 63

'Caesar', photographer 488
Cairo 74–5, 298
Cairo Unity Talks (1963) 329–30
Camp David Accords 367, 413
Carbillet, Gabriel, governor of Jabal al-Duruz 117–19, 120, 121
Carter, Jimmy, US president 432–3
casino, Damascus 477
Catroux, General George 109–110, 168–9
Cemal Pasha 82–5
censorship 74, 210, 305
censuses
1910-11: 80–81
1942: 170
of Kurds in al-Hassakeh (1962) 385–7
Central Bank 325, 424, 457
Central Crisis Management Cell (CCMC) 487–8, 494
Cereals Office 264
al-Cham holding company 460, 461
chambers of commerce 266
charities 462–3
religious 472–3
Chechens 28
chemical weapons, regime use of (civil war) 504–5, 515, 520
Christians xvii, 2, 26, 35, 297
in Aleppo 24–5
charities 473
HTS and 523
as refugees in Jazira 157
relaxation of constraints on 472
special status 56, 57
see also Maronite Christians
Cilicia 101
Circassians xvii, 1, 28
Civil Code (1949) 260
civil service 115
Ba'th attack on 338
political polarization 284, 286
reforms 233
civil society movement (2000-2001) 445–8
relaxations on associations 462
repression of 478–9
civil war (2012-2020) xvi–xvii, 496–505
beginnings 495–6
ceasefire (2016) 513
ceasefire (2020) 523–4
de-escalation zones 515
foreign support for opposition 497, 510
Islamization of uprising 498–500
Local Administrative Councils (self-government) 497–8

local reconciliation agreements 519–20
move to normalization (2020-2024) 524–6
regime use of chemical weapons 504–5, 515, 520
territorial divisions 507–9
zones of control (2020) 524
Clément-Grandcourt, General 109
Clinton, Bill, US President 438
Cold War 278, 301, 427
colonialism xv, xviii, 10
French doctrine 102–5
Colvin, Marie 491
Committee of Union and Progress (CUP) 75–6, 79–81, 82
Committees for the Revival of Civil Society 446
communications
mobile phones 448, 459
postal services 53
Radio Damascus 202, 210, 226, 354
satellite television 430–31
social media 481
telegraph 53, 60
see also newspapers
Constituent Assembly
1928 elections 134–6
1931-32 elections 136–7
and 1950 constitution 220–21
reinstated (1954) 269–70
constitutions
1928 (republic) 136
1950: 220–23, 269
1953: 236–7
1961 provisional 321
1973: 363–4
HTS promise of 528
Ottoman 57, 74, 79
consultative assemblies, *Bilad al-Sham* 13, 14
consumerism 454, 465
Contrôle Bédouin (CB) 115
Corrective Movement (*al-Haraka al-Tashihiya*) 357, 363
corruption
Assad regime 416, 421, 435, 436
campaign against 443
Quwwatli's regime 177–8, 179–81, 198–9, 200–201
cotton industry 64
crops 141–2, 256–7
nationalized 342
Cotton Office 263–4
coups d'état
against UAR (1961) 317–18
Ba'th Party (1963) 325–31
Hafiz Assad (1970) 356–7
al-Hinnawi (1949, 2nd) 213–15
Iraqi plot (1956) 289–91
Jadid (1966) 344–6
Nahlawi (1962) 322–3
Nasserist attempt (1963) 330
removal of Shishakli 246–9, 250–51
al-Shishakli (1949, 3rd) 215, 217–18
al-Za'im (1949, 1st) 202–212
Covid-19 pandemic (2020) 524
Craig, James 409–410
Crane, Charles 108

Crimean War 20
currency
  devaluation (1980s) 422
  dinar 98
  single UAR 309, 310–311
  'Syrian pound' (French) 98, 101, 139
  Turkish pound 139
Czechoslovakia, arms shipments from 286

Daghestanis 28
Damascus 5, 32, 137, 139
  1860 massacre 25–6
  1928 conference 134
  1936 protests 149
  2011 protests 485
  al-Merjeh Square 124
  aqueduct 143
  Arab Government 87–95
  as capital 98, 221, 379–80
  car bombs 494
  French bombardment (1925) 125–6
  French bombardment (1944) 171–2
  French occupation 101–2
  French State of 107, 114
  and Great Syrian revolt 121, 122–7
  hanging of Arabists 83
  Maydan commercial quarter 38, 63
  Mezzeh prison 357, 407, 446
  migrants in 469–70
  and Ottoman opposition 76–7, 79
  population 338, 379–80
  relations with Druze elites 38, 63, 122, 152
  Yarmouk Camp 379, 509, 520
Damascus Chamber of Commerce 426
'Damascus Declaration for Democratic National Change' (2005) 478
Damascus province 6, 7, 54–5
'Damascus Spring' 444–7, 448–9
Dar'a military base 292
al-Dardari, Abdullah 458, 463, 481
David, Jean-Claude 380
al-Dawalibi, Ma'rouf, prime minister 225, 226, 320, 322
Declaration of the Islamic Revolution 400–401
Defence Companies
  brutality of 393, 399, 402
  and Hama massacre 402–3
  Rif'at al-Assad and 369, 389
Deir al-Qamar 8
Deir al-Zour 28, 94, 246, 430
  2011 protests 485
  Ba'th Party in 327
  garrison 14, 49
  ISIS control over 501
  poverty in 466
  as provincial centre 56
  taken by HTS (2024) 526
  violence against demonstrators 398
Dentz, General 167
Der'a 192, 327, 381
  al-Umari Mosque 483

held by regime (2015) 491–2, 509
protests 482–4
retaken by regime 521
al-Dibs, Yusuf, *History of Syria* 73
Dictionary of Damascene Industries (1890-1905) 68–9
al-Din, Abd al-Baqi Nizam 385
al-Din, Adnan Sa'd 397
Diyab, Izz al-Din 273
Douba, Ali 370
Dreykish 381
drought
1929: 147
1958-60: 314–15, 319
2006-2010: 466–7
drugs
captagon trade 525
hashish 184, 190
Druze xvii, 1, 15, 36–42
and Ba'th Party 276, 335, 347–8
conflict with Bedouin 470, 474
and Damascene merchants 38, 63, 122, 152
and education system 59
emigration 474
and French Mandate 100, 109–110
and Great Syrian Revolt (1925-27) 117–23
and al-Hinnawi coup 213
HTS and 523
Mount Lebanon 8, 34, 35
opposition to Ibrahim Pasha 37–8
opposition to Shishakli 241–6
rebellion against 1910-11 census 80–81
response to integration 152–3
see also Jabal al-Duruz

earthquake (2023) 526
East Jerusalem 197, 353
Ecochard, Michel 379
economy
1950s boom 219, 253, 254–69
1955 crisis 285–6
1960 crisis 314–16
1964 crisis 341
1980s crisis 406, 420–27
Assad's policies 363, 423–6
austerity programmes 320, 422
Ba'thist state controls 340–41, 342, 349
defence spending 224, 286, 371
denationalizations 319, 321
'economic pluralism' 425
finance infrastructure 264–5
financial crises xix, 64–6, 468
food shortages 420
and Great Depression 147–8
import substitution 374
inequality xvi, 144, 530
inflation 255, 375–6, 463
nationalism of elite 144–5
nationalizations 228, 315–16, 319
oil crises 374–5, 420–21
Ottoman Empire changes 68–70
private investment 257, 265, 424–5
private sector 368, 373, 423–6
state-led industrialization 373–4
Syrian Arab Kingdom problems 98–9

economy – *cont.*
under French Mandate 139–40
see also agriculture; industry; Social Market Economy
education 59, 223, 228, 378
Imperial School for Tribes 59
military schools 59
missionary schools 59, 228
secular 53, 69–70, 477
Sharia high schools 471
state 58–9, 84, 377
Egypt xv, xviii, 254, 297–300
and 1948 war with Israel 299
2011 uprising (Arab Spring) 479–80
and Arab nationalism 70, 299
Aswan Dam project 288
British occupation 297, 298, 300
and control of *Bilad al-Sham* 12–18
Coptic Christians 297
and Czech arms supplies 286
and Iraq 279
and League of Arab States 206–7
literacy 298–9
mutual defence pact (1955) 286–7
and October War 365–6
and Palestine 299
peace deal with Israel 413
relations with Syria 278, 324–5, 391, 432
rise of 9–12
Syrian dissidents in 298
and United Arab Republic 253–4, 295
withdrawal from Syria (1840) 17–18, 24
see also Cairo; United Arab Republic
elections
1928: 135
1931-32: 136–7
1936: 152
1947: 188
1949: 210
1953: 238–9
1954: 269–77
1961: 320–21
1990: 425–6
2003: 455–6
HTS promise of 528
see also referendum(s)
electricity 264, 377
elites (grand families)
and 1954 elections 277
alienated by Shishakli 249
economic nationalism 144
effect of Land Code on wealth of 29
and Egyptian policy towards Syria 325
financial investment 265
and Higher National Committee (1919) 93
and integration 154
Jabal al-Ansariya 47
Lebanon 35–6
loss of power 291, 328
and nationalist movement 134–6
in Ottoman Empire 4–5

and Quwwatli government 180–81
rich entrepreneurs 373
and social reform 269
and Syrian Arab Kingdom 99–100
and UAR land reforms 306–7
urban view of rural populations 21–2
see also business elites; intellectuals
embezzlement, of military funds 198–9
Erdoğan, Recep Tayyip, Turkish president 518–19, 523
ethnicity
and identity 45, 77, 110–111, 155
in Ottoman Empire 2–3
Euphrates River Dam 349, 383–4
Euphrates Valley 27–8, 48–9
European Union, sanctions 525
eyalat (provinces) 54–5

Fadl Allah, Abu Mansur 213–14
Fallaha, Badi 426
families, grand *see* elites
famine, First World War 84–5
Fansah, Nadhir 212
al-Farfour, Shaykh Salih 429
Faris, Salim 75–6
Farouq, King of Egypt 207
Farzat, 'Ali 376
Fatah, Palestinian faction 351, 355, 413
al-Fatat society 81, 87
al-Fath Institute 429
Faysal al-Awwal bin Husayn bin 'Ali al-Hashimi, king of Syria 86, 87–95, 97, 99–102
death 165, 189
Faysal II, king of Iraq 219
overthrown by 1958 coup 311–12
'February Crisis' (2001) 447–8
Federation of Arab Republics, proposed 363
Federations of Employers' Syndicates 266
feudalism, *iqta'* system 31–2, 33
Fid'an tribe 48
Fighting Vanguard of the Mujahidin 393–4
and Muslim Brotherhood 396, 397, 400–401, 402–3
films, film-makers, documentaries 377–8, 381–2
financial crises, international xix
1873: 64–6
2008-09: 468
First World War xiv, xvii, 81–2, 84–7
food processing 143, 264
foreign relations 278–87
after Cold War 432–40
Assad and 411–16
Ba'th radicalism 350–51
and conspiracies 288–91, 293
with Iraq 450
mutual defence pact with Egypt (1955) 286–7
with Palestine 351
Fourier, Jean-Baptiste 9

France
army in the Levant 113, 165
collapse of franc (1924) 114
colonial administration of Syria 113–17
colonial doctrine 102–5, 117–18, 156
declaration of martial law (1940) 165
divide-and-rule policy 106–112, 151
interests in Syria 60–61, 84, 88, 140
and Lebanon 145–7, 151
mandatory powers in Syria 100–101, 102–5
and Mehmed Ali 17
Napoleonic occupation of Egypt 9–10
nation-building reforms 23
occupation of Syria xix, 89–90, 92–5, 101–2
and Ottoman provincial administration 56
peasants 21–2
Popular Front government 151, 163
relations with Britain 108–9
and Sanjak of Alexandretta 160, 162–4
Suez Crisis 288
and Syrian civil war 520
and Syrian independence 151–2, 168–72
Vichy regime 167, 168–9
franchise, universal 214, 239
Franco, General Francisco 235
Franco-Syrian treaty
Paris negotiations 150–52
proposed 137–8, 163–4
Franjiyeh, Suleiman, President of Lebanon 391
Free French, invasion of Syria (1941) 167–8
free speech, suppression of 410–411
Free Syrian Army (FSA) 490–92, 496
control of Hawran region (2015) 508–9
guerrilla tactics 491–2
and Islamist support 498–9
Free Syrian Forces 244
Fu'ad Pasha, Ottoman governor of Damascus 27
fuel prices 463, 467–8, 470–71
al-Fursan magazine 416

Galliéni, Joseph-Simon 103, 104
Gamelin, General 121, 126, 128
Gaulle, General Charles de 167–8
Gaza, Israeli occupation 353
Gaziantep, Turkey 465
gendarmerie
military control over 225–6
Quwwatli and 194–5
General Federation of Trade Unions 324, 339, 423, 439
German nationalism 273–4
Germany, investment in railways 61
Ghab marshes 209
reclamation 258–9, 382–3

Ghadaq, agro-company 426
Ghalyoun, Burhan 448, 454–5, 490
al-Ghanim, Abd al-Wahib 284
al-Ghanim, Wahib 361
al-Ghazali, Nawas 251
Ghazzi family 32
al-Ghazzi, Sa'id, prime minister 272, 285, 287
Ghiyath tribe 243
Ghouta district 32, 124, 126, 128
  chemical attack 504–5
  expansion of Damascus into 379
  held by rebels 509
  regained by regime 520
globalization xviii–xix
  and Long Depression (1873-1896) 64–6
  nineteenth-century 61, 62–70
Golan Heights 245
  and civil war 520–21
  Israeli annexation (1981) 412–13
  Israeli occupation 37–8, 353, 364, 367–8
gold standard 65–6
Gouraud, General 101–2, 105, 106–7
grain trade 63, 66
  French Mandate and 140–41
  imports (1960) 314
  Wheat Office (Second World War) 169–70
  and wheat production 256
Great Britain
  and Arab League proposal 245
  and Arab Revolt (1916-18) 85–7, 88
  bombing of Aleppo (1850) 25
  free trade 62–3
  improved relations with 433
  and Iraq 137, 278
  and Jabal al-Duruz uprising 245–6
  mandatory powers in Syria 100–101
  occupation of Egypt 75
  occupation of Syria 89–95
  and Ottoman Empire 16, 56
  relations with France 108–9
  and Shishakli regime 228–9
  Suez Crisis 288
  and Syrian civil war 520
  and Syrian independence 168–72
  trade with Syria 61, 68
Great Depression (1929-39) 147
Great Syrian Revolt (1925-27) 117–31
  French counter-insurgency 129–30
  guerrilla warfare 127–30
  legacy of Syrian unity 131
  rebel organization 127–9
  Revolutionary Council 129
  violence of French repression 130–31
Greater Lebanon 107–8, 133, 136
  see also Lebanon, State of; Mount Lebanon
Greater Syria, Jordanian project 177, 189–93
Gulf States 391–2
  aid from 369, 375, 406, 433
Gulf War, First 433
Gulf War, Second 450–51

Habannaka, Shaykh Hasan 350
Habash, Muhammad 477
Haddadin, Alawi tribe 44
al-Hadi, Daham, Shammar shaykh 158, 159
Hadid, Marwan 393, 397
Hadidiyyin tribe 192
Hadiqat al-Akhbar, newspaper 73
al-Haffar, Lutfi 117, 135, 143, 164, 166, 271
Hafiz al-Assad Institute for the Memorization of the Qur'an 430
al-Hafiz, General Amin, as president 334–5, 336–7, 344–5, 346–7
Hague, William 480
Haifa, access to port 139, 259
al-Hajj Salih, Yasin 408, 411, 479
al-Hakim, Hasan 189, 225, 240
Halabi family 153, 187
al-Halabi, Muhammad Izz al-Din 123
Hama
  and 1964 anti-Ba'th uprising 341–2
  1982 uprising 402–3, 405
  2011 protests 485
  expansion 380–81
  feudal landowners 32, 229–30, 231–2
  Great Syrian Revolt 123–4
  peasant sharecroppers 30–31, 262
  and radical Islamism 397–8
  taken by HTS (2024) 526
Hamdan family, Hawran 38
Hamdoun, Mustafa 250, 272, 306
Hamsho, Muhammad 459–60
Hananu, Ibrahim 99, 110, 137
Hanna, Abdullah 31
Harb al-'Isabat, guerrilla warfare doctrine 127
Harik, Ilya 300–301
al-Hariri, Colonel Ziyad 328, 330
al-Hariri, Rafiq 435, 456
al-Hariri, Wahbah 198
Harmoush, Lieutenant Colonel Hussein 490
Hasan, Baha al-Din 426
al-Hasani, Shaykh Taj al-Din, as Syrian president 168–9, 170
Hashemite dynasty 165–6, 190
al-Hashimi, Yasin 90
hashish, ban on cultivation 184, 190
al-Hassakeh, held by PYD (2015) 508
al-Hassakeh province 466, 470, 476
  census 385–7
  Kurds 474–5
Hassoun, Shaykh Ahmad Badr al-Din, grand mufti 429, 471
Hatay
  as Turkish province 163
  see also Alexandretta, Sanjak of
Hatum, Salim 347–8
Hawran region 67–8, 147, 276, 483
  civil war 520–21
  and Jordan 192–3
  village shaykhs 36–42

al-Hawrani, Akram 171, 205, 211, 213, 243, 245, 250
and 1954 elections 277
Arab Socialist Party 231, 270, 276
and Ba'th Party 326, 327–8
career 230–31
exile 235–6, 239
and Shishakli's reforms 219, 229–33, 249
and social reform 232–3
vice president of UAR 304
al-Hawrani, Rashid 230
Hawwa, Sa'id 397
al-Hayat newspaper 445
Hay'at Tahrir al-Sham (HTS) rebel group *see* HTS
al-Hayati, Colonel Yahya 127
Haydar, Ahmad 426
Helbaoui, Yousef 262
Higher Military Council, and Hinnawi coup 214
Higher Ministerial Committee (UAR) 311
Higher National Committee (1919) 93–4
Hijaz railway 61, 80, 85, 461
Hijaz region 78, 166
Hilal, Muhammad Talab 387–8
al-Hinnawi, Colonel Sami, coup (1949) 213–15, 217
Hisbah religious police, Islamic State 502
al-Hizb al-'Arabi al-Ishtiraki see Arab Socialist Party
Hizb al-Istiqlal (Independence Party) 91
Hizb al-Ittihad al-Suri (Syrian Union Party) 91
al-Hizb al-Qawmi al-Suri (Syrian Social Nationalist Party, SSNP) 211–12, 221, 230, 239, 281
banned 283–4
and Iraqi coup plot 289–90
in parliamentary coalition (2003) 457
Hizb al-Sha'b see People's Party
al-Hizb al-Watani (National Party) *see* National Party
Hizbullah party (anti-colonial movement, Hama (1925)) 123, 438, 526
and Syrian civil war 512
Syrian support for 434
Hmaymim, Russian use of airbase 512
Homs 32, 240, 262, 430
1936 protests 150
2011 protests 484, 491
bombardment 491
civil war 520
expansion 380–81
oil refinery 375
redevelopment project 469
taken by HTS (2024) 526
al-Homsi, Ma'moun 426, 448–9
hotels 464
housing
effect of Social Market Economy deregulation 467
mukhalafat informal settlements 469

housing – *cont.*
speculative property boom 468–9
HTS (Hay'at Tahrir al-Sham) (Organization for the Liberation of Syria) xii–xiii, 522–3
in government 527–9
and normalization 525–6
overthrow of Assad regime 526
Hububati, Khalid 477
al-Hula, sectarian violence 494
Hula Valley 225
Husayn ibn Ali al-Hashimi, Sharif, and Arab Revolt 85–7, 88, 89
al-Husayni, Lieutenant Colonel Faysal 241–2
al-Husayni, Lieutenant Colonel Ibrahim 208, 240
al-Husri, Sati' 299
Hussein, King of Jordan 87, 219, 245, 287
and PFLP hijacking 355–6

Ibn Abidin, Shaykh Muhammad Amin 14–15
Ibn Nusayr 43
Ibn Sa'ud, King Abd al-Azzi, Saudi Arabia 166, 192, 206, 291
Ibn Sha'lan, Fawaz 192
Ibrahim Pasha, governor of *Bilad al-Sham* 12–16, 17, 46
identity xv
Arab 77
and ethnicity 45, 77, 110–111, 155
late Ottoman 54, 77
and national civil society 72–3
see also sectarianism
Idlib 381, 466
and earthquake (2023) 526
HTS in 522–3, 526
Jabal al-Zawiya region 491–2
rebels in xi, 508, 519, 520, 521
regime attacks 514, 515
al-Ilah, Abd, regent of Iraq 219
al-'Ilm newspaper 232
al-Imadi, Muhammad, minister of economy 423
Imperial Edict (1856) 18
Independent Liberals 284
industry 264–8
artisanal 68–9, 142
Ba'th factory constructions 349
Ba'th nationalizations 342
cotton 64, 142
and French Mandate 142–4
import substitution 374
modernization 368
new light industries 143–4
silk 8, 34, 64
state regulation 267
textiles 142–3, 264, 265
UAR five-year plan 311
see also agriculture
inequality
economic xvi, 144
persistence 530
regional 466–70
under Social Market Economy 463–4, 465–6
inflation 255, 375–6, 463, 468
property prices 469–70

infrastructure
civil war destruction 528
early development xiv, 8
French 103, 117–18
independent Syria 179
Ottoman investment in 53–4
under Assad regime xvi, 377–8, 380
institutions of government 178–9
Shishakli and 218–19, 227, 258
Za'im and 205
see also state administration
intellectuals
and 2011 protests 490
and prospect of reform (from 2000) 443–9
restrictions on 477–8
intelligence officers
Bashar's purge of 455
French 115–16
International Monetary Fund (IMF) 320
Iran 472, 526
Assad and 414–16
and peace negotiations (2017) 514–15
Revolutionary Guard 513
and Russian intervention 512–13
Iraq xviii, 5
1958 coup 311–12
1963 Ba'th coup 325, 326, 331
Anglo-Iraq Treaty 137
and Axis powers 167
Bashar Assad and 450
Ba'th regime (1968) 354, 415
British mandate over 101
and Egypt 279
Hafiz Assad and 415–16
Hashemite throne 165
and al-Hinnawi coup 213
invasion of Kuwait 433
ISIS in 501
and Kurds 385
and Lebanese civil war 391
oil pipeline from 375, 450
and opponents of Syrian centralization 177
plans for coup 289–90
proposals for union with 214–15, 312
proposed agreement (Za'im) 206
and second-generation al-Qaeda 499–500
and Shishakli regime 219–20, 225, 244–5
and Six-Day War 352–3
US-led invasion (2003) 450–51
Iraqi Communist Party 312
Iron Hand Society 108
Islam 1–2, 71, 78
as main religion 221
see also Islamism; Sharia law; Shia Muslims; Sunni Muslims
'Islamic Front in Syria' 400
Islamic State of Iraq (ISI) 500–501
Islamic State of Iraq and Syria (ISIS) (Islamic State) 501–2, 503
areas of control (2015) 508
coordinated fight against 503–4
Hisbah religious police 502
remnants of 529

Islamic State of Iraq – *cont.*
retreat of 516–17
Salafi Sharia courts 502
United States war against 510, 515–16
Islamism
civil war armed opposition 498–9
radical 397–8, 471–2
rise of 394
Ismail, Khedive of Egypt 74
Isma'ilis, conflict with Alawis 470
Israel, State of 195, 436–9
clashes 225, 351
conflict with 286
and Egypt 299, 413
and Jabal al-Duruz uprising 245
and Lebanon 391
Operation Grapes of Wrath 438
Six-Day War 352–3, 412
and Suez Crisis 288
UN Security Resolutions and 412–13
Yom Kippur War 365–7, 412

Jabal al-Ansariya 6, 43–7, 106
Jabal al-Duruz 6, 38, 42, 187–8
1954 uprising 241–6, 251
and French occupation 106, 109–110, 114
and French treaty negotiations 138, 151
and Great Syrian Revolt 117–21
and Greater Syria project 190–91
and Syrian Arab Kingdom 99
trade 190–91
see also Druze
al-Jabal, Badawi 182
Jabal Hawran 36
al-Jabarti, Abd al-Rahman 10
Jabbour tribe 470
Jabiri family 32
al-Jabiri, Sa'dallah 108, 135, 150, 170–71, 181
Jablah 43
Jadid, Major Ghassan 281, 289
Jadid, Salah 328, 351
and Assad 354, 356–7, 362
coup (1966) 344–6
radicalism of regime 349–51
Jamal al-Atasi Forum 447
al-Jamali, Fadil, Iraqi prime minister 244–5, 271
Jamil, Naji 392
Jam'iyyat al-Bustan al-Khayri (The Garden Charitable Association) 473
Jarablus, taken by Turkey from Islamic State 518
Jaramana, Druze settlement 124
al-Jawa'ib, newspaper 71
Jaysh al-Sha'b, armed forces magazine 349–50
al-Jaza'iri family 88–9
al-Jaza'iri, Tahir 75, 76–7
al-Jazira region 5, 49, 50–51, 474
cotton production 256–7, 259
new villages 157
resistance to reunification 156–9
state-run farms 349
and UAR land reforms 306–8

Jerusalem 55, 86
see also Israel
Jews 2, 26, 143
jihad
in Iraq 472
and Islamist terrorism 393–400
jihadis, released by Assad regime (2011) 499
al-Jinan, newspaper 74
Jisr al-Shughur, 2011 protests 485, 490–91
al-Jolani, Abu Muhammad (Ahmad al-Shara'), HTS 500, 522, 523, 527
Jordan xv, 177, 525
Black September 355–6
and Greater Syria project 189–93
and Jabal al-Duruz uprising 245–6
Palestinian refugees 353
and PLO 437
and Six-Day War 352–3
and State of Israel 197
see also Transjordan
Joud family, Latakia 460
Joud, Haytham 461
journalism
Arab 79
see also Al Jazeera; newspapers
Junayd family, Jabal al-Ansariya 47
Jundi family 32
al-Jundi, Abd al-Karim 355
al-Jundi, army magazine 282
Junior Chamber International 462
Kaftaro, Shaykh Ahmad, grand mufti 342, 389, 429
Kalbiyyah, Alawi tribe 44
Kan'an, Ghazi 435, 436, 456
Kasm, Abd al-Ra'uf 395, 424
al-Kawakibi, Abd al-Rahman, *Umm al-Qura* 78
Kaylani family 32, 232
al-Kaylani, Rashid 167
Kayyali family 32
Kemal, Mustafa (Kemal Atatürk) 93, 110
Khaddam, 'Abd al-Halim 341–2, 478
as foreign minister 392, 417–18
vice president 370, 431, 440, 444, 447, 455, 456
Khalas, Ibrahim 349–50
Khan al-Shaykh refugee camp 197
Khan Maysaloun, battle at 102
al-Khani, Abdullah Fikri 222, 234–5
al-Kharrat, Fakhri 126
al-Kharrat, Hasan 126
Khayr Bek, Ismail 46–7
Khayyatin, Alawi tribe 44, 154
al-Khaznawi, Muhammad Mashuk 476
al-Khouri, Faris 116, 143, 150, 152, 203, 278, 280
Khoury, Philip 136
Khulayfawi, Abdul Rahman, prime minister 376
al-Khuli, Muhammad 356–7, 369–70

Khumasiya industrial conglomerate 315–16, 317, 321, 323
al-Khuri, Khalil, *Kharabat Suriya* 73
al-Kikhia, Rushdi 181, 243, 320–21
Kikhya family 306
Kilani family 32, 124
Kilo, Michel 400, 444, 445, 446–7, 448
King-Crane Commission (1919) 91–2, 100
al-Kinj, Ibrahim 154, 183
Kisrawan rebellion (1858-59), Mount Lebanon 34–5
Kissinger, Henry 366, 413
Kobanî (Ayn al-Arab) 503–4, 508
Kulthoum, Umm 301
Kurd 'Ali, Muhammad 79, 179, 181
Kurd Dagh region 387
Kurdish Democratic Party 387
Kurdish National Congress (KNC) 502–3
Kurds xvii, 1, 3
  and Assad regime 385–9
  and citizenship 471, 486
  and education system 59
  effect of 1962 census on 385–7, 471
  and fight against Islamic State (ISIS) 502–4
  in Jazira 50, 156–7, 159
  and resettlement of Weldeh tribe 384–5, 388
  security forces and 474–6
al-Kutla al-Wataniyya see National Bloc
Kuwait, and Syrian civil war 498
Kuzbari family 460
al-Kuzbari, Colonel Haydar 317
al-Kuzbari Ma'moun 248, 266, 317
  Arab Liberation Movement 270
  prime minister (1961) 319–20

labour relations, agricultural 309
labour rights 268
Labour and Social Welfare Directorate 268
labour unions, militancy 285–6
Land Code, Ottoman (1858) 19, 23, 260
  effect on Syrian interior 30–33
  and Hawran 36–42
  and Jabal al-Ansariya 43–7
  and Mount Lebanon 33–6
  and property rights 28–51
land reforms
  Ba'th redistribution 349, 467
  French 141–2
  UAR 306–9
  Za'im's proposed 208, 232–3
land tenure
  cadastral surveys 141, 261–2
  forms of 260–61
  limits on holdings 306, 321, 324, 340
  national survey (1953) 263
  pre-1955 (table) **307**
  and property rights 23, 260–64
  and rural poverty 262–3
Latakia 43, 99, 187, 512

and 1990 election 430
al-Nusra control 508
Ba'th Party in 276, 327, 354
cotton production 64
population growth 381
port facilities 208–9, 259
response to integration 151, 153–4
shabbiha groups 493
law
secular civil (under Za'im) 207–8
Sharia 58, 207–8
Le Commerce du Levant 310
League of Arab States 206–7
League of Higher Graduates 416
League of National Action (*'Usbat al-'Amal al-Qawmi*) 148–9
League of Nations
mandatory powers and responsibilities 91, 101, 113, 133
and Turkish claims to Alexandretta 160–61
Lebanon 107–8, 133, 138
banks 310, 315
civil war (1975-76) 390–92, 413
economy 146–7, 435
elites 35–6
prospect of unification with 145–7, 151
recognition of Syrian hegemony over 433–6
trade with 212, 267
Levant, colonial settlement 54
Lisan al-Sha'b newspaper 282
Liwa al-Islam, Islamist group 499, 503
Local Administrative Councils 497
Long Depression (1873-1896) 64–6
Lyautey, Hubert, and French colonial Morocco 103–5, 117
Lyde, Samuel 44–5

Ma'arrat al-Numan 485, 491
McMahon, Sir Henry 86, 88
Madrid peace conference (1991) 437
Mahayni family 63
Majalla, Ottoman law code 19
Majdal al-Shur Declaration 40–41
Majjar brothers 256
Makhlouf, Adnan 370
Makhlouf, Ihab 459
Makhlouf, Rami 448, 459, 460, 473, 493, 524
al-Malki, Colonel Adnan 272
assassination (1955) 280–83
Mamarbachi, Pierre 256
Mamlukes, Egypt 10–11
Manouliyan, Hrant 194
Mardam, Fu'ad 201
Mardam, Jamil 116–17, 135, 163, 166
and 1936 general strike 150
and French treaty negotiations 137–8, 163–4
as prime minister 152, 164
Mardam-Beg family 32
Maronite Christians
colleges 70–71
and French Greater Lebanon 107
and French Mandate 100
Israel and 391

Maronite Christians – *cont.*
Kisrawan rebellion 34–5
Mount Lebanon 8, 14, 15
relations with Druze 35, 38
Martel, Charles de 138, 150
Marxism–Leninism, Ba'th Party 334
Matar, Ilyas, *The Pearl Necklace of the Syrian Kingdom* 73
Matawira, Alawi tribe 44
matrouka, land tenure 260–61
matrouka mahmiyya, land tenure 261
Mawali tribe 48, 123, 192
mawat, land tenure 261, 263
media, and 2011 uprising 492
Mehmed Ali Pasha 8, 12, 70
ejection from Syria 16–17
as governor of Egypt 10–11, 22
Mezzeh prison, Damascus 357, 407, 446
Michaud, General 120–21
Middle East Defence Pact 225
Middle East Supply Centre 255, 264
Migdal, Joel 23
migration
Druze emigration 474
Egyptian immigrants 309
rural–urban 378–81, 466–7, 469–70
millet system, Ottoman Empire 2
minibuses, strikes 470–71
Miqdad, Faysal 483
miri, land tenure 260
Mishaqa, Mikhail 8
Mistura, Staffan de, UN Special Envoy 515
Misyaf 116
mobile phones 448, 459
Mohammed, Ossama, *Khutwa Khutwa* (film) 377–8
monarchism, monarchists 189
Morocco, French colonial occupation 103–4, 112, 130
Mount Hermon 353, 366
Mount Lebanon region 6, 7–8
effect of Land Code in 33–6
and French Mandate 100
and origins of Arab renaissance 70–71
Règlement organique (1861) 35
see also Lebanon, State of
Mubarak, Hosni, Egyptian president 432, 479–80
Mudarris family 32, 306
Mudrus, Armistice of (1918) 87
mukhabarat 405, 410, 454
and Kurds 474, 475–6
use of torture 475–6
mulk, land tenure 260
al-Muqtabas, newspaper 79, 80
al-Muqtataf, newspaper 74
Murad, Leila 301
Muraywid, Isam 214, 244
al-Murshid, Fatih 184
al-Murshid, Sulayman, rebel leader 45, 182–5, 194
Muslim Brotherhood 171, 221, 227, 396–400
and 1954 elections 273
and 2011 protests 490

death penalty for membership 400
and Fighting Vanguard of the Mujahidin 396, 397, 400–401, 402–3
and Hama massacre 402–3, 405
and National Salvation Front 478
Muslim Brotherhood, Egyptian 396–7
Muslims xvii, 1
parliamentary majority 239
and violence against Christians 26
see also Islam; Shia Muslims; Sunni Muslims

al-Nadhir newspaper 400–401
al-Nadi al'Arabi organization 90–91
Nahda (Arab Renaissance) 70–75, 77
Islamic strand 74–5
Nahhas, Sa'ib, Transtour 373, 426
Nahlawi, Colonel Abd al-Karim 317
Najib, Atif 482, 483
Napoleon Bonaparte, and Egypt 9–10
al-Nasr newspaper 282
al-Nasser, Gamal Abd xv, 234, 278–9, 299
and Arab defence pact 279–80
death (1970) 356
economic policies 305–6, 312–13
popularity of 300–305
rapprochement with Jadid 351
and Six-Day War 352
and Suez crisis 288
and Syrian secession 323, 329–31
threat of invasion (1961) 318
and United Arab Republic 294–5, 301–6
Nasserists, Syrian army 328, 330
National Bloc (*al-Kutla al-Wataniyya*) 135–8
erosion of confidence in 159, 164–5
and Lebanon 145–6
and proposed treaty with France 137–8
Second World War 170–71
and youth groups 149–50
National Cement Company 143
National Charter (1961) 319
National Coalition 490, 497
National Council for the Revolutionary Command (1963) 328–9
National Democratic Gathering 447
National Dialogue conference 486
National Dialogue Forum (*Muntada al-Hiwar al-Watani*) 444
National Guard (*al-Haras al-Qawmi*) 330
National Pact (1953) 240
National Party (*al-Hizb al-Watani*) 180–81, 328
and 1954 elections 277
coalition with People's Party 270

National Party – *cont.*
ideological divisions 284
relations with Egypt and Saudi Arabia 278
and Shishakli regime 218
National Progressive Front 362, 368, 395, 425–6
National Salvation Front 478
nationalist movement (from 1927) 134–5
Nayrab Camp, Aleppo 197
Netanyahu, Benjamin, Israeli prime minister 438
newspapers 53, 72, 73–4, 79, 232–3, 282
al-Ahram (Egypt) 74
al-Ba'th 344, 354, 376
Hadiqat al-Akhbar 73–4
al-Jawa'ib 71
al-Muqtabas 79
Palestine 79
al-Thawra 344, 354–5, 376, 441, 446, 448
al-Nidal newspaper 282
Niéger, Colonel Paul 111
Nile, river 297–8, 308
Nineveh province, ISIS in 501
Noble Edict of the Rose Chamber (1839) 18, 24
non-governmental organizations (NGOs), under Social Market Economy 461–2, 473
Normand, General 120
Nuri family 63
al-Nusra, Jabhat (Victory Front)
break with al-Qaeda 521–2
control of Idlib (2015) 508
and Hay'at Tahrir al-Sham (HTS) 522
and ISI 500–501

Obama, Barack, US President 480, 510
and Syrian use of chemical weapons 504–5
October War (Yom Kippur) 365–7
oil crisis (1973) 374–5
oil crisis (1980s) 420–21
oil pipelines 209, 288, 375, 421, 450
oil production 421
Operation Peace Spring (2019) 523
Oslo Accords 437
Ottoman Army, use against protesters 25, 26–7, 42, 80–81
Ottoman Empire 1–4, 5, 6, 22
constitution 57, 74, 79
debt crisis 64, 66–7
declaration of bankruptcy (1875) 67
and First World War xiv–xv, 81–2
and great powers 16, 20–21
modernization 53–4
parliament, first (1876) 57, 80
provincial administration 54–61
secret organizations 75–6, 81, 85, 90–91
and secularization 20
social and economic change 68–70
and Syrian provinces 24–6, 48–9, 53–6

Tanzimat reforms
(1839-1876) 18–24
see also Turkey
Ottoman Public Debt
Administration 66–7

Palestine xix, 86
and 1948 War 195–9
British mandate over 101
guerrilla attacks on Israel 355
newspapers 79
trade with 139
Zionist settlers 84, 88
see also Hamas; Hizbullah
Palestine Liberation Organization
(PLO) 355, 390–91, 437
Palestinian refugees, Six-Day
War 353
Palmerston, Viscount 16–17
Palmyra 192, 407
Islamic State destruction 508
massacre (1980) 399, 407
recaptured by regime 514
Paris Peace Conference
(1919-20) 90–92
Paris, Treaty of (1856) 20
parliament 221, 226
independent businessmen
in 425–6
religious shaykhs in 430, 471
tribal independents 430
Peasant Bureau, Ba'th Party 372
peasants
Bilad al-Sham 13–14, 15
Egyptian 12, 300–301
elite views of 21–2
and French land reforms 141
Ghab reclaimed lands 382–3
in Hawran 36–42
lack of legal rights 268, 309
and Majdal al-Shur
Declaration 40–41
and modernization
programmes 381–2
and National Bloc 135
political support for 232–3
as tenant sharecroppers 30–31,
262
see also agriculture
Peasants' Union 339, 368,
372, 463
People's Party (*Hizb al-Sha'b*)
116–17, 121, 181, 214–15, 328
and 1954 elections 277
coalition with National Party
270, 278
ideological divisions 284
and Iraq 271, 278
relations with army 225–6
and secession government
320–22
and Shishakli regime 218, 228
Peres, Shimon 438
PKK, Turkish Kurdish movement
475, 517–18
polarization, political xv, 278–87,
292, 293–5
political left
and 1954 elections 277
move towards Soviet
Union 293
rise of 269, 270, 291, 292

political organizations
Arab Liberation Movement (ALM) 227, 234
secret 75–6, 81, 85, 90–91
political parties 214, 362
and 1954 elections 269, 272–7
abolition by Za'im 209–210
disbanded at union with Egypt 301–2, 303–4
early 90–91, 94
factionalism 180, 223
new 446
promise of restoration 457, 478
political prisoners 481
release of 428, 445–6
political reconstruction (from 2024) xii, 525, 527–9
political violence 529–30
mass executions 399, 400
massacres 398, 399, 400
state repression 394–6
targeted 282, 289
as tool of Assad regime 392–400, 405–6, 488–9
Ponsot, Henri 133, 135, 137–8
popular culture, Egypt 301
Popular Front for the Liberation of Palestine (PFLP) 355–6
popular politics, 1930s 147–52
'Populars', the (*al-Sha'biyun*) movement 187–8
population
densities 308
diversity of xvii–xviii, 1
growth 148, 377
postal services 53
Poulleau, Alice 124–5
poverty 466–8
rural 47, 262–3
Prebisch, Raúl 374
president
powers of 221–2
term of office 181, 428
prisons 407–8
secret 488
torture 405, 407–8, 475–6, 488–9
'Programme for Workers and Peasants' (1952) 232–3
property rights 23, 222–3, 260–64
Tanzimat reforms 28–51
protests and demonstrations
against Ba'th regime 392–6, 398–400
against intervention in Lebanon 392–3
at Ba'th attack on religion 350
bread riots (Hama 1920) 98
CCMC campaign against 487–9
increasing (2011) 481–7
lawyers' syndicate 393
Palestinian militants 392
'rally against feudalism' (1951 Aleppo) 232
at secession from UAR 322, 323
students (1956) 287
violent repression of 482–3, 484, 485, 487–9
see also rebellions; strikes; terrorism
public health 377
charities and 473

Putin, Vladimir, Russian president 510, 511
PYD (*Partîya Yekîtî ya Dêmokrat*), Syrian Kurdish movement 475
  area of control (2015) 508
  and fight against Islamic State 502–4, 517–19
  and normalization 525–6
  and PKK 517
  Rojava project (local administration) 503, 517–18
  US support for 510
  YPG (People's Protection Units) 503–4, 516

Qabbani, Nizar, *Marginalia* 365
Qadmous, Alawi–Isma'ili conflict 470
Qamishli 157, 385
  Arab–Kurd conflict 470, 474–5
  under PYD control 508
al-Qa'qa, Abu 471–2
al-Qassab, Shaykh Kamal 94
Qatana, prison 407
Qatana Mutiny 291
Qatar, and Syrian civil war 498
al-Qawuqji, Fawzi 123–4, 196
Qubaysiyat, women's network 471
Qudsi family 32
al-Qudsi, General Rasmi 242–3
al-Qudsi, Nazim 181
  as president 320, 322–3
  as prime minister 220, 224, 228
Qunaytra, Golan region 353, 367
  taken by HTS (2024) 526
Qusayr 512
Qutb, Sayyid 394
Quwwatli family 32
al-Quwwatli, Shukri 144, 164, 292
  administration of 177–81
  and ALA 195–7
  and armed forces 193–202
  centralization policies 177, 178–81
  and Druze 186–8
  in Egypt 271
  external threats 189–93
  and Greater Syria project 191
  increasing discontent with 198–202, 203
  and independence 175–6
  leader of National Bloc 166–7
  and Murshid 183, 184–5
  and Nasser 302
  new National Party 180–81
  as president 170, 181, 285, 287
  return (1954) 277
  and Soviet Union 288
  and United Arab Republic 302

Rabat, French segregation in 105
Rabin, Yitzhak, Israeli prime minister 437–8
Radio Damascus 202, 210, 226, 354
Rahim, Yunis Abd al-Rahman 281
railways 53, 60–61
Ramadi, Iraq 508
Raqqa 27, 466
  agricultural cooperatives 339–40
  devastation 516–17
  ISIS control over 501
  under Islamic State control 508
  United States recapture of 515–16

Ras al-Ayn 523
Rastan 485, 491, 520
Rathmell, Andrew 281
al-Rayyis, Munir 116, 179
rebellions and uprisings
  1939: 165
  1949: 199–200
  1964 anti-Ba'th uprising 341–2
  against 1910-11 census 80–81
  against foreign rule (1919) 92–3, 99
  against Ibrahim Pasha (1830s) 15–16
  against Ottomans 25–8
  'Ammiyya Revolt (1888) 41–2, 67
  descent into civil war (2012) 495–6
  development of (2011) 490–96
  Great Syrian Revolt (1925-27) 116, 117–31
  Hama uprising (1982) 402–3, 405
  Kisrawan rebellion (1858-59) 34–5
  use of *shabbiha* loyalist thugs against 492–4, 495
  see also protests and demonstrations; terrorism
referendum(s)
  1953: 236–7
  Assad's presidency 419, 428
  on union with Egypt 301–2
refugees
  1870s 28
  internally displaced by civil war 521, 528–9
  in Iraq 244
  from Jabal al-Duruz to Jordan 243
  in Jazira 156–7
  Palestinian 197–8, 209, 353
  returning 525
regionalism xix, 529
  Ba'th Party and 276
  improved connections 60–61
  Ottoman provincial administration 7–9, 54–61
  Shishakli and 250–51
regions
  rural–urban migration 378–81, 466–7, 469–70
  transformation of rural life 377–8
  variations in inequality 466–70
religions
  and 1990s toleration 429–30
  Ottoman Empire 1–2
  see also Christians; Islam
religious establishment
  Ba'th Party and 342, 350
  reassertion of controls 477
  relaxation of restrictions 471–3
Republican Guard 370
Revolutionary Command Council 292
Rida, Rashid 75, 78
Rifa'i family 32, 306
Rifa'i order of Sufis 230
rights
  of citizens 222
  labour 268
  peasants' 268, 309
  property 23, 28–51, 222–3, 260–64

al-Rikabi, Ali Rida 89, 97
Riyad, Mahmud, and UAR 304–5
roads 179, 377
  1950s investment 259
  Ottoman investment 53, 60
Rumsfeld, Donald, US Secretary of Defence 450
Russia
  expansion into Caucasus 28
  and Islamist threat to Caucasus 511–12
  military intervention (2015) xx, 510, 511–15
  and Ottoman Empire 16, 18
  and overthrow of Assad regime 526
  and peace negotiations 513, 514–15
  relations with Iran 512–13
  and Syrian civil war 505
  see also Soviet Union
Ruwala tribe 48, 192

Sa'adah, Antun 211–12, 213, 221
Sabbagh family 63
Sadat, Anwar, Egyptian president 363, 365–6
Saddam Hussein
relations with Assad 415–16, 433
and Second Gulf War 450–51
al-Sadr, Musa, Imam 414
Safa, Colonel Muhammad 244
Safadi, Muta' 336, 337
safarbarlik (trauma of First World War) 85
al-Sa'id, Nuri, Iraqi prime minister 166, 279
Salafi Sharia courts, Islamic State 502
Salameh, Mahmud 446, 448
Salamiyya 27
Salkhad 120
samneh affair 200, 205, 420
San Remo Conference (1920) 100–101
sanctions 449–51, 525
Sanqar, Ihsan 426
Saqba village 128
Saraqib, 2011 protests 485
Sarrail, General Maurice 119–20, 125, 133
Sarraj, Abd al-Hamid 272, 302
  and Iraqi coup plot 289–90
  and UAR Special Bureau 305, 312, 314, 316, 320
satellite television 430–31
  see also Al Jazeera
Saudi Arabia 166, 278, 291, 525
  Rif'at Assad and 417
  and Syrian civil war 498
  and Syrian independence 177
Saudis, relations with Ottoman Empire 78
Sawt al-'Arab, Egyptian radio station 301
Saydnaya, prison 407
al-Sayyid, Jalal 386
al-Sayyid, Sa'id 385–6
Sba' tribe 48
Schad, Geoffrey 143
Seale, Patrick 200, 250, 289
Second World War 164–72

Second World War – *cont.*
Egypt and 298
food shortages 169–70, 255
sectarian conflict, 2005-06 killings 470
sectarianism xvii, xviii, 251
in 2011 uprisings 492–5
Ba'th Party 335–6
French policy 106–112
security agencies
Assad's 369–70
mukhabarat 405, 410, 454, 474–6
report-writing 410
UAR Special Bureau 305, 312, 314, 316
Seif, Riyad, and Damascus Spring 444–5, 446–9
Selu, Colonel Fawzi 220, 266
as president 218, 227, 238
September 11, 2001 attacks 449
Service des renseignements (SR), French intelligence 115, 130, 156
Seurat, Michel 399
shabbiha (loyalist thugs) 492–4, 495
Shahba Spinning and Weaving Company 142, 265
al-Shahbandar, Abd al-Rahman 79, 116, 121, 166, 186
and nationalist movement 108, 134, 164
proposed confederation of Arab states 165–6
Shallah, Badr al-Din 398
al-Shallash, Ramadan 94, 122, 129
Sham'a family 32
Shamir, Yitzhak, Israeli prime minister 436–7
Shammar tribe 50, 158, 470
Shara' family 527
al-Shara', Ahmad (Abu Muhammad al-Jolani) 500, 522, 523, 527
al-Shara', Farouq 437, 438, 486
Sharabati, Ahmad 194, 198–9, 224
Sharett, Moshe, Israeli prime minister 245
Sharia law 58, 207–8
Sharif Husayn *see* Husayn
Sharon, Ariel, Israeli prime minister 448
al-Sharq al-Awsat newspaper 447
Shawkat, Assef 440, 487, 494
Sheikh Bader, population growth 381
Shia Muslims, and Assad's alliance with Iran 414–15, 472
al-Shidyaq, Ahmad Faris 71–2, 76
al-Shihabi, Amir Bahjat 158–9
al-Shihabi, Hikmat 389, 417–18, 436
al-Shishakli, Adib 205, 211
analysis of failure of 249–51
and Arab Liberation Movement (ALM) 227, 234
assassination 251
coup (1949) 215
coup (1951) 226
curbs on foreign influence 228–9
and economy 266–7
influence of Hawrani on 229–33

institution building 218–19, 227
military dictatorship (from 1951) 226–39
new constitution (1953) 236–7
opposition to 240–49, 250
personal power 235, 236–7
as president and prime minister 238
reform agenda 218–19, 237–9
relations with army 225, 239, 249–50
removed by coup (1953) 246–9, 250–51
al-Shishakli, Adib (brother of Salah) 289
al-Shishakli, Captain Salah 242–3, 289
Shone, General Terence 172
Shufi family 187
Shuqayr, Shawkat 248, 272, 281, 282
Sidon province 6
silk industry 8, 34, 64
Sinai Peninsula 353, 365–6
Six-Day War (1967) 352–3
Syrian aftermath 354–7, 364
Sixth National Congress, Ba'th Party 332–4, 340–41
'Some Theoretical Points of Departure' 333–4, 340
smuggling 395
see also corruption
Social Market Economy xvi, xx, 454–5, 457–64
'build–operate–transfer' (BOT) model 461
foreign investment 458, 466
free trade agreements 458, 465
holding companies 460
inflation 255, 375–6, 463
monopolies 461
non-governmental organizations 461–2
poverty 466
private sector 457–8
public–private partnerships 461
and social control strategy 470–71
and social reforms 481–2
social media, ban lifted 481
social reform 222, 268
after end of Cold War 427–32
Bashar Assad and 481–2
see also Social Market Economy
social welfare
charities 472–3
NGOs 461–2
socialism xv
Ba'th radical policies 331–4, 335, 349–51, 372
Solidere, company 435
Souria Holding company 461
Southern Front coalition (Free Syrian Army) 508–9
Soviet Union xviii, 288
aid from 369
Assad and 365, 414, 511
Ba'th Party and 349
dissolution 427
and Egypt 286
and Euphrates Dam 383
invasion of Afghanistan 413–14

Soviet Union – *cont.*
and Lebanese civil war 392
and Six-Day War 352, 353
and Syrian Communist Party 270, 277
and UAR 320
see also Russia
Spain, Franco regime 235
Spears, General 169–70, 172
'Special Bureau', UAR security agency 305, 312, 314, 316, 319–20
state administration
industrialization 373–5
public sector 368, 374
regulation of industry 267
and Social Market Economy 458
state building, Ba'th Party 331–43
state of emergency (from 1963) 199, 364, 393, 398
'frozen' (2001) 449
strikes 285–6, 324
1936 general 150, 158
1949 general 199
1954: 272
Struggle Companies 370
Sudan 22
Suez Crisis 288–9
Sukkar family 127
Sukkar, Nabil 428
Sulayman, Ali, father of Hafiz Assad 361
Sulayman Pasha 7
Sultan Pasha *see* al-Atrash, Sultan
Sunni Muslims xvii, 1, 14–15
and Ba'th Military Committee 336–7
French view of 108–9, 114
Jabal al-Ansariya 43, 44, 45
Suqur al-Sham, Islamist group 499
al-Suri, Abu Mus'ab 403
Suwayda (Suweida) 120–21, 241, 242
Ba'th Party and 276, 327, 347–8
Bedouin–Druze conflict 470, 474
military base 292
parliamentary independents 430
population 381
taken by HTS (2024) 526
Suwaydan family 36
Suwaydani, Ahmad 348
Sykes, Mark 49–50
Sykes-Picot Accord (1916) xvii, 88, 92
Syria xiii–xv, xvii
and Arab–Israeli War (1948) 178
declaration of independence (1920) 92–5, 97
French colonial state xix, 113–17
future prospects for (2024-25) 529–30
geographical boundaries xiv, 73
independence (1946) 172, 175–6, 177, 178–81, 255
and Lebanese civil war 390–92
as Ottoman province (1864) 53, 55, 57, 74, 79
secessionist regime 318–25
and unification 145, 151, 162–4
as US 'rogue state' 449–50

see also Bilad al-Sham ('lands of Damascus'); constitutions; United Arab Republic
Syria Accountability and Lebanese Sovereignty Restoration Act (US, 2003) 450
'Syria' (*Suriya*), name xiv, 7, 16, 73
Syria Trust for Development (*al-Amana al-Suriya li'l-Tanmiya*) 462–3
Syrian Agricultural Bank 264
Syrian Arab Kingdom 97–102
Syrian army 175, 231
  and 1948 war 178, 195–7
  and 1956 coup plot 290
  and 1962 coup 322–3
  and assassination of Malki 282, 283
  Ba'thist Military Committee 328, 343–4
  Ba'thists in 325–6
  budget 224, 371
  and civil war 504–5
  defections to FSA 490, 492
  expansion under Assad 368, 370–71
  expansion under Za'im 205–6
  intervention in politics 223–6, 271–2
  Nasserists 328, 330
  October War 367
  political factions 284, 291, 294–5
  purges 348
  Qatana Mutiny 291
  Quwwatli and 193–202
  and secession government 319, 320–21
  and Shishakli regime 218, 233–4, 239
  and Syrian independence 271, 279
Syrian Communist Party 171, 209–210, 270
  and 1954 elections 277
  and Ba'th Party 349
  and Soviet Union 270, 277
  and UAR 303, 312
Syrian Communist Party League of National Action 165
Syrian congress (1919) 91–3, 94–5, 97–8, 99–100
Syrian Conserves Company 144
Syrian Defence Forces (SDF) 516
Syrian Democratic Forces (SDF) 504
'Syrian Interim Government' (2013) 498
Syrian Islamic Front 499
Syrian Islamic Liberation Front 499
Syrian National Army, Turkish support for 518–19, 523
Syrian National Council (SNC) 490, 494
Syrian Patriotic Party (*al-Hizb al-Watani al-Suri*) 94
Syrian Press Office 210
Syrian Protestant College 59
Syrian Regional Congress 335
Syrian Salvation Government 522

Syrian Society for the Arts and
 Sciences 72
Syrian steppe (*al-badiya*) 48–9
Syrian Union Party (*Hizb al-Ittihad al-Suri*) 91
Syrian University, Damascus
 207, 228
Syrian Young Entrepreneurs 462
Syrian–Saudi Company for
 Industrial and Agricultural
 Investments (1976) 375
Syriatel, mobile phone network
 459, 483, 495

al-Tahtawi, Rif'at 21
Taif Accord (1989) with
 Lebanon 434
Talal, King of Jordan 219
Talas, As'ad 217
Talbiseh 520
Tansiqiyat (Local Coordination
 Committees) 489–90, 494, 497
Tanzimat reforms, Ottoman
 Empire (1839-1876) 18–24, 53
 aligned with global
 modernization 22–3
 effect on social relations 53
 equality before law 19
 implementation 23–4
 law of nationality 19
 Majalla law code 19
 and property rights 28–51
 see also Land Code (1858)
tariffs 267, 285, 341
Tartous 154, 381, 511
tax collection 4, 11
 tax farming 13, 35
taxation 20, 24
 exemptions 425
 increased 98–9
 progressive direct 223
Tayfur family 32, 232
Tayy tribe 50, 158
telegraph 53, 60
television 430–31
 miniseries (*musalsalat*) 431–2
Tell Abyad 508, 523
terrorism, Islamic jihadi 393–400
textile industry 142–3, 264, 265
Thamarat al-Funun, newspaper 74
al-Thawra newspaper 344, 354–5,
 376, 441, 446, 448
Tishrin newspaper 427–8
Tlass, Abd al-Razzaq 491
Tlass, Mustafa 336–7, 345, 356, 359,
 455, 456
 as defence minister 370, 393,
 417–18
torture, in prisons 405, 407–8,
 475–6, 488–9
tourism industry 373, 425,
 459–60, 464–5
trade
 deficit (1961) 319
 effect of French Mandate
 borders 139
 free trade 62–3
 free trade agreements 458, 465
 international 26, 143
 and markets 267–8
 nineteenth-century
 globalization 61, 62–70

protectionism 266–7
and Second World War rationing 180
UAR import restrictions 311
trade routes 6, 8, 139
trade unions 319, 324, 339–40
Transjordan 27, 28, 101, 107
see also Jordan
tribal law 309
Tripoli province 6
Trump, Donald, US President 515, 517
Tunisia, and Arab Spring 479
al-Turk, Riyad 400, 408, 444, 448
Turkey 107, 279, 465
interventions in Syria (2018-19) 518–19, 523
and peace negotiations (2017) 515
and Russian intervention in Syria 514
and Sanjak of Alexandretta 160–63
support for Syrian rebels 510
see also Ottoman Empire
Turkish language 2, 80, 161

'Ubayd, Hamad 342, 347
'Umran, Muhammad 272, 328, 337, 344–5, 362–3
unemployment 468
United Arab Company for Industry 265
United Arab Republic (1958-61) (UAR) 302–318
changes in Syria 303
economic unification 305–317
Egyptianization 304–5
secession 317, 318–25
Syrian alienation 316–17
United Commercial and Industrial Company 265
United Constitutional Front 284
United Nations
and Iraq 450
and State of Israel 195, 366, 412–13, 437
Syrian peace negotiations 513
United Nations Relief and Works Agency (UNRWA) 235
United States of America xviii, 65, 283
and Aswan Dam project 288
and Eisenhower Doctrine 293
and Jordan 356
King-Crane Commission 91–2
and Lebanon 391
and Middle East Defence Pact 225
relations with Syria 432–3, 436–7, 480
sanctions on Syria 449–51, 525
support for anti-Islamic State forces 503–4, 510, 516, 518
Syrian air attacks (2017) 515, 516
and Syrian use of chemical weapons 504–5, 520
and 'war on terror' 449–50
'Uqaydat tribe 50, 94, 192
Uqla, Adnan 400, 401–3
urban redevelopment 465
al-'Utri, Naji, prime minister 456

Vienna, Stock Exchange collapse (1873) 65

Wadi al-Taym 15
Wagner Group, Russian military company 512
al-Wahhab, Muhammad Abd 301
Wahhabis 7, 14, 78
Wall Street Journal, Bashar Assad interview 480
Warriner, Doreen 257
water supplies 377
  irrigation 258, 467
Weldeh tribe 383–4, 388
West Bank 197, 353
wilaya, provincial administration 55–6
Wilson, Woodrow, US President 91–2
women
  right to vote 207, 214, 239
  Tansiqiyat activists 489
  wearing of head-scarves 430, 483
  wearing of veil 209, 477
Women's Union 340, 368
World Bank (International Bank of Reconstruction and Development) 286, 311
World Trade Organization 458

Yanni, Jurji, *History of Syria* 73
Yarmouk 379, 509, 520
Yemen (*al-Yaman*) 5, 78
Yezidis, Islamic State genocide of 502, 503
Yom Kippur War (October War) 365–7
Young Turks 76, 79
youth organizations 148–50, 165
YPG (People's Protection Units) 503–4, 516
al-Yusuf, Captain Ibrahim 393

al-Za'im, Husni 199, 200–202, 204
  abolition of political parties 209–210
  and army 205–6, 209–210
  character 204, 210
  coup 201, 202–212
  execution 213–14
  external threats 206–7
  and Sa'adah 211–12
  social policy 207–9, 232
al-Za'im, Isam 443
al-Za'im, Muhammad Sa'id 266
al-Zarqawi, Musam, al-Qaeda 499–500
al-Zawahiri, Ayman 521
Zayd movement, Damascus 472
Zionists, Zionism 84, 88, 147–8, 149
Zu'ayyin, Yusuf 346
al-Zu'bi family 36
al-Zu'bi, Mahmoud 443